UPON THEIR LAWFL

C000023815

Vernon Upton, G.M.

UPON THEIR LAWFUL OCCASIONS

Reflections of a Merchant Navy Officer During Peace and War

Matador
9 De Montfort Mews
Leicester LE1 7FW, UK
Tel: (+44) 116 255 9312 / 9311
Fax: (+44) 116 255 9323
Email: books@troubador.co.uk
Web: www.troubador.co.uk/matador

ISBN 1 904744 25 7

Cover illustration: R. Bartelt Design

Typeset in 11pt Hoefler Text by Troubador Publishing Ltd, Leicester, UK
Printed by Cromwell Press Ltd, Trowbridge, Wilts

Matador is an imprint of Troubador Publishing

CONTENTS

DEDICATION

I dedicate this book firstly to my wife Betty, to whom I owe 62 years of unbelievably happy married life, and whose constant love and loyalty, care during illness and support at all times, have been indispensable elements in my life.

Also my mother, Rose, whose courage and determination saved my life and the life of my brother, Franklyn, when Yokohama was devastated by the great Kanto earthquake; and whose dedication to our family continued throughout our lives.

To my son, Robert Gordon Upton, M.A., M.Sc. (Oxon), A.C.A., who helped me in the proof reading of the drafts, and whose critique was of invaluable assistance.

My grand daughter, Lucy, with her computer skills, has been an enthusiastic helper, in the initial design of the cover, and in her project to promote the sale of the books.

Finally, I remember with gratitude the sacrifice of those seamen of the Merchant Navy and our comrades in the Regular and Reserve Naval forces, and the seamen of other nationalities, the airmen of Coastal Command, the gunners of the Royal Maritime Artillery and naval D.E.M.S personnel, and all others who died during the long and unremitting Battle of the Atlantic, and other theatres of war. The restless oceans are their shrouds, and their final resting places known only to the God they worshipped.

Vernon G.A. Upton
May 2004

FOREWORD

Captain N. Lloyd-Edwards, GCStJ, RD*, JP, RNR,
H.M. Lord-Lieutenant for the County of South Glamorgan

The Welsh Festival of Remembrance is held in St. David's Hall, Cardiff, each year one week before the Festival in the Royal Albert Hall, London. The format of both is very similar. Some four years ago, the author attended the Welsh Festival and was saddened to hear a small group of younger service personnel make derogatory remarks about the civilian status of the Merchant Navy when the audience gave a standing ovation when their banner party entered the arena. Earlier that year they had been awarded the Freedom of the City of Cardiff, the first City to do so in recognition of their contribution to our country, particularly in times of war.

The author was so aggrieved that people should be so ignorant of what the Merchant Navy had done that he resolved to write this book. Research took over four years, and there is no doubt that this will be a source of reference to historians. But more than that, it is a story of human endeavour in some of the worst possible scenarios.

As with all human nature, there is a mixture of courage and inadequacy, of brilliant leadership and indifferent command, of devotion to duty and self-interest, pigheadedness and tolerance. But through it all, one cannot but be impressed that so many ordinary men should have risen to the challenges which few could have anticipated and, drawing upon their training, discipline and devotion to the cause, managed to carry out their duty, sometimes in the most horrendous circumstances.

Young readers will have difficulty in understanding the primitive and dangerous conditions in which these men had to work, be it manual handling of heavy anchor cables in a dark chain locker, to fighting the onslaught of ice, turbulent seas and enemy submarines.

As one who served under the White Ensign, I also salute our brothers who have served under the Blue and Red Dusters.

I am proud to know the author who, in a typically self-effacing way, is donating any surplus over production costs to charitable causes, and I wholeheartedly commend it to you.

May 2004

SHIP LOSSES

U-BOAT SINKINGS AND LOSSES

1

INTRODUCTION AND ACKNOWLEDGEMENTS

The title of this narrative is derived from the Naval Prayer, which is read or recited by the Captain, Chaplain, First Lieutenant, or other officer, on the quarter decks of ships of the Royal Navy when the ships' companies are mustered for Divisions.

Even now, when I recite the Prayer to myself, I sustain sentiments of nostalgia, and of intense pride, to have served at sea when the fleets of our Royal Navy made our country pre-eminent throughout the world, and the ships of our Mercantile Marine probably outnumbered the combined fleets of all other nations.

> "O Eternal Lord God, who alone spreadeth out the Heavens and ruleth the raging of the sea; who hast compassed the waters with bounds until day and night come to an end: be pleased to receive into Thy Almighty and most gracious protection the persons of us, Thy servants, and the fleet in which we serve. Preserve us from the dangers of the sea and from the violence of the enemy, that we may be a safeguard to our most gracious Sovereign Lord, King George (Sovereign Lady, Queen Elizabeth) and his (her) Dominions, and a security for such as pass on the seas upon their lawful occasions; that the inhabitants of our island may in peace and quietness serve Thee, our God, and that we may return in safety to enjoy the blessings of the land, with the fruits of our labours, and with a thankful remembrance of Thy Mercies, to praise and glorify Thy Most Holy Name. Through Jesus Christ, our Lord. Amen".

I am proud to have known, and revere the memory of, so many fine shipmates with whom I served during nine years service in the Merchant Service (re-named and now known as the Merchant Navy), who were lost at sea during World War II.

The names of over 25,000 merchant seamen who died in the service of our country in World War Two are recorded around the perimeter of the memorial amphitheatre at Tower Hill, and the names of 14,879 who died during the 1914-1918 war are engraved on plaques within the columns of the enclosure overlooking the amphitheatre. The official publication "British Vessels Lost at Sea 1939-45" shows the losses in merchant seamen killed as 29,994. Captain S.W. Roskill, D.S.C., R.N., in his admirable book "The Navy at War 1939 -1945", gives the totals as 30,248 merchant seamen and 51,578 Royal Navy personnel killed.

We should also remember with gratitude and pride, our allies, particularly the fine Scandinavian and Greek seamen who shared with us the horrors of the war at sea from the earliest period of hostilities, and later, the seamen of the U.S.A. The sea provides a common resting place for all those brave and dedicated men.

I dedicate this account of what has been a fruitful and eventful life, firstly to my devoted wife, Betty, whose constant love, care, companionship and support have been an inspiration to me, and which have been indispensable elements in my life. She has been like a ray of sunshine in my life, from the moment when we met.

When I met Betty quite by chance on 11 January 1941, I was captivated by her charm, happy disposition, and irrepressible good humour. As I became more closely acquainted with her, I discovered her courage in adversity, constant loyalty, and strong moral fibre and character. I have no doubt that I owe to her the long life I have enjoyed. When I was discharged medically unfit for further sea service in 1945, her dedicated nursing and care helped to restore me to better health. Her constant devotion enabled me to enter into what was – for me – the uncharted arena of life ashore, so remote from the regime of life at sea. Throughout a life of over fifty years in industry and commerce, Betty has always been there, through periods of depressing poverty, and times that have been happier and more plentiful. During our happy marriage extending for over sixty years, she has been the indispensable element. I owe everything to Betty.

I also pay tribute to my mother, Rose Upton, whose memory I will always cherish. When by a miracle my brother Franklyn and I survived the holocaust of the catastrophic Great Kanto earthquake (Kanto Dai - Shinsai) that occurred at noon on Saturday 1 September 1923, the devotion and courage of our mother undoubtedly saved our lives. She protected her two infant children with her body, when our home disintegrated and burst into flames. Although a tiny woman, she drew on reserves of strength and determination to carry us to safety through the inferno and devastation of what was left of Yokohama. Our cook and amahs were trapped in the ruins of the kitchen of our house, and perished in the fire. Over 140,000 people died in the earthquake that destroyed half of Yokohama, and devastated seven square miles of Tokyo. The dedication and love of our mother continued throughout the days of our childhood and youth, and have been an example and an inspiration to us.

My father instilled in me by example his loyalty to our country, and a fierce independence and honesty. Although we were in fundamental disagreement on some aspects of attitude, there was much in him that I admired and respected.

My son, Robert Gordon Upton, M.A., M.Sc. (Oxon), A.C.A., has been of great help to me in the proof reading of this narrative. One of my ambitions has been to secure for him the benefit of the highest standard of education. His recommendations, suggestions and critique, based on his academic training, have been invaluable; and for which I record my grateful thanks.

I also record my thanks to John and Marion Clarkson of Ships in Focus, Alex Duncan (deceased) and the National Maritime Museum, for their permission to use ship photographs from their libraries.

I am indebted to one of my close friends, Wing Commander John Irfon Davies, C.B.E., who stimulated me into writing this narrative, as the result of our conversation over the dinner table. Since then, he has persisted in his encouragement.

During my life at sea, I served with many fine shipmates, some of whom became my close friends. The closest were my two fellow apprentices, who shared the confines of the cramped amidships accommodation in the half deck of *Appledore*. William Phillip (Jumbo) James, my cabin mate from 1936 until 1938, when he completed his period of four years on indentures; and Phillip Gordon Harris, who joined the ship in Vancouver, and with whom I served from 1938 until 1940. Both lost their lives during the war. They were good friends and shipmates.

This narrative traces in brief detail the history of my family, and our early lives in Japan and Canada. However, its main theme has been to present a perspective of life in merchant ships in times of peace and war; initially through the eyes of an apprentice officer, and then from the

3

bridge of a merchant ship throughout 20 ocean passages before 3 September 1939 and 27 during the war period from 1939 until 1945.

Very few officers of merchant ships kept diaries. Therefore, I have had to carry out substantial research, through the medium of a number of publications, and to delve into the innermost elements of memory. This has not been an easy task, because no publication encapsulates the information in complete detail. I have referred to nine books on the subject, in order to prepare a chronological record of events in which I was closely involved, or which occurred in the ocean areas at the time when ships in which I served were at sea. These books were:

Lloyd's War Losses, Volume 1 lists in chronological order losses by war causes of ships of all nationalities.

British Vessels Lost at Sea 1939–45 by H.M.S.O., covers in detail the losses of British Royal Navy and merchant ships

The Navy at War 1939–1945 by Captain S.W. Roskill, D.S.C., R.N. (Retired), has been a most helpful source of information and research.

The World's Merchant Fleets 1939 by Roger Jordan, provides even more comprehensive detail in covering ships of non-UK registry, but is restricted to those afloat prior to World War Two. It records losses due to maritime hazards, collisions in convoy, vessels sunk as the result of weather hazard, and other causes not resulting from enemy action.

The Allied Convoy System 1939–1945 by Arnold Hague, gives useful information on convoys and their losses, but does not include stragglers or ships otherwise detached or dispersed from convoy.

British Merchant Ship Losses to Axis Submarines by Alan J. Tennent, is a most comprehensive and informative publication, but omits ships lost to aircraft, mines, or surface ship attack.

Axis Submarine Successes of World War Two by Jurgen Rohwer, presents the perspective from under water, and helps to fill the gaps in other records. This is useful, because the U-Boat reports show the time of attack, which has been very helpful.

Business in Great Waters by John Terraine, not only covers naval events in the 1914–1918 and 1939–1945 wars in comprehensive detail, but also provides a wealth of background information.

U-Boats Destroyed by Paul Kemp, presented the final and very useful avenue in the chain of research.

Reference to, and cross-reference between, these publications has enabled me to clarify events that occurred during the periods when my name was included on the articles of the ships on which I served during the war. Many other publications, too numerous to mention, provided an insight into the war at sea. The narrative therefore covers events that occurred during the ocean passages of the nine ships in which I served; and other significant maritime events. Some of the events that are related were well publicised at the time – and since – but may not be known to those to whom the war at sea has been something to read about, or watch on television.

All the books to which I have referred have been written by able individuals well qualified in research, and some by those who experienced life at sea. In this book, I have tried to portray my life at sea before the war, and as an officer from the bridge of a merchant ship under war conditions.

The exercise of the rigid censorship rules during the war ensured that knowledge of events was restricted to news reports, our own personal experiences, or the experiences of others as recounted to us. Our ignorance of the overall picture of the enormous casualties in ships and men served to maintain the morale of the participants at a relatively high level. However, towards the end of the war there were significant indications of what may be termed "fraying around the edges", particularly among officers, who were more conversant with events than other ranks. In particular, the strains imposed on Masters of merchant ships were immense, coupled with the lonely nature of life in command. Hence, a number resorted to the comfort of the bottle. In addition, the substantial difference in ages between Masters and their subordinates may have made them less able, physically, to withstand the stresses they had to sustain.

There did not appear to be an intense hatred of the officers and crews of the enemy U-Boats. In total war, merchant ships and their crews are conceived to be legitimate targets. A steel sheet carried by a merchant ship is a potential plate for a warship, and an aluminium ingot contains sufficient material from which to manufacture many fighting aircraft. International convention demanded that submarines were obliged to surface and warn merchant ships before attacking them. However, immediately after the declaration of war, ships were armed with anti-submarine and anti-aircraft weapons. The threat of such weaponry made surfacing to challenge a merchant ship extremely hazardous, even though the defensive armaments were obsolete weapons manned by relatively unskilled gunners.

Admiral Donitz perceived from the beginning that the war would be won or lost on the shipping lanes leading to our island. The U-boats under his command came very close to achieving success. Moreover, in 1942, when he was given the infamous order by Hitler that survivors were to be killed, the order given to the U-boat commanders was of such an ambiguous nature that the instruction did not result in the elimination of all survivors, as intended by Hitler. However, during my researches into the sinking of merchant ships, there is evidence of atrocities that were not, or could not, be recorded because there were no survivors. It is recorded that one submarine commander was duly indicted for war crimes and executed. I have no doubt that a substantial number of the perpetrators of heinous atrocities were neither indicted nor punished. The German U-boats were well commanded – certainly in the first two years of the war – and bravely fought. We had no love for them, and certainly did not mourn their loss.

The enemy had built 1,162 U-Boats by the end of the war, of which 784 were sunk or destroyed. The enemy records reflect that 40,100 officers and men had passed through U-boat training, and undertook operational service. Their casualties amounted to 30,246 killed or died of their wounds.

The conditions, under which we lived, particularly on North Atlantic convoys, were sometimes indescribable. They were even worse for our escorts, particularly the corvettes. There is no doubt that these tiny escort vessels were a significant element in our winning the Battle of the Atlantic. Those who have served at sea in the tempestuous weather of the North Atlantic, where ships and seamen encounter eight months of winter and four months of awful weather, can never cease to marvel at the sea-keeping qualities of these sturdy craft and the courage and fortitude of their brave and dedicated crews. On many occasions, all we could see of them was the tops of their masts in a maelstrom of mountainous seas, rolling almost on their beam-ends, and pitching so heavily that they showed their keels as far aft as their bridges.

When we were keeping watch during blinding snowstorms, hurricane force winds and precipitous seas, we remarked to each other "what must it be like for the poor devils in the Jerry U-boats?" However, bad weather was sometimes a blessing, because it made the buggers shelter from the weather, well below the surface.

Many statistics have been compiled, and can be found in the publications that have provided reference elements in my research. I am indebted to the authors for their painstaking research, which has helped to stimulate apparently long-lost memories of events.

Without intending to subject a reader to pages of statistics, I have endeavoured to cover each ocean passage with a statistical record and a brief analysis of events that occurred in a convoy passage of between two and three weeks. The casualties in seamen killed were truly awesome. It is helpful – perhaps essential – for a reader to know something of life at sea between the wars, the rigorous regime under which we worked, the intense training to which we were subjected, and the great pride which we sustained towards our ships and the service in which we served. Our country was fortunate to have possessed a Merchant Navy of over 100,000 professional seamen at the start of hostilities. The basic skills of their profession had been learned. The special skills of handling large numbers of ships in close formation in convoy had to be assimilated, together with training in the use of defensive armaments. Always there was the uncompromising North Atlantic weather of frequent gales, fog, blinding snowstorms and precipitous seas. We had all that in times of peace. The war added the combined hazards of the normally unused northern route, darkened ships, and the constant menace of attack. This made life at sea during the war a physical and mental stress.

We shared a common bond with the officers and men of the regular Royal Navy, R.N.R. and R.N.V.R. Life at sea was our chosen profession and we were intensely proud of the fact that our training in terms of competence and discipline was of the highest standard. If we survived, we hoped to resume in the careers interrupted by the war.

Regrettably, a very high percentage of those who were in the services before the war were killed, severely injured, or made unfit for further service, as the result of injury, stress or illness. The survivors were treated in a most callous manner by the establishment represented by the Ministry of War Pensions, and other government departments. It was a tragic indictment on our system.

Some of the opinions and comments expressed about the dinosaurs in Whitehall may be extreme. These were the views of officers and men being hacked to pieces by a remorseless and implacable enemy. It is the widely held opinion of officers of merchant ships that those in Whitehall did not appreciate the vital importance of proper convoy protection until

Phillip Gordon Harris
Date and name of ship unknown

William Phillip 'Jumbo' James
Date and name of ship unknown

Johnny Hay
Lady Glanley – Convoy HX90
Lost with all hands, 2/12/40

Good friends and fine shipmates, all killed during the war
"We shall remember them"

late in 1942, when they woke up and began to implement effective countermeasures. They had on record the U-Boat onslaught of 1917 and 1918 as a model, yet were unprepared for the inevitable repetition of those events on a massively increased scale. It was Field Marshall Haig and his "Somme complex" repeated. It was no picnic for those of us who served and suffered. Our story should be told, and I hope that this narrative will fulfil that requirement.

Edward Carpenter. a seaman, expresses the sentiments of Merchant seamen poignantly in the book of poems by Dr. Ronald Hope entitled *Voices from the Sea*. Harrap of London first published the book in 1977 in association with the Marine Society. The poem is reproduced with the permission of the Director of the Marine Society, Captain J.J. Howard, M.B.E., F.N.I., R.N.

Merchant Seamen
Edward Carpenter, Seaman

I've read about soldiers and sailors,
Of infantry, airmen and tanks,
Of battleships, corvettes and cruisers,
Of Anzacs, and Froggies and Yanks:
But there's one other man to remember
Who was present at many a fray,
He wears neither medals nor ribbons
And derides any show or display.

I'm talking of A.B.'s and firemen,
Of stewards and greasers and cooks,
Who manned the big steamers in convoy
(You won't read about them in books).
No uniform gay were they dressed in,
Nor marched with their colours unfurled:
They steamed out across the wide oceans
And travelled all over the world.

Their history goes back through the ages –
A record of which to be proud –
And the bones of their forefathers moulder
With naught but the deep for a shroud.
For armies have swept on to victory
O'er the bodies of those who have died;
'Tis thus that the nations do battle
For country, and freedom and pride.

In thousands they sailed from their homeland,
From Liverpool, Hull, and the Clyde;
To London, and Bristol, and Cardiff
They came back again on the tide.
An old "four-point-seven" their safeguard–
What nice easy prey for the Huns
Who trailed them with bombers and U-boats
And sank them with "tin fish" and guns".

The epic of gallant *Otaki*,
That grim forlorn hope *Jervis Bay*,
Who fought to the last and were beaten-
But they joined the illustrious array
Whose skeletons lie 'neath the waters,
Whose deeds are remembered today,
And their glory will shine undiminished
Long after our flesh turns to clay.

They landed the Anzacs at Suvla
And stranded the old *River Clyde*,
Off Dunkirk they gathered the remnants
(And still they were not satisfied),
They battled their way through to Malta
And rescued the troops off Malay;
They brought the Eighth Army munitions
And took all the prisoners away.

And others "signed on" in the tankers
And loaded crude oil and octane–
The lifeblood of warships and engines,
Of mechanised transport and plane.
But these were the U-Boats chief victims;
What death they were called on to face
As men were engulfed by infernos
In ships that were "sunk without trace."

They were classed a non-combatant service
Civilians who fought without guns–
And many times they'd have welcomed
A chance of a crack at the Huns.
But somehow in spite of this drawback
The steamers still sailed and arrived,
And they fed fifty millions of people–
And right to the end we survived.

And now that the turmoil has ended,
Our enemies vanquished and fled,
We'll pray that the living will foster
The spirit of those who are dead.
When the next generation takes over,
This country we now hold in lease
Will be theirs – may they cherish its freedom
And walk down the pathways of peace.

When the Master of Masters holds judgment
And the Devil's dark angels have flown,
When the clerk of the heavenly council
Decrees that the names shall be shown,
They will stand out in glittering letters
Inscribed with the blood they have shed:
Names of ships – and the seamen who manned them;
Then the ocean can give up its dead.

2

EARLY LIFE IN JAPAN

My parents had told me that their respective families settled in the Far East in the middle of the nineteenth century; but as a youth I did not question them about specific details. Therefore, the information I have derived is the result of my researches into various sources, and is not complete.

The members of the Whymark family of my maternal grandmother had been prominent Freemasons. Reference to the Grand Librarian of the United Grand Lodge of England proved to be fruitful. It is recorded that my great great uncle, George Whymark, was initiated in O Tentosama Lodge, Yokohama, on 23 March 1870, being then described as a Chief Steward, P. & O. ship *Ottowa*. He is then recorded as joining Nippon Lodge, Yedo, on 17 June 1871, and is described as a Teacher of English, so by that time he had taken up residence in Japan. He then joined Rising Sun Lodge, Kobe, in 1873, and was Master of the Lodge in 1875.

His son, George Harvey Whymark, was born in 1865 in the United Kingdom, and was initiated by his father in Rising Sun Lodge on 15 January 1887, being described as a Merchant aged 22. He was Master of the Lodge in the years 1888, 1890 and 1905, so his progression was meteoric. He was a Founder Master of Albion in the Far East Lodge, Kobe, and became a member of Tokio Lodge and Lodge Hiogo and Osaka. He was installed as District Grand Master, Japan, in 1911 and held office until 1923.

He initiated my father, Gordon Nelson Roderigue Upton, in Rising Sun Lodge on 21 May 1913, my father being described as a Clerk age 23. After returning following military service during the 1914–1918 war, my father was installed as Master of the Lodge in 1921, the date of my birth.

Japan was ruled by feudal Shoguns until the accession of the Emperor Mutsuhito (Meiji Tenno) in 1868, when the country was opened to Western trade and industrial influence. George Whymark and his family, which included his daughter, my paternal grandmother, were among the

Right Worshipful Brother George Harvey Whymark
District Grand Master, Japan, 1911 to 1923

first European settlers in Japan.

My paternal grandfather, Franklin Upton, was a quartermaster on one of the British ships that began to trade regularly after Japan was opened to western influence. He settled in the country with his wife. He appears to have been an itinerant character, and the last record I have of him is in 1914, when he was resident in Seoul, Korea, described as a merchant. He was an inveterate gambler, gaining and losing fortunes, and I understand that he died in Shanghai in China.

My father was born in Japan on 3 March 1889 as one of a number of brothers. His mother died when he was an infant; and he was taken into the care of his uncle, George Harvey Whymark and their family, with whom he stayed until adulthood.

My maternal grandfather, David James, was a Master Mariner, serving in command of vessels engaged in trade with the Far East. He settled in Japan, where he was appointed as the first Inland Sea Pilot. His family consisted of eight sons and four daughters, of whom my mother was the third eldest daughter, born in Kobe on 19 August 1898. I know very little about my uncles, but enjoyed a close relationship with my Aunt Dorothy after she had settled in England and Wales after World War Two; and also with my Aunt Margaret, who had married an American businessman, Louis Howe, and settled in California. Aunt Margaret spent several months as a guest in our home when on holiday in the United Kingdom. Her eldest son, Milton, distinguished himself in the United States Marine Corps in the war in the Pacific, and continued serving during the war in Korea, where he was wounded and invalided out of service. His mother told me that he had been awarded the Medal of Honour, the highest American gallantry award, but I have never verified this.

Captain David James was known to be a typical Victorian martinet head of his family, and was held in great respect in the Far East, particularly by the Japanese. He remained in Japan after the outbreak of hostilities following the attack on Pearl Harbour, and died during the war. He was well treated by the Japanese, because of their great respect for him. The earthquake divided his large family. Three of his sons remained in Japan, three settled in the U.K., and one in Australia. One daughter – Elizabeth – remained in Japan: Margaret settled in California: Dorothy settled in Australia, and my mother, Rose, settled in Vancouver, Canada.

The strong seafaring traditions, and association with the shipping industry throughout our families, were strong influences that stimulated my interest in the sea and ships early in life; and eventually resulted in my deciding to pursue a career at sea. I have never regretted having made that decision.

3

THE GREAT WAR
1914–1918

During his childhood, youth, and early adulthood, my father lived with the Whymark family, enjoying the typical privileged life of a member of the European community. He joined the shipping and ship-owning company of Dodwells, where he was employed in 1913 as a mercantile assistant and was in that job on the date of the outbreak of the war on 4 August 1914.

He and my uncles, David and George James, took passage on a ship to Vladivostock, and travelled by the Trans Siberian Railway to Moscow, and thereafter to England, where they all joined army infantry units. It is possible that my uncle, Walter James, may have been a member of the party, but I am not certain. My uncles distinguished themselves during the war and David James was awarded the Military Cross for gallantry in action.

My efforts to trace the war record of my father have been hampered by the fact that the Ministry of Defence have stated that it was necessary to "weed" the personal files of officers during the inter war period, particularly in the 1930's, mainly to save storage space, due to the large numbers of files and documents held. Hence, the information extracted from their records has been meagre.

THE ROYAL IRISH FUSILIERS

The Ministry of Defence records show that Gordon Nelson Roderique Upton, born 3 March 1889, place of birth Kobe, Japan, trade Japanese Merchant, height 5 ft. 9 1/2 inches, weight 156 lbs, enlisted in the Royal Fusiliers at London as number 19/5803 on a Short Service Engagement on

17

28 December 1914. He was posted to the 19th Battalion on the same date. His next of kin is recorded as his father, Franklin Upton of Kavanaugh & Co. Seoul, Korea, Japan.

After basic training he was posted to a Commission on 13 May 1915, and on the following day was appointed to a Short Service Commission as a Second Lieutenant in the Royal Irish Fusiliers 3rd (Reserve Battalion). From then the Ministry of Defence records show a gap of two and a half years to 28 November 1917, but the records of the Royal Irish Fusiliers show my father as one of the officers of the 1st Battalion under the command of Lieutenant Colonel A.R. Burrowes (later Major General A.R. Burrowes, C.M.G., D.S.O.) However, on tracing the actions in which the regiment participated in the 1914-1918 war, and from the information derived from conversations with my father, it is clear that his service with the 1st Battalion was of short duration; and that he served as an officer in the 2nd Battalion from late 1915 until 1917.

The 1st Regular Battalion formed part of 10th Brigade, 4th Division, and the 2nd Battalion part of the 82nd Brigade, 27th Division, of the British Expeditionary Force, the 1st Battalion being thrown into the line at Le Cateau, to cover the retreat from Mons.

The 2nd Battalion joined the B.E.F. at the end of 1914, and acquitted itself with distinction in the bayonet charge counter attack at St. Eloi, of which Rudyard Kipling wrote:

There were lads from Galway, Louth and Meath,
Who went to their death with a joke in their teeth.

The regiment originated as the 87th and 89th Regiments of Foot in 1793, and subsequently have distinguished themselves as the 1st and 2nd Battalions of the Royal Irish Fusiliers. Known as the *Faughs* from their battle cry *Faugh-a-ballagh*, meaning "Stand aside", the regiment distinguished itself in one of the most terrible bayonet fights ever witnessed, at the Battle of Barrosa in 1811, where Sergeant Masterson wrested the Imperial Eagle standard from a French officer, with the immortal words "Be Jabers, boys, I have the cuckoo".

My father went into the line late in May 1915 in the area of St. Julien, where the 1st and 2nd Battalions were on the right and left of their divisional fronts, with a cavalry regiment between them. On 24 May, the enemy attacked with heavy artillery and small arms fire, accompanied by billowing clouds of chlorine gas. It was here that the order was given "piss on your blankets, boys", and the infantry held their positions with this

Captain Gordon Nelson Roderique Upton
Royal Irish Fusilliers and
Rose Upton
Kobe, Japan, 11 May 1919

makeshift protection from the poison gas. Intense trench fighting continued through to July, when the whole division moved to the less active Somme sector; and in September the 2nd Battalion was moved to Marseilles, en route to Salonika in Macedonia, with the 27th Division. The 1st Division remained on the Western Front.

Throughout most of 1915 the 5th and 6th Battalions formed part of 31st Brigade, 10th Irish Division, during the campaign in Gallipoli, where both regiments were decimated by casualties and disease and were withdrawn for re-grouping in September 1915. Subsequently, the two battalions moved to Salonika, where they joined the 2nd Battalion, then part of 82nd Brigade. During most of 1916 and 1917 the 2nd, 5th and 6th Battalions remained in contact with the Bulgar forces in Macedonia; and on 1 November orders were given to amalgamate the decimated 5th and 6th Battalions, and the three battalions were incorporated into the 10th Irish Division.

The records show that my father was promoted to Lieutenant on 13 December 1916, when serving on the Macedonian front, where he was mentioned in despatches.

The 10th Irish Division, including the 2nd and 5th/6th Battalions, left for Egypt in August and September 1917, and joined the army of General Sir Edmund Allenby in the line between Beersheba and Gaza. There the two Battalions, as part of 31st Brigade, distinguished themselves again in the charge on the Turkish positions at Wadi-esh-Sheria on 6 November 1917. The division continued in action against the Turkish army, until the capture of Jerusalem in December 1917.

My father had been suffering severely from the effects of the chlorine gas attacks, to which the battalion had been subjected at Ypres in May 1915, and from the privations suffered on the Western Front and during nearly two years in the disease ridden area of the Struma front in Macedonia. The records show that he disembarked at Boulogne on 28 November 1917. He was initially posted to the Labour Corps 13th Depot and was then posted to the Chinese Depot on 15 December 1917. I have to presume that this posting constituted retirement from front line duties, due to serious deterioration in his health. My father spoke fluent Japanese and was able to converse in Chinese, so it is likely that these attributes prompted his transfer to the Chinese Labour Battalion, which undertook road making and trench digging on the Western Front, under the command of Chinese speaking British officers.

He then held the rank of Captain, but the date of his promotion is not shown in the Ministry of Defence records. He was invalided out on 17 May 1918, suffering from the effects of chlorine gas, shell shock, and the privations suffered in the campaigns in Macedonia and Palestine. After a period in military hospitals, he returned to Japan in early 1919 and married my mother in Kobe on 10 May 1919.

My earliest recollections as a child of six years of age were when my mother was forced to call upon her two young children to assist her in restoring my father's breathing when he was gasping for breath. This occurred frequently, usually during the night. We would help our mother to lift our father to a sitting position, with one child on each arm and my mother pumping his chest, until he started breathing normally. This continued throughout our early lives but became easier for us as we grew older and stronger and more capable of dealing with his weight.

Despite his experiences, he volunteered again in 1939, at the age of 50; but was rejected because he was over age for military service. In any case, he did not stand a chance of passing the medical inspection. However, when Pearl Harbour was attacked on 7 December 1941, he volunteered again; and was accepted by the Royal Canadian Navy in its Intelligence Section, in view of his fluency in the Japanese language and intimate knowledge of its written characters. He held rank as a Lieutenant in the R.C.N.V.R. for over three years, during which time his intelligence signals unit kept track of Admiral Yamamoto until he was hunted down and killed when his aircraft was intercepted by U.S.A. aircraft.

He related a traumatic and unforgettable experience, which occurred when his regiment was in the line on the Western Front. This caused him severe nightmares. His platoon was engaged in a trench-raiding excursion, which usually involved an officer, a non-commissioned officer and a small detachment of about six private soldiers. The usual weapons for an officer were a revolver, trench dagger and a club designed by the armourer – an entrenching tool handle weighted with a ball of lead and wrapped in barbed wire. The trench dagger was in the form of a knuckle-duster, to which was fixed a short blade. The other ranks carried rifles, fixed bayonets and grenades. The aim was to isolate a section of enemy trench, throw grenades down the dugouts, and hope to capture a Jerry for interrogation and unit identification.

When returning to our lines, the party was illuminated by star shells and attacked by the enemy, suffering a number of casualties. My father was caught in the barbed wire in no-man's-land and attacked by an enemy soldier who attempted to bayonet him. Instinctively, he grasped the rifle and fixed bayonet of a dead comrade, and propped this up to parry the attack. The momentum of the charge of the enemy soldier caused him to fall on the point of the upright bayonet, which penetrated his throat, and drove though his skull and out through the back of his head. This left the two combatants face-to-face, and covered with blood. My father remembered in vivid detail that the soldier was a young man, and his recollection of the event haunted him for the rest of his life. As a youth, I could envisage the macabre scenario – the mud and desolation of no-man's-land, dimly lit by the guttering light of a flare, and the two combatants locked in a struggle to the death.

Although he had suffered during the 1914 – 1918 War, my father remained intensely patriotic, and this patriotism was instilled into me. From an early age, we attended the annual Memorial in Victory Park in North Vancouver on Armistice Day. He also selected innumerable books on military history and supplemented these with his own experiences.

He was an accomplished raconteur, relating his experiences as a platoon and company officer of an infantry regiment. His two favourite stories related to the ubiquitous character, "Tommy Atkins".

A battalion moving up to the line near Ypres met a battalion moving into reserve billets. The following conversation took place between one private soldier wearily trudging through the pouring rain towards the line, and another private soldier, equally wearily trudging into reserve.

First Soldier:	*"'ow far is it to bleedin' Wipers, mite ?"*
Second Soldier:	*"Five kilometres as the crow flies, mite".*
First Soldier:	*"We don't want to know 'ow far the bleeder flies, mite, but 'ow far he f———g 'ops".*

Another story, about a private soldier in the trenches, who had received a cake from his mother.

Soldier without cake:	*"'Ow about a piece of your cike, mite?"*
Soldier with cake:	*"Yus, mite, but do you like ends?"*
Soldier without cake:	*"Not much".*

Soldier with cake removes bayonet from scabbard and cuts cake in half. *"Ard luck then, mite, 'cos me and me mite does".*

My father was an unforgettable character, but an enigma. I was influenced by his inherent honesty and unswerving loyalty to our country but disagreed vehemently with his Victorian attitude towards those whom he perceived to be his inferiors, which included all who had not enjoyed his relatively privileged background. He sustained a particularly cavalier and condescending attitude towards the female sex. I was aggravated beyond measure when he once said of my mother "What does she know about that, son? She is only a woman". He averred that marital infidelity was the natural prerogative of husbands, but was a heinous sin when committed by their wives. In this element of his character, we disagreed profoundly, and we tended to grow apart, particularly when he objected to my friends, who were in his words, "working class". This may have been the rule in the attitudes that prevailed in the Victorian and Edwardian eras, and in the Far East. However, they could not be tolerated in the egalitarian society in western Canada where we lived. Despite his eccentricity, and a forthright manner approaching rudeness, he was a respected member of the community in which we lived, where he was known as "Snob Upton". My mother adapted to Canadian society, but my father never changed throughout his life.

4

THE GREAT KANTO EARTHQUAKE, 1 SEPTEMBER 1923

Before and after my birth in January 1921, and the birth of my brother, Franklyn Nelson in March 1922, our family lived at 17 Kitano-2-Chome, in the city of Kobe. We moved to Yokohama, when my father transferred his place of work to the city of Tokyo. He commuted daily by train between Yokohama and Tokyo. We lived a relatively affluent life, employing a cook, house amah and baby amah – Kani-San. My parents enjoyed a wide social life in common with the non-oriental residents of the country, mainly British, American and European. Our servants spoke only a little English, so the domestic conversation was in the Japanese language. I can still remember the few words of Japanese taught to me as a child by Kani-San, to whom I was joined by a mutual devotion. She taught we a few words of greeting and how to count from one to ten. It must have been an idyllic life, but I was too young to remember much.

By all accounts, Saturday 1 September was an oppressively hot and sultry day. My father had travelled to Tokyo by train in the morning. In the late morning, the cook and amahs were in the kitchen preparing lunch. It was the usual custom for the baby amah, Kani-San, to wash my brother and myself before our meals; but on that occasion, she was helping the cook and house amah, while my mother was in the bathroom washing us.

The great Kanto Earthquake (Kanto-Dai-Shensai) that occurred at two minutes before noon on 1 September 1923 has been described as the worst natural calamity in history, particularly when taking into account the subsequent destructive after shocks, tidal waves, land slides, explosions and fires. It is recorded that 140,000 people died; but in view of the elementary census records kept at that time, this is bound to be an understatement. The devastation was catastrophic, with 7 square miles of Tokyo burned, and half of Yokohama destroyed.

Our fragile Japanese built house collapsed within minutes of the commencement of the first tremor. From early childhood, my mother had been taught the elementary precautions to be taken in the event of earthquakes, and had experienced many minor earth tremors during her lifetime. Although then only 25 years old, she possessed an inherent calmness under stress; and moved into the doorway of the bathroom to stand within the door frame, protecting her children with her body. The house collapsed about us, and the door frame protruded through the roof, enabling her to pull herself and her children through the wreckage and into the garden. Although bruised and shaken, we were not seriously injured.

The severe tremor had turned the hot cooking stove over, trapping the cook. The house amah and baby amah tried to free the cook; but they were all trapped in the wreckage of the kitchen, which immediately caught fire. Within minutes, the whole house was a blazing inferno, with the hapless servants trapped in the kitchen, screaming in the conflagration.

Several neighbours arrived on the scene, but nothing could be done to save the servants, or others trapped in the blazing ruins of adjacent houses. By then the electric cables, gas mains and oil tanks had ruptured, huge fissures had opened up in the roads and fires were raging everywhere.

My mother was a tiny woman, only 4 ft 11 inches in height and weighing less than 8 stones (under 100 pounds), but possessing astonishing courage. I was then 2 years and 9 months old, and able to walk, but my brother was only 1 year and 6 months old. My mother carried Franklyn and led me by the hand. She made the decision to make for the Bluff, an area of high ground several miles away on the outskirts of the city. After hours of staggering with one child in her arms and the other holding her hand, she reached the top of the Bluff, overlooking Yokohama Bay. Here, a group of men had organised rescue equipment, including ropes, which they used to lower survivors to the edges of the bay. Lifeboats from ships in the harbour then carried the survivors to the ships, which provided medical and other help.

The oil and gas tanks had then caught fire, and Yokohama was a sea of flames. Thousands of people sought refuge in one of the main open spaces of the city, but the heat of the conflagration was so intense that huge numbers perished from suffocation due to the lack of oxygen.

Tokyo was almost destroyed at the same time. My father encountered similar devastation in the streets: buildings demolished, power lines destroyed, oil tanks and gas reservoirs smashed and burning, and everywhere huge fires. Since all road and rail transport facilities had been destroyed, he decided to walk to Yokohama, arriving at the ruins of our home on the following morning. He was unable to obtain any information about the fate of his family. Therefore, he joined in the rescue work in the hope that he might find someone who was able to give him information about our fate or whereabouts. In the meantime, we were aboard R.M.S. Empress of Canada, at anchor in Yokohama harbour.

All ships had been instructed to remain at their anchorages or berths, because of the dangers of fire in the huge quantities of floating oil on the sea. All flames on board had been extinguished because of fire and explosion risk. I have been told that we remained in this volatile environment for a number of days, but not exactly how long. Then, fortuitously, my father boarded Empress of Canada, where he remained for several days among the many hundreds of survivors, without knowing that his family were aboard the same ship. Eventually, when on the open deck, he encountered us; and our family was quite miraculously re-united.

A number of members of our respective families chose to remain; but many decided to leave. My uncles Ernest, Frederick, Leonard and Walter remained in Japan. Uncles George and David travelled to the United Kingdom. Uncle Albert and Aunt Dorothy settled in Australia, Aunt Margaret and her family in the U.S.A. Most of the Whymark families settled in the United Kingdom and South Africa. Therefore, our large combined families eventually settled in many parts of the world, and as the result the large close family community was dispersed, and as the result lost contact with each other.

The family members who had not resided in Tokyo and Yokohama had been relatively unaffected by the trauma of the great Kanto earthquake. Those who had survived the holocaust, and who had lost their worldly possessions, remained on the ships that had provided refuge for them. My parents decided to leave Japan, and took passage on R.M.S. Empress of Canada, bound for Vancouver.

5

EARLY YEARS IN CANADA
THE GREAT DEPRESSION

R.M.S. Empress of Canada arrived in Vancouver late in the month of September 1923. Our family had lost all their possessions in the disastrous earthquake, and my parents did not intend to return to Japan after the ordeal that they had suffered. Although we possessed no material resources, there were limited funds available, and this enabled my parents to rent a small house in the Dunbar area.

My brother, Alan George, was born in 1926, when we lived in Dunbar. In the meantime, my father had engaged in a partnership with a man named Field. The basis of their partnership was obscure to me; but it appeared that the arrangement concluded between them was that my father would draw a salary from the partnership income, his duties being in the field to attract business to the joint venture. Field attended to the office management and its costs. Field mismanaged the financial affairs, resulting in the insolvency of the partnership, and absconded, leaving the creditors to sue the other partner. An arrangement was made with the creditors, which absorbed much of the income of our family for many years, and kept us close to poverty for the whole of my life in Canada.

During our early years in Canada, throughout the years of the great depression, life was hard beyond measure; but despite the indescribable hardships and constant poverty, my parents maintained their inherent dignity and fierce independence. The natural born Canadians did not take kindly to the cultured English accents of my parents, which they regarded as condescending and snobbish.

After moving from our first modest but comfortable house, we rented a series of dilapidated three-roomed apartments in the city of Vancouver, finally descending to the indignity of a ramshackle tiny wooden shack in North Vancouver, where we lived from hand to mouth for a time. We lived in an unsympathetic and unremitting era. I well remember looking through the window with my brothers, waiting for my father to return, our noses pressed to the panes. The inevitable question was "Does he have a parcel in his hand?" If he was carrying a brown paper parcel, we knew that there would be a meal on the table for supper. He never disappointed us, even though the fare was meagre. Potato soup, liver and onions, and sausage and mashed potatoes sustained us.

My mother had to learn to cook and undertake household duties; but despite the vicissitudes of our life, she maintained a happy disposition, and it was a delight to hear her singing. She made the most delicious potato and onion soup, and when we were able to afford minced steak, her curried meatballs were magnificent. Nettles grew everywhere in profusion, and the leaves and stems boiled and flavoured, tasted like spinach. Blueberries and salmonberries were plentiful in the spring and summer, and were used to make jams and jellies. When I was about seven years old, I was taught how to fish for trout in the streams in North Vancouver, and when older we fished in Burrard Inlet for flat fish, tommy cod and rock cod. So there was always the likelihood of a fish in the pan for a meal.

It was then that my father returned to the profession for which he had been trained, when he was employed as manager of Harvey Shipping Company, on a modest salary. His employers were agents for a number of European shipping companies including W.J. Tatem Ltd., Andrew Weir & Co (Bank Line Ltd.), Evan Thomas Radcliffe, and Compagnie Maritime Belge (Lloyd Royal) S.A. Because of his range of contacts, the number of shipping companies for which his employers acted as agents expanded, and we began to enjoy a modest but infinitely better standard of living. However, the payments of the partnership debt and accrued interest, continued to erode our income until the commitment was cleared in 1934. We had that burden for nearly ten years. I was then working as my father's office boy at a pay of $ 10 per month, most of which I had to give to our mother to supplement her housekeeping allowance.

I had started my education in Lord Kitchener and Lord Roberts schools in Vancouver, then Lonsdale School in North Vancouver, and finally North Star School, when we moved to the district of North Lonsdale. The Principal of North Star School was Charles Darwin, who was related to the author of the same name. Mr. Darwin had lost an eye and an arm when serving on the Western Front during the 1914 – 1918 war, the arm being replaced by a hook. He used this to great effect to hook an erring boy by the collar, while he applied a strap to the buttocks of his victim with his other arm. Notwithstanding his strictness and firm discipline, he was respected by all, and was undoubtedly a fine tutor.

Charles Darwin administered a team of teachers, four in the lower school, Misses Angus, Hamilton, Hardacre and Frith, all maiden ladies, who enforced strict discipline in their own several distinctive ways. The one other male teacher in the upper school was Mr. Swanson, a huge man, who once picked me up bodily and wiped the blackboard with my mop of curly hair to eradicate a mistake I had made. He was indeed an unforgettable character

At the age of twelve, I graduated to North Vancouver High School. Here, I fell foul of the chemistry and physics teacher, one Wilfrid R. McDougall. He had delegated to me the task of finding an empty Flit tin, which we would fill with water in the laboratory, steam the water out, screw back the top and watch the tin collapse due to the atmospheric pressure acting on the vacuum created within the tin. Unfortunately, I tried the experiment at home and it worked, with the result that I had only a flattened tin left to take to the classroom.

This enraged McDougall to the extent that he threw a laboratory flask at me in his rage. I reacted to this indignity by pushing him over. I left his class determined that I would never attend the school again. He was a very unpleasant and extremely ill tempered individual. Although eventually he was promoted to the office of Principal of the North Vancouver High School, and was held in respect by his contemporaries and certain pupils and others, certainly he was never my favourite tutor. He had a propensity for granting his favours to, and bestowing his patronage on, the subservient sycophants in his classes. Most of his female pupils were afraid of him, and many of his male pupils held him in awe. I may have been the exception, but to me he was one individual whom I found it impossible to like, and difficult to respect.

My father very reluctantly agreed that I could finish my high school tuition, when it became clear to him that I was determined not to deviate from my decision, permanently to separate myself from the awful Wilfrid R. McDougall. He made the one provision that I enrol as a part time pupil in the Sprott Shaw School of Business, and start working as an office boy in the shipping company that he managed. By that time, Mr. Harvey had died, and my father assumed complete charge of the company for his widow. My office duties were of a menial nature: licking the postage stamps, running messages to the offices of the ships' chandlers, sending telegraph messages, and the limited typing of letters written in draft by my father in long hand.

The Sprott Shaw School of Business was a private educational establishment where female stenographers were trained. The subjects included in its curriculum were Pitman shorthand, touch-typing and double entry book keeping, all taught by females in their late twenties and early thirties, and usually to female pupils. I was the only male pupil, and therefore something of a novelty to them. Later, on reflection, I am convinced that they connived between them to teach me as little as possible, and create in me the maximum sexual stimulation.

One teacher in particular would wear her blouse partly unbuttoned, and would hang her body over me to show as much of herself as was possible without undressing. The ladies did not wear brassieres in that era, so I was presented with an unobstructed view. She was quite well blessed above the waist, and after a session with her, I was just about ready to jump into a freezing cold lake. I am sure that the ladies must have had a great deal of fun when they broke off from teaching for their coffee and biscuits. I could hear them screaming with laughter, no doubt at my expense.

The Harvey Shipping Company employed contract supercargoes, whose duties were to accompany the ships around the loading ports in southern British Columbia, including the ports on Vancouver Island. The original intention was that after the appropriate training, experience, and qualifications, I would be employed as one of the company supercargoes.

As part of an indoctrination process, I was allowed to accompany the supercargo allocated to *Appledore* after her arrival in Vancouver in 1934. *Appledore* carried three apprentices, Hector Ling – the senior – William Phillip (Jumbo) James, and "Tich" Jefferies. This left a spare bunk for me in their four-berth cabin in the half deck. After loading the customary stabilising cargo of grain at New Westminster, we loaded lumber in the ports of Nanoose, Chemainus, and finally the deck cargo in Port Alberni. Here I left the ship. The apprentices were particularly considerate and friendly, and the short time I spent on *Appledore* prompted my decision to ask my father if he could arrange for my apprenticeship at sea. I was then over a year short of the minimum age of fifteen years, so I continued in my work in the offices of Harvey Shipping Company.

After I had been working in the shipping office for about nine months, I realised that future did not lie in the arena of menial office duties, and I could not aspire to promotion to the appointment as a supercargo without practical training. Moreover, my relationship with my father had become strained because of his attitude to what he termed as my "unsuitable working class friends", and his condescending attitude to the female sex, which I found to be intolerable. Our relationship had deteriorated from the early stages of father worship. Notwithstanding this, he applied for a berth for me as an apprentice in one of the ships of Tatem Steam Navigation Co. Ltd. of Cardiff, when I reached the age of fifteen. I doubt whether my mother ever forgave him for the fact that I went to sea.

With no income at all, I had to look for work during the ensuing period of over a year. I visited the local sawmills, but they hired mainly experienced adults, usually Scandinavians. Prospects were very remote, but an opportunity presented itself when I was out in the local woods and came upon a number of piles of cordwood stacked by the trail, about a half a mile from our small settlement of houses. I called at all the houses in the neighbourhood and eventually learned that the cordwood (about 25 cords in all) belonged to a neighbour, who agreed to pay me a dollar a cord to carry it to his house and stack it in his yard. My father openly scoffed at the idea of a 13-year old boy attempting such a project, and told me that I would never complete the work.

This made me even more determined to succeed. Using an old wheelbarrow, I made hundreds of journeys along the trail from the pile in the woods, and after months of backbreaking toil, I completed the work and was rewarded with the promised payment of $ 25. Our neighbour then suggested that he would buy more firewood from me if I would cut down the trees and prepare the wood for burning in the domestic stoves and central heating furnaces. The area abounded with stands of spruce, hemlock, cedar and groves of alder, and all that was necessary was to obtain a permit to fell the trees from what is now known as the Department of Mines and Resources. Permission was granted free of charge, and I was in the lumber business. The cedar was used for kindling wood, and the other trees for firewood, particularly the alder, fir and hemlock.

The equipment was quite elementary: a good quality double bladed axe, hollow ground on one blade for felling trees and convex ground on the other blade for splitting; an eight-foot cross cut saw; a sledge hammer; a number of steel splitting wedges; and a wheelbarrow. These could be bought cheaply from the local second hand shops, and the cost was covered by the $ 25 I had earned. I spent over a year on this positively backbreaking work.

I selected the trees with the straightest grain, generally up to two feet in diameter, which I felled with the axe, and swamped (removed the branches). Using the cross cut saw, I cut the trees into four-foot lengths

S.S. Appledore, built in 1929. 5218 gross registered tonnage
16 June 1936 to 9 July 1940
Homeward bound from Western Canada with a cargo of grain and timber
(Photograph by John and Marion Clarkson: Ships in Focus)

which were then split into cordwood of manageable weight, generally less than one hundred pounds. A cord was a pile of 128 cubic feet of four-foot lengths of wood, namely four feet wide, four feet high and eight feet long, stacked between four four-foot high stakes driven in pairs into the ground eight feet apart. That was the measurement method traditionally used.

Firewood was the main fuel in those times. Depending on the wood type, a cord would sell for between $12 and $15 delivered from the sawmill, and most homes used between ten and twelve cords a year. My aim was to produce enough for our own use, and sufficient for two more homes in a year of work, about 40 cords.

When I had cut and split a cord of wood, I would carry it to the nearest road, where I cut it with a buck saw on a sawhorse, ready for transportation. Sometimes, I was able to hire a "buzz-saw", a circular saw fixed on a cart and powered by a car engine. A local man owned some carts, which were pulled by horses, and I used this cheap method of transportation. Most users carried their firewood to their basements, where it was split and stacked, but I offered this service at 25 cents an hour, and also did odd jobs for our friends at the same charge. Not all could afford to pay, and two ladies paid me respectively in home baked bread and home made jam and preserves.

My production during a year produced a modest income, which I shared with my mother. My father did not pay me for the firewood cut for our own use, considering this be payment for my accommodation and food. I also picked and sold blueberries during the summer, and had a Vancouver Daily Province paper route in the evenings. This covered deliveries to over sixty customers over a wide area. All this paid for my hobbies of fishing and shooting. The very hard work at such an early age developed substantial muscular strength and stamina, which stood me in such good stead in future years.

When I see the teenage louts from the local secondary modern school in our village during their lunch break, I reflect on my heavy and unremitting labour when I was fourteen years old. Their most strenuous exercise is stuffing their mouths with chipped potatoes and tossing the plastic containers and plastic bottles on the street, itself strewn with the chewing gum carelessly spewed from their vacuous mouths. They and their doting parents would be better citizens if they had been subjected to the rigid discipline and rigours of that era.

During this period in my life I grew closer to my mother, and it was a terrible wrench for both of us when we parted when I joined *Appledore* on 6 June 1936, to commence my life at sea. My relationship with my father during those two years was not as cordial as it had been in the early days of father worship. He had so many fine attributes, but for me the chink in his armour was the cavalier attitude he showed towards what I had conceived to be the sanctity of marriage. My relationship with my mother had been so close that I could never condone this. However, my father and I parted on friendly terms, and we maintained regular correspondence throughout my life at sea. We never agreed on one particular aspect of his life, but I always respected him for his forthright and honest attitudes towards the important ethics of his business life, his unswerving loyalty to his Sovereign and native country, and his inalienable financial integrity. So it was that I embarked on my career at sea.

6

EARLY LIFE AT SEA AS A MIDSHIPMAN, 1936–1937

APPLEDORE – VOYAGE 20

Homeward Bound – Vancouver to U.K.
16 June 1936 to 20 August 1936

I joined *Appledore* on 9 June 1936, when I signed articles. My apprentice-ship indentures were dated 16 June 1936. We put to sea from the Vancouver Island harbour of Victoria in the last week of June 1936. *Appledore* was a typical general cargo carrier of the era, flush deck fore and aft with a raised forecastle head, 3,149 nett registered tons, 5,218 gross registered tons, with a cargo capacity of a nominal 10,010 tons, carried in five main holds and their 'tween decks. Her dimensions were: length 418 feet 8 inches, beam 56 feet. Her designed speed was 10 knots loaded and her loaded draught was 25 feet 10 inches. She was built in 1928 by Furness Shipbuilding Co. Ltd. in Haverton Hill on Tees, and registered in Bideford, North Devon, registered number 161611, call sign GPTD.

My cabin mates in the amidships accommodation were Hector Ling, from Barry Dock, the senior apprentice, William Phillip (Jumbo) James, from Cardigan, and Arthur Hall, from Newport. Hector would complete his term of four years on indentures within four months, "Jumbo", had served two years, and Arthur was the junior – before I joined the ship. The other apprentice, who had served in *Appledore* when I was a supernu-merary, "Titch" Jeffries, had left the ship without completing his period on indentures.

The accommodation for four apprentices in the fleet of company ships was almost identical, being situated on the forward port side of the amidships deck house over the engine room. Access was along the port

Senior Apprentice Hector Ling

(Back from left) **Able Seaman 'Tassy' Brennan, Apprentice 'Jumbo' James, Able Seaman 'Maltie' Joe Grech,** (Front from left) **Able Seaman Lewis, Carpenter Lewis, Bosun 'Paddy' Hennessey**

Appledore 1936 – Fine shipmates all

inside alleyway opposite the door that led to the engine room companionways. The accommodation comprised two rooms: a mess room opening off the alleyway, from which a door gave access to the sleeping cabin. Here there were four bunks lying fore and aft in two pairs one over the other, with wooden benches alongside the lower bunks. Two pairs of drawers were situated under the port and starboard lower bunks. Two full-length vertical lockers were fitted at the after end of each pair of bunks. A dressing table, with four drawers and mirror, was situated on the forward bulkhead. There were two portholes on the forward bulkhead and one on the port bulkhead over the top bunk. The senior apprentice claimed the top port bunk, the next senior the top starboard bunk, then in order of seniority, the bottom port and bottom starboard bunks. The priorities had been long established to take advantage of the coolest parts of the accommodation in hot weather. The cramped accommodation was about nine feet square.

The mess room was equally cramped, and consisted of four narrow vertical lockers for stowage of oilskins, sea boots and outside gear, a small four section food locker, and wooden slatted benches along the port and after bulkheads, around a table bolted to the deck. The area was about nine by seven feet. The forward section of the engine room alleyway provided space for buckets for ablutions and cleaning. There was one porthole on the port bulkhead of the mess room. This was to be my home for over four years.

The deck hands were a motley group of seamen: the bosun, Paddy Hennessey, a tough barrel of a man, who had served as a deck hand on the fishing boats of his native Kinsale, in Ireland; Michael O'Driscoll, another Kinsale fisherman, a gentle giant of a man; Joe Grech (Maltie Joe) a Maltese fisherman; John (Tassie) Brennan, a Tasmanian who had served in the union-dominated ships trading around the Australian coast and Indian Ocean; an able seaman, Lewis, and the carpenter, also a Lewis, both Cardigan Welshmen. I cannot remember the names of them all. The doyen of this deck crew was William Ross, a tough able seaman, who had run away to sea from his native Shetland Islands at the turn of the century and served as a boy, ordinary seamen and able seaman on the huge windjammers that plied the route to Australia around the Cape of Good Hope. These vessels, mainly barque or ship-rigged vessels of five or six masts, could carry 5,000 tons of cargo, and spread a massive area of sail.

Bill Ross had served on one of these barques, *Speke* of Liverpool, which carried a main yard 90 feet long and spread not only upper and lower topgallant and mizzen sails, but also skysails. Reefing the main course sails in a Cape Horn gale required crawling out to the end of the yard 45 feet away from the mast and about 20 feet out from the ship's side, supported precariously only by the foot ropes leading from the mast to the yard end. Such was the early life of one of the finest seamen with whom I was privileged to serve. He became my tutor and mentor, and I was privileged to share a watch with him when I was trained to be a sufficiently competent helmsman. Bill Ross and I developed a close friendship, which was to last for the three years in which we served together. From our first ocean passage together he taught me the skills of a seaman, and no officer could have had a more patient or proficient mentor. I was an avid pupil. Able seaman Tassie Brennan and I also became close friends. He was my best man when Betty and I married in 1942.

The First Mate was Mr. Rice. As far as we were concerned, we never knew whether he had a Christian name. We knew him as "that bugger Rice, or that sod Rice". We never knew nor cared where he came from. It may have been Cornwall. I cannot remember the name of the Second Mate. I believe that it was Pengelly. The recently qualified Third Mate was William Ewart Scobie, whose home was in Cardiff. Bill Scobie was an unusually talented officer. "Best cadet of the year" in the Reardon Smith Nautical School in Cardiff in 1931, he joined *Umberleigh* as a 16-year old deck boy, and remained in the ship as ordinary seaman and able seaman, before sitting the examination for his certificate of competency as Second Mate in 1936, when he joined *Appledore*.

He was what we in the half deck knew as a "hawsepipe officer", a term used by midshipmen for officers who came from the ranks. We midshipmen felt that "hawsepipe officers" entertained antipathy towards us. We believed that we received better and more considerate treatment from officers who had served their apprenticeship in the half deck. Bill Scobie was an exception, and was admired and popular.

It was soon made clear to me that the junior apprentice constituted the lowest form of life on the planet. It was so with "Titch" Jeffries during his short period of service on *Appledore*. Very shortly after I settled in I was singled out for the same treatment. In the case of Titch, the First Mate, Mr. Rice, treated him in a particularly repressive and obnoxious manner. Apart from the usual indignity of ensuring that the bosun would allocate to the boy the most menial and filthy tasks, Mr. Rice would go out of his way to try to catch Jeffreys off his course, so that he could implement the traditional punishment of imposing an extra two-hour trick on the helm during his watch below.

Rice had a hooked nose, and reminded me of a heron, as he stalked back and forth on the bridge during his watches. Working watch and watch, four hours on and four hours off, the helmsman would usually find it difficult to keep from dozing off towards the end of his trick on the helm. Usually, the officers were tolerant, and the reprimand would be "Watch your course, son". However, tolerance was not a characteristic that Rice possessed. He would creep up to the wheel house door, push his face up to the compass binnacle, and if the apprentice was guilty of the crime of being more that two degrees off course either way, he would declare gleefully "Got you, you bugger, three degrees off to starboard. Two hours extra trick for you in your watch below." During day working hours this would mean that the helmsman, who would normally take the first trick at the helm during the next watch, would be employed on deck duties, giving the bosun an extra hand on deck.

This happened on a voyage home from Vancouver, during the morning watch, when the Master was enjoying his constitutional walk back and forth on the lower bridge. Jeffreys was a tiny individual, who was so short that he had to stand on a box to see the compass. Rice saw the uneven wake when he looked astern, rushed into the wheelhouse, and caught Jeffries off his course. As usual, he gleefully announced the imposition of the customary penalty. By that time, Jeffries had suffered enough indignity, and he had already had enough of the sea. Previously he must have contemplated asking his father to buy him out of his indentures.

He shouted back at the First Mate, "F— you, Mr. Mate", and put the helm hard a starboard, so the ship steamed in a wide circle. The Master screamed, "For Christ's sake, Mr. Rice, you have taken a round turn out of her. We have burned a couple of tons of bloody coal steaming in circles!" The First Mate answered, "It's the bloody apprentice at the helm, Sir. The bugger has gone mad!" The response was, "For Christ's sake relieve the wheel, or we will run out of coal". The First Mate blew the whistle for the standby man to take the wheel, and as Jeffries made his way down the companion ladder, he aimed a kick at him, which connected.

Eventually a complaint was lodged with the Board of Trade. Jeffries left the ship at the end of that voyage. His replacement was Arthur Hall. This event was related to me in lurid detail, as a warning as to what I could expect when I was considered proficient enough to steer the ship.

The senior apprentice, Hector Ling, was a tolerant individual and treated me with consideration and kindness; but during the early days of my apprenticeship, both Arthur Hall and Jumbo James gave me a hell of a time. Firstly, they attempted to sequester my "going ashore gear" of grey flannels and sports jacket – unsuccessfully – because I was of substantially bigger and stronger physique. They then resorted to trying to goad me by referring to the fact that I had been born in Japan, with nicknames such as "you bloody Jap" and then "Tojo". The goading culminated just before we reached the Panama Canal on the southward passage along the west coast of Central America. I had just finished my rota of "peggy", which was the name given to the cleaning of the cabins – on this occasion before the usual Sunday routine of Captain's weekly inspection.

It was a sweltering hot day, and I was sitting on the mess room settee stripped to the waist and running with sweat from my exertions. James had just completed his trick on the helm and was coming off watch. He greeted me with the words "Finished your bloody peggy, Tojo? Just the job for a bloody slant-eyed Jap". I replied, "Better to be a Jap than a bloody Cardigan bastard", whereupon he smashed me behind the right ear with a vicious right hook, when I was in a seated position; and I crashed into the locker. My father had been a useful boxer; and had installed a ring in our basement, where my brothers and I had to fight out our differences under his expert tuition. His advice had been "a left to the jaw and a right to the pit of the stomach". When I managed to stagger to my feet and recover, that is the treatment I served out to my roommate, plus several body blows and an uppercut, which knocked him out.

He was lying in a dazed condition on the deck between the cabin and the alleyway, with his head across the brass splashboard, when Captain Swindell arrived for his Sunday inspection. His words were "Christ Almighty, Upton, you have bloody well killed James!" James was taken forward and patched up. From then on, I was never goaded again by him, and we remained good friends and shipmates until he finished his time several voyages later

Arthur Hall tried his hand about a week later, and again it was over the "peggy" rota. It was his turn to clean the accommodation, but he ordered me to do the work, because he felt that his seniority entitled him to order me around – as the junior apprentice. I told him to go to hell, which prompted him to invite me to "meet him on deck". We roped off a ring on the deck cargo over No. 3 hatch, and some of the crew formed an audience. As soon as we squared up to each other, it was clear that he would have profited from the rigorous and expert training regime, to which my father had subjected his sons.

He ended up going through the ropes of the makeshift ring, and head first down the gap in the deck cargo left open for the port No. 3 derrick. His left arm was broken in the fall, and again he had to be treated by Captain Swindell, who put the arm in splints and a sling. His comment to me was, "Not you again, Upton"; but he did not put either of us in the logbook. Fights aboard ships were commonplace events.

I felt so contrite about this that I undertook his peggy until he was able to use his arm again. I had no trouble from Arthur Hall or any other member of the crew from then on, and my nickname changed to "the mad Canuck", which lived with me for the rest of my time aboard.

My first encounter with the food was far from encouraging. Our usual breakfast was poor quality porridge, (burgoo) usually speckled with weevils, very occasionally followed by curry and rice, (dog shit and hail-stones). Sometimes it was rissoles (arseholes), made from scraps of meat off cuts. Tea was used over-and-over again, by adding to the pot. The cocoa was quite palatable, particularly when condensed milk was added. Bread was baked daily, usually speckled with weevils, but provided a staple diet, spread with salt butter (which became progressively more rancid) and the very good jam.

The main meal was lunch. The fresh meat was kept in an icebox, which preserved the carcases for about ten days; but it was used until the last stinking slice, sometimes over two weeks old. The salt beef was preserved in barrels. It came to the table when the last supply of the so-called fresh meat was exhausted. The salt beef (salt horse) was awful, a mixture of skin, fat and gristle. The salt pork (salt pig) was even worse, more like blubber. Vegetables consisted of dried peas and haricot beans, with fresh cabbage for a short time after leaving port. There was an apparently inexhaustible supply of potatoes in the lazarette (spud locker) aft, that kept the galley boy (spud basher) almost continuously employed, exhorted by the cook, "Peel them thin you little bugger, or I'll have your guts for garters". We also had tins of corned beef (corned dog), which was quite good, and what was called minced collops, termed "dogs' vomit". Very occasionally, we had bacon and eggs for breakfast, but the eggs became rotten within a week.

Rice pudding was one of the desserts. Another was "apple daddy", made from stewed dried apples and a stodgy pastry. We used to save the rice, when curry and rice (dog shit and hailstones) was on the table, spread it with condensed milk and put it in the oven. This made a very palatable rice pudding.

The soup was popular, if that term could be used in reference to the food. There was always a huge cauldron on the galley stove, and, although it was filled with all the scraps, recovered by the cook (grub spoiler), in the preparation of the food, it provided nourishment for the hungry hard-working crew. Most of the potato peelings and cabbage stems went into the soup. Nothing was wasted. Surprisingly, we remained reasonably healthy and fit.

We received our statutory allocation of a pint of limejuice daily, partly as an anti-scorbutic, and partly to dampen the male sex urge. As one steward put it, "This will keep your cocks in check, boys."

The ship had a spare cabin in the bridge accommodation, which could be used as the hospital room. My father had been requested by the owners to advertise accommodation for two passengers for the passages to Vancouver and return to the U.K. As the result, we usually carried two passengers, generally married couples. The fare was set at £ 25, which was quite reasonable, because the cabin was comfortable and the food in the officers' saloon was basic. On the passage home, we accommodated a parson and his wife. The clergyman immediately got into trouble with the Master, by attempting to coerce the crew into attending divine service on Sundays. The problem was that many of the crew were Roman Catholics, and the Somali firemen were Muslims.

In his bigoted enthusiasm, he attempted forcefully to convert members of the crew to what he termed the "true faith". Eventually he was ordered to remain within the bridge accommodation as otherwise he may have disappeared "over the wall" one dark night.

Between those events, we passed through the Panama Canal. The canal fascinated me then, and continued to fascinate me on the many subsequent passages. The canal was a colossal engineering achievement in the construction of the locks, and the efficiency of the mooring and berthing, by the use of the electric "mules". The beauty of the Miraflores Lakes and the awesome grandeur of the cut through the mountain at Culebra. Here a plaque commemorated the deaths of a great number of workmen who perished in its construction, being overwhelmed in the huge landslip, which occurred when part of the excavations caved in.

After the short passage through the Caribbean Sea, we made port in Port Royal in Jamaica, where we moored alongside the bunkering wharf, and replenished our coal bunkers. Most of the crew had saved their jam ration – in seven-pound tins – which they bartered, mainly for stalks of bananas brought alongside by the "bumboat men". Jam was the favourite bartering commodity, and a seven-pound tin would not only secure a stalk or two of bananas, but sometimes also the favours of some of the females who would ply their wares from the bumboats. The officers were under strict orders to keep the bumboats at the end of a heaving line, and no rope ladders over the side because of the prevalence of V.D. among the local females. The term they used was, "We want no sour cigars under your trousers, boys".

We put to sea from Port Royal, and entered the Atlantic in the area of the Gulf Stream, through the Mona Passage, probably the most spectacularly beautiful area of the world that I have ever known. The passage across the Atlantic was the usual homeward bound routine of washing and painting the bulkheads, awning spars and ventilators and other top hamper. Subsequently, when favoured with a following wind, the mainmast, and, with a head wind, the foremast and yardarm. Finally, the funnel in its three colours, black with a red band and the large white "M" for Maritime Shipping and Trading Company Ltd.

Great care was taken with the teak brightwork hand rails on the bridges, which were carefully scraped to the bare wood with a piece of broken glass, given two coats of a mixture of red lead and paraffin, and finally a coat of copal varnish. The brass work on the bridges: compasses, binnacles, engine room telegraphs, and the steam whistle, were cleaned using a mixture of colza oil and ground pumice.

Juniors were not allowed to go aloft or to use the white Lagoline paint on the awning spars or upper works, or the mast colour paint used on the ventilators and lower bulkheads; so my work was confined to chipping, scraping, and washing paintwork. The teak decks of the bridges were cleaned and burnished by the use of "holy stones", the term being derived from the attitude of prayer, on hands and knees. It was back breaking work, on hands and knees is the sweltering heat.

After an uneventful passage, we made port in Southampton. When alongside, I was detailed to go over the side on staging to paint the hull black, down to the boot topping line. Here my naivety really got me into serious trouble. When we were over the side painting the ship, Arthur Hall told me that it was the customary practice to paint the name of the ship on the quayside, whereupon I painted "*APPLEDORE of BIDEFORD*" in large black letters on the stonework. We were then moored between the huge 52,000-ton Cunard liner *Berengaria* and the even larger White Star liner, the 56,000-ton *Majestic*. When we had discharged our deck cargo of timber, and part of our lower-hold cargo, we moved berth.

The port authorities then discovered my handiwork with the paint-brush, and all hell broke loose. I was summoned to the bridge to be confronted by furious port officials and an even more irate and embar-rassed Master, and was asked what I had been up to. I was then set-to to brush caustic on the offending painted characters and scrape the stonework clean, and not to knock-off until the work had been completed to the satisfaction of the port officials. It was one hell of a job because the paint had penetrated the stonework, and each character had to be chipped and scraped laboriously from the stonework. It was my own fault for being so gullible as to listen to Arthur Hall, who was a thor-oughly irresponsible character.

We put to sea from Southampton bound for London, where we berthed in Surrey Commercial Docks, firstly at the buoys to discharge the remainder of our timber cargo into barges, and then alongside to discharge the lower hold cargo of grain. We then put to sea bound for Barry Docks, for the routine repairs, bunkering and stores replenishment. The ship paid off on 20 August 1936, and signed on the following day.

When we were in the graving dock the wives of the Master and officers came aboard for a short stay. Mr. Rice ordered me to go ashore to meet his wife at the station and escort her aboard the ship. She was a pleasant lady, who offered me sixpence to carry her suitcase. I did not accept this money for a service to a lady. I escorted the lady to the cabin of the First Mate, and before I had time to deposit her suitcase on the deck the randy bugger was undressing her; so I beat a hasty retreat to let them get on with it. He was never our favourite officer. So ended my first ocean passage in *Appledore*. I was at the beginning of a very long learning curve.

APPLEDORE – VOYAGE 21

U.K. to British Columbia
21 August 1936 to 20 December 1936

The ship underwent repairs and the re-painting of her bottom in the Barry Graving Dock, as well as the other usual work when in dry dock – the fleeting of the chain cable and the statutory testing in the Lloyds' Proving House in Cardiff. In addition, the stern gland was replaced. The Third Mate, Bill Scobie, was transferred to another company ship, and replaced by Owen Rowlands, a native of Amlwch in Anglesey.

I first encountered the Marine Superintendent, when the ship was in the dry dock. He was an individual who held arbitrary power over the fleet of ships and the men who served in them. He would rarely deign to speak to, or even acknowledge, junior officers or apprentices; but the Masters, First Mates, Chief, and Second Engineers held him in almost abject terror of summary dismissal. He was in charge of the employment of all officers, stores procurement, and all other operational elements. The man was universally detested throughout the fleet for his coarse and overbearing manner, foul language, and the total absence of any human feelings towards those subordinate to him.

His background was as an ambitious engineer who had succeeded by kicking others around and licking boots. These were the ideal characteristics for a Marine Superintendent in a shipping line whose owners and directors put profits and dividends before the welfare of their employees. Privately he was known as an "arsehole licker" or "brown tongue". When he came aboard, the senior officers ran around like headless chickens; and were usually subjected to his invective, either in private, or more often in public in the presence of their subordinates. The man did not have a redeeming feature. He was awful.

The owner of the shipping line was William James (known as Bill) Tatem, knighted in 1916 as Lord Glanely of St. Fagans, ostensibly in recognition of his contribution to the 1914–1918 war effort. Certainly, his contribution did not include war service in the armed services, or at sea in merchant ships, so he never experienced the dangers and trauma of life at sea, or the waterlogged trenches of Flanders. The future Lord Glanely was a native of *Appledore* in North Devon. He started work as a clerk in a Cardiff shipping family business, and then went into business on his own account in 1897. Undoubtedly, he must have been an individual of determined character and sound business acumen; but humanity was not an element in his character. His ventures prospered throughout the shipping boom prior to and after the 1914–1918 war, and by 1936, the company possessed a fleet of quite modern general traders.

The last consideration of ship owners generally, and South Wales owners in particular, was the welfare of the men who served in their ships. The employment of unscrupulous sycophants such as the Marine Superintendent typified a poor and oppressive management structure. As a result, the conditions in the ships varied from indifferent to appalling.

Similar regimes and conditions prevailed in the other basic industries in South Wales, Tyne and Wear side, and on the Clyde – steel, tinplate, coal and ship building and repair, with low paid workers operating in unsafe and dangerous environments for pittance rewards while the owners lived in glorious luxury. When I joined *Appledore*, the established victualling costs stood at one shilling and one penny per day per man. By 1938, the bullying of Masters and Chief Stewards by the Marine Superintendent had reduced the costs to eleven pence three farthings per man per day, a reduction of one penny one farthing. This equated to a paltry saving in victualling costs over a four-month voyage of about £ 23 per ship, in a regime in which the racehorses in the stables of ship owners fed better that the crews of the ships.

When Lord Glanely was killed in 1942, in an air raid, when staying in a luxury hotel in Weston Super Mare, one of my fellow officers put the reaction of us all into appropriate terms when he said that his epitaph should be "Under the sod lies another". Such was our opinion of the First Baron Glanely of St Fagans.

Lord Glanely was not alone in attracting the detestation of those who served in our merchant ships. Tatem ships were known as "T on the funnel but not on the table". The prominent "S" on the funnels of ships of the Reardon Smith Line earned them the title of "Starvation Smiths". Two white bands and one red band on the funnels of the Harrison Line qualified them to the title of "Two of fat and one of lean". H. Hogarth & Sons ships were known by the alliterative term of "Hungry Hughie Hogarth."

Bunkering was always a frantic and filthy operation, with the Marine Superintendent invoking every epithet in his vocabulary to bully the Master and senior officers into turning the ship around, whether ready or not. If it meant catching the tide, he dispensed with the services of coal trimmers to save money. The ships would be singled up fore and aft, with coal still being tipped into the bunkers, minutes before the dock gates were opened. We would put to sea with a huge pile of coal on No. 3 hatch and on deck amidships. This was dangerous, particularly in heavy weather; but the safety of the crew was immaterial to the owners.

Even in the face of severe gale warnings, we frequently put to sea in such an unsafe and dangerous condition. Then the deck hands and firemen would be turned-to to trim the coal to the wings of the lower holds and into the 'tween decks, hopefully before we reached the Bay of Biscay or southwestern approaches. Negotiating this pile of coal amidships, which reposed at bulwark level, was very dangerous, despite lifelines, particularly when the ship was rolling almost on her beam-ends. Then it was possible to invoke the "safety of the ship" rule, which permitted work without overtime.

This was just one more example of the draconian regime to which British seamen were then subjected. On one occasion, the bosun went on the bridge just after 1600 on a wild day with a falling barometer and a rough beam sea breaking aboard amidships. He suggested to Mr. Rice "She is taking water amidships, Sir. Shall I put the day men to battening down the saddleback and port Tee hatches?" The immediate answer was "Not bloody likely, Bosun. Turn the buggers to at 5.00 p.m. after working hours, on safety of the ship emergency work."

It usually took three days to trim the coal into the bunkers, and cover and batten down the hatches, followed by a thorough washing down of the ship. Then we were able to clean our accommodation and ourselves and return to a more ship shape condition.

Hector Ling had completed his period on indentures during the previous voyage, but remained in the amidships accommodation until the end of the voyage, but on articles as an able seaman. He signed on as able seaman for voyage 21, but moved to the forecastle accommodation aft. He had been very kind to me, and I was pleased that he would be my shipmate for the voyage. It was the usual custom for apprentices who had served their period on indentures to sign on articles as an able seaman, quartermaster, or bosun for at least a voyage. They would then accumulate sufficient pay to fund their accommodation ashore during the customary three months final tuition at Smith Nautical College in Cardiff. Hence, Hector Ling had signed for a four-month voyage at the pay of an able seaman, a paltry £ 9 2s 6d per month, which would have funded three months accommodation when preparing for his examinations for a certificate of competency as Second Mate (Foreign Going Steamship).

During the period of apprenticeship, correspondence course tuition was provided by the Merchant Navy Officers Training Board, which set the curricula and periodic examination papers for study and completion at sea. I embarked on the first year curriculum at the beginning of the voyage. When we were not occupied on watch, usually the officers on watch would help with tuition during the dog watches of 1600 to 1800 and 1800 to 2000, for those apprentices on watch below. It was the rule that such tuition was not undertaken in ship's time. The experienced seamen provided practical training during routine working periods.

Officers were expected to work "field days", usually in the dog watches, mainly sewing canvas – lifeboat, ventilator or engine room telegraph covers, awnings and other work of a manageable size. They undertook this work when sitting on a deck chair on the navigating or lower bridges in their watch below, and during their normal watches, when the ship was well out of the dense traffic in coastal waters. Such was the routine on most general traders or "tramp" ships. All canvas work used aboard was hand sewn, although main hatch tarpaulins were machine stitched in the sail makers' lofts ashore. However, we always maintained large stocks of tarpaulin canvas, from which we made hand sewn hatch tarpaulin covers, as well as bolts of repairing canvas and cotton duck canvas. Bill Ross was a most expert sail maker, and during the dog watches, I was thoroughly indoctrinated into the craft, and became proficient. He averred that he could *hear* a proficient sail maker at work by the sound of the stitches being pulled tight.

Bill Ross was not only a seaman of superlative knowledge and experience, but he had an almost uncanny ability to predict weather conditions. He had studied the behaviour patterns of sea birds, particularly the Albatross of the southern hemisphere, the porpoises and dolphins, even the flying fish. Every cloud pattern had its meaning. Even without the benefit of a barometer, thermometer or barometric pressure chart, he would forecast the trend and intensity of a tropical revolving storm with unerring accuracy. I sat for many hours under the awnings aft on the poop, listening with avid interest to his encyclopaedic knowledge, and his apparently endless store of stories and doggerels connected with life at sea generally, and his own life in particular.

It was not enough for him for his pupil to be able learn how to splice, or make a knot, bend, or hitch. He demanded an ambidextrous ability to make a bend or hitch left or right handed, behind the back, or in the dark. Moreover, every bend or hitch had its own special use. He was expert in the making of what were termed "fancy knots", sennit, Turk's Heads, cross pointing, what he called "sailorising". He taught me how to make dog leads, bell toggle lanyards and sea bags – both the conventional type using longitudinal flat seams joining several pieces of canvas – and the unique method of making the bag from one piece of canvas, using a spiral flat seam.

All the time he would be recounting his stories. There was one about an old shellback holding forth during a dog watch to an audience of boy cadets. The dictionary defines a shellback as "an expert seaman, especially one who has crossed the Equator." We preferred the definition as "one who has rounded the Horn under sail". Bill Ross was one such shellback:

Shellback to his audience, *"When I first went to sea, men were men, and boys were boys. It was all rum, bum and baccy. Now it is soda, cigarettes and self abuse"*. Shellback follows this with, *"Well what do you think about that, lads?"*

Boy cadet answers, *"That's all very well, sir, but now those boys are men, and the men are silly doddering old buggers"*.

I will never be able to express my thanks to this fine seaman, for his tuition, assistance, and patience in instilling into me part of his vast knowledge.

The ship was well into the Atlantic Ocean by the time we had trimmed down the bunkers, battened down the amidships hatches, and washed down fore and aft. We then settled into the usual outward bound routine of washing the paintwork, ready for painting homeward bound, first the bridges, awning spars, alleyways and accommodation. Most ships had their upperworks and outboard bulwark fish plates painted white, with the mast houses, inside bulwark fish plates, and the lower sections of accommodation painted mast colour. The cargo from the Canadian west coast ports always included a deck cargo of timber. The mast houses, derricks, and those bullheads, which would be obstructed by the deck cargo, were also painted outward bound.

As the ship made southerly progress, the holds were opened, and washed down ready for the grain cargo. This necessitated the filthy work of "bilge diving", to clear the strum boxes situated at the after ends of the holds, to allow free access for the bilge water to the bilge pumps. There was no other way but to lay face down with our heads in the bilges over a stinking morass of rotten grain, and decomposing rats, scraping out the filthy mess with our hands, and depositing it in buckets for dumping over the side. This work was usually reserved for deck boys, ordinary seamen and apprentices, while the more experienced men were set to erecting the lower hold shifting boards, and the 'tween deck feeder boxes, for the lower hold bulk grain cargo.

The complement of deck hands on merchant ships, of the type most in service, was usually a bosun and carpenter, nine able seamen, two ordinary seamen and a deck boy. Apprentices with under a year of service counted as deck boys, those with eighteen months service as ordinary seamen, and those with over two years service as able seamen. The three apprentices counted respectively as: Jumbo James as an A.B., Arthur Hall as an O.S. and myself as a deck boy, thus reducing the complement of hands in the forecastle by one of each of those ratings. This satisfied the Board of Trade, and stimulated ship owners to endeavour to maintain a complement of four apprentices on each of their ships, thus saving the pay of four deck hands. Apprentices were a form of cheap labour.

The pay of a bosun or carpenter was £ 10 2s 6d per month, an able seaman between £ 9 2s 6d and £ 9 10s 0d per month, an ordinary seaman about £ 4 2s 6d a month and a deck boy would earn about £ 2 10s 0d a month. Food – of a sort – was provided on all Shipping Federation articles covering foreign going steamships.

Most apprentices were bound by the terms of the standard Shipping Federation indentures, £ 10 in the first year, £ 12 in the second year, £ 18 in the third year, and £ 20 in the fourth year. On satisfactory completion of the four-year term, they were paid a bonus of one shilling for each month in service, in lieu of laundry, and a good conduct bonus of £ 5, a grand total of £ 67 8s 0d for four years of hard labour. British ship owners could never qualify as benevolent institutions.

A story often related on ships involves a First Mate, bosun, and apprentice. Possibly the name of the First Mate could, or should have been Rice. The apprentice had been put to work in the weather outside

Painting the winch under parts with
black lead and paraffin

After painting the funnel in
tropical weather

Two of the dirtier jobs of an apprentice on *Appledore*

alleyway, washing the accommodation and the inside of the bulwarks with
the customary bucket of "soogie moogie", (fresh water and soda crystals)
and bucket of fresh water. A heavy sea broke aboard in the alleyway,
washing the apprentice overboard. The bosun communicated the news to
the First Mate on the bridge with the words. "Christ, Sir, the apprentice
washing the bulkheads in the port alleyway has been washed overboard!"
The reply from the mate, "Bloody hell, bosun, I hope his buckets didn't
go over the side with him!" Apprentices were expendable. Buckets cost
money.

The normal routine in 1936 was that six deck hands worked watch and
watch, four hours on and four off, when at sea, with the bosun and
carpenter and the remainder of the deck hands on day work. Three men
constituted a watch, namely helmsman, lookout (at night), and a standby
man. The lookout and standby man worked with the day work hands
during the day. The night routine was for each man respectively, two
hours on the helm, followed by one hour on standby and one hour look-

out. This routine rotated between each watch member and from watch to watch. During 1937, the Board of Trade articles terminated the four hours on and four off watches and replaced them with the four hours on and eight off routine.

During our passage across the North Atlantic, our work had been devoted mainly to cleaning up the ship, including my indoctrination into "bilge diving". It seemed that Mr. Rice, the First Mate, had developed an antipathy towards me, possibly because he may have disliked what were then termed "colonials", because my family lived in Canada. It is more likely that he chose to single out the junior apprentice to satisfy the bully in is nature. Although it was usual for the bosun to allocate the work, I heard him on a number of occasions say "Bosun, put Upton on that job", usually the dirtiest work on the duty roster. Hence, once the weather had improved, I was introduced to the work of scraping the eccentric straps under the steam winches.

This necessitated crawling into the space under the winch between the angle brackets that secured the winch to the deck, and scraping the thick mixture of oil, coal dust and muck which had accumulated on the eccentric straps and other moving parts. The restricted space admitted only the arms, head and shoulders, when lying face upwards, so all the muck fell into the eyes, nose, and ears. There was no escape from what was a hot and filthy hellhole.

After crawling out of the tiny space, the filthy mess was removed, using a triangular scraper, then deposited in a bucket, and dumped over the side. It was then necessary to crawl back under the winch, and coat the moving parts with a mixture of black lead and paraffin with a wad, so that the filthy concoction again covered all the parts of the face. The black lead and paraffin mixture burned and stung all the parts of the face and arms. Altogether, it was the filthiest work. It took about a day for each pair of winches, so the work took about five days to complete. The only way to clean the parts of the body and face was to wipe down with paraffin, followed by a thorough wash in Lifebuoy soap.

Here again, I was a victim of the callous policies of the wealthy owner of the ships under the Tatem house flag, and those of his equally callous directors and their subservient sycophants. The domestic fresh water capacity of the ships was restricted to a small 15 ton capacity tank situated in the tween decks under the galley, and served by a hand operated pump on the after bulkhead of the galley. The handle was secured by a chain and padlock, custody of the key being in the hands of the cook.

A capacity of 15 tons equates to 3,360 gallons, so a crew of 37 men

'Bilge diving' with Apprentice
Phillip Harris

The filthiest job of all, painting after
peak with hot Camrex paint

More filthy work for the Apprentices on *Appledore*

would have a proportion of just over 3 gallons a day each over a 30-day passage, reducing to half this amount for the 60-day non stop passages from the U.K. to Australia. A substantial proportion was used in cooking, and an even greater amount for the washing of paintwork. The "soogie moogie" used for this work required common soda crystals dissolved in fresh water, plus an equal amount of fresh water for washing off. Therefore, each man was rationed to a bucket of water or less per day for ablutions and the washing of clothing.

Hot fresh water was available from a huge cauldron permanently secured by "fiddles" on the galley stove. The allowance was restricted to a dipper of water a day from this reservoir, and the protocol was that a man drawing a dipper of water would replace the quantity with a dipper of cold water from the pump. The dipper was made from seven-pound jam tin with a handle soldered to it. Each time this silly, wasteful and time-consuming process was repeated, the pump had to be unlocked and locked, and water would drip on the deck. The ridiculous aspect of all this was that there was sufficient space above the main deck in the amidships superstructure to accommodate a domestic water tank of 100 tons capacity, feeding taps in the galley by gravity.

The hot water supply could be supplemented by cadging a bucket of condenser water from the engineer on watch – depending on his mood at the time. We lived and worked in an era in which it was likely that more water was used in one day to wash out the racehorse stables of Lord Glanely, than the niggardly quantity measured out in a week to the men who served in one ship. I was fast learning the facts of life aboard a Tatem ship.

The passage across the Atlantic was uneventful. I had settled into the daily shipboard routine, and was learning rapidly what my indentures termed "the business of a seaman as practised in steamships."

As soon as we were within the area of warmer and more settled weather, the experienced hands were employed in erecting shifting and feeder boards for the lower hold grain cargo. This was exceptionally heavy work. The juniors would be put to work on their knees chipping and scraping the steel main decks, preparatory to treating the decks with a mixture of crude oil, fish oil, and Terebene. This was hot and very dirty work; and left the decks very slippery, until the mixture had oxidised. The sticky mixture was picked up on our shoes and carried into the internal alleyways and our accommodation. A red oxide based deck paint was used on some ships, but this was a far more expensive treatment, which would not be tolerated in the stringent economy regime in Tatem ships.

After leaving the Panama Canal a party of deck hands was allocated the work of painting the No. 5 lower hold deck heads with an obnoxious bitumen based paint under the trade name of Presomet. This burned the skin on contact, and when painting the deck heads overhead, there was no way to prevent the paint from running down the arms and on the face. It was filthy work, particularly in the oppressive heat under the deck heads. Hector Ling, Arthur Hall and I had spent the morning on this work in No. 5 hold, and were knocking off prior to lunch. We had been working from staging hanging from the deck heads, to which we climbed by ropes from the floor of the lower hold. The ropes were rove through snatch blocks hanging from the lower hold beams, and used to lift the staging planks into position. Both ends of the ropes were free, so that in sliding to the lower hold floor it was necessary to hold both parts.

Both Arthur and I did this, and descended safely. However, Hector must have had a mental aberration, for he stepped off the stage plank, took hold of one part only, so the other part was free to run over the sheave of the snatch block; and dived head first about 25 feet to the floor of the hold. It was fortunate that his fall was partially arrested by the curve of the counter of the ship in No. 5 hold, but he ended up, head down, in the starboard bilge, wedged between two frames.

A batten cleat had penetrated his face and torn his cheek and lip open badly, and he had suffered a broken leg and arm in the fall, as well as suffering severe concussion. We rigged a heaving line, and lifted him to the main deck. The Master set his arm and leg in splints, swabbed the facial injuries with hydrogen peroxide, and stitched the gaping wound, then covered his whole face with a bandage, except for his eyes, nose and mouth. Typical of the callous regime of Mr. Rice, in the afternoon Hector was carried out to the main deck amidships, sat on the deck, where he was put to work chipping rust with the chipping hammer in the hand of his sound arm. To add insult to injury, Captain Swindell shouted to him from the bridge, "Well, Ling, you will have a bloody hard job kissing your girl friend in Barry with a lip like that". There was no point in seeking sympathy, because it was not there. I believe that Captain Swindell was trying to be humorous, because he was not a callous man.

On the voyage along the Pacific coast, I began my instruction on the helm in ideal conditions, a ship in ballast in nearly smooth conditions. *Appledore* was not an easy ship to steer, and constant vigilance was necessary to prevent her wandering off course. However, I progressed rapidly into becoming a competent helmsman, although my tricks on the helm were then restricted to tuition under supervision during the dog watches.

On one occasion when I had been allowed to take the helm in my time off on a Sunday morning during the forenoon watch, the ship was approaching the vicinity of San Francisco, but well off shore. The Third Mate, Owen Rowlands, was on watch, and Captain Swindell had joined him on the bridge for a chat. Captain Swindell looked into the wheelhouse, and remarked, "Oh, it's you, Upton. How would you like to see the Golden Gate Bridge?" whereupon the Third Mate interjected, "We are too far out, sir." Captain Swindell responded, "Put her to starboard, Mr. Rowlands. I want Upton to see the bridge".

He then walked out to the starboard wing of the bridge and let out a reverberating fart. The result was a combination of a flat calm, the confines of the bridge under the awnings, and a hearty breakfast of curry and rice. The stench was overpowering, even permeating into the wheelhouse. Captain Swindell then countermanded his order with the words "Perhaps you are right, Mr. Rowlands. We are too close. I can smell the sewers of San Francisco this far out." Owen Rowlands was a North

Welshman from Amlwch in Anglesey, possessing a dry wit and great sense of humour. He responded, "Captain, I believe that the shit house is a lot closer than San Francisco." Both he and Captain Swindell were quite unforgettable characters.

We docked in Vancouver several days later, and I was released on leave to enjoy the luxury of my home. After loading part cargo of grain in North Vancouver, the ship moved to New Westminster and then to Victoria, where I rejoined her about two weeks later. We put to sea shortly afterwards.

Again, we carried passengers for the return passage, a married couple. The husband conceived that he had freedom of the ship to fraternise with the crew, and on a number of occasions went aft to chat with the deck hands and firemen. When the Master and officers remonstrated with him, he took offence because he felt that such a restriction consti- tuted racial and class discrimination against the lower deck personnel. It was pointed out to the passenger that it was not easy for an inexperienced person to negotiate the journey along the deck cargo aft and amidships, during the hours of darkness, or in bad weather.

As a compromise, he was permitted to go aft as far as the galley during the daylight hours, when he could be observed by the officer of the watch and members of the watch on deck. This was conditional upon the under- standing that he was not permitted to distract men who were undertak- ing their duties. He was also enjoined to return to his cabin in the bridge accommodation before nightfall. This seemed to satisfy him.

Our passage to the Panama Canal was relatively uneventful except for one incident. Sunday afternoon after lunch was allocated to lifeboat drill, weather permitting. Although the weather conditions were not severe, on the first Sunday at sea the ship was pitching quite heavily into a moderate head sea. The First Mate gave the bosun the instruction to lift the port lifeboat out of her chocks, swing out the davits, secure the boat outboard, and then swing it back inboard, and return the boat to its chocks. The bosun protested that it would be dangerous to do so because the boat could take charge with the ship pitching so heavily. He received the answer "You do as you are bloody well ordered", so we got on with it.

It took all the deck hands to lift the heavy 27-foot long class 1A lifeboat from its chocks, manning the forward and after falls. The boat was lifted, and the forward and after guys manned preparatory to swing- ing it outboard. Then the after guy tackle parted as the boat took charge with the forward pitch of the ship, and the boat swung outboard through the radial movement of the davits, and then as violently inboard again, on the upward pitch of the bows, scattering the crew members like ninepins, and pinning the bosun to an awning spar by one hand. We then managed to get the boat under control and lower it to the chocks.

Miraculously, the only casualty was the bosun, Paddy Hennessey. The thumb of his right hand was almost severed at the knuckle. He turned to me and said, "Hold the end of the thumb, son", whereupon he took his knife from its sheath, and with one stroke chopped off the end of his thumb. He then unbuttoned his trousers, took out his stubby little penis, piddled on the bleeding stump of his thumb, and wrapped it in a dirty handkerchief. "I won't be needing that again". The end of his thumb went overboard, and we secured the boat and knocked off. The Kinsale Irish fishermen were a tough lot.

After traversing the Panama Canal, we bunkered at Port Royal as usual, and put to sea in the evening after a short stay. The first night in the Caribbean Sea after clearing Port Royal was quite wild, with a strong wind on the port bow, a rough breaking sea, and heavy rain squalls. Occasional seas were breaking over the forecastle head, and coming aboard in the waist amidships.

I went into the galley at about 1945, to make a cup of tea before turning in, just as one bell was rung, and the night watch were going on duty. The male passenger was sitting on the galley bench having a chat with the "black pan" firemen before they went below on watch. A member of the deck watch suggested to him that he should go forward to his cabin, and he agreed to do so. I then turned in. At about eight bells (2000), a sea came aboard amidships and filled the port outside alleyway right up to porthole level. I then went to sleep, but was awakened about an hour later by the sound of commotion in the alleyway. The wife of the passenger had gone to the cabin of the Master believing that her husband was with him, whereupon a search was made, and the passenger could not be found.

A crew member had seen him moving forward along the port alleyway at just about eight bells, so he must have been either in the alleyway or on the amidships deck cargo when the sea broke aboard. He had not only disregarded the instruction to return to his cabin in daylight, but had used the weather instead of the lee alleyway. His wife was in a state of hysteria by then and, although it was hopeless, we rigged cargo light clusters in the rigging and reversed our course for two hours. It was a hopeless search, which we abandoned at about midnight.

Although the passenger had disregarded many exhortations not to go aft to fraternise with the crew, this did not serve to alleviate the problems faced by the Master, after having lost a passenger overboard. He had to face the problem of completing the fateful voyage with the distraught widow as the only female on board the ship. No doubt, he would have been forced to face an official inquiry into the event, but we never learned about the findings.

The ship docked in London and discharged her cargo, following which we made passage to South Wales, where we paid off on 20 December 1936. Hector Ling paid off. I lost contact with him. He was then very much smitten by a girl in his native Barry Docks, and I believe that she may have induced him to "swallow the anchor" and take up life ashore. He never maintained contact with us from the day when he left the ship. Arthur Hall "jumped ship", and his parents or his surety will have paid what the indentures termed "the penal sum of £ 20." Two voyages later he boarded the ship in Newport and burst into our cabin like a whirlwind, dressed in the uniform of an ordinary seaman in the Royal Navy. I reflect on whether he survived the war.

The First Mate, Mr. Rice, just disappeared from the scene. He went ashore, ostensibly going on leave, and did not return. During the Spanish civil war in 1938, we received a report that Mr. Rice was killed in a Fascist bombing raid on a Spanish port. Mr. D.J. Davies, a native of Cardigan, signed on as First Mate. Johnny Hay, the son of a Treorchy clergyman, signed on as Second Mate. We were not sorry to lose Mr. Rice, who seemed to have an antipathy towards apprentices. Certainly, he showed neither concern for us, nor any vestige of consideration.

APPLEDORE – VOYAGE 22

U.K. to River Plate
21 December 1936 to 4 April 1937

Our stay in Barry Docks followed the usual pattern. The marine superintendent boarded the ship as soon as she was made fast, and the customary routine of invective and bullying commenced as soon as he stepped aboard. I made a vow that I would never allow myself to suffer the indignities meted out by this thoroughly reprehensible character. In my lowly rank, I was below the level of recognition. As usual, we put to sea with the customary huge pile of bunker coal on No. 3 hold and on deck amidships. This was now in the winter season, so we rigged lifelines over the coal before reaching Lundy Island.

1937 – Bay of Biscay
Rolling her gunwales under. Rolling
to port 60 degrees

1940 – Hove to in fierce gale
Taking a heavy sea over the forecastle head

Appledore in very heavy weather, Bay of Biscay and North Atlantic

When we had cleared the Bristol Channel, the wind was increasing, and we encountered winds of strong to whole gale strength, force 9 to 10 on the Beaufort scale, in the Bay of Biscay. The huge seas on the starboard beam caused the ship to roll so violently, that it was difficult to retain a footing on the decks, and made crossing the coal on deck amidships very hazardous. Despite this, the bunkers had to be trimmed below decks, and the deck hands had to undertake this dangerous work in the appalling conditions, with the ship rolling on her beam-ends, storm force winds and frequent violent squalls of rain, sleet and snow. We had completed this work by the time we cleared the Bay of Biscay, when the weather had moderated.

I had then been allocated to duties in a watch, taking my turns on the helm, lookout and on standby. During one night, when on lookout on the forecastle head, I reported that the foremast light was not showing, to receive the answer by megaphone from the bridge "Come to the bridge, son". When I reached the bridge, the officer of the watch greeted me by handing me a light bulb, with the instruction "Replace the foremast light bulb". Fortunately, the ship was rolling gently in the beam swell, but this was the first time when I had been ordered to go aloft, and I was quietly shitting myself as I climbed the fifty feet to the fore cross trees in pitch darkness.

When I reached the cross trees, I sat there with my legs around the mast and my feet braced against the handrail stanchions, while I tried to unscrew the brass wing nuts securing the cover of the lamp casing. Quite miraculously, this was not difficult, but there was a problem in what to do with the cover when I replaced the lamp bulb, so I shoved it under one leg, and eventually the work was completed. I descended to the main deck, and was bloody glad to be there.

The routine was similar to that on all outward-bound passages: trimming down the bunkers, battening down, washing down, cleaning paintwork, bilge diving, and the erection of shifting boards and feeder boards. I was now deemed sufficiently experienced to work on the erection of the shifting and feeder boards. Compared with bilge diving, this was relatively clean work. Two men were required to sit in rope ladders suspended from the main deck hatch beams. The heavy shifting boards were lifted by tackles, and guided into place between vertical members, where they were bolted together, and the ends secured in grooves in the forward and after bulkheads.

Enormous physical effort was required to handle the heavy boards, when sitting on the rungs of a rope ladder, swinging violently from the lower hold deck heads. It was a strenuous and exhausting task. Despite the arduous and potentially dangerous nature of the work of erecting shifting boards, we escaped serious injury, apart from bruising and abrasions, and other physical damage mainly to fingers and hands.

Overcoming the rust deposits was a perennial activity, requiring the systematic chipping, painting and scraping of the decks, deck heads and bulkheads, to be painted with a first coat of a mixture of red lead, red oxide, boiled linseed oil and Terebine. First Mates and bosuns had their own particular paint mixing formulae for priming, undercoat and finishing paintwork, and rigidly insisted that we follow them. The mixture for undercoat usually included white lead, white zinc, raw linseed oil and turpentine, in whatever proportions suited the formula of each individual. In this, as always, Bill Ross was a master.

We encountered mostly fine weather on the passage to the River

Plate, passing east of the Azores, west of the Canary Islands and west of St. Paul Rocks, making landfall near the island of Fernando Norohna off the coast of Brazil. We then continued on a southerly course along the coast of Brazil to the delta of Rio de la Plata, where we anchored. The short stay at anchor in the estuary off Buenos Aires was pleasant. The estuary of the huge river was almost free of salt water; so all the restrictions that had been imposed on the use of fresh water were eliminated during our time there. In addition, the hoses were able to pump fresh water on deck, another luxury.

While at anchor in Buenos Aires Roads, I was introduced to the positively terrifying work of stowing the anchor cables. The term cable is a misnomer, being usually descriptive of a wire hawser. When associated with the usual bower anchors fitted to ships, the term chain cable is used. The heavy stud links of the chain were forged in lengths of 15 fathoms or 90 feet, and connected by shackles. Each length was termed a shackle of cable. Ships usually carried nine or ten shackles in each of their port and starboard chain lockers under the forecastle head. Most modern ships incorporated self-stowing chain lockers. These were so constructed as to obviate the necessity for human assistance in stowing the chain cable. The ships of the Tatem fleet did not possess the luxury of self-stowing chain lockers. As usual in their regimes, apprentices were given the incredibly dangerous work, usually working in pairs.

The port and starboard chain lockers were situated immediately under the steam windlass on the forecastle head. They were deep narrow dungeons extending from the double bottom to the forecastle deck. Chain cable led from each locker through the spurlingate pipes, over the port and starboard gypsies of the windlass, and down the port and starboard hawse pipes to the five-ton bower anchors. When heaving anchor, the sprockets of the gypsies engaged each link of chain in turn, and the chain cable passed down the spurlingate pipes into the locker. In self-stowing lockers, the spurlingate pipes canted away from the centre line of the ship, so that the chain cable entered the lockers on their centre line, where it lay in relatively symmetrical piles, ready for letting go of the anchor.

In *Appledore* and her type, the spurlingate pipes lay in a vertical plane, depositing the chain cable against the bulkhead separating the port and starboard chain lockers. Therefore, it was necessary for men to enter the lockers, physically to coil the very heavy links of chain cable. For this purpose, one man had to stand successively on one of a number on a precarious shelves secured to the ship's side in the locker. As the chain was piled in the locker, he climbed upwards from one shelf to the other. He was furnished with a stout hook on a shaft about four feet long that he used to pull the chain cable away from the central bulkhead. The other man stood on the pile of chain in the bottom of the locker, near the central bulkhead, and pushed the chain towards his companion, using his shoulder. He tried to maintain a foothold on the uneven pile of chain that was covered by mud and slime, and avoid being trapped under the large and very heavy links of chain cable. It was very dangerous work.

The lockers were invariably overpoweringly hot, and the only light was provided by a hurricane lamp secured to the deck head. The stench from accumulated mud and slime and decaying shellfish was unbelievable. By means of one man pushing the chain cable with his shoulder, and the other pulling with his hook, the huge links of chain were coiled around the lockers. Despite the hosing down of the chain cable as it emerged from the hawse pipes, the links in the lockers and those being stowed were covered in slime and stinking mud; so it was precarious to stand, either on the chain links or the shelf.

It was extremely difficult to communicate with those on deck, above the noise of the windlass and the clanking and banging of the chain; so in the event of a mishap in the locker the hapless victim stood a chance of being buried under tons of chain. Many able seamen refused to work in such lockers, but apprentices did not enjoy any rights at all, and this work was usually undertaken by the apprentices on *Appledore*. We dreaded the task, and despite having to undertake the work many times, on each occasion we faced with great apprehension the prospect of being crushed by tons of chain cable.

We berthed for a short time in Buenos Aires for the Master to go ashore, and then received orders to move up river above Rosario to the small port of San Nicholas on the Parana' River. San Nicholas was a small community situated on a hill above a backwater off the main river. The approach was difficult, and necessitated dropping the stream anchor from the stern in mid river, and moving slowly ahead to the loading berth, paying out the anchor warp wire as the ship moved ahead.

The ship carried a small kedge anchor weighing about one and a half tons, and a larger stream anchor, which was a heavy brute weighing over three tons. Both were of the old fashioned stocked type in use for hundreds of years, and were housed in a vertical position on the bulkhead of the poop accommodation superstructure, and secured by clamps. A heavy davit, to lift them and swing them outboard, was situated on the starboard side of the poop deck.

I was detailed to work with the after mooring party with the Second Mate, Johnny Hay, and a number of seamen. We cleared away the stream anchor and shackled on the after Board of Trade wire. These mooring wires were of three and a half inches circumference, and were stored respectively on drums on the forecastle head and poop. They were used as additional mooring wires of greater strength than the seven and a half inch circumference Manila hemp mooring ropes, and the smaller diameter flexible wire rope spring wires. The anchor was lifted by a three-fold tackle with the hauling part led through snatch blocks to the drum end of the starboard No. 5 hold winch.

It was then swung outboard, lowered below deck level and secured to a pair of mooring bollards. That was when we encountered trouble. The bulb on the end of the anchor stock obstructed on the lip of one of the accommodation portholes. The anchor was hanging on this precarious support, and the wire on the bollards became slack. I was ordered to shake the wire turns on the bollards, and take in the slack, when suddenly the three ton stream anchor freed itself from the porthole ledge, and fell about six inches until it was arrested by the turns of wire on the bollard.

My right hand was on one of the turns of wire, and the jerk carried my hand between the tightening wire and the bollard, trapping four fingers between the top and middle knuckles. I could feel the bones being crushed by the heavy weight and the pain was excruciating; but the only way that my fingers could be extricated was to slack the wire with the full weight of the anchor, and allow my fingers to be carried right around the bollard, until they would be freed at the other side. One of the deck hands slacked away on the wire, and after the anchor had been lowered about another two feet, my mangled fingers were freed. The four fingers were in a hell of state, the nails torn off, the broken bones of the fingers exposed, and the whole mess covered in grease, dirt, and oozing blood.

I was ordered to go forward to report to the First Mate. He took out a basin, poured in some iodine, and held my fingers in the antiseptic solution. The fingers were then swabbed with hydrogen peroxide, and bandaged firmly together. All he said was, "You silly bugger. You should have kept your hands clear of the wire. Now, off to work." I then returned to my duties. We paid away on the warp, and berthed alongside the jetty under the cliffs on which San Nicholas was situated.

I was then put to work preparing the No. 4 derricks. The topping lifts were permanently attached to the winches, but the guys and tackles had to be secured to the derricks, before they were hoisted. Unfortunately, I hoisted the derrick without having fitted its flexible steel wire rope preventer and hoisted the derrick minus its preventer. When the First Mate saw this, he ordered me to shin up the guy rope of the port derrick, dragging the heavy preventer behind me. I managed to climb to the derrick head about 25 feet above deck, and secured the preventer over the derrick head, with great difficulty with one good left hand, and the right hand quite useless. Then I lost my grip, and fell headlong. Fortunately, my fall was arrested by the main topmast forestay, and I slid down the stay, and ended in a heap on the boat deck. I was taken to hospital, but the damage had been limited to severe bruising. That was the first and last time I forgot to fit the preventer to a derrick.

The ship remained in San Nicholas for several weeks, when a cargo of part bulk and part bagged grain was loaded by the most archaic of methods. Grain in bags was carried in carts drawn by mules to an area on the cliff top above the berth, where it was unloaded by hand onto wooden chutes. Each of the five cargo holds was served by chutes, which terminated at benches on the hatch boards. The bags of grain slid down the chutes, coming to rest by benches. A number of hatch boards had been removed adjacent to the benches, giving access to the holds. Stevedores sat on the benches and bled the grain from the sacks into the holds by cutting the twine binding of the sacks. The empty sacks were then bundled and returned to the cliff top, and taken back to the grain silos for re-filling. Then the tedious process was repeated. We loaded grain in bags in the 'tween decks.

After loading deeper than our fresh water marks – to compensate for the fuel to be burned on our passage down river – the ship was warped out of her berth on the stream anchor, into mid river, the stream anchor was lifted, and we made passage down river to Buenos Aires. We then put to sea, interrupting our passage at Las Palmas, where we received orders, and re-fuelled. The passage to the U.K. was uneventful. We followed the usual homeward bound routine of painting the accommodation, masts, rigging and funnel, different sections of the ship being covered on each voyage.

We made port in London and docked in Surrey Commercial Docks. After we had discharged our cargo of grain, we put to sea for South Wales, where we paid off on 4 April 1937.

By the end of the voyage, the mangled fingers of my right hand had healed, and new nails were growing. The little finger had retained its shape, but the top joint had been broken so badly that the finger could not be bent. The middle and fourth fingers were twisted and misshapen, and movements of the top joints were ruined. The joints of the index finger had escaped damage, but the finger had been twisted, when the other fingers were trapped in the turns of wire on the bollard.

I was very fortunate to have escaped more serious injury, when the fingers of my right hand had been trapped in the turns of the warp of the stream anchor. The strain of the three ton weight compressing four fingers between the wire warp and the bollard could have severed the fingers; so I had escaped with relatively modest injury. It was an excruciatingly painful experience, when my fingers were carried, under enormous pressure, all round the circumference of the bollard. Although the four fingers were permanently misshapen, the use of my right hand has never been seriously impaired.

7

LATER YEARS AS A MIDSHIPMAN, 1937–1939

Captain John Swindell left the ship, and was relieved in command by Captain D.P. James, a native of Cardigan. Captain D.P. James proved to be a martinet of the old school, always immaculate in his appearance. Regardless of weather conditions, when in blue uniform he always wore a tie, and when in white uniform, his tunic was buttoned to the top, and even clipped at the throat. Although ships were usually kept in smart condition, the dress code of the officers had been relaxed, and varied appreciably from ship to ship. They usually wore blue serge trousers and blue patrol jackets, over an open neck shirt or roll-neck pullover. Captain James insisted on collars and ties in the mess. He was also very particular about the meticulous care of HIS domain, the lower bridge. Any traces of salt spray had to be washed off the handrails, and HIS awnings had to be scrubbed by hand, using soft soap, to give them a gleaming white appearance.

Moreover, he was equally meticulous in the observance of naval protocol when we encountered ships of war. Our Red Ensign was always hoisted at the flagstaff aft at daybreak, and lowered at sunset when the ship was in port. Immediately the last mooring rope was cast off, the ensign was transferred and flown from the gaff halyard on the mainmast, when the ship was under way.

As soon as a warship was observed, the standby man was summoned by one blast of the whistle of the officer of the watch, and ordered to stand by the gaff halyards. As the ships drew abeam of each other, a whistle signal ordered the dipping of our ensign, which was held in the dipped position while the warship dipped her ensign in acknowledgement. A further whistle signal ordered the hoisting of our ensign, which followed that of the warship, as her ensign was returned to its fully hoisted position.

This protocol of dipping the ensign to a ship of war had to be timed exactly, to the complete satisfaction of the Master. His weekly inspections of his ship were also undertaken with similar care and attention, and woe betide the cook or steward who had a greasy or dirty cooking utensil. He wore white gloves when on inspections, which found every vestige of dirt and grease, even on the tops of doors. On one occasion, he detected a small trace of grease in a cooking pot, with the comment to the cook "What's this I have found, Cookie?"

With Captain David P. James, excellence was deemed the norm, and perfection the constant aim. He forbade the use of Christian name terms between brother officers on the bridge or at the mess table. When addressing an officer, he was meticulous in the use of MISTER, except in the case of the Chief Engineer, whom he always addressed as "Chief". Although he was a strict disciplinarian, his judgements were always fair and objective; and his care for injured or sick subordinates was kind and considerate. Captain James was in every way an ideal ship's Master, and an individual whom I will always remember with respect and admiration.

The passage to Sydney New South Wales in ballast, and the return passage loaded with grain, was the longest and most monotonous voyage during my life at sea. We put to sea as usual with untrimmed bunkers on deck amidships. The passage to the Cape of Good Hope took about 28 days, without sight of land. We rounded the cape out of sight of land, and after a further passage of over a month made landfall in the Bass Strait between Tasmania and Australia, the total passage to Sydney New South Wales taking over 60 days.

The passage to the Cape of Good Hope was as uncomfortable as it could be sailing in ballast, with the ship alternating between violent rolling, to pitching so heavily that the bows and the propeller were out of the water alternately as she pitched. This was termed "hitting the milestones". The ship was shaking from stem to stern, and seemed to be falling apart. Then on the passage from the Cape of Good Hope to Australia, "running down the easting" in the Roaring Forties, we encountered continuous huge following seas that never relented. Although the ship was usually dry when in ballast, there were times when we were taking green water aboard forward and over the quarter in the winter seas of the southern hemisphere. The almost constant gales were accompanied by rain squalls so fierce that the amidships scuppers and wash ports were unable to clear the water on deck.

I suffered another accident as we were entering Sydney harbour. It was my trick at the helm as we approached the harbour entrance. I was awakened by the standby man later than usual, and was attempting to drink a very hot mug of cocoa as eight bells sounded. In my haste, I scalded my mouth and throat in gulping down the cocoa, then slipped as I raced for the lower bridge ladder, cracking my kneecap open on the serrated brass step of the ladder. The bone was broken right across, the knee was bleeding profusely, and it was very painful. However, I took the helm, and stood on one leg for the rest of my trick. There was no alternative. A cracked kneecap was an unimportant event. Fortunately, the pilot had boarded, and we were soon alongside.

It was usual for ships loading grain at the elevators in Sydney to be turned around in about 36 hours. From the time when we berthed until the time we put to sea fully loaded with over 9,000 tons of grain, less than 48 hours had elapsed, and less than a week after traversing the Bass Strait on the outward passage, we were traversing the Great Australian Bight, homeward bound.

We were now deeply loaded, and pitching into the continuous westerly gales and heavy seas, with lifelines rigged fore and aft and heavy seas breaking aboard continuously. The westerly winds had unobstructed passage around the circumference of the earth, creating huge head seas. It was mid-winter in the Roaring Forties, with frequent rain, sleet and snow showers and always the gale force winds. The outside alleyways were constantly awash, and the access doors to the accommodation were always shut, so the damp permeated into every part of the accommodation. Our cabins stank of damp clothing, soaking oilskins and sea boots.

We were over a month on passage to South Africa, where we made port at Durban on the south east coast, for a short stay to replenish bunkers. After less than a day we put to sea in the face of a severe westerly gale, with the seas breaking green over the forecastle head, even as we cleared the breakwater. We carried the gale with us until we had rounded the Cape of Good Hope, and commenced our northerly passage in the Atlantic Ocean. About two weeks later we made port in Dakar in West Africa, where we again replenished our bunkers, remaining at anchor in the roads for a day. Once again, Jumbo James and I were detailed to the filthy and dangerous work of stowing the chain cable.

On the passage between Dakar and the U.K., I was deemed sufficiently experienced to be given the work of painting down the main topmast. This was a comparatively uncomplicated task, because the mainmast did not carry a long signal yard, only a gaff. The gaff could be topped to a vertical posture, making it easy for painting, without leaving the bosun's chair, as was the case when painting the foremast signal yard. The mainmast was painted black down to the crosstrees, and mast colour from the cross trees to the deck. Once hoisted aloft, the bosun's chair was secured by a sheet bend through the harness of the chair and around the body. Thus, the man working aloft was able to feed the slack of the gantline through the sheet bend, and lower himself.

The first element of work was the painting of the four topmast stays from their seizings at the mast head to the deck, using a mixture of white lead and tallow, applied by a wad. This required being hoisted to the mast head, about 85 feet above deck level, four times, shackling on to each stay in turn, and being lowered slowly to the deck. When the fore and after stays and two back stays had been completed, the gaff topping lift was treated, followed by the gaff and mast down to the crosstrees, in black paint. Next the six shrouds for the lower mainmast were treated with white lead and tallow, followed by the lower mast, painted mast colour, and finally the stay and shroud seizings at deck level, painted black.

Four hours was the time allocated for the work. It was frightening to go aloft on the first occasion, but afterwards I found it exhilarating. After painting the mainmast, other seamen were aloft on the foremast. I was put to work painting the funnel, with one other deck hand. The funnel was of single plate construction, so the lee side was always very hot. Many ships of the era were fitted with funnels of double plate construction, with a cowl at the top. These were known as "foreskin funnels", and were reputed to be relatively cool.

Juniors were always allocated the most uncomfortable work, so I went aloft on the lee side of the funnel. The bosun's chairs were suspended by hooks over the top lips of the funnel, and could be worked around its circumference by swinging the chair outwards, and kicking along on the funnel. Working on the weather side was hot, dirty work, but the lee side in a fresh breeze was purgatory, particularly near the top of the funnel, where a combination of blinding fumes and the hot plates of the funnel scorched arms and legs. It was just another task in the constant battle against corrosion.

By the time we made land in the English Channel, all the top works had been painted, and the ship was in immaculate condition, except for the hull.

We made port in London early in the month of August 1937, after being at sea for 137 days with 48 hours in port. I had then completed just over my first year at sea. After discharging our cargo in London, we put to sea for the passage to Newport in South Wales, where we paid off on 16 August 1937. During our stay in London, the deck hands and apprentices were put to work over the side on stages, painting the hull black down to the level of the boot topping at water level.

APPLEDORE – VOYAGE 24

Voyage 24 – U.K./Genoa/Licata to Geraldton
17 August 1937 to 19 February 1938

We signed on the following day, 17 August 1937. The ship was dry docked for bottom painting and engine repairs, after our long period at sea, and the anchors, chain cables and their shackles were again tested at the Lloyd's Proving House. We then loaded bunkers and a cargo of Welsh steam coal.

Appledore put to sea at the end of August 1937, bound for the Italian port of Genoa. All the cargo was battened down below decks, and on this occasion, the bunkers were properly trimmed below and battened down. Even our cheeseparing marine superintendent appeared to have appreciated just how dangerous it would have been to put to sea in a loaded condition with bunker coal loose on deck. Our passage to the Straits of Gibraltar was uneventful.

The Spanish Civil War was raging on land, and there had been engagements between the naval forces of the protagonists, and bombing attacks on ships by German and Italian aircraft; but the bombing attacks had been generally restricted to ships in port, or approaching port with the intention of running the blockade. Ships passing well clear of the coast were usually unmolested. *Appledore* was the exception, because as we approached the Straits of Gibraltar in darkness, we were challenged by the Spanish cruiser *Canarias*. Searchlights were trained upon our ship, a shot was fired across our bows, and we were ordered to stop, by command delivered over a megaphone.

We were not certain whether *Canarias* was in the armed forces of the Republicans or Nationalists. It appeared to us that the civil war was a convenient excuse for the intervention of the Communists on one side and the Fascists on the opposite side. The Spanish people were the sufferers, regardless of the faction they appeared to support. There was then a great deal of blockade running by a number of smaller British

ships, and one Master achieved temporary publicity in the trade in potatoes to northern Spain, earning himself the nickname of "Potato Jones".
It is likely that our wireless operator sent a general signal reporting the
event of our being challenged by a Spanish warship. This may have
resulted in the prompt intervention of *H.M.S. Hood.*

We were about to comply with the challenge when a huge shape
loomed through the darkness, and *Canarias* was intercepted by the battle
cruiser *H.M.S. Hood.* There would have been nicotine stains on the underpants of a few Spaniards, if they had persisted in challenging a British
ship in the face of such force, particularly the most powerful British
warship. *Canarias* withdrew and we continued without further challenge.

The rest of the passage was without incident, and we made port in
Genoa in about the middle of September 1937, where we discharged our
cargo. The government of Italy had been taken over by the Fascist regime
of Benito Mussolini. The people were oppressed, frightened, and poverty
stricken. Before I joined *Appledore*, the ship had been impounded for 100
days in the Eritrean port of Massowa by the Italian forces then attacking
Abyssinia, and in partial occupation of the country.

The ship had carried a cargo of oats loaded in Odessa, and destined
for feeding the mules used by the Italian army during its campaign. The
crew had suffered severely from malnutrition and disease during their
period of over three months in captivity, and when they were released
only a handful of men were fit enough to take the ship to sea. Jumbo
James, who was one of them, related the details of their 100 days in
captivity. He had no love for the Italians, or our government, which stood
aside while a British ship was so flagrantly held captive by a foreign
power. After release, *Appledore*, with its skeleton crew, and over 30 men in
their bunks due to sickness, made port in Aden. There they recovered.
Jumbo James recounted to me how the very few able men had worked the
ship on the passage in the Red Sea, from Massowa to Aden. They all
worked in the stokehold to shovel coal into the three fires to raise steam
in one boiler. The engines were started, and the ship moved at slow speed
for a short distance. The ship was anchored for enough time to raise
steam again, and so the process was repeated until they made port in
Aden. This happened in temperatures of over 100 degrees Fahrenheit

We put to sea after about two weeks in Genoa, destination Licata in
Sicily. The distance between ports is less than 400 miles, a steaming time
of just over 36 hours, during which time all deck hands worked night and
day to prepare the ship for its next cargo. It was necessary to wash down
the five cargo holds and pump out the bilges, re-cover the bilges with

burlap, and have the ship ready for loading, in less than two days. With the bilge pumps and hoses working continuously washing down all five holds, the ship left a huge black slick in its wake.

Someone had bought a demijohn of inexpensive raw Italian brandy, which served to keep us going during our hectic work. This large bottle of firewater was passed from hand to hand, and helped to keep us awake during nearly two days of continuous arduous work.

Licata is a small seaport on the west coast of Sicily, protected by a breakwater. The water is relatively shallow alongside, so only a small part of our cargo of bulk sulphur could be loaded when berthed at the quay. This was brought to the ship on donkey carts in large wicker baskets, two baskets to each cart, each weighing about a half a ton. The derricks were rigged outboard in single gear, and the baskets were whipped aboard and emptied into the holds. When we had loaded an amount of cargo limited by our draft in the shallow water, we moved into deeper water; with both bower anchors out and two stern ropes secured to the breakwater.

Moving berth to deeper water every day again required the apprentices to stow the chain cable in the frightening confines of our chain lockers. On this occasion, the chain cables in both lockers were stowed simultaneously as we heaved both bower anchors; so two able seamen were detailed to work with us.

The baskets of bulk sulphur were then carried to the ship on open boats about 30 feet long, under sail, a single lateen sail on a long spar, with two baskets on each boat, on platforms laid across the thwarts. The manner in which the Sicilian seamen handled the boats was nothing short of uncanny; and despite the fact that dozens of boats were plying back and forth and luffing into the wind, to wait their turn alongside, they never collided with each other. It was a revelation for even our experienced seamen to observe the proficiency of the Sicilian seamen.

As the ship loaded deeper, we moved further away from the breakwater, until the cargo was fully loaded. By then, we had used up all of our mooring ropes, rigged end to end, and were moored at a substantial distance from the shore.

The poverty suffered by the most charming and friendly Sicilians was unbelievable. As the galley garbage of potato peelings, stale bread, salt pork and beef fat, and other rubbish was dumped over the side, hordes of children would be swimming alongside gobbling it up as it floated away. The people were terrified of Mussolini and his secret police; but occasionally, we would hear the words "Mussolini no f——g bueno". After about two weeks loading, we put to sea, destination Geraldton in

Western Australia.

We arrived in Port Said about the third week in October 1937, traversed the Suez Canal, and reached the Indian Ocean a week later. The Suez Canal was fascinating. A powerful searchlight was loaded aboard in Port Said, to be used during the night passage of the canal. The channel navigating buoys were fitted with reflectors instead of the usual electric lights, and in the beams of the searchlights showed up like the cats eyes on our roads. The passages through the Red Sea and Indian Ocean were uneventful, and we berthed in Geraldton, Western Australia after a passage of about three weeks.

Geraldton appeared to be a hotbed of homosexual men. A number of them boarded the ship in order to develop relationships with the crew. They gave themselves exotic names such as "Annie Laurie", "Dulcie the Duchess" and "Dolores". They were referred to as "brown hatters" or "two men looking the same way" in the vernacular of the forecastle.

After discharging cargo, we put to sea, destination Geelong, near Melbourne. On passage through the Great Australian Bight, we encountered fierce gales with tumultuous seas and violent rain squalls. During one squall, lightning struck the foremast, tearing away the lightning conductor and demagnetising the ship. This affected all the magnetic compasses, except for a lifeboat compass, which worked in reverse. This was rigged in the wheelhouse, and we steered by this means until we reached Geelong, where the compass adjuster boarded the ship and corrected the steering and other compasses. The ship eventually recovered its polarity, but the compasses had to be adjusted again in U.K. port.

While we were berthed in Geelong, *Harbledown* of J. & C. Harrison Line, and the almost new Alfred Holt Liner *Charon* were lying respectively across the berth and ahead of us. *Charon* was a particularly smart ship, all "spit and polish", with a Lascar crew. Every morning, one of the quartermasters climbed the masts and polished the lightning conductors with Brasso. The brass lightning conductors extended from the deck to the trucks at the tops of the masts. However, if you gave a Lascar some polish and a rag, he would happily rub away on the same place forever.

A cadet in white uniform was stationed at the bottom of the companionway, saluting the officers, ladies and others who boarded the ship. The Blue Funnel Line of Alfred Holt Ltd, and the P.& O. Line were reputed to be the "crème de la crème" of the British Merchant Navy. It had been alleged that they requested permission to wear swords, and were given the Royal Assent on the condition that the sword and scabbard had to be worn on the right side; a polite way of telling them to bugger off. I have never ascertained whether this was true.

Harbledown was also a modern ship, a typical Harrison general trader with what we termed a "foreskin funnel", because it was a double-skin stack with a cowl on the top. When the Master of *Harbledown* and our Master observed the cadets of *Charon* on gangway duty, the apprentices on *Appledore* and *Harbledown* were detailed to similar duty. Captain James ordered us to wear our white uniforms, Blanco our shoes and stand at the foot of the companionway, tunics buttoned to the throat and clipped at the collar. It was purgatory for us in the oppressive heat and humidity.

It proved to be a somewhat futile exercise, because very few people boarded the ship, with the exception of the Master and officers and the occasional port official or ship chandler. Although *Charon* was a relatively small ship, she carried 120 passengers, so the cadets were kept saluting all and sundry.

Sadly, *Harbledown* did not survive the war. She was torpedoed and sunk by U-94 in the North Atlantic in convoy SC26 on 4 April 1941, with the loss of 14 crew and 2 gunners. We had developed friendships with our fellow cadets and apprentices on the two ships, and I reflect upon whether they survived the loss of their fine ship. *Charon* survived the war.

We put to sea after about two weeks in Geelong, loaded with about 9,000 tons of grain. Although it was then the summer season in the southern hemisphere, the strong winds and heavy seas, so prevalent in the Roaring Forties, persisted, and the ship was buffeted by head winds and seas for the passage to Durban. When loaded, *Appledore* was a wet ship amidships, with seas almost constantly breaking aboard in the waist. The passage across the southern Indian Ocean took nearly a month. Because the ship was too wet for painting, we spent most of the time washing the paintwork, except on those days when the interminable westerly winds abated sufficiently.

We made port at Durban, where we stayed for a short time to replenish our bunkers. I visited members of the Whymark family, relatives through my paternal grandmother, who had settled in South Africa, after escaping as refugees from the Great Kanto earthquake in Yokohama in 1923.

After a short stay, we put to sea, destination Dakar in Senegal. When we entered the Atlantic Ocean and were on a northerly course, we encountered better weather. I was then ordered to work aloft again, being given the task of painting the foremast and rigging. I was instructed and supervised by Bill Ross, who had been promoted, and signed on as bosun.

The topmasts were constructed from pitch pine, with steel lower parts. They were designed so that they could be lowered by telescoping into the lower mast, to clear the bridges spanning the Manchester Ship Canal and other canal bridges.

The topmasts rested on heavy steel fids through the lower masts, and were lowered by wire ropes and sheaves on the bottom of the topmast and on the lower masts, after the fids had been removed. At the level of the crosstrees, the topmasts were wedged in place in the lower masts, and the joint kept watertight by a canvas gaiter, bound around the joint and painted. Dummy gantlines of ratline rope were permanently rove through the masthead sheaves of the two topmasts, a short distance above the circular band carrying the brackets for the rigging.

The first invariable rule was that the gantline, from which the seaman was suspended in the bosun's chair, had to be taken from an unused coil of best quality Manila hemp rope two and a half inches in circumference. This was married to the dummy gantline, and pulled through the masthead sheave.

Another rule that was enforced strictly, was that the seaman who would use the bosun's chair had to secure the gantline to his chair. No other person would be permitted to do so. Even when we relieved each other when working aloft, the chair would be disconnected from its gantline, and re-secured by the seaman who would continue the work. The rule was, "If you are going to get killed, it will be your own bloody fault."

The seaman working aloft would be hoisted to the masthead, where he secured himself by holding the two parts of the gantline above him with one hand to keep him in position. He then passed the hauling part of the gantline through the ropes of the bosun's chair, and carried the loop around his body, legs and feet, forming a sheet bend with the gantline around the ropes of the bosun's chair. He was then held by the sheet bend, through which he was able to slacken the gantline rope, and control his descent in short stages. Although working at a height of over eighty feet above deck, and sometimes swinging back and forth with the motion of the ship, an experienced seaman was not in serious danger when using sound gear secured expertly – *by himself*.

The fore topmast carried a huge pitch pine signal yard about 25 feet long. Why the otherwise niggardly Tatem Company incurred the expense of what was a relatively useless spar was a mystery. A steel wire jackstay between the fore topmast and the funnel would have been a far more practical method of carrying signal flags. However, the spar had to be washed and painted regularly, and this was a very difficult and potentially dangerous task. I had already worked aloft on a previous voyage, and had overcome my first apprehensions.

Washing and painting the foremast was similar to the work on the mainmast. The huge yard presented problems for even the most experienced seaman. Before going aloft, I was coached by Bill Ross, who also stood by, attending to the gantline. Firstly, I was hoisted to the masthead, where I shackled the chair to the yard arm topping lifts in turn, and treated them with white lead and tallow out to the ends of the yard arm. When this had been completed, I was lowered to the junction bracket between topmast and yard, and Bill Ross made fast the gantline to the drum end of No. 2 starboard winch.

The difficult task then began. It was necessary for the man aloft to lie over the yard, with a bucket of soogie moojie hanging on the right side of his chair, and a bucket of fresh water on the left side, and gradually inch himself the distance of about 12 feet to the end of the yard. His supporting gantline rope then constituted the hypotenuse of a right angled triangle, so it was necessary for the man attending the gantline on deck to feed slack, inch-by-inch, as the man made his precarious way to the end of the yard. By careful and constant adjustments, the chair was kept against the seat of the man aloft.

The washing process commenced at the end of the yard, and continued until the man aloft inched his way back to the mast. However, as he did so, the process reversed, because the gantline became slack, as he made his way inwards. Therefore, his attendant had to take in slack carefully, again inch-by-inch, to keep the chair on his seat. After the completion of the washing of the topmast and yard, the buckets were lowered to the deck, and the paint pots and brushes hoisted aloft to the man in the bosun's chair. The whole process was then repeated as the yards were painted.

With the constant attention of the experienced bosun I was kept on the seat of the chair, although lying over the spar; and I accomplished the washing and painting of the starboard and port sections of the yard. It was undoubtedly unnerving work. Like the chain lockers, the long yards on *Appledore* did not meet with unqualified favour. Once, in Barry Dock, when a number of new deck hands had signed on and were boarding the ship, an able seaman looked aloft, and, observed the exceptional length of the signal yard. He remarked, "If they bloody well believe that I will crawl out to the end of that f——g yard, they have no bloody hope". The foremast could not be completed in a watch of four hours, so the lower mast was finished in the following watch.

The passage from Dakar to the English Channel was uneventful. We encountered moderate weather and sea conditions. The ship arrived in the U.K., as usual in a smart condition, and discharged her cargo in Hull. Following discharge, we made passage to Barry Docks, where we paid off on 19 February 1938 after a voyage that had lasted for six months and three days.

Jumbo James had finished his time during the voyage, and left the ship to return to his home in Cardigan. He did not sign on as A.B. for a subsequent voyage. Although we had been close companions and friend for twenty months, I never heard from him again. During the war, I learned that he had been killed when his ship was lost. He was a good friend and fine shipmate.

APPLEDORE – VOYAGE 25

U.K. to British Columbia
28 February 1938 to 20 June 1938

The new First Mate, John Davies, was typical of many of the men who were natives of the Cardigan Bay sea-faring villages; clannish and nepotistic. It was not long before he began to replace our deck hands, as they paid off, with natives of the villages of Cardigan, St. Dogmaels, Llangranog and Newquay.

After the ship had spent nine days in dry dock, having her bottom scraped and painted, anchor cables and shackles tested, stern gland re-packed, and engines serviced, a new crew was engaged on 28 February 1938, for a voyage to British Columbia.

True to form, the First Mate had replaced a number of able seamen, an ordinary seaman and a deck boy with chums from the Cardigan Bay villages, namely able seamen Davie John Grey, John Bowen, Ivor Owen and David Davies, also Hodges, the new carpenter The deck boy was a daft chap whom we immediately called "Floppy". He had been taken from a farm, and was unbelievably dirty, scruffy and unintelligent. The First Mate also arranged to sign on his stepson, who had qualified for the degree of B.A. at Aberystwyth University. He was signed on ostensibly as a supernumerary with the pay of an ordinary seaman. A voyage in a merchant ship was supposed to broaden his knowledge. He had no nautical knowledge or experience, but had the nepotistic patronage of the First Mate. I recall one hard-bitten A.B. saying to him, when he made a mess of some work, when helping to splice a mooring wire. "You may be a B.A., but you will never make a f——g A.B."

Two close friends, with whom I had served since joining the ship, paid off in Barry. John ("Tassie") Brennan, the Tasmanian A.B., had met his future wife, Marie, in Newport at the end of the previous voyage, and settled ashore. Michael O'Driscoll, the giant A.B., also paid off. I maintained contact with John Brennan, but was sad to learn during the war that Michael O'Driscoll had lost his life when his ship was torpedoed and caught fire. He was burned to death. He was a fine seaman and good friend.

We put to sea, as customary with bunker coal on deck, and the usual routine followed during the next week. The passage to the Panama Canal was uneventful. I had now become a proficient helmsman, with greater experience of the vagaries of the steering behaviour of the ship than the newly signed deck hands. Therefore, I was detailed to helm duties when the ship was traversing the Culebra Cut in the canal.

Several days after leaving Cristobal, when on lookout one night, I was suddenly oppressed by shivering fits and profuse perspiration. The only way to keep warm was to stand in the forecastle head ventilator in the warm air rising from the forepeak. When the bells were struck, and I did not answer them, the officer of the watch sent the standby man forward to investigate. He found me slumped unconscious in the ventilator. I was carried to a spare cabin and the Master diagnosed malaria. His attention was considerate and dedicated, and within ten days, I was well enough to resume my duties, although still very weak. Captain David P. James was an exceptional Master, combining strict discipline with care and consideration for those subordinate to him. The after effects persisted periodically for many years, with attacks of jaundice, shivering and profuse perspiration.

My father and mother boarded the ship when we arrived in Vancouver, and were greeted by the Master. My mother asked him "May I please have my son for a while?" The answer was "The First Mate makes the decision concerning leave for the apprentices." An approach to John Davies received the answer that he could not release me from my duties. After twenty months without leave, this was monstrous, but the bugger would not relent, and I was kept aboard. Shortly afterwards, I observed his stepson leaving the ship on his way to attend the University of B.C., to visit the faculty as part of his ongoing educational experience. When my father learned of this, he was furious, and told the Master that he would immediately telephone the ship owners to report this blatant example of nepotism in favour of a supernumerary ordinary seaman, who was related

Appledore, Voyage 25, June 1938
Working aloft in tropical weather. Washing down the fore topmast 60 feet above decks

to John Davies. The result was that the stepson was recalled and kept aboard, and I was given leave. John Davies never forgot or forgave that incident. I enjoyed two weeks in the comfort of my home.

During my absence, Phillip Gordon Harris, a native of Vancouver, signed indentures and joined the ship. We were to serve together for over two years. We became very close friends.

I rejoined the ship in Victoria. Our passage to the Panama Canal was uneventful. My proficiency at the helm had come to the attention of the canal pilots, one of whom requested that I take the helm through the lakes and Culebra Cut. A rather amusing incident occurred when the pilot boarded just before lunchtime. The pilots usually brought their own food aboard in an icebox, because they did not trust the quality of the food on British general traders. Captain James told the pilot that we would be eating salt pork, which he really believed to be very good. The pilot agreed, and a plate of salt pork was brought to the bridge, all blubber and gristle, and accompanied by the inevitable haricot beans and potatoes. The pilot tried one mouthful, and said to the Master, "For Jesus Christ's sake Captain, how do you expect a human being to eat such bloody crap?" The pilot allowed me to share the contents of his icebox, fresh chicken sandwiches and salad, followed by ice cream. I enjoyed this sumptuous repast as we were waiting for the locks to fill. Captain James was not amused.

The passage to Port Royal and on to the U.K. was uneventful. In his typical clannish manner, the First Mate, John Davies, favoured the two able seamen from his Cardigan hometown with navigational instruction, although he left his junior officers to provide tuition for the apprentices. He did not like us at all, and the feelings were mutual. However, the Second Mate, Johnny Hay, was most helpful. I had then served for over two years, had achieved good results in the examinations set by the Merchant Navy Officers Training Board, and was able to take a sight and work the calculations for latitude and longitude. Phillip Harris was also proving to be an excellent pupil, and he and I practised semaphore signalling in our watches below, eventually achieving speeds well in excess of Board of Trade requirements.

On the return passage, the masts were not painted, only washed clean with soogie moogie, and I went aloft on the foremast for the second time. The bosun, Bill Ross, tended the gantline when I was aloft. He would not delegate this work on the fore topmast and yard arms to any able seaman, however competent. Though the work was hazardous, I was as safe as it was possible to be, and completed the work without any great difficulty. Otherwise, the work was typical homeward bound routine. We discharged in Surrey Commercial Docks in London, lying at the buoys and discharging into lighters and Thames barges.

During the stay at the buoys in London, it was the duty of the apprentices to ferry the crew ashore in one of the jolly boats, which were propelled by sculling with a single oar from a crutch in the transom. It was backbreaking work, sculling the heavy boat with its load of passengers to and from the jetty many times a day. We established a routine of leaving the ship at hourly intervals from 1800 to midnight, collecting our mainly drunken passengers as they arrived on the jetty. By a miracle, they were conveyed safely to the ship, where they lurched their uncertain ways aft to their drunken slumbers. The Master and officers had the privilege of breaking the routine. They carried whistles, which they blew to summon the jolly boat.

After two weeks in London, we put to sea for South Wales, and paid off in Barry Docks on 20 June 1938.

APPLEDORE – VOYAGE 26

U.K. to Texas City
21 June 1938 to 20 August 1938

Voyage 26 commenced at Barry Dock on 21 June 1938, destination the American Gulf of Mexico port of Texas City. The weather was reasonably moderate for our passage into mid-Atlantic, and we made good progress at an average speed of about 11 knots, passing west of the Azores Islands. After about ten days on passage, when in a position between Bermuda and the Bahamas Islands, we exchanged wireless signals with *Iddesleigh*, then on passage homeward bound from the Mexican Gulf, under the command of Captain J.H. Swindell, who had previously been in command of *Appledore*. Captain James permitted me to send a wireless message to Captain Swindell. The signal read, "Best wishes from Upton, apprentice on *Appledore*." The response was "Captain Swindell lost overboard 30 June 1938, signed J.P. Herbert First Mate".

I have since learned that Captain Swindell was last seen walking aft, and the manner of his loss is still a mystery. The position given in the official Log was shown as 25 – 35 north latitude, 79 – 58 west longitude, placing the ship west of the area known as the Bermuda Triangle, not a great distance off the coast of Florida, between Florida and the Bahamas Islands. This news came as a great shock, because Captain Swindell had been well liked and respected in the half deck of *Appledore*.

We had burned the bunker coal from our No. 3 cargo hold en route, and for about two days before arriving in Texas City all the deck hands were working around the clock to clear the hold ready for our grain cargo. The residue of the bunker coal was transferred to the other fuel bunkers. The hold was then washed down thoroughly, bilge boards lifted, and the bilges pumped out. This work had not been completed when we had arrived alongside. By then, we were exhausted.

We arrived alongside early in the morning. I worked with the forward mooring party with the First Mate, bosun and carpenter on the forecastle head. Phillip Harris was in the after mooring party with the Second Mate. When the ship was secure, the First Mate gave the order to the bosun that the men could knock off after opening the hatches and hoisting the derricks, but the boys would be employed cleaning the No. 3 bilges until the work had been completed. I asked Bill Ross the bosun whether I was classified as a man or a boy, and he replied that I was equivalent to an able seaman in experience. He deemed me a man, equivalent to an able seaman. Therefore, after the holds and derricks were ready for cargo, I drew hot water, and had a wash.

As I left the washroom, I encountered the First Mate by No. 4 hatch. He held a heavy hammer in his hand, which he had used to knock out the wedges securing the hatch battens. He greeted me with the words, "Upton, what the hell are you doing having a wash", to which my reply was, "The bosun gave me permission to knock off with the men, sir." His response was "You young bugger, get down with the boys and clean No. 3 bilges". He moved towards me, brandishing the hammer in a threatening manner. By then I had suffered enough of him, and my reaction to his aggressive attitude was, "Take a step towards me sir, and you and your bloody hammer are going over the wall." Thereupon, I walked away from him, went to our cabin, and turned in.

About ten minutes later, the bunk curtains were parted to reveal the livid ugly face of the First Mate, who shouted, "The Captain wants to see you now!" Captain James was at the top of the ladder leading to the lower bridge as I went forward, and greeted me with the words, "What the hell are you up to, refusing to obey an order from your superior officer?" I tried to explain the circumstances, but all he said was, "Do as you are bloody well told, and get down to the bilges right away." I refused, whereupon his parting words were, "You are shitting in your own nest, young man."

After returning to our cabin and reflecting on the incident, I returned to the bridge. The Master was in a more receptive and reasonable mood. He listened to my version of the event, which was that the First Mate had given the bosun an unequivocal order, which he had then countermanded. I told the Master that I would be posting a letter to my father, reporting the full circumstances, and requesting release from indentures on payment of the stipulated cash penalty.

The alternative was a request for transfer to a ship where the second in command behaved more like an officer, and less like a thug and bully, bestowing favours on his select clique and treating his apprentices like pieces of shit. I was entitled to request that my complaint and request be recorded in the Official Log, together with the version of the First Mate. John Davies had gone too far in his oppressive treatment, particularly in making threatening gestures with a hammer. It was fortunate for both of us that he had stepped back when I responded, because I was strong enough to have thrown him overboard, and was furious enough to have done so. Fortunately, I had resisted the temptation.

The Master did not repeat the order to clean the bilges. His only reaction was that he would speak to the First Mate. Therefore, I was allowed to return to our cabin and turn in. The following day, the First Mate entered our cabin, just before we turned to for work, greeting me with a most cordial expression and the words "Good morning bosun." He then told me that the bosun, Bill Ross, had been pinned to No. 5 hatch coaming by a hatch beam, and had suffered a severe compound fracture of his leg, which necessitated hospitalisation in Texas City. After the accident, the Master had conferred with the First Mate, and they had decided that I was the most appropriate member of the crew to serve as a replacement for the injured bosun.

It was positively astonishing to be confronted by such a change of attitude, but I agreed to undertake the duties of bosun. Following this, I encountered the Master amidships. His attitude was also most affable. He greeted me with "Have you written to your father yet, Upton?" When I said that I had not done so, he said, "Let us all forget what went on yesterday, and chuck it overboard with the slops, shall we?"

We signed on a British able seaman who had lost his ship when stranded ashore drunk, or more likely, had jumped ship and run out of money. I was promised the difference in pay between a bosun and an A.B., £ 1-10-0 a month, but this was never paid. My total cash advanced during voyage 26 amounted to eighteen shillings and two pence.

My first attempt to turn the crew to the following day was not an outstanding success. Although four of the able seamen were natives of Cardigan, with quite temperate habits, we had signed on in Barry two very tough Irishmen in the persons of Jimmy Greenaway and Paddy Courtney, together with a mad character from Glasgow. They had returned from a binge ashore in the early morning, and had turned in fully clothed. They were still half drunk when I entered the forecastle in the morning, and attempted to shake them out of their stupor. The decks were slippery with vomit and urine and the stench was overpowering. Then they decided to jump me, to take down my trousers.

"Let's have a look at the wedding tackle of the new bosun!" This resulted in a violent struggle in the hot and stinking forecastle. I managed to fight them off, and relief came when they started fighting among themselves. Eventually they turned to, but were not much use until they had sobered up. After that encounter, the deck hands were their usual grumbling, boisterous and hard-working selves.

We were alongside in Texas City for about ten days, loading a cargo of grain, following which we put to sea, destination Manchester, where we arrived in the first week of August 1938. After ten days in Manchester, we put to sea bound for South Wales, and paid off in Barry Docks on 20 August 1938.

A substantial number of British ships were being laid up in the immediate pre-war period, many lying at anchor in Falmouth Bay, and a great number in South Wales ports. About half the Tatem fleet lay side by side at the buoys in Barry Docks. The masters, mates and most engineers were sent on unpaid leave and the crews paid off. The apprentices serving in the ships, which were laid up at the buoys, remained aboard. Food was supplied by a stand-by cook. The stokehold fires were drawn, so we had neither steam nor electricity. I was then the senior in our group of ships, with their total complement of about fifteen apprentices, so was ordered to take charge and organise the various working parties.

We lay at the buoys for over a month, our working hours occupied by chipping, scraping and painting most of the time. During our spare time, we swung out a number of jolly boats and engaged in pulling and sailing races in the large area of the docks. We also formed a soccer team which we named "Tatem's Terriers", playing matches with the local clubs. Then there was the distraction of Barry Island, and its fairground, especially the Dodgems. We visited the fairground en masse, converging on any group of the young girls, who frequented the area. They pretended to play hard to get, but they loved being chased.

APPLEDORE – VOYAGE 27

U.K. to British Columbia
22 September 1938 to 9 January 1939

The short but idyllic interlude terminated when the master, officers and many of our previous crew rejoined the ship. We signed articles on 22 September 1938, and berthed alongside the coal tips, where we bunkered, took on stores and attended to the servicing of the engines. We put to sea several days later bound for British Columbia. The deck crew were unchanged, with the exception of the wild Scottish A.B., who went on a wild drunken binge, and never returned. John Davies remained as First Mate, and Owen Rowlands was promoted to Second Mate. Johnny Hay was transferred to the newly built motor ship, *Lady Glanely,* as Second Mate. The First Mate had selected one of his favourites, Davie John Grey to be bosun, a most inappropriate choice. I had served in a watch with Davie Grey on the previous voyage. He was an amenable companion, a talkative and innocuous little man, but a mediocre seaman. Compared with seamen like Paddy Hennessey and Bill Ross, he was a joke as a bosun, lacking the authority necessary for the rank.

However, he seemed to suit John Davies, who was now able to converse with his bosun in the Welsh language. Indeed, we had by then reached a situation in which even helm orders were given in Welsh. This caused problems when a seaman who was not conversant with the language manned the helm. Those of us who did not understand Welsh decided to put an end to this silly nonsense, which could have had serious consequences. When on watch, when I was manning the helm one night, the First Mate gave me an order in Welsh, without realising that the helmsman did not understand the language. I put the helm hard over, and the result was a scream from the wing of the bridge in English "What the f——g hell are you up to?"

There was no Welsh equivalent to the epithet he had expressed. My answer was "I thought you said hard a starboard, sir." John Davies looked through the wheelhouse door and said, "Oh, it's you, Upton. For God's sake, why didn't you tell me? Get back on your course". My response was, "How about speaking English, sir. Most of us will understand you then." I have never entertained sentiments adverse to any language, including Welsh, but when a small clique on a ship converse in the presence of those who cannot understand what they are saying, it is an ignorant, inconsiderate and rude practice.

Almost without exception, the seamen from Welsh speaking areas were fine shipmates, usually friendly, courteous and capable. Most were courteous enough to stop speaking in Welsh when in the presence of those not conversant with the language. John Davies was the exception, but soon changed his ways, certainly in respect of helm orders.

The passage to Vancouver was uneventful. Phillip Harris and I were allowed leave when the ship was loading in British Columbia, and after the customary period of about two weeks, we returned and the ship put to sea.

The only incident affecting me was when we were on homeward passage from the West Indies to the U.K. I was detailed to wash and paint the foremast, which I had accomplished without problems on two previous occasions. As usual an A.B. was detailed to man the gantline, and was stationed at the drum end of the No. 2 starboard winch where the gantline was belayed, to give and take in slack to ensure that the chair was always under control. The bosun, Davie Grey, instructed him to make fast the gantline and undertake other work, just at the critical time when

I was lying over the yard near its end on the starboard side. Therefore, as I inched my way back along the yard, painting my way towards the mast, the gantline became progressively slack. I had reached the lashing securing the yard to the backstay, when I found that the seat of the chair had lowered to my feet, and I was completely unsupported. Being precariously suspended eighty feet above the deck cargo was a terrifying and very dangerous predicament.

I managed to force my right arm over the yard and under the lashing to the backstay, as the chair and paint pot swung away from me against the topmast. I was then hanging by my right arm, swaying and twisting with the movement of the ship, and without any support from the chair. The head wind carried the paint down to the top and lower bridges, where the Master, Second Mate and two passengers were standing.

Fortunately, when he saw my predicament, the Second Mate took immediate action. The bosun's chair was lowered to the deck, and immediately an experienced A.B. was hoisted aloft, carrying a heaving line. He stood on the junction bracket between topmast and yard, and secured himself to the mast; then secured the chair to the heaving line, which he threw out over the yard topping lift. This enabled the men on deck to pull the chair out to where I was hanging, by then almost exhausted by the effort. I was then able to push my feet into the chair harness and release my grip on the lashing to the backstay.

The gantline was then hauled in until I was seated in the chair, supported by the gantline again, and held out at the end of the yard by the heaving line. They then slacked out the heaving line, and I swung slowly back to the mast, and was lowered to the crosstrees. The chair was then sent back aloft and the seaman, who had undoubtedly saved my life, was lowered to the deck.

When I reached the safety of the crosstrees, after the stupid action of Davie Grey had caused what would have been almost certain death, I called him everything I could summon from my vocabulary, using every epithet in the book, and was only stopped by the Master, who shouted, "Enough of that, Upton. Come on the bridge!" I was then severely reprimanded for using foul language within the hearing of a female passenger. Later, I was set to work scraping off the paint that had been spilt on the bridge handrails and decks, when my paint pot overturned. The work was done in my watch below, using a piece of broken glass as a scraper. The bloody fool of a bosun escaped without even mild reprimand. This was just one example of the sheer incompetence of the man whom John Davies had selected as bosun. Davie Grey was so anxious to ingratiate himself with the First Mate, that he placed the life of a shipmate in jeopardy. He was a very poor choice as bosun, but such was the nepotistic attitude of the First Mate. Fortunately, I was saved by the prompt action of the Second Mate, and the shipmate who went aloft at appreciable personal risk to help me.

A Swedish able seaman, named Oscar Lundgren, had signed articles in Barry at the beginning of the voyage. He was detailed to stand a watch with me. Oscar possessed a most unusual physique: a huge barrel chest and long, very muscular arms, supported on a pair of very short spindly legs. However, the predominant feature of his body was his huge penis, of which he was – justifiably – very proud. It was our usual custom to urinate over the side (on the lee side of course) when at sea, but not in port – certainly not during daylight hours. If spotted by the Dock Police an offender would have been taken before a magistrate and fined five shillings for "urinating in public".

Oscar disregarded this convention. The result was that when he would hang his huge "wedding tackle" over the side, the Cockney stevedores would stop work to have a look. One made the remark "He's unreeling the bleedin' fing like a fire 'ose!" Another described it as "Look mites, 'e got more to piss with than we 'ave to f.....g walk with!" and another, "Look, e's wringing it out like a bleedin' sweat rag!" Oscar proved to be a fine seaman, and an amenable watch mate.

During passage from the Panama Canal, in oppressively hot weather, the First Mate decided that the after peak ballast tank required painting. This work had never been undertaken previously in my experience. The paint used for this treatment was a product called Camrex, which had to be heated to boiling point on a brazier, and applied when scalding hot. When it oxidised, it left a sticky covering skin on the steel plates.

Access to the after peak was through one small manhole, through which our party of four was lowered, to stand on the stern tube. There were narrow gaps between the stern tube and the ship's side plates on both sides. These were only just sufficiently wide to admit the body of a man, and gave access to a very confined triangular space under the stern tube. Oscar just squeezed into the space. The buckets of Camrex were boiled on a brazier on deck, and lowered into the after peak, where the bubbling boiling liquid was applied to the plates with tar brushes. When it touched the cold plates, boiling Camrex particles spattered everywhere, and blistered any exposed skin. We protected ourselves with gunnysacks with holes for the head and arms, worn upside down. It was pure hell in a temperature of about 130 degrees F.

When Oscar had finished in the space under the stern tube, he became stuck between the ship's side and the stern tube, due to his body having swollen in the heat. With two men on each arm, he could not be moved. We then tried a handy billy tackle, with a strop around his outstretched arms, but failed. Finally, his body was greased, and buckets of water were thrown over him to cool him down, while we hauled on the tackle. Eventually, Oscar squirted out of the aperture, like a cork out of a bottle. Fortunately, his huge penis was undamaged! We made port in London in late December 1938. We spent Christmas in London, after discharging our cargo at the buoys and alongside, and made passage to Barry Docks, where we signed off on 9 January 1939.

APPLEDORE – VOYAGE 28

U.K. to Vancouver
10 January 1939 to 7 May 1939

We signed on at Barry on 10 January 1939. After having completed bunkering, the usual repairs, and the loading of stores, we put to sea in the middle of January 1939, for our destination of British Columbia.

As we reached mid Atlantic, we encountered freshening winds, and received warnings of a hurricane moving northeast from the West Indies. All preparations were made for exceptionally severe weather, and by 6 February, the ship was hove to at steerage speed in the face of force 12 winds, and precipitous seas. The seas were breaking about sixty feet high from trough to crest, and despite our high freeboard in ballast, we were shipping green seas fore and aft, in winds approaching hurricane force 12, "that which no canvas can withstand."

Maria de Larrinaga had put to sea from Houston, Texas on 24 January 1939. She was in sight of *Appledore*, and had been running before the increasingly tempestuous weather, on a northeasterly course, when we hove to. We encountered her for a very short time, hove to at a distance of about six miles from our ship, and on our starboard beam.

Maria de Larrinaga and *Appledore* were ships of similar dimensions and tonnage. In her deeply loaded condition, with over 8,000 tons of cargo below decks, she was making very heavy weather in the exceptional sea conditions, with huge seas breaking aboard fore and aft. We lost sight of her during the frequent heavy and tempestuous squalls of rain, sleet and snow. We then received a series of general distress messages from her, reporting that one of her forward hatches had been stove-in. We responded indicating that we would endeavour to stand by her, although she was no longer in sight. However, by the strength of her wireless signals she was not far away. In our hove-to state, just making steerageway in the huge seas and torrential squalls, there was nothing more that we could do.

During the day of 8 February, we remained hove to and in wireless contact with *Maria de Larrinaga*. Then during the evening, in darkness, her distress signals ceased, and our wireless operator failed to regain contact. At daybreak the following day, we attempted to contact her by wireless signals. There was no response, and we had to assume that *Maria de Larrinaga* had foundered with all hands, about 37 men. She was a well-found and modern ship that must have been overwhelmed by an exceptionally heavy sea, which stove in her forward hatches. The official records show that she was declared missing, believed foundered, on Wednesday, 8 February 1939, after her final distress message had given her position as 42 – 15 N. 46 – 50 W. This was a horrifying experience for us, and one never forgotten; particularly because we were so close to the stricken ship, but powerless to give assistance. The North Atlantic Ocean was always an implacable and remorseless enemy.

The remainder of our passage to Vancouver was relatively uneventful. As was now my good luck, the Panama Canal pilot selected me to take the helm in the lakes and Cullebra Cut, for which I was rewarded with a share of his food, a luxury I had begun to anticipate with relish. Phillip Harris and I were given leave while the ship loaded at ports along the coast, and rejoined in New Westminster. *Appledore* put to sea in the third week of March 1939.

During the passage south along the west coast of the U.S.A. and Central America, we attempted desperately to catch one of the large Kingfish, which were showing in the smooth seas. We had seen these fish following and attacking the rotator of the log line, streamed astern from the taffrail on the poop. One of these would have provided a welcome change of diet from the foul smelling and tasting salt pig and salt horse.

The day before we arrived at the Panama Canal, our efforts were rewarded, but not with the capture of a Kingfish, but with a very large shark. This took the bait of a hunk of salt pork fat impaled on a large hook attached to the deep-sea sounding wire. The huge fish was dragged to the ship by the winch on the sounding machine, hoisted aboard from a davit, and duly despatched. It was hanging from the davit, stinking, in the hot sun, with a heaving line attached to its tail, when the pilot boarded.

The pilot ordered it to be cut loose. As it was released from the falls of the davit, the heaving line caught around the feet of a seaman, who was carried overboard with the fish. Fortunately, he was rescued before being caught by a shark or other predator.

We replenished bunkers in Port Royal, bought bananas from the bumboat men, and gorged on the fruit for most of the Atlantic passage. We discharged our cargo of grain and timber at Surrey Commercial Docks in London. As usual, we put to sea, bound for South Wales, where we paid off on 7 May 1939.

APPLEDORE – VOYAGE 29

U.K. to the River Plate
8 May 1939 to 28 July 1939

After signing articles on 8 May 1939, followed by the usual routine of bunkering, the replenishing of stores, and engine and general mainte-nance, we put to sea, bound for the River Plate. The passage was without incident. During the passage, I completed the third year of my period on indentures, and was well advanced in the subjects of navigation, chart work, ship construction and the other subjects in the syllabus for the examination for the certificate of competency of Second Mate.

We anchored for a short time in the estuary of the River Plate off Buenos Aires, where we received orders to proceed to Bahia Blanca, to load a cargo of grain. During the period when the ship was berthed in the port, the Third Mate formed a passionate attachment for a local senorita. Shortly afterwards, we found his cabin empty, and he was missing, having jumped ship. In most ports, there were always numbers of British seamen and seamen of other nationalities stranded ashore, usually having missed their ships after drunken sprees; but the Master could find no officers among their numbers. Therefore, I was summoned to his cabin, to be informed that I would be signed on as acting Third Mate. I was permitted to mess with the officers, but remained in our amidships accommodation. An able seaman was signed on, to maintain the statutory deck comple-ment. This was a wonderful and most welcome opportunity for me.

We put to sea in the second week of June 1939, destination Las Palmas for bunkers and orders. During passage, I stood watch during the morn-ing and night watches, 0800 to noon and 2000 to midnight – always under the watchful eye of Captain James. It was such a privilege to stand on the bridge under the guidance and supervision of a Master of such extensive experience. He was a seaman of great ability, but also possessed kindliness within a strict regime of discipline.

Despite his age, his eyesight was uncanny, and he would often test mine. He would suddenly appear on the bridge by my side, after I had been scanning the horizon, with the words, "Well, young Upton, what do you see?" to which I would reply "Nothing, sir." "What about that ship, hull down on the starboard beam? I saw her ten minutes ago from the lower bridge." It was quite incredible that he had seen a ship hull down, with only the mast tops above the horizon, from the lower bridge, ten feet below my eye level. As I conditioned my vision to a greater level of concentration, he caught me out on fewer occasions.

It was not that his eyesight was better than mine, but experience had trained his vision to a higher standard of concentration than mine. Later in my career as an officer, I remembered the practical lessons of Captain James, and passed them on to apprentices who stood watches with me.

He also permitted me to take the morning longitude and noon latitude sights with his sextant, and work out the mathematical calculations. The masters and officers of the older school used what was then called the "cosine formula" for working the longitude calculations. This had been superseded by the "haversine formula", incorporated into the syllabus of the Merchant Navy Officers Training Board. The old timers would have nothing to do with the new method of calculation. Therefore, those who had been indoctrinated into the use of the "cosine formula" were unable to check the work of users of the "haversine formula". The Board of Trade no longer recognised the older method in its examinations. The results were the same, whichever formula was used. I gained further practical experience from the vast skill of Captain James in the use of the sextant. Usually, the positions resulting from the simultaneous sights of the three officers and the master were very close to each other. However, early on in my indoctrination I was never within five miles of their positions.

Captain James was very patient in standing by my side as he and I took sights with his sextant, and compared the angles that we read from the vernier on the graduated scale of the sextant arc. Our angles varied appreciably on every reading, the difference being the result of my lack of experience in viewing the exact location of the lower limb of the sun in the mirror, as superimposed upon the visible horizon. This was caused by inexperience in the use of the shades, and in the care to be used in sweeping the lower limb of the sun over the horizon. Patient practice resulted in my positions gradually coinciding more closely with those of the others.

Between Bahia Blanca and Las Palmas, one of the Nigerian firemen named Robert Adolphus John became desperately ill. Shortly afterwards, after having relieved the First Mate for his evening meal, I was sitting in the mess, eating my meal, in the company of the Second Mate. The Master entered the mess to tell us that the fireman had died during the afternoon. We were ordered to go aft to the firemen's forecastle to prepare the corpse for burial at sea the following day. When we entered the forecastle, it was unbearably hot, and the dead man had already begun to smell of decomposition. The stench was overpowering.

The Second Mate ordered "Get on with it, Upton. I will go forward to get some fire bars and ratline." We had drawn two lengths of repairing canvas, each about a fathom and a half long, from the bosun; so I set to, in the oppressive heat, sowing the lengths of canvas side by side. This made the shroud wide enough to accommodate the body. The next task was to roll the body off the lower bunk onto the canvas on the deck. The dead man was well over six feet tall, and substantially built; but after great effort, he was lying on the canvas, ready for the sewing of the shroud, starting at the feet. It was a hell of a job, flopping the body off the bunk, and rolling it onto the canvas, in the oppressive tropical heat of the forecastle. I was using a large roping needle, so the stitches were not tidy. "Homeward bounder stitches" is the term.

This did not take very long, and the nearer the stitches came to the head of the corpse, the more obnoxious became the smell, and the longer the stitches. The Second Mate arrived, with a seaman carrying three fire bars and a length of ratline. By then, only the face of the corpse was showing. The Second Mate ordered, "Last stitch through the nose, Upton".

My reply was "Bloody well do it yourself." The purpose was to make sure that the corpse was dead. We dispensed with that traditional practice. The fire bars were the oldest and most corroded that that the Second Engineer could find in the pile of scrap in the stokehold. Tatem ships did not use new fire bars to weigh down corpses. We lashed the fire bars, one on each side, and one on the top of the body, and left the forecastle. By then I was in a bath of perspiration, and ready for a thorough wash down.

Early the following morning, a stage had been erected on the port side alongside No. 3 hatch, with a hatch board supporting the corpse, and a clean Red Ensign covering him. The engines were stopped and the

Master called all hands to the after deck. He the read the Service for the Burial of Dead at Sea, and the corpse was tipped into the sea. Captain James was quite moved as he read the burial service, but the First Mate was unmoved. As the body entered the water, he said, "Watch the bugger now. He will come up for his last look". This was true, because the body plunged vertically into the sea, feet first, submerged for several feet, rose to the surface, and then plunged down out of sight.

After the usual short stay in Las Palmas for coal and orders, we put to sea bound for Rotterdam. My first experience of standing a watch on the bridge was ending all too quickly. As Captain James and I stood together on the bridge as we entered Rotterdam, he asked me how I had enjoyed the experience. My reply was that it was not only a memorable experience, but rewarding in financial terms, to receive the pay of a Third Mate for one month, namely £ 13 2s 6d. The response was that I was under a misapprehension. I would be paid the difference between the pay of an A.B., and the pay of a Third Mate, because an A.B. had been signed on to replace me on deck. The difference would be £ 4 0s 0d for the month. I cannot remember whether I ever received this extra pay. It was never recorded on my indentures.

My indentures showed that no cash was advanced to me on voyage 29, due to my having drawn £ 40 4s 1d by the end of the previous voyage; so I had commenced the voyage overdrawn on my pay by the princely sum of £ 1 18s 7d. This was the miserly regime of the standard Shipping Federation indentures for apprentices. On reflection, although the pay for the month did not show on my indentures, it is likely that I received payment when the ship paid off, because I had signed the articles as acting Third Mate.

The speed of discharge of grain cargoes in the port of Rotterdam was phenomenal, and we put to sea several days after arrival, bound for South Wales, where we paid off on 28 July 1939. By that date, it seemed to us that war would be inevitable. I had then completed my nineteenth ocean passage in time of peace.

8

WARTIME LIFE AT SEAS AS A MIDSHIPMAN, 1939–1940

We signed articles on 28 July 1939, and put to sea shortly afterwards. The passage from the U.K. was uneventful, following the pattern of the previous voyages. We received wireless news of the events which were unfolding in Europe, and the apprehensions that a confrontation between Germany, and the alliance of France and Great Britain, could develop into a conflict between the powers.

Before we arrived in Vancouver, we had learned about the German attack on Poland. We arrived on 1 September 1939, and Phillip Harris and I were given leave. I was at home on the evening of 1 September 1939. My father, as always belligerent, was certain that we would soon "have a crack at the bloody Bosche!" The memories of the barbaric chlorine gas attack at Ypres in 1915 had never been effaced from his memory, or the physical effects that had so damaged his lungs.

The following day I luxuriated in the comforts of my home, and enjoyed the wonderful food prepared by my mother. I shared a bedroom in our small bungalow with my younger brothers. Very early in the morning of 4 September 1939, my father burst into our bedroom with the news that we were at war. He had never lost his pathological hatred of the Germans, and I still remember his words, "Boys, we are going to fight the bloody Bosche again. We can hold up our heads again as Englishmen." He never used the term "British".

Later in the morning of Monday 4 September 1939, my father, my brother Frank and I travelled by streetcar and ferry to Vancouver to the Canadian Recruiting Office. My father was rejected because he was deemed too old at 51 years of age, and Frank was too young. I was interviewed by a recruiting sergeant who questioned me about my education and any special qualifications, in view of the fact that I had expressed a preference for aircrew training. My response was that I had studied navigation, signals and meteorology for over three years; whereupon his reply was "Where the hell did you learn all that, son?" "I am an apprentice on a ship in port, sir." "Then you had better bugger off and stay on your ship, where you will be of more use. Now clear off". My ambitions to become a fighter pilot had been short-lived.

Eventually, my father succeeded in realising his ambition to wear a uniform again. When the Japanese attacked Pearl Harbour on 7 December 1941, an appeal was made for those possessing fluent knowledge of the Japanese language to assist the intelligence service. My father not only had a fluent command of the language, but also was able to speak in the various Japanese dialects, and write and understand the written characters. Firstly, he was engaged as an interpreter for the Royal Canadian Mounted Police, when the members of the large ethnic Japanese community in British Columbia were interrogated and interned. After the war, when the native Japanese were released from internment, he worked on the reparations tribunals.

He had been commissioned as a Lieutenant in the Royal Canadian Naval Volunteer Reserve in 1942, in charge of a detachment responsible for monitoring the signals of the Japanese fleet, eventually specialising in a surveillance watch on the signals traffic of the flagship, and particularly Admiral Yamamoto. This was of inestimable value, because eventually he and his team of W.R.C.N.S. were able to identify the touch of the wireless key of the personal signalmen who accompanied Admiral Yamamoto. Good intelligence led to the assassination of the villain of Pearl Harbour by the U.S. Air Force. My father was always proud to believe that his services had proved to be so useful. Indeed, they must have been.

During the time Phil Harris and I spent on leave, the hull of the ship had been painted grey, in a colour termed-in the vernacular of the lower deck- "crab fat". It was never explained to me how this term originated, because I have never associated any shade of grey with crabs in general, or their fat in particular. Massive quantities of grey paint were taken aboard for the painting of the superstructure, but it was necessary to paint the hull down to the boot-topping line while the ship was in port. The First Mate had also procured four long baulks of timber, for the "chippie" to shape into griping spars for the lifeboats, that were to be swung outboard on their davits, and secured by griping bands.

We returned to duty on about 20 September 1939 and put to sea, carrying our usual Canadian west coast cargo of about 3,000 tons of grain in the five lower holds and 6,000 tons of timber in the upper lower holds, 'tween decks and on deck. This mix of cargo made the ship very tender in a seaway, despite the relatively dense and heavy lower hold cargo. We never relished the Atlantic crossing in this condition of reduced stability – particularly in the winter months.

Shortly after putting to sea, we received a wireless signal instruction that the outside of the deck cargo had to be painted grey, to coincide with the hull colour. The officers could not believe that this would make a ship less visible to the enemy submarines, whether submerged or on the surface, and in either day or night visibility conditions. Clearly, the white superstructure had to be camouflaged, but the colour of the sides of the deck cargo was already unobtrusive.

It was well known that the German optical equipment in the form of binoculars, telescopes, range finders and periscopes, was of superb quality. Therefore, it seemed to be nothing short of preposterous that some naval officers in Whitehall could believe that painting a timber deck cargo grey would improve our chances of survival in the event of contact with enemy forces. This attitude was typical of their failure to appreciate, from a desk in the centre of London, practical conditions on the bridge, or in the engine room, of a merchant ship. Despite the stupidity of the order, we undertook the painting of the outside of the timber deck cargo.

Rigging stages outboard was very difficult and dangerous work when the ship was at sea. Eventually we shackled snatch blocks to the links of the deck cargo securing chains and went over the side individually in bosun's chairs. It was necessary to complete the work during the passage to the Panama Canal, because the weather in the Caribbean Sea was usually temperamental, but more so as the hurricane season approached. The painting of the timber was not easy because of the uneven and absorbent nature of the surface. When we reached the canal, the work had been completed, after the use of huge quantities of grey paint.

During the passage the "chippie" had roughed out the shape of the griping spars with his adze, planed, tapered, and finished them. The grip-ing spars were necessary as a support for the lifeboats when swung outboard from the radial davits. It was my work to fashion the eight kapok "puddings", which were fixed on the griping spars, to cushion the weight of the swung-out lifeboats. I was also detailed to make the canvas and rope belly bands, which held the boats to the spars. The "puddings" consisted of large quantities of cotton waste wadding, fixed around the

Appledore in her first convoy, November 1939
H.M.S. Ramilles our 'mother hen' in the centre column

griping spars, then covered by canvas and painted. The griping bands
were made from several sections of repairing canvas, about six inches
wide, sewn together, with strong rope grommets at each end. They were
made long enough to embrace the hulls of the lifeboats. Wire "snotters"
were spliced to each end, the top end being shackled to the top of each
davit, and the bottom end secured inboard to a bollard on the boat deck
by a bottle screw, and a quick-release attachment. These acted as cush-
ions for the gunwales and planking of the boats. All this work was
completed by the time that we reached Port Royal in Jamaica, where we
replenished our bunkers.

After putting to sea from Port Royal, the two class 1A lifeboats amidships, and the two jolly boats on the lower bridge were swung out board
and secured. The lifeboat falls had been fleeted and stretched, secured to
their bollards, and coiled ready for emergency use. Blackout switches had
been fitted to the doors and a blackout regime practised.

The passage from the West Indies to Halifax was uneventful, and we
arrived in Halifax about the third week in October 1939. We had learned
of the sinking of *Athenia* by the submarine U-30, commanded by O.-
Leutnant Fritz-Julius Lemp, on 3 September, an act of callous disregard
for the conventions of war. This was followed by the sinking of the
aircraft carrier *Courageous* on 17 September by U-29, commanded by O.-
Leutnant Otto Schuhart. On 14 October 1939, U-47, commanded by K.-
Lt. Gunther Prien, penetrated the fleet anchorage in Scapa Flow, and

torpedoed and sank the battleship *Royal Oak* with massive casualties. This was an outstanding achievement. The exceptional record of Gunther Prien and U-47 continued, until he and his crew were killed on 7 March 1941. Reports differ, one version attributing the loss either to accidental causes, or to striking a drifting mine. The attack reports of the destroyers *H.M.S. Wolverine* and *Verity* clearly confirm that their attacks resulted in the destruction of U-47.

The casualties suffered in the sinking of these two major naval units, and a clearly identified passenger ship, emphasised to us that the impending war at sea would be a costly and unremitting struggle. We were soon to experience the extent of the horrors and privations that ensued during the five years of conflict.

The anchorage at Halifax was crowded with ships. The first trans Atlantic convoy HX1 of 15 ships had assembled and put to sea on 30 September 1939, followed by HX2 of 15 ships on 10 October, and then the combined convoys HX3 and HX3S, totalling 24 ships, on 14 October. The convoys put to sea at regular intervals of between 6 and 10 days, gradually clearing the accumulation of ships in the anchorage; and then at regular short intervals during the war.

The first Halifax convoy to suffer a loss was HX 5, which put to sea on 17 October, and lost *Malabar* to U-34 in the south western approaches on 27 October, with the loss of 5 of her ship's company.

CONVOY HX9

Appledore lay at anchor for over two weeks, and finally put to sea on 18 November in convoy HX9 of 30 ships, escorted by the battleship, *H.M.S. Ramilles*. Although she was no protection against submarine attack, it was a comfort to be protected by her eight 15-inch guns, because it was known that both *Admiral Graf Spee* and *Deutschland* had been at large. The former had been active in the North Atlantic, where she sank *Stonegate*, south east of Bermuda, on 5 October, and then later in the South Atlantic, where she sank *Clement, Newton Beech, Ashlea* and *Hunstman* in the first ten days of October. Although we had learned about the loss of most of those ships in the radio news bulletins, we were not able to appreciate at that time the full impact of the events that had occurred.

Later in the war, the strict censorship denied us direct information on the extent of the losses as they occurred. However, through personal experience, or the experiences of others related to us, or learned through the scuttlebutt news relayed through the shipping offices, we were always well informed about ship losses and human casualties. Furthermore, the losses of major naval units could not be suppressed, and made the headlines when they occurred.

Convoy HX9 was commanded by a retired naval officer, who was accommodated in one of the Manchester Liners. The use of active service or retired naval officers in command of convoys was necessary, but most had never commanded slow moving, cumbersome and heavily laden merchant ships. This fundamental lack of knowledge of conditions in merchant ships caused many problems and misunderstandings. Notwithstanding this, the naval convoy commodores were brave and dedicated men, who served their country well. A substantial number of these elderly naval officers lost their lives during the war, when younger and able-bodied men enjoyed the relative luxuries of "reserved occupations".

The Master had returned from the convoy conference laden with all the documentation appertaining to the convoy. We had been provided with the codebooks entitled "Consigs", together with the weighted box for the disposal of confidential documents in emergency. We were also supplied with a book of zig-zag patterns. Although it was likely that convoy commodores brought zig-zag clocks on board the ships in which they were accommodated, they were not universally issued to merchant ships until later. We received our zig-zag clock when the ship was fitted out at the end of the voyage.

When the convoys were ordered to zig-zag, the procedure would be to watch the commodore ship when the signal to execute was shown, noting the time. Then, by consulting the zig-zag book for the consecutive deviations from the mean course of the convoy, watching the commodore ship, and monitoring the time, zig-zag patterns could be maintained quite accurately. It required great concentration to maintain station when on a zig-zag, and at the end of a four hour watch, officers would retire to their cabins seeing double.

The apprentices were each allocated a watch on the bridge for signalling duties during the day, so we were on signalling duties on alternate watches. Although some ships had been equipped with the powerful Aldis signalling lamps, we relied on flag signals and semaphore, with which Phillip Harris and I had become proficient.

The convoy put to sea in remarkably good order, each ship commanded by a fiercely independent Master, who, previously, had spent a lifetime keeping well clear of other vessels. Now they would live in their close company. The first night, in the close company of other ships in darkness, produced many near misses, but no collisions; and we gradually settled into convoy routine. The great problem, which faced those on the bridges was then, and continued to be, station keeping in convoy. There were no revolution counters on the bridges, and communication between bridge and engine room for many years had been by the manually operated engine room telegraph, with segments for Dead Slow, Slow, Half, and Full Speed ahead and astern. A frantic double ring on the telegraph signified to the engineer that a state of emergency existed.

There was a voice tube from the bridge to the engine room, with a whistle plugged in at each end of the tube. Blowing down one end of the tube or the other sounded the whistle. However, at a distance of about a hundred and fifty feet, a fart on the bridge would usually be more audible to the other end than the feeble whistle. The tedious process was achieved by blowing down the tube, and then holding one ear to the bell mouth of the speaking tube, waiting for an answer that rarely materialised. In strong to gale force winds, the wind would actuate the whistles, causing false alarms, so the speaking tubes were not a reliable method of communication.

We had to improvise a better method of communication between bridge and engine room. The "chippie" fashioned a board, painted black, on which was painted "UP" and "DOWN" in white characters. This contraption was attached to a length of heaving line. A deck hand was stationed on the top of the engine room skylight, in the lee of the funnel, awaiting the megaphone instructions from the officer of the watch.

This would be either "UP TWO", or "DOWN ONE" or whatever, indicating the change in the number of revolutions, to be increased or decreased. When the shouted order was received, the standby man chalked the number against either UP or DOWN on the board, and lowered the board through one of the open lee flaps of the engine room skylight, to the engineer on watch.

The engineer acknowledged by either a tick mark or O.K., or sometimes an epithet like "f— off!" He then conformed, by increasing or decreasing the engine speed by the requisite number of revolutions. The engineers suffered appreciably, and in so many ways. I will never cease to admire their patience and courage. The Second, Third and Fourth Engineers were usually alone in the engine room during their respective watches. A donkey man helped them on day work.

The duties of the engineer on watch included monitoring the steam pressure, attending to the pumping equipment, ascending to, and descending from, the various platforms, for periodic lubrication of the pistons, eccentrics, and other components of the engines. They had to visit the stokehold periodically and, during each watch, undertake at least one excursion along the propeller shaft tunnel through numbers 4 and 5 holds to the stern tube, to lubricate the propeller shaft bearing journals.

The necessity for the sole engineer on watch to attend to these important tasks would almost invariably cause delays in altering the speed of the engines, a fact that naval convoy commodores appeared to find difficult to appreciate or tolerate. Moreover, the governors fitted to the reciprocating steam engines, with which most merchant ships were powered, were far from accurate. Speed was usually adjusted by reducing or increasing steam pressure, an equally inaccurate method.

To naval officers, who were trained and served in an environment in which substantial numbers of personnel were on duty on the bridges, and in the engine rooms, of warships, it had to be impossible to appreciate the conditions under which our officers worked. We received a constant barrage of signals "The ship or ships indicated are out of station, and must immediately, repeat immediately, recover their stations" followed later by "The ship or ships indicated have not obeyed my previous instruction, etc." "The ship or ships indicated are making too much smoke."

All the time the poor officer on the bridge and the engineer on watch endeavoured to cope with everything that was going on. The deck officer had to be alert for the almost constant signals from the commodore, at the same time watching for the ship astern that had overlapped in the column, or the ship ahead that had lost steam pressure and was getting perilously close. The engineer on watch may have been 100 feet down the propeller shaft tunnel, or up one of the platforms in the engine room, trying to cope, single handed, under enormous difficulties. It was very difficult for us, and did not improve much during the war.

Unfortunately – or perhaps, fortunately – the codebook "Consigs" did not include what would have been appropriate signals in response, such as, "Bugger off, you silly sod. The poor bloody engineer is up to his arse in grease at the end of the tunnel, repairing an overheated bearing journal!" Alternatively, "For Christ's sake, we have lost steam pressure due to fire cleaning. Do you think we are doing this for bloody fun!" The commodores usually chose oil-fired, or diesel engine powered ships, so the difficulties inherent in keeping station in coal burning vessels were not in their textbooks.

The most acute problem, apparently never appreciated by our naval commodores, was the essential routine of periodic cleaning of the stoke hold fires. Most merchant ships were powered by water tube boilers, usually three boilers, each with three fires, burning steam coal. These were served by three firemen per watch, each attending three fires, and one trimmer working in the bunkers. It was routine to draw one fire at the end of each watch in rotation, raking out the ash, and slicing and removing the clinker. This residue was lifted to the main deck by hoist, and dumped over the side.

Appledore burned about 50 tons of coal per day, so the clinker and ash for each watch represented the residue from between 8 and 10 tons of coal. In peacetime, the glowing clinker and ashes were dumped immediately. During the war, in blackout, the glowing embers would have been visible for miles. Therefore, the clinker was allowed to cool, and the clinker and ash were dumped during daylight hours.

Fire cleaning posed a serious problem, when attempting to maintain a constant speed. The temporary loss of part of the heating capacity of three fires during this process resulted in a loss of steam pressure. Ships would overlap in the columns as the result of reduction in speed, resulting in much frantic signalling between ships and from the commodore.

All these problems were further aggravated by zigzagging. Ships reacted differently when the angles of their rudders altered, and lost speed at different rates, as they altered course. Moreover, with ships turning together, instead of consecutively, ships were in line neither ahead nor beam to beam, so station keeping resulted in a haphazard formation. When a zigzag pattern terminated, the convoy had to be re-formed.

The convoy commodores were used to the handling of oil-burning naval ships of approximately equal propulsive power, and similar revolution control equipment, with adequate numbers of subordinate staff to increase or decrease the revolutions at the turn of a valve. In a predominately coal burning fleet of merchant ships, the problems of accurate station keeping were never overcome.

On 23 November 1939, we learned by wireless signal of the sinking of the armed merchant cruiser *H.M.S. Rawalpindi* by the battle cruiser *Scharnhorst*, after a courageously fought action against overwhelming odds. This underlined the fundamental difference between British and German surface forces. A German raider, if confronted by a British capital ship would have opened the sea cocks and been scuttled rather than join action against such odds. The Jerries never subscribed to the "Nelson Touch". *H.M.S. Rawalpindi* closed the enemy in true Royal Navy tradi-

Port lifeboat wrecked and hanging
precariously by one davit

Starboard lifeboat swept overboard,
boat deck devastated

Daylight after the great storm of November 1939
Appledore still afloat after nearly foundering

tion, and sacrificed herself to save the convoy.

This emphasized the value of our ocean escort of *H.M.S. Ramilles*. The German battle cruisers were of recent design and build, and armed with eight superb eleven-inch guns, controlled by the most modern fire control equipment. Notwithstanding this, they would never join action, even with an old British battleship built in 1916. If the positions had been reversed, a British warship captain would not have hesitated to join action, regardless of the odds.

Two days later, on 25 November, when our convoy was in mid Atlantic, U-28 sank *Royston Grange*, and U-43 sank *Uskmouth*, again in the southwestern approaches. Both U-Boats had achieved previous successes. From then on, everything was quiet except for the weather.

During the afternoon watch, when I was on signal duty, the officer of the watch observed a dramatic fall in barometric pressure. This was accompanied by an increasing southwesterly swell, which was developing

Nos. 4 and 5 deck cargo partly swept
overboard

Damage to No. 4 and 5 deck cargo
No. 5 port derrick twisted

Daylight after the great storm of November 1939
Appledore still afloat after nearly foundering

almost astern of us, together with a wind increasing to force 7, moderate gale. Our heavily loaded ship, with its substantial deck cargo, was already beginning to labour heavily in the high following sea. The Master was called to the bridge; by which time the barometer had fallen below 29.50 inches and was continuing to fall rapidly. Clearly, exceptionally severe weather was imminent.

The commodore was notified by flag signal that the ship was becoming unmanageable, and was asked for permission to heave to before the onset of darkness. Other ships made similar requests. The response signal was, "All ships will maintain convoy course and speed." By then, signalling was becoming increasingly more difficult, with the ships obscured by rain and snow squalls and fading light. By the onset of darkness, the ship was wallowing heavily in a high following breaking sea, in winds that had reached force 9, strong gale.

The barometer was then close to 29 inches and was still falling. The

No. 3 deck cargo devastated
Viewed from port boat deck

Damage to No. 5 deck cargo
Viewed from port side of poop

Daylight after the great storm of November 1939
Appledore still afloat after nearly foundering

other ships in the convoy were making very heavy weather, including *H.M.S. Ramilles*, which was shipping heavy seas fore and aft. Most of the ships had lost station in the convoy, and others had straggled out of sight. The only recourse in the exceptionally severe weather conditions would have been for the convoy to spread out in formation and heave to together. The codebook "Consigs" provided for this contingency in a number of signal hoists. "The convoy will heave to together." "The ships will heave to independently without further orders," or similar. The naval commodore had ample precedent in the codebooks, to take action in the face of such conditions.

We faced the hours of darkness, blacked out, with ships altogether too close to each other, a rapidly falling barometer, and weather conditions that were likely to reach force 11, storm, or even force 12, hurricane. By 1800, in rapidly deteriorating light conditions and frequent violent rain, hail and sleet squalls, the obdurate commodore failed to take action. By the time of the night watch, the barometer fell to under 28.50 inches, and the wind increased to force 11, storm force, and in gusts to nearly force 12, with a precipitous sea on our starboard quarter.

It was my first trick at the helm at 2000, and at one bell, 1945, I had dressed in oilskins and sea boots, ready to go on watch. Phillip Harris was already finishing the second dogwatch, and was either at the helm or on lookout. As I was leaving the cabin, a huge sea came aboard with a thunderous crash. I did not witness this, but it was clear that substantial damage had been caused. Our cabin was immediately beneath the port lifeboat, and I could hear the noise of splintering of wood overhead, and a grinding noise from the davits.

The ship was thrown over violently, resulting in a substantial list to port. The outside working alleyway was completely submerged over porthole level. It was difficult to open the accommodation alleyway door, which was partly obstructed by the timber deck cargo, stowed over No. 4 hold, that had shifted forward bodily. There was only sufficient room to squeeze between the cargo and bulkhead. Access forward was impossible through the flooded port alleyway or the starboard windward alleyway, which was washed by seas; so I climbed on the boat deck, and made my way forward through the shambles amidships. Even in the pitch-black darkness, it was a scene of devastation.

The starboard lifeboat was no longer in its davits, having been washed overboard from starboard to port, carrying away most of the awning spars and ventilators. The port lifeboat forward falls had parted, and the boat had been thrown violently against its davits, smashing in its bows and gunwales. The boat was hanging at an angle, precariously from the after davit, supported partly by its griping bands. The engine room skylight had been stove in, leaving water waist-deep in the engine room. The boat deck was devastated.

A number of boat deck ventilators had been sheered off at their bases, and the main stokehold ventilators had been severely buckled. The damage amidships was catastrophic. The deck cargo over No. 3 Hold had shifted bodily about four feet to port, and had jammed the control rods for the steering engine, where their stanchions were situated in spaces prepared within the deck cargo, and shored up by baulks of timber. The force of the movement of the cargo had splintered the shoring timbers, and the universal couplings connecting the sections of the steering rods had jammed solid. The ship had been carrying port helm when the huge sea broke aboard, and had veered to port into a broached-to position. The substantial list to port had submerged the port alleyways up to boat deck level.

The only way to cross the amidships deck cargo from the boat deck to the bridge was to lie on the splintered remains of the deck cargo and crawl from one securing chain to another along the sloping and damaged deck cargo. This was difficult, not only because of the severe list to port and uneven surface, but also because a violent snow squall had covered the deck cargo with a coating of ice. When I reached the bridge, the Master ordered me to go aft to instruct the bosun to set the deck hands and donkeyman to disconnect the control rods from the steam valve of the steering engine, and to stay aft until this had been done. Philip Harris remained at the wheel. I was also given a number of whistles, to be used for signalling.

While I was on the bridge, the ship broached to, to port, with the wind and sea on the port beam. A succession of precipitous seas broke aboard fore and aft. The ship heeled over to starboard, almost to the point of capsizing, and slowly recovered, returning to its heavy list to port. Most of the damage was caused aft, over No. 4 and No. 5 hatches, where the chains securing the deck cargo had parted. A large section of cargo over No.5 hatch moved bodily to starboard, and before going over-board, it was held in the starboard mainmast shrouds. The shrouds held under the weight, but the displaced deck cargo imposed a great strain on the lower mainmast. The port shrouds then parted, so the weight of cargo held by the starboard shrouds bent the mainmast to starboard. The port main topmast stay held, so the topmast was bent to port at the crosstrees, and this carried away the wireless aerials.

The eye of the depression must have passed through our position with the last violent snow squall, and the wind veered to the northwest. The relaxation in the intensity of the weather enabled me to go aft, although with difficulty in pitch-black darkness. The bosun and crew then went to work. It did not take us long to disconnect the linkage to the steering engine, so we were able to control the steering of the ship by manual control of the steering engine valve. The further orders were to station a number of deck hands, to form a chain of communication, from the after accommodation to the bridge. Men were positioned respectively by the after accommodation, on the main mast house, and the after and forward ends of the boat deck. Each man was issued with a whistle and a length of ratline to lash him in place.

The code of signals was simple. One blast on the whistle for hard a starboard, two for hard a port, and three for amidships. On receiving the signal, the steering engine was operated by manual control, by its steam valve. The first whistle signal, relayed to the steering engine, was to port, and gradually we turned to the ideal heaving-to course, with the wind and sea about a point on the port bow. Engine speed was then reduced to slow or dead slow. We rode out the rest of the night still listing heavily to port, but out of the danger of being overwhelmed in a broached-to condition. The storm began to abate during the middle watch, accompanied by violent squalls and a high breaking sea. By morning, the wind was about force 8, fresh gale, and wind and sea moderating. No ships were in sight.

Daylight showed us the devastation caused by the first sea, which disabled the steering gear, and the subsequent seas, which came aboard when we were lying partly on our side in a broached-to condition. When the violent pitching and rolling had subsided sufficiently, we released the bottle screws on the cargo securing chains on No. 3 hatch, and removed the timber surrounding the amidships steering rods, where we found the damage repairable. The cargo securing chains, which had broken when part of the deck cargo over No. 4 and No. 5 hatches went overboard, were replaced. These held in place a substantial quantity of timber, which was hanging precariously outboard on both sides.

The "chippie" then re-constructed the gaps in the deck cargo where the steering control rods had been situated. The damaged steering gear rods were then heated in the forge, straightened and re-coupled. The timber deck cargo was again shored up, and we were enabled to restore normal connection with the steering engine. When we lost steering the previous night, it was decided that it would be impossible to man the large emergency steering wheel on the after docking bridge. It would have taken several men to turn the wheel, and in the huge following seas that were breaking aboard, we would have lost them overboard. The port lifeboat was secured as best we could, but was a write off. A jury aerial was then rigged. The flooded accommodation was pumped and baled out, and we were back in business, but in a state of devastation on deck.

There was no sign of the convoy, so we made independent passage through the English Channel to the Thames estuary. Another mishap occurred after the pilot boarded. The ship grounded on the Goodwin Sands. Fortunately, the ship was not heavily aground, and was re-floated on the flood tide, with the assistance of the engines. We anchored off Southend, waiting for a north bound convoy, and the next day put to sea in a North Sea convoy, and arrived in Hull on 7 December 1939, where we discharged our cargo and paid off.

Appledore and her crew were very fortunate to have survived the passage across the North Atlantic. Almost certainly we would have capsized and foundered if the first enormous sea had broken aboard when we were in a broached-to condition. The account given by those on the bridge, when the huge sea broke aboard, was that the stern was lifted by one large sea, veering the ship violently to port, with the bows down at a steep angle, and a substantial list to port. As the sea passed under, the bows lifted, the stern dipped at a steep angle, and the ship veered and heeled to starboard. With the ship in the trough between two enormous seas, the second sea broke aboard.

The sea overwhelmed the ship over the starboard quarter to a depth estimated as forty feet. The full impact of the crest then broke over the boat deck, amidships forward of the funnel, and over the bridge, flooding the wheelhouse, which was about 30 feet above sea level. It was a gigantic sea.

The ships in the convoy should never have been placed in such exceptional danger. The naval commodore must have known that with a barometer falling to below 28.50 inches, exceptionally severe weather had to be expected. He should have turned all the ships into the wind and sea during the daylight hours, increased the distance between ships, and hove to together. To attempt to maintain course, speed and station keeping, had to be irresponsible and stupid. I reflect on how many other merchant ships, faced with similar conditions, failed to survive. The publication *British Vessels Lost at Sea 1939 – 1945* lists 411 British ships as lost due to *cause uncertain*. The prompt and effective reaction of our Master and his crew, under such extremely hazardous conditions, ensured that we were not included in the total as number 412.

I do not condemn naval convoy commodores as a body by this criticism. However, in their remit from the Admiralty they should have been instructed that, when in weather conditions which hazarded the safety of merchant ships, they should allow greater flexibility of action to the experienced Masters who commanded those ships. Later in the war, we experienced occasions when a convoy commodore issued the instruction for ships to heave to collectively, and sometimes at the discretion of individual Masters. Therefore, lessons were learned.

Notwithstanding this, I am sure that every officer who served in merchant ships would join with me in paying tribute to the retired senior naval officers who answered the call of their country, and shared with us the discomforts of weather and the violence of an implacable and determined enemy. A substantial number were lost, together with their supporting staff. They were brave and dedicated men.

Captain James left the ship at the end of the voyage. He had been an inspiration during over three years under his command, and was a model of all that is fine and commendable in a commanding officer. My lasting memory of Captain David P. James was a conversation between us that occurred early in our long association.

It took place on a very hot tropical day when the ship was on passage between the Panama Canal and Vancouver, with a temperature of over 100 degrees Fahrenheit, in calms, with a smooth sea. I was lying on my back under No. 2 port cargo winch, scraping the eccentric straps, covered in grease, oil and the residue of coal dust, and covered in sweat and grime.

I had been suffering from constipation as the result of the awful food, and was sick after trying to eat the fat and greasy salt pork provided for lunch, when I heard the words, "What do you think of life at sea now, Upton?" On crawling out of the confines of the hot and filthy prison, I was confronted by the person of the Master, immaculate in white patrol jacket, shorts, socks and shoes. The answer was "Not much, sir. I am sick, constipated, and fed up." The response was, "Have you looked at the rivet spacing on the angle irons securing the winches to the decks? When you dive in the bilges, do you examine the construction of the frames, margin plates, and tank side brackets?" On receiving a negative answer, he offered profound advice, never forgotten.

The exact words may have been different, but the import is as clear now, as it was then. "Young man, every officer who stands a watch on the bridge of a ship, including myself, has been subjected to similar dirty and demeaning work. Remember that even when in such circumstances, he should learn something new every day. When you are examined on the subject of Ship Construction and Stability, your knowledge of beams, frames, margin plates, and tank side brackets will be tested. Look, listen and learn."

Captain D.P. James had served as an apprentice in the early years of the twentieth century, in the huge windjammers, many of which were still in service then. His ship-handling capability was remarkable. When approaching Barry Roads, with the ship "flying light" in ballast, beset by a westerly gale and a fierce six-knot flood tide, he would manoeuvre his unwieldy ship to make a perfect lee for the pilot cutter. When hove to in storm force winds, his judgement of the best speed and course in relation to the wind direction was superb.

He was not without a dry humour. When I stood a watch with him as acting Third mate, we were talking about life in windjammers. He then related an anecdote about the windjammer Master who had assumed command of his first steamship. A dialogue had ensued between the Master, First and Second Mates, who were respectively on the bridge, forecastle head and poop. The Third Mate on the bridge relayed his orders.

"Order the mates to cast off the bow ropes and springs fore and aft." With the ship then singled up fore and aft, the next order was, "Cast off breast ropes." When the ship was free from her moorings, the new Master remarked to the Third Mate, "Now let us see how good these new-fangled engines are." When the Chief Engineer answered through the speaking tube, "Is that you, Chief? We have cast off. Now give this bloody ship a touch sideways!"

During the period between the outbreak of hostilities and the date when convoy HX9 arrived in U.K. port, the casualties in ships and seamen were severe. They were the forerunner of calamitous losses in the five years of war that followed.

APPLEDORE – VOYAGE 31

United Kingdom to New Orleans
8 December 1939 to 15 April 1940

Captain D.P. James was relieved as Master by Captain J.P. Herbert, who had been First Mate of *Iddesleigh* when Captain J.H. Swindell was lost overboard, and had held command of the ship until he joined *Appledore*

The ship was berthed in Hull for over a month. A great deal of work was undertaken to prepare the ship for wartime service. The chartroom and wheelhouse were given protection by the fixing of slabs of what appeared to be tarmac, which were bolted to the bulkheads. The after accommodation was strengthened to accept the defensive weapons that were to be situated on the after docking bridge. A 4-inch breech-loading gun and a 12-pounder quick firing dual-purpose gun were bolted to platforms on the after docking bridge. Magazines and ready-use ammunition lockers were constructed. For anti-aircraft protection, we were equipped with single Lewis machine guns, fixed on each wing of the bridge.

Phillip Harris and I, together with a number of members of the crew, were enrolled for training for a Merchant Seaman Gunners' Course, and, on passing the tests, were issued with a certificate of proficiency. My certificate is No. 3425, issued by the M.N.D.I.O. in Hull on 15 December 1939. The course was elementary, but thorough. The instructors were petty officer gunnery instructors of long service and inexhaustible knowledge. They had a vernacular all of their own.

Our Royal Marine Gunlayer
'Guns'

Phillip Harris, Trainer (left)
and Vernon Upton,
breechworker (right)

Appledore December 1939. Members of the guns crews

"Now this 'ere is a 4-inch B.L. gun. B.L. to you ignorant sods means breech-loadin'. This is the catch retainin' breech screw open, and this is the f——— striker. When the gun layer pulls the trigger, the f——— striker 'its the percussion cap on the tube, which fires into the cordite end of the charge, which blows the projectile out of the f——— spout of the bloody gun. Get it? The vernacular used in the descriptions of misfires, and other instructions was equally lurid and profane, and quite unforgettable.

A regular lieutenant commander gunnery officer attended the final passing-out practice sessions on the 4-inch B.L., 12-pounder Q.F., and Lewis machine guns. Each member of the gun crew was observed in his respective gun positions, layer, trainer, breech worker, and ammunition/rammer numbers. When it was my turn as breech worker on a 4-inch B.L. gun, the gun was elevated well above the horizontal. The

Appledore, January 1940. 4 inch B.L. gun crew
Anti U-Boat action stations

drill ammunition consisted of dummy wooden shells for both guns, and dummy wooden charges.

The dummy shells were rammed into the breech, followed by the charges, which were pushed in by hand, successively forming a chain along the barrel of the gun. As successive dummy shells and charges were pushed along, they fell from the muzzle of the gun into a net, and were collected by the ammunition numbers and used again. The breech worker held the breech open by the B.M. (breech mechanism) lever. The ammunition number shoved the shell into the breech, while the other ammunition number held the ram.

After the ram had been lifted from its position in the quenching bucket, the ammunition number turned to grasp the handle of the ram, and both ammunition numbers rammed the shell into the breech accompanied by the shout of "HOME, OUT, UNDER!"

The head of the ram was then placed under the mushroom head of the breech, to prevent it from being closed inadvertently before the charge was inserted in the breech. The other ammunition number then placed the charge in the breech, and shouted "IN!" when his hands were clear of the breech screw. The ram was returned to its quenching bucket under the gun, and the breech worker slammed the screw breech closed, cocking the striker.

This all happened in accordance with routine, but, as the dummy charge was resting in the breech, the elevated angle of the gun caused it to start sliding out of the aperture. Following the shout of "IN!" and as the breech was being slammed closed, the ammunition number attempted to stop the dummy charge sliding out. His right hand was trapped in the breech as the heavy screw mechanism turned. His hand was mangled and almost severed at the wrist. The reaction of the officer was typical of the regular Royal Navy. He said to me, "It's not your fault, son. You did what we have trained you to do. Take him to the medical officer, and carry on." The navy did everything by the book, and that is why they were so good, but sympathy was not their strong point. Despite the fact that I had been exonerated from blame, I felt awful about the accident.

The pay for a Merchant Seaman Gunner possessing the certificate was sixpence per day. Shortly after our training, our gun layer joined the ship. He was a retired colour sergeant of the Royal Marines, who had been pensioned out of regular service. I cannot remember his name, because we called him "Guns." He had a quite phenomenal knowledge of naval weapons, from small arms to 16-inch naval guns, which he had been trained to strip and assemble to the last nut and bolt, when blindfolded. He was always immaculate in his uniform, and his weapons were equally pristine in appearance. He was an unforgettable character.

Another remarkable character was Hamat Bin Samat, a Malay serang or bosun, who was engaged with a deck crew of Malay seamen. They were fine seamen and excellent shipmates, always happy and full of humour. Hamat Bin Samat was unable to pronounce the letter "F", substituting the letter "P" in his aspiration. He used to refer to Phil Harris and me as the "Puckin' 'prentices." We soon realised that he was very learned in all aspects of weather at sea, and we used to ask him, "How will the weather be, Hamat?" The answer would be, "Soon come plenty pog. We carry puckin' pog two days. Then puckin pog clear, get plenty puckin' pine weather." After we had asked him the same question on several occasions, just to listen to his response, he said "You puckin 'prentices ask me about puckin' pog just to pull my puckin' leg." We enjoyed a happy voyage with Hamat Bin Samat and his Malay compatriots.

After about six weeks in Hull, we put to sea. Our signalling capability had been improved quite substantially. The ship was issued with two Aldis lamps, which enabled us to communicate by morse code over distances of several miles. The whole suit of signal flags was replaced by flags that could be secured together by quick-release brass clips, vastly superior to the previous flags, which had been fitted with wooden toggles at the head, and an eye on the tail rope. When the tail ropes became wet, the eyes swelled around the toggles, making it very difficult to separate

Appledore, January 1940
12-pounder quickfiring gun crew. Anti-aircraft action stations

the flags. It had been a nuisance trying to assemble a number of flag hoists together on the signal halyards, in a gale of wind and pouring rain, with each flag jammed solid.

Our zig-zag clock made life on the bridge more bearable. It was no longer necessary to keep a constant watch on the ship of the commodore. The hands of the clock were set to electrodes that actuated a loud bell outside the wheelhouse, at the time intervals of the course alterations. Communications between bridge and engine room were improved by the fitting of telephones. Cranking the handle produced a ringing at the other end, but not always a reply, if the engineer was not near the telephone. It improved verbal communication quite substantially, giving a wider scope for personal contact between the respective officers. When several attempts at ringing had been abortive, the conversation would be, "Where the bloody hell have you been? I am stuck up the arse of the ship ahead. For Christ's sake, down two". The response would be, "I have been down the f——g tunnel. Do you think that all I have to do is sit by this bloody telephone, and wait for you to call me?"

Despite the frequency of such lurid exchanges, the relationship between the bridge and engine room was remarkably good. We knew that they had a tough job to do, and they knew that it was not funny for us, standing sometimes nearly frozen, trying to keep station in heavy seas, mist and fog. Notwithstanding all this, the telephones were a great improvement over the speaking tubes and wooden boards lowered through the engine room skylights. We were beginning to improve.

Convoy OB79

Our route outward bound was south about in North Sea convoy to Southend, and independently through the English Channel to St. Georges Channel. We made rendezvous with convoy OB79 of 16 ships that had assembled in Liverpool on 25 January 1940. Convoy OB79 dispersed on 28 January 1940 – my nineteenth birthday – in about 15 degrees west longitude. We did not encounter any enemy activity, and the ships continued independently to their various destinations. We arrived in New Orleans in the second week of February 1940, and commenced loading a cargo of scrap iron and steel.

During the outward-bound passage of *Appledore* to the U.S.A., U-Boats sank 31 ships, all in the southwestern approaches and Bay of Biscay between 38 and 57 degrees north latitude and between 6 and 15 degrees west longitude, indicating the concentration of enemy activity.

There could be two reasons for the heavy loss of life. The weather was cold, with heavy seas, which would have eliminated or reduced the chances of survival in life saving craft. Moreover, two of the ships sunk with all hands, or with heavy fatal casualties, were Greek, one was Swedish, three Danish and one Norwegian. All were of neutral nationality, on independent passage. It is likely that the crews were not sufficiently prepared and equipped for emergency. The French ship P.L.M. 15 was attacked in daylight by U-37 in the Bay of Biscay in heavy weather, so it is probable that she sank very rapidly, before life saving craft could be launched, resulting in her loss with all 37 crew. *Stanholme* was mined with the loss of 13 out of 26 crew.

Again, the successful U-Boats were U-48, with five ships, U-44 five ships, U-53 five ships and U-37 four ships. Miraculously, neither U-48 nor U-37 are recorded as having been sunk by Allied forces. The last record of Herbert Schultze and U-48 is dated 12 June 1941, when his attack report indicated the sinking of *Empire Dew* at 0251 hours. It is interesting to follow Werner Hartmann, commander of U-77, who later assumed command of U-198. An attack report dated 01 August 1943 signalled the sinking of the Dutch ship *Mangkalihat* in the Indian Ocean. It appears that he returned to Germany, and relinquished command to Heusinger von Waldegg. The U-Boat returned to the Indian Ocean, where she was sunk with all hands on 12 August 1944, by a combined force of two escort carriers, seven frigates and two sloops.

How times had changed by then! In 1940, we were lucky to have one elderly sloop to cover a convoy of 30 ships, and four years later 11 naval units and many aircraft could be devoted to the hunting down and destruction of one U-Boat!

Convoy HX31

After over two weeks in New Orleans, we made passage to Halifax, where we assembled in convoy HX31 of 30 ships. We encountered no enemy activity on the Atlantic passage. The weather was atrocious, with severe gales, heavy rain, sleet and snow squalls, and poor visibility.

On a filthy day, I was on watch with the newly joined Third Mate. He was an elderly man, who had been retired for a number of years, and answered the call for experienced officers to return to sea duties. He was huddled in the wing of the lee side of the bridge with a scarf covering his mouth and both nostrils running, a forlorn figure. His eyesight was suspect, and he found it difficult to distinguish flag signals, even when using a telescope. He had said to me "Will you be my eyes, son? I cannot see too well." He had qualified as a Master, but I never knew whether he had held command. He was a kindly officer, whom we respected.

We had to admire his guts, leaving the comfort of his home, to return to the freezing bridge of a ship beset by the dangers of war. Despite all this, the Master seemed to take a perverse pleasure in treating this grand old man like a piece of shit on every opportunity. This animosity came to a climax when the Third Mate was standing on the lee side of the bridge and I was on the windward side on lookout and signal watch.

I saw and read a signal, which was hoisted on the ship of the commodore, on our starboard side. I moved around to the port side to inform the Third Mate, who was busy with station keeping, so I carried on, acknowledging the signal. Therefore, for a short time the Third Mate had left the signalling to me, as we had agreed.

As the flag group acknowledging the signal was bent on the halyards, the Master arrived on the navigating bridge, and shouted to the Third

Mate, "What's that signal showing from the Commodore?" The Third Mate was not able to tell him immediately, and the Master did not give him time to explain. The Master then subjected the old "shellback" to an abusive tirade. This was just too much for the fine old man. I cannot remember the exact words, but they could be translated as "Don't shout at me like that, you bloody young pup. I was standing a watch when you were shitting in your nappies, you bloody ignorant bugger!" Miraculously, this silenced the Master, who remained on the lee side of the bridge with the Third Mate but said nothing more.

The Master then moved to the weather side and engaged in conversation with me. He brought up the subject of Captain Swindell, with whom we had both served, and started to make derogatory remarks about him. I told him that I had respected Captain Swindell as a Master and a person, and would prefer not to hear him slandered. The Master terminated the conversation, and ordered me to go to his cabin and bring his greatcoat to the bridge. On my return, I handed him his greatcoat, and made to return to my station on the weather wing of the bridge, whereupon he said "Upton, don't you think that you should help your Captain on with his greatcoat?" The response was, "I believed that you were capable of doing that yourself, sir."

He looked in the face and said, "You don't like me, Upton, do you?" The answer was, "No sir, I do not. Captain Swindell was a good Master who is now dead. He should not be slandered by you," to which his response was, "Get on with your duties." I was then allowed to resume my duties. Our exchange did not affect his attitude towards me. I paid due deference to his rank and authority, and he treated me in a scrupulously correct and fair manner. In his testimonial he stated, "I herewith testify to his sterling qualities with regard to character, ability and devotion to duty. He is a lad with great promise for the profession he has chosen."

Captain J.P. Herbert was not a petty man, and despite the events I have related, was a competent and very efficient Master. Moreover, his attitude towards the elderly Third Mate was far more tolerant after the altercation between them. I served with him for one voyage, and after our exchange, our relationship was formal, but cordial.

Convoy HX31 dispersed in the southwestern approaches on 12 April 1940. The ships bound for the English Channel and North Sea dispersed in the St. Georges Channel, and continued independently to their destinations. We joined a North Sea convoy at Southend, and arrived at Hull on 15 April 1940, where the ship paid off and discharged our cargo.

During our stay in port, the ship was fitted with de-gaussing cables to counteract the magnetic mines, which were being laid in U.K. shipping lanes.

APPLEDORE – VOYAGE 32

U.K. to Charleston, South Carolina
16 April 1940 to 26 June 1940

The voyage commenced when articles were signed in Hull on 16 April 1940. Captain Adam Leask assumed command from Captain J.P. Herbert. I did not have time to get to know him well, but found him to be an excellent Master. He was a native of the Shetland Islands, a large hard-bitten character.

It was the practice of apprentices to cross off each day from the decreasing total of days in the four-year period covered by their indentures. I had started with 1,461 days on 16 June 1936, and at the commencement of voyage 32, exactly 60 days were left on my dog-eared sheet. The song of an apprentice, sung to the tune of "What a friend we have in Jesus", was:

"When I finish my indentures,
Oh, how happy I will be,
No more chipping, painting and scraping,
On the *Appledore* for me.
No more cleaning out the bilges,
No more taking wheels at night,
When I finish my indentures,
Oh how happy I will be !"

The new First Mate, Mr. Sorenson, was an interesting character, originally trained as a cadet in H.M.S. Conway. He was an individual with a very posh accent – a dramatic change from some of the "Hawse Pipe Officers", with whom we had served previously. He was a firm disciplinarian, with a perverse sense of humour. His opening remarks when we met were, "Good morning, lads. What felony have you been up to today?" He was a popular officer, and held in great respect.

CONVOY OB136

We put to sea from Hull, on a route south about through the North Sea swept channel and the English Channel to join outward-bound convoy OB136 of 18 ships that left Liverpool on 25 April, and dispersed at sea on 28 April 1940. The convoy was not attacked by the enemy. After dispersing from the convoy, we made a good passage in fine weather, and arrived in Charleston in the second week of May 1940. Our cargo was again a lethal combination of mixed steel, and iron and steel scrap. However, at that time we were not aware of the potential dangers, because we had neither encountered enemy action, nor learned much from the experiences of others. That was to come.

During the passage of convoy OB136, no ships were sunk in the North Atlantic. Five ships were lost in the North Sea and English Channel, three by submarine attack, and one to a mine laid by U-9. The number of seamen killed was 67 out of 148, a very high fatal casualty rate of over 45 percent.

Convoy HX49

We completed loading and put to sea, arriving in Halifax in the first week of June 1940, where we joined convoy HX49 of 30 ships. The convoy put to sea on 9 June 1940.

Our fragile escort consisted of two sloops. We encountered no enemy action during our passage to the southwestern approaches. However, the activity of U-Boats had begun to intensify, but was concentrated entirely in the western approaches east of the line of longitude 15 degrees west; and in the Bay of Biscay and approaches to the English Channel. U-Boats sank 33 ships, the raider *Widder* one ship, and an E-Boat and aircraft one ship each.

Sierra Leone convoy SL34, from Freetown, lost *Willowbank* and *Barbara Marie* in the Bay of Biscay. *Barbara Marie*, carrying a cargo of iron ore, was sunk with 32 dead out of her crew of 37. Both ships were sunk by U-46, which had previously sunk *Margareta*, and which subsequently sank *Elpis*. Convoys HX47 and HX48 lost two ships each. *Antonis Georgandis*, a Greek ship loaded with a cargo of bulk grain, was lost with all 37 hands, sunk by U-101. The homeward bound Gibraltar convoy HG34F lost five ships out of 21.

Our convoy HX49 lost the first of four ships, when the Dutch tanker, *Moordrecht*, with a cargo of over 11,000 tons of fuel oil, was sunk with heavy loss of life, torpedoed in the early night of 20 June 1940, exploding in an inferno of flames. The tanker *San Fernando* was torpedoed the following day. I was on watch when I saw the huge columns of water as the torpedoes struck. Fortunately, she did not catch fire. *San Fernando* was sunk by U-47, which sank *H.M.S. Royal Oak* in Scapa Flow. She was a large

S.S. Fernando, an Eagle Oil Tanker, built in 1919. 13,056 gross registered tonnage
Torpedoed and sunk by U-47 on 21 June 1940, in convoy HX49
(*Photograph by John and Marion Clarkson – Ships in Focus*)

tanker of 13,056 gross tons carrying nearly 20,000 tons of crude oil, taken in tow, but foundered on 22 June. On the same day, the large Norwegian tanker, *Eli Knudsen*, carrying over 13,000 tons of fuel oil, was torpedoed by U-32, and sank after having been taken in tow. There were no fatal casualties. Finally, the Norwegian ship *Randsfjord*, with a general cargo, was sunk by U-30. Four of her crew of 33 were killed.

A most catastrophic loss occurred on 17 June 1940, when the liner Lancastria was bombed and sunk by aircraft, when endeavouring to evacuate service personnel and refugees from the French port of St. Nazaire. Accounts of the losses vary, but Lloyds' records the death of 66 of her crew of 306, and about 3,000 troops and refugees.

Convoy HX49 dispersed in the western approaches to the English Channel, and its two sections separated and continued independently at their individual maximum speeds, respectively north through the St. Georges Channel, and east through the English Channel. Soon the faster ships were out of sight. We encountered sporadic enemy air activity in the English Channel. Although we observed signs of action in the distance in the form of anti-aircraft fire, explosions, and diving aircraft, our ship was not attacked

We joined a North Sea convoy at Southend, and arrived in Middlesbrough on 27 June 1940 where we paid off. I remained on board for about two weeks, to work on deck as a rigger, and to form part of the stand-by gun crew for our quick firing 12-pounder gun. This handy weapon could be worked by a crew of three, gun layer, trainer, and breech worker/ammunition number.

Our Royal Marine gunner, "Guns", served as the gun layer, Phillip Harris as trainer, and I stood in as the breech worker and ammunition number. There were numerous air attacks on the ports of the Tyne and Tees, and we stood by our anti-aircraft weapons to repel any direct attacks on the ships in port. Phillip Harris, our Royal Marine gun layer and I had gone ashore one night to what turned out to be a binge in the Vane Arms in Stockton-on-Tees, when the air raid alert sirens sounded.

We returned to the ship, suffering very much from our session in the pub, to be confronted by Spencer, the Third Mate, who ordered us to go aft and man the 12-pounder. As we arrived aboard, one large bomb exploded on or near the transporter bridge over the river, and another exploded in the mud of the other side of the River Tees. The fragments from this bomb had struck *Brika*, which was moored to our starboard side, killing one man, and blowing the arm off another. The wives of some of the officers of *Brika* were staying aboard, and there was hysterical screaming and shouting aboard.

The gun layer ordered the loading with high explosive from our ready use lockers, but in the confusion, I selected shrapnel shells. I should have known better, because the two shells were of different shapes. They were also marked differently and in different colours, so in daylight there could have been no mistake. In the darkness, and not sober, I made the mistake. The shrapnel shells went into the breech, and we fired several rounds. The high explosive shells, which we should have been using, were fused to burst at a distance of about 1,000 yards, whereas the shrapnel shells burst at close range. A number of barrage balloons caught fire and fell to earth. It is likely that our shrapnel shells had done the damage. We ceased firing, and shortly afterwards the all clear siren sounded. Thereafter we heard nothing from official sources about the event.

During my wartime service in *Appledore*, my researches have revealed the following statistics of casualties in ships, seamen and U-Boats during the period from 3 September 1939 to 24 June 1940, the date when we arrived in Middlesbrough after voyage 32. They include only those ships lost in deep-sea waters.

Ships sunk as the result of U-Boat attack.
Seamen killed – 1,292 out of 7,049.
Ratio of fatal casualties to seamen at risk – over 18 percent.
German U-Boats that undertook successful attacks – 33.
German U-Boats destroyed by our counter measures – 15.
U-Boat personnel killed – 445.
U-Boat personnel who survived – 212.
U-Boat personnel fatal casualty rate – 47.64 percent.

Casualties – Ships and Personnel
3 September 1939 to 7 December 1939

Ships sunk – 60 by 32 successful U-Boats.
Surface ships accounted for six merchant ships
Scharnhorst sank *Rawalpindi*, 238 dead out of 275

Ten convoys were attacked, HG33 losing three ships,
OB17 two ships, and KF4 two ships

Lost with all hands

Loire, cargo iron ore, 37 dead.

Lost with very heavy casualties

Kenebec, cargo fuel oil, 14 dead out of 40.
Aviemore, cargo tinplate, 23 dead out of 34.
Hazelside, cargo, pulp and wheat, 11 dead out of 34.
Yorkshire, general cargo and passengers, 58 dead out of 278.
Menin Ridge, iron ore, 20 dead out of 34.
Thrasyvoulos, cargo coal, 23 dead out of 35.
Arlington Court, cargo maize, 12 dead out of 34.
Sliedrecht, cargo benzene, 26 dead out of 35.
Darino, cargo general, 16 dead out of 27.
Navasota, in ballast, 37 dead out of 74.
Thomas Walton, in ballast, 13 dead out of 34.

Merchant seamen and killed – 380 – out of 2547, a fatal casualty rate of 15 percent. Over 86 percent of the ship's company of *Rawalpindi* were lost. The *Athenia* losses were 102 out of 1402 passengers and crew.

APPLEDORE - VOYAGES 30 TO 32

APPLEDORE - VOYAGE 30 - RECORD OF MERCHANT SHIPS SUNK IN ATLANTIC - 03/09/39 TO 07/12/39

DATE	SHIP	NAT.	CONVOY NO.	CAUSE OF LOSS	POSITION		CARGO	CASUALTIES CREW	DEAD
03/09/39	ATHENIA	BRITISH		U-30	56-42 N.	14-05 W.	PASS	1,402	102
05/09/39	BOSNIA	BRITISH		U-47	45-29 N.	09-45 W.	SULPHUR	34	1
05/09/39	ROYAL SCEPTRE	BRITISH		U-48	46-23 N.	14-59 W.	GRAIN	34	1
06/09/39	RIO CLARO	BRITISH		U-47	46-30 N.	12-00 W.	COAL	41	0
06/09/39	MANAAR	BRITISH		U-38	39-00 N.	11-00 W.	GENERAL	92	7
07/09/39	PUKKASTAN	BRITISH		U-34	49-23 N.	07-49 W.	MAIZE	34	0
07/09/39	OLIVEGROVE	BRITISH		U-33	49-05 N.	15-58 W.	SUGAR	34	0
07/09/39	GARTAVON	BRITISH		U-47	47-04 N.	11-32 W.	GENERAL	34	0
08/09/39	KENNEBEC	BRITISH		U-34	49-18 N.	08-13 W.	FUEL OIL	40	14
08/09/39	REGENT TIGER	BRITISH		U-29	49-47 N.	15-34 W.	GASOLENE	40	0
08/09/39	WINKLEIGH	BRITISH		U-48	48-06 N.	18-12 W.	GRAIN	37	0
11/09/39	BLAIRLOGIE	BRITISH		U-30	54-59 N.	15-08 W.	SCRAP	34	0
11/09/39	FIRBY	BRITISH		U-48		13-50 W.	BALLAST	34	0
11/09/39	INVERLIFFFEY	BRITISH		U-38	48-18 N.	11-48 W.	GASOLENE	49	0
13/09/39	NEPTUNIA (TUG)	BRITISH		U-29	49-28 N.	15-03 W.		21	0
14/09/39	VANCOUVER CITY	BRITISH		U-28	51-23 N.	07-03 W.	SUGAR	33	3
14/09/39	FANAD HEAD	BRITISH		U-30	56-43 N.	15-21 W.	GRAIN	50	0
14/09/39	BRITISH INFLUENCE	BRITISH		U-29	49-43 N.	12-49 W.	FUEL OIL	42	0
15/09/39	CHEYENNE	BRITISH		U-53	50-20 N.	13-30 W.	GASOLENE	43	6
16/09/39	ARKLESIDE	BRITISH		U-33	48-00 N.	09-30 W.	COAL	30	0
16/09/39	AVIEMORE	BRITISH	OB4	U-31	49-11 N.	13-38 W.	TINPLATE	34	23
16/09/39	RUDYARD KIPLING	BRITISH		U-27	53-50 N.	11-10 W.	FISH		
17/09/39	KAFIRISTAN	BRITISH		U-53	50-16 N.	16-55 W.	SUGAR	35	6
18/09/39	KENSINGTON COURT	BRITISH		U-32	50-31 N.	08-27 W.	CEREALS	35	0
18/09/39	ARLITA	BRITISH		U-35	57-51 N.	09-28 W.	FISH		
18/09/39	LORD MINTO	BRITISH		U-35	57-51 N.	09-28 W.	FISH		
24/09/39	CALDEW (TUG)	BRITISH		U-33	60-47 N.	06-20 W.			
24/09/39	HAZELSIDE	BRITISH		U-31	51-17 N.	09-22 W.	WHEAT	34	11

APPLEDORE - PASSAGE FROM VANCOUVER TO HALIFAX - 24/09/39 TO 17/11/39

DATE	SHIP	NAT.	CONVOY NO.	CAUSE OF LOSS	POSITION		CARGO	CASUALTIES CREW	DEAD
30/09/39	CLEMENT	BRITISH		GRAF SPEE	09-05 S.	34-05 W.	GENERAL	34	0
01/10/39	SUZON	BELG.		U-35			PITPROPS	20	0
03/10/39	DIAMANTIS	GREEK		U-35			IRON ORE		
05/10/39	STONEGATE	BRITISH		DEUTSCHLAND	31-10 N.	54-00 W.	NITRATE	34	0
05/10/39	NEWTON BEECH	BRITISH		GRAF SPEE	09-35 S.	06-30 W.	MAIZE	34	0
07/10/39	ASHLEA	BRITISH		GRAF SPEE	09-00 S.	03-00 W.	SUGAR	34	0
10/10/39	HUNTSMAN	BRITISH		GRAF SPEE	08-30 S.	05-15 W.	GENERAL	40	0
12/10/39	ARIS	GREEK		U-37	53-28 N.	14-30 W.	BALLAST	34	2
12/10/39	EMILE MIGUET	FRENCH	KJ2	U-48	50-00 N.	14-30 W.	GASOLENE	35	2
13/10/39	HERONSPOOL	BRITISH	OB17	U-48	50-13 N.	14-48 W.	COAL	35	1
13/10/39	LOUISIANE	FRENCH	OB17	U-48	50-15 N.	15-05 W.	GENERAL	29	1
14/10/39	BRETAGNE	FRENCH	KJF3	U-45	50-20 N.	12-45 W.	GENERAL	35	7
14/10/39	LOCHAVON	BRITISH	KJF3	U-45	50-25 N.	13-10 W.	GENERAL	60	0
14/10/39	LAURENTZ W. HANSEN	NOR.		DEUTSCHLAND	49-05 N.	43-44 W.	TIMBER	35	3
14/10/39	SNEATON	BRITISH		U-48	49-05 N.	13-05 W.	COAL	30	1
15/10/39	VERMONT	FRENCH		U-37	48-01 N.	17-22 W.	BALLAST	34	2
17/10/39	CITY OF MANDALAY	BRITISH	HG3	U-46	44-57 N.	13-36 W.	GENERAL	80	7
17/10/39	CLAN CHISHOLM	BRITISH	HG3	U-48	45-00 N.	15-00 W.	GENERAL	45	4
17/10/39	YORKSHIRE	BRITISH	HG3	U-46	44-52 N.	14-31 W.	PASS	278	58
24/10/39	LEDBURY	BRITISH		U-37	36-01 N.	07-22 W.	BAUXITE	31	0
24/10/39	MENIN RIDGE	BRITISH		U-37	36-01 N.	07-22 W.	IRON ORE	34	20
24/10/39	TAFNA	BRITISH		U-37	35-44 N.	07-23 W.	IRON ORE	33	2
27/10/39	BRONTE	BRITISH	OB25	U-34	49-30 N.	12-15 W.	GENERAL	42	0
29/10/39	MALABAR	BRITISH	HX5	U-34	49-57 N.	07-37 W.	GENERAL	76	5
30/10/39	THRASYVOULOS	GREEK		U-37	49-25 N.	11-18 W.	COAL	35	23
31/10/39	BAOULE	FRENCH	20K	U-25	43-48 N.	09-08 W.	GENERAL	35	13
12/11/39	ARNE KJODE	NOR.		U-41	58-45 N.	07-09 W.	GAS OIL	35	5
12/11/39	LOIRE	FRENCH		U-26	36-16 N.	02-16 W.	IRON ORE	37	37
16/11/39	ARLINGTON COURT	BRITISH	SL7	U-43	48-14 N.	11-42 W.	MAIZE	34	12
16/11/39	SLIEDRECHT	DUTCH		U-28			BENZENE	35	26
	APPLEDORE		**HX9**						
19/11/39	DARIN0	BRITISH		U-41	44-12 N.	11-07 W.	GENERAL	27	16
19/11/39	PENSILVA	BRITISH	HG7	U-49	46-51 N.	11-36 W.	MAIZE	30	2
23/11/39	H.M.S. RAWALPINDI	BRITISH		SCHARNHORST				275	238
25/11/39	ROYSTON GRANGE	BRITISH		U-28	49-15 N.	09-00 W.	GENERAL	35	0
25/11/39	USKMOUTH	BRITISH		U-43	43-22 N.	11-27 W.	COAL	30	2
26/11/39	GUSTAF E. REUTER	SWED.		U-48	43-30 N.	11-30 W.	BALLAST	35	1
05/12/39	NAVASOTA	BRITISH	OB46	U-47	50-43N.	10-16W.	BALLAST	74	37
06/12/39	BRITTA	NOR.		U-47				35	6
07/12/39	THOMAS WALTON	BRITISH		U-38	67-52N.	14-28E.		34	13
							TOTALS	**4,224**	**720**

Casualties – Ships and Personnel
8 December 1939 to 15 April 1940

Ships sunk – 48 – by 18 successful U-Boats.

Lost with all hands

Flora, cargo coal, 25 dead.
Norma, cargo not recorded, 25 dead.
Maryland, cargo not recorded, 32 dead.
P.L.M. 15, cargo iron ore, 37 dead.
Castlemoor, cargo not recorded, 40 dead.
Navarra, cargo coal, 12 dead.

Lost with very heavy casualties

Eleni Stathatou, in ballast, 12 dead out of 37.
Martin Goldschmidt, cargo phosphates, 15 dead out of 20.
Aase, cargo fruit, 15 dead out of 16.
Steinstad, cargo not recorded, 13 dead out of 25.
Stancliffe, cargo iron ore, 20 dead out of 37.
Thurston, cargo manganese ore, 29 dead out of 32.
Bothal, in ballast, 15 dead out of 20.
Viking, in ballast, 15 dead out of 17.
Britta, in ballast, 13 dead out of 18.

Merchant seamen killed – 429 out of 1632 –
a fatal casualty rate of over 26 percent.

Convoys attacked – OB48, OG16, OG18, OA80G,
and OA84 OG19F and HX22.

The records show no specific details of the loss of *Castlemoor*. The only reference to the ship is shown in "Britain's War at Sea", 27th April 1940. The report states that she was "last seen 25 February 1940 by *Merchant Royal*, 800 miles west of Ushant," and another, "*Castlemoor*, 6,574 tons (Runciman Shipping Co.) was presumed lost with 40 crew on board." The weather was not exceptionally severe, although the seas were heavy. She was a well-found diesel-engined ship, built in 1922, of 10,785 tons dead-weight capacity, that left Halifax on 16 February 1940 bound for the River

Tees. Therefore, the loss of *Castlemoor* is still a mystery. Possibly, she struck a floating mine that had broken adrift from the English Channel barrage in heavy weather.

APPLEDORE - VOYAGES 30 TO 32

APPLEDORE - VOYAGE 31 - RECORD OF MERCHANT SHIPS SUNK IN ATLANTIC - 08/12/39 TO 15/04/40

APPLEDORE - BERTHED IN HULL - 08/12/39 TO 22/01/40

DATE	SHIP	NAT.	CONVOY NO.	CAUSE OF LOSS	POSITION		CARGO	CASUALTIES CREW	DEAD
08/12/39	BRANDON	BRITISH	OB48	U-48	50-06N.	09-10 W.	BALLAST	37	9
09/12/39	SAN ALBERTO	BRITISH	OB48	U-48	49-20 N.	09-45 W.	BALLAST	37	1
15/12/39	GERMAINE	GREEK		U-48	51-00 N.	12-18 W.	MAIZE	25	0
25/12/39	STANHOLME	BRITISH		MINED	51-20 N.	03-39 W.	COAL	26	13
14/01/40	FAGERHEIM	NOR.		U-44	47-20 N.	06-16 W.	ORE	25	14
15/01/40	ARENDSKERK	DUTCH		U-44	46-55 N.	06-34 W.	GENERAL	25	0
20/01/40	E. DRACOULIS	GREEK		U-44	40-20 N.	10-07 W.	WHEAT	25	6
24/01/40	ALSACIEN	FRENCH		U-44	38-00 N.	09-55 W.	GENERAL	30	4
	APPLEDORE		**OB79**						
25/01/40	TOURNY	FRENCH		U-44	38-09 N.	09-55 W.	GENERAL	30	8
28/01/40	ELENI STATHATOU	GREEK		U-34			BALLAST	37	12
28/01/40	FLORA	GREEK		U-44			COAL	25	25
30/01/40	KERAMIAAI	GREEK	OA80G	U-55	48-37 N.	07-45 W.	BALLAST	28	0
30/01/40	VACLITE	BRITISH	OA80G	U-55	49-20 N.	07-04 W.	BALLAST	35	0
03/02/40	ARMINISTAN	BRITISH	OG16	U-25	38-15 N.	11-15 W.	GENARAL	37	0
05/02/40	BEAVERBURN	BRITISH	OA84	U-41	49-19 N.	10-08 W.	GENERAL	50	1
10/02/40	BURGERDIJK	DUTCH		U-48	49-45 N.	06-30 W.	WHEAT	37	0
11/02/40	SNESTAD	NOR.		U-53	58-40 N.	13-40 W.	BALLAST	30	2
12/02/40	DALARO	SWED.		U-53	56-35 N.	11-50 W.	LINSEED	30	1
12/02/40	NIDARHOLM	NOR.		U-26	50-10 N.	14-09 W.	GENERAL	25	0
13/02/40	NORMA	SWED.		U-53	55-30 N.	11-00 W.		25	25

APPLEDORE - BERTHED IN NEW ORLEANS - 14/02/40 TO 05/03/40

DATE	SHIP	NAT.	CONVOY NO.	CAUSE OF LOSS	POSITION		CARGO	CASUALTIES CREW	DEAD
14/02/40	LANGLEEFORD	BRITISH		U-26	51-40 N.	12-40 W.	WHEAT	34	4
14/02/40	MARTIN GOLDSHMIDT	DANISH		U-53	55-53 N.	12-37 W.	PHOSPHATES	20	15
14/02/40	SULTAN STAR	BRITISH		U-48	48-54 N.	10-03 W.	GENERAL	76	1
15/02/40	MARYLAND	DANISH		U-50	57-09 N.	12-00 W.		32	32
15/02/40	AASE	DANISH		U-37	49-17 N.	08-15 W.	FRUIT	16	15
15/02/40	STEINSTAD	NOR.		U-26				25	13
15/02/40	DEN HAAG	DUTCH		U-48	48-02 N.	08-26 W.	OIL	37	0
17/02/40	ELLIN	GREEK		U-37			COAL	37	0
17/02/40	PYRRHUS	BRITISH	OG18	U-37	44-02 N.	10-18 W.	GENERAL	85	8
17/02/40	WILJA	FINNISH		U-48	49-24 N.	07-10 W.	GENERAL	27	0
18/02/40	BANDERAS	SPAN.		U-53			PHOSPHATES	29	7
18/02/40	P.L.M. 15	FRENCH		U-37	43-37 N.	09-15 W.	ORE	37	37
21/02/40	TARA	DUTCH		U-50	42-45 N.	10-25 W.	GRAIN	30	0
22/02/40	BRITISH ENDEAVOUR	BRITISH	OG19F	U-50	42-11 N.	11-35 W.	BALLAST	38	5
01/03/40	LAGAHOLM	SWED.		U-32	59-34 N.	05-10 W.	GENERAL	25	1
04/03/40	THURSTON	BRITISH		U-29	50-23 N.	05-49 W.	MANGANESE	29	26
08/03/40	COUNSELLOR	BRITISH	HX22	U-32	53-38 N.	03-23 W.	GENERAL	78	0
11/03/40	EULOTA	DUTCH		U-28	48-35 N.	08-22 W.	BALLAST	42	0
19/03/40	MINSK	DANISH		U-19	51-20 N.	03-39 W.	COAL	20	11
20/03/40	ALGIER	DANISH		U-38	60-17 N.	02-49 W.	GENERAL	25	5
20/03/40	BOTHAL	DANISH		U-19	58-08 N.	02-38 W.	BALLAST	20	15
20/03/40	VIKING	DANISH		U-19	58-08 N.	02-38 W.	BALLAST	17	15
21/03/40	CRISTIANSBORG	DANISH		U-38	60-17 N.	02-49 W.	MAIZE	25	1
	APPLEDORE		**HX30**						
25/03/40	BRITTA	DANISH		U-47	60-00 N.	04-19 W.	BALLAST	18	13
25/03/40	DAGHESTAN	BRITISH		U-57	NEAR ORKNEYS		CRUDE OIL	34	4
27/03/40	CASTLEMOOR	BRITISH			NO DETAILS			40	40
06/04/40	NAVARRA	NOR.		U-59	59-04 N.	04-00 W.	COAL	12	12
10/04/40	SVEABORG	SWED.		U-37	62-52 N.	06-34 W.	DIESEL OIL	34	5
10/04/40	TOSCA	NOR.		U-37	62-52 N.	07-34 W.	GENERAL	34	2
12/04/40	STANCLIFFE	BRITISH		U-37			IRON ORE	37	20
							TOTALS	**1,632**	**428**

Casualties – Ships and Personnel
16 April 1940 to 8 July 1940

Ships sunk – 72 by 23 successful U-Boats.
Raiders sank two ships.
Aircraft sank five ships.
Light surface ships sank two ships.
One ship sunk by a mine.

Lost with all hands

Lily, cargo unknown, 20 dead.
Antonis Georgandis, cargo grain, 37 dead.
British Monarch, cargo iron ore, 40 dead.
The Monarch, cargo not recorded, 12 dead.

Lost with heavy casualties

Tringa, cargo iron ore, 17 dead out of 23.
Sheaf Mead, in ballast, 32 dead out of 37.
Uruguay, cargo maize, 15 dead out of 28.
Telena, cargo crude oil, 18 dead out of 54
Orangemoor, cargo iron ore, 18 dead out of 40.
Barbara Marie, cargo iron ore, 32 dead out of 37.
Italia, cargo gasoline, 19 dead out of 35.
Moordrecht, cargo fuel oil, 25 dead out of 29.
Tilia Gorthon, cargo coal, 10 dead out of 21.
Otterpool, cargo iron ore, 23 dead out of 38,
Elmcrest, in ballast, 16 dead out of 38.

Passenger ships

Arandora Star – 860 dead out of 1,555.
The fatal casualties that occurred when *Arandora Star* was sunk were
mainly passengers, 713 German and Italian internees and German
prisoners-of-war and 109 military guards.

Merchant seamen killed – 1,355 out of 4323 – a fatal casualty rate
of over 31 percent.

Convoys attacked – HGF31F, HX47, HX48, HX49, SL34, HG34F, 65X,
OA172, SL36, OB176, OA178, HX52 and HX53.

WARTIME LIFE AT SEA, 1939–1940

APPLEDORE - VOYAGES 30 TO 32

APPLEDORE - VOYAGE 32 - RECORD OF MERCHANT SHIPS SUNK IN ATLANTIC - 16/04/40 TO 08/07/40

APPLEDORE - BERTHED IN HULL - 16/04/40 TO 30/04/40

DATE	SHIP	NAT.	CONVOY NO.	CAUSE OF LOSS	POSITION		CARGO	CASUALTIES CREW	DEAD
21/04/40	CEDARBANK	BRITISH		U-26	62-49 N.	04-10 E.	GENERAL	45	15
24/04/40	HAXBY	BRITISH		A.M.C.	31-30 N.	51-30 W.	BALLAT	37	17
26/04/40	LILY	DANISH		U-13	NORTH SEA			20	20
	APPLEDORE		**OB140**						
03/05/40	SCIENTIST	BRITISH		A.M.C.	20-00 S.	04-30 E.	GENERAL	50	3
10/05/40	SAN TIBURCIO	BRITISH		U-9			FUEL OIL	40	0
11/05/40	VIJU	EST.		U-9				20	15
11/05/40	TRINGA	BRITISH		U-9	51-21 N.	02-25 E.	ORE	23	17

APPLEDORE - BERTHED IN CHARLESTOWN - 18/05/40 TO 02/06/40

DATE	SHIP	NAT.	CONVOY NO.	CAUSE OF LOSS	POSITION		CARGO	CASUALTIES CREW	DEAD
19/05/40	ERIK FRISELL	SWEDISH		U-37	57-25 N.	09-15 W.	FODDER	34	0
24/05/40	KYMA	GREEK		U-37	48-30 N.	09-30 W.	MAIZE	30	7
27/05/40	SHEAF MEAD	BRITISH		U-37	43-48 N.	12-32 W.	BALLAST	37	32
27/05/40	URUGUAY	ARG.		U-37	43-40 N.	12-16 W.	MAIZE	28	15
28/05/40	BRAZZA	FRENCH		U-37	42-43 N.	11-00 W.	GENERAL		
29/05/40	TELENA	BRITISH		U-37	42-25 N.	09-08 W.	CRUDE OIL	54	18
30/05/40	STANHALL	BRITISH		U-101	48-59 N.	05-17 W.	SUGAR	37	1
31/05/40	ORANGEMOOR	BRITISH	HG31F	U-101	49-47 N.	03-20 W.	IRON ORE	40	18
01/06/40	ASTRONOMER	BRITISH		U-58	58-04 N.	02-12 W.	STORES	100	4
02/06/40	POLYCARP	BRITISH		U-101	49-19 N.	09-19 W.	GENERAL	43	0
	APPLEDORE		**HX49**						
09/06/40	MARGARETA	FINN.		U-46	45-00 N.	14-30 W.	PEANUTS	25	5
10/06/40	V.N. GOULANDRIS	GREEK		U-48	46-00 N.	12-30 W.	WHEAT	28	6
11/06/40	MOUNT HYMETTUS	GREEK		U-101	43-13 N.	11-20W.	BALLAST	24	0
12/06/40	WILLOWBANK	BRITISH	SL34	U-46	44-16 N.	13-54 W.	MAIZE	51	0
12/06/40	BARBARA MARIE	BRITISH	SL34	U-46	44-16 N.	13-54 W.	IRON ORE	37	32
12/06/40	EARLSPARK	BRITISH		U-101	42-26 N.	11-33 W.	COAL	38	7
13/06/40	BRITISH PETROL	BRITISH		A.M.C.	20-00 N.	50-00 W.	BALLAST	46	2
13/06/40	SCOTSTOUN	BRITISH		U-25			A.M.C.		6
14/06/40	BALMORALWOOD	BRITISH	HX48	U-47	50-19 N.	10-28 W.	WHEAT	41	0
14/06/40	ITALIA	NOR.	HX47	U-47	50-37 N.	08-44 W.	GASOLENE	35	19
14/06/40	A. GEORGANDIS	GREEK		U-101	42-45 N.	16-20 W.	GRAIN	37	37
14/06/40	MOUNT MYRTO	GREEK	HX48	U-38	50-03 N.	10-05 W.	GENERAL	24	4
15/06/40	ERIK BOYE	BRITISH	HX47	U-38	50-37 N.	08-44 W.	WHEAT	22	0
16/06/40	ANDANIA	BRITISH		UA	62-36 N.	15-09 W.	A.M.C.		0
16/06/40	ELPIS	GREEK		U-46	43-46 N.	14-06 W.	WHEAT	28	0
16/06/40	WELLINGTON STAR	BRITISH		U101	42-39 N.	17-01 W.	GENERAL	69	0
17/06/40	LANCASTRIA	BRITISH		AIRCRAFT					3,006
18/06/40	ALTAIR	NOR.		U-32	49-35 N.	11-00 W.		25	0
18/06/40	SARMATIA	FINN.		U-28	49-04 N.	12-00 W.	BALLAST	23	0
19/06/40	BARON LOUDOUN	BRITISH	HG34F	U-48	45-00 N.	11-25 W.	IRON ORE	33	3
19/06/40	TUDOR	NOR.	HG34F	U-48	45-10 N.	11-50 W.	STEEL	39	1
19/06/40	A. GEORGIOS	GREEK		U-28	49-35 N.	11-15 W.	GRAIN	30	1
19/06/40	BRITISH MONARCH	BRITISH	HG34F	U-48	45-00 N.	11-25 W.	IRON ORE	40	40
19/06/40	THE MONARCH	BRITISH		E-BOAT	47-20 N.	04-40 W.		12	12
19/06/40	LABUD	YUGO.		U-32	51-06 N.	08-38 W.	MAIZE	34	0
20/06/40	EMPIRE CONVEYOR	BRITISH		U-122	56-16 N.	08-10 W.	WHEAT	41	3
20/06/40	MOORDRECHT	DUTCH	HX49	U-48	43-34 N.	14-20 W.	FUEL OIL	29	25
20/06/40	TILIA GORTHON	SWED.	HG34F	U-38	48-50 N.	07-21 W.	COAL	21	10
20/06/40	OTTERPOOL	BRITISH	HG34F	U-30	48-47 N.	07-50 W.	IRON ORE	38	23
21/06/40	LUXEMBURG	BELG.		U-38	47-25 N.	04-55 W.	GENERAL	35	0
21/06/40	YARRAVILLE	BRITISH	65X	U-43	39-40 N.	11-34 W.	BALLAST	54	5
21/06/40	SAN FERNANDO	BRITISH	HX49	U-47	50-20 N.	10-24 W.	CRUDE OIL	49	0
22/06/40	ELI KNUDSEN	NORW.		U-32	50-36 N.	08-44 W.	FUEL OIL	37	0
22/06/40	NEION	GREEK	HG34F	U-38	47-09 N.	04-17 W.	GENERAL	35	1
22/06/40	RANDSFJORD	NORW.	HX49	U-30	50-29 N.	05-56 W.	GENERAL	33	4
24/06/40	CATHRINE	PAN.		U-47	50-08 n.	15-00 W.		19	0
25/06/40	CRUX	NOR.		UA	36-52 N.	14-00 W.		30	0
25/06/40	SARANAC	BRITISH	OA172	U-51	48-24 N.	15-05 W.	BALLAST	44	4
25/06/40	WINDSORWOOD	BRITISH	OA172	U-51	48-24 N.	15-05 W.	COAL	40	0
26/06/40	DIMITRIS	GREEK		U-29	44-23 N.	11-41 W.	CEREALS	30	0
27/06/40	LENDA	NOR.		U-27	50-12-N.	13-18 W.	TIMBER	26	1
27/06/40	LETICIA	DUTCH		U-47	50-11 N.	13-15 W.	GAS OIL	30	2
27/06/40	LLANARTH	BRITISH		U-30	47-30 N.	10-30 W.	FLOUR	35	0
29/06/40	EMPIRE TOUCAN	BRITISH		U-47	49-20 N.	13-52 W.	BALLAST	34	3
29/06/40	F.B. GOULANDRIS	GREEK		U-26	49-59 N.	11-24 W.	BALLAST	38	6
30/06/40	AVELONA STAR	BRITISH		U-43	46-46 N.	12-17 W.	MEAT	84	4
30/06/40	BELMOIRA	NOR.		U-26	48-15 N.	10-30 W.	BALLAST	30	0
30/06/40	G. KYRIAKIDES	GREEK		U-47	50-25 N.	14-33 W.	SUGAR	30	0
30/06/40	MERKUR	EST.		U-26	48-26 N.	10-58 W.	TIMBER	30	4
01/07/40	ADAMASTOS	GREEK		U-29	46-20 N.	14-30 W.	GRAIN	25	0
01/07/40	BEIGNON	BRITISH	SL36	U-30	47-20 N.	10-30 W.	WHEAT	33	3
01/07/40	CLEARTON	BRITISH	SL36	U-102	47-53 N.	09-30 W.	CEREALS	34	8
02/07/40	AENEUS	BRITISH		AIRCRAFT			TROOPS	143	21
02/07/40	ARANDORA STAR	BRITISH		U-47	55-20 N.	10-33 W.	PASS.	1,555	860
02/07/40	ATHELLAIRD	BRITISH	OB176	U-29	47-24 N.	16-49 W.	BALLAST	42	0
02/07/40	STA. MARGARETA	PAN.		U-29	47-10 N.	16-10 W.	COAL	39	3
04/07/40	BRITSUM	DUTCH	OA178	AIRCRAFT	50-40 N.	01-55 W.	BALLAST	35	9
04/07/40	DALLAS CITY	BRITISH		AIRCRAFT	50-09 N.	02-01 W.	SULPHATE	37	0
04/07/40	DEUCALIAN	DUTCH	OA178	AIRCRAFT	50-11 N.	02-35 W.	BALLAST	27	0
04/07/40	ELMCREST	BRITISH		E-BOAT			BALLAST	38	16
05/07/40	DELAMBRE	BRITISH		A.M.C.	04-00 S.	26-00 W.	GENERAL		
05/07/40	MAGOG	BRITISH	HX52	U-99	50-31 N.	11-05 W.	TIMBER	23	0
06/07/40	VAPPER	EST.		U-34	49-02 N.	09-29 W.	COAL	33	1
07/07/40	BISSEN	SWED.		U-99	50-06 N.	10-23 W.	TIMBER	20	0
07/07/40	LUCRETIA	DUTCH		U-34	49-50 N.	08-07 W.	GAS OIL	32	2
08/07/40	HUMBER ARM	BRITISH	HX53	U-99	50-40 N.	09-10 W.	LUMBER	43	0
							TOTALS	4,410	1,375

APPLEDORE - VOYAGES 30 TO 32

SHIP AND U-BOAT LOSSES - WHEN SERVING ON *APPLEDORE* - 03 SEPTEMBER 1939 TO 08 JULY 1940

GERMAN U-BOATS NUMBER	TOTALS C/F	B/F	TOTAL	03/09/39 07/12/39	08/12/39 12/04/40	13/04/40 08/07/40
UA			2			2
U-9			3			3
U-13			1			1
U-19			3		3	
U-25			3	1	1	1
U-26			8	1	3	4
U-27			2	1		1
U-28			6	3	1	2
U-29			8	3	1	4
U-30			7	3		4
U-31			2	2		
U-32			6	1	2	3
U-33			3	3		
U-34			7	4	1	2
U-35			4	4		
U-37			19	6	7	6
U-38			10	3	2	5
U-41			3	2	1	
U-43			4	2		2
U-44			6		6	
U-45			2	2		
U-46			5	2		3
U-47			14	5	1	8
U-48			22	9	7	6
U-49			1	1		
U-50			3		3	
U-51			2			2
U-53			7	2	5	
U-55			2		2	
U-57			1		1	
U-58			1			1
U-59			1		1	
U-99			3			3
U-101			7			7
U-102			1			1
U-122			1			1
	180	0	180	60	48	72
HEAVY SHIPS	7	0	7	7		
RAIDERS	4	0	4			4
LIGHT WARSHIPS	2	0	2			2
AIRCRAFT	5	0	5			5
ITALIAN SUBMARINES	0	0	0			
OTHER CAUSES	2	0	2		2	
	20	0	20	7	2	11

ENEMY U-BOAT LOSSES — DETAILS OF LOSS

	DATE	CAUSE	DEAD	SAVED
U-1	16/04/40	MINE	24	0
U-12	08/10/39	MINE	27	0
U-13	31/05/40	D/C	0	26
U-15	01/02/40	COLL.	25	0
U-16	24/10/39	D/C	28	0
U-22	25/04/40	MINE	27	0
U-26	03/07/40	D/C	0	48
U-27	20/09/39	D/C	0	38
U-33	12/02/40	D/C	25	11
U-35	29/11/39	D/C	43	0
U-36	04/12/39	SUB.	40	0
U-39	14/09/39	D/C	43	3
U-40	13/10/39	MINE	38	0
U-41	05/02/40	D/C	49	17
U-42	13/10/39	D/C	25	0
U-44	20/03/40	MINE	47	0
U-45	14/10/39	D/C	38	0
U-49	15/04/40	D/C	1	41
U-50	06/04/40	MINE	44	0
U-53	24/02/40	D/C	42	0
U-54	13/02/40	MINE	41	0
U-55	30/01/40	D/C	1	40
U-63	25/02/40	D/C	1	24
U-64	13/04/40	AIR	8	34
U-122	22/06/40	???	48	0
TOTALS		25	665	282
B/F		0	0	0
C/F		25	665	282

During my wartime my service in *Appledore*, our forces had accounted for 14 U-Boats, 9 by depth charge attack, one by aircraft, 2 by mines, and one combined aircraft and depth charge attack. One U-Boat was lost due to unknown causes.

When *Appledore* was at sea as part of convoy HX9, only nine merchant ships were sunk. Prior to the date of the departure of convoy

HX9, 58 merchant ships had been sunk between the outbreak of hostilities and the date of our departure from Halifax. The most successful U-Boat was U-48, under the command of Herbert Schultze, credited with eight ships.

The early statistics prove that there was heavy loss of life in ships carrying bulk cargoes and oil products. Statistics, which I have compiled and produce within the body of this narrative, underline the lethal nature of such cargoes, particularly when the attack occurred during darkness and in tempestuous weather conditions.

The majority of losses had occurred in the southwestern approaches and Bay of Biscay, to unescorted ships on independent passage. The losses during the passage of convoy HX9 were relatively low due to the tempestuous weather conditions that were encountered in the western approaches. This very nearly caused the foundering and loss of *Appledore*. Undoubtedly, none of us would have survived

Now, many years after those early days of the war, and with the experience of an officer who served on the bridges of merchant ships throughout the conflict, I am able to reflect on how unprepared we were for hostilities. The war at sea during the Great War from 1914 to 1918 is well documented in the many books on the subject. During my youth, my father had encouraged me to read books from his own comprehensive personal library, and selected books from the Vancouver lending library. He induced me to read the five volumes of "Naval Operations", and all the volumes of "World Crisis" by Winston Churchill, as well as books by Mahan, Bywater, Sir Julien Corbett and many others.

The records reflected in graphic detail the threat to our survival caused by the unrestricted U-Boat attacks in 1917 and 1918; and the lessons that should have been learned from those events. Moreover, many of those who had held high authority twenty years previously served in the precincts of power between the wars, and in 1939.

From 1935 until the outbreak of hostilities, it was certainly clear to Winston Churchill – and should have been to the Admiralty – that war with Germany was almost inevitable. It should have been equally clear that the German navy would commence hostilities, using the same naval weapons that nearly brought them success in 1917. Despite all this, we were woefully unprepared.

Details of the navies of the world were regularly published, as far as was permissible, in *Janes' Fighting Ships,* and new construction reviewed in *The United Services Review.* It was therefore well known that massive naval rearmament was being undertaken throughout the world, after the original restrictions imposed by the Washington Conference were lifted. The Royal Navy programme for warship building included the five *King George V* class of battleships, the *Town, Colony* and *Dido* cruisers, and the powerful fleet destroyers of the *Tribal, J, K, L* and *M* classes.

However, the building of the most important units to counteract the potential U-Boat threat to our vitally important merchant ships appeared to be completely overlooked. This massive misjudgement nearly resulted in disaster on our shipping lanes. Those who sought funds for naval ship-building had to be aware that massive numbers of cruisers would not combat the obvious menace of U-Boats. Neither would great numbers of destroyers, capable of nearly 40 knots in smooth seas, but with high fuel consumption and relatively poor sea-keeping qualities, when faced by North Atlantic weather conditions.

Even after Winston Churchill assumed office as the First Lord of the Admiralty, and the famous signal "Winston is back!" was transmitted to the Fleet, it seemed that no lessons had been learned from the massive losses of merchant ships in 1917. Certainly very few steps appear to have been taken to prepare for what must have been the inevitable repetition of events. It is understandable that the alteration in U-Boat tactics in 1940, when they changed to night attacks on the surface by co-ordinated flotillas, had been unforeseen. However, even with the knowledge of these "wolf pack attacks", effective countermeasures had not been implemented until 1943 – two and a half years later.

We urgently needed vessels with good sea-keeping characteristics, long-range fuel capacity, and a speed capability of about 20 knots, sufficient to run down a surfaced U-Boat. Two dual-purpose primary armament guns, 4-inch, 4.5-inch, or 4.7-inch, and a number of Bofors and Oerlikon quick-firing automatic weapons were sufficient to deal with surfaced U-Boats. Regrettably, for a long time, the vital defence of merchant shipping was undertaken by the small 1914-1918 war destroyers of the "V", "W" and "S" classes, the *Fowey* class of sloops, and the very seaworthy *Algerine* class of minesweepers. Destroyers, in the classes built between 1930 and 1935, performed sterling service. *H.M.S. Bulldog* was one destroyer that seemed to be everywhere. The corvettes bore the almost insuperable burden for a long time, but because of their speed limitations, they needed the support of vessels of twice their speed.

The experiences of 1917 should have convinced the Admiralty that defending convoys was infinitely more important than protecting capital ships at anchor in Scapa Flow and Rosyth. The sad facts are that the naval officers in the Admiralty were unprepared for the U-boat attacks, either on ships on independent passage, or in convoy.

Our convoy escorts were supplemented by the fifty obsolete "four-stack" American 1914-1918 destroyers bartered for British bases. Although they were modified to the point of being almost rebuilt, they were not suitable ships for defence of convoys against the modern, fast U-boats, in the exceptionally severe conditions in the North Atlantic. These obsolete vessels, narrow in the beam, and with very poor sea-keeping capability and endurance, were berthed almost immediately in dockyards for massive structural and armament modifications.

The American shipyards, with their massive building capacity, could have produced fifty purpose-built modified larger corvettes in the time taken to modify the unsuitable American "four-stackers". A stretched version of the corvette, fifty feet longer to accommodate a much more powerful engine and greater fuel capacity, would have provided the speed capability, and better ability to operate in the usually heavy seas of the North Atlantic. The large, ocean going, American Coastguard cutters, the destroyer escorts, and the "Bird" class sloops, in service later in the war, were ideal convoy escort vessels. They arrived on the scene almost too late.

The same military leaders who decided our destinies had immediate and comprehensive knowledge of the dispositions of the small number of active U-boats on station in the southwestern approaches. It did not require a genius to appreciate that those were our areas of greatest vulnerability. Early in the war, the number of U-Boats disposed in those areas of concentration for homeward bound merchant shipping amounted to 17 in total out of the 29 in the numbering sequence U-25 to U-53. The records reflect the fact that the German U-Boat arm numbered 57 operational submarines.

The number of U-Boats likely to be operational was no secret, and it should have been clear where they would be concentrated. The Western Approaches was the funnel through which all traffic to and from our islands had to pass. A convoy of 30 ships would be entrusted to one sloop of the *Fowey* class. When the aircraft carrier *Ark Royal* was threatened by U-Boat attack, the action of the Admiralty in disposing the modern destroyers *Faulknor, Foxhound* and *Firedrake* to hunt down and destroy U-39 proved that the Admiralty had the resources and resolve, when one of our capital ships was threatened. It was in the area of priorities that they were adrift.

When the Home fleet provided heavy units for the distant cover for the Arctic convoys, an escort of fleet destroyers screened the capital ships. When *H.M.S. King George V* and *Rodney* put to sea to hunt down

Bismarck, the battleships were accompanied by flotillas of modern fleet destroyers, and similar escorts were provided for aircraft carriers. The destroyers that were deemed as unsuitable escorts for merchant ships, put to sea in all weathers to protect capital ships. This must have seemed puzzling to an officer on a merchant ship. When the Master brought aboard the convoy escort dispositions, the first question asked was "are there any destroyers with us, sir?" Usually, between 1939 and early 1943, we were lucky to have a destroyer and three or four corvettes.

The two German capital ships at sea had in that time disposed of only five ships, whereas the U-Boats had accounted for over 50. Indeed U-37 and U-48 probably sank more ships than the combined total achieved by *Scheer* and *Graf Spee*. Moreover, the 17 U-boats probably accounted for more merchant ships in a period of 74 days than all the capital ships and heavy cruisers of the German navy sank in the whole war.

The events of the 1914 to 1918 war proved that German capital ships usually presented their sterns to British ships of war, and surface raiders had achieved relatively insignificant success. There was no sense in protecting our capital ships, if they and their escorts were confined to port because their oil supplies were going up in flames in tankers that were not being properly protected.

During the 1914 to 1918 war, and the early years of World War Two, there was ample evidence of the lack of resolve in German surface warships. The pocket battleship *Graf Spee*, if more resolutely commanded, should have overwhelmed *Ajax* and *Achilles*, after the disabled *Exeter* withdrew from the battle. Instead, the powerful pocket battleship skulked into Buenos Aires, with her main and secondary armament intact, where she was ignominiously scuttled. After sinking *Hood*, the relatively undamaged *Bismarck* possessed the speed and armament capability to despatch *Prince of Wales*, but with typical lack of resolve broke off the action.

The R.A.F., with its jealously preserved compartments of Fighter, Bomber and Coastal Commands, starved Coastal Command of suitable aircraft until it was almost too late. It seemed that there was no co-ordinated strategic plan in the R.A.F. for merchant ship protection by aircraft. In the early months of the war, the Wellington, Whitley and Hampden aircraft of Bomber Command could have been modified by using part of their bomb-carrying capacity for the fitting of long-range fuel tanks. This would have bolstered the woefully weak capability of Coastal Command, which had to satisfy its operational requirements with the obsolete squadrons of Airspeed Oxford and Avro Anson aircraft, followed by the admirable Hudson, all short range aircraft.

The usefulness of the Whitley and Wellington bombers was proved when they achieved significant successes in anti U-Boat operations over the Bay of Biscay and the western approaches later in the war. They should have been released from leaflet dropping and tactical bombing of Berlin early, when they were desperately needed, and not later, when they were relatively obsolete, and not considered to be suitable for tactical bombing duties.

Later, massive numbers of Lancaster, Halifax and Sterling bombers were used by Air Chief Marshall Arthur Harris in the inaccurate bombing of mainly non-military targets in Germany and occupied Europe, at a massive cost in aircraft, and their brave and dedicated personnel. These large aircraft, with their huge bomb load capacity, could have been modified to carry enormous quantities of fuel, and deployed in bases on the Hebrides and in Northern Ireland, to close the "black hole" between 15 and 45 degrees west longitude, where our major losses occurred. A half a dozen squadrons of heavy bombers, suitably modified for long-range anti-U-Boat operations, would have made an immense impact in the years 1939 to 1942. Regrettably, Bomber Command did not make them available, and Winston Churchill did not order Air Chief Marshall Harris to do so. They both seemed imbued with the passionate misconception that Germany could be forced into submission by destroying civilians and their homes.

Incredibly, it has been recorded that when the thousand-bomber air attack on Germany was being planned by "Bomber" Harris, with the support of Winston Churchill, aircraft were transferred from Coastal Command to Bomber Command to make up the numbers to the "magic" thousand. A practical seaman on a merchant ship may have been excused if he had said, "What the hell was the difference between 950 and 1,000 bombers over Berlin, if all the high octane gasoline to fuel them was burning in funeral pyres on the Atlantic Ocean?" The extra 50 bombers would have made no difference over Berlin, but would have had a significant effect if they had been deployed over the Western Approaches.

It is significant of the neglect that the very long-range Liberator bombers of 120 Squadron R.A.F., based in Northern Ireland, were not operational until May 1943. Even then, only 17 aircraft were so deployed. It is an example of deplorable inaction that ASVIII centimetre radar was not authorised for use by Coastal Command until February 1943. It was almost too late then.

No individual in high authority, in his own personal cocoon, seemed to appreciate the facts known to all of us, and amply underlined by our massive losses. They did not seem to understand that it requires aluminium to construct aircraft and steel to build ships, petrol and oil to fuel their engines, and food and supplies to support their personnel and the people of our country. They appeared to look no further than the limits of their own operation commands.

Unfortunately, the merchant seamen suffered grievously from this neglect, which persisted until 1943. It was a tragic case of persistent lack of appreciation of priorities, and could have resulted in the annihilation of our convoys, and the eventual strangulation of the supplies that were so vital for the promotion of the war.

Those who served throughout nearly six years of the terrible battles on the sea routes of the Atlantic, and elsewhere, know just how close we came to defeat, and to the physical and mental breakdown of those who participated. It was a narrow escape

The Master, Captain Adam Leask, went on leave immediately after the ship berthed. Regrettably, I did not obtain a reference from him for my service during voyage 32. A written reference, or a watch-keeping certificate, signed by the Master, was necessary for officers between the qualifications of Second and First Mate. The signed indentures were all that was required for the qualification of Second Mate. Nevertheless, I regretted not having applied to Captain Leask for a reference, to complete my records.

I paid off on Monday 8 July 1940, with 23 days pay as an A.B. in my pocket. With war bonus and an additional sixpence a day for M.N. Seaman Gunner, this would have been between £ 10 and £ 12, enough for the fare to Cardiff, and several weeks lodgings. I travelled to Cardiff on Tuesday 8 July, and was ensconced in a modest but tidy boarding house in Beauchamp Street, ruled by a landlady named Mrs. Gall, the charge for bed and breakfast and evening meal being 25 shillings a week.

On Wednesday 10 July, I travelled to the docks. My first visit was to the nautical opticians, T.J. Williams, where I bought a new octant for £ 5. My very limited resources would not fund even a second-hand sextant, so the octant would have to suffice, until I had obtained a berth, hopefully as an un-certificated Third Mate. My next visit was to the offices of the ship owners in Bute Street, where H.G. Cox, the Managing Director, interviewed me. The parchment original of my apprentice's indentures was produced. On the back were details of the money I had drawn during thirteen voyages – four years hard labour for a pittance.

The total amount drawn was £ 69 15s 2d over a period of four years.

During my period as an apprentice, my indentures were kept in the custody of the Master, and I had never kept a record of the sums that I had drawn, so without my knowledge, I had accumulated a debt. The only explanation I could conceive was that the additional pay, promised for the periods when I had undertaken the duties of bosun and Third Mate, had not been included as additional credits during each voyage, and marked on my indentures. Effectively, I had not been paid, so that when I thought I was receiving extra pay at the end of the voyage, I was deluded.

Completion of the period on indentures paid a satisfactory service bonus of £ 5, and one shilling a month in lieu of laundry, so I was under the delusion that I would be collecting £ 7 8s od above my pay of £ 60. The funds I had overdrawn had resulted in a debt of £ 9 15s 2d on my indentures. Instead of receiving the much-needed payment, I was forced to repay £ 2 7s 2d; which I had not anticipated, and did not have.

Relaxing after work in port

Before Sunday lunch
with the Master and Officers

The cleaner aspects of life as an apprentice on *Appledore*

I told H.G. Cox that I had already paid for the fare to Cardiff, lodgings in advance, and the purchase of the octant, and had only a few shillings for fares in Cardiff. Despite the fact that he was living in relative luxury, and could have covered the debt from his own pocket, or through the office petty cash, the miserable skinflint refused to sign the indentures until I repaid the paltry sum of the debt. This forced me to leave his office and return to the nautical optician, where they very kindly permitted me to return the octant, and refunded the £ 5.

I was then in the shit, because the instrument was essential, if I was to obtain a berth as an uncertificated Third Mate. On returning to the office, the debt was paid in cash, and is reflected on the indenture document as "Cash Refunded £ 2 7s 2d." The miserly bugger then gave me the change of £ 2 12s 10d, and endorsed the indentures, "We hereby certify the within written Indenture has been well and faithfully performed by Apprentice Upton who completed his term of service with good reports from Masters and Officers under whom he has served." This was endorsed "For The Maritime Shipping & Trading Co. Ltd," and signed "H.G. Cox, Director" and dated 10th July 1940.

Further indignity from them was to follow. They knew that I had no sextant (octant) and no money. I was then told that the company would be assuming management of an American ship on behalf of the Ministry of War Transport. A crew was being selected to man Onomea, and would travel to New York to join the ship. I was offered the berth of Third Mate, and promised an advance note of £ 10, if I agreed to sign on. In completely impoverished circumstances, I had no option but to agree. On Wednesday 24 July 1940, I signed articles as Third Mate of *Onomea*. in Cardiff Shipping Office.

During the two weeks when I was standing by *Appledore*, 24 ships were sunk by U-Boats, one by a surface raider, one by an E-Boat and four by aircraft.

9

THE WAR AT SEA: ISTOK
24 JULY–8 OCTOBER 1940

PASSAGE TO NEW YORK AND PHILADELPHIA AND RETURN IN ISTOK

The first entry in my new Continuous Certificate of Discharge book No. R198560 reflects the name of the ship *Istok*, date of engagement 24 July 1940 at Cardiff. My instructions were that I would serve as Third Mate in *Onomea*, an American ship acquired under Lease Lend arrangements concluded between our respective governments. *Onomea* had been owned by Matson Navigation Company of San Francisco. Their fleet consisted of mainly older cargo ships built before 1920, with the exception of the passenger ships *Lurline* of 18,009 gross registered tons built in 1932, and *Matsonia* of 17,226 gross registered tons, built in 1927.

Although I had been loath to continue employment with the Maritime Shipping and Trading Co. Ltd, owned and managed by individuals whom I saw as being bereft of any decent human attributes, my impecunious situation gave me little alternative. At least I had a berth as an officer in the profession in which had trained for so long. I would at last stand on the bridge of a ship, albeit "in effective charge of a watch", until I had qualified. It was with a great sense of achievement that I signed articles for service in *Onomea*. My little octant had been recovered by repayment of the cost of £ 5, and served me well for two voyages. Although I was without the full scope of a sextant, my sights with the instrument were satisfactory. Later, I traded it in for a second hand Hughes "Three Circle" sextant, which served me well for the remainder of my service at sea. The advance note of £ 10 enabled me to replenish items of uniform and other clothing.

Onomea was acquired in a deal between the governments of the U.K

S.S. Istok, ex *Verdala*, ex *Mongolian Prince*
In pre-war Prince Line livery as the *Mongolian Prince*
(*Photograph by A. Duncan, Cowes, I.O.W.*)

and U.S.A., probably the beginning of Lease Lend. She had been completed in 1917 under the name *War Flame*, as part of the First World War building programme, re-named respectively *West Haven* in 1929 and *Marion Otis Chandler* in 1938, before being acquired by Matson Navigation Company. She was typical of the "War" series of ships, known as "Three Islanders", two long well decks separating the three superstructures, represented by the forecastle head, poop, and amidships bridge and boat decks. They were wet and dangerous ships in heavy weather, hence the name "Three Islanders".

Onomea had a length of 424 feet, beam of 54 feet one inch, loaded draught of 24 feet, 5,520 gross registered tonnage, 8,820 deadweight tonnage and designed loaded speed of 11 knots.

After signing on in Cardiff, we travelled by train to Liverpool, where we were accommodated in the Adelphi Hotel for about a week.

PASSENGER ON SCYTHIA

We then boarded Scythia as passengers for the passage to New York. *Scythia* was one of the less modern elements of the fleet of Cunard White

S.S. Istok, ex *Verdala*, ex *Mongolian Prince*
Built in 1913, 5904 gross registered tonnage.
In wartime livery with defensive armament, re-named *Maycrest*
(Photograph by National Maritime Museum)

Star Ltd, built in 1920, 19,761 gross registered tons, with a length of 624 feet, beam of 73 feet 10 inches, draught of 32 feet 8 inches and a designed speed of 16.5 knots.

She had accommodation for 330 cabin class, 313 tourist class and 533 third class passengers. With 1,176 passengers and a crew of about 300 aboard, the ship represented a potential nightmare in the event of enemy attack. Her modest speed made her vulnerable, even to attack by a surfaced U-Boat.

Many of the passengers were of continental European origin, Poles, Austrians, French, and various Slovenian countries, mostly refugees seeking asylum in the U.S.A. and Canada. The majority were either middle-aged or elderly couples, and children, with a small number of teenage or young females. The female passengers of marriageable age were a nuisance. They may have thought that it would be advantageous for them to capture young American or Canadian males as potential husbands, thereby enabling them to secure accelerated access through United States and Canadian immigration.

When they heard English spoken, in what they believed to be North

American accents, woe betide the unfortunate young (or not so young) males they set their sights on. There were a number of crews travelling to join ships in the U.S.A. and Canada, so the ladies had plenty of potential victims. However, the unsophisticated creatures failed to distinguish between the U.K. and American accents, so some of our officers and other ranks were fair game. The enthusiasm of the eager females was immediately quenched if the response to the question "Are you English?" was in the affirmative. They were looking for Americans. We gave them a wide berth.

Our trans Atlantic passage was north about, south of the Hebrides and Iceland, and then by a substantial deviation to the south, nearly as far as Bermuda, before altering course to the westward. We arrived in New York at the end of the second week in August 1940. The refugees were landed at Ellis Island. We were accommodated in a hotel in Manhattan. Our orders had been changed, and we were ordered to join the Yugoslav ship, *Istok*, then loading a cargo of pig iron in Philadelphia.

Istok was owned by Jugoslavenski Lloyd Ackionarsko Drustvo of Zagreb, built in 1913 under Lithuanian registry (name unknown), re-named respectively *Verdala* in 1917, *Mongolian Prince* in 1928, and then Istok. She was a typical well-decked three island ship of the era, 5,904 gross registered tons, 9,670 deadweight tons, 438 feet length, 56 feet beam, loaded draught 25 feet 4 inches and designed speed 9 knots. The ship was registered in Dubrovnik.

The Yugoslav crew jumped ship when they learned that the ship would carry the lethal cargo of pig iron. A skeleton crew under my command travelled to Philadelphia to commission the ship and complete loading. The Master, senior officers and remainder of the crew joined a week later, and we put to sea bound for Halifax, arriving at the end of August 1940. Two Irishmen, members of the original crew, had remained aboard. They were given passage to Halifax in the capacity of supernumeraries. It was intended that they would leave the ship in Canada.

Early on the day after our arrival in Halifax, I was awakened by an officer of the Royal Canadian Mounted Police, who was tapping on the door of the cabin. He had been told that I had been the first officer to board *Istok* with the skeleton crew, and asked me for information about the crew, and whether I had any suspicions about the integrity of any members of the crew. An amount of explosive had been found aboard, and had been taken ashore. I stated that I could vouch for the integrity of the British crew, but had found it strange that our two supernumeraries had stayed on board for the short passage to Halifax. They were not British nationals, yet had remained with a potentially lethal cargo.

They were arrested, and placed in custody ashore. We heard no more about the incident. *Istok* was granted British registration in Halifax on 31 August 1940.

The Maritime Shipping & Trading Co. Ltd of Cardiff transferred another crew to commission *Onomea* under the British flag, and continued to manage the ship for the Ministry of War Transport under the name *Empire Leopard*. Her Master was Captain John Evan Evans, who was known to many of us. *Empire Leopard* was one the of ships that constituted convoy SC107, which was attacked by the 13 U-Boats of the "Veilchen" (Violet) group, stationed in the western North Atlantic.

During concerted attacks over several days, convoy SC107 lost 13 out of its 41 ships. *Empire Leopard* was sunk by U-402 at 0804 on 2 November 1942, suffering catastrophic casualties. The Master, 31 crew and 7 gunners were killed. Only 3 of the complement of 42 were saved. The salvo of torpedoes from U-402 sank *Empire Antelope* at the same time and in the same position, 52 – 26 North, 45 – 22 West. Quite miraculously, only one member of the crew of *Empire Antelope* was lost out of her complement of 50. Such are the fortunes (or misfortunes) of war.

During the thirty-one days between our boarding Scythia in Liverpool, and the date of British registration of Istok, the casualties in ships, seamen and passengers had been very heavy.

The catastrophic casualties, so disastrous in terms of ships and material, and the loss of so many trained officers and men must have begun to cause concern, even to the dinosaurs in Whitehall. The losses, particularly the human casualties, were not publicised, so the members of the public were unaware of the events. There was no way in which the knowledge of such casualties could be suppressed from the participants. Strict censorship prevented the public from learning of losses at sea, but could not keep the personal tragedies from the close-knit communities in the ports, including the bereaved families. Moreover, the effect on morale aboard ships was beginning to show. Officers and men knew that bulk cargoes – steel, scrap, ores and phosphates- as well as oil, particularly high-octane and other volatile liquids, presented the likelihood of the risk of high fatalities. They knew that such cargoes constituted their death warrants.

All these risks were multiplied by darkness, heavy weather conditions, temperature of atmosphere and water, and the presence or absence of arrangements for rescue operations. The paucity of escorts was universally known to the crews of merchant ships, as was the hopeless inadequacy of any planning for the clear inevitability of unrestricted U-Boat attacks. We needed properly designed escort vessels; but we did not have them; and so the massive casualties continued. Once the convoy had been assembled and put to sea, the question would be asked, "Where are the bloody destroyers, sir?"

The Press made a great fuss about the wonderful deal Winston Churchill had concluded for the transfer of the obsolete "four-stacker" American destroyers. If we had traded our bases for fifty of the large ocean going U.S. Coastguard Cutters, it would have made sense. It would have taken less time, and cost infinitely less if, in 1940, fifty standard merchant ship hulls had been converted to small aircraft carriers with flight decks of approximately 600 feet length, carrying a dozen aeroplanes. It was pathetic, as convoy after convoy was escorted by a River Class sloop and two corvettes.

That was the tragic scenario when *Istok* put to sea on 17 September 1940, in convoy HX74 of 33 ships. The ship was in an awful state of disrepair, having been neglected by her Yugoslav owners for many years. The engines were in need of overhaul, and the ship was rust-ravaged from truck to keel. We did not have the time to inspect the lifesaving equipment or undertake repairs, and lived in the hope that they would not be needed. Given the state of the ship and a cargo of pig iron, there was little prospect of the ship staying afloat long enough to launch the boats and rafts.

There was a telephone between bridge and engine room, and we were furnished with Aldis lamps and a zig-zag clock, so at least the ship could be kept in station as long as the engines kept working.

Convoy HX74

When convoy HX74 put to sea, three Halifax convoys, HX71, HX72 and HX73, and one Sydney Cape Breton convoy, SC3, were at sea and approaching U.K. waters. Convoy HX 73 lost only one ship, *Dalveen*, sunk by aircraft north of the British Isles, with the loss of 11 of her crew of 43. Our convoy was not attacked directly, although there were many alarms and the dropping of depth charges.

The main convoy arrived in Liverpool on 2 October, and we berthed in Swansea on 4 October 1940. As we were approaching the lock gates in

Swansea, with the pilot aboard and the engines at dead slow ahead, the order was given for half astern. As was the custom, to create a loud ring at the other end, I cranked the handle full ahead first, and then back to half astern. The handle jammed on full ahead, but before the engineer could react, there was a frantic ring by telephone, and the verbal order of, "For Christ's sake. The bloody telegraph has jammed on full ahead. Put her full astern!" Fortunately, prompt reaction by the engineer preventing our ramming the lock gates. We berthed without further mishap.

An examination of the engine telegraph cables in the 'tween decks revealed that the covers had been removed and the cables cut partly through. This act of sabotage must have been perpetrated at the same time and by the same individuals who had planted the explosives that were discovered in Halifax. There was an inquiry by intelligence officials, but by then the saboteurs must have been identified, and, hopefully, hanged or shot. We never learned about their fate.

I paid off on 8 October 1940. I intended having a few days leave before reporting to the Merchant Navy Officers Reserve Pool, but this was prevented by urgent orders to join *Filleigh*, which was bunkering, after the discharge of a cargo of steel in Avonmouth. The Third Mate had failed to re-join after leave of absence, so I was the nearest available replacement. I joined her on 9 October 1940, and we put to sea the following day, bound for the Canadian St. Lawrence ports.

Istok was re-named *Maycrest* under the ownership of the Ministry of War Transport, and managed by Maritime Shipping and Trading Co. Ltd. for the remainder of her life. She was requisitioned by the Admiralty on 30 June 1944, and on 4 August 1944 was sunk as a breakwater component in Mulberry Harbour, Normandy.

During the passage of *Istok* in convoy HX74, no losses were sustained by its 33 ships. Once again, the most successful U-Boats were those that had been on active service at the beginning of hostilities.

During a period of 66 days, Hans Jenisch in U-32 sank 10 ships. He survived the sinking of his U-Boat by H.M.S. *Harvester* and *Highlander* on 30 October 1940. Werner Hartmann in U-37 sank 11 ships. Herbert Sohler in U-46 sank 4 ships and a further 4 several weeks later. Herbert Schultze in U-48 sank 6 ships and a further 6 several weeks later. Otto Kretchmer in U-99 sank 6 ships, plus a further 9 later. He too survived when U-99 was sunk on 17 March 1941 by H.M.S. *Walker*. Joachim Schepke in U-100 sank 13 ships and a further 7 later. He was killed when U-100 was sunk on 17 March 1941 by H.M.S. *Vanoc* and *Walker*. Other successful U-Boats were the newer craft, U-137, Herbert Wuhlfarth, 3 ships sunk, and U-138, Wolfgang Loth, 4 ships sunk. He had commanded, respectively, U-9, U-138, U43 and U-181. We were not sorry to learn that Prien, Shepke and Kretchmer had been either killed or taken prisoner.

Although convoy HX74 was not attacked, the losses in the Atlantic during the passage of the convoy were severe. Enemy tactics had changed to well-organised night attacks by flotillas of surfaced U-Boats, against lightly protected convoys. The corvettes did not possess sufficient speed to run down the enemy, and we were still woefully weak in destroyers.

The statistics of losses again underline the very high casualties in ships carrying the most lethal cargoes. Undoubtedly, iron ore and mainly steel and scrap cargoes were infinitely the most hazardous, and this was now well known throughout the merchant ships.

An almost fatalistic attitude had developed. From 1940 until the end of the war, most ships in which I served carried substantial tonnages of steel as lower hold cargo. Fortunately, I seem to have borne a charmed life for most of the time, but the stress on all of us was severe. The records must reflect the number of men who cracked up, but I encountered no incidences.

The statistics that I have compiled underline the lethal nature of cargoes of steel, pig iron, iron ore, or similar bulk cargo constituents. Most general traders carried part cargoes of steel, combined with war materials. The details of losses cover only those ships that were sunk in convoy over a relatively short period, in ideal circumstances for rescue.

The fatal casualties in ships that were sunk when on independent passage, or dispersed or detached from convoys, were substantially higher. As an example, the total number of men killed in the 17 ships shown on the schedule represented the equivalent complement of 100 heavy bombers or 7 infantry companies. Such losses in service units would have made those in Whitehall devote a greater measure of priority to convoy protection.

Casualties – Ships and Personnel
24 July 1940 to 30 August 1940

Ships sunk – 57 by 21 successful U-Boats.
Surface raiders sank three ships.

Aircraft sank six.
Italian submarines sank two ships.
Light surface warships sank two ships.

Lost with all hands

Statira, general cargo and phosphates, 31 dead.
Aspasia, cargo not recorded, 37 dead.
Fircrest, cargo iron ore, 40 dead.
Dalblair, in ballast, 42 dead.
Millhill, cargo steel, 34 dead.

Lost with very heavy casualties

Upwey Grange, cargo meat, 36 dead out of 86.
Canton, general cargo, 16 dead out of 32.
Clan McPhee, general cargo, 67 dead out of 92.
Leonidas M. Valmas, cargo timber, 16 dead out of 30.
Anglo Saxon, cargo coal, 39 dead out of 41.
Severn Leigh, in ballast, 33 dead out of 42.
Keret, in ballast, 13 dead out of 20.
Athelcrest, cargo fuel, 30 dead out of 36.
Empire Merlin, cargo sulphur, 32 dead out of 33.
Harpalyce, cargo steel, 37 dead out of 47.
Pecten, cargo fuel oil, 49 dead out of 57.
Chelsea, cargo maize, 24 dead out of 35.
Har Zion, general cargo, 36 dead out of 37.
Ali El- Kebir, carrying 860 crew and troops, 60 dead.

Merchant seamen, naval personnel and passengers killed – 811 out of 3,671, a fatal casualty rate of 22 percent.

Passenger ships lost 443 killed out of 2,141, and armed merchant cruisers lost 67 killed out of 616.

Eighteen convoys were attacked. The worst casualties occurred in convoys HX60 (3 ships), HX65 (8 ships) and HX66 (4 ships).

U-Boats U-107 and U-48 sank nine ships each, U-38 seven, and U-46 and U-124 six each.

SCYTHIA,ONOMEA AND ISTOK - 24 JULY 1940 TO 30 AUGUST 1940

RECORD OF MERCHANT SHIPS SUNK IN ATLANTIC - 24/07/40 TO 30/08/40

ONOMEA - SIGNED ARTICLES AT CARDIFF - 24/07/40

DATE	SHIP	NAT.			CONVOY			CAUSE	POSITION		CARGO	CASUALTIES	
			NO.	SHIPS	DEP.	ARR.	DISP.	OF LOSS				CREW	DEAD
24/07/40	MEKNES	FRENCH						E-BOAT	50-04 N.	02-15 W.	TROOPS	1281	383
26/07/40	ACCRA	BRITISH	OB188	37	23/7/40		27/7/40	U-34	55-40 N.	16-28 W.	GENERAL	953	24
26/07/40	SAMBRE	BRITISH	OB188					U-34	56-37 N.	17-53 W.	GENERAL	43	4
28/07/40	ORLOCK HEAD	BRITISH						AIRCRAFT	58-44 N.	04-21 W.	CEMENT	25	6
29/07/40	CLAN MENZIES	BRITISH						U-99	54-10 N.	12-00 W.	GENERAL	94	6
29/07/40	CLAN MONROE	BRITISH						E-BOAT	51-52 N.	01-48 E.	ORE	79	13
30/07/40	JAMAICA PROGRESS	BRITISH						U-99	56-26 N.	08-30 W.	FRUIT	53	7
31/07/40	DOMINGO DE LARRINAGA	BRITISH						A.M.C.	05-26 S.	18-06 W.	GRAIN	38	8
31/07/40	JERSEY CITY	BRITISH	OB191	29	30/7/40		2/8/40	U-99	55-47 N.	09-18 W.	BALLAST	45	2

SCYTHIA - ON PASSAGE TO NEW YORK - 01/08/40 TO 15/08/40

01/08/40	SIGYN	SWED.						U-59	56-10 N.	09-25 W.	TIMBER	23	0
03/08/40	ATOS	SWED.						U-57	56-00 N.	07-00 W.	GENERAL	28	1
03/08/40	RAD	YUGO.						UA	11-20 N.	21-00 W.	CHEM.	29	0
03/08/40	STATIRA	BRITISH						AIRCRAFT			GENERAL	31	31
04/08/40	BEAULIEU	NOR.						A.M.C.	26-30 N.	48-00 W.		37	3
04/08/40	GERALDINE MARY	BRITISH	HX60	60	23/7/40	7/8/40		U-52	56-58 N.	15-55 W.	PAPER	51	3
04/08/40	GOGOVALE	BRITISH	HX60					U-52	56-59 N.	17-38 W.	FLOUR	39	3
04/08/40	KING ALFRED	BRITISH	HX60					U-52	56-59 N.	17-38 W.	TIMBER	39	5
04/08/40	PINDOS	GREEK	SL40	24	16/7/40	8/8/40		U-58	55-22 N.	08-50 W.	GRAIN	35	3
05/08/40	BOMA	BRITISH	OB193	48	4/8/40		7/8/40	U-56	55-44 N.	08-04 W.	COAL	56	3
07/08/40	MOHAMED ALI EL-KEBIR	BRITISH						U-38	55-22 N.	13-18 W.	GENERAL	860	60
08/08/40	UPWEY GRANGE	BRITISH						U-37	54-20 N.	15-28 W.	MEAT	86	36
09/08/40	CANTON	SWED.						U-30	55-04 N.	11-21 W.	GENERAL	32	16
10/08/40	TRANSYLVANIA (A.M.C.)	BRITISH						U-56	55-50 N.	08-03 W.	A.M.C.	340	40
11/08/40	LLANFAIR	BRITISH	SL41	39	25/7/40	14/8/40		U-38	54-48 N.	13-46 W.	SUGAR	32	3
12/08/40	BRITISH FAME	BRITISH	OB193	28	29/6/40		2/7/40	MALASPINA	37-44 N.	22-56 W.	BALLAST	49	3
13/08/40	NILS GORTHON	SWED.	HX62	76	31/7/40	15/8/40		U-60	55-45 N.	07-30 W.	PULP	21	4
15/08/40	SYLVAFIELD	BRITISH	HX62	76	31/7/40	15/8/40		U-51	56-39 N.	11-15 W.	FUEL OIL	42	3
15/08/40	ASPASIA	GREEK						UA	35-00 N.	20-00 W.		37	37

ISTOK - BERTHED PHILADELPHIA - 16/08/40 TO 26/08/40

16/08/40	CLAN McPHEE	BRITISH	OB197	54	13/8/40		16/8/40	U-30	57-30 N.	17-14 W.	GENERAL	92	67
16/08/40	EMPIRE MERCHANT	BRITISH	OA198	10	13/8/40		18/8/40	U-100	55-21 N.	13-40 W.	GENERAL	55	7
16/08/40	HEDRUN	SWED.	OB197					U-48	57-10 N.	16-37 W.	COAL	30	10
18/08/40	AMPLEFORTH	BRITISH	OA199	29	15/8/40		20/8/40	U-101	56-10 N.	10-40 W.	BALLAST	37	9
18/08/40	VILLE DE GAND	BELG.						U-48	55-28 N.	15-10 W.	EXPL.	53	15
19/08/40	KELET	HUNG.						UA	50-00 N.	22-00 W.	BALLAST	33	0
19/08/40	TUIRA	PAN.	OB198					UA	55-28 N.	15-10 W.	BALLAST	53	0
20/08/40	LEONIDAS M. VALMAS	GREEK						U-46	53-20 N.	20-30 W.	COAL	30	2
21/08/40	ANGLO SAXON	BRITISH						U-46	55-13 N.	10-38 W.	TIMBER	30	16
22/08/40	KERET	NOR.	OA200	40	16/8/40		20/8/40	A.M.C.	26-10 N.	34-09 W.	COAL	41	39
23/08/40	BROOKWOOD	BRITISH	OA200					U-37	54-16 N.	23-08 W.	BALLAST	20	13
23/08/40	CUMBERLAND	BRITISH	OB202	32	22/8/40		26/8/40	U-57	54-40 N.	27-56 W.	BALLAST	37	1
23/08/40	ST. DUNSTAN	BRITISH	OB202					U-57	55-43 N.	07-33 W.	GENERAL	58	4
23/08 40	SEVERN LEIGH	BRITISH	OA200					U-57	55-43 N.	08-10 W.	BALLAST	63	14
24/08/40	BLAIRMORE	BRITISH	SC1	40	15/8/40	29/8/40		U-37	54-31 N.	25-41 W.	BALLAST	42	33
24/08/40	LA BREA	BRITISH	HX65	51	12/8/40	27/8/40		U-37	56-00 N.	27-30 W.	TIMBER	34	4
25/08/40	ATHELCREST	BRITISH	HX65					U-48	57-24 N.	11-21 W.	FUEL OIL	33	2
25/08/40	EMPIRE MERLIN	BRITISH	HX65					U-48	58-24 N.	11-25 W.	DIESEL OIL	36	30
25/08/40	FIRCREST	BRITISH	HX65					U-48	58-30 N.	10-15 W.	SULPHUR	33	32
25/08/40	GOATHLAND	BRITISH						AIRCRAFT	58-52 N.	06-34 W.	IRON ORE	40	40
25/08/40	HARPALYCE	BRITISH						U-124	50-21 N.	15-08 W.	IRON ORE	36	0
25/08/40	JAMAICA PIONEER	BRITISH						U-124	58-52 N.	06-34 W.	STEEL	47	37
25/08/40	PECTEN	BRITISH	HX65					U-100	57-02 N.	11-04 W.	BANANAS	64	2
25/08/40	YEWCREST	BRITISH	OB201	31	20/8/40		25/8/40	U-57	56-22 N.	07-55 W.	FUEL OIL	57	49

ISTOK ON PHILADELPHIA TO HALIFAX - 25/08/40 TO 30/08/40

26/08/40	CAPE YORK	BRITISH	HX65A					U-37	55-10 N.	25-02 W.	BALLAST	38	1
26/08/40	ILVINGTON COURT	BRITISH						AIRCRAFT	57-45 N.	01-48 W.	GENERAL	33	0
26/08/40	REMEURA	BRITISH						DANDOLO	37-14 N.	21-52 W.	IRON ORE	39	0
27/08/40	A.M.C. DUNVEGAN CASTLE	BRITISH	SL43	47	11/8/40	31/8/40		AIRCRAFT	57-50 N.	01-54 W.	GENERAL	94	0
27/08 40	EVA	NOR.	SC1	40	15/8/40	29/8/40		U-46	54-50 N.	11-00 W.	ESCORT	276	27
27/08/40	THEODOROS T.	GREEK						U-28	57-50 N.	11-15 W.	LUMBER	30	1
28/08/40	DALBLAIR	BRITISH	OA204	43	25/8/40		29/8/40	U-37	50-10 N.	19-50 W.	MAIZE	35	0
28/08/40	ELLE	FINN.						U-100	56-06 N.	13-33 W.	BALLAST	42	42
28/08/40	KYNO	BRITISH	HX66					U-101	57-43 N.	12-18 W.	TIMBER	29	2
29/08/40	ASTRA II	BRITISH	OA204					U-28	58-06 N.	14-34 W.	GENERAL	37	5
29/08/40	ALIDA GORTHON	SWED.	OA204					U-100	56-09 N.	12-14 W.	BALLAST	26	5
29/08 40	EMPIRE MOOSE	BRITISH	OA204					U-100	59-09 N.	12-14 W.	BALLAST	24	11
30/08/40	CHELSEA	BRITISH	HX66					U-100	56-06 N.	14-00 W.	BALLAST	36	0
30/08/40	MARSTENEN	NOR.						U-32	59-45 N.	06-49 W.	MAIZE	35	24
30/08/40	MILL HILL	BRITISH	HX66					AIRCRAFT	58-23 N.	02-37 W.	PULP	20	0
30/08/40	NORNE	NOR.	HX66					U-32	58-48 N.	06-49 W.	STEEL	34	34
30/08/40	VILLE DE HASSELT	BELG.						U-32	58-48 N.	06-49 W.	SCRAP	34	34
30/08/40	SAN GABRIEL	GREEK	OB205	33	29/8/40		30/8/40	U-46	57-40 N.	09-00 W.	GENERAL	63	0
								U-59	56-04 N.	09-52 W.	BALLAST	24	2

| | | | | | | | | | | | TOTALS | 6428 | 1321 |

Casualties – Ships and Personnel
31 August 1940 to 08 October 1940

Ships sunk – 61 – by 21 successful U-Boats.
Italian submarines sank three ships.
Aircraft sank two ships.
Raiders sank two 2 ships.

Lost with all hands

Bibury, cargo coal, 36 dead.
Magdalena, cargo iron ore, 31 dead.
Baron Blythswood, cargo iron ore, 34 dead.
Darcoila, in ballast, 31 dead.
Georges Mabro, cargo not recorded, 30 dead.
Bassa, in ballast, 48 dead.
Samala, cargo bananas, 67 dead.
Kayeson, cargo coal, 38 dead.
British General, cargo crude oil, 47 dead.
Nina Borthen, cargo not recorded, 37 dead.

Lost with very heavy casualties

Posidon, cargo sulphur, 17 dead out of 32.
Maas, in ballast, 28 dead out of 30.
Lotos, cargo not recorded, 17 dead out of 25.
City of Benares, general passengers, 253 dead out of 401.
Tregenna, cargo steel, 33 dead out of 37.
City of Simla, passengers, 260 dead out of 407.
Empire Adventure, in ballast, 21 dead out of 39.
Invershannon, cargo fuel oil, 17 dead out of 47.
Empire Airman, cargo iron ore, 33 dead out of 37.
Frederick S. Fales, cargo fuel oil, 20 dead out of 48.
Eurymedon, general cargo, 29 dead out of 93.
Mabriton, in ballast 12 dead out of 37.
Manchester Brigade, general cargo, 58 dead out of 62.
Benlawers, general cargo, 24 dead out of 52.

Merchant seamen killed – 871 out of 2764,
a fatal casualty rate of 31.5 percent.

Four passenger ships were lost with 519 out of a total complement of 1301.

Ten convoys were attacked, SL46 (one ship), SC3 (6 ships), OB213 (2 ships), HX71 (6 ships), HX72 (11 ships), OB217 (2 ships), OB218 (5 ships), OB220 (one ship), OB221 (one ship)

ISTOK - 24 JULY 1940 TO 8 OCTOBER 1940

RECORD OF MERCHANT SHIPS SUNK IN ATLANTIC - 31/08/40 TO 0810/40

ISTOK - SIGNED ARTICLES AT HALIFAX - 31/08/40

DATE	SHIP	NAT.	CONVOY NO.	CAUSE OF LOSS	POSITION		CARGO	CASUALTIES	
								CREW	DEAD
31/08/40	EFPLOIA	GREEK		U-101	55-27 N.	13-17 W.	BALLAST	37	0
31/08/40	HAR ZION	BRITISH	OB205	U-38	56-20 N.	10-00 W.	GENERAL	37	36
02/09/40	CYMBALINE	BRITISH		A.M.C.	28-00 N.	35 W.	BALLAST	37	7
02/09/40	THORNLEA	BRITISH	OB206	U-46	55-15 N.	16-40 W.	COAL	36	3
02/09/40	VILLE DE MONS	BELG.		U-47	58-20 N.	12-00 W.	GENERAL	54	0
02/09/40	BIBURY	BRITISH	OB205	U-46	55-14 N.	16-40 W.	COAL	36	36
03/09/40	ULVA	BRITISH		U-60	55-45 N.	11-45 W.	COAL	20	3
03/09/40	TITAN	BRITISH	OA207	U-47	58-14 N.	50-50 W.	BALLAST	96	6
04/09/40	LUIMNEACH	BRITISH		U-46	47-50 N.	09-12 W.	PYRITES	18	6
07/09/40	GRO	NOR.	SC2	U-47	58-30 N.	16-10 W.	WHEAT	32	11
08/09/40	ANTONIS CHANDRIS	GREEK		A.M.C.	11-25 N.	34-10 W.	COAL	32	0
08/09/40	POSIDON	GREEK	SC2	U-47	56-43 N.	09-16 W.	SULPHUR	32	17
09/09/40	MARDINIAN	BRITISH	SC2	U-28	56-37 N.	09-00 W.	PITCH	38	6
11/09/40	MAAS	DUTCH	OA210	U-28	55-34 N.	15-56 W.	BALLAST	30	28
14/09/40	ALEXANDROS	GREEK	SC3	U-48	56-30 N.	16-30 W.	TIMBER	30	5
14/09/40	ST. AGNES	BRITISH	SL46	EMO	41-27 N.	21-50 W.	LINSEED	64	0
15/09/40	ALEXANDROS	GREEK	SC3	U-48	56-30 N.	16-30 W.	TIMBER	30	5
15/09/40	EMPIRE VOLUNTEER	BRITISH	SC3	U-48	56-43 N.	15-17 W.	IRON ORE	33	0
15/09/40	HIRD	NOR.	SC3	U-65	58-00 N.	12-20 W.	GENERAL	37	0
15/09/40	KENORDOC	BRITISH	SC3	U-99	57-42 N.	15-02 W.	TIMBER	20	7
16/09/40	LOTOS	NOR.	SC3	U-99	N.W. OF ROCKALL		TIMBER	25	17
	ISTOK		HX74						
17/09/40	CITY OF BENARES	BRITISH	OB213	U-48	56-48 N.	21-15 W.	PASSENGERS	401	253
17/09/40	MARINA	BRITISH	OB213	U-48	56-46 N.	21-15 W.	COAL	36	2
17/09/40	CROWN ARUN	BRITISH	HX71	U-99	58-02 N.	14-18 W.	PITPROPS	25	0
17/09/40	TREGENNA	BRITISH	HX71	U-65	58-22 N.	15-42 W.	STEEL	37	33
18/09/40	CITY OF SIMLA	BRITISH	OB216	U-138	55-55 N.	21-15 W.	GENERAL	407	260
18/09/40	CABO TORTOSA	SPAN.		BAGNOLINI	41-20 N.	09-16 W.	PYRITES	30	0
18/09/40	MAGDALENA	BRITISH	SC3	U-48	57-20 N.	20-16 W.	IRON ORE	31	31
20/09/40	BOKA	PAN.	OB216	U-138	55-54 N.	07-24 W.	COAL	34	8
20/09/40	EMPIRE ADVENTURE	BRITISH	OB216	U-128	55-48 N.	07-22 W.	BALLAST	39	21
20/09/40	INVERSHANNON	BRITISH	HX72	U-99	56-00 N.	23-00 W.	FUEL OIL	47	17
20/09/40	NEW SEVILLA	BRITISH	OB216	U-138	55-50 N.	07-30 W.	STORES	285	2
21/09/40	CITY OF SIMLA	BRITISH	OB216	U-138	55-55 N.	08-20 W.	GENERAL	350	3
21/09/40	BLAIRANGUS	BRITISH	HX72	U-99	55-18 N.	22-21 W.	PITPROPS	34	7
21/09/40	CANONESA	BRITISH	HX72	U-100	55-45 N.	18-25 W.	GENERAL	63	1
21/09/40	BARON BLYTHSWOOD	BRITISH	HX72	U-99	56-00 N.	23-00 W.	IRON ORE	34	34
21/09/40	DALCAIRN	BRITISH	HX72	U-100	59-00 N.	19-00 W.	WHEAT	42	0
21/09/40	ELMBANK	BRITISH	HX72	U-99	55-20 N.	22-30 W.	TIMBER	56	1
21/09/40	EMPIRE AIRMAN	BRITISH	HX72	U-100	54-00 N.	18-00 W.	IRON ORE	37	33
21/09/40	FREDERICK S. FALES	BRITISH	HX72	U-100	55-30 N.	13-40 W.	FUEL OIL	48	20
21/09/40	SCHOLAR	BRITISH	HX72	U-100	55-11 N.	17-58 W.	GENERAL	45	0
21/09/40	TORINIA	BRITISH	HX72	U-100	54-47 N.	18-00 W.	FUEL OIL	55	5
22/09/40	SIMLA	NOR.	HX72	U-100	55-08 N.	17-40 W.	STEEL	35	5
25/09/40	EURYMEDON	BRITISH	OB217	U-29	53-36 N.	20-25 W.	GENERAL	93	29
25/09/40	MABRITON	BRITISH	OB216	U-32	56-12 N.	23-00 W.	BALLAST	37	12
25/09/40	SULAIRIA	BRITISH	OB217	U-43	53-43 N.	20-10 W.	GENERAL	57	1
26/09/40	CORRIENTES	BRITISH	OB217	U-32	53-47 N.	24-19 W.	GENERAL	40	0
26/09/40	MANCHESTER BRIGADE	BRITISH	OB218	U-137	54-53 N.	10-22 W.	GENERAL	62	58
26/09/40	STRATFORD	BRITISH	OB218	U-137	54-50 N.	10-40 W.	BALLAST	34	2
26/09/40	SILJAN	SWED.		U-46			COAL	25	9
26/09/40	DARCOILA	BRITISH	OB217	U-32	53.32 N.	26-00 W.	BALLAST	31	31
26/09/40	TANCRED	NOR.	OB217	U-32	53-32 N.	24-35 W.	BALLAST	36	0
27/09/40	ASGERD	NOR.	OB218	U-137	56-35 N.	09-10 W.	BALLAST	25	0
27/09/40	VESTVARD	NOR.		U-31			BALLAST	29	1
27/09/40	GEORGES MABRO	EGYPT.		U-37	52-00 N.	09-00 W.		30	30
28/09/40	DALVEEN	BRITISH	HX73	AIRCRAFT	58-10 N.	02-19 W.	WHEAT	43	11
28/09/40	EMPIRE OCELOT	BRITISH	OB218	U-32	54-37 N.	21-30 W.	BALLAST	35	2
29/09/40	BASSA	BRITISH		U-32	54-00 N.	21-00 W.	BALLAST	48	48
30/09/40	SAMALA	BRITISH		U-37	53-00 N.	18-00 W.	BANANAS	67	67
30/09/40	HAULERWIJK	DUTCH	OB218	U-132	54-28 N.	26-33 W.	BALLAST	31	4
30/09/40	HEMINGE	BRITISH	OB220	U-37	53-26 N.	18-33 W.	COAL	26	1
01/10/40	AGHIOS NICOLAOS	GREEK		BARACCA	40-00 N.	16-55 W.	BULK ZINC	26	0
01/10/40	HIGHLAND PATRIOT	BRITISH		U-38	52-20 N.	19-04 W.	GENERAL	143	3
02/10/40	KAYESON	BRITISH		U-32	51-12 N.	24-22 W.	COAL	38	38
02/10/40	LATYMER	BRITISH		AIRCRAFT	51-20 N.	10-30 W.	GENERAL	28	6
06/10/40	BENLAWERS	BRITISH	OB221	U-123	53-20 N.	26-10 W.	GENERAL	52	24
06/10/40	BRITISH GENERAL	BRITISH		U-37	51-42 N.	24-03 W.	CRUDE OIL	47	47
06/10/40	NINA BORTHEN	NOR.		U-103	54-00 N.	26-00 W.		37	37
							TOTALS	**4,065**	**1,390**

THE WAR AT SEA: ISTOK

ISTOK - 24 JULY 1940 TO 8 OCTOBER 1940

SHIP AND U-BOAT LOSSES - WHEN SERVING ON *ISTOK* - 24 JULY 1940 TO 08 OCTOBER 1940

GERMAN U-BOATS			SHIPS SUNK IN PERIOD			ENEMY U-BOAT LOSSES			
NUMBER	TOTALS C/F	B/F	TOTAL	24/07/40 30/08/40	31/08/40 08/10/40	DETAILS OF LOSS DATE	CAUSE	DEAD	SAVED
UA			4	4		U-25 03/08/40	MINE	49	0
U-28			4	2	2	U-51 20/08/40	SUB.	43	0
U-29			1	0	1	U-57 03/09/40	COLL	6	19
U-30			2	2		U-102 05/07/40	???	43	0
U-31			1		1				
U-32			10	3	7				
U-34			2	2					
U-37			11	7	4				
U-38			4	2	2				
U-43			1		1				
U-46			7	3	4				
U-47			4		4				
U-48			12	5	7				
U-51			1	1					
U-52			3	3					
U-56			2	2					
U-57			4	4					
U-58			1	1					
U-59			2	2					
U-60			2	1	1				
U-65			2		2				
U-99			9	3	6				
U-100			13	6	7				
U-101			3	2	1				
U-103			1		1				
U-123			1		1				
U-124			2	2					
U-128			1		1				
U-132			1		1				
U-137			3		3				
U-138			4		4				
	298	180	118	57	61	**TOTALS** 4		141	19
						B/F 25		665	282
HEAVY SHIPS	7	7	0			**C/F** 29		806	301
RAIDERS	9	4	5	3	2				
LIGHT WARSHIPS	4	2	2	2					
AIRCRAFT	13	5	8	6	2				
ITALIAN SUBMARINES	5	0	5	2	3				
OTHER CAUSES	2	2	0						
	40	20	20	13	7				

10

THE WAR AT SEA: FILLEIGH

9 OCTOBER–22 DECEMBER 1940

I joined *Filleigh* on 9 October 1940 as Third Mate, immediately after paying off *Istok* the previous day. Although I had vowed not to serve in Tatem ships again, the Merchant Navy Officers Reserve Pool gave officers little choice generally, and in cases of emergency, they gave no option. It was a change to board a well-found and well-equipped ship again after *Istok*, which had suffered from years of neglect under the Yugoslav flag. It was a case of packing my kit and moving across the Swansea Docks.

Joining *Filleigh* was like coming home. She was so similar to *Appledore* in accommodation layout and build. A fine ship with handsome lines, *Filleigh* was the smallest ship in the fleet, 4,856 gross registered tons: 395 feet 6 inches long: 55 feet 4 inches beam: 25 feet 9 inches loaded draught: and 9,100 deadweight tons. Her designed speed was 9.75 knots. She was known to be a faster ship than most of the others. Her shorter length and broad beam gave her exceptionally good sea-keeping qualities.

Her Master, Captain A. Harp, had served in her for many years. The Second Mate, Ivor Day, was also a long-serving officer. Both had served all their life at sea in ships of the Tatem fleet. The Third and First Mates had paid off, and the new First Mate was Mr. Thomas, I believe to have been a native of Barry Docks. They were good officers. Captain Harp was a meticulous Master. However, he, the Second Mate, and other officers and seamen who had served on the ship for the previous voyage, had been severely unnerved by the catastrophic loss of *Tregenna*, on the homeward bound Atlantic passage.

During our passage to the U.K. in *Istok* in convoy HX74, the previous Halifax convoys HX71, HX72 and HX73 were at sea, together with convoy SC3, which put to sea from Sydney Cape Breton. Freetown

S.S. Filleigh, built in 1928, 4856 gross registered tonnage
Torpedoed and sunk by U-245 on 18 April 1945 off Normandy Beaches
(*Photograph by John and Marion Clarkson, Ships in Focus*)

convoy SL46 and outward bound convoys OB213, OB217, OB218, OB220 and OB221 were also at sea. There were 408 ships at sea, either in, or dispersed from the 12 convoys.

The number of escort vessels allocated for the protection of merchant ships was woefully week – even then – over a year after the commencement of hostilities. The south western approaches had been closed by the occupation of the French Biscay ports, so all our traffic would have to be channelled through a narrow gap north or south of the Hebrides, east of 15 degrees west longitude.

Those who survived the slaughter will always reflect on the loss of 1,226 men in 48 ships in a period of 27 days, so close to U.K. bases, and ask why merchant ship protection had not improved perceptively in over a year of hostilities. Yet, suitable aircraft were still not showing overhead, even close to shore, and convoy protection was undertaken by the dedicated personnel in a small number of sloops and older destroyers.

Filleigh had put to sea from Halifax in convoy HX71 on 5 September 1940 in company with 33 ships. She was stationed in the outer starboard column of the convoy, with *Tregenna* the next ship ahead. At 2318 on 16 September 1940, *Crown Arun*, which had become detached from convoy HX71, was torpedoed by U-99 (Otto Kretchmer), and despatched by gunfire. She was south and east of the convoy.

The following day, 17 September 1940, the ships in the convoy were pitching violently in a heavy sea and swell. *Filleigh* was in station astern of Tregenna, at the distance of three cables length, stem to stem. *Tregenna* carried about 8,500 tons of steel in her five lower holds. During the afternoon watch, it would have been likely that no more than four men would have been on deck on each ship – officer of the watch, helmsman, lookout and standby man. Hans-Gerrit von Stockhausen, in command of U-65, avoided the escort screen, and a spread of torpedoes was fired at the outside starboard column of ships. It is likely that two struck Tregenna between Numbers 1 and 2 holds, and possibly also in Number 3 hold, just as the ship pitched heavily forward.

Tregenna did not recover, and plunged downwards, standing vertically for about thirty seconds before sinking. The ships were travelling at about 8 knots, which would equate to a speed of 13.5 feet per second. *Filleigh* was about 1800 feet astern, stem-to-stem. Given the length of *Tregenna* as 413 feet, the ships were about 1400 feet apart, separated in time by under two minutes. *Filleigh* passed over the stricken ship, without having time to alter course to avoid her. According to the Second Mate, Ivor Day, *Tregenna* had sunk in forty seconds.

Filleigh was ordered to rescue survivors, and made a wide turn to starboard around where the sinking occurred, lowering a lifeboat. The lifeboat rescued four men, the Second Mate, helmsman and lookout, all of whom jumped from the bridge, and a standby man, who jumped clear just as the stern was submerged. *Filleigh* stood by at dead slow speed ahead, and made a lee for an injured seaman, who was floating nearby. Blood was pouring from a huge wound in his head.

A rope ladder was lowered and an officer sat in the rungs, where he managed to hold the seaman with one arm around his body, waiting for a heaving line to be lowered. Then a tragedy occurred. A heavy sea washed the hat off the head of the rescuer: whereupon he instinctively released his grip on the man to save his cap. The injured man was carried into the propeller of the ship, and cut to pieces. I do not know whether the officer who attempted the rescue was the Third Mate or First Mate, because neither remained on the ship for the next voyage. The effect on him must have been traumatic. Although It is very doubtful whether the injured seaman would have survived if he had been rescued, the feeling of personal guilt regarding this instinctive action must have remained with the officer for the rest of his life.

Out of a complement of 37, The Master, and 32 of the crew of *Tregenna* had perished in less than a minute. This awful tragedy exemplified the

S.S. Tregenna, ex-war bulldog, built in 1919, 5242 gross registered tonnage
S.S. Filleigh rescued four survivors, 33 killed
(*Photograph by A. Duncan, Cowes, I.O.W.*)

lethal nature of steel cargoes. The four survivors were landed at Avonmouth on 22 September where *Filleigh* discharged her cargo, and then put to sea for Swansea, for bunkers.

Convoy OB227

We put to sea on 11 October, and joined outward bound convoy OB 227 on 13 October 1940, our destination the St. Lawrence ports. During our passage in convoy OB227, Halifax convoys HX76, HX77, HX78, HX79, HX80, HX81 and HX82 were at sea, 269 ships, and Sydney Cape Breton convoys SC6, SC7 and SC8, 112 ships. Also outward-bound convoys OB228, OB229, OB230 and OB231, 137 ships. Fifteen U-Boats made successful attacks on the 518 ships in 14 convoys. The attacks were devastating, HX77 losing six ships, and HX79 losing 12 ships. Convoy SC6 lost three ships, but the most devastating losses occurred in SC7, which lost 21 ships out of 34, probably the heaviest loss in one Atlantic convoy during the war.

Blairspey, in convoy SC7, was hit by four torpedoes, two from U-101 and two from U-100. Her cargo of timber saved the ship, but she broke her back and the bow section sank. Despite the heavy casualties, the stern section was towed to port. A new bow section was constructed, and the ship rebuilt under the name *Empire Spey*. I was posted to her as First Mate in June 1944.

A report on the attack on SC7 sums up the impoverished state of our convoy protection. "The escort was lamentably thin, an armed yacht, which left two days after leaving Sydney, and the sloop H.M.S. Scarborough, although an escort group of two sloops and two corvettes was due to meet the convoy." The protection of merchant ships was certainly not a priority in Whitehall!!

Once again, the massive losses had occurred in a relatively compact area of ocean, between 56 and 59 degrees north latitude and 10 and 20 degrees west longitude, an area of 180 miles between north and south and 300 miles between east and west. This was well within the range of the heavy bombers in the command of Air Chief Marshall Arthur Harris. If only a few squadrons of suitably modified bombers had been released, to patrol the concentrated area of enemy activity – well within their range – the losses in ships and men would have been dramatically reduced. All that was required was the modification of the bomb capacity to increase the quantity of fuel. Indeed, aircraft stationed in the Outer Hebrides, could have covered the area without modification. With leaders like that, who needs enemies?

Our convoy OB227 had not been attacked, and dispersed early on 15 October, after crossing 15 degrees west longitude. During the middle watch, I was awaked with orders to join the Master on the bridge. The First Mate was also given the same orders, and we both arrived on the bridge at the same time. The ship was at dead slow speed in a fresh wind, with rough sea and frequent sleet and snow squalls. It was bitterly cold.

The Master and Second Mate were on the port weather side of the bridge. In that period of the war, the cabins were not equipped with red night acclimatisation lights, so for the first few minutes, neither the First Mate nor I had acclimatised our sight to the darkness. The Master handed me his Bulldog night binoculars, with the words, "What do you make of that on the port beam, Mr. Upton?"

He repeated the question to the First Mate, who had been given binoculars by the Second Mate. "It appears to be a ship in distress, sir." We could see a ship on the port beam, apparently stopped, and well down by the head. There were several flickering lights close to the ship. "What do you make of the lights?" We both answered that they appeared, either to be lights on lifeboats, or on the lifejackets of survivors in the water; probably the former. The response from the Master was astonishing, "I believe that they are two U-Boats signalling to each other. They have not seen us. Mr. Day agrees with me." The First Mate replied, "For Christ's sake sir, if we can see the buggers, how in hell can they not see us? They are survivors, and we must rescue them."

The reaction of the Master was even more incredible. He persisted with his interpretation of what we had seen, which was corroborated by the Second Mate. He ordered full speed ahead, and we left the ship and resumed our passage; despite the vehement protestations of two officers, the First Mate and myself. I will never forget the event. With the benefit of the statistics and records now available, it seems clear that the ship could have been *Trevisa*, recorded to have been a straggler from convoy SC7. Georg Wilhelm Schulz, commander of U-124, reported having attacked *Trevisa* on 16 October 1940 at 0350 hours, their time. This would have been an hour earlier by G.M.T. The position given was 57 – 28 N. latitude, 20 – 30 west longitude. *Trevisa* carried a cargo of lumber, so it is likely that she did not sink immediately, which would account for the fact that she was afloat when we encountered her.

It is on record that the casualties on *Trevisa* were 7 men killed out of a crew of 21. The survivors were rescued by the corvette *H.M.S. Bluebell*, and landed at Gourock. The only reason that can be advanced for the attitudes of the Master and Second Mate, was that they must have been unnerved by the sinking of *Tregenna* on the previous Atlantic passage. The fact that our ship was on dead slow speed, and as vulnerable as if we were stopped, made the whole event almost unbelievable. We had to live with, and conform to the orders of our Master, but could not forget or forgive the incident.

The convoy close astern of us, OB228, sustained the loss of five ships, the first being *Hurunui*, on 14 October, by U-93, then *Bonheur* on 15 October. The next casualty was *Dokka*, sunk by U-93 on 17 October, with the deaths of 10 out of 17 crew. Then, *Uskbridge* was sunk by U-93, two dead out of 29. Finally, *Sandsend* on 18 October, sunk by U-48 with the loss of 5 men out of 39. Two ships were sunk when in convoy, one on the night after dispersal, and one the following day. All the ships were sunk by surfaced U-Boats between midnight and 0600.

The night attacks were fearful events. Firstly, during the day the U-Boats would shadow the convoy well out of sight, reporting to each other and consolidating their attack positions. Our wireless operators could listen to their signals traffic. One "Sparks" remarked, "Listen to them. The bastards are all around us!" Then we suffered hours of apprehension, waiting for darkness, and the inevitable attacks.

The ships in the outer columns of the convoy, the "windy corners", were usually the first to suffer. It was eerie, waiting in pitch darkness for the first flash and explosion. In our convoy OB227, *Thistlegarth* was sunk by U-103 on 15 October, with the loss of 30 out of a complement of 39. All that we saw was a violent flash, flickering lights in the vicinity, then stygian darkness again.

After having sustained the loss of *Thistlegarth*, we encountered no further enemy action, although we received numerous distress messages from the ships engulfed in the slaughter of convoys SC7 and HX79, in which 33 ships were sunk in a period of eleven days of constant attacks.

During the 18 days on passage, the casualties were heavy. Enormous casualties were again sustained in ships carrying steel cargoes. Indeed most general cargoes included large parcels of steel in the lower holds, which would account for heavy casualties in ships carrying general cargo. However, the loss of *Sulaco* must be a mystery to any experienced officer.

Sulaco was an Elders & Fyffes Ltd banana carrier of 5,389 gross registered tons, with an excellent speed of 13.5 knots, on independent passage in ballast, one day after convoy dispersal. The weather was typically cold, with freezing snow squalls, a rough sea and heavy swell. The report of U-124 shows the time of attack as 0229 on 20 October 1940. With a ship in ballast, the crew of *Sulaco* should have had time to launch lifeboats, yet only one man survived out of 67. Later in the war, many ships were sunk in ballast under similar suspicious circumstances, always when unescorted. The conclusion to be drawn is that they were subjected to gunfire attack to prevent the launching of life-saving craft. This was later advocated by both Hitler and Donitz, and there seems little doubt that such action was encouraged, but suppressed in the German records.

We developed a fatalistic attitude. It was all so impersonal, if it was happening to someone else. There would be a blinding flash, the roar of the explosion, and always the impenetrable darkness. "Some poor bastards have had the hammer over in the port windy corner. Thank Christ it was not us!" The darkness was like a guardian angel, protecting us from the horrific tragedies that were occurring so close, but a world away. It was only occasionally that ships in convoy were sunk in daylight. That is why the sinking of *Tregenna* had such a profound effect on the officers and crew of *Filleigh*. Survivors from sunken ships could never forget such events. The screams of drowning or burning shipmates: the scramble to escape from cabins: to man lifesaving craft in a chaos of flames and escaping steam: and all in the dark. It was sheer hell; yet, throughout all this, there were few instances of panic due to cowardice. Nevertheless, the strain was almost unbearable: and men kept a brave face because they did not want to betray their fear to their shipmates.

Casualties - Ships and Personnel
09 October to 13 November 1940

Ships sunk – 56 by 16 successful U-Boats.
Italian submarines sank three merchant ships.

Lost with all hands

Creekirk, cargo iron ore, 36 dead.
Beaverford, general cargo, 77 dead.
Balmore, cargo pyrites, 37 dead.

Lost with very heavy casualties

Davanger, cargo fuel oil, 17 dead out of 29.
Port Gisborne, general cargo, 26 dead out of 64.
St. Malo, cargo steel, 28 dead out of 44.
Thistlegarth, in ballast, 30 dead out of 39.
Dokka, in ballast, 10 dead out of 17.
Assyrian, general gargo, 17 dead out of 47.
Fiscus, cargo steel, 38 dead out of 39.
Thalia, cargo steel, 22 dead out of 26.
Ruperra, cargo steel, 30 dead out of 37.
Sulaco, in ballast, 66 dead out of 67.
Whitford Point, cargo steel, 37 dead out of 39.
Kenbane Head, general cargo, 23 dead out of 44.
Scottish Maiden, cargo fuel oil, 16 dead out of 44.
Trewellard, cargo steel, 16 dead out of 41.

Merchant seamen killed – 668 out of 2677, a fatal casualty rate of 25 percent. In the 12 ships carrying high-risk cargoes, 357 seamen had been killed out of a total complement of 484. a fatal casualty rate of 74 percent.

Two armed cruisers, *H.M.S. Patroclus* and *Jervis Bay* lost respectively 76 dead out of 339 and 190 dead out of 255.
Seven convoys were attacked, SC6 losing 3 ships, SC7 21ships, OB227 one ship, OB228 5 ships, HX77 6 ships and HX79 12 ships.

Successful U-Boats were – U-47 (*Gunther Prien*), U-48 and U-99 (*Otto Kretchmer*), 6 ships each, U-100 (*Joachim Schepke*) and U-101 – 5 ships each, U-46 and U-103 – 4 ships each. Once again, the most experienced U-Boat commanders were the more successful.

FILLEIGH - 09 OCTOBER 1940 TO 22 DECEMBER 1940

RECORD OF MERCHANT SHIPS SUNK IN ATLANTIC - 08/10/40 TO 13/11/40

FILLEIGH - SIGNED ARTICLES AT SWANSEA - 09/10/40

DATE	SHIP	NAT.	CONVOY NO.	SHIPS	CAUSE OF LOSS	POSITION		CARGO	CASUALTIES CREW	DEAD
08/10/40	CONFIELD	BRITISH	HX76	38	U-58	56-48 N	10-17 W	GENERAL	37	1
09/10/40	ZANNES GOUNARIS	GREEK	SC6	38	U-103	58-11 N	13-57 W	PHOSPHATE	37	1
09/10/40	GRAIGWEN	BRITISH	SC6		U-103	58-11 N	13-57 W	MAIZE	34	7
09/10/40	DELPHIN	GREEK	SC6		U-103	58-11 N	13-57 W	MAIZE	34	0
	FILLEIGH		OB227	47						
11/10/40	BRANDANGER	NOR.	HX77	39	U-48	57-00 N	17-42 W	LUMBER	30	6
11/10/40	DAVANGER	NOR.	HX77		U-48	57-00 N	19-10 W	FUEL OIl	29	17
11/10/40	PORT GISBORNE	BRITISH	HX77		U-48	56-38 N	16-40 W	GENERAL	64	26
12/10/40	ORAO	YUGO.			TAZZOLI	35-41 N	10.53 W	WHEAT	35	2
12/10/40	PACIFIC RANGER	BRITISH	HX77		U-59	56-20 N	11-43 W	GENERAL	53	0
12/10/40	ST. MALO	BRITISH	HX77		U-101	57-58 N	16-32 W	STEEL	44	28
13/10/40	STANGRANT	BRITISH	HX77		U-37	58-27 N	12-36 W	STEEL	38	8
14/10/40	HURUNUI	BRITISH	OB228	47	U-93	58-58 N	09-54 W	BALLAST	75	2
15/10/40	BONHEUR	BRITISH	OB228		U-138	57-10 N	08-36 W	GENERAL	37	0
15/10/40	KABALO	BELG.	OB223	25	CAPPELLINI	31-59 N	31-21 W	GENERAL	38	0
15/10/40	THISTLEGARTH	BRITISH	OB227	24	U-103	58-43 N	15-00 W	BALLAST	39	30
16/10/40	TREVISA	BRITISH	SC7	34	U-124	57-28 N	20-30 W	LUMBER	21	7
17/10/40	AENOS	GREEK	SC7		U-38	59-00 N	13-00 W	WHEAT	29	4
17/10/40	DOKKA	NOR.	OB228		U-93	60-46 N	16-30 W	BALLAST	17	10
17/10/40	LANGUEDOC	BRITISH	SC7		U-48	59-14 N	17-51 W	FUEL OIL	41	0
17/10/40	SCORESBY	BRITISH	SC7		U-48	59-14 N	17-51 W	TIMBER	37	0
17/10/40	USKBRIDGE	BRITISH	OB228		U-93	60-40 N	15-50 W	COAL	29	2
18/10/40	ASSYRIAN	BRITISH	SC7		U-101	57-12 N	10-43 W	GENERAL	47	17
18/10/40	BEATUS	BRITISH	SC7		U-46	57-31 N	13-10 W	LUMBER	37	0
18/10/40	BOEKELO	DUTCH	SC7		U-100	56-40 N	10-45 W	LUMBER	25	0
18/10/40	CONVALLARIA	SWED.	SC7		U-46	57-22 N	11-11 W	PULP	27	0
18/10/40	CREEKIRK	BRITISH	SC7		U-101	57-30 N	11-10 W	IRON ORE	36	36
18/10/40	EMPIRE BRIGADE	BRITISH	SC7		U-99	57-12 N	10-43 W	GENERAL	41	6
18/10/40	EMPIRE MINIVER	BRITISH	SC7		U-99	56-40 N	10-45 W	STEEL	38	3
18/10/40	FISCUS	BRITISH	SC7		U-99	57-29 N	11-10 W	STEEL	39	38
18/10/40	GUNBORG	SWED	SC7		U-46	57-14 N	10-48 W	PULP	23	0
19/10/40	MATHERAN	BRITISH	HX79	49	U-38	57-00 N	17-00 W	GENERAL	81	9
18/10/40	NITRITOS	GREEK	SC7		U-99	57-14 N	10-48 W	SULPHUR	28	1
18/10/40	SANDSEND	BRITISH	OB228		U-48	58-15 N	21-29 W	COAL	39	5
18/10/40	SHEKATIKA	BRITISH	SC7		U-101	57-29 N	11-10 W	TIMBER	36	0
18/10/40	SOESTERBERG	DUTCH	SC7		U-101	57-12 N	10-43 W	TIMBER	23	6
18/10/40	THALIA	GREEK	SC7		U-99	57-00 N	11-30 W	STEEL	26	22
19/10/40	BILDERDIJK	DUTCH	HX79		U-47	56-35 N	17-15 W	GRAIN	39	0
19/10/40	CAPRELLA	BRITISH	HX79		U-100	56-37 N	17-15 W	FUEL OIL	53	1
19/10/40	CLINTONIA	BRITISH	SC7		U-123	57-10 N	11-20 W	PULPWOOD	35	1
19/10/40	CUBANO	NOR.	OB229	35	U-124	57-55 N	25-00 W	BALLAST	33	2
19/10/40	LA ESTANCIA	BRITISH	HX79		U-47	57-00 N	17-00 W	SUGAR	34	1
19/10/40	RUPERRA	BRITISH	HX79		U-46	57-00 N	16-00 W	STEEL	37	30
19/10/40	SEDGEPOOL	BRITISH	SC7		U-123	57-20 N	11-22 W	WHEAT	39	3
19/10/40	SHIRAK	BRITISH	HX79		U-47	57-00 N	16-35 W	GASOLENE	37	0
19/10/40	SITALA	BRITISH	HX79		U-100	56-28 N	16-23 W	CRUDE OIL	44	1
19/10/40	SNEFJELD	NOR.	SC7		U-99	57-28 N	11-10 W	LUMBER	21	0
19/10/40	SULACO	BRITISH	OB229	35	U-124	57-25 N	25-00 W	BALLAST	67	66
19/10/40	UGANDA	BRITISH	HX79		U-38	56-37 N	17-15 W	LUMBER	40	0
19/10/40	WANDBY	BRITISH	HX79		U-47	56-45 N	17-07 W	LUMBER	34	0
20/10/40	WHITFORD POINT	BRITISH	HX79		U-47	56-38 N	16-00 W	STEEL	39	37
20/10/40	JANUS	SWED.	HX79		U-47	56-36 N	15-03 W	FUEL OIL	37	4
20/10/40	LOCH LOMOND	BRITISH	HX79		U-100	56-15 N	15-24 W	LUMBER	40	1
27/10/40	MEGGIE	SWED.			NANI	OFF AZORES		COAL	20	0
30/10/40	VICTORIA	GREEK	OB244	46	U-103	54-42 N	13-32 W	SUGAR	29	0

FILLEIGH - BERTHED AT SOREL. MONTREAL AND ST. JOHNS - 31/10/40 TO 18/11/40

DATE	SHIP	NAT.	CONVOY NO.	SHIPS	CAUSE OF LOSS	POSITION		CARGO	CASUALTIES CREW	DEAD
01/11/40	EMPIRE BISON	BRITISH	HX82	39	U-124	59-30 N	17-40 W	SCRAP	36	32
03/11/40	CASANARE	BRITISH	HX83	36	U-99	53-58 N	14-13 W	BANANAS	62	9
03/11/40	H.M.S. PATROCLUS	BRITISH	HX83		U-99	53-43 N	14-41 W	ESCORT	339	76
05/11/40	BEAVERFORD	BRITISH	HX84	38	SCHEER	52-26 N	32-34 W	GENERAL	77	77
05/11/40	FRESNO CITY	BRITISH	HX84		SCHEER	51-47 N	33-29 W	MAIZE	37	1
05/11/40	H.M.S. JERVIS BAY	BRITISH	HX84		SCHEER	52-26 N	32-34 W	ESCORT	255	190
05/11/40	KENBANE HEAD	BRITISH	HX84		SCHEER	52-26 N	32-34 W	GENERAL	44	23
05/11/40	MOPAN	BRITISH	HX84		SCHEER	52-31 N	32-15 W	BANANAS	68	0
05/11/40	SCOTTISH MAIDEN	BRITISH	HX83		U-99	54-40 N	14-08 W	FUEL OIL	44	16
05/11/40	TREWELLARD	BRITISH	HX84		SCHEER	52-26 N	32-34 W	STEEL	41	16
06/11/40	NALON	BRITISH			AIRCRAFT	53-57 N	15-05 W	GENERAL	72	0
06/11/40	CLAN MacKINLAY	BRITISH			AIRCRAFT	58-35 N	02-53 W	GENERAL	83	5
08/11/40	VINGALAND	SWED.			AIRCRAFT	55-41 N	18-24 W	STEEL	25	6
11/11/40	BALMORE	BRITISH			AIRCRAFT	52-00 N	17-00 W	PYRITES	27	27
13/11/40	CAPE ST. ANDREW	BRITISH	OB240	57	U-137	55-14 N	10-29 W	BALLAST	68	15
13/11/40	EMPIRE WIND	BRITISH			AIRCRAFT	53-48 N	15-52 W	BALLAST	41	0
							TOTALS		3341	934

During this period, successful U-Boats were – U-47 (*Gunther Prien*), U48, and U-99 (*Otto Kretchmer*), 6 ships each, U-100 (*Joachim Schepke*), and U-101 – 5 ships each, U-46 and U-103 – 4 ships each. Once again, the most experienced U-Boat commanders were the more successful.

We encountered several days of dense fog in the western Atlantic, but, for us, the remainder of the passage was uneventful. We arrived at Sorel, at the mouth of the St. Lawrence River, late in October 1940, where we began loading a part cargo of grain. After loading part cargo at Sorel, *Filleigh* moved to Montreal, where we finished loading general cargo, with army transport vehicles as deck cargo.

During our stay in port we learned about the attack by the pocket battleship, *Admiral Scheer*, on the Halifax convoy HX 84, of 38 ships, in which 5 ships were sunk in convoy, *Beaverford, Fresno City, Kenbane Head, Maidan* and *Trewellard*, with the loss of 214 officers and men. *Mopan* was sunk, when detached from the scattered convoy, and *San Demetrio*, damaged in the attack, re-boarded, and brought to port.

The courageous defence of the convoy by the ocean escort, the armed merchant cruiser, *H.M.S. Jervis Bay*, delayed the enemy attack long enough to enable the convoy to disperse, and preserved 28 of the ships, including *San Demetrio. Admiral Scheer* then moved south, where she sank *Port Hobart* on 24 November, *Tribesman* on 1 December 1940, *Duquesa* on 18 December and *Stanpark* on 20 January 1941.

We put to sea from Montreal on 18 November 1940, and made port in St. Johns, Newfoundland on 23 November, where we remained for a day.

CONVOY HX91

Convoy HX90 of 35 ships left Halifax on 21 November, and convoy HX91 left 4 days later. The St. Johns section, including *Filleigh*, made rendezvous with convoy HX 91 on 27 November, increasing the number of ships in the convoy to 29. We made contact with the convoy in dense mist, with the ships barely discernible in the gloom, and took station in our allotted position. The convoy then encountered dense fog, with visibility so poor that even the ships ahead and astern could not be discerned. Ships signified their proximity to each other by blasts on their whistles or sirens in morse code, using their convoy position numbers. Fog buoys were streamed.

Fog buoys were wooden contraptions, in the form of a "T". They were towed with the cross member of the "T" leading. A metal scoop was fitted to the leading end of the fog buoy, and this was connected to a spout at the trailing end. The forward movement of the fog buoy collected water in the scoop, and this was forced by pressure to the spout, where a column of water was ejected to a height of several feet. The distance between ships in columns was 3 cables or 1818 feet, stem to stem, so the calculation for the distance to be streamed astern of the towing ship was 1818 feet, minus the length of the towing ship.

After streaming, the following ship endeavoured to keep the fog buoy alongside, between the bows and bridge, on the lee side, where the officer of the watch would be stationed. That was easy for the designers of the fog buoys, who had no experience of station keeping in close proximity, in mainly coal burning ships, all with different handling characteristics. For the officers on watch, station keeping in fog was an unmitigated nightmare.

During fire cleaning, the ship ahead would suddenly lose speed, and the first indication would be a rapid overtaking of the fog buoy. Next, the ship ahead would loom out of the dense fog, and it would be necessary to alter course to overlap, thus losing the fog buoy. This would happen all down a column of five ships, so the combined overlaps would intrude the ships into the adjacent column. This brought ships, not only dangerously close astern and ahead; but added the danger of collision with ships abeam.

When the leading ship in a column recovered steam pressure, the officer on watch had the problem of identifying the ships abeam on both sides, using morse code on the whistle or siren to signal the convoy position number. The following ships had the equally difficult problem of recovering sight of the fog buoy: and identifying whether they had made contact with the correct one. Usually, if ships were even vaguely discernible, a signal by Aldis lamp, "What bloody ship are you? I have lost the buoy of number nine two," would result in the response. "We are eight one. You are in the wrong bloody column, and ahead of station!" Then you would be up the proverbial shit creek, without a paddle. Miraculously, by the use of whistle signals, and Aldis lamp – if close enough to see the other ship – we managed to recover station – until the next time. Although there were a number of collisions, some with disastrous and fatal consequences, it was incredible how well we managed under almost impossible conditions. The design of fog buoys never improved, but we became more experienced.

Fog during the day was enervating enough. The problems were aggravated during the night. After being relieved, officers would return to their cabins fatigued almost to the point of collapse, after four hours of constant eye and mental strain. Fortunately, we cleared the areas of more prevalent fog after leaving the Grand Banks. When the fog cleared, miraculously, the convoy was still there, usually with ships in incorrect stations, but in a very short time, order was restored.

The convoy schedule showed the height of the top of the mast of each ship, measured from the waterline. This enabled the officer of the watch to prepare a table of sextant angles related to distance in feet, so that the use of the sextant in daytime would identify the distance astern or abeam rapidly and accurately.

The weather was, as usual, bitterly cold with strong winds, heavy seas, and frequent sleet and snow squalls. During the early period of the war, almost all of the many distress messages had been from ships attacked in positions close to Northern Ireland, east of 17 degrees west longitude. The attacks had not been limited by our counter measures, but by the shortage of U-Boats: and the fact that they had innumerable targets concentrated within three days' passage from their French bases. For about ten days on passage, we could be reasonably certain that we would not be attacked in mid ocean.

During the passage of convoy HX91 to the U.K., 260 ships were at sea in eight homeward-bound convoys, HX88 to HX92, SC12 and 13, and Freetown convoy SL56. A further 323 ships were at sea in ten outward-bound convoys, OB249 to OB256, and Gibraltar convoy OG46. Therefore, the U-Boats were presented with a massive target of 583 ships in eighteen ocean convoys: all of which would have to concentrate upon, or were leaving, the narrow seas of the western approaches. Only fifteen U-Boats, out of the number disposed in the western approaches, made successful attacks. They sank 51 ships between 17 November and 14 December 1940.

The pocket battleship, *Admiral Scheer,* sank one ship, Italian submarines, two, and aircraft, two. The massive number of 46 ships out of 51, were sunk in an area between 51 degrees and 60 degrees north latitude, and 9 degrees and 18 degrees west longitude.

Merchant seamen were bound to reflect with dismay that numbers of Hampden, Whitley and Wellington heavy bombers had been employed in the early days of the war in dropping leaflets, for the German people to use as toilet paper. However, Bomber Command would not release them for Coastal Command anti-U-Boat countermeasures, even though the distance from bases in the Hebrides and Northern Ireland could have been no greater than the distance to the Ruhr Valley. In 1942, two years later, the same heavy bomber types achieved notable successes in the same areas that were not covered in 1940. By that time, they would have been surplus to the requirements of Bomber Command and the aspirations of Air Chief Marshall Arthur Harris, to bomb the German people into submission. They were then discarded into the wastebasket represented by the defence of merchant ships.

During the time when we were loading in the St. Lawrence ports, and on passage to join convoy HX91, 17 ships were sunk, including *King Idwal*. I learned the details of the loss of *King Idwal,* and the deaths of 12 of her crew of 40, later in the war from the surviving Third Mate, Frank Bernard Howe. From the day we put to sea we were inundated with distress messages, many from ships we had known well.

Aracataca was the first ship from convoy HX90 to be sunk. I learned the details from a surviving wireless operator. *Aracataca* was a banana carrier owned by Elders & Fyffes Ltd, a fine ship with a designed speed of 13.5 knots, but capable of higher speed. The ship became detached from the convoy in heavy weather and frequent squalls; and was on a broad zigzag at her maximum speed. Ernst Mengersen, commander of U-101, reports an attack at 0041 on 30 November 1940, U-Boat time. Official British records show 29 November, due to the time difference. At least one, and probably two torpedoes struck *Aracataca*, and 36 out of her complement of 70 were killed. Mengersen was one of the more capable of the U-Boat commanders, and it must have been a very skilful feat to have torpedoed a relatively fast ship, on a broad zigzag, in such awful weather.

From then on the slaughter of convoy HX 90 continued, with the sinking of *Appalache, Conch*, and the armed merchant cruiser escort, *H.M.S. Forfar,* with heavy loss of life, 173 dead out of a complement of 194. Then we received the signals of distress from *Goodleigh*, a newly built Tatem line ship. Many of those who were our friends and had been our shipmates, served on *Goodleigh*. In addition, two South Wales ships, *Lady Glanely* and *Victoria City*, had been sunk on 2 December 1940, in convoy HX90, both lost with all hands. *Victoria City* did not have the time to transmit a distress signal. We picked up the distress message of *Lady Glanely*. We learned details of her loss when we made port. The carnage in convoy HX90 continued with the sinking of *Kavak, Stirlingshire, Tasso, Wilhelmina* and *W. Hendrik*. Earlier heavy losses had been incurred in convoy SC11, six ships, and later in convoys OB244, OB248 and OB252. The loss of the ships was, for us, a series of distress messages. It was not until later that we learned of the full horrors of the nights of 1 to 5 December 1940.

M.V. Lady Glanely, built in 1938, 5497 gross registered tonnage
Torpedoed and sunk by U-101 on 2 December 1940 in convoy HX90
All hands lost, 33 men killed
(*Photograph by National Maritime Museum*)

After leaving the fog and strong winds that we encountered in the western Atlantic, we experienced improved weather conditions for a few days in mid Atlantic, with moderate to fresh winds and moderate seas. A very heavy swell was developing from a southerly direction. We entered the area where convoy HX90 and other convoys had suffered such disastrous losses, on about 7 December, passing through areas of debris, smashed life saving rafts, and flotsam from the ships that had been sunk.

On that day, we crossed an area where many corpses were floating. There must have been fifty dead naval personnel in one small area, all wearing Royal Navy inflatable life preservers, some in almost vertical positions, many lying face up or face down. They must have been part of the 173 who died when U-99 sank *H.M.S. Forfar*. We passed very close to a number of very young ratings, floating on their backs, as if asleep, and reflected sadly that each one represented a grieving wife, mother, or other loved one. Every man who witnessed the scenes of destruction and death would be moved at the time, and carry an indelible memory throughout his life. My only regret was that Otto Kretchmer and 37 of the crew of U-99 eventually survived.

Then the weather intervened. The tempestuous gales that followed must have caused the deaths of many survivors who had not been rescued. No lifesaving craft or humans could have survived in the hurricane force winds and huge seas. However, It provided a temporary respite from the U-Boats. Convoy HX91 was not attacked; and all ships entered the western approaches individually, or in small groups.

We did not have the benefit of the system of weather analysis of pre-war years, when reports from a number of ships would enable us to plot the direction, course and severity of tropical revolving storms. Without accurate reports, we relied almost entirely on monitoring barometric pressure, to identify the paths and strength of hurricanes. It was clear from the rapid fall in pressure that our convoy was in the path of a depression of exceptional depth, as the pressure fell through 29 inches, eventually to a low of under 28.50 inches. This was lower than when *Appledore* had nearly foundered a year earlier. This time we were over 500 miles north, where the seas were massively more severe.

The wind increased rapidly to force 8 from the south west, with a heavy following sea developing on the starboard quarter, and during the day of 9 December, it was clear that we had to heave to. The convoy was making heavy weather, and the ships had spread without orders. By after-noon, the frequent squalls of rain, sleet and snow obscured the commodore ship, making signalling almost impossible.

The convoy had been executing a number of emergency turns for a period of a week previously, because there were a substantial number of U-Boat position reports. These turns were discontinued as the weather deteriorated, but we had not received a signal for the convoy to heave to.

Captain Harp, had ordered the officers to double watches, during the period of U-Boat attacks, so the Master and Second Mate, and the First Mate and I, shared watch and watch respectively

After over a year of experience of convoys, the Masters of merchant ships realised that their knowledge of the handling of their ships in heavy weather was infinitely superior to the judgement of naval commodores. There may have been a signal, "The convoy will maintain course and speed," but it is unlikely that the Masters would have taken any notice in the positively perilous weather that we faced; particularly with darkness approaching. We hove to during daylight hours on 7 December, in a force 8 gale and heavy sea. It would have been foolhardy to have remained on convoy course in the rapidly developing following sea, whatever the commodore may have decided to do.

Captain Harp handled his ship with great skill, and never left the bridge until the weather had abated. The weather continued to deteriorate dramatically during the night, with force 12 winds and huge breaking seas. Standing on the bridge of little *Filleigh*, as the ship first plunged into the

S.S. Goodleigh, built in 1938, 5445 gross registered tonnage
Torpedoed and sunk by U-52 on 2 December 1940 in convoy HX90
(Photograph by National Maritime Museum)

troughs of the precipitous head seas, and then struggled slowly to weather the crest of the following sea, it was difficult to believe that the ship would survive. At daylight on the following day, we were hove to north west of Tory Island and the Bloody Foreland, close enough to land to have the chart "Inistrahull to Bloody Foreland" on the chartroom table.

We could see a ship in the distance, well to the westward of our position. We were making just sufficient speed to keep the ship from drifting onto a lee shore, but the other ship was making very heavy weather, and drifting closer to us. Although *Filleigh* took a substantial number of heavy seas aboard, no damage occurred to the ship. However, the deck cargo of army lorries on No. 2 hatch began to shift. We were forced to make a decision, whether to try to re-secure them, or cut them loose. In either case, a party of men would have to undertake the dangerous work on the exposed foredeck.

I was ordered to assemble a small party of able seamen, and attempt to secure the cargo. If this proved to be too difficult, we were to cut the lorries loose. The Master reduced speed to steerageway. Firstly, we rigged lifelines on the lee side from the mast house to the starboard alleyway bulwarks. We secured ourselves to the heavy lifeline by individual short lines, giving us scope for limited movement on the foredeck alongside No. 2 hatch. We arranged that a violent blast on a whistle, from the bridge, would warn us of the arrival of a sea that was likely to break aboard. Securing the cargo was not as difficult as we had anticipated, requiring a combination of wire strops, chains and bottle screws, to strengthen the original lashings, some of which had parted. It took about an hour to complete the work, during which time a number of heavy seas broke over us.

Despite being secured to lifelines, several of us were washed violently against the bridge bulkhead by the heavy seas. I sustained severe injury to my lower back. At the time, it was painful, and made walking and even standing, very difficult. It was a struggle to ascend and descend the ladders to the bridge, and to stand a four-hour watch, but in our situation of emergency, there was no other option. I wedged my body between the engine room telegraph and the forward bridge handrail, and kept watch propped in that position. The hurricane force winds and precipitous seas continued throughout the day, but, apart from the problem with the deck cargo, we never broke a rope yarn.

The ship that we had seen in the distance had drifted to within several miles of *Filleigh*. We identified her as a Greek ship, *Dionyssios Stathatos*. We had received a distress call from her, reporting damage to the rudder. *Dionyssios Stathatos* was wallowing uncontrollably, broached to, in the huge seas that were breaking aboard from stem to stern. We then received a signal that she had lost her rudder completely. The seas were so enormous that when we were on the crest, we were looking down on her, and it was clear that she could never last for long in a broached-to condition in such weather.

The ship was completely overwhelmed by a succession of huge seas, rolled over on her beam-ends, capsized and sank with all hands on 12 December. The seas were then running at about 60 feet in height from trough and crest, with enormous breakers on the crests. We were powerless to assist. *Filleigh* was maintaining only sufficient speed to prevent our being driven on a lee shore. We were spectators to a ghastly tragedy.

Records reporting the loss of *Dionyssios Stathatos* differ appreciably in terms of date and position. "The World's Merchant Fleets 1939" reflects the date of loss as 12 December 1939 in a position 58-31 N. 21-55 W., and reports that the ship was abandoned after losing her rudder. This is incorrect in terms of date and position.

"The Allied Convoy System 1939 – 1945" reports the date of loss as 12 December 1940, caused of loss "foundered", showing the ship as an element of convoy HX91. This report is accurate. *Dionyssios Stathatos* was one of the many older ships built in 1919, and launched with the name *War Cadet*. It is likely that she would have been poorly maintained, which was usual for Greek-owned ships.

Filleigh handled very well in the tempestuous weather, and Captain Harp never left the bridge, or handed over the ship to his officers during the whole period, making adjustments in engine revolutions, even a revolution at a time, just to maintain steerage way. He was an excellent Master, and we were fortunate to have him in command.

When the weather abated, we made contact with the sloop, *H.M.S. Fowey*, which had collected a number of ships from our convoy HX91, and some stragglers from convoy SC14. *Fowey* escorted us to Belfast Lough, where we made port in Belfast. After a week in Belfast we made passage to Cardiff, where the ship paid off on 22 December 1940. It was miraculous that on both Atlantic passages the ship had passed through the area where 114 ships had been sunk by U-Boat attack, as well as with those sunk by Admiral Scheer: and we arrived home unscathed, but psychologically scarred. We were very fortunate.

During the 27 days between 14 November 22 December 1940, our losses in ships and men were enormous. They were exaggerated by the tempestuous weather during early December 1940. It would have been impossible for the crews of ships that had been sunk or badly damaged to have survived such weather conditions. We were fortunate.

Filleigh was torpedoed and sunk on 18 April 1945 by U-245 commanded by Friedrich Schumann-Hindenberg in position 51-20 north latitude, 01-42 east longitude. Schumann-Hindenberg and U-245 survived the war. Five of the complement of 52 on *Filleigh* were lost. One of the letters that my father had written to me during the war, had informed me that Phil Harris, my fellow apprentice on *Appledore*, had been killed when *Filleigh* was lost. I have not verified whether he was lost in *Filleigh*.

During the time I served in *Filleigh*, only three U-Boats were lost, U-31 and U-32 by depth charge attack, and U-104 by an unknown cause. The 23 successful U-Boats had sunk 114 ships, so the success rate of the U-Boats was proportionately high.

When I paid off on 22 December 1940, the war had lasted for 476 days, and I had served on articles for 461 days, covering nine Atlantic crossings in three ships. We had lost 414 ships sunk, mainly in the Atlantic Ocean. The enemy U-Boats had paid for their success with the loss of 32 of their number, in which 866 of their crews had been killed and 377 rescued. The British Merchant Navy had suffered the deaths of 5,905 officers and other ranks, out of a total complement of 19,996, a fatal casualty rate of 29.53 percent. It had been a bloody and uneven struggle, and I was in need of a rest.

Casualties – Ships and Personnel
14 November 1940 to 22 December 1940

Ships sunk – 58 by 15 successful U-Boats.
Italian submarines sank six ships.
Admiral Scheer sank two ships.
Aircraft sank two ships.

Lost with all hands

Lillian Moller, cargo iron ore, 37 dead
Cree, cargo iron ore, 43 dead.
Samnanger, in ballast, 37 dead.
Gwalia, cargo coal, 16 dead.
Pacific President, in ballast, 50 dead.
Lady Glanely, cargo grain and lumber, 33 dead.
Victor Ross, in ballast, 44 dead.
Empire Seaman, cargo unknown, 35 dead.
Skrim, cargo unknown, 35 dead.
Victoria City, cargo steel, 43 dead.
Empire Jaguar, in ballast, 37 dead.
Empire Statesman, cargo iron ore, 31 dead.
Stureholm, cargo unknown, 37 dead.
Dionyssios Stathatos, cargo wheat, foundered, 40 dead.
Kyleglen, in ballast, 36 dead.
Euphorbia, cargo coal, 34 dead.
Amicus, cargo phosphates, 37 dead.

Lost with very heavy casualties

Veronica, cargo iron ore, 17 dead out of 20.
Bradfyne, cargo grain, 39 dead out of 43.
Oakcrest, in ballast, 35 dead out of 41.
Bruse, cargo lumber, 16 dead out of 22.
Leise Maersk, cargo grain, 17 dead out of 24.
Salonica, cargo pit props, 16 dead out of 25.
Tymeric, cargo coal, 72 dead out of 75.
Glenmoor, cargo coal, 31 dead out of 33.
Mount Athos, cargo coal, 19 dead out of 30.
St. Elwyn, cargo coal, 29 dead out of 40.

Aracataca, cargo bananas, 36 dead out of 70.
Tribesman, cargo unknown, 53 dead out of 135.
Kavak, cargo bauxite, 25 dead out of 31.
Daphne, in ballast, 18 dead out of 19.
Silverpine, in ballast, 36 dead out of 55.
Farmsum, cargo coal, 16 dead out of 35.
Ashcrest, cargo steel, 36 dead out of 37.
Calabria, cargo general, 360 dead out of 381.
Towa, cargo grain, 18 dead out of 37.
Anastassia, cargo timber, 18 dead out of 28.
Duquesa, general cargo, 79 dead out of 99.
Carlton, cargo coal, 31 dead out of 35.

Merchant Seamen killed in cargo carrying ships – 1428 out of 2599, a fatal casualty rate of 55 percent.

Casualties in five mainly passenger carrying ships – 473 dead out of 1187, a fatal casualty rate of 40 percent.

Lost in the armed merchant cruiser, *H.M.S. Forfar*, ocean escort for convoy HX90 – 173 dead out of 194.

Although the fatal casualty rate continued to be very high in ships carrying high-risk cargoes, there were high casualties in grain and coal – and even lumber carriers. However, the number of ships in ballast that were either lost with all hands or with high casualties, is astonishingly high. This must have been due to survivors in lifesaving craft having been overwhelmed by the mountainous seas and gales that we encountered for over a week.

Successful U-Boats were – U-100, Joachim Schepke, 9 ships sunk, U-103, Victor Schutze, 7 ships and U-96, Heinrich Lehmann-Willenbrock, and U-123, Karl-Heinz Mohle, 5 ships each.

Joachim Shepke was lost with U-100 on 17 March 1941, and Gunther Prien with U-47 on 7 March 1941. The other "U-Boat Ace", Otto Kretchmer was saved after the sinking of U-99 on 17 March 1941. We wept no tears for their loss.

Seventeen convoys were attacked, HX90 losing 12 ships OB244 6 ships, SC11 5 ships, HX92 5 ships, and OB252 5 ships.

THE WAR AT SEA: FILLEIGH

FILLEIGH - 09 OCTOBER 1940 TO 22 DECEMBER 1940

RECORD OF MERCHANT SHIPS SUNK IN ATLANTIC - 14/11/40 TO 22/12/40

FILLEIGH - ON PASSAGE FROM MONTREAL TO ST. JOHNS - 18/11/40 TO 22/11/40

DATE	SHIP	NAT.	CONVOY NO.	SHIPS	CAUSE OF LOSS	POSITION		CARGO	CASUALTIES CREW	DEAD
15/11/40	APAPA	BRITISH			AIRCRAFT	54-31 N.	16-34 W.	GENERAL	253	23
15/11/40	HAVBOR	NOR.			U-65	04-24 N.	13-46 W.	CRUDE OIL	37	34
15/11/40	KOHINUR	BRITISH	OB235	35	U-65	04-24 N.	13-46 W.	GENERAL	85	48
16/11/40	FABIAN	BRITISH	OB234	26	U-65	02-49 N.	15-29 W.	GENERAL	39	6
16/11/40	PLANTER	BRITISH	SL53S	6	U-137	55-38 N.	08-27 W.	GENERAL	73	13
17/11/40	SAINT GERMAIN	BRITISH	HG46	51	U-137	55-40 N.	08-40 W.	PIT PROPS	18	0
17/11/40	VERONICA	SWED.	HG46		U-137	55-20 N.	08-45 W.	IRON ORE	20	17
18/11/40	CONGONIAN	BRITISH			U-65	08-21 N.	16-15 W.	BALLAST	39	1
18/11/40	LILIAN MOLLER	BRITISH	SL53S	6	BARACCA	52-57 N.	18-00 W.	IRON ORE	37	37
18/11/40	NESTLEA	BRITISH			AIRCRAFT	50-38 N.	10-00 W.	ORE	39	0
21/11/40	CREE	BRITISH	SL53	24	U-123	54-39 N.	18-50 W.	IRON ORE	43	43
21/11/40	DAYDAWN	BRITISH	OB244	46	U-103	56-30 N.	14-10 W.	COAL	38	2
21/11/40	VICTORIA	GREEK	OB244		U-103	56-17 N.	14-12 W.	BALLAST	37	10
22/11/40	BRADFYNE	BRITISH	SC11	34	U-100	55-04 N.	12-18 W.	GRAIN	43	39
22/11/40	JUSTITIA	BRITISH	SC11		U-100	55-00 N.	13-10 W.	GENERAL	39	13
22/11/40	OAKCREST	BRITISH	OB244		U-123	53-00 N.	17-00 W.	BALLAST	41	35
23/11/40	ANTEN	SWED.	OB244		U-123	56-57 N.	18-18 W.	BALLAST	33	1
23/11/40	BRUSE	NOR.	SC11		U-100	55-04 N.	12-15 W.	LUMBER	22	16
23/11/40	BUSSUM	DUTCH	SC11		U-100	55-39 N.	08-58 W.	GRAIN	29	0
23/11/40	LEISE MAERSK	BRITISH	SC11		U-100	55-30 N.	11-00 W.	GRAIN	24	17
23/11/40	SALONICA	SWED.	SC11		U-100	55-16 N.	12-14 W.	TIMBER	25	16
23/11/40	KING IDWAL	BRITISH	OB244		U-123	56-44 N.	19-13 W.	BALLAST	40	12
23/11/40	TYMERIC	BRITISH	OB244		U-123	57-11 N.	20-32 W.	COAL	75	72
	FILLEIGH		HX91	29						
27/11/40	DIPLOMAT	BRITISH	HX88	51	U-104	55-42 N.	12-38 W.	GENERAL	53	14
27/11/40	GLENMOOR	BRITISH	OB248	44	U-103	54-35 N.	14-24 W.	COAL	33	31
28/11/40	MOUNT ATHOS	GREEK	OB248		U-103	54-30 N.	15-25 W.	COAL	30	19
28/01/40	ST. ELWYN	BRITISH	OB249	53	U-103	53-30 N.	19-00 W.	COAL	40	29
29/11/40	ARACATACA	BRITISH	HX90	35	U-101	57-08 N.	20-50 W.	BANANAS	70	36
30/11/40	TRIBESMAN	BRITISH			SCHEER	15-00 N.	15-35 W.		135	53
01/12/40	APPALACHE	BRITISH	HX90		U-101	54-30 N.	20-30 W.	GASOLENE	39	7
01/12/40	CONCH	BRITISH	HX90		U-47	55-40 N.	19-00 W.	FUEL OIL	53	0
01/12/40	H.M. A.M.C. FORFAR	BRITISH	HX90		U-99	55-23 N.	20-11 W.		194	173
01/12/40	PALMELLA	BRITISH			U-37	40-30 N.	13-30 W.	GENERAL	29	1
02/12/40	SAMNANGER	NOR.			U-99	55-26 N.	16-50 W.	BALLAST	37	37
02/12/40	GOODLEIGH	BRITISH	HX90		U-52	55-02 N.	18-45 W.	LUMBER	37	1
02/12/40	GWALIA	SWED.			U-37	39-22 N.	14-22 W.	COAL	16	16
02/12/40	JEANNE M.	BRITISH	OG46	39	U-37	39-19 N.	13-54 W.	COAL	26	7
02/12/40	KAVAK	BRITISH	HX90		U-101	55-00 N.	19-30 W.	BAUXITE	31	25
02/12/40	VICTORIA CITY	BRITISH	HX90		U-140	56-00 N.	19-30 W.	STEEL	43	43
02/12/40	PACIFIC PRESIDENT	BRITISH	OB251	34	U-43	56-04 N.	18-45 W.	BALLAST	50	50
02/12/40	LADY GLANELY	BRITISH	HX90		U-101	55-00 N.	20-00 W.	LUMBER	33	33
02/12/40	STIRLINGSHIRE	BRITISH	HX90		U-94	55-42 N.	16-13 W.	GENERAL	73	0
02/12/40	TASSO	BRITISH	HX90		U-52	55-03 N.	18-04 W.	LOGS	32	5
02/12/40	VICTOR ROSS	BRITISH	OB251		U-43	56-04 N.	18-40 W.	BALLAST	44	44
02/12/40	WILHELMINA	BRITISH	HX90		U-94	55-43 N.	15-06 W.	GENERAL	38	5
03/12/40	DAPHNE	SWED.	OG46		U-37	38-12 N.	09-26 W.	BALLAST	19	18
03/12/40	W. HENDRIK	BRITISH	HX90		AIRCRAFT	56-26 N.	12-20 W.	LUMBER	35	5
04/12/40	EMPIRE SEAMAN	BRITISH			U-52	NOT KNOWN			35	35
05/12/40	SILVERPINE	BRITISH	OB252	44	ARGO	54-14 N.	18-08 W.	BALLAST	55	36
06/12/40	SKRIM	NOR.			U-43	53-00 N.	23-00 W.		35	35
07/12/40	FARMSUM	DUTCH	OB252		U-99	52-11 N.	22-56 W.	COAL	37	16
08/12/40	ASHCREST	BRITISH	SC13	32	U-140	54-35 N.	09-20 W.	STEEL	37	36
08/12/40	CALABRIA	BRITISH	SL56	42	U-103	52-43 N.	18-07 W.	GENERAL	381	360
08/12/40	EMPIRE JAGUAR	BRITISH	OB252		U-103	51-34 N.	17-35 W.	BALLAST	37	37
11/12/40	ROTORUA	BRITISH	HX92	30	U-96	58-56 N.	11-20 W.	GENERAL	150	23
11/12/40	EMPIRE STATESMAN	BRITISH	SL56		U-94	NOT KNOWN		IRON ORE	31	31
11/12/40	TOWA	DUTCH	HX92		U-96	58-50 N.	10-10 W.	GRAIN	37	18
12/12/40	STUREHOLM	SWED.	HX92		U-96	57-50 N.	08-40 W.		37	37
12/12/40	MACEDONIER	BELG.	HX92		U-96	57-52 N.	08-42 W.	PHOSPHATE	41	4
12/12/40	DIONYSSIOS STATHATOS	GREEK	HX91		FOUND.			WHEAT	40	40
14/12/40	KYLEGLEN	BRITISH	OB256	30	U-100	58-00 N.	25-00 W.	BALLAST	36	36
14/12/40	WESTERN PRINCE	BRITISH	HX92		U-96	59-32 N.	17-47 W.	GENERAL	268	14
14/12/40	EUPHORBIA	BRITISH	OB256		U-100	59-04 N.	15-30 W.	COAL	34	34
18/12/40	ANASTASSIA	GREEK	SC15	21	VENIERO	54-24 N.	19-04 W.	TIMBER	28	18
18/12/40	DUQUESA	BRITISH			SCHEER	00-57 N.	22-42 W.	GENERAL	99	0
18/12/40	NAPIER STAR	BRITISH			U-100	58-58 N.	23-13 W.	GENERAL	99	79
19/12/40	AMICUS	BRITISH	SC15		BAGNOLINI	54-10 N.	15-50 W.	PHOSPHATE	37	37
20/12/40	CARLTON	BRITISH	OB260	29	CALVI	58-18 N.	18-49 W.	COAL	35	31
21/12/40	CHARLES PRATT	PAN.			U-65	08-26 N.	16-50 W.	FUEL OIL	52	2
21/12/40	MANGEN	SWED.			MOCENIGO	40-27 N.	16-47 W.	COAL	20	8
							TOTALS		3980	2074

UPON THEIR LAWFUL OCCASIONS

FILLEIGH - 9 OCTOBER 1940 TO 22 DECEMBER 1940

SHIP AND U-BOAT LOSSES - WHEN SERVING ON *FILLEIGH* - 09 OCTOBER 1940 TO 22 DECEMBER 1940

GERMAN U-BOATS NUMBER	TOTALS C/F	B/F	TOTAL	SHIPS SUNK IN PERIOD 09/10/40 13/11/40	14/11/40 22/12/40	ENEMY U-BOAT LOSSES	DATE	CAUSE	DEAD	SAVED
U-37			5	1	4	U-31	02/11/40	D/C	2	43
U-38			3	3		U-32	30/10/40	D/C	9	33
U-43			3		3	U-104	27/11/40	???	49	0
U-46			4	4						
U-47			7	6	1					
U-48			6	6						
U-52			3		3					
U-58			1	1						
U-59			1	1						
U-65			5		5					
U-93			3	3						
U-94			3		3					
U-96			5		5					
U-99			12	9	3					
U-100			13	4	9					
U-101			9	5	4					
U-103			12	5	7					
U-104			1		1					
U-123			7	2	5					
U-124			4	4						
U-137			4	1	3					
U-138			1	1						
U-140			2		2					
	412	298	114	56	58					

						TOTALS	3	60	76
						B/F	29	806	301
						C/F	32	866	377

	TOTALS C/F	B/F	TOTAL	09/10/40 13/11/40	14/11/40 22/12/40
HEAVY SHIPS	15	7	8	6	2
RAIDERS	9	9	0		
LIGHT WARSHIPS	4	4	0		
AIRCRAFT	21	13	8	5	3
ITALIAN SUBMARINES	14	5	9	3	6
OTHER CAUSES	3	2	1		1
	66	40	26	14	12

11

BETWEEN SHIPS FOR EXAMINATIONS

CERTIFICATE OF COMPETENCY – SECOND MATE

After I paid off from Filleigh, my lower spine, which had been injured in the severe weather, was causing me great pain, so I visited the Shipping Federation doctor in Cardiff. I had no sooner entered his consulting room, when I was confronted by the words "If you are going to complain about a pain in the back, you can forget about getting a voyage off. You have sciatica. Here is a prescription for some painkillers. Off you go!" The bugger did not even bother to examine me.

During that period of the war, not all merchant seamen were breaking their necks to get back to the Western Ocean and its submarine wolf packs. Despite this, "swinging the lead" was not then a prevalent practice. Even later, when the casualties were very much higher, there were very few malingerers. It was priceless that this relatively young medical practitioner in his reserved occupation, presumed to sit in judgement over us. He was one of many, to whom the war was a continuation of an already comfortable and risk-free existence.

Over thirty years later, specialist and ex-ray examination diagnosed massive damage to the lumbar vertebrae, which required major surgery in 1984. In 1995, after sustained resistance, the Ministry of War Pensions finally, and very reluctantly, approved a war disability pension, for that injury and other injuries sustained later during the war.

After paying off, I found lodgings in 9 Park Grove, near the centre of Cardiff, in a modest establishment under the command of a Mrs. Tiley. I was ensconced in a room with a smoky open coal fire. The smoke from the chimney overwhelmed the room when the wind was in certain direc-

173

tions, and everything in the room was covered in smuts. I was asked if I liked fish and chips; and that became my staple diet when Mrs. Tiley received a reply in the affirmative. I had learned from Shipping Office scuttlebutt that *Appledore* was berthed in Newport, so I travelled by bus to visit my old ship.

Phillip Harris was standing by the ship. Most of the officers were on leave for the Christmas holiday. There were spare bunks in the amidships accommodation, so I stayed aboard with Phil over the holidays. He had received a food parcel from his mother in Vancouver, so we fed well, and it was an enjoyable stay. We also spent our evenings ashore in the local watering holes, the notable one being the Bodega.

Appledore had been an element in the ill-fated convoy HX90, with *Goodleigh* and *Lady Glanely*. Two ships of the Tatem fleet had been stationed in the port "windy corner" side of the convoy. *Lady Glanely* was the leading ship in column 1, with *Jersey* in position "12", and *Appledore* in position "13". *Dunsley*, in position "14" had been designated as the rescue ship, with *Goodleigh* in column 2. During the afternoon of 1 December 1940, *Lady Glanely* lost station, due to the diesel engine reaching its critical speed during an emergency turn. After the engine stalled, the ship fell astern, but shortly afterwards regained her speed and rejoined the convoy. As *Lady Glanely* passed *Appledore* in recovering station, the ever-irrepressible Second Mate, Johnny Hay shouted across on the megaphone "Do you want a bloody tow?" He and the crew of *Lady Glanely* would be dead within twelve hours. In 1939, four Canadian apprentices signed indentures for service in *Lady Glanely*, all natives of Vancouver. During the pre-war period, there were large numbers of young men unemployed in western Canada, with remote prospects of finding work. It is likely that they learned about the employment as indentured apprentices from Phil Harris, because I had neither met nor knew them. All were lost with *Lady Glanely*. Phil Harris was killed later in the war, leaving me as the only survivor of six.

The first casualty was the armed merchant cruiser, *H.M.S. Forfar*, followed by *Appalache*, torpedoed by U-101 at 2112 in the night watch of 1 December, followed by *Kavak* at 0306 in the middle watch of 2 December. Gunther Prien in U-47 reported sinking the Belgian ship, *Ville d'Arlon*, but there is no official record of even the existence of a ship of that name, despite the fact that an eye witness gave an account of the ship of that name as having straggled from the convoy due to steering gear malfunction. However, U-101 reported sinking *Lady Glanely* at 0407 in the middle watch. Two heavy explosions and a bright blue flash were seen from *Appledore*. There was a fitful moon showing, and in the faint light, *Lady Glanely* was seen to capsize.

James Slater, Second Mate of *Jersey*, gave an account of the sinking of *Lady Glanely*, in a letter to a mutual friend, Edward Driscoll, dated 20 September 1994. He gave a graphic account of U-47 surfacing in the convoy and engaging *Dunsley* by gunfire. *Dunsley* returned fire with her four-inch gun, and according to his account, the two lifeboats containing survivors from *Lady Glanely* were struck by shells from either U-47 or *Dunsley*, or both. Although James Slater had seen two lifeboats leave the sinking *Lady Glanely*, they were not seen after the surface action ceased. *Lady Glanely* was followed by *Conch* and *Tasso*, and then *Goodleigh* at 0628 in the morning watch of 2 December.

Both *Goodleigh* and *Lady Glanely* were on homeward passages from New Westminster and Vancouver respectively, *Lady Glanely* carrying the usual cargo of about 3000 tons of wheat and over 6,125 tons of lumber, and Goodleigh carrying a cargo of 1,000 tons of spelter and 8,400 tons of lumber. *Appledore* had always been in a "tender" condition of stability with similar cargoes, due to the higher centre of gravity imposed by the deck cargo. The other ships would have been in a similar state of reduced stability

The more dense mass of the spelter carried in the lower holds of *Goodleigh* may have improved stability. Conversely, the burning of oil fuel from tanks with a lower centre of gravity may have made *Lady Glanely* more tender, and caused her to capsize. From the description of the violence of the explosion, *Lady Glanely* may have been struck by a spread of several torpedoes, turning the ship over. The First Mate of *Goodleigh* was the only fatal casualty. He would have been on watch at the time of attack, so must have been caught on the open bridge by the blast of the explosion.

The following day and night the slaughter of ships continued, right into the North Channel. Convoy HX90 made port in Liverpool on 5 December 1940. *Appledore* docked in Newport the following day. Phil Harris and the crew of *Appledore* had been severely affected by the events. I never saw Phil Harris again, after our short reunion in Newport.

I returned to my lodgings on 28 December 1940, and on Monday 30 December enrolled for a course of refresher studies at the Smith Nautical School of Navigation and Seamanship in the Cardiff Technical College. The courses usually covered a period of ten weeks. Officers were released by the Merchant Navy Officers' Reserve Pool for a maximum of three months of unpaid study leave.

My service in *Istok* had covered a period of two months and fourteen days, during which I earned pay of about £ 50, a proportion of which I spent in the Adelphi Hotel in Liverpool, and aboard *Scythia*. Pay from two months and twenty-two days on *Filleigh* would have amounted to about £ 55. After the heavy drinking excursions with Phil Harris, I would have been left with about £ 75 out of the pay from the two ships. The cost of lodgings was 25 shillings a week for twelve weeks. I had traded in my octant for a second hand Hughes "Three Circle" sextant, so had a reserve of about £ 35. This made it vitally important to rush through the refresher course in order to sit the examination for a certificate of competency as Second Mate of a Foreign Going Steamship. My deadline was Monday 3 March 1941.

There were about twenty aspiring pupils in the class, under the tutelage of two Master Mariners of vast experience. Signals instruction was provided by a wonderful character, given the nickname of "Guv" by his pupils. "Guv" was a legend, not only in South Wales, but also in the wider seafaring community. He was a retired Royal Navy Chief Petty Officer Signalman, a "C.P.O. Bunting Tosser" in Royal Navy vernacular. When addressed, he usually preceded his response with the words "Cor, stiffen a bug, Guv!" which accounted for his nickname.

"Guv" had served in the Royal Navy when ships signalled to each other by huge semaphore arms attached to the topmasts. These were operated by a linkage leading to the decks, and actuated by large levers manhandled by several signallers. He boasted that ships would be able to communicate with each other when hull down, and only the topmasts visible. We loved this unforgettable individual.

Four days after enrolling in the Technical College, on Thursday 2 January 1941, I was studying in my room when the air raid alert was sounded. We had experienced many alarms in port previously, and I paid little attention at first. However, on this occasion a heavy air raid had developed. It was not until the following morning that I appreciated fully the severity of the air raid, which caused considerable damage to residential areas and resulted in the deaths of over 300 people. The city centre and Technical College had not suffered damage, and we attended for tuition as usual. I had completed my second complete week of study on Friday 10 January 1941.

Saturday, 11 January 1941 was the most memorable and important day of my life. At about 9 p.m., I had been studying and revising for several hours after high tea – fish and chips as usual from the nearest takeaway shop. Quite suddenly, I decided to stop studying, and to walk into Queen

Vernon Upton
January 1941, aged 19

Betty Mitchell
January 1941, aged 18

Street for a drink. A shrouded sign indicated a dance hall, the Connaught Rooms, so I paid my shilling, or whatever the cost, and entered.

My dancing capability consisted of shuffling very roughly in time to the music, on two right feet. Soon I found myself endeavouring to dance in a milling throng, attached to a nondescript female. Then the band-leader announced a "ladies' excuse me dance", and that is when my life changed. The most lively and vivacious person I had ever encountered then accosted me! When I looked into a pair of mischievous blue eyes, my fate was sealed for the rest of my life.

Betty Mitchell and two friends had decided to go dancing at the Connaught Rooms on the evening of 11 January 1941. When they were due to travel by bus, the transport services were discontinued, because an air raid alert was sounded, probably due to aircraft bound for Liverpool crossing Cardiff en route. The all clear was sounded at about the time when I left my lodgings, and the bus service was resumed, so we arrived at the dance hall almost simultaneously. We like to believe that fate took a hand, and that we were destined to meet.

Whatever the circumstances, I made an immediate decision that I would marry this 18-year old lovely. After the dance, we walked to her home, during which time I was teased remorselessly. After four and a half years continuously on a ship with all male companionship, I must have appeared to be exceptionally naïve. I certainly was in a state of bewilderment as I walked back to my lodging house, after arranging to meet Betty for tea the following Monday.

The Continental Restaurant, was the venue for our assignation; where we fed on Spam and an omelette made from reconstituted egg powder, followed by watching a film at the Capitol Cinema. Then the long walk to Betty's home, and back to my lodgings. Thereafter, we met twice weekly, following the same routine. During our long walks, I recited to Betty all the Articles for the Prevention of Collisions at Sea, which aspiring officers were required to know word perfect. Eventually, she became almost as conversant with them as most Second Mates.

We celebrated our birthdays shortly afterwards, my 20th, and Betty her 19th. Shortly afterwards, I proposed on a number of occasions, without success; but after further persistent attempts, was accepted. There were insufficient funds for even a modest engagement ring, so it was decided that a ring would be bought after service in my next ship. By then, I had "met the family", who were not exactly overjoyed with the prospect of the marriage of their young daughter.

Betty was engaged full time in caring for her mother, who had been stricken by acute rheumatoid arthritis, was unable to walk, dress or wash, and required almost constant attention. It was a great burden for one so young as Betty, particularly during the frequent air raid alarms, during which she showed great courage in her concern for her mother.

The date of the examination was Monday 3 March 1941. The Cardiff examiner for Masters and Mates was Captain Burgess. Most examiners carried formidable reputations, and emphasised certain special aspects of the examinations, which were held in twice daily sessions over a period of five days. Captain Burgess was known to be a "bugger on Articles", usually expecting a candidate to recite them in full, odds first 1 to 31, and evens from 30 back to 2. He was known to dwell inordinately on Article 9 concerning fishing vessels and fishing boats, particularly the section on the seas of Japan and Korea. However, Captain Keeting, the examiner in Liverpool had a frightening reputation. It was unfortunate – for some – that he had the same name as the well-known insecticide Keetings' Powder. A wag had written in the toilet, "Keetings kills bugs, fleas, moths, flies and cockroaches – AND SECOND MATES". When Captain Keeting saw this, he failed all the aspiring Second Mates before him for the examination, in the oral section.

After several weeks with Mrs. Tiley, I was disenchanted with the filthy coal fire and smuts on everything, and the interminable fish and chips. A number of fellow students were accommodated with Mrs. Southall and her husband in Colum Road, so I changed lodgings. Mrs. Southall charged 30 shillings a week, but provided scrupulously clean rooms, and excellent food. She was a motherly character, and loved by the nautical students.

I presented myself on Monday 3 March 1941 for my examinations in Knowledge of Principles, followed by Navigation I and Navigation II, and was anticipating the chartwork examination. This was a 3-hour paper and we were not aware of the chart to be covered until we saw it on the chart table; usually some obscure part of the world like the Straits of Malacca, which most of had never traversed.

There was a severe air attack on the night before the day when the chartwork examination was set. When I arrived at the city end of Bute Street, where I usually boarded a tram to the docks, the service was discontinued. Bute Street was closed due to unexploded bombs. Access to James Street by a deviation down Tresillian Terrace was also blocked. Therefore, I had to walk to the Shipping Federation Offices by a circuitous route, a distance of several miles.

Captain Burgess, and the other examinees, had arrived by routes not obstructed, but I was 40 minutes late for the examination. I was greeted by "You are disqualified for late attendance, Upton!" Faced with the traditional penalty of six months at sea before I could sit the examination again, I tried to explain the circumstances to Captain Burgess. He relented to the extent of permitting me to sit the chartwork paper, but stipulated that I would have to finish with the rest, precisely on the bell.

Losing 40 minutes in a 3-hour paper was bad enough, but now my apprehensions were increased by the prospect of identifying a chart of some obscure part of the world. Here again, fate took a hand. There on the chart table was the most familiar chart in my recent memory, "Northern Ireland – Inistrahull to Bloody Foreland!" That chart had been on the chart table of *Filleigh* for several days when we had been hove to during the previous voyage. I knew the variations, soundings, landmarks, and tidal currents intimately. It was a massive stroke of luck; and I finished the paper with time to spare, much to the astonishment of Captain Burgess.

Seamanship I and Seamanship II, and Ship Construction, Stability and Cargo Work followed. Oral examinations were usually held on the Friday and Saturday; and examinees were selected in alphabetical order.

The results of the written papers were notified on the Saturday. Captain Burgess had just completed the oral examination of a man named James, and had failed the candidate. James came out of the examination room in a very crestfallen state with the words, "The bugger has failed me, and sent me back to sea for six months!" He had passed his written papers, but failed the oral examination. If a candidate had passed the written section but failed the oral section, he was required to serve a further six months on articles before presenting himself for re-examination in the oral section. If he failed the oral section again, a further six months on articles was required, but he would then have to sit both the written and oral sections again.

One could not blame Captain Burgess. He had a difficult job, and undertook his work with impartiality and according to the rules. The sad result was that James went back to sea as a Third Mate and, regrettably, he was killed shortly afterwards.

After James had left, I was admitted to the examination room. Captain Burgess confronted me with the astonishing news that I had passed all the written examinations with the highest marks in the country, including – miraculously – chartwork. In alphabetical order, my name was at the bottom of his list. As there was insufficient time for an oral examination on the Saturday, this was scheduled for the Monday. He then made the remark, "With luck, you will have your Certificate on Monday afternoon." He was most affable, a characteristic not usually associated with examiners of Masters and Mates.

I presented myself on Monday morning 10 March 1941 at the board of Trade offices. "Guv" conducted an examination in morse code, semaphore, and the International Code of Signals, which I passed. Then it was the orals examination conducted by Captain Burgess. True to form, the articles were recited, followed by practical seamanship, particularly appertaining to clearing a foul hawse. These elements of the examination were not troublesome. Then the room was darkened, and Captain Burgess switched on various steaming and sailing lights out of a myriad of combinations, barking a sequence of questions "What is that light?" "Who gives way?" "Why? " "What article?"

We came to a steam trawler under way, on our starboard side, showing the red section of its tri-coloured lantern. The answers were "Steam trawler, fishing, showing its red light. We would give way according to steering and sailing rules." "What is its fog signal?" My answer was incorrect. "One long and two short blasts on the whistle or siren, sir." Captain Burgess did not say anything. I had given the signal for a vessel manoeuvring with difficulty. He then switched on a series of other lights, with similar questions, finally returning to the steam trawler, this time showing the green section of the tri-coloured lantern on our port side. My answers were, "Steam trawler fishing, showing its green light. Although I would not be bound to give way under the steering and sailing rules, I would conform to the ruling of an Admiralty Court". (An officer of a merchant ship had obeyed the steering and sailing rules by standing on when on a collision course with a steam trawler on his port side, showing the green section of the tri-coloured light. There was a collision. The judge in an Admiralty Court had ruled that although the merchant ship may have had right of way under the steering and sailing rules, the steam trawler was hampered by its nets. He ruled that the officer on the merchant ship should have given way under Article 29 of The Regulations for the Prevention of Collisions at Sea, which referred to the necessity to conform to "The ordinary practice of seamen.") Clearly, the ordinary practice of seamen was to avoid colliding with another ship, whether in the right or wrong. This was covered by a short doggerel that we learned when we were apprentices:

"This is the tale of Captain Grey,
Who died asserting his right of way,
He was right, dead right, as he sailed along,
But just as dead as if he were wrong."

The next question was, "What is the fog signal?" The reply was "A prolonged blast on the whistle or siren, followed by a ringing of the bell, sir." "So, Upton, when a steam trawler shows its red light, it gives a different fog signal from the signal when it shows its green light. Is that so?" "No, sir, I made a mistake the first time." The response was "That was the reason why I brought the trawler back the second time!" I really thought that I had cocked it all up, and had visions of reporting at the Shipping Office the following day to serve the customary penalty of six months sea time. In any case, in dense fog both ships should have been stopped or travelling at slow speed; and a merchant ship hearing either fog signal would have exercised proper caution. That was the view taken by Captain Burgess, and that is why he passed me. He was a fearsome character, but scrupulously fair.

My Certificate of Competency as Second Mate of a Foreign Going Steamship No. 46226 was issued to me at the Board of Trade offices in Cardiff on 14 March 1941. I had made it!

12
THE WAR AT SEA: HADLEIGH
18 MARCH–4 SEPTEMBER 1941

After I was issued with my Certificate of Competency, I was ordered to report to the Merchant Navy Officers Reserve Pool offices across the road in Bute Street. This was controlled by a Captain Skee. The spelling of the name may not be correct. He was a man in younger middle age, so was lucky to be ashore when many Master Mariners of greater age were at sea in command of their ships. He was not liked by Masters and officers, because he held almost arbitrary authority over their appointment to ships. This offended their inherent independence. However, someone had to take on the onerous task of allocating Masters and mates to their ships. We did not envy him, although we believed that an older man should have done the work. He would have been more useful in command of a ship.

Although I had vowed never to serve in another Tatem ship, the advent of the M.N. Officers Reserve Pool had largely eliminated any choice. Usually officers were allocated to the type of ship with which they were familiar, which was logical. An officer who was familiar with tankers would require a period of familiarisation, if detailed to serve on a general trader; and vice versa. Similarly, officers were allocated to ships within a company fleet, because the ships conformed to similar specifications and characteristics. Hence, when *Hadleigh* reported a vacancy for a Third Mate, it is likely that I was the most suitable officer available. *Hadleigh* and *Appledore* were sister ships, almost identical in every respect. *Everleigh* was also one of three sister ships, in which the specifications were identical. Therefore, in joining *Hadleigh* it was almost like stepping aboard *Appledore* again. She had been built by Furness Shipbuilding Co. Ltd of Haverton Hill on Tees, with a gross tonnage of 5,222 tons, length 418 feet 8 inches, beam 56 feet, loaded draught of 25 feet 10 inches and a designed loaded speed of 10 knots. She was also very similar to *Filleigh*. I was

S.S. Hadleigh, built in 1930, 5,222 gross registered tonnage
Torpedoed by U-77 on 16 March 1945, beached and became a total loss.
(*Photograph by Joan and Marion Clarkson, Ships in Focus*)

ordered to join *Hadleigh* on 17 March 1941.

After bidding farewell to Betty and her family, I travelled overnight to Hull on Sunday 16 March, and boarded the ship the following day. The Master was Captain W.H. Gould, a man of substantial bulk, both fore and aft and across the beam. He was an excellent Master. I signed articles on 18 March 1941. The ship remained in Hull for a week, and put to sea on the early morning of 26 March 1941, joining a northbound North Sea convoy off Spurn Head. The North Sea convoys were of great length, disposed in two columns, restricted between the coast and the minefields. The swept channel was relatively narrow, so there was very little sea room in which to manoeuvre. When passing each other, southbound and northbound convoys kept to starboard.

I stood my first watch on *Hadleigh* at 0800. The Master had ordered me to stamp on the navigating bridge deck in the event of an emergency. Flamborough Head was well astern, and we were almost abeam of the Tees estuary. We were in the starboard column, well astern of the leading ships. Escort was usually provided by armed trawlers, commanded by fishing trawler skippers, commissioned in the R.N.R. These independent characters made their own rules, as they had been used to doing in peacetime.

The convoys were frequently subjected to night attacks by E-Boats, and day attacks by aircraft. Restricted between the coast and the minefields, with convoys passing in opposite directions, North Sea convoys presented relatively easy targets for the enemy forces, particularly the aircraft, and suffered almost daily severe losses.

Hadleigh had been ordered to launch its anti-aircraft kite when we joined the convoy, and this was flying at maximum height. The kite wire was rove through a sheave at the fore topmast head, and raised or lowered by No. 2 starboard winch. A speed of about six knots was required to keep the kite airborne.

At about 1100, after I had been on watch for three hours, we heard the sound of an aircraft, but none was visible. An enemy aircraft had crossed the convoy well ahead of us and disappeared inland. It must have turned sharply, and commenced a shallow dive from over the land, appearing at low level just over the point of land on our port bow. The JU88 then turned to starboard and flew directly down the port column of the convoy, dropping a stick of bombs on the P&O ship *Somali*, several ships ahead of us. The aircraft then flew between the columns of ships, opening fire from its bow and stern machine guns, and within 30 seconds was lost from sight astern of the convoy. Although *Hadleigh* and other ships were flying anti-aircraft kites and balloons, the JU88 passed by without striking the kite wires. There was some desultory anti-aircraft small arms fire, but no heavier calibre weapons opened fire. It all happened too quickly.

Somali turned to port, with a huge fire blazing on the foredeck, and stopped athwart of the port column. The ship astern of *Somali* in the port column turned hard-a-starboard, to avoid the stricken ship, and forced the ship abeam in the starboard column to turn hard-a-starboard as well. Both then turned hard-a-port, because of the proximity of the minefield, and lost way. The distance between us was so short that I had to turn the ship hard-a-starboard, towards the minefield, to avoid a collision. *Somali* had then stopped, between the port column of the convoy and the land.

I stamped on the bridge to summon the Master, and turned hard-a-port, to avoid the minefield. However, we were then in trouble. The sudden avoiding manoeuvre had taken the way off the ship, and the kite fell into the sea a good distance off our starboard quarter. Captain Gould had then arrived on the bridge. The kite was being towed astern, with the wire leading from the masthead, diagonally down around the bridge, and under the gunwale of the starboard bridge jolly boat. The gunwale of the lifeboat was beginning to collapse under the strain, and was creaking ominously.

The Master took over the bridge of the ship and ordered me to clear the wire. In the meantime, the First Mate was organising a party to cut loose the kite. I jumped into the lifeboat, but as I was attempting to clear the wire, it broke loose, and I was flung violently backwards, damaging my left arm. As I returned to the bridge, the fore topmast gave way under the massive strain, and fell on the bridge, with the heavy pitch pine yardarms attached. The huge bulk of the Master was right in the path of the falling topmast.

He was so busy with conning the ship that I saw the danger first, and took emergency action by pushing him violently out of the path of the falling mass. We both fell to the deck, but my left arm was pinned between the bridge rail and falling mast and yard. When we extricated ourselves, my left arm was very badly crushed, from the wrist almost to the elbow, and the whole mess was spurting blood profusely.

I went below, where the Steward applied a tourniquet to staunch the severe bleeding. The left arm was swabbed with hydrogen peroxide, and bound tightly with bandages, to keep the whole mess together. The arm was put in a sling, and I returned to the bridge and finished my watch. The Master was shaken, but unscathed. By then, the kite had been cut loose, and a party of seamen were unravelling the mass of rigging and spars on the bridge. The carpenter later re-fitted the parts of the topmast that had remained intact.

Somali had originally lain athwart of the convoy course, and had moved clear of the following ships. She lay stopped, with a huge fire burning forward and amidships, causing a series of explosions. The convoy passed her off the port of Blyth in Northumberland. She was still burning fiercely, with an escort trawler in attendance. We learned later that she had sunk the following day, 27 March, one mile off Snoop Head near Sunderland. Miraculously, only one man was killed out of a complement of 79.

Convoy OB304

The convoy proceeded to Methil, where we anchored. We then put to sea through the Pentland Firth and Minches to Loch Ewe. From Loch Ewe we joined outward bound convoy OB 304 of 41 ships, which took the northerly passage through the Minches and north of the Hebrides. Convoy OB304 dispersed on 4 April 1941 in position 62-20 north latitude, 20-15 west longitude. We made port in the U.S.A. on 17 April 1941.

Immediately after putting to sea in convoy OB304 we received distress messages from 36 ships, 10 of which were concentrated in a compact sea area between 58 and 59 degrees north latitude, and 22 and 29 degrees west

Second Mate   Third Mate
First Mate

The Officers of *Hadleigh*

longitude. Our convoy, OB304 lost only one ship, *Conus*, sunk by U-97 in the night watch on 4 April, shortly after the convoy was dispersed.

The loss of *Conus* in our convoy OB304 is a great mystery. The only explanation I can advance for the loss of this large ship with all hands is that U-97 surfaced and opened fire, destroying the lifecraft, and killing all hands when they were abandoning ship.

Ten convoys were attacked during our passage to New York. The ships sunk were: SL69 (five ships), OG56 (two ships), SC25 (one ship), HX115 (three ships), OB302 (two ships), OB304 (one ship), OB306 (four ships), OG57 (five ships) and HX117 (one ship). However, convoy SC26 suffered the greatest casualties, with 12 ships lost out of 23, a catastrophic massacre.

One of the casualties was *Harbledown*, which had been moored close to *Appledore* in Geelong in 1938. We had made friends with our fellow apprentices on the ship. *Harbledown* was an element in convoy SC26, sunk on 4 April 1941 by U-94 with the loss of 16 of her complement of 39. Although *Hadleigh* was not attacked on the trans Atlantic passage, we were inundated by distress messages, and surrounded by enemy attacks on convoys and ships that had been dispersed from convoys or were on independent passage.

By that time, those of us who had served at sea from the outbreak of hostilities were in no doubt as to the fate of ships carrying steel or similar cargoes. These were usually torpedoed during the night by surfaced U-Boats. Many had seen the rapid sinking of such ships, and others had heard accounts from their shipmates. I had learned about the loss of *Tregenna* from the officers of *Filleigh*.

An analysis of casualties on a small but representative sample of ships sunk in convoy, when carrying full, or substantial part, cargoes of steel, bulk iron ore, scrap, phosphates, or pig iron makes sombre reading.

From a sample of 22 ships sunk in HX convoys, with approximate total crew numbers of 880, 733 officers and men were lost, a fatal casualty rate of over 83 percent.

An analysis of 32 ships sunk in the slower SC convoys with approximate crew numbers of 1,240, reflects 922 were lost, a fatal casualty rate of over 74 percent. The combined losses represented a quite appalling fatal casualty rate. Only 465 men survived out of over 2,120, the casualty rate being over 78 percent.

Although we did not know the statistics at the time, we knew by then that the chance of survival when carrying such cargoes was minimal. Prospects of survival by day were very slim; by night death was almost a certainty.

Hadleigh was berthed at New York from 17 April to 6 may 1941. Our cargo included as a base element various amounts of steel or steel-based products: coiled sheet, plate, billets, and blooms or sections, in the lower holds. We carried general cargoes of all types in the upper sections of the holds and in the 'tween decks, and usually lorries or other vehicles or cases on deck. The smaller proportion of steel the better. With such cargoes a torpedo hit forward of the bridge usually had disastrous results, so we always slept "fully booted and spurred", and with our cabin and alleyway doors partly open on the hook to prevent them jamming completely in their frames, thereby trapping the occupants. It was a precarious existence, which we endured passage after passage. The faster HX convoys usually took 15 to 18 days and the slower SC convoys 16 to 19 days for the Atlantic crossings, depending on the routing, number of emergency turns, and, of course, the weather.

Casualties – Ships and Personnel
18 March 1941 to 6 May 1941

Ships sunk – 59 by 22 successful U-Boats.

Italian submarines sank two ships.
Surface raiders sank three ships.
Aircraft sank 13 ships.
One ship lost in collision in convoy.
One ship lost by causes unknown.

Lost with all hands

Chama, in ballast, 58 dead.
Agnete Maersk, in ballast, 28 dead.
Koranton, general cargo, 34 dead.
Conus, in ballast, 59 dead.
Venezuela, in ballast, 40 dead

Lost with very heavy casualties

Benvorlich, general cargo, 20 dead out of 52.
Benwyvis, general cargo, 34 dead out of 54.
Clan Ogilvy, general cargo, 61 dead out of 82.
Millisle, cargo unknown, 10 dead out of 13.
Britannia, troopship, 249 dead out of 484.
Empire Mermaid, cargo steel, 22 dead out of 41.
Limbourg, cargo phosphates, 28 dead out of 30.
Liguria, cargo unknown, 19 dead out of 29.
Umona, general cargo, 100 dead out of 105.
Castor, cargo fuel oil, 15 dead out of 42.
Beaverdale, general cargo, 21 dead out of 79.
British Viscount, cargo fuel oil, 28 dead out of 48.
Daphne, cargo coal, 18 dead out of 25.
Indier, cargo steel, 42 dead out of 46.
Westpool, cargo scrap, 35 dead out of 43.
Harbledown, cargo wheat, 16 dead out of 39.
Welcombe, cargo grain, 20 dead out of 42.
Duffield, cargo fuel oil, 25 dead out of 52.
Helena Margareta, in ballast, 26 dead out of 36.
British Endurance, general cargo, 65 dead out of 94.
Oilfield, cargo benzene, 47 dead out of 55.
Nerissa, passengers, 207 dead out of 287.

Merchant seamen killed – 1308 out of 4243,
a fatal casualty rate of 31 percent.

Passengers killed – 252 out of 730, a fatal casualty rate of 35 percent.

HADLEIGH - 18 MARCH 1941 TO 4 SEPTEMBER 1941

RECORD OF MERCHANT SHIPS SUNK IN ATLANTIC - 18/03/41 TO 06/05/41

HADLEIGH - SIGNED ARTICLES AT HULL - 18/03/41

DATE	SHIP	NAT.	CONVOY NO.	CAUSE OF LOSS	POSITION		CARGO	CASUALTIES CREW	DEAD
18/03/41	MEDJERDA	BRITISH	SL68	U-105	17-00 N.	21-00 W.	IRON ORE	54	1
18/03/41	MANDALIKA	DUTCH	SL68	U-105	18-16 N.	21-26 W.	SUGAR	62	3
18/03/41	CLAN McNAB	BRITISH		COLLISION	17-13 N.	21-22 W.	GENERAL	82	0
19/03/41	BENVORLICH	BRITISH		AIRCRAFT	54-48 N.	13-10 W.	GENERAL	52	20
20/03/41	BENWYVIS	BRITISH	SL68	U-105	20-00 N.	25-00 W.	GENERAL	54	34
20/03/41	CLAN OGILVY	BRITISH	SL68	U-105	20-00 N.	25-45 W.	GENERAL	82	61
21/03/41	JHELUM	BRITISH	SL68	U-105	21-00 N.	25-00 W.	GENERAL	54	8
21/03/41	LONDON II	BRITISH		AIRCRAFT	51-24 N.	04-30 W.	STEEL	19	4
21/03/41	MILLISLE	BRITISH		AIRCRAFT				13	10
22/03/41	AGNITA	BRITISH		A.M.C.	02-30 N.	25-00 W.	BALLAST	38	0
23/03/41	CHAMA	BRITISH	OG56	U-97	49-35 N.	19-30 W.	BALLAST	58	58
24/03/41	AGNETE MAERSK	BRITISH	OG56	VENIERO	49-00 N.	21-55 W.	BALLAST	28	28
25/03/41	BEAVERBRAE	BRITISH		AIRCRAFT	60-38 N.	08-44 W.	GENERAL	84	0
25/03/41	BRITANNIA	BRITISH		A.M.C.	07-24 N.	24-03 W.	TROOPS	484	249
25/03/41	TROLLEHOLM	SWED.		A.M.C.					
26/03/41	EMPIRE MERMAID	BRITISH		UNKNOWN	58-36 N.	10-00 W.	STEEL	41	22
26/03/41	FARADAY	BRITISH		AIRCRAFT			CABLE SHIP	125	8
26/03/41	SOMALI	BRITISH		AIRCRAFT	55-23 N.	01-21 W.	GENERAL	79	1
27/03/41	KORANTON	BRITISH	SC25	U-98	59-00 N.	27-00 W.	GENERAL	34	34
29/03/41	GERMANIC	BRITISH	HX115	U-48	61-18 N.	22-05 W.	WHEAT	40	5
29/03/41	HYLTON	BRITISH	HX115	U-48	60-02 N.	18-10 W.	LUMBER	36	0
29/03/41	LIMBOURG	BELG.	HX115	U-48	61-18 N.	22-05 W.	PHOSPHATE	30	28
29/03/41	LIGURIA	SWED.	OB302	U-46	60-00 N.	29-00 W.	BALLAST	29	19
30/03/41	COULTARN	BRITISH	OB302	U-69	60-3- N.	29-30 W.	BALLAST	42	3
30/03/40	UMONA	BRITISH		U-124	07-25 N.	13-55 W.	GENERAL	105	100

HADLEIGH — **OB304**

31/03/41	CASTOR	SWED.		U-46	57-59 N.	32-08 W.	FUEL OIL	42	15
01/04/41	BEAVERDALE	BRITISH	SC26	U-48	60-15 N.	29-19 W.	GENERAL	79	21
02/04/41	BRITISH RELIANCE	BRITISH	SC26	U-46	58-21 N.	28-30 W.	GAS OIL	50	0
03/04/41	ALDERPOOL	BRITISH	SC26	U-46	58-21 N.	27-59 W.	WHEAT	41	0
03/04/41	BRITISH VISCOUNT	BRITISH	SC26	U-73	58-12 N.	27-40 W.	FUEL OIL	48	28
03/04/41	DAPHNE	FINNISH	SC26	U-76	60-00 N.	20-00 W.	COAL	25	18
03/04/41	HELLE	NOR.	SC26	U-98	59-00 N.	24-30 W.	PULP	24	0
03/04/41	INDIER	BELG.	SC26	U-73	58-40 N.	27-28 W.	STEEL	46	42
03/04/41	LEONIDAS Z. ZAMBANIS	GREEK	SC26	U-73	58-12 N.	27-40 W.	WHEAT	29	2
03/04/41	WESTPOOL	BRITISH	SC26	U-74	58-12 N.	27-40 W.	SCRAP	43	35
04/04/41	ATHENIC	BRITISH	SC26	U-73	58-32 N.	20-13 W.	BRAIN	40	0
04/04/41	CONUS	BRITISH	OB304	U-97	56-14 N.	31-19 W.	BALLAST	59	59
04/04/41	MARLENE	BRITISH		U-124	08-15 N.	14-19 W.	GENERAL	60	13
04/04/41	HARBLEDOWN	BRITISH	SC26	U-94	58-30 N.	23-00 W.	WHEAT	39	16
04/04/41	WELCOMBE	BRITISH	SC26	U-98	59-07 N.	23-42 W.	GRAIN	41	20
05/04/41	ENA DE LARRINAGA	BRITISH		U-105	01-10 N.	26-06 W.	GENERAL	43	5
06/04/41	DUNSTAN	BRITISH	OB306	AIRCRAFT	59-09 N.	08-22 W.	GENERAL	48	2
06/04/41	LINCLON ELLSWORTH	NOR.		U-94	62-37 N.	27-06 W.	BALLAST	29	0
06/04/41	NICOLAOU ZOGRAFIA	GREEK		AIRCRAFT	57-10 N.	12-30 W.	GENERAL	32	0
06/04/41	OLGA S.	DANISH		AIRCRAFT	55-48 N.	09-45 W.	GENERAL	31	1
06/04/41	DUNSTAN	BRITISH	OB306	AIRCRAFT	59-09 N.	08-22 W.	GENERAL	48	2
08/04/41	TWEED	BRITISH	OG57	U-124	07-43 N.	15-11 W.	BALLAST	31	3
08/04/41	DUFFIELD	BRITISH	OG57	U-107	31-13 N.	23-40 W.	FUEL OIL	52	25
08/04/41	ESKDENE	BRITISH	OG57	U-107	34-24 N.	23-51 W.	COAL	39	0
08/04/41	HARPATHIAN	BRITISH	OG57	U-107	32-22 N.	22-53 W.	STORES	43	4
08/04/41	HELENA MARGARETA	BRITISH	OG57	U-107	33-00 N.	23-32 W.	BALLAST	36	26
08/04/41	PRINS WILLEM II	DUTCH	HX117	U-98	59-50 N.	24-25 W.	SUGAR	34	12
10/04/41	SALEIER	DUTCH	OB306	U-52	58-04 N.	30-48 W.	COAL	63	0
11/04/41	AEGEON	GREEK		U-124	06-55 N.	15-38 W.	WHEAT	34	5
12/04/41	ST. HELENA	BRITISH		U-124	07-50 N.	14-00 W.	GENERAL	40	0
12/04/41	KEXHOLM	SWED.	OB306	AIRCRAFT	59-50 N.	08-22 W.	COFFEE	35	0
13/04/41	H.M.S. RAJPUTANA	BRITISH	HX117	U-108	64-50 N.	27-25 W.		263	41
14/04/41	CORINTHIC	BRITISH		U-124	08-10 N.	14-40 W.	GRAIN	40	2
15/04/41	AURILLAC	BRITISH		TAZZOLI	37-09 N.	18-43 W.	ORE	41	1
17/04/41	VENEZUELA	SWED.		U-123	53-00 N.	18-00 W.	BALLAST	40	40

HADLEIGH - BERTHED AT NEW YORK - 19/04/41 TO 10/05/41

20/04/41	EMPIRE ENDURANCE	BRITISH		U-73	50-05 N.	23-14 W.	GENERAL	94	65
21/04/41	CALCHAS	BRITISH		U-107	23-50 N.	27-00 W.	GENERAL	113	32
26/04/41	MOUNTPARK	BRITISH		AIRCRAFT	56-21 N.	11-57 W.	GRAIN	41	6
27/04/41	BEACON GRANGE	BRITISH		U-552	62-05 N.	16-26 W.	BALLAST	82	2
27/04/41	CELTE	BRITISH		AIRCRAFT	61-20 N.	11-00 W.	FISH	24	0
28/04/41	CALEDONIA	NOR.	HX121	U-96	60-03 N.	16-16 W.	FUEL OIL	37	12
28/04/41	CAPULET	BRITISH	HX121	U-512	61-10 N.	16-55 W.	FUEL OIL	44	9
28/04/41	OILFIELD	BRITISH	HX121	U-96	60-05 N.	16-00 W.	BENZENE	55	47
28/04/41	PORT HARDY	BRITISH	HX121	U-96	60-05 N.	16-00 W.	GENERAL	98	1
29/04/41	CITY OF NAGPUR	BRITISH		U-75	52-30 N.	26-00 W.	GENERAL	478	16
30/04/41	NERISSA	BRITISH	HX121	U-552	55-57 N.	10-08 W.	GENERAL	287	207
30/04/41	LASSELL	BRITISH	OB309	U-107	12-55 N.	28-56 W.	GENERAL	53	17
01/05/41	SAMSO	BRITISH		U-103	08-35 N.	16-17 W.	CEREALS	20	1
02/05/41	TARANGER	NOR.		U-95	61-07 N.	25-20 W.	BALLAST	34	2
03/05/41	WRAY CASTLE	BRITISH		U-103	06-48 N.	13-55 W.	SUGAR	44	1
04/05/41	JAPAN	SWED.	OB310	U-38			GENERAL	54	0
05/05/41	QUEEN MAUD	BRITISH	OB309	U-38	07-54 N.	16-41 W.	GENERAL	39	1
06/05/41	CAMITO	BRITISH		U-97	50-34 N.	21-40 W.	ADMIRALTY		
06/05/41	DUNKWA	BRITISH	OB310	U-103	08-49 N.	16-52 W.	GENERAL	47	8

| | | | | | | | **TOTALS** | **5,003** | **1,560** |

An analysis of the activities of individual U-Boats shows the high success rate of a relatively small number of the regular service U-Boat commanders, who had been trained in the pre-war years, 37 ships sunk by 8 U-Boats, out of the 59 ships sunk by 22 U-Boats.

Successful U-Boats

U-124	Six ships sunk.
U-107	Six ships sunk.
U-105	Five ships sunk.
U-73	Five ships sunk.
U-48	Five ships sunk.
U-46	Four ships sunk.
U-98	Three ships sunk.
U-96	Three ships sunk.

Three ships were lost in very doubtful and disturbing circumstances. The British ship *Chama*, in ballast, on independent passage after having straggled from convoy OG56, was torpedoed by U-97 at 2226 on the night of 23 March 1941. The ship sank with the loss of the entire complement of 58. The position was 49-35 N. 19-13 W. in the northern part of the Bay of Biscay. *Chama* was a large modern tanker. It appears to be nothing short of incredible that a modern tanker in ballast would sink in relatively moderate weather conditions without any survivors. Although it will never be proved, I am certain that the U-Boat probably subjected the life craft and the survivors to gunfire attack. The commander of U-97 was Kapitanleutnant Siegfried "Udo" Heilmann. It is likely that this event was never investigated.

Agnete Maersk was a small British ship, also in ballast, and detached from convoy OG56. The ship was attacked by the Italian submarine *Veniero* at 1509 on the afternoon of 24 March 1941 in position 49-00 N 22-55 W. The ship sank with the loss of her complement of 28. A report states that she was subjected to gunfire, most likely directed on the survivors. The Commander of *Venerio*, Manlio Petroni, also appears to have escaped investigation for war crimes.

Another mysterious sinking was the loss of *Conus*, which had accompanied us, and which had dispersed with convoy OB304 on 4 April 1941. The wind and sea conditions were moderate. *Conus* was a large and well-found tanker of the Anglo Saxon Fleet on passage in ballast, yet was sunk with the loss of her entire complement of 59 men. Once more, the perpetrator of what I believe was another atrocity was U-97. Again, the villain was Kapitanleutnant Siegfried "Udo" Heilmann. Later, he had been transferred to the command of U-389, in which he and his crew were lost on 5 October 1943. It is gratifying to me that he paid the price. I have no doubt that the survivors of many ships on independent passages met a similar fate, not reported in the accounts of the enemy.

My knowledge now of exact dates is not completely accurate, because my ships made so many similar Atlantic voyages. I can only relate my periods of service to events that are on record, and identify my personal experiences in relation to them. It was so on my first voyage in *Hadleigh*. We would have arrived at our port of loading on about 17 April 1941, and remained for the usual two to three weeks, departing for Halifax during the second week in May. *H.M.S. Hood* was sunk on the morning of 24 May 1941, after we were about four days on passage. Therefore, it is almost certain that our ship was part of convoy HX128, a nine-knot convoy of 56 ships that left Halifax on 20 May. The main body arrived at Liverpool on 7 June 1941.

Convoy HX128

Before the night of 22/23 May 1941, we received a signal from the convoy commodore for a series of emergency turns to port. During the night, we maintained a westerly course at reduced speed. We were also ordered to switch off all radio equipment, even for listening. We believed that this manoeuvre was intended to divert us from an anticipated U-Boat concentration. The menace was the presence in the Denmark Strait of the battleship *Bismarck*, and the heavy cruiser *Prinz Eugen*, both of which had been found, and were being shadowed by the cruisers *H.M.S. Norfolk* and *Suffolk*. The following morning we resumed a course north of our original projected track, returned to convoy speed, and maintained this course until 27 May 1941. Then the radio silence order was rescinded, and we were again able to listen to wireless traffic.

In the forenoon watch of 27 May, the apprentice who was on signal watch brought me a plain language flag signal, which he had written in the signal log "BISMARCK SLNK". The weather was typically filthy for that part of the Atlantic, with patches of thick mist and rain, and occasional blinding snow storms, a strong wind and heavy seas. By then the signal flags were dirty and ragged, so I looked for the ship flying the cleanest flags, and identified the signal as "BISMARCK SUNK". The error in the reading of the signal by the apprentice had been that he had mistaken the flag "L" (black and yellow quarters) for the "U" (red and white quarters). I relayed the message to the Master, and there was great rejoicing and relief to learn that such a massive threat had been eliminated. It was only after the wireless operator tuned in to the B.B.C. Overseas News that we learned of the tragic loss of *H.M.S. Hood* and over 1,400 officers and men, in a naval engagement that occurred so close to the path of advance of the convoy. What the *Bismarck* and *Prinz Eugen* would have done to our convoy is unimaginable.

Once again, the ship in which I served had crossed the Atlantic without being attacked, and had avoided what would have been annihilation by the very powerful enemy squadron of surface ships.

Those elements of the convoy, with destinations on the east coast of the U.K., including *Hadleigh*, were detached, and passed through the Pentland Firth and along the east coast to the convoy assembly port of Methil. Thence we proceeded to South Shields. We were then on 6-month articles, so the ship did not pay off. I travelled to Cardiff on a short leave during the middle of June 1941.

The company Marine Superintendent boarded the ship in South Shields. He has been described earlier in this narrative; and had lost none of his obnoxious characteristics with the passage of time. The fear of marine superintendents was endemic throughout the Tatem line and many other shipping lines. This fear of authority dated back to the depression days. During that era, masters, deck officers and engineers lived in apprehension of losing their livelihoods, at the whims of these oppressive tyrants, who had no conception of decency or humanity.

I had applied to the First Mate for my entitlement to leave of absence, which amounted to two and a half days for each month on articles. He had given me permission, so, I cleaned up and packed my bag, and reported to him before going ashore. The marine superintendent was in the cabin of the First Mate as I entered, sitting in a chair like a bloated toad. They had been checking his list of deck stores. He greeted me with the words, "Where the bloody hell do you think you are going?" "Cardiff on leave", I replied. "You are, like hell. I want all the mates to stand by the ship, so you can forget about any tarts in Cardiff". I hated his guts, and would never have paid deference to his authority. My response was, "You have no authority on this ship, you pig", and I was down the gangway and away. He could have his ship, for all I cared. There is no way in which I would have demeaned myself by deference to such an example of the worst type of mankind.

I found it quite incredible that experienced and qualified deck and engineer officers allowed themselves to be browbeaten by such obnoxious sycophants. It only required a small number of strong-willed Masters, backed up by their officers, to walk off their ships just as they were ready to catch the tide and sail, to put such individuals right in the shit of their own making. Owners like Lord Glanely and his directors would have learned quickly where they stood financially, as the result of the loss of revenue that such a rebellion would have provoked. In wartime the Ministry of War Transport would have been far from pleased.

Even in wartime, the inherent fear of the Marine Superintendent remained. It was tragic, when good men were dying at sea in quite appalling circumstances in thousands; only to suffer the indignity meted out by such petty tyrants, when they made port.

Casualties – Ships and Personnel
7 May 1941 to 6 June 1941

Ships sunk – 66 by 25 successful U-Boats.
Italian submarines sank six ships.
Aircraft sank five ships.

Lost with all hands

Starcross, general cargo, 40 dead.
British Security, cargo benzene, 53 dead.
Tregarthen, cargo coal, 45 dead.

Lost with very heavy casualties

Ramilles, cargo coke, 29 dead out of 41.
Empire Caribou, cargo chalk, 29 dead out of 40.
Empire Ridge, cargo iron ore, 31 dead out out of 33.
Darlington Court, cargo wheat, 25 dead out of 37.
Harpagus, cargo grain, 32 dead out of 50.
John P. Pedersen, cargo fuel oil, 22 dead out of 38.
Norman Monarch, cargo wheat, 26 dead out of 48.
Rothermere, cargo steel, 22 dead out of 56.
Marionga, general cargo, 26 dead out of 31.
Empire Protector, general cargo, 29 dead out of 60.
Rinda, general cargo, 13 dead out of 31.
Glenhead, cargo coal, 27 dead out of 36.
Taberg, in ballast, 15 dead out of 21.
Yselhaven, in ballast, 24 dead out of 34.

Merchant Seamen killed – 652 out of 3609,
a fatal casualty rate of 18 percent.

Between 18 March 1941 and 6 June 1941, nine U-boats had been sunk
with the loss of 143 out of a total complement of 243.

During the periods when I had been borne on ships' articles,
from 3 September 1939 to 6 June 1941, a total of 537 ships had been sunk,
against a total of 41 U-Boats sunk.

HADLEIGH - 18 MARCH 1941 TO 4 SEPTEMBER 1941

GERMAN U-BOATS	SHIPS SUNK IN PERIOD					ENEMY U-BOAT LOSSES			
NUMBER	TOTALS C/F B/F	TOTAL	18/03/41 06/05/41	07/05/41 06/06/41		DETAILS OF LOSS DATE	CAUSE	DEAD	SAVED
U-38		9	2	7		U-47 07/03/41	D/C	45	0
U-43		1		1		U-65 28/04/41	D/C	50	0
U-46		5	4	1		U-70 07/03/41	D/C	20	25
U-47						U-76 05/04/41	D/C	1	40
U-48		9	5	4		U-99 17/03/41	D/C	3	40
U-52		1	1			U-100 17/03/41	RAM	38	6
U-65		0				U-110 09/05/41	D/C	15	32
U-69		3	1	2		U-147 02/06/41	D/C	26	0
U-73		5	5			U-551 23/03/41	D/C	45	0
U-74		1	1						
U-75		2	1	1					
U-76		1	1						
U-93		2		2					
U-94		7	2	5					
U-95		1	1						
U-96		4	3	1					
U-97		4	3	1					
U-98		5	3	2					
U-99		0							
U-100		0							
U-101		1		1					
U-103		9	3	6					
U-105		11	6	5					
U-106		3		3					
U-107		13	6	7					
U-108		4	1	3					
U-109		1		1					
U-110		2		2					
U-111		2		2					
U-123		1	1						
U-124		6	6						
U-138		1		1					
U-147		1		1					
U-201		1		1					
U-512		1	1						
U-551									
U-552		2	2						
U-553		0							
U-556		5		5					
U-557		1		1					
	537 412	125	59	66		TOTALS	9	243	143
						B/F	32	866	377
HEAVY SHIPS	15 15	0				C/F	41	1,109	520
RAIDERS	12 9	3		3					
LIGHT WARSHIPS	4 4	0							
AIRCRAFT	39 21	18	13	5					
ITALIAN SUBMARINES	22 14	8	2	6					
OTHER CAUSES	5 3	2	2						
	97 66	31	20	11					

UPON THEIR LAWFUL OCCASIONS

HADLEIGH - 18 MARCH 1941 TO 4 SEPTEMBER 1941

RECORD OF MERCHANT SHIPS SUNK IN ATLANTIC - 06/05/41 TO 06/06/41

HADLEIGH - ON PASSAGE FROM NEW YORK TO HALIFAX - 11/05/41 TO 15/05/41

DATE	SHIP	NAT.	CONVOY NO.	CAUSE OF LOSS	POSITION		CARGO	CASUALTIES CREW	DEAD
06/05/41	OAKDENE	BRITISH	OG59	U-105	06-19 N.	27-55 W.	COAL	35	0
06/05/41	SURAT	BRITISH		U-103	08-23 N.	15-17 W.	GENERAL	37	3
07/05/41	EASTERN STAR	NOR.	OB318	U-94	61-29 N.	22-40 W.	GENERAL	37	0
07/05/41	FERNLANE	BRITISH		TAZZOLI	10-02 N.	20-17 W.	GENERAL	35	0
07/05/41	IXION	BRITISH	OB318	U-94	61-29 N.	22-40 W.	GENERAL	105	0
08/05/41	RAMILLES	BRITISH	OB317	U-97	48-05 N.	32.26 W.	COKE	41	29
09/05/41	ALFRED OLSEN	NOR.		TAZZOLI	02-59 N.	20-26 W.	BALLAST	34	0
09/05/41	BENGORE HEAD	BRITISH	OB318	U-110	60-28 N.	32-40 W.	COAL	41	1
09/05/41	CITY OF WINCHESTER	BRITISH	OB313	U-103	08-20 N.	26-14 W.	GENERAL	97	6
09/05/41	ESMOND	BRITISH	OB318	U-110	60-28 N.	32-40 W.	BALLAST	50	0
09/05/41	GREGALIA	BRITISH	OB318	U-201	60-34 N.	32-37 W.	BALLAST	66	0
10/05/41	EMPIRE CARIBOU	BRITISH	OB318	U-556	59-28 N.	35-44 W.	CHALK	40	29
10/05/41	GAND	BELG.	OB318	U-556	57-54 N.	37-34 W.	BALLAST	44	1
11/05/41	SOMERSET	BRITISH		AIRCRAFT	54-54 N.	16-20 W.	GENERAL		
13/05/41	BENVRACKIE	BRITISH	OB312	U-105	00-49 N.	20-15 W.	GENERAL	60	13
13/05/41	SHROPSHIRE	BRITISH	SC30	U-98	56-43 N.	38-57 W.	ESCORT	278	0
13/05/41	SOMERSBY	BRITISH	SC30	U-111	60-39 N.	26-13 W.	GRAIN	43	0
14/05/41	KARLANDER	NOR.		AIRCRAFT	55-38 N.	13-38 W.	BALLAST	26	0
15/05/41	BENVENUE	BRITISH	OB314	U-105	04-27 N.	18-25 W.	GENERAL	58	2
16/05/41	MARISA	DUTCH		U-107	06-24 N.	18-34 W.	BALLAST	49	3
16/05/41	RODNEY STAR	BRITISH		U-105	05-03 N.	19-02 W.	GENERAL	83	0
17/05/41	STATESMAN	BRITISH		AIRCRAFT	56-44 N.	13-45 W.	GENERAL	51	1
18/05/41	PIAKO	BRITISH		U-107	07-52 N.	14-57 W.	GENERAL	73	10
19/05/41	EMPIRE RIDGE	BRITISH	HG61	U-96	55-18 N.	10-49 W.	IRON ORE	33	31
	HADLEIGH		**HX128**						
20/05/41	STARCROSS	BRITISH	SL73	OTARIO	51-45 N.	20-45 W.	GENERAL	40	40
20/05/41	RADAMES	EGYPT.		U-103	06-00 N.	12.00 W.		25	1
20/05/41	BRITISH SECURITY	BRITISH	HX126	U-556	57-28 N.	41-07 W.	BENZENE	53	53
20/05/41	COCKAPONSET	BRITISH	HX126	U-556	57-28 N.	41-07 W.	GENERAL	41	0
20/05/41	DARLINGTON COURT	BRITISH	HX126	U-556	57-28 N.	41-07 W.	WHEAT	37	25
20/05/41	HARPAGUS	BRITISH	HX126	U-109	56-47 N.	40-55 W.	GRAIN	50	32
20/05/41	JAVANESE PRINCE	BRITISH	OB322	U-138	59-55 N.	10-50 W.	BALLAST	60	6
20/05/41	JOHN P. PEDERSEN	NOR.	HX126	U-94			FUEL OIL	38	22
20/05/41	MARCONI	BRITISH	OB322	U-94	58-00 N.	41-00 W.	BALLAST	78	22
20/05/41	NORMAN MONARCH	BRITISH	HX126	U-94	56-41 N.	40-52 W.	WHEAT	48	26
20/05/41	ROTHERMERE	BRITISH	HX126	U-98	57-53 N.	41-39 W.	STEEL	56	22
20/05/41	STARCROSS	BRITISH	HX126	U-93	51-45 N.	20-45 W.	GENERAL	40	0
21/05/41	ELUSA	DUTCH	HX126	U-93	59-00 N.	38-05 W.	FUEL OIL	52	3
21/05/41	ROBIN MOOR	U.S.A.		U-69	06-15 N.	25-30 W.	GENERAL	46	0
21/05/41	TEWKESBURY	BRITISH		U-69	05-49 N.	24-09 W.	GENERAL	42	0
22/05/41	BARNBY	BRITISH	HX126	U-111	60-30 N.	34-12 W.	FLOUR	45	2
22/05/41	BRITISH GRENADIER	BRITISH		U-103	06-15 N.	12-59 W.	BALLAST	46	0
23/05/41	BERHALA	DUTCH	OB318	U-38	09-50 N.	07-10 W.	GENERAL	62	3
24/05/41	MARIONGA	GREEK		U-38	05-42 N.	10-29 W.	STORES	31	26
24/05/41	***HOOD* SUNK**								
24/05/41	VULCAIN	BRITISH		U-38	09-20 N.	15-35 W.	COAL	46	7
25/05/41	WANGI WANGI	DUTCH		U-103	05-24 N.	12-00 W.	GENERAL	93	1
26/05/41	COLONIAL	BRITISH		U-107	09-13 N.	15-09 W.	GENERAL	93	0
27/05/41	***BISMARCK* SUNK**								
28/05/41	PAPALEMOS	GREEK		U-107	08-06 N.	16-18 W.	CEREALS	29	2
29/05/41	EMPIRE STORM	BRITISH	HX128	U-557	55-00 N.	39-50 W.	FLOUR	43	3
29/05/41	TABARISTAN	BRITISH		U-38	06-32 N.	15-23 W.	GENERAL	60	21
30/05/41	CAIRNDALE	BRITISH		MARCONI	35-19 N.	8-33 W.	BALLAST	46	4
30/05/41	EMPIRE PROTECTOR	BRITISH		U-38	06-00 N.	14-25 W.	GENERAL	60	29
30/05/41	RINDA	NOR.		U-38	6-52 N.	15-14 W.	GENERAL	31	13
30/05/41	SILVERYEW	BRITISH		U-106	16-42 N.	25-29 W.	GENERAL	60	3
31/05/41	CLAN MacDOUGAL	BRITISH		U-106	16-50 N.	25-10 W.	GENERAL	85	2
31/05/41	GRAVELINES	BRITISH	HX127	U-147	56-00 N.	10.00 W.	LUMBER	36	11
31/05/41	SIRE	BRITISH		U-107	08-50 N.	15-30 W.	BALLAST	49	3
01/06/41	ALFRED JONES	BRITISH		U-107	08-00 N.	15-00 W.	GENERAL	35	2
01/06/41	PRINCE RUPERT CITY	BRITISH		AIRCRAFT	58-47 N.	4-42 W.	BALLAST	49	4
01/06/41	SCOTTISH MONARCH	BRITISH		U-105	12-58 N.	27-20 W.	COAL	49	1
02/06/41	INVERSUIR	BRITISH	OB327	U-48	48-28 N.	28-20 W.	BALLAST	45	0
02/06/41	MICHAEL E.	BRITISH	OB327	U-108	48-50 N.	29-00 W,	BALLAST	51	4
03/06/41	EIBERGEN	DUTCH	OB327	U-75	48-02 N.	25-06 W.	BALLAST	39	4
04/06/41	TRECARRELL	BRITISH	OB327	U-101	47-10 N.	31-04 W.	BALLAST	43	4
04/06/41	WELLFIELD	BRITISH	OB328	U-48	48-34 N.	31-34 W.	BALLAST	41	8
06/06/41	BARON LOVAT	BRITISH	OG63	MARCONI	35-30 N.	11-30 W.	COKE	35	0
06/06/41	GLEN HEAD	BRITISH	OG63	AIRCRAFT	35-40 N.	10-30 W.	COAL	36	27
06/06/42	SACRAMENTO VALLEY	BRITISH	OB324	U-106	17-10 N.	30-10 W.	COAL	49	3
06/06/41	TABERG	SWED.	OG63	MARCONI	35-36 N.	11-12 W.	BALLAST	21	15
06/06/41	TREGARTHEN	BRITISH	OB329	U-48	46-17 N.	36-20 W.	COAL	45	45
06/06/41	YSELHAVEN	DUTCH	OB328	U-43	49-25 N.	40-54 W.	BALLAST	34	24
							TOTALS	**3,609**	**652**

The Ministry of War Transport had established compulsory six-month periods on articles for Merchant Seamen. Although on some ships the usual custom of signing on and off articles continued, *Hadleigh* did not pay off and sign on when we arrived in Newcastle. Hence, I am unable to establish from my records the dates when we arrived at and left Newcastle. By reference to other events, the date of arrival would have been 9 June 1941, and the date of departure 24 June 1941.

CONVOY OB314A

We made passage northbound by North Sea convoy to Methil, and through the Pentland Firth, and Minches to Loch Ewe. We joined convoy OB341A of 42 ships, which sailed from Liverpool on 2 July 1941. *Hadleigh* joined the convoy in the North Channel. The convoy arrived at Halifax on 18 July 1941, and thence we proceeded independently to Philadelphia. The ships were not attacked when in convoy, but two British ships were sunk on 9 July after dispersal: *Designer*, with the loss of 26 of her crew of 77, and *Inverness*, with the loss of 6 of her crew of 41. Both ships were sunk by U-98.

During the period when *Hadleigh* was discharging in Newcastle, and on passage to the U.S.A., thirteen Atlantic convoys were attacked: OB323, OB324, OB328, OB329, OB330, OB336, OB337, OB341, SL75, SL76, SL78, HX133 and OG67, the heaviest casualties being six ships in HX133, four in SL78 and three each in SL76 and OB336. The casualties in seamen killed were substantial.

After a relatively uneventful Atlantic passage, *Hadleigh* arrived in the U.S.A. on 20 July 1941, where we loaded the usual composite cargo of steel products in the lower holds, and general war materials, equipment and vehicles in the upper hold space, 'tween decks, and as deck cargo. We remained in the port of Philadelphia for about three weeks.

Casualties – Ships and Personnel
7 June 1941 to 17 July 1941

Ships sunk – 50 by 24 Successful U-Boats.
Italian submarines sank six ships.
Aircraft sank five ships.
One ship was lost due to unknown cause.

Lost with all hands

Trevarrack in ballast, 45 dead.
Silverpalm, general cargo, 68 dead.
Christian Krogh, in ballast, 23 dead.
Eirini Kyriakidou, cargo iron ore, 31 dead.
Arakaka, meteorological ship, 46 dead.
Anna Bulgari, in ballast, 37 dead.
Nicolas Pateras, in ballast, 30 dead.
Schie, in ballast, 35 dead.
Ellinico, in ballast, 35 dead.
Kalypso Vergoti, general cargo, 37 dead.
Toronto City, meteorological ship, 35 dead.
Robert L. Holt, in ballast, 49 dead.

Lost with very heavy casualties

Baron Carnegie, in ballast, 25 dead out of 39.
Chinese Prince, general cargo, 45 dead out of 63.
Empire Dew, in ballast, 23 dead out of 41.
Djurdjura, cargo iron ore, 33 dead out of 38.
Cathrine, cargo iron ore, 23 dead out of 27.
Vigrid, general cargo, 26 dead out of 47.
Malaya II, general cargo, 39 dead out of 45.
River Lugar, cargo iron ore, 41 dead out of 47.
PLM22, cargo iron ore, 32 dead out of 43.
Auris, cargo fuel oil, 32 dead out of 59.
Pluto, cargo grain, 12 dead out of 30.
Grayburn, cargo scrap metal, 35 dead out of 53.
Hekla, in ballast, 14 dead out of 20.
Rio Azul, cargo iron ore, 33 dead out of 42.
St. Anselm, cargo pig iron, 34 dead out of 67.
Malvernian, passengers, 107 dead out of 164.
Anselm, troopship, 254 dead out of 1,308.
Designer, general cargo, 26 dead out of 77.

Merchant seamen killed – 985 out of 2,451,
a fatal casualty rate of 40 percent. Killed in troop
and passenger ships – 361 out of 1,472.

THE WAR AT SEA: HADLEIGH

HADLEIGH - 18 MARCH 1941 TO 4 SEPTEMBER 1941

RECORD OF MERCHANT SHIPS SUNK IN ATLANTIC - 07/06/41 TO 17/07/41

HADLEIGH - BERTHED AT NEWCASTLE - 09/06/41 TO 24/06/41

DATE	SHIP	NAT.	CONVOY NO.	CAUSE OF LOSS	POSITION		CARGO	CASUALTIES CREW	DEAD
07/06/41	BARON NAIRN	BRITISH	OB328	U-108	47-36 N.	39-02 W.	BALLAST	40	1
07/06/41	KINGSTON HILL	BRITISH		U-38	09-35 N.	29-40 W.	COAL	46	14
08/06/41	ADDA	BRITISH	OB323	U-107	08-30 N.	14-39 W.	GENERAL	417	9
08/06/41	DIRPHYS	GREEK		U-108	47-44 N.	39-02 W.	COAL	25	6
08/06/41	ELMDENE	BRITISH	OB324	U-103	08-47 N.	16-37 W.	COAL	36	0
08/06/41	TREVARRACK	BRITISH	OB329	U-46	48-46 N.	29-14 W.	BALLAST	45	45
08/06/41	PENDRECHT	DUTCH	OB329	U-48	45-18 N.	36-40 W.	BALLAST	36	0
09/06/41	PHIDIAS	BRITISH	OB330	U-46	48-25 N.	26-12 W.	GENERAL	51	8
09/06/41	SILVERPALM	BRITISH		U-101	51-00 N.	26-00 W.	GENERAL	68	68
09/06/41	DAGMAR	BRITISH		AIRCRAFT	50-35 N.	01-48 W.	COAL	18	3
09/06/41	DIANA	BRITISH		AIRCRAFT			FISH	28	1
09/06/41	FENIX	FINN.		AIRCRAFT	61-56 N.	12-14 W.	GENERAL	25	2
09/06/41	MERCIER	BELG.		U-204	48-30 N.	41-30 W.	GENERAL	68	7
10/06/41	AINDERBY	BRITISH		U-552	55-30 N.	12-10 W.	IRON ORE	40	12
10/06/41	CHRISTIAN KROGH	NOR.		U-108	47-00 N.	42-20 W.	BALLAST	23	23
11/06/41	BARON CARNEGIE	BRITISH		AIRCRAFT	52-03 N.	05-25 W.	BALLAST	39	25
11/06/41	HAVTOR	NOR.		U-79	63-35 N.	28-05 W.	BALLAST	20	6
12/06/41	CHINESE PRINCE	BRITISH		U-552	56-12 N.	14-18 W.	GENERAL	63	45
12/06/41	EMPIRE DEW	BRITISH		U-48	51-09 N.	30-16 W.	BALLAST	41	23
12/06/41	RANELLA	NOR.		U-553			BALLAST	29	0
12/06/41	TRESILLIAN	BRITISH	OB330	U-77	44-40 N.	45-30 W.	BALLAST	44	0
13/06/41	DJURDJURA	BRITISH		BRIN	38-53 N.	23-11 W.	IRON ORE	38	33
13/06/41	EIRINI KYRIAKIDOU	GREEK	SL75	BRIN	38-53 N.	23-11 W.	IRON ORE	31	31
13/06/41	PANDIAS	GREEK		U-107	07-49 N.	23-28 W.	COAL	34	11
17/06/41	CATHRINE	BRITISH	SL76	U-43	49-30 N.	16-00 W.	ORE	27	23
18/06/41	NORFOLK	BRITISH		U-552	57-17 N.	11-14 W.	GENERAL	71	1
20/06/41	GANDA	PORT.		U-123	34-00 N.	11-40 W.	GENERAL	66	5
21/06/41	CRITON	BRITISH			06-06 N.	13-40 W.	IRON ORE	34	10
22/06/41	CALABRIA	SWED.	SL75	U-141			GENERAL	24	3
22/06/41	ARAKAKA	BRITISH		U-77	47-00 N.	40-00 W.	MET. SHIP	46	46
24/06/41	BROCKLEY HILL	BRITISH	HX133	U-651	56-13 N.	37-31 W.	GRAIN	42	0
24/06/41	ANNA BULGARI	GREEK		U-77	55-00 N.	48-00 W.	BALLAST	37	37
24/06/41	SOLOY	NOR.	HX133	U-203	54-39 N.	39-31 W.	WHEAT	29	0
24/06/41	NICOLAS PATERAS	GREEK	OB336	U-108	55-00 N.	38-00 W.	BALLAST	30	30
24/06/41	VIGRID	NOR.	HX133	U-371	54-30 N.	41-30 W.	GENERAL	47	26
24/06/41	KINROSS	BRITISH	OB336	U-203	55-23 N.	38-49 W.	BALLAST	37	0
24/06/41	SCHIE	DUTCH	OB336	U-203	55-23 N.	38-49 W.	BALLAST	35	35
25/06/41	ELLINICO	GREEK		U-108	55-00 N.	38-00 W.	BALLAST	35	35
26/06/41	MAASDAM	DUTCH	HX133	U-564	60-00 N.	30-35 W.	GENERAL	79	2
26/06/41	MALAYA II	BRITISH	HX133	U-564	59-56 N.	30-35 W.	GENERAL	45	39
26/06/41	RIVER LUGAR	BRITISH	SL78	U-69	24-00 N.	21-00 W.	IRON ORE	47	41
27/06/41	EMPIRE ABILITY	BRITISH	SL78	U-69	23-50 N.	21-10 W.	GENERAL	114	2
27/06/41	OBERON	DUTCH	SL78	U-123	25-43 N.	22-47 W.	GENERAL	34	6
27/06/41	P.L.M. 22	FRENCH	SL78	U-123	25-43 N..	22-47 W.	IRON ORE	43	32
28/06/41	AURIS	BRITISH		DA VINCI	34-27 N.	11-57 W.	FUEL OIL	59	32
28/06/41	PLUTO	FINNISH		U-146	59-39 N.	08-20 W.	GRAIN	30	12
29/06/41	G.J. GOULANDRIS	GREEK	SL76	U-66	29-05 N.	25-10 W.	SUGAR	28	0
29/06/41	KALYPSO VERGOTTI	GREEK	SL76	U-66	29-00 N.	25-00 W.	GENERAL	37	37
29/06/41	GRAYBURN	BRITISH	HX133	U-651	59-30 N.	18-07 W.	SCRAP	53	35
29/06/41	HEKLA	DANISH		U-564	59-15 N.	34-05 W.	BALLAST	20	14
29/06/41	RIO AZUL	BRITISH	SL 76	U-123	29-00 N.	25-00 W.	IRON ORE	42	33
	HADLEIGH		OB341						
30/06/41	ST. ANSELM	BRITISH		U-66	31-00 N.	26-00 W.	PIG IRON	67	34
01/07/41	TORONTO CITY	BRITISH		U-108	47-03 N.	30-00 W.	MET. SHIP	35	35
04/07/41	ROBERT L. HOLT	BRITISH	OB337	U-69	34-15 N.	20-00 W.	TROOPS	49	49
01/07/41	MALVERNIAN	BRITISH		AIRCRAFT	47-37 N.	19-07 W.	PASS.	164	107
04/07/41	AUDITOR	BRITISH		U-123	25-47 N.	28-25 W.	GENERAL	71	1
05/07/41	ANSELM	BRITISH		U-96	44-25 N.	28-35 W.	TROOPS	1,308	254
09/07/41	DESIGNER	BRITISH	OB341	U-98	42-59 N.	31-40 W.	GENERAL	77	26
09/07/41	INVERNESS	BRITISH	OB341	U-98	42-46 N.	32-45 W.	GENERAL	42	6
14/07/41	RUPERT DE LARRINAGA	BRITISH	OG67	MOROSINI	36-18 N.	21-11 W.	COAL	43	0
15/07/41	LADY SOMERS	BRITISH		MOROSINI	37-12 N.	20-32 W.		175	0
17/07/41	GUELMA	BRITISH		MALASPINA	30-44 N.	17-33 W.	GENERAL	41	0
						TOTALS		3,923	1,346

199

CONVOY HX145

Hadleigh put to sea from Philadelphia in the first week of August 1941, and made passage to Halifax, where we joined convoy HX145 of 83 ships, which left Halifax on 16 August. The HX convoys were then experiencing a respite from attack, eighteen convoys having passed through the submarine cordons without loss to ships in convoy. The Freetown to Liverpool SL convoys had been suffering massive losses well to the south of the route of the SC and HX convoys, SL 81 losing 5 ships out of 18 and SL87 suffering the disastrous loss of 7 ships out of 11. In convoy SL81, the British ships *Belgravian, Cape Rodney, Harlingen, Kumasian,* and *Swiftpool* were lost. The greatest death toll was in *Swiftpool,* sunk by U-372, with the loss of 42 officers and men. Once again, the lethal cargo was iron ore. Three U-boats combined in the attacks, U-74, U-75 and U-372. SL87 lost seven British ships, *Dixcove, Edward Blyden, John Holt, Lafian, Niceto de Larrinaga, Silverbelle* and *St. Clair II,* to U-67, U-68, U-103 and U-107. Fortunately, the fatal casualties in these seven ships were restricted to 18 officers and men. This was because they were carrying cargoes that gave their crews a chance of getting away from the ships in time.

However, outward bound convoy OS4 suffered enormous fatal casualties. U-557 and U-558 accounted for the British ships *Tremoda* (32 dead), *Sangor* (59 dead), *Embassage* (39 dead), *Otaio* (26 dead), and the Norwegian *Segundo* (7 dead).

Almost all the ships were sunk in convoy: Gibraltar convoys OG67 (one ship), OG69 (seven ships), OG71 (eight ships); convoy OS1 (three ships) and convoy OS4 (six ships). Sierra Leone convoy SL81 lost six ships.

The most tragic casualties occurred when the Yeoward Line ship *Aguila* was sunk by U-201, with the loss of 89 passengers out of 91. Many of the passengers were W.R.N.S. personnel on passage to Gibraltar. The survivors from *Aldergrove* and *Aguila* were rescued by the small ocean-going tug, *Empire Oak,* which, was torpedoed with the loss of 23 survivors and crew. Later in the war, I served with a survivor of convoy OG71, who gave me a graphic account of the catastrophic events.

Despite the large number of ships in convoy HX145, the Atlantic crossing was free from enemy attacks, and the main body of the convoy made port in Liverpool on 31 August 1941. *Hadleigh* and the ships destined for the east coast ports dispersed in the North Channel, and made passage through the Minches and Pentland Firth. We berthed in West Hartlepool, where the ship paid off on 4 September 1941.

The compulsory six-month period on articles had terminated, and I was due for leave. Also, my badly smashed left arm, which had never received professional medical attention, was giving a great deal of pain, and I had almost lost the use of the hand; so medical attention was necessary.

The marine superintendent boarded the ship in West Hartlepool, with the news that the great Lord Glanely would visit the ship several days later. The Master was instructed to prepare the ship for the visit. The deck hands had paid off, so the Master and officers who were remaining with the ship were expected to wash and clean the ship for the visitor. The marine superintendent had the audacity to ask me if I would stand by the ship for a few days to assist the others. Although I had paid off, my compensation would have been several days accommodation and food, and what he termed the "honour" of being introduced to the First Baron Glanely of St. Fagans! I told the bugger to hire a gang of riggers to do the work, or better still, to don a pair of sea boots, and join the work party. That was the last I saw – or wanted to see – of the dreadful marine superintendent.

My last memory of *Hadleigh* was the Master, First and Second Mates, and several engineers in dungarees and sea boots, washing the ship down fore and aft. The Tatem line possessed a fleet of fine, well-found ships, manned by good men, but spoiled by the rule of niggardly and oppressive tyrants, devoid of any decent human attributes. I did not serve in another of the ships of the Tatem fleet.

Casualties – Ships and Personnel
18 July 1941 to 4 September 1941

Ships sunk – 34 by 18 successful U-Boats.
Italian submarines sank four ships.
Aircraft sank two ships
Raiders sank one ship

Lost with very heavy casualties

Holmside in ballast , 21 dead out of 37.
Horn Shell, in ballast, 17 dead out of 41.
Kellwyn, cargo coke, 14 dead out of 23.
Hawkinge, cargo coal, 15 dead out of 31.
Shahristan, general cargo, 65 dead out of 138.
Tunisia, cargo iron ore, 38 dead out of 43.
Swiftpool, cargo iron ore, 42 dead out of 44.
Empire Hurst, cargo iron ore, 28 dead out of 35.
Sessa, general cargo, 24 dead out of 27.

Aguila, general cargo and service personnel, 157 dead out of 167.
Alva, cargo coal, 16 dead out of 25.
Ciscar, general cargo, 16 dead out of 39.
Clonlara, cargo coal, 11 dead out of 19.
Empire Oak (Tug), 23 dead out of 37.
Inger, cargo coal, 9 dead out of 23.
Stork, cargo gasoline, 19 dead out of 22.
Embassage, general cargo, 39 dead out of 42.
Saugor, general cargo, 59 dead out of 82.
Tremoda, general cargo, 32 dead out of 53.
Fort Richepanse, general cargo, 41 dead out of 63.

Merchant seamen and Service personnel killed –
750 out of 1,824, a fatal casualty rate of 41 percent.

HADLEIGH - 18 MARCH 1941 TO 4 SEPTEMBER 1941

RECORD OF MERCHANT SHIPS SUNK IN ATLANTIC - 18/07/41 TO 04/09/41

HADLEIGH - BERTHED IN PHILADELPHIA - 18/07/41 TO 07/08/41

DATE	SHIP	NAT.	CONVOY NO.	CAUSE OF LOSS	POSITION		CARGO	CASUALTIES CREW	DEAD
19/07/41	HOLMSIDE	BRITISH	OG67	U-66	19-00 N.	21-30 W.	BALLAST	37	21
21/07/41	IDA KNUDSEN	NOR.		TORELLI	34-34-N.	13-14 W.	GASOLENE	37	5
24/07/41	MACON	BRITISH		BARBARIGO	32-48 N.	26-12 W.	GENERAL	62	2
26/07/41	BOTWEY	BRITISH	OS1	U-141	55-42 N.	09-53 W.	BALLAST	52	0
26/07/41	HORN SHELL	BRITISH		BARBARIGO	33-23 N.	22-18 W.	BALLAST	41	17
26/07/41	KELLWYN	BRITISH	OG69	U-79	43-00 N.	17-00 W.	COKE	23	14
27/07/41	HAWKINGE	BRITISH	OG69	U-203	44-55 N.	17-44 W.	COAL	31	15
28/07/41	INGA I	NOR.	OG69	U-126	43-10 N.	17-30 W.	COAL	19	3
28/07/41	ERATO	BRITISH	OG69	U-126	43-10 N.	17-30 W.	GENERAL	36	9
28/07/41	LAPLAND	BRITISH	OG69	U-203	40-26 N.	15-30 W.	GENERAL	25	0
28/07/41	NORITA	SWED.	OG69	U-203	40-10 N.	15-30 W.	GENERAL	20	2
28/07/41	WROTHAM	BRITISH	OG69	U-561	43-00 N.	17-00 W.	BALLAST	26	0
29/07/41	CHAUCER	BRITISH		A.M.C.	16-46 N.	38-01 W.	BALLAST	48	0
29/07/41	SHAHRISTAN	BRITISH	OS1	U-371	35-13 N.	23-57 W.	GENERAL	138	65
30/07/41	SITOEBONDO	DUTCH	OS1	U-371	35-19 N.	23-53 W.	GENERAL	83	19
04/08/41	ROBERTMAX	BRITISH		U-126	36-47 N.	21-15 W.	FISH	6	0
04/08/41	TUNISIA	BRITISH	SL81	AIRCRAFT	53-53 N.	18-10 W.	ORE	43	38
05/08/41	BELGRAVIAN	BRITISH	SL81	U-372	53-03 N.	15-54 W.	GENERAL	50	2
05/08/41	CAPE RODNEY	BRITISH	SL81	U-75	53-26 N.	15-40 W.	GENERAL	39	0
05/08/41	HARLINGEN	BRITISH	SL81	U-75	53-16 N.	15-40 W.	GENERAL	44	2
05/08/41	KUMASIAN	BRITISH	SL81	U-74	53-11 N.	15-38 W.	GENERAL	51	1
05/08/41	SWIFTPOOL	BRITISH	SL81	U-372	53-02 N.	15-58 W.	IRON ORE	44	42
11/08/41	EMPIRE HURST	BRITISH		AIRCRAFT	36-48 N.	09-50 W.	IRON ORE	35	26
14/08/41	SUD	YUGO.		U-126	41-00 N.	17-41 W.	BALLAST	33	0
	HADLEIGH		HX145						
17/08/41	SESSA (LONGTAKER)	PAN.		U-38	61-26 N.	30-50 W.	GENERAL	27	24
19/08/41	AGUILA	BRITISH	OG71	U-201	49-23 N.	17-56 W.	GENERAL	167	157
19/08/41	ALVA	BRITISH	OG71	U-559	48-48 N.	17-46 W.	COAL	25	16
19/08/41	CISCAR	BRITISH	OG71	U-201	49-10 N.	17-40 W.	GENERAL	39	16
19/08/41	SILDRA	NOR.		TAZZOLI	05-30 N.	12-50 W.	BALLAST	40	0
22/08/41	CLONLARA	BRITISH	OG71	U-564	40-43 N.	11-39 W.	COAL	19	11
22/08/41	EMPIRE OAK	BRITISH	OG71	U-564	40-43 N.	11-39 W.		37	23
23/08/41	ALDERGROVE	BRITISH	OG71	U-201	40-43 N.	11-39 W.	FUEL OIL	32	1
23/08/41	INGER	NOR.		U-143	58-58 N.	07-50 W.	COAL	23	9
23/08/41	SPIND	NOR.	OG71	U-564	40-43 N.	11-39 W.	COAL	25	0
23/08/41	STORK	BRITISH	OG71	U-201	40-43 N.	11-39 W.	GASOLENE	22	19
27/08/41	EMBASSAGE	BRITISH	OS4	U-557	54-00 N.	13-00 W.	GENERAL	42	39
27/08/41	SAUGOR	BRITISH	OS4	U-557	53-36 N.	16-40 W.	GENERAL	82	59
27/08/41	SEGUNDO	NOR.		U-557	53-36 N.	16-40 W.	BALLAST	34	7
27/08/41	TREMODA	BRITISH	OS4	U-557	53-42 N.	15-43 W.	GENERAL	53	32
28/08/41	OTAIO	BRITISH	OS4	U-558	52-16 N.	17-50 W.	GENERAL	71	13
03/09/41	FORT RICHEPANSE	BRITISH	OS4	U-567	52-15 N.	21-10 W.	GENERAL	63	41
							TOTALS	**1,824**	**750**

HADLEIGH - 18 MARCH 1941 TO 4 SEPTEMBER 1941

SHIP AND U-BOAT LOSSES - WHEN SERVING ON *HADLEIGH* - 07JUNE 1941 TO 04 SEPTEMBER 1941

GERMAN U-BOATS			SHIPS SUNK IN PERIOD			ENEMY U-BOAT LOSES			
NUMBER	TOTALS C/F	B/F	TOTAL	07/06/41 17/07/41	18/07/41 04/09/41	DATE	CAUSE	DEAD	SAVED
U-38			2	1	1	U-138 18/06/41	D/C	0	27
U-43			1	1		U-144 28/07/41	SUB	28	0
U-46			3	3		U-207 11/09/41	D/C	41	0
U-48			2	2		U-401 03/08/41	D/C	44	0
U-66			4	3	1	U-452 03/08/41	AIR	42	0
U-69			3	3		U-501 10/09/41	D/C	37	0
U-74			1		1	U-556 27/06/41	D/C	5	40
U-75			2		2	U-570 27/08/41	AIR	0	44
U-77			3	3		U-651 29/06/41	D/C	0	44
U-79			2	1	1				
U-96			1	1					
U-98			2	2					
U-101			1	1					
U-103			1	1					
U-107			2	2					
U-108			6	6					
U-123			5	5					
U-126			4		4				
U-141			2	1	1				
U-143			1		1				
U-146			1	1					
U-201			4		4				
U-203			6	3	3				
U-204			1	1					
U-371			3	1	2				
U-372			2		2				
U-552			3	3					
U-553			1	1					
U-557			4		4				
U-558			1		1				
U-559			1		1				
U-561			1		1				
U-564			6	3	3				
U-567			1		1				
U-651			1	1					

	C/F	B/F			
	621	537	84	50	34

		DEAD	SAVED
TOTALS	9	197	155
B/F	41	1,109	520
C/F	50	1,306	675

	C/F	B/F			
HEAVY SHIPS	15	15	0		
RAIDERS	13	12	1		1
LIGHT WARSHIPS	4	4	0		
AIRCRAFT	46	39	7	5	2
ITALIAN SUBMARINES	32	22	10	6	4
OTHER CAUSES	6	5	1	1	
	116	97	19	12	7

13

ON SHORE LEAVE FOR
MEDICAL TREATMENT

After paying off from *Hadleigh* I returned to Cardiff, arriving on 5 September 1941. I was accommodated in a spare bedroom in Betty's family home. She and I travelled to the resort of Weston-Super-Mare on the following day for a short holiday. We were engaged to be married, and set the date for the wedding for the spring of 1942. I was then suffering appreciable pain and loss of movement in my left arm and hand. This was aggravated when I strained the arm accidentally, when my left wrist failed with a resounding crack. When we returned from holiday, I visited the Shipping Federation medical office, where they arranged for X-ray examination in the Royal Hamadryad Hospital for Seamen. The Medical Superintendent, Doctor Longmore, identified the injury as a comminuted fracture of the arm, and severe damage to the carpal scaphoid bones in the wrist. His diagnosis was not encouraging. The fractures to the arm had occurred five and a half months earlier, and had not been set by a medical practitioner, so the lower arm and wrist were badly misshapen. He decided that they should attempt to rectify the damage under anaesthetic.

When I recovered consciousness, my left arm was encased in a heavy plaster, from the elbow to the base of the fingers. Unfortunately, the nurse or V.A.D. who applied the plaster did not shave the arm, so the hairs on the arm had been embedded in the wet plaster. This caused great irritation until the plaster had been removed.

Doctor Longmore could not give me a definite prognosis, except that I would be unfit for sea service for at least three months, ten weeks in plaster and two weeks of daily physiotherapy. However, he was optimistic that I would recover the use of the arm, with no lasting damage. His optimism was justified, because sixty years later the arm seems to be as strong as ever.

I had nothing to do during the following ten weeks, except to endeavour to alleviate the itching and discomfort caused by the trapped hairs of the arm in the plaster. I even resorted to inserting the blade of a carving knife between the plaster and the arm, and this helped. It was sheer bliss when the plaster was removed. I then attended for daily physiotherapy sessions at the hospital clinic in the charge of a blind physiotherapist, a Mr. Capel. His treatment worked wonders. The severe pain had been alleviated, and after several weeks of strengthening exercises, normal movements in the arm and wrist were restored.

It was strange to be within brick walls after the constrictions of a ship for an almost continuous period of over five years. I found it very difficult to sleep, without the sound of the engines, and the other familiar noises on board ship. In addition, when at sea during the war, we had slept "fully booted and spurred", ready for the sound of an explosion or of the alarm bells to summon us to the bridge or gun or boat stations. It was eerie. Despite the occasional air raid alarms, and the food rationing, my period ashore was a welcome return to civilisation, despite the financial vicissitudes.

I occupied myself with assisting Betty's mother to walk. She had developed into a veritable cripple since the onset of rheumatoid arthritis in 1939, and required assistance with most normal functions. She was altogether too heavy for Betty to cope with, and required daily exercise as a therapy. I endeavoured to instil in her the determination to walk down the aisle on the day of our wedding, unaided except for her walking stick. By increasing the distance and duration of exercise each day, we were well on the way towards achieving our objective.

Air raid warnings were always a problem. It was necessary to navigate Betty's mother from her chair to a seat under the stairs. Betty then lay on the floor under the table. I preferred to go outside on fire watching duty. There were no serious attacks on the city, but almost daily warnings, due to aircraft passing over the city en route to Liverpool, Belfast and Glasgow.

It was only a short walk from the house to the Shipping Office and the offices of the Navigators and Engineer Officers Union on Bute Street. Therefore, I was able to make frequent visits to renew acquaintances with previous shipmates and to receive news of events at sea, which were not publicised in the newspapers or over the radio. The massive volume of maritime losses showed no sign of diminishing, and reports from participants indicated no significant improvement in the protective measures, particularly aircraft cover. Apparently no lessons had been learned from the unrestricted U-Boat attacks of 1917 and 1918. Looking at the scenario with hindsight, it seemed incredible that both "Bomber Harris" and Winston Churchill conceived that they could continue with thousand bomber air raids on targets such as Cologne, when millions of gallons of oil fuel were being lost in conflagrations at sea.

Moreover, even with their limited intelligence, the dinosaurs in Whitehall should have realised that they would be confronted with a serious manpower problem because of an average fatal casualty rate of over 30 percent in the Merchant Navy. We knew from bitter experience that the only way to combat night surface attacks by U-Boats would be to keep them well away from convoys by day, preferably submerged. During our passages at sea, we received almost continuous reports of concentrations of U-Boats. "There are now twelve (or whatever) enemy submarines in your area". If a Lancaster bomber with a bomb load of ten tons had sufficient range to cover the round trip to Berlin or Dresden, the aircraft could be suitably modified for anti U-Boat long range surveillance operations. It did not happen in 1941 because of tunnel vision in Whitehall.

In April 1918, an Admiralty "think tank" had laid down certain rules.

The normal number of ships in any convoy to be 20 (26 maximum; any increase requiring special Admiralty approval).
Escort for a convoy of over 22 ships 8 destroyers.
Escort for a convoy of between 16-22 ships 7 destroyers.
Escort for a convoy of under 16 ships 6 destroyers.

In 1941 and 1942, a convoy of over 50 ships would be very fortunate to have an escort of two relatively old destroyers and two corvettes.

The immense value of aircraft for anti-U-Boat operations was perceived most clearly in 1917 and 1918, not so much for aggressive attacks, but to "keep their heads down". We knew the U-Boat tactics all too well. They would shadow the convoy at a safe distance, and concentrate their groups during the day. Our wireless operators would pick up their signals, and Admiralty direction finders could obtain positional cross bearings. Then, during the night the U-Boat groups would use their greater speed to take up position ahead of the convoy, where they would launch their high-speed surface attacks.

The prerequisite in all this was the necessity to keep the buggers well away from the convoys, preferably a hundred miles. This represented five hours for a destroyer at an economical speed of 20 knots, or 8 hours for a corvette at 12 knots; but only 20 minutes for an aircraft flying at 300 miles an hour.

Every time I visited the docks area, I received news of well-known ships sunk, and the loss of so many fine men and shipmates. The Bristol Channel Ports of Newport, Cardiff, Penarth, Barry and Swansea represented for us a close community, which existed in the years well before the war. We were like a family. It is difficult to dwell upon the tragic situation that existed without sustaining sentiments of great anger and frustration that such lack of forward planning appeared to have existed prior to the war, and so little had been done to rectify a perilous situation two years after the outbreak of hostilities.

I had received no compensation payments for my injuries, so my pay on signing off from *Hadleigh* had to be conserved. We were therefore on a tight budget, which allowed one excursion to the cinema each week, and a weekly visit to the dance hall in town. We usually walked on these excursions, to conserve funds.

The arm in plaster and a sling provided an unexpected bonus. Most commodities were either rationed or in short supply, including sweets and chocolates. A request to the assistant in a confectionery shop usually resulted in the response, "Sorry, sir, no sweets or chocolates". Unashamedly, I invoked the principle of "all's fair in love and war", being well qualified in both elements, namely we were at war and I was madly in love. If I showed my injured arm conspicuously, the usual reaction of the shop assistant was "A box of Kunzle you wanted, was it, sir? I think I have just one left".

The catastrophic attack on the American fleet at Pearl Harbour on 7 December 1941, had brought the U.S.A. into the war. Those of us who had close contacts with the American people knew the huge potential and resources of the country, the fierce patriotism of its people, and their industrious resolve. We had been alone for over a year, but now we knew that the tide had begun to turn, and victory would be achieved.

I was deemed fit for duty at sea by 10 December 1941, and was ordered to report to the Merchant Navy Officers Reserve Pool offices. Although I had hoped for a berth as Second Mate after over a year as Third Mate, including six months as a certificated officer, I was allocated the berth of Third Mate of *Barrwhin*. I packed my bags, made my farewells, and boarded the 0055 train in the early morning of 14 December 1941, destination Newcastle-upon-Tyne. After the customary seven changes en route, the train reached its destination at 1300 on 15 December 1941. There were changes at Crewe, Stockport, Stalybridge, Leeds, York, Northallerton and Darlington. As usual, the carriages and corridors were crammed with standing, seated, and prostrate service personnel, and were permeated with the smell of urine and ordure from the overworked and filthy toilets.

The conditions on the train to the north had not changed, except that the discomfort, smell, and perpetual noise seemed to be worse. It was over twelve hours of purgatory. Leaving the carriage to visit the stinking toilets usually took a half an hour, stumbling over prostrate passengers in the corridors, kit bags, steel helmets, gas masks, rifles and accoutrements. Then there was the rush for the doors at each of the seven changes, when the whole process of trying to find a few square inches of space in more overcrowded compartments, had to be repeated. If there was time, there may have been a cup of tea on the railway station platform. Incredibly, the trains ran closely to their timetables, despite everything.

Those of us entitled to first class rail vouchers fared slightly better, because we were able to alternate between standing between the seats, sitting, and lying for short periods in the luggage racks. Despite the inconvenience, the atmosphere was always friendly and helpful between travellers, regardless of rank.

14

THE WAR AT SEA:
BARRWHIN

15 DECEMBER 1941–
8 SEPTEMBER 1942

PREPARING FOR CONVOY TO MURMANSK

I met the Master of *Barrwhin* at the Shipping Office in the early after-noon of 15 December 1941, signed on, and boarded the ship. *Barrwhin* was in most respects very similar to the vessels in which I had served previously, *Appledore*, *Filleigh* and *Hadleigh*. A general trader of a type constructed in great numbers between 1925 and 1935. *Barrwhin* was built in 1929 for the Barr Crombie Line of Glasgow, 2,970 nett registered tonnage, 4,998 gross registered tonnage, and a designed cargo capacity of 9,100 tons. Her specifications were a length of 421 feet, beam of 55 feet 9 inches, and a designed speed of 10.5 knots. Registered in Glasgow, number 161890, she was a flush decked vessel with a raised forecastle head and five main holds, powered by coal fired boilers and reciprocating steam engine, with power boosted by a Bauer-Wach exhaust turbine. When the exhaust turbine was connected, she was capable of a speed of over 12 knots. Sir William Reardon Smith & Sons Ltd managed the ship on behalf of the Ministry of War Transport.

The ship was berthed at South Shields, where she was undergoing extensive modifications, preparatory for service on the convoy route to North Russia. This included extra heating and insulation, strengthening of the forepeak with concrete to withstand the pressure of ice, the construc-tion of additional accommodation in No. 4 and No. 5 'tween decks for the additional D.E.M.S. gunners, installation of an additional 3" dual purpose gun, Oerlikon and Marlin machine guns, and a "Pillar Box" on the stern

S.S. Barrwhin, built in 1929, 4998 gross registered tonnage
Torpedoed and sunk by U-436 on 29 October 1942, in convoy HX212 – 24 men lost
(*Photograph by A. Duncan, Cowes, I.O.W.*)

docking bridge. This carried sixteen high explosive armed rockets in four banks of four, which could be fired eight at a time. Launchers for "Snowflake" illumination rockets were fitted on each side of the navigating bridge, and radio telephone equipment was installed in the chart room.

The modification work took very much longer than should have been the case, having regard to the urgency and importance of the work. This was due to the quite astonishing indifference, and lack of any vestige of patriotism displayed by many of the ship repair workers. It was not unusual to find them loafing in secluded and sheltered parts of the ship, malingering, working to rule, playing cards in obscure corners, or sleeping when they should have been working. As a result, progress was very slow. When I encountered a party of workmen playing cards while sitting in coils of mooring rope, smoking, and drinking bottles of beer; it so infuriated me that I confronted them, in an attempt to shame them into some semblance of responsibility or contrition for what they were doing. The response was, "We hope that the f——— war goes on for ever". When they were reminded that good men were dying in their thousands, while they were enjoying their huge pay packets, and the safety of their reserved occupations, with the benefits of their homes and families, while slacking in their work, the answer was "Let the poor bastards die if they want to". It did no good to report them to supervisory authority, because they appeared to be indifferent. The situation was tolerated.

Later in the war in New York, the work of constructing more accommodation in the after 'tween decks was completed by American workmen within 24 hours. Similar work undertaken by Tyneside workmen took six weeks. When I reflected on the huge losses sustained by our Western Ocean convoys, and the sacrifices of the R.A.F. and other armed forces, it made me sick to my guts. Perhaps the men I encountered were exceptions. I hope that was the case.

After completion of the modification work, we loaded a mixed cargo of ammunition, case oil, crated Hurricane fighter planes and a number of Valentine tanks, stowed in No. 2 hold where they could be unloaded by ships' gear by our jumbo derrick.

My fellow officers were the Master, Captain T.S. Dixon, M.M., the First Mate, Ron Shilstone, and the Second Mate, Cecil Sanders, plus two apprentices. Captain Dixon had been awarded the Military Medal for gallantry during the 1914-1918 war, when he left his career at sea to join the army after learning that his brother had been killed in action on the Western Front. Ron Shilstone was a most amusing character, a native of Babbacombe. Cecil Sanders had served his term of apprenticeship in ships in the Far East, and had qualified for his certificates of competency in India, known as "curry and rice tickets". Those of us who had qualified in the United Kingdom tended to denigrate the curry and rice qualifications. Cecil Sanders had returned from the Far East only recently, and had never stood a watch in a convoy. In addition, because he had not experienced enemy action, he did not take the precautions, which had become second nature to us. He slept in his pyjamas in his bunk, and shut the door of his cabin. He was a very heavy sleeper, probably lulled by his lack of experience of the realities of enemy attack.

He usually relieved me on watch up to a half an hour late, and then only after I had sent the stand by man to his cabin several times to wake him. He would arrive on the bridge, usually rubbing the sleep from his eyes, and I had to wait a further ten minutes for him to acclimatise himself. I did not give him full marks as a shipmate. Captain Dixon was a fine Master in every respect, and Ron Shilstone was an officer of great ability. *Barrwhin* was a very happy and efficient ship, despite my personal problems with the timekeeping of the Second Mate.

The crew were furnished with the special clothing necessary for service in Arctic waters, consisting of two of each long john underpants and matching long sleeved vests, thick knee length stockings, a thick pullover, a fleece lined leather jerkin, a balaclava, a fleece lined duffel coat with hood and face mask, and woollen and fleece lined gloves. I never wore the underwear, preferring more conventional vest and short pants, followed by two pairs of serge trousers. The fleece lined leather knee boots were the most important articles of cold weather clothing. We were also given tins of whale oil and were told how to apply the oil to our limbs. Most of us never bothered with the whale oil. There were also comprehensive instructions on the precautions to be taken to identify and treat frostbite. In particular I recall the passage "When urinating, carefully shield the penis with the hand".

We put to sea from South Shields in the last week of January 1942, after six weeks spent in modification work and cargo loading, and joined a northbound North Sea convoy. We stopped at Methil, where the officers had a short course of training in the use of the twin Marlin machine guns that were fitted on each wing of the bridge.

Our instructor was a typical R.N. Chief Petty Officer gunner, with the usual patter associated with the rank. "Now this 'ere is a bleedin' Marlin point three inch twin machine gun. The ammo belt carries 120 rounds of tracer and ball bullets. It was used by the Yanks in their aircraft in the 1914-1918 war." He followed this with the instructions for loading and firing the weapon. "You pushes the tongue of the ammo belt through the breech, gives it a tug, and pulls back on the bleedin' cockin' 'andles." Then came the priceless instructions. "The aircraft is coming at you, thowin' a lot of shit your way. It's 'im or you, see. You pulls the triggers and nothin' 'appens, and you says to yourself, Christ Almighty, the f——— stroiker's broken. Then you bleedin' well ducks." On 29 January 1942, the day after my 21st birthday, I was duly qualified in the firing, cleaning and oiling of a Marlin machine gun in the D.E.M.S. Training Centre in Leith.

Barrwhin made passage through the Pentland Firth and Minches to the convoy assembly anchorage in Loch Ewe, where convoy PQ11 assembled and put to sea on 6 February 1942, for Kirkwall in the Shetland Islands, where the ships lay at anchor for a week.

Casualties – Ships and Personnel
15 December 1941 to 6 February 1942

Ships sunk – 55 by 23 successful U-Boats.

Lost with all hands

Culebra general cargo, 45 dead.
D.G. Thermiotis, general cargo, 33 dead.
Caledonian Monarch, cargo wheat, 41 dead.
Alexandra Hoegh, cargo crude oil, 28 dead.
Traveller, general cargo, 26 dead.
Tacoma Star, general cargo, 85 dead.
Major Wheeler, cargo unknown, 35 dead.

Lost with very heavy casualties

Annavore, cargo pyrites, 34 dead out of 38.
Cardita, cargo gasoline, 27 dead out of 60.
Cyclops, general cargo, 87 dead out of 182.
Frisco, cargo lumber, 13 dead out of 16.
Yngaren, general cargo, 38 dead out of 40.
Friar Rock, general cargo, 25 dead out of 37.
Chepo, general cargo, 17 dead out of 38.
Dayrose, in ballast, 38 dead out of 42.
Empire Surf, in ballast, 47 dead out of 53.
Coimbra, cargo crude oil, 36 dead out of 46.
Diala, in ballast, 57 dead out of 65.
Nyholt, in ballast, 20 dead out of 40.
Allan Jackson, cargo crude oil, 22 dead out of 35.
City of Atlanta, general cargo, 44 dead out of 47.
Lady Hawkins, passengers, 252 dead out of 322.
William Hansen, cargo unknown, 10 dead out of 19.
Gandia, cargo potash, 66 dead out of 79.
Inneroy, cargo gasoline, 31 dead out of 36.
V.A. Polemis, in ballast, 21 dead out of 33.
Empire Gem, cargo gasoline, 49 dead out of 51.
Ringstad, cargo china clay, 30 dead out of 43.
San Arcadio, cargo gas oil, 41 dead out of 50.
W.L. Steed, cargo oil, 34 dead out of 38.
Amerikaland, cargo unknown, 29 dead out of 40.
Montrolite, cargo crude oil, 28 dead out of 48.
India Arrow, cargo oil, 26 dead out of 38.
Opawa, general cargo, 56 dead out of 71.

Merchant seamen killed – 1,399 out of 2,468, a fatal casualty rate of nearly 57 percent. Passengers killed – 163 out of 212.

UPON THEIR LAWFUL OCCASIONS

BARRWHIN - 15 DECEMBER 1941 TO 8 SEPTEMBER 1942

RECORD OF MERCHANT SHIPS SUNK IN ATLANTIC - 15/12/41 TO 06/02/42

BARRWHIN - SIGNED ARTICLES AT NEWCASTLE 15.12.41 - BERTHED AT SOUTH SHIELDS

DATE	SHIP	NAT.	CONVOY NO.	CAUSE OF LOSS	POSITION		CARGO	CASUALTIES CREW	DEAD
15/12/41	EMPIRE BARRACUDA	BRITISH	HG76	U-77	35-30 N.	06-17 W.	GENERAL	52	13
19/12/41	RUCKINGE	BRITISH	HG76	U-108	38-15 N.	17-16 W.	GENERAL	41	2
21/12/41	ANNAVORE	NOR.	HG76	U-567	43-55 N.	19-50 W.	PYRITES	38	34
21/12/41	HELEN	NOR.		U-573	35-31 N.	05-10 W.	BALLAST	41	0
31/12/41	CARDITA	BRITISH	HX166	U-87	59-18 N.	12-50 W.	GASOLENE	60	27
11/01/42	CYCLOPS	BRITISH		U-123	41-51 N.	63-48 W.	GENERAL	182	87
12/01/42	FRISCO	NOR.		U-130	45-50 N.	60-20 W.	LUMBER	16	13
12/01/42	YNGAREN	SWED.	HX168	U-43	57-00 N.	26-00 W.	GENERAL	40	38
13/01/42	FRIAR ROCK	PAN.		U-130	45-30 N.	50-40 W.	GENERAL	37	25
14/01/42	CHEPO	PAN.	ON55	U-43	58-30 N.	19-40 W.	GENERAL	38	17
14/01/42	DAYROSE	BRITISH		U-552	46-32 N.	53-00 W.	BALLAST	42	38
14/01/42	EMPIRE SURF	BRITISH	ON55	U-43	58-41 N.	19-16 W.	BALLAST	53	47
14/01/02	NORNESS	PAN.		U-123	40-28 N.	70-50 W.	FUEL OIL	41	1
15/01/42	COIMBRA	BRITISH		U-123	40-25 N.	72-21 W.	CRUDE OIL	46	36
15/01/42	DIALA	BRITISH	ON52	U-553	44-50 N.	46-50 W.	BALLAST	65	57
17/01/42	NYHOLT	NOR.	ON52	U-87	45-46 N.	54-18 W.	BALLAST	40	20
17/01/42	CULEBRA	BRITISH	ON53	U-123	40-00 N.	50-00 W.	GENERAL	45	45
18/01/42	D. G. THERMIOTIS	GREEK	SC63	U-86	47-30 N.	52-20 W.	GENERAL	33	33
18/01/42	CALEDONIAN MONARCH	BRITISH	SC63	U-333	57-00 N.	26-00 W.	WHEAT	41	41
18/01/42	ALLAN JACKSON	U.S.A.		U-66	35-00 N.	74-22 W.	CRUDE OIL	35	22
19/01/42	CILTVAIRA	LATV.		U-123	35-25 N.	75-23 W.	PAPER	31	2
19/01/42	CITY OF ATLANTA	U.S.A.		U-123	35-42 N.	75-21 W.	GENERAL	47	44
19/01/42	LADY HAWKINS	BRITISH		U-66	35-00 N.	72-30 W.	GENERAL	322	252
20/01/42	MARO	GREEK	ON55	U-43	40-00 N.	50-00 W.			
21/01/42	ALEXANDRA HOEGH	NOR.		U-130	40-54 N.	66-03 W.	CRUDE OIL	28	28
21/01/42	WILLIAM HANSEN	NOR.		U-754	46-56 N.	52-47 W.		19	10
22/01/42	ATHELCROWN	BRITISH	ON56	U-82	45-06 N.	40-56 W.	BALLAST	50	4
22/01/42	GANDIA	BELG.	ON54	U-135	45-00 N.	41-00 W.	POTASH	79	66
22/01/42	INNEROY	NOR.		U-553	41-16 N.	60-32 W.	GASOLENE	36	31
22/01/42	V.A. POLEMIS	GREEK	ON53	U-333	42-32 N.	52-38 W.	BALLAST	33	21
23/01/42	LEIESTEN	NOR.	ON56	U-82	45-27 N.	43-19 W.	BALLAST	29	6
23/01/42	THIRLBY	BRITISH	SC66	U-109	43-20 N.	66-15 W.	MAIZE	45	3
24/01/42	EMPIRE GEM	BRITISH		U-66	35-06 N.	74-58 W.	GASOLENE	51	49
24/01/42	EMPIRE WILDEBEESTE	BRITISH	ON53	U-106	39-30 N.	59-54 W.	BALLAST	31	9
24/01/42	RINGSTAD	NOR.	ON55	U-335	45-50 N.	51-04 W.	CHINA CLAY	43	30
25/01/42	MOUNT KITHERON	GREEK		U-754	47-32 N.	52-31 W.	COAL	36	12
25/01/42	VARANGER	NOR.		U-130	38-58 N.	74-06 W.		38	0
26/01/42	ICARION	GREEK		U-754	46-02 N.	52-22 W.	BALLAST	29	9
26/01/42	PAN NORWAY	NOR.		U-123	35-56 N.	50-27 W.	BALLAST	41	0
26/01/42	REFAST	BRITISH	ON56	U-582	42-41 N.	53-02 W.	BALLAST	43	10
26/01/42	TRAVELLER	BRITISH		U-106	39-30 N.	64-20 W.	GENERAL	26	26
27/01/42	FRANCIS E. POWELL	U.S.A.		U-130	31-45 N.	74-53 W.		32	4
30/01/42	ROCHESTER	U.S.A.		U-106	37-10 N.	73-58 W.		33	3
31/01/42	SAN ARCADIO	BRITISH		U-107	38-10 N.	63-50 W.	GAS OIL	50	41
01/02/42	TACOMA STAR	BRITISH		U-109	37-33 N.	69-21 W.	GENERAL	85	85
02/02/42	W.L. STEED	U.S.A.		U-103	38-25 N.	73-00 W.	OIL	38	34
03/02/42	AMERIKALAND	SWED.		U-106	36-36 N.	74-10 W.		40	29
04/02/42	MONTROLITE	BRITISH		U-109	35-14 N.	60-15 W.	CRUDE OIL	48	28
04/02/42	SAN GIL	PAN.		U-103	38-05 N.	74-40 W.	OIL	42	2
04/02/42	SILVERAY	BRITISH	SL99	U-751	43-54 N.	64-16 W.	GENERAL	58	8
05/02/42	CHINA ARROW	U.S.A.		U-103	37-44 N.	73-18 W.	OIL	37	0
05/02/42	HALCYON	PAN.		U-109	34-20 N.	59-16 W.	BALLAST	30	3
05/02/42	INDIA ARROW	U.S.A.		U-103	38-48 N.	59-16 W.	OIL	38	26
06/02/42	OPAWA	BRITISH		U-106	38-21 N.	61-13 W.	GENERAL	71	56
06/02/42	MAJOR WHEELER	U.S.A.		U-107				35	35
							TOTALS	**2,680**	**1,562**

From 15 December 1941 to 6 February 1942, eleven convoys with 320 ships were attacked. Their losses were: HG76 (four ships), HX166, HX168 ON54, SC66 and SL99 (one ship each), ON52 (two ships), ON53 (three ships), ON55 (four ships), ON56 (three ships), SC63 (two ships). The most successful U-Boats were: U-123 (seven ships), U-108 (six ships),

U-106 and U-130 (five ships each) and U-43, U-103 and U-109 (four ships each). A total of 23 ships were sunk in convoy and 32 when dispersed or on independent passage, mainly near the American coasts, West Indies, and in the Caribbean Sea. The American ships on the coastal routes began to suffer severely. The ships were unprepared for war. It was a slaughter.

CONVOY PQ11

The ships of convoy PQ11 put to sea from Kirkwall on Saturday 14 February 1942. The previous day had been Friday the 13th, and I well recall that a number of crew, including Captain Dixon, had been loath to put to sea on that unlucky day. Perhaps the convoy commodore shared such superstitions, because the orders indicated that we were scheduled to sail on the previous day. We left Kirkwall accompanied by a modest escort, and were joined by our ocean escort at Hvalfjord, an anchorage on the east coast of Iceland. The escort consisted of two destroyers, *H.M.S. Airedale* and *Middleton*, minesweepers *H.M.S. Niger* and *Hussar*, trawlers *H.M.S. Blackfly, Cape Arcona* and *Cape Mariato*, and the corvette *H.M.S. Oxslip*. When compared with the escorts that had accompanied Atlantic convoys of over 50 ships, this was a large escort for a convoy of 13 ships. We were indeed travelling first class.

The convoy consisted of eight British ships, two Russian, and one of each American, Honduran and Panamanian. The Americans owned substantial fleets of merchant ships under flags of convenience, so it is likely that all three ships under Panamanian flags were American owned. Our convoy escorts were relieved on passage by the minesweepers *H.M.S. Salamander, Harrier* and *Hazard* and the Russian destroyers *Gromki* and *Grozni*. It is likely that our original escort joined homeward bound convoy QP7, which crossed PQ11 on passage.

The convoy was not attacked by the enemy, and arrived at the mouth of Kola Inlet on 22 February 1942. The weather on passage was indescribable, with fierce gales, high seas, almost constant blizzards, and low visibility. The relatively shallow waters in the Arctic area kicked up short steep seas in the constant gales, rather like the North Sea, but infinitely worse. The heavily laden ships were taking green water aboard fore and aft, and the bridges and upper works were constantly drenched with huge volumes of spray. This froze immediately on everything, including those on watch who were cowering behind frail canvas dodgers on the open bridges. It was sheer hell, standing a watch under such conditions, in ambient temperatures of up to 30 degrees below freezing, with the strong winds doubling the wind chill factor.

The masts, rigging, derricks, deck cargo, and bulkheads became massively covered with thick ice, which had to be cut away with steam lances. Conditions were even worse for the smaller warships, which suffered icing to the point when stability would have been jeopardised. After being relieved from watch keeping duty, it took fully a half an hour to chip the coating of ice from duffel coats in order to release their fastening toggles, while suffering agony as the circulation slowly returned. The accommodation became rank from the smell of melting ice and wet clothing. This was all aggravated by the almost constant darkness of the northern latitudes. In the unlikely event of clear weather, a fitful sun occasionally rose on the southern horizon at about 1100, and set at 1300.

Murmansk – a frozen hell!

A Russian pilot boarded the ship at the entrance to Kola Inlet. We learned from him that the enemy had established an air base in Petsamo in Finland, about 40 miles from Murmansk. As we arrived off Murmansk, an air raid was in progress. A small number of JU87 and JU88 aircraft were bombing the harbour facilities and town. I had been detailed by the Master as gunnery officer, a duty usually allocated to the Second Mate. However, the Second Mate had received no training in fire control, so I had the duty. We closed up the guns' crews manning the three-inch and Oerlikons, and cleared away the bridge twin Marlin machine guns. We fired a few rounds of high explosive projectiles. The attack was short-lived, and by the time we anchored the aircraft had returned to base. By then, the short period of daylight was over, and we were again in darkness. *Barrwhin* remained at anchor for several days until a berth was vacant alongside the damaged Fish Factory wharf. The date was 25 February 1942.

The Russians treated us abominably. All they wanted was the equipment and supplies we were carrying. They showed us no friendship or gratitude. They took great pains to obliterate any markings that might show that aircraft, tanks or supplies had not come from Russian manufacturing sources. Markings, instruction plates, and other data in English were removed as soon as the equipment, tanks or aircraft were landed, and were replaced by marks, instructions and labels in Russian. There was no discrimination between the sexes in the military personnel or stevedores. Everywhere, the invasive and oppressive influence of the political commissars was apparent.

Their treatment of their own people was callous and indifferent. In the sub-zero temperature, derrick rigging, particularly guy ropes, became so brittle that they tended to part under stress. On one occasion, the jumbo derrick guy rope parted while a 16-ton Valentine tank was suspended from the derrick. The swinging load took charge, and pinned a workman against the bulwark close to No. 2 hatch, causing appalling injuries. The commissar, believing that the workman had caused the mishap, commenced hitting the poor dying wretch with a club, until the First Mate and I restrained him. Then he showed no interest in the man, while he examined the small dent in the tank. We had the man carried to our sick room, but he was beyond help, and died of his injuries.

When we arrived, I attempted to carry out my customary duty of going ashore to read the draft markings fore and aft; but was prevented by a female soldier pushing a bayonet under my nose, accompanied by the words "niet, niet," and words in Russian probably translated as "bugger off aboard". I reported to the First Mate that a bayonet had almost transfixed me, whereupon he protested to the translator and commissar. He was told that his officers could read the draught marking by hanging over the bows and counter. When he heard this, Ron Shilstone was furious. His reaction was "I'll settle the Bolshie sods". He instructed the duty engineer to turn the steam off deck.

This attracted an immediate reaction from the commissars, who were confronted by the First Mate with the words "when you buggers let my officers go ashore to read the bloody draft marks, we will start discharging your f—— cargo". We had no more trouble of that sort from then on. The buggers would have been put against the wall and shot, if the discharge of the cargo had been delayed by our lack of co-operation, as the result of their intransigence.

Then we had a visit from a Russian naval officer, who had seen our guns' crews closed up for action when we were arriving. He demanded to know who had given us authority to man our weapons when in Russian territory. He was told clearly that we would defend our ship against enemy attack, certainly when under way. He demanded the immediate removal of the strikers from all our weapons with the exception of the two twin Marlin machine guns on the bridge wings. These we would be allowed to fire, if we sustained a direct close level attack on our ship. The reason he gave was that we could do damage to Russian property, or hazard lives, when firing our heavier weapons.

The strikers were retained in Russian custody until we had discharged and anchored in Kola Inlet prior to return. The Russians were morose, unfriendly and thoroughly uncooperative. On reflection, they led a miserable existence within a regime in which human beings did not matter, living in squalid conditions in appalling weather.

During our passage from Loch Ewe and Kirkwall in convoy PQ11, between 7 February and 15 February 1942, the situation in the North Atlantic had shown no sign of improvement. Seven convoys with 209 ships, had been attacked with major losses: ON60 (two ships), ON62 (two ships), ON63 (two ships), ON66, SC67 and HX174 (one ship each), ON67 (nine ships). Incredibly, the majority of ships lost were elements in the outward bound convoys, sixteen outward bound and two homeward bound.

The main pattern of attacks occurred in the area around Bermuda and the West Indies, where there were a large number of ships on independent passage in ballast. Casualties to crews of ships remained well above the usual 30 percent. The total of British ships sunk was 24, and 23 from other flags.

The total of U-Boats which were sunk in the period between 15 December 1941 and 25 February 1942 was 23, 11 by depth charge attack, one by gunfire (probably after depth charge attack), three by ramming (probably after depth charge attack), three in collision with their own forces, two by our submarines and three by air attack. This was an encouraging improvement in the effectiveness of our counter measures, particularly in convoy protection by surface ships.

Only three U-Boats were destroyed by air attack, U-206 by a Whitley bomber on patrol over the Bay of Biscay, U-577 by a Swordfish in the Mediterranean, and U-451 by a Swordfish in the Straits of Gibraltar. The fact that a Whitley on anti U-Boat patrol intercepted and sank U-206 proves that our heavy bombers had the capability. It was tragic that so few were deployed.

The disturbing element was the high proportion of ships on independent passage in ballast that were lost with all hands. This leads me to the conclusion that U-Boats were surfacing when no escorts were present, and were firing upon ships before, and when the crews were abandoning ship. To an experienced officer there can be no other conclusion.

Casualties – Ships and Personnel
7 February 1942 to 25 February 1942

Ships sunk – 47 by 23 successful U-Boats.
Three ships sunk by Italian submarines.

Lost with all hands

Tolosa, cargo unknown, 22 dead.
Victolite in ballast, 47 dead.
Biela, general cargo, 49 dead.
Empire Spring in ballast, 53 dead.
Ramapo, cargo unknown, 30 dead.
Somme, general cargo, 48 dead.
Empire Komet, general cargo, 46 dead.
Nordvangen, cargo unknown, 37 dead.
Azalea City, cargo unknown, 38 dead.
Torungen, cargo fuel oil, 19 dead.
Empire O'Hail, in ballast, 49 dead.
Andara, in ballast, 62 dead.
White Crest, cargo coal, 41 dead.
Cabedelo, cargo unknown, 35 dead.

Lost with very heavy casualties

Ocean Venture, general cargo, 31 dead out of 45.
Blink, cargo phosphates, 24 dead out of 30.
Merpi, in ballast, 26 dead out of 40.
Oranjestad, cargo fuel oil, 15 dead out of 25.
Tia Juana, cargo crude oil, 17 dead out of 26.
Pan Massachusetts, cargo gasoline, 22 dead out of 40.
J.N. Pew, cargo gasolens, 33 dead out of 36.
Kongsgaard, cargo crude oil, 38 dead out of 46.
Adellen, in ballast, 36 dead out of 48.
George L. Torian, cargo bauxite, 26 dead out of 30.
Kars, cargo gasoline, 46 dead out of 47.
Sama, cargo china clay, 20 dead out of 38.
W.D. Anderson, cargo crude oil, 34 dead out of 36.
Finnanger, in ballast, 39 dead out of 53.
La Carriere, in ballast, 15 dead out of 41.

Merchant seamen killed – 1,065 out of 2,126,
a fatal casualty rate of 50 percent.

BARRWHIN - 15 DECEMBER 1941 TO 8 SEPTEMBER 1942

RECORD OF MERCHANT SHIPS SUNK IN ATLANTIC - 07/02/42 TO 25/02/42

BARRWHIN - ON PASSAGE FROM SOUTH SHIELDS TO LOCH EWE AND KIRKWALL

DATE	SHIP	NAT.	CONVOY NO.	CAUSE OF LOSS	POSITION		CARGO	CASUALTIES CREW	DEAD
07/02/42	EMPIRE SUN	BRITISH		U-751	44-08 N.	64-17 W.	GRAIN	65	11
08/02/42	OCEAN VENTURE	BRITISH		U-108	37-05 N.	74-46 W.	GENERAL	45	31
09/02/42	TOLOSA	NOR.		U-108	34-40 N.	73-50 W.		22	22
09/02/42	EMPIRE FUSILIER	BRITISH	ON60	U-85	44-45 N.	47-25 W.	BALLAST	47	9
10/02/42	VICTOLITE	BRITISH		U-564	36-12 N.	67-14 W.	BALLAST	47	47
11/02/42	BLINK	NOR.		U-108	35-00 N.	72-27 W.	PHOSPHATE	30	24
11/02/42	HEINA	NOR.	SC67	U-591	56-10 N.	21-07 W.	GENERAL	30	0
	BARRWHIN		PQ11						
14/02/42	BIELA	BRITISH	ON62	U-98	42-55 N.	45-40 W.	GENERAL	49	49
14/02/42	EMPIRE SPRING	BRITISH	ON63	U-576	42-00 N.	55-00 W.	BALLAST	53	53
15/02/42	BUARQUE	BRAZ.		U-432	36-35 N.	75-20 W.	GENERAL	85	2
15/02/42	MEROPI	GREEK		U-566	44-14 N.	62-41 W.	BALLAST	40	26
16/02/42	MONAGAS	VEN.		U-502	12-03 N.	70-25 W.	FUEL OIL	31	5
16/02/42	RAMAPO	PAN.		U-108	35-10 N.	65-50 W.		30	30
16/02/42	ORANJESTAD	BRITISH		U-156	12-25 N.	69-55 W.	FUEL OIL	25	15
16/02/42	SAN NICOLAS	BRITISH		U-502			CRUDE OIL	26	7
16/02/42	TIA JUANA	BRITISH		U-502			CRUDE OIL	26	17
16/02/42	SOMME	BRITISH	ON62	U-108	40-00 N	55-00 W.	GENERAL	48	48
18/02/42	OLINDA	BRAZ.		U-432	37-30 N.	75-00 W.	BEANS	47	0
19/02/42	EMPIRE SEAL	BRITISH		U-96	43-14 N.	64-45 W.	STEEL	57	1
19/02/42	PAN MASACHUSETTS	U.S.A.		U-128	28-27 N.	80-08 W.	GASOLENE	40	22
19/02/42	EMPIRE COMET	BRITISH	HX174	U-136	58-15 N.	17-10 W.	GENERAL	46	46
20/02/42	NORDVANGEN	NOR.		U-129	10-50 N.	60-54 W		37	37
20/02/42	DELPLATA	U.S.A.		U-156	14-55 N.	62-10 W.	GENERAL	52	0
20/02/42	SCOTTISH STAR	BRITISH	ON63	TORELLI	13-24 N.	49-36 W.	GENERAL	73	4
21/02/42	AZALEA CITY	U.S.A.		U-432	38-00 N.	78-00 W.		38	38
21/02/42	CIRCE SHELL	BRITISH	ON60	U-161	10-59 N.	62-05 W.	BALLAST	58	1
21/02/42	J.N. PEW	U.S.A.		U-67	12-40 N.	74-00 W.	GASOLENE	36	33
21/02/42	KONGSGAARD	NOR.		U-67	OFF CURACAO		CRUDE OIL	46	38
22/02/42	TORUNGEN	NOR.		U-96	44-00 N.	63-30 W.	FUEL OIL	19	19
22/02/42	ADELLEN	BRITISH	ON67	U-155	49-21 N.	38-15 W.	BALLAST	48	36
22/02/42	CITIES SERVICE EMPIRE	U.S.A.		U-128	28-25 N.	80-02 W.	FUEL OIL	50	12
22/02/42	GEORGE L. TORIAN	BRITISH		U-129	09-13 N.	59-04 W.	BAUXITE	30	26
22/02/42	KARS	BRITISH	ON67	U-96	44-15 N.	63-25 W.	GASOLENE	47	46
22/02/42	REPUBLIC	U.S.A.		U-504	27-05 N.	80-15 W.	OIL	34	5
22/02/42	SAMA	NOR.	ON67	U-155	49-30 N.	38-30 W.	CHINA CLAY	38	20
22/02/42	W.D. ANDERSON	U.S.A.		U-504	27-09 N.	80-15 W.	CRUDE OIL	36	34
22/02/42	EMPIRE HAIL	BRITISH	ON66	U-94	44-48 N.	40-21 W.	BALLAST	49	49
23/02/42	LENNOX	BRITISH		U-129	09-15 N.	58-30 W.	BAUXITE	20	2
23/02/42	LIHUE	U.S.A.		U-161	14-30 N.	64-45 W.	BALLAST	45	0
23/02/42	THALIA	PAN.		U-129	13-00 N.	70-45 W.	BALLAST	41	1
23/02/42	WEST ZEDA	U.S.A.		U-129	09-13 N.	59-04 W.	GENERAL	35	0
24/02/42	EIDANGER	NOR.	ON67	U-158	44-12 N.	43-25 W.	BALLAST	39	0
24/02/42	FINNANGER	NOR.		U-558	44-12 N.	43-25 W.	BALLAST	53	39
24/02/42	EMPIRE CELT	BRITISH	ON67	U-558	43-50 N.	43-38 W.	BALLAST	53	6
24/02/42	INVERARDER	BRITISH	ON67	U-558	44-34 N.	42-37 W.	BALLAST	42	0
24/02/42	LA CARRIERE	BRITISH		U-156	16-53 N.	67-05 W.	BALLAST	41	15
24/02/42	ANADARA	BRITISH	ON67	U-558	43-35 N.	42-15 W.	BALLAST	62	62
24/02/42	WHITE CREST	BRITISH	ON67	U-162	43-45 N.	42-15 W.	COAL	41	41
25/02/42	CABEDELO	BRAZ.		DA VINCI	16-00 N.	49-00 W.		35	35
25/02/42	ESSO COPENHAGEN	PAN.		TORELLI	10-04 N.	53-28 W.	FUEL OIL	39	1
							TOTALS	**2,126**	**1,065**

BARRWHIN - 15 DECEMBER 1941 TO 8 SEPTEMBER 1942

SHIP AND U-BOAT LOSSES - WHEN SERVING ON *BARRWHIN* - 15 DECEMBER 1941 TO 25 FEBRUARY 1942

GERMAN U-BOATS			SHIPS SUNK IN PERIOD			ENEMY U-BOAT LOSSES				
	TOTALS		TOTAL	15/12/41	07/02/42		DETAILS OF LOSS			
NUMBER	C/F	B/F		06/02/42	25/02/42		DATE	CAUSE	DEAD	SAVED
U-43			4	4		U-75	28/12/41	D/C	14	30
U-66			3	3		U-79	23/12/41	D/C	0	44
U-67			2		2	U-82	06/02/42	D/C	45	0
U-77			1	1		U-93	15/01/42	RAM	6	40
U-82			2	2		U-95	28/11/41	SUB	33	12
U-85			1		1	U-111	04/10/41	D/C	9	44
U-86			1	1		U-126	15/12/41	D/C	51	0
U-87			2	2		U-127	15/12/41	D/C	51	0
U-94			1		1	U-131	17/12/41	GUN	0	55
U-96			3		3	U-204	19/10/41	D/C	46	0
U-98			1		1	U-206	30/11/41	AIR	46	0
U-103			4	4		U-208	07/12/41	D/C	45	0
U-106			5	5		U-374	12/01/42	SUB	43	1
U-107			2	2		U-433	16/11/41	D/C	6	38
U-108			6	1	5	U-434	18/12/41	D/C	2	44
U-109			4	4		U-451	21/12/41	AIR	44	1
U-123			7	7		U-557	16/12/41	COLL	43	0
U-128			2		2	U-567	21/12/41	D/C	47	0
U-129			5		5	U-574	19/12/41	RAM	27	20
U-130			5	5		U-577	15/01/42	AIR	43	0
U-135			1	1		U-580	11/11/41	COLL	20	32
U-136			1		1	U-581	02/02/42	RAM	4	39
U-155			2		2	U-583	15/11/41	COLL.	45	0
U-156			3		3					
U-158			1		1					
U-161			2		2					
U-162			1		1					
U-333			2	2						
U-335			1	1						
U-432			3		3					
U-502			3		3					
U-504			2		2					
U-552			1	1						
U-553			2	2						
U-558			4		4					
U-564			1		1					
U-566			1		1					
U-567			1	1						
U-573			1	1						
U-576			1		1					
U-582			1	1						
U-591			1		1					
U-751			2	1	1					
U-754			3	3						

723	**621**	**102**	**55**	**47**	

HEAVY SHIPS	15	15	0		
RAIDERS	13	13	0		
LIGHT WARSHIPS	4	4	0		
AIRCRAFT	46	46	0		
ITALIAN SUBMARINES	35	32	3		3
OTHER CAUSES	6	6	0		
119	**116**	**3**	**0**	**3**	

TOTALS	23	670	400
B/F	50	1,306	675
C/F	73	1,976	1,075

We remained berthed at the Fish Factory wharf for about twenty relatively uneventful days. *Barrwhin* carried two apprentices, one a Scot, with rabid Scottish Nationalist tendencies. He was inflicted on me for signals duty and lookout. I cannot remember his name, but he became something of a nuisance, airing his anti-English sentiments. He soon shut up when I posted him permanently to the weather side of the bridge, to freeze. The other apprentice was a very small individual whose home was in North Wales, a diligent and competent boy. I learned many years later that he had distinguished himself in his profession, having served in command at sea, and having held supervisory posts ashore, until he retired. His name was Robert George Owen-Ffoulkes.

The Scottish apprentice was an ebullient, aggressive and quite irresponsible character, not only very fond of himself, but also of the female sex. Many of the Russian stevedores were females, who were barely discernible from the men, and then only by their higher pitched voices. They were something of a pest with their demands "Tommy, you got cigarettes". Our apprentice decided to obtain the favours of one of these Amazons, in exchange for a tin of fifty Players cigarettes; and was successful in inducing a "lady" to accede. The question was where to perform the amorous adventure in the freezing weather. The rendezvous for the act of unrequited love would be the warm secluded stokehold.

They both disappeared down the ladder to the stokehold; but shortly afterwards the amorous apprentice arrived on deck in a somewhat crestfallen state. His account of events was "She started to peel off the layers of clothing, sir, and as she did so, the stench of unwashed flesh became more obnoxious. Before I was completely overcome, I gave her the cigarettes to induce her to put her clothes on again". This was the end of the first and only potential Romeo and Juliet episode between a merchant seaman and a member of the opposite sex of our ally.

When alongside the Fish Factory discharging cargo, the ship parted her forward spring and breast rope, and stern rope, during a violent gale, which occurred suddenly when I was officer of the deck. The ship took charge, and gained momentum along the quayside, until the after breast rope and bow rope just took the strain, and partially arrested the forward movement. I rushed forward, and released both bower anchors, which stopped the ship. We then put out mooring ropes, and warped the ship back to its berth. Then, when we raised the anchors, we found that I had released them to fall through two small Russian fishing boats, which had moored ahead of us to discharge their fish. Fortunately, their crews had gone ashore. The companion ladder fell away from the quayside, when the ship broke loose, and was dragged along as the ship moved. Incredibly, the Russian female soldier on sentry duty followed the gangway all through this event, as if nothing had happened. She even tried to stop our seamen from going ashore to replace the mooring ropes. The Russians were impossible.

After we had completed discharge, the ship moved to an anchorage in Kola Inlet, where we remained until 21 March 1942. It was bitterly cold, with frequent sudden fierce winds, accompanied by heavy snow squalls. The Kola Inlet was free from heavy ice, but there were many small fragments of ice floating around the ship. Apart from the duty deck officer, we all played cards in the officers' mess.

One day, when the officers had completed lunch, a seaman burst into the mess telling us that a fireman had gone mad and jumped overboard. The Master ordered the Second Mate to launch the port jolly boat, and try to rescue the man. I was on deck making my rounds, and was on the after deck when I heard the commotion on the poop. When I arrived aft, I saw the man in the water near our port quarter, and immediately threw him a lifebuoy attached to a heaving line. The shock of immersion in the freezing water must have brought the man to his senses, because he held on to the life buoy, and was hauled aboard. Within five minutes, we had him stripped and wrapped in a blanket, in the officers' mess, with a huge measure of whisky aboard.

The jolly boat had been lowered and launched, and was being pulled under oars through the ice fragments, with the Second Mate shouting to the Master, "I can't find him sir. He must have drowned." The Master ordered him to return, and the jolly boat was hoisted and secured. By that time, the Second Mate was in almost a worst condition than the fireman who had jumped overboard. He and his boat crew were frozen to the marrow. The Master ordered that the fireman be locked away in a spare cabin in the No. 4 'tween deck accommodation, and I was entrusted with the key to the door.

The routine that we followed was for a steward to bring food to the fireman at meal times, when I would open the door, and wait while the food was eaten. At regular intervals during the day, I opened the door, escorted the prisoner to the toilet, and stood outside while he attended to his personal needs. The Master visited the cabin usually once a day. The fireman, who was a West African, started to protest to the Master that he was not a loony, and wanted to return to the forecastle. Notwithstanding his protestations of a return to sanity, he was kept locked in the cabin while we were at anchor, and after we put to sea.

The rest of the period when we lay at anchor was uneventful. The weather remained awful. During that time, the pattern of U-Boat attacks in the Atlantic changed dramatically. Only three ships were sunk in the three convoys that were attacked, one each in convoys ON66, OS19 and OS20. However, an astonishing number of 51 ships were sunk when on independent passage, the majority off the eastern seaboard of the U.S.A., the West Indies, and in the Caribbean Sea.

This was the beginning of what the U-Boat commanders termed their "Happy Time", when they had it their own way. Undoubtedly, one of the contributory factors to what proved to be a holocaust was the intransigent attitude of Admiral Ernest L. King, who was in command of the American Atlantic naval operations. It has been averred that he had a profound dislike of the British, and this may explain his attitude. He refused to set up a convoy system, to take heed of the advice of experienced Royal Navy officers, or to accept the offer of the small but necessary number of British escort units.

Undoubtedly, Admiral Ernest King faced a dilemma. After the treacherous attack on the American fleet at Pearl Harbour, Japan was seen as the main enemy; and the threat of the German U-Boats on the eastern seaboard as a sideshow. The resources available to Admiral King were limited at that early stage of their war, particularly long range aircraft. However, apparently to fail to heed the advice of British naval experience because of a petty antipathy was unworthy of a man of his ability. Many brave and dedicated American merchant seamen lost their lives in appalling circumstances as the result of his intransigence.

Most naval historians now seem to concur in opinion that the stubborn, even stupid intransigence of three individuals delayed the establishment of effective countermeasures to defeat the U-Boat peril. On the British side, we had Winston Churchill over-ruling every opinion contrary to his own, and Air Chief Marshall Arthur Harris steadfastly pursuing his obsession that Germany could be defeated by carpet-bombing. He was supported by Winston Churchill. Despite intelligence indicating the building of U-Boat pens in the French Biscay ports, these two leaders waited until the pens were protected by massive layers of concrete, before ordering bombing raids.

On the American side, Fleet Admiral Ernest L. King stood by while ships were being sunk and American seamen were killed in huge numbers, right under his nose. Incredibly, there was no blackout regime, either on American ships or on shore. The dinosaurs were not only confined to Whitehall, but Washington had its share of obdurate leaders.

The American crews suffered tremendously due to the quite astonishing lack of preparation for hostilities, which must have been seen as inevitable. Their ships were not armed or equipped, and their crews exercised no blackout control regimes. It was a tragic situation.

Casualties – Ships and Personnel
26 February 1942 to 20 March 1942

Ships sunk – 54 by 23 successful U-Boats.
Ten ships sunk by Italian submarines.
Two ships sunk by aircraft.

Lost with all hands

Carperby, cargo coal, 47 dead.
Mariana, cargo unknown, 36 dead.
Ingerto, cargo unknown, 31 dead.
Manaqui, general cargo, 35 dead.
Sarniadoc, in ballast, 19 dead,
Stangarth, general cargo, 45 dead.
Ranja, cargo fuel oil, 34 dead.
Mount Lycabettus, cargo bauxite, 30 dead.

Lost with very heavy casualties

R.P. Resor, cargo gasoline, 41 dead out of 43
Bayou, cargo unknown, 29 dead out of 30.
Leif, cargo cement, 18 dead out of 28.
Gunny, cargo iron ore, 14 dead out of 26.
Steel Age, cargo iron ore, 35 dead out of 36.
Sydhav, cargo crude oil, 12 dead out of 36.
Barbara, cargo unknown, 34 dead out of 88.
Cayrou, general cargo, 60 dead out of 92.
Tyr in ballast, 13 dead out of 31.
Gulftrade, cargo fuel oil, 19 dead out of 35.
Caribsea, cargo unknown, 23 dead out of 30.
John D. Gill, cargo crude oil, 23 dead out of 49.
Tolten, in ballast, 25 dead out of 27.
British Resource, cargo benzene, 46 dead out of 51.
Lemuel Burrows, general cargo, 20 dead out of 34.

Baron Newlands, cargo iron ore, 18 dead out of 38.
San Demetrio, cargo gasoline, 19 dead out of 53.
Ceiba, general cargo, 44 dead out of 50.
W.E. Hutton, cargo fuel oil, 13 dead out of 36.

Merchant seamen killed – 909 out of 2,679,
a fatal casualty rate of 34 percent.

BARRWHIN - 15 DECEMBER 1941 TO 8 SEPTEMBER 1942

RECORD OF MERCHANT SHIPS SUNK IN ATLANTIC - 26/02/42 TO 20/03/42

BARRWHIN - BERTHED IN MURMANSK AND KOLA INLET - 25/02/42 TO 21/03/42

DATE	SHIP	NAT.	CONVOY NO.	CAUSE OF LOSS	POSITION		CARGO	CASUALTIES CREW	DEAD
27/02/42	R.P. RESOR	U.S.A.		U-578	40-06 N.	73.56 W.	GASOLENE	43	41
28/02/42	BAYOU	PAN.		U-129	08-08 N.	55-14 W.		30	29
28/02/42	EVERASMA	LATV.		DA VINCI	17-00 N.	48-00 W.		15	0
28/02/42	LEIF	NOR.		U-653	34-45 N.	69-20 W.	CEMENT	28	18
28/02/42	OREGON	U.S.A.		U-156	20-44 N.	67-52 W.	FUEL OIL	37	7
01/03/42	CARPERBY	BRITISH	ON66	U-558	39-57 N.	55-40 W.	COAL	47	47
02/03/42	GUNNY	NOR.		U-126	27-09 N.	66-33 W.	ORE	26	14
03/03/42	MARY	U.S.A.		U-129	08-25 N.	52.50 W.	GENERAL	34	1
05/03/42	BENMOHR	BRITISH		U-505	05-10 N.	13-15 W.	GENERAL	56	0
05/03/42	COLLAMER	U.S.A.		U-404	44-19 N.	63-09 W.	GENERAL	38	7
05/03/42	O.A. KNUDSEN	NOR.		U-128	26-17 N.	75-50 W.	GASOLENE	41	1
05/03/41	MARIANA	NOR.		U-126	22-14 N.	71-23 W.		36	36
06/03/42	ASTREA	DUTCH		TAZZOLI	29-12 N.	64-29 W.	GENERAL	27	0
06/03/42	MELPOMENE	BRITISH	OS19	FINZI	23-35 N.	62-39 W.	BALLAST	49	0
06/03/42	SKANE	SWED.		FINZI	22-50 N.	60-10 W.	GENERAL	36	0
06/03/42	STEEL AGE	U.S.A.		U-129	06-45 N.	53-15 W.	IRON ORE	36	35
06/03/42	SYDHAV	NOR.		U-505	04-47 N.	14-57 W.	CRUDE OIL	36	12
06/03/42	TONGSBERGFJORD	NOR.		TAZZOLI	31-22 N.	68-05 W.	GENERAL	33	1
07/03/42	ARABUTAN	BRAZ.		U-155	35-15 N.	73.55 W.	COAL	55	1
07/03/42	BARBARA	U.S.A.		U-126	20-10 N.	73-05 W.		88	34
07/03/42	CARDONIA	U.S.A.		U-126	19-53 N.	73-27 W.		38	1
07/03/42	UNIWALECO	BRITISH		U-161	13-25 N.	61-31 W.	FUEL OIL	51	18
08/03/42	BALUCHISTAN	BRITISH		U-68	04-13 N.	08-32 W.	GENERAL	71	3
08/03/42	CAYROU	BRAZ.		U-94	39-10 N.	72-02 W.	GENERAL	92	60
08/03/42	HENGIST	BRITISH		U-569	59-31 N.	10-15 W.	FISH	29	3
08/03/42	MONTEVIDEO	URUG.		TAZZOLI	29-13 N.	69-35 W.	GENERAL	49	14
09/03/42	HANSEAT	PAN.		U-126	20-25 N.	74-07 W.		38	0
09/03/42	LILY	GREEK		U-578	43-32 N.	54-14 W.	BALLAST	32	3
09/03/42	TYR	NOR.		U-96	43-40 N.	61-10 W.	BALLAST	31	13
10/03/42	CHARLES RACINE	NOR.		FINZI	23-10 N.	60-28 W.	BALLAST	41	0
10/03/42	GULFTRADE	U.S.A.		U-588	39-50 N.	73-52 W.	FUEL OIL	35	19
11/03/42	CARIBSEA	U.S.A.		U-158	34-40 N.	76-10 W.		30	23
11/03/42	HVOSLEF	NOR.		U-94	38-27 N.	74-54 W.	SUGAR	20	6
12/03/42	CYGNET	PAN.		TAZZOLI	24-05 N.	74-20 W.	BAUXITE	30	0
12/03/42	OLGA	U.S.A.		U-126	21-32 N.	76--24 W.	BALLAST	33	1
12/03/42	TEXAN	U.S.A.		U-126	21-34 N.	76-28 W.		56	9
12/03/42	INGERTO	NOR.		U-578	29-35 N.	66-30 W.		31	31
13/03/42	DAYTONIAN	BRITISH		TAZZOLI	26-33 N.	74-43 W.	GENERAL	59	1
13/03/42	JOHN D. GILL	U.S.A.		U-158	33-55 N.	77-37 W.	CRUDE OIL	49	23
13/03/42	TOLTEN	CHILIAN		U-404	40-10 N.	73-50 W.	BALLAST	27	25
13/03/42	TREPCA	YUGO.		U-332	37-00 N.	73-25 W.	BAUXITE	37	4
14/03/42	BRITISH RESOURCE	BRITISH		U-124	36-04 N.	65-48 W.	BENZINE	51	46
14/03/42	LEMUEL BURROWS	U.S.A.		U-404	39-21 N.	74-13 W.	GENERAL	34	20
14/03/42	PENELOPE	PAN.		U-67	15-00 N.	64-20 W.	CRUDE OIL	49	2
15/03/42	MANAQUI	BRITISH		U-504	17-00 N.	61-00 W.	GENERAL	35	35
15/03/42	ARIO	U.S.A.		U-158	34-37 N.	76-20 W.	BALLAST	36	8
15/03/42	SARNIADOC	BRITISH		U-161	15-45 N.	65-00 W.	BALLAST	19	19
15/03/42	ATHELQUEEN	BRITISH	OS20	TAZZOLI	26-50 N.	75-40 W.	BALLAST	49	3
15/03/42	DAGO	BRITISH		AIRCRAFT	39-19 N.	09-27 W.	GENERAL	37	0
16/03/42	AUSTRALIA	U.S.A.		U-332	35-07 N.	75-23 W.	FUEL OIL	40	4
16/03/42	BARON NEWLANDS	BRITISH		U-68	04-35 N.	08-32 W.	ORE	38	18
16/03/42	STANGARTH	BRITISH		U-504	22-00 N.	65-00 W.	GENERAL	45	45
16/03/42	OSCILLA	DUTCH		MOROSINI	19-15 N.	60-25 W.	BALLAST	54	4
17/03/42	ALLENDE	BRITISH		U-68	04-00 N.	07-44 W.	GENERAL	38	5
17/03/42	RANJA	NOR.		U-71	38-00 N.	65-20 W.	FUEL OIL	34	34
17/03/42	ILE DE BATZ	BRITISH		U-68	04-04 N.	08-04 W.	GENERAL	44	4
17/03/42	KASSANDRA LOULOUDI	GREEK		U-124	35-04 N.	75-25 W.	GENERAL	35	0
17/03/42	SAN DEMETRIO	BRITISH		U-404	37-02 N.	73-50 W.	GASOLENE	53	19
17/03/42	SCOTTISH PRINCE	BRITISH		U-68	04-10 N.	08-00 W.	GENERAL	38	1
17/03/42	MOUNT LYCABETTUS	GREEK		U-373	40-15 N.	61-00 W.	BAUXITE	30	30
17/03/42	CEIBA	HOND.		U-124	35-43 N.	73-49 W.	GENERAL	50	44
18/03/42	E.M. CLARK	U.S.A.		U-124	34-50 N.	75-35 W.	FUEL OIL	41	1
19/03/42	LIBERATOR	U.S.A.		U-332	35-05 N.	75-30 W.	FUEL OIL	35	5
19/03/42	PAPOOSE	U.S.A.		U-124	34-17 N.	76-39 W.	BALLAST	34	2
19/03/42	W.E. HUTTON	U.S.A.		U-124	34-25 N.	76-50 W.	FUEL OIL	36	13
20/03/42	OAKMAR	U.S.A.		U-71	36-27 N.	68-46 W.	GENERAL	36	6
20/03/42	RISOY	GREEK		AIRCRAFT	50-40 N.	05-01 W.	BALLAST	18	0
							TOTALS	**2,679**	**909**

The dramatic increase in fatal casualties on ships sailing independently strengthens even further the suspicion that not only the sinking of ships, but the destruction of life craft and seamen, was now part of the U-Boat strategy. A fatal casualty rate of between 30 and 50 percent was then the norm, and, incredibly, priority for aircraft was still devoted to strategic bombing. It was a quite unbelievable scenario.

CONVOY QP9

We cleared Kola Inlet on 21 March 1942, and assembled at sea in convoy QP9 of 18 ships, of which 11 were British, 4 Russian, and one each American, Honduran and Panamanian. Therefore, the homeward bound convoy included an additional three British and two Russian ships, added to the ships of convoy PQ11. The minesweepers *H.M.S. Speedwell, Gossamer, Harrier, Hussar, Niger* and the Russian destroyer *Gremaschi*, provided local escort. Convoy PQ13 of 19 ships had left Loch Ewe on 10 March 1942 and Reykjavik on 20 March 1942. We crossed convoy PQ13 en route. It was usual practice to exchange escorts about mid way. The destroyer *H.M.S. Offa* and the minesweepers, *H.M.S. Sharpshooter* and *Britomart* relieved our escorts. The cruiser *H.M.S. Nigeria* provided distant cover.

During our passage, my orders were to ensure the safe custody of the fireman locked in the 'tween deck accommodation. I would unlock the door when his food was brought to him, or when he attended to his personal needs; and would lock him in the accommodation when he was not attended. After several days, he convinced the Master that his sanity had returned, after the shock of being immersed in the icy waters. Captain Dixon gave orders that he be allowed to return to the forecastle crew accommodation. Shortly after his release, the First Mate received a message by Aldis lamp from the ship astern "Have you lost a man overboard?" which he entered in the signal log. Believing that they were having a joke, the First Mate replied, "Yes, but only one", which he also logged. When I relieved the First Mate, I read the signals and, after a search, the crazy fireman could not be found. I signalled the ship astern by Aldis lamp, to ask them about their previous message. The answer was to confirm that they had seen a man in the water; and assumed that he had jumped overboard or had fallen from one of the ships ahead of them in the column. In those conditions, there was no chance that we could have saved his life.

On the return passage, we encountered even worse gales and blizzards than on the outward passage, but otherwise the return voyage in convoy QP9 was relatively uneventful. An attack on the convoy was attempted by U-655 on 24 March 1942, but the U-Boat was sighted by *H.M.S. Sharpshooter*, and rammed and sunk with her complement of 45 officers and men. We felt no remorse about the event.

North of Iceland, the convoy dispersed, with some ships making rendezvous with westbound Atlantic convoys, and others proceeding independently to Reykjavik. During the night watch on the route along the west coast of Iceland, the visibility was very poor, with a strong wind and frequent heavy snow squalls. According to our instructions, certain coastal lights would be switched on for short intervals, to aid navigation. Therefore, I was expecting to encounter a coastal light with certain characteristics. During a short period of better visibility, I sighted a light on the port bow, and when abeam, altered course to port to make the next point of land. I believed that I had seen the light earlier than anticipated, but I attributed this to a strong favourable southerly coastal current. At about 2200, Captain Dixon arrived on the bridge.

We sighted a dark mass on the port bow, which appeared to be another heavy snow squall. Fortunately, Captain Dixon was not satisfied. I had missed a footnote on the instruction orders, which read "Mariners should not confuse shore lights for marine navigational purposes, with aircraft beacons". The beacons were provided for the aircraft ferry pilots flying from Canada to Iceland. We immediately altered course to starboard away from the land, and shortly afterwards sighted the loom of the correct light. This event was a lesson for me. Although Captain Dixon was a strict disciplinarian, he behaved with great tolerance on that occasion.

We arrived in Reykjavik on 3 April 1942; and after a day at anchor made rendezvous with an eastbound convoy, which dispersed in the North Channel. We paid off in West Hartlepool on 13 April 1942. During our passage from Murmansk to the U.K., 22 March 1942 to 13 April 1942, the pattern of U-Boat activity had not changed. Only four convoys were attacked, namely Halifax convoy HX181, which lost one ship, outward bound convoy ON80, which lost one ship, and two Murmansk convoys, PQ13, which lost seven out of nineteen ships, and QP10 which lost four out of fifteen ships. Aircraft accounted for six ships, U-Boats for five ships, and the German destroyer Z26 for one ship in the two Arctic convoys.

The following Arctic convoys PQ14, PQ15, PQ16 and PQ17 suffered grievous losses of 35 ships in total, of which 24 ships were sunk in convoy PQ17, out of its 39 ships. Convoy PQ18 also suffered very heavy losses, 13 out of 44 ships. During the period from late 1941 until mid 1945, 104 ships were sunk in Arctic convoys, 46 American, 37 British, 11 Russian, 8 Panamanian, 1 Norwegian and 1 Dutch. Of the 17 ships, which had accompanied *Barrwhin* in convoys PQ11 and QP9, 7 were sunk subsequently. Allied losses were 2 cruisers, 7 destroyers, 3 sloops, 1 frigate, 3 corvettes, 1 submarine and 4 minesweepers. German losses were the battle cruiser *Scharnhorst*, 2 destroyers, 2 escorts, 31 submarines and many aircraft. The greatest loss of life occurred in *Scharnhorst*, from which only 35 of her complement of nearly 1,500 survived.

Many of my contemporaries believe that the Arctic convoy veterans deserve a special medal, issued by the Crown, distinct from the Atlantic Star. I do not share that point of view. The war at sea was bloody awful, in the Atlantic, Arctic, Mediterranean or eastern waters. The fundamental difference in the Arctic convoys was the quite appalling weather conditions.

During our passage home, 40 ships were lost when on independent passage in the West Indies, Caribbean Sea, Mexican Gulf and along the eastern seaboard of the U.S.A., where the U-Boats wrought havoc among the huge traffic in oil tankers. Three ships were sunk in very suspicious circumstances, all lost with all hands: *Muskogee*, sunk by U-123 south of Bermuda, *Fanfjeld* sunk by U-252 "west of Iceland", and *Chr. Knudsen*, sunk by U-85, with the vague attack report "New York to Capetown". U-85 and U-252 were subsequently sunk with all hands. We do not mourn their passing.

Only eight U-Boats were destroyed between 15 February 1942 and 13 April 1942. The reason was that they were operating in undefended areas. Moreover, the shipping traffic was not only dense, but lit up like Christmas trees. The American seamen stood this massive onslaught with courage and great fortitude, but their losses were enormous. Unfortunately, the slaughter was to continue for many months, until forceful measures were undertaken to organise proper and effective protection.

The American naval command eventually woke up to reality, and with their customary drive and huge manufacturing and ship construction capability, established a programme for the building of destroyer escorts and escort aircraft carriers, as well as hundreds of mass-produced merchant ships.

The American destroyer escorts and their large Coast Guard cutters, as well as our frigates and Bird class sloops, were ideal ocean-going escort vessels. The American task forces consisting of an escort carrier and a group of destroyer escorts, proved to be effective hunter/killer groups, and when eventually combined with aircraft, the allied toll of U-Boat kills began to increase. Our hunter/killer groups of sloops soon made a tremendous impact.

Unfortunately, our casualties in merchant ships and seamen continued at an appalling rate. However, our pre-war regime for officer training had resulted in a continuing supply of trained deck officers. In this respect the American Merchant Marine suffered, but with their characteristic drive and energy they established a massive programme of short-term training.

We filled the gaps in the shortages of engineer officers from the factories and workshops, and established training programmes for other deck and engine room ratings. Sometimes the junior engineers had been employed previously as motor – even bicycle mechanics, but with the backing of certificated second and chief engineers, they did a good job.

Casualties – Ships and Personnel
21 March to 13 April 1942

Ships sunk – 53 by 24 successful U-Boats.
Six ships sunk by Italian submarines.
Three ships sunk by raiders.
Six ships sunk by aircraft.
One ship sunk by enemy destroyer.

Lost with all hands

Muskogee, cargo unknown, 34 dead.
Narragansett, cargo fuel oil, 49 dead.
Tredinnick, general cargo, 52 dead.
Carolyn, naval auxiliary, 47 dead.
Fanfjeld, cargo unknown, 25 dead.
Empire Prairie, general cargo, 48 dead.
Chr. Knudsen, cargo unknown, 37 dead.

Lost with very heavy casualties

Thursobank, general cargo, 30 dead out of 64.

Naeco, cargo fuel oil, 24 dead out of 38.
Empire Steel, cargo gasoline, 39 dead out of 47.
Ocana, cargo fuel oil, 49 dead out of 57.
Dixie Arrow, cargo crude oil, 11 dead out of 33.
Equipoise, general cargo, 40 dead out of 53.
City of New York, general cargo, 26 dead out of 144.
Induna, general cargo, 31 dead out of 50.
Muncaster Castle 24 dead out of 350.
Menominee, tug, 16 dead out of 18.
San Gerardo, cargo fuel oil, 51 dead out of 57.
T.C. McCobb, in ballast, 24 dead out of 39.
Rio Blanco, cargo iron ore, 19 dead out of 40.
David H. Atwater, cargo coal, 24 dead out of 27.
Otho, cargo iron ore, 31 dead out of 53.
San Delfino, cargo gasoline, 28 dead out of 49.
Gulfamerica, cargo fuel oil, 19 dead out of 48.
Empire Amethyst, cargo gasoline, 41 dead out of 46.
El Occidente, cargo iron ore, 20 dead out of 41.

Merchant seamen killed – 1,004 out of 3392,
a fatal casualty rate of 30 percent.

Two passenger ships were sunk, *Ulysses* (all rescued) and *Muncaster Castle*
(19 passengers lost out of 246)

UPON THEIR LAWFUL OCCASIONS

BARRWHIN - 15 DECEMBER 1941 TO 8 SEPTEMBER 1942

RECORD OF MERCHANT SHIPS SUNK IN ATLANTIC - 21/03/42 TO 13/04/42

DATE	BARRWHIN SHIP	NAT.	QP9 CONVOY NO.	CAUSE OF LOSS	POSITION		CARGO	CASUALTIES CREW	DEAD
22/03/42	THURSOBANK	BRITISH		U-373	38-05 N.	68-30 W.	GENERAL	64	30
23/03/42	PAGASITIKOS	GREEK		A.M.C.	31-00 S.	11-55 W.	COAL	35	0
22/03/42	MUSKOGEE	U.S.A.		U-123	28-00 N.	58-00 W.		34	34
23/03/42	BRITISH PRUDENCE	BRITISH	HX181	U-754	45-28 N.	56-13 W.	FUEL OIL	50	3
23/03/42	NAECO	U.S.A.		U-124	33-59 N.	76-40 W.	FUEL OIL	38	24
23/03/42	PEDER BOGEN	BRITISH		MOROSINI	24-43 N.	57-44 W.	FUEL OIL	53	0
24/03/42	EMPIRE STEEL	BRITISH		U-123	37-45 N.	63-17 W.	GASOLENE	47	39
25/03/42	NARRAGANSETT	BRITISH		U-105	34-46 N.	67-40 W.	FUEL OIL	49	49
25/03/42	OCANA	DUTCH		U-552	42-36 N.	65-25 W.	FUEL OIL	57	49
25/03/42	TREDINNICK	BRITISH		CALVI	27-15 N.	49-15W.	GENERAL	52	52
26/03/42	DIXIE ARROW	U.S.A.		U-71	34-55 N.	75-02 W.	CRUDE OIL	33	11
26/03/42	EQUIPOISE	PAN.		U-160	36-36 N.	74-45 W.	GENERAL	53	40
26/03/42	CAROLYN	U.S.A.		U-123	36-00 N.	70-00 W.	AUXILIARY	47	47
27/03/42	SVENOR	NOR.		U-105	35-35 N.	69-20 W.	FUEL OIL	37	8
28/03/42	EMPIRE RANGER	BRITISH	PQ13	AIRCRAFT	72-10 N.	30-00 E.	GENERAL	56	1
28/03/42	RACELAND	PAN.	PQ13	AIRCRAFT	72-40 N.	20.20 E.	GENERAL	45	13
29/03/42	BATEAU	PAN.	PQ13	Z-26	72-00 N.	33-00 E.	GENERAL	46	0
29/03/42	CITY OF NEW YORK	U.S.A.		U-160	35-16 N.	74-25 W.	GENERAL	144	26
29/03/42	HERTFORD	BRITISH		U-571	40-50 N.	63-31 W.	GENERAL	61	4
30/03/42	EFFINGHAM	U.S.A.	PQ13	U-435	70-28 N.	35-44 E.	GENERAL	32	0
30/03/42	INDUNA	BRITISH	PQ13	U-376	70-55 N.	37-18 E.	GENERAL	50	31
30/03/42	MUNCASTER CASTLE	BRITISH		U-68	22-00 N.	12-02 W.	GENERAL	350	24
31/03/42	MENOMINEE	U.S.A.		U-754	37-34 N.	75-25 W.	TUG	18	16
31/03/42	EASTMOOR	BRITISH		U-71	37-33 N.	68-18 W.	GENERAL	52	16
31/03/42	SAN GERARDO	BRITISH		U-71	36-00 N.	67-00 W.	FUEL OIL	57	51
31/03/42	T.C. McCOBB	U.S.A.		CALVI	07-10 N.	45-20 W.	BALLAST	39	24
01/04/42	RIO BLANCO	BRITISH		U-160	35-16 N.	74-18 W.	IRON ORE	40	19
01/04/42	LOCH DON	BRITISH		U-202	37-05 N.	61-40 W.	GENERAL	47	3
01/04/42	TIGER	U.S.A.		U-754	36-50 N.	75-49 W.	FUEL OIL	42	1
01/04/42	WILLESDEN	BRITISH		A.M.C.	16-00 S.	16-00 W.	GENERAL	47	5
03/04/42	DAVID H. ATWATER	U.S.A.		U-552	37-57 N.	75-10 W.	COAL	27	24
03/04/42	OTHO	U.S.A.		U-754	36-25 N.	72-22 W.	ORE	53	31
03/04/42	EMPIRE STARLIGHT	BRITISH	PQ13	AIRCRAFT	MURMANSK		GENERAL	50	1
03/04/42	NEW WESTMINSTER CITY	BRITISH	PQ13	AIRCRAFT	MURMANSK		GENERAL	50	2
03/04/42	WEST IRMO	U.S.A.		U-505	02-10 N.	05-35 W,	GENERAL	99	10
04/04/42	COMOL RICO	U.S.A.		U-154	20-46 N.	66-46 W.	MOLASSES	42	3
04/04/42	ALPHACCA	DUTCH		U-505	01-50 N.	07-40 W.	GENERAL	72	15
05/04/42	CATAHOULA	U.S.A.		U-154	19-16 N.	68-12 W.	MOLASSES	45	7
05/04/42	BYRON D. BENSON	U.S.A.		U-552	36-08 N.	75-32 W.	CRUDE OIL	37	9
06/04/42	KOLL	NOR.		U-571	35-00 N.	68-24 W.	GAS OIL	36	3
06/04/42	KOLLSKEGG	NOR.		U-754	35-01 N.	68-49 W.	CRUDE OIL	42	4
07/04/42	BRITISH SPLENDOUR	BRITISH		U-552	35-07 N.	75-19 W.	BENZINE	53	12
07/04/42	LANCING	NOR.		U-552	35-08 N.	75-22 W.	FUEL OIL	50	1
08/04/42	NEMANJA	YUGO.		U-84	40-30 N.	64-50 W.	SUGAR	47	13
09/04/42	ATLAS	U.S.A.		U-552	34-37 N.	76-16 W.	GASOLENE	34	2
09/04/42	ESPARTA	U.S.A.		U-123	30-46 N.	81-11 W.		40	1
09/04/42	MALCHASE	U.S.A.		U-160	34-28 N.	75-56 W.	SODA ASH	29	1
09/04/42	FANFJELD	NOR.		U-252				25	25
10/04/42	EMPIRE PRAIRIE	BRITISH		U-654	35-00 N.	60-00 W.	GENERAL	48	48
10/04/42	KIRKPOOL	BRITISH		A.M.C.	33-00 S.	07-00 W.	COAL	44	0
10/04/42	TAMAULIPAS	U.S.A.		U-552	34-25 N.	76-00 W.	GAS OIL	37	2
10/04/42	EUGENE V.R. THAYER	U.S.A.		CALVI	02-12 S.	39-35 W.	BALLAST	39	0
10/04/42	BALKIS	NOR.		CALVI	02-30 S.	38-00 W.	PAPER	35	8
10/04/42	SAN DELFINO	BRITISH		U-203	35-35 N.	75-06 W.	GASOLENE	49	28
10/04/42	CHR. KNUDSEN	NOR.		U-85				37	37
.11/04/42	EMPIRE COWPER	BRITISH	QP10	AIRCRAFT	71-01 N.	36-00 E.	GENERAL	57	8
11/04/42	GULFAMERICA	U.S.A.		U-123	30-10 N.	81-15 W.	FUEL OIL	48	19
11/04/42	ULYSSES	BRITISH		U-60	34-23 N.	75-35 W.	GENERAL	289	0
11/04/42	GRENANGER	NOR.		U-130	22-45 N.	57-13 W.	GENERAL	36	0
12/04/42	ESSO BOSTON	U.S.A.		U-130	21-42 N.	60-00 W.	FUEL OIL	37	0
12/04/42	DELVALLE	U.S.A.		U-154	16-51 N.	72-25 W.	GENERAL	63	2
12/04/42	BEN BRUSH	PAN.		CALVI	04-32 S.	35-03 W.	FUEL OIL	35	1
13/04/42	HARPALION	BRITISH	QP10	AIRCRAFT	73-33 N.	27-19 E.	ORE	78	0
13/04/42	EMPIRE AMETHYST	BRITISH		U-154	17-40 N.	74-50 W.	GASOLENE	46	41
13/04/42	EMPIRE PROGRESS	BRITISH	ON80	U-402	40-29 N.	52-35 W.	BALLAST	50	12
13/04/42	LESLIE	U.S.A.		U-123	28-35 N.	80-19 W.	SUGAR	32	4
13/04/42	KORSHOLM	SWED.		U-123	28-21 N.	80-22 W.	PHOSPHATE	26	9
13/04/42	EL OCCIDENTE	PAN.	QP10	U-435	73-28 N.	28-30 E.	ORE	41	20
13/04/42	KIEV	RUSS.	QP10	U-435	73-22 N.	28-48 E.			

TOTALS   3,733   1,023

BARRWHIN - 15 DECEMBER 1941 TO 8 SEPTEMBER 1942

SHIP AND U-BOAT LOSSES - WHEN SERVING ON *BARRWHIN* - 26 FEBRUARY 1942 TO 13 APRIL 1942

GERMAN U-BOATS			SHIPS SUNK IN PERIOD			ENEMY U-BOAT LOSSES				
NUMBER	TOTALS C/F	B/F	TOTAL	26/02/42 20/03/42	21/03/42 13/04/42		DATE	CAUSE	DEAD	SAVED
U-60			1		1	U-85	14/04/42	D/C	45	0
U-67			1	1		U-133	14/03/42	MINE	45	0
U-68			6	5	1	U-503	15/03/42	AIR	51	0
U-71			5	2	3	U-585	30/03/42	MINE	44	0
U-84			1		1	U-587	27/03/42	D/C	42	0
U-85			1		1	U-655	24/03/42	RAM	45	0
U-94			2	2		U-656	01/03/42	AIR	45	0
U-96			2	1	1	U-702	10/04/42	???	44	0
U-105			1		1					
U-123			7		7					
U-124			7	6	1					
U-126			7	7						
U-128			1	1						
U-129			3	3						
U-130			2		2					
U-154			4		4					
U-155			1	1						
U-156			1	1						
U-158			3	3						
U-160			4		4					
U-161			2	2						
U-202			1		1					
U-203			1		1					
U-252			1		1					
U-332			3	3						
U-373			2	1	1					
U-376			1		1					
U-402			1		1					
U-404			4	4						
U-435			3		3					
U-504			2	2						
U-505			4	2	2					
U-552			7		7					
U-558			1	1						
U-569			1	1						
U-571			2		2					
U-578			3	3						
U-588			1	1						
U-653			1	1						
U-654			1		1					
U-754			5		5					
	830	723	107	54	53					

			TOTALS	8	361	0
			B/F	73	2,021	1,075
			C/F	81	2,382	1,075

	C/F	B/F	TOTAL	26/02-20/03	21/03-13/04
HEAVY SHIPS	15	15	0		
RAIDERS	16	13	3		3
LIGHT WARSHIPS	5	4	1		1
AIRCRAFT	54	46	8	2	6
ITALIAN SUBMARINES	51	35	16	10	6
OTHER CAUSES	6	6	0		
	147	119	28	12	16

LEAVE ASHORE FOR MARRIAGE

Barrwhin paid off immediately after arriving in Newcastle, and signed on the following day, 14 April 1942. We anticipated a stay in port of at least two weeks, because we believed that we would load war supplies, and return to service in the Arctic convoys. I applied for leave, and was granted ten days.

I sent a telegram to Betty, who had made plans for our wedding, but could not fix the date. She was unable to arrange for the banns to be read, so we had to apply for a special licence. Betty was a minor, so she needed to obtain parental consent. I left Newcastle on 14 April 1942, and after the usual uncomfortable 12-hour train journey, arrived in Cardiff at noon the following day. The special licence was dated 17 April, and the wedding was arranged for noon on Saturday 18 April 1942.

Because of the stringent rationing and the scarcity of clothes coupons, weddings were very much utility affairs. Betty had saved eight clothing coupons for her dress, and had borrowed her wedding shoes and a veil respectively from a friend and her sister. The dress cost 30 shillings. She managed to scrounge a chocolate cake from the local baker, and pestered the off-licence proprietor for one bottle of port.

Then the bombshell burst! On the evening of the day before the wedding, I received a telegram "Return to ship immediately – signed Shilstone, First Mate". I replied, "Wedding tomorrow. Is ship proceeding to sea?" The reply from Ron Shilstone was, "Rejoin ship Monday 1300 latest".

We travelled to Weston-Super-Mare in the afternoon of our wedding day and arrived in the early evening. I gave Betty all my money except £1-10s-4d, and bade farewell to my bride at 1800 the following day, Sunday 19 April. She remained in Weston-Super-Mare overnight. I travelled to Cardiff, and then boarded the 0055 train to the north, with its usual seven changes and smelly and uncomfortable carriages. We arrived in Newcastle on time at 1300, when I took a taxi to the dock.

To my horror, the ship was not at the berth; but a stevedore informed me that she had left only a few minutes before. My only recourse was to travel by taxi to Jarrow Staithes, where it was likely that the dock pilot would leave the ship. There were a number of boatmen stationed at the staithes. The taxi agreed a charge of one pound for the journey. We soon caught up with the ship, and passed her. I opened the sunshine roof of the antiquated Austin taxi and waved my hat. The Master indicated that he had seen me. On arrival at the staithes, I found a boatman who agreed

St Paul's Church, Cardiff
18 April 1942

Weston-Super-Mare
One day honeymoon
19 April 1942

to scull me to the centre of the river for ten shillings, leaving me with only four pence in my pocket. The ship put out a boat rope and rope ladder, and I clambered aboard, much relieved, but not in favour with Captain Dixon.

Although the ship had been prepared for service in Arctic conditions, and it was intended that we were return to Murmansk, urgent orders had been received that a part cargo of cased wines and spirits would be loaded.

Barrwhin put to sea and joined a northbound North Sea convoy on the evening of Monday 20 April 1942. During the passage, I was taken quite seriously ill, with a high temperature, and was unable to stand my watch. A number of others who had served on the previous voyage were similarly afflicted. The common symptoms of bleeding gums and loose teeth identified the disease as scurvy. After several days of treatment by anti scorbutics, we were fit for duty, although rather groggy.

Convoy ON89

After an uneventful passage to Loch Ewe, we joined outward bound convoy ON89 in the North Channel on the evening of 23 April 1942. The only casualty to the convoy on passage was *British Workman*, torpedoed and sunk by U-455 on 3 May 1942, after being dispersed from the convoy.

During the last week of our passage, we encountered the dense fog that was prevalent on the Grand Banks and in the Denmark Strait. The convoy had dispersed, partly because ships became detached in the fog, but also because they were proceeding independently to different destinations. We were unable to obtain an accurate position, because we could not see any heavenly bodies, or obtain a clear view of the horizon. The Master relied upon wireless cross bearings, which were very inaccurate. The cross bearings resulted in large "cocked hats" on the chart, where the position lines crossed; and the only recourse was to place the ship somewhere in the centre of the triangle formed by three inaccurate position lines.

When we were less than a day away from New York, we encountered a short period of clear sky and horizon, when I was standing the night watch I was able to identify two stars of high magnitude, probably Arcturus or Spica, and the planet Venus. When the Second Mate relieved me on watch – usually fifteen to thirty minutes late – I worked up the sight, which gave me simultaneous position lines. This placed the ship well ahead of our dead reckoning position. The fog had shut down as thick as previously. Although we had not anticipated being in soundings, by the previous calculations, I turned on the echo sounder, and obtained a line of soundings. This verified the accuracy of the position.

Most of the older Masters entertained an inordinate suspicion of lunar or stellar sights. Younger officers, who had been trained in the immediate pre war era, did not share this concern. The potential hazards in taking lunar and stellar sites in moonlight were of obtaining "ghost horizons"; but experienced seamen could obtain accurate positions by taking advantage of two simultaneous position lines from separate heavenly bodies. This was not possible with solar sights.

Captain Dixon appeared to share the views of contemporaries of his age. He relied on the customary solar sight for an approximate longitude at 0800, based on dead reckoning latitude, followed by an accurate sight for latitude at noon, when the sun was on the meridian.

I entered the position and the soundings in the scrap log, and called the Master to the bridge. He accepted my position without question, and ordered reduced speed. The anchor cable was cleared, and shortly afterwards we anchored. The fog cleared completely at daybreak, and we berthed in New York in the forenoon of 8 May 1942. When we anchored, we were about twenty miles from the Ambrose Light Vessel, on the Nantucket Shoals.

During the 24 days between signing on and arrival at New York the pattern of U-Boat activity had not changed. Ships on passage in the West Indies, Caribbean, eastern seaboard of the U.S.A, and Mexican Gulf suffered severely. The rate of losses remained consistent at about ten ships every four days. Thirty merchant seamen were being killed every day. Only eight ships were sunk in six ocean convoys.

During our passage, only four U-Boats were destroyed against the loss of 59 ships, U-74 and U-573 by air attack, and U-252 and U-352 by depth charge attack. The two sunk by air attack were destroyed in the Bay of Biscay and Mediterranean respectively. *H.M.S. Vetch* and *Stork* destroyed U-252, while the U-Boat was preparing to attack outward bound Gibraltar convoy OG82. The U.S. Coastguard Cutter *Icarus* destroyed U 352 off the coast of North Carolina. The reason for the apparent lack of success against U-Boats is not attributable to any lack of effort by, or dedication of, our anti U-Boat forces, but rather to the lack of intelligent planning and resolute action in higher levels of command on both sides of the Atlantic. They did not seem to be prepared for eventualities.

Of the 59 ships sunk, 26 were American or American owned, 20 British, and 13 of other nationalities. The majority were sunk near the American coast. The U.S.A. had then been at war for five months, but had failed to implement any effective measures for merchant ship protection. The result was the heavy casualties suffered by the seamen in their ships. We felt great sadness that so many fellow merchant seamen were being killed in the blazing infernos of American tankers.

I believe that in areas where countermeasures were either non-existent or fundamentally ineffective, there can be no doubt that many U-Boat commanders surfaced and attacked their targets by gunfire with the intention of eliminating the crews of ships. One U-Boat commander is alleged to have stated that he had "not seen any men killed", when confronted with the accusation that he had committed an atrocity. A laconic report "vessel sunk by torpedo and gunfire" would have been guaranteed to satisfy a receptive Admiral Donitz, who would have been very unlikely to call for more comprehensive attack reports. Later in the war, central U-Boat headquarters openly advocated a policy of attacks on personnel, ie. the "destruction of lifesaving equipment" and "the sinking of rescue vessels." It was not until recently that I learned about the sinking of *Laconia*, the event that stimulated the furious intervention of Hitler, and the issuing by Donitz of the "Laconia Order" and the "Rescue Ship Order".

These instructions to U-Boat commanders were sufficiently ambiguous to generate serious misinterpretations of their import and intention. By that time, many of the original regular U-Boat commanders had been replaced by more ardent and less scrupulous Nazi-indoctrinated officers. Moreover, Gestapo personnel were being incorporated into the U-Boat complements. I believe that these circumstances resulted in many war crimes that never reached the tribunals, and whose perpetrators were not punished. It was poetic justice that so many did not survive the slaughter of enemy U-Boats and their crews that occurred between 1943 and 1945, which was appropriate retribution and punishment.

The account of the sinking of the Greek ship *Peleus* gives an insight into not only the types of U-Boat commanders, but also the regime in which they were members. The villainous Kapitan-Leutnant Heinz Eck, in command of U852, not only gave the orders to his subordinates to fire on the survivors with machine guns and machine pistols, but grenades were thrown at the survivors as well.

The fact that grenades were part of the armoury of U852 indicates that their intention was to attack survivors in life craft from very short ranges. It is unlikely that individual U-Boat commanders would have equipped their armouries with close range infantry weapons without official approval. The Germans do everything by the book, and there can be little doubt therefore, that grenades must have been standard equipment on U-Boats in 1943. Every box of grenades would take up useful space that could be devoted to food or useful supplies, and the Germans would be unlikely to sacrifice sausages for grenades, unless they were ordered to do so.

The villain, Eck, and two of his subordinates, Hoffman and Weisspfennig, were tried, convicted of war crimes, and executed by firing squad. They were a disgrace to their service, and to the memory of the many fine U-Boat commanders and their crews who died, and those who survived, such as Hartenstein, Karl Friedrich Mertens and Ulrich Heyse.

Casualties – Ships and Personnel
14 April 1942 to 8 May 1942

Ships sunk – 59 by 27 successful U-Boats.
One ship sunk by a raider.
One ship sunk by destroyers.
Four ships sunk by aircraft.

Lost with all hands

Margaret, cargo unknown, 27 dead.
Frank Seamans, cargo bauxite, 27 dead.

Lost with very heavy casualties

Korthion, cargo bauxite, 14 dead out of 23.
Robin Hood, cargo iron ore, 14 dead out of 40.
Empire Howard, general cargo, 25 dead out of 62.
Empire Dryden, general cargo, 26 dead out of 51.
Harpagon, general cargo, 41 dead out of 49.
Steelmaker, general cargo, 26 dead out of 44.

Chenango, cargo iron ore, 36 dead out of 37.
Derryheen, cargo fuel oil, 37 dead out of 55.
Lammot du Pont, cargo linseed, 18 dead out of 56.
Modesta, cargo bauxite, 18 dead out of 41.
Taborfjell, cargo sugar, 17 dead out of 20.
Tsiolkovsky, in ballast, 27 dead out of 41.
Cape Corso, cargo munitions, 50 dead out of 56.
Botavon, cargo war materials, 21 dead out of 72.
Eastern Sword, in ballast, 11 dead out of 29.
Munger T. Ball, cargo gasoline, 33 dead out of 37.
Joseph M. Cudahy, cargo fuel oil, 27 dead out of 37.
Amazone, general cargo, 14 dead out of 34.
Mount Louis, in ballast, 15 dead out of 21.
Ohioan, cargo iron ore, 15 dead out of 37.

Merchant seamen killed – 684 out of 2,855, a fatal casualty rate of 24 percent. The passenger ship Lady Drake was sunk with the loss of 6 of her 141 passengers.

Convoys attacked – ON89 (one ship lost) and OS25 (one ship lost): and Arctic convoys PQ13 (one ship lost): PQ14 (one ship lost): PQ15 (three ships lost) and QP11 (one ship lost.

Successful U-Boats – U507 (seven ships): U-66 (six ships): U-125 and U-162 (five ships each) and U-108 (four ships).

BARRWHIN - 15 DECEMBER 1941 TO 8 SEPTEMBER 1942

RECORD OF MERCHANT SHIPS SUNK IN ATLANTIC - 14/04/42 TO 08/05/42

BARRWHIN - SIGNED ARTICLES AT NEWCASTLE - 14/04/42 - BERTHED AT NEWCASTLE - 14/04/42 TO 20/04/42

DATE	SHIP	NAT.	CONVOY NO.	CAUSE OF LOSS	POSITION		CARGO	CASUALTIES CREW	DEAD
14/04/42	EMPIRE THRUSH	BRITISH		U-203	38-08 N.	75-18 W.	PHOSPHATE	62	0
14/04/42	KORTHION	GREEK		U-66	12-50 N.	60-30 W.	BAUXITE	23	14
14/04/42	LANCASTER CASTLE	BRITISH	PQ13	AIRCRAFT	MURMANSK ROADS			57	10
14/04/42	MARGARET	U.S.A.		U-571	E. COAST U.S.A.			27	27
15/04/42	ROBIN HOOD	U.S.A.		U-575	38-45 N.	66-46 W.	ORE	40	14
16/04/42	EMPIRE HOWARD	BRITISH	PQ14	U-403	73-50 N.	21-40 E.	GENERAL	62	25
16/04/42	AMSTERDAM	DUTCH		U-66	12-00 N.	62-45 W.		40	2
16/04/42	DESERT LIGHT	PAN.		U-572	35-35 N.	72-48 W.	GENERAL	31	1
17/04/42	ALCOA GUIDE	U.S.A.		U-123	35-34 N.	70-08 W.	BALLAST	34	7
17/04/42	HEINRICH VON RIEDEMANN	PAN.		U-66	11-55 N.	63-40 W.	CRUDE OIL	44	0
20/04/42	EMPIRE DRYDEN	BRITISH		U-572	34-21 N.	69-00 W.	GENERAL	51	26
20/04/42	HARPAGON	BRITISH		U-109	34-35 N.	65-50 W.	GENERAL	49	41
20/04/42	VINELAND	BRITISH		U-154	23-05 N.	72-20 W.	BALLAST	35	1
20/04/42	STEELMAKER	U.S.A.		U-654	33-48 N.	70-36 W.	GENERAL	44	26
20/04/42	CHENANGO	U.S.A.		U-84	36-25 N.	74-55 W.	ORE	37	36
20/04/42	AGRA	SWED.		U-654	34-40 N.	69-35 W.	GENERAL	39	6
21/04/42	WEST IMBODEN	U.S.A.		U-752	41-14 N.	65-55 W.	GENERAL	34	0
21/04/42	PIPESTONE COUNTY	U.S.A.		U-576	37-43 N.	66-16 W.	GENERAL	45	0
21/04/42	BRIS	NOR.		U-201	33-35 N.	69-38 W.	FLOUR	25	5
22/04/42	SAN JACINTO	U.S.A.		U-201	31-10 N.	70-45 W.	GENERAL	183	14
22/04/42	DERRYHEEN	BRITISH		U-201	31-20 N.	70-55 W.	GENERAL	47	0
22/04/42	CONNECTICUT	U.S.A.		A.M.C.	11-13 N.	61-35 W.	FUEL OIL	55	37
	BARRWHIN		ON89						
23/04/42	LAMMOT DU PONT	U.S.A.		U-125	27-10 N.	57-10 W.	LINSEED	56	18
24/04/42	EMPIRE DRUM	BRITISH		U-136	37-00 N.	69-15 W.	GENERAL	41	0
25/04/42	MODESTA	BRITISH		U-108	33-40 N.	63-10 W.	BAUXITE	41	18
26/04/42	ALCOA PARTNER	U.S.A.		U-66	13-32 N.	67-57 W.	BAUXITE	46	10
28/04/42	ARUNDO	DUTCH		U-136	40-11 N.	73-44 W.	GENERAL	43	6
29/04/42	ATHELEMPRESS	BRITISH	OS25	U-162	13-21 N.	56-15 W.	BALLAST	57	3
29/04/42	MOBILOIL	U.S.A.		U-108	25-35 N.	66-18 W.	FUEL OIL	52	0
29/04/42	HARRY G. SEIDEL	PAN.		U-66	11-50 N.	62-50 W.	BALLAST	50	2
30/04/42	TABORFJELL	NOR.		U-576	41-52 N.	67-43 W.	SUGAR	20	17
30/04/42	ASHKABAD	RUSS.		U-402	34-19 N.	76-31 W.	BALLAST	47	0
30/04/42	FEDERAL	U.S.A.		U-507	21-13 N.	76-05 W.	BALLAST	33	5
01/05/42	LA PAZ	BRITISH		U-109	28-30 N.	80-10 W.			
01/05/42	PARNAHYBA	BRAZ.		U-162	10-12 N.	57-16 W.	GENERAL	75	4
01/05/42	BIDEVIND	NOR.		U-752	40-13 N.	73-46 W.	GENERAL	36	0
01/05/42	TSIOLKOVSKY	RUSS.	QP11	Z-24/25	73-23 N.	25-30 E.	BALLAST	41	27
02/05/42	CAPE CORSO	BRITISH	PQ15	AIRCRAFT	73-02 N.	19-46 E.	MUNITIONS	56	50
02/05/42	BOTAVON	BRITISH	PQ15	AIRCRAFT	73-02 N.	20-22 E.	GENERAL	72	21
02/05/42	JUTLAND	BRITISH	PQ15	AIRCRAFT	73-02 N.	19-46 E.	GENERAL	53	1
02/05/42	SANDAR	NOR.		U-66	11-42 N.	61-10 W.	FUEL OIL	27	2
03/05/42	BRITISH WORKMAN	BRITISH	ON89	U-455	44-07 N.	51-53 W.	BALLAST	53	7
03/05/42	OCEAN VENUS	BRITISH		U-564	28-23 N.	80-21 W.	GENERAL	47	5
03/05/42	SAN RAFAEL	DOM.		U-125	18-36 N.	79-12 W.	BALLAST	38	1
03/05/42	LAERTES	DUTCH		U-564	28-21 N.	80-23 W.	GENERAL	66	18
03/05/42	SAMA	NIC.		U-506	25-04 N.	79-45 W.	BANANAS	14	0
04/05/42	EASTERN SWORD	U.S.A.		U-162	07-10 N.	57-58 W.	BALLAST	29	11
04/05/42	MUNGER T. BALL	U.S.A.		U-507	25-24 N.	83-46 W.	GASOLENE	37	33
04/05/42	JOSEPH M. CUDAHY	U.S.A.		U-507	25-57 N.	83-57 W.	FUEL OIL	37	27
04/05/42	TUSCALOOSA CITY	U.S.A.		U-125	18-25 N.	81-31 W.	GENERAL	34	0
04/05/42	NORLINDO	U.S.A.		U-507	24-57 N.	84-00 W.	BALLAST	28	5
05/05/42	STANBANK	BRITISH		U-103	34-55 N.	61-47 W.	GENERAL	49	9
05/05/42	LADY DRAKE	BRITISH		U-106	35-43 N.	64-43 W.	PASS.	261	12
05/05/42	AFOUNDRIA	U.S.A.		U-108	20-00 N.	73-30 W.	BALLAST	37	0
06/05/42	EMPIRE BUFFALO	BRITISH		U-125	19-14 N.	82-34 W.	BALLAST	42	13
06/05/42	HALSEY	U.S.A.		U-333	27-20 N.	80-03 W.	FUEL OIL	32	0
06/05/42	ALCOA PURITAN	U.S.A.		U-507	28-35 N.	88-22 W.	BAUXITE	54	0
06/05/42	GREEN ISLAND	U.S.A.		U-125	18-25 N.	81-30 W.	GENERAL	22	0
06/05/42	AMAZONE	DUTCH		U-333	27-21 N.	80-05 W.	GENERAL	34	14
06/05/42	ABGARA	LATV.		U-108	20-45 N.	72-55 W.	SUGAR	34	0
07/05/42	FRANK SEAMANS	NOR.		U-162	06-21 N.	55-38 W.	BAUXITE	27	27
07/05/42	ONTARIO	HOND.		U-507	28-12 N.	87-32 W.	BANANAS		
08/05/42	MOUNT LOUIS	BRITISH		U-162	08-23 N.	58-44 W.	BALLAST	21	15
08/05/42	OHIOAN	U.S.A.		U-564	26-31 N.	79-59 W.	ORE	37	15
08/05/42	TORNY	NOR.		U-507	26-40 W.	86-40 W.	NITRATE	26	2
						TOTALS		**2,969**	**690**

We were carrying a part cargo of various spirits in thousands of cases, including Scotch whisky, vintage port and brandy, and champagne, stowed in No. 2 and No. 4 holds. I was responsible for the supervision of the discharging of cargo in the forward holds, and the Second Mate was in charge of the after holds. When the foreman stevedore became aware of the nature of the cargo, he came to me to ask if his gang could have a couple of cases of whiskey, putting his request in the terms "You would not want the cargo to be broached, or a couple of slings break loose, would you, sir?" I had gained substantial experience of American steve-dores; and although they were unmitigated rogues, I had learned that they subscribed to their own code of honour.

When I put it to the First Mate that they would be content with two cases of whisky, he agreed. The result was that we discharged Nos. 1 and 2 hold without pilfering or "accidental" breakage. The Second Mate had spent his seagoing life on the far eastern trade, and had not encountered the New York stevedore gangs. He very unwisely refused to comply with the request for two cases of whisky for the gangs working the after holds. The inevitable result was broached cargo and substantial breakage. Incredibly, the stevedores were not at all interested in the vintage spirits that we carried. They wanted Scotch whisky.

Whilst we were lying in Brooklyn, and when I was duty officer, there was a commotion on deck. The carpenter, who had always appeared to be a rational individual, suddenly went mad, struck the American night watchman on the head with a heavy hammer, fracturing his skull. Then, he jumped into the harbour water just where the sewers were being discharged. We never saw him again. He was the second member of the crew to commit suicide.

We loaded a part cargo of steel sections in the lower holds, with general cargo in the upper holds and 'tween decks, and vehicles and cases on deck. We put to sea from New York on 24 May, joining convoy SC86 of 35 ships, which sailed from Sidney Cape Breton on 5 June.

During the 15 days when *Barrwhin* was berthed in New York and load-ing cargo, U-Boats made successful attacks on four convoys. Outward bound convoys ON 93 and OS 28 lost one ship each and convoy ON 92 lost 8 ships out of 46. Homeward bound Freetown convoy SL109 lost one ship. Out of 68 ships lost, 57 were sunk when on unescorted or independ-ent passage. The U-Boat "happy time" continued, apparently without restraint, or the implementation of effective counter measures. By that time, no amount of censorship could obscure the serious situation from the public. Crowds of American people were able to see the tankers burning and exploding close to their coasts, and the survivors being landed in their ports. Belatedly, a blackout of coastal towns had been enforced, and the rudiments of a coastal convoy system had been established.

Casualties – Ships and Personnel
9 May 1942 to 24 May 1942

Ships sunk – 68 by 28 successful U-Boats.
One ship sunk by a raider.
One ship sunk by an Italian submarine.

Lost with all hands

Torondoc, cargo bauxite, 21 dead.
Zurichmoor, in ballast, 38 dead.

Lost with very heavy casualties

Lubrafol, cargo fuel oil, 13 dead out of 44.
Lise, in ballast, 12 dead out of 33.
Leto, cargo grain, 12 dead out of 47.
Virginia, cargo gasoline, 26 dead out of 40.
Denpark, cargo iron ore, 21 dead out of 46.
Norlantic, general cargo, 11 dead out of 30.
Gulfpenn, cargo fuel oil, 13 dead out of 38.
David McKelvy, cargo crude oil, 17 dead out of 40.
Portrero del Llano, cargo crude oil, 13 dead out of 35.
San Victorio, cargo benzine, 51 dead out of 52.
Fort Qu'appelle, general cargo, 14 dead out of 47.
Gulfoil, cargo crude oil, 21 dead out of 40.
Heredia, cargo probably fruit, 30 dead out of 48.
Ogonitz, cargo nitrates, 19 dead out of 41.
Halo, cargo crude oil, 39 dead out of 42.
Presidente Trujillo, general cargo, 24 dead out of 39.

Merchant seamen killed – 545 out of 3042,
a fatal casualty rate of 18 percent.

Convoys attacked – ON92 (eight ships lost): SL109 (one ship lost):
ON93 (one ship lost): and OS28 (one ship lost).

Successful U-Boats -U-156 (eight ships): U-103 (six ships): U-155 (five
ships): U-124, U-125, U-506 and U-588 (four ships each.

Ships lost – British (24 ships sunk): American or American owned (24 ships sunk): other nationalities (20 ships sunk).

No U-Boats were sunk in the period of fifteen days.

BARRWHIN - 15 DECEMBER 1941 TO 8 SEPTEMBER 1942

RECORD OF MERCHANT SHIPS SUNK IN ATLANTIC - 09/05/42 TO 24/05/42

BARRWHIN - BERTHED IN NEW YORK - 09/05/42 TO 24/05/42

DATE	SHIP	NAT.	CONVOY NO.	CAUSE OF LOSS	POSITION		CARGO	CASUALTIES CREW	DEAD
09/05/42	CALGAROLITE	BRITISH		U-125	19-24 N.	82-30 W.	BALLAST	45	0
09/05/42	LUBRAFOL	PAN.		U-564	26-26 N.	80-00 W.	FUEL OIL	44	13
10/05/42	KITTYS BROOK	BRITISH		U-588	42-56 N.	63-59 W.	GENERAL	52	9
10/05/42	CLAN SKENE	BRITISH		U-333	31-43 N.	70-43 W.	ORE	82	9
11/05/42	CAPE OF GOOD HOPE	BRITISH		U-502	22-48 N.	58-43 W.	GENERAL	37	0
11/05/42	EMPIRE DELL	BRITISH	ON92	U-124	53-00 N.	29-57 W.	BALLAST	63	2
12/05/42	CRISTALES	BRITISH	ON92	U-124	52-55 N.	29-50 W.	GENERAL	82	0
12/05/42	LLANOVER	BRITISH	ON92	U-124	52-50 N.	29-04 W.	BALLAST	46	0
12/05/42	COCLE	PAN.	ON92	U-94	52-37 N.	29-13 W.	BALLAST	42	4
12/05/42	MOUNT PARNES	GREEK	ON92	U-124	52-31 N.	29-20 W.	COAL	33	0
12/05/42	NICOYA	BRITISH		U-553	49-19 N.	61-51 W.	GENERAL	85	6
12/05/42	LISE	NOR.		U-69	13-53 N.	68-20 W.	BALLAST	33	12
12/05/42	LETO	DUTCH		U-553	49-32 N.	65-19 W.	GRAIN	47	12
12/05/42	BATNA	BRITISH	ON92	U-94	52-09 N.	33-56 W.	COAL	43	1
12/05/42	VIRGINIA	U.S.A.		U-507	28-53 N.	89-29 W.	GASOLENE	40	26
12/05/42	DENPARK	BRITISH	SL109	U-128	22-28 N.	28-10 W.	ORE	46	21
13/05/42	ESSO HOUSTON	U.S.A.		U-162	12-12 N.	57-25 W.	FUEL OIL	42	1
13/05/42	KOENJIT	DUTCH	ON92	U-156	15-30 N.	52-40 W.	GENERAL	37	0
13/05/42	NORLANTIC	U.S.A.		U-69	12-13 N.	66-30 W.	GENERAL	30	11
13/05/42	TOLKEN	SWED.	ON92	U-94	51-50 N.	33-35 W.	BALLAST	34	0
13/05/42	BRITISH COLONY	BRITISH		U-162	13-12 N.	58-10 W.	FUEL OIL	44	4
13/05/42	GULFPENN	U.S.A.		U-156	28-29 N.	89-17 W.	FUEL OIL	38	13
13/05/42	CITY OF MELBOURNE	BRITISH		U-156	15-00 N.	54-40 W.	GENERAL	78	1
14/05/42	BRABANT	BELG.		U-155	11-32 N.	62-43 W.	BALLAST	33	3
14/05/42	DAVID McKELVY	U.S.A.		U-506	28-30 N.	89-55 W.	CRUDE OIL	40	17
14/05/42	POTRERO DEL LLANO	MEX.		U-504	25-35 N.	80-06 W.	CRUDE OIL	35	13
14/05/42	COMAYAGUA	HON.		U-125	19-00 N.	81-37 W.	BALLAST	42	6
14/05/42	SILJESTAD	NOR.		U-156	15-20 N.	52-40 W.	GENERAL	33	2
15/05/42	KUPA	YUGO.		U-156	14-50 N.	52-50 W.	GENERAL	41	2
15/05/42	AMPALA	HON.		U-507	26-30 N.	89-17 W.	GENERAL	57	1
16/05/41	NICARAO	U.S.A.		U-751	25-20 N.	74-19 W.	BANANAS	39	8
16/05/41	RUTH LYKES	U.S.A.		U-103	16-36 N.	82-25 W.	COFFEE	32	6
17/05/42	SAN VICTORIO	BRITISH		U-155	11-40 N.	62-33 W.	BENZENE	52	51
17/05/42	FORT QU'APPELLE	BRITISH		U-135	39-50 N.	63-30 W.	GENERAL	47	14
17/05/42	GULFOIL	U.S.A.		U-506	28-08 N.	89-46 W.	CRUDE OIL	40	21
17/05/42	CHALLENGER	U.S.A.		U-155	12-11 N.	61-18 W.	GENERAL	71	8
17/05/42	SKOTTLAND	NOR.		U-588	43-07 N.	67-18 W.	TIMBER	24	1
17/05/42	PEISANDER	BRITISH		U-653	37-24 N.	65-30 W.	WHEAT	64	0
17/05/42	BARRDALE	BRITISH		U-156	15-15 N.	52.27 W.	GENERAL	53	1
18/05/42	BETH	NOR.		U-162	48-00 N.	57-32 W.	FUEL OIL	31	1
18/05/42	MERCURY SUN	U.S.A.		U-125	21-01 N.	84-26 W.	FUEL OIL	35	6
18/05/42	FAUNA	DUTCH		U-558	22-10 N.	72-30 W.	GENERAL	29	2
18/05/42	QUAKER CITY	U.S.A.		U-156	14-55 N.	51-40 W.	ORE	40	10
19/05/42	WILLIAM J. SALMAN	U.S.A.		U-125	20-08 N.	83-46 W.	GENERAL	28	6
19/05/42	TISNAREN	SWED.		CAPPELLINI	03-38 N.	32-01 W.	GENERAL	40	0
19/05/42	HEREDIA	U.S.A.		U-506	28-53 N.	91-03 W.		48	30
19/05/42	ISABELLA	U.S.A.		U-571	17-50 N.	75-00 W.	GENERAL	37	3
19/05/42	OGONITZ	U.S.A.		U-103	23-30 N.	86.37 W.	NITRATES	41	19
20/05/42	HALO	U.S.A.		U-506	28-42 N.	90-08 W.	CRUDE OIL	42	39
20/05/42	DARINA	BRITISH	ON93	U-158	29-17 N.	54-25 W.	BALLAST	56	6
20/05/42	SYLVAN ARROW	PAN.		U-155	11-22 N.	62-14 W.	CRUDE OIL	44	1
20/05/42	NORLAND	NOR.		U-108	31-22 N.	55-47 W.	BALLAST	48	0
20/05/42	GEORGE CALVERT	U.S.A.		U-753	22-55 N.	84-26 W,	GENERAL	50	3
20/05/42	KATTEGAT	NOR.		A.M.C.	28-11 S.	11-30 W.	BALLAST	35	0
21/05/42	NEW BRUNSWICK	BRITISH	OS28	U-159	36-53 N.	22-55 W.	GENERAL	62	3
21/05/42	MONTENOL	BRITISH	OS28	U-159	36-41 N.	22-45 W.	BALLAST	64	3
21/05/42	CLARE	U.S.A.		U-103	21-35 N.	84-43 W.	BALLAST	40	0
21/05/42	FAJA DE ORO	MEX.		U-106	23-30 N.	84-24 W.	BALLAST	37	10
21/05/42	ELIZABETH	U.S.A.		U-103	21-35 N.	84-48 W.	GENERAL	42	9
21/05/42	TORONDOC	BRITISH		U-69	14-45 N.	62-15 W.	BAUXITE	21	21
21/05/42	TROISDOC	BRITISH		U-558	18-15 N.	79-20 W.	CEMENT	18	0
21/05/42	PRESIDENTE TRUJILLO	DOM.		U-156	14-38 N.	61-11 W.	GENERAL	39	24
22/05/42	PLOW CITY	U.S.A.		U-588	38-53 N.	69-57 W.	BAUXITE	31	1
22/05/42	FRANK B. BAIRD	BRITISH		U-158	28-03 N.	58-50 W.	BAUXITE	23	0
22/05/42	ZURICHMOOR	BRITISH		U-432	39-30 N.	66-00 W.	BALLAST	38	38
23/05/42	SAMUEL Q. BROWN	U.S.A.		U-103	20-15 N.	84-37 W.	FUEL OIL	55	2
23/05/42	MARGOT	BRITISH		U-588	39-00 N.	68-00 W.	GENERAL	40	1
23/05/42	WATSONVILLE	PAN.		U-155	13-12 N.	61-20 W.	GENERAL	30	0
24/05/42	HECTOR	DUTCH		U-103	20-03 N.	81-50 W.	GENERAL	21	2
24/05/42	GONCALVES DIAZ	BRAZ.		U-502	16-09 N.	70-00 W.	COFFEE	51	6
							TOTALS	**3,042**	**545**

BARRWHIN - 15 DECEMBER 1941 TO 8 SEPTEMBER 1942

SHIP AND U-BOAT LOSSES - WHEN SERVING ON *BARRWHIN* - 14 APRIL 1942 TO 24 MAY 1942

GERMAN U-BOATS	SHIPS SUNK IN PERIOD				ENEMY U-BOAT LOSSES				
NUMBER	TOTALS C/F B/F	TOTAL	14/04/42 08/05/42	09/05/42 24/05/42		DATE	CAUSE	DEAD	SAVED
U-66		6	6		U-74	02/05/42	AIR	46	0
U-69		3		3	U-252	14/04/42	D/C	44	0
U-84		1	1		U-352	09/05/42	D/C	13	33
U-94		3		3	U-573	01/05/42	AIR	1	43
U-103		7	1	6					
U-106		2	1	1					
U-108		5	4	1					
U-109		2	2						
U-123		1	1						
U-124		4		4					
U-125		9	5	4					
U-128		1		1					
U-135		1		1					
U-136		2	2						
U-154		1	1						
U-155		5		5					
U-156		8		8					
U-158		2		2					
U-159		2		2					
U-162		8	5	3					
U-201		3	3						
U-203		1	1						
U-333		3	2	1					
U-402		1	1						
U-403		1	1						
U-432		1		1					
U-455		1	1						
U-502		2		2					
U-504		1		1					
U-506		5	1	4					
U-507		9	7	2					
U-553		2		2					
U-558		2		2					
U-564		4	3	1					
U-571		2	1	1					
U-572		2	2						
U-575		1	1						
U-576		2	2						
U-588		4		4					
U-653		1		1					
U-654		2	2						
U-751		1		1					
U-752		2	2						
U-753		1		1					
	**957	830**	**127**	**59**	**68**				

						TOTALS	4	104	76
						B/F	81	2,382	1,075
						C/F	85	2,486	1,151

	C/F	B/F	TOTAL	14/04/42 08/05/42	09/05/42 24/05/42
HEAVY SHIPS	15	15	0		
RAIDERS	18	16	2	1	1
LIGHT WARSHIPS	6	5	1	1	
AIRCRAFT	58	54	4	4	
ITALIAN SUBMARINES	52	51	1		1
OTHER CAUSES	6	6	0		
	**155	147**	**8**	**6**	**2**

CONVOY SC86

Barrwhin put to sea on 25 May 1942, bound for Halifax, and arrived there two days later. We joined Sydney Cape Breton convoy SC86 of 35 ships on 5 June. The weather on passage from New York was typical for the time of year, with alternative banks of dense fog. This brought the usual appalling conditions of station keeping in fog. The dense fog continued intermittently across the Grand Banks and into the Atlantic. On the remainder of the passage, we encountered moderate winds and seas, and no enemy activity.

Only two ocean convoys were attacked when we were on passage to Halifax. Outward bound convoy OS28 lost one ship, the tanker *Athelknight*, on 27 May, by U-457, after detachment from the convoy. Arctic convoy PQ16 of 36 ships lost seven ships, six to aircraft and one sunk by U-703. The convoys lost 66 seamen dead out of a total complement of 352. The relatively lower fatal casualty rate can be attributed to the fact that the majority of the ships were sunk by aircraft attack during the warmer weather of early summer. Out of the total of 39 ships sunk during the period, 8 were sunk when in, or dispersed from, convoys, and 31 when unescorted, mainly in the areas close to the U.S.A., of which 22 were American owned or manned.

During our 18-day passage from Halifax to Immingham, seven ocean convoys were attacked. Moreover, the attacks on ships on independent passage in the western Atlantic continued without apparent respite. Of 67 ships that were sunk, 15 were in or detached from convoys, and 52 when unescorted. The greatest losses occurred in convoys ON100 (four ships) and HG84 (five ships). Convoys RU71, TA5, XB25 and ON102 were also attacked, losing five ships between them. Once again, the ship in which I served made the passage without suffering enemy attack. Despite this, carrying lethal cargoes on successive ocean passages imposed a severe strain on officers and men.

Significantly, although the war had reached its 33rd month, there was no evidence of air protection for convoys, and our escorts rarely exceeded two older class destroyers and two corvettes. This was a poor show, bearing in mind the fact that Allcock and Brown had crossed the Atlantic non-stop in 1919 in an antiquated Vickers Vimy 1914 to 1918 war bomber, and Charles Lindbergh had negotiated the same ocean crossing in 1927. Later in the war I was to serve as Second Mate of *Pilar de Larrinaga*, which had been bombed and damaged by a Focke Wulf Condor aircraft in a position 54-23 north, 16-53 west, on 18 July 1941, eleven months earlier.

Therefore, the enemy possessed the technology to produce aircraft with long-range capability, and the resolve to attack ships in an area where we never saw aircraft cover until 1943. We possessed the technology to attack long-range targets, but appeared to be decidedly lacking in resolve, or in the establishment of priorities.

Casualties – Ships and Personnel
25 May 1942 to 23 June 1942

Ships sunk – 106 by 38 successful U-Boats.
Four ships sunk by raiders.
Six ships sunk by Italian submarines.
Six ships sunk by aircraft.

Lost with all hands

Poseidon, cargo fuel oil, 31 dead.
L.J. Drake, cargo fuel oil, 41 dead.
Merrimack, cargo unknown 25 dead.
Frimaire, cargo fuel oil, 50 dead.
Tillie Lykes, cargo unknown, 33 dead.

Lost with very heavy casualties

Carrabule, cargo asphalt, 22 dead out of 40.
Jack, cargo sugar, 41 dead out of 63.
Alamar, cargo war materials, 23 dead out of 45.
Alcoa Pilgrim, cargo bauxite, 31 dead out of 40.
Norman Prince, in ballast, 16 dead out of 49.
Western Head, cargo sugar, 24 dead out of 30.
Allister, cargo bananas, 15 dead out of 23.
Dinsdale, cargo gasoline, 13 dead out of 44.
Bushranger, cargo bauxite, 17 dead out of 43.
Illinois, cargo bauxite, 32 dead out of 38.
City of Alma, in ballast, 29 dead out of 39.
M.F. Elliott, in ballast, 15 dead out of 45.
Gemstone, cargo iron ore, 19 dead out of 43.
Nidarnes, cargo fuel oil, 13 dead out of 25.
Velma Lykes, general cargo, 15 dead out of 32.
Castilla, cargo flour, 24 dead out of 59.

Sicilien, general cargo, 46 dead out of 77.
Ramsay, in ballast, 40 dead out of 49.
Lylepark, general cargo, 23 dead out of 46.
Dartford, in ballast, 30 dead out of 47.
Pelayo, general cargo, 21 dead out of 42.
Regent, general cargo, 11 dead out of 25.
Thurso, general cargo, 13 dead out of 42.
Bennestvet, general cargo, 12 dead out of 25.
Cherokee, in ballast with passengers, 86 dead out of 169.
San Blas, in ballast, 33 dead out of 47.

Merchant seamen and passengers killed – 1,242 out of 5,609, a fatal casualty rate of 22 percent

BARRWHIN - 15 DECEMBER 1941 TO 8 SEPTEMBER 1942

RECORD OF MERCHANT SHIPS SUNK IN ATLANTIC - 25/05/42 TO 05/06/42

BARRWHIN - ON PASSAGE NEW YORK TO HALIFAX AND WAITING FOR CONVOY SC86 - 25/05/42 TO 05/06/42

DATE	SHIP	NAT.	CONVOY NO.	CAUSE OF LOSS	POSITION		CARGO	CASUALTIES CREW	DEAD
25/05/42	BEATRICE	U.S.A.		U-558	17-21 N.	76-07 W.	SUGAR	31	1
25/05/42	PERSEPHONE	PAN.		U-593	39-44 N.	73-53 W.	CRUDE OIL	37	9
26/05/42	ALCOA CARRIER	U.S.A.		U-103	18-45 N.	79-50 W.	BALLAST	37	0
26/05/42	CARRABULE	U.S.A.		U-106	26-18 N.	89-21 W.	ASPHALT	40	22
26/05/42	SYROS	U.S.A.	PQ16	U-703	72-35 N.	05-30 E.	GENERAL	40	12
26/05/42	POYPHEMUS	DUTCH		U-578	38-12 N.	63-22 W.	WHEAT	61	15
27/05/42	ATHELKNIGHT	BRITISH	OS28	U-172	27-50 N.	46-00 W.	BALLAST	52	5
27/05/42	JACK	U.S.A.		U-558	17-36 N.	74-42 W.	SUGAR	63	41
27/05/42	HAMLET	NOR.		U-753	28-32 N.	91-30 W.	CRUDE OIL	36	0
27/05/42	EMPIRE PURCELL	BRITISH	PQ16	AIRCRAFT	73-57 N.	26-18 E.	GENERAL	56	8
27/05/42	EMPIRE LAWRENCE	BRITISH	PQ16	AIRCRAFT	73-57 N.	25-10 E.	GENERAL	68	19
27/05/42	LOWTHER CASTLE	BRITISH	PQ16	AIRCRAFT	73-57 N.	25-10 E.	GENERAL	47	1
27/05/42	CITY OF JOLIET	U.S.A.	PQ16	AIRCRAFT	73-50 N.	26-06 E.	GENERAL	48	0
27/05/42	ALAMAR	U.S.A.	PQ16	AIRCRAFT	73-57 N.	25-10 E.	GENERAL	45	23
27/05/42	MORMACSUL	U.S.A.	PQ16	AIRCRAFT	73-57 N.	25-10 E.	GENERAL	48	3
28/05/42	YORKMOOR	BRITISH		U-506	29-55 N.	72-26 W.	BAUXITE	46	0
28/05/42	ALCOA PILGRIM	U.S.A.		U-502	16-28 N.	67-33 W.	BAUXITE	40	31
28/05/42	MENTOR	BRITISH		U-106	24-11 N.	87-02 W.	GENERAL	85	7
28/05/42	POSEIDON	DUTCH		U-155	36-00 N.	71-00 W.	FUEL OIL	31	31
28/05/42	NEW JERSEY	U.S.A.		U-103	19-10 N.	81-50 W.	BALLAST	62	0
28/05/42	CHARLBURY	BRITISH		BARBARIGO	06-22 S.	29-44 W.	COAL	42	2
28/05/42	NORMAN PRINCE	BRITISH		U-156	14-40 N.	62-15 W.	BALLAST	49	16
29/05/42	WESTERN HEAD	BRITISH		U-107	19-57 N.	74-18 W.	SUGAR	30	24
29/05/42	ALLISTER	BRITISH		U-504	18-23 N.	81-13 W.	BANANAS	23	15
30/05/42	BAGHDAD	NOR.		U-155	14-15 N.	54-30 W.	GENERAL	30	9
30/05/42	ALCOA SHIPPER	U.S.A.		U-404	37-49 N.	65-15 W.	GENERAL	32	7
30/05/42	FRED W. GREEN	BRITISH		U-506	30-20 N.	62-00 W.	GENERAL	41	5
31/05/42	LIVERPOOL PACKET	BRITISH		U-432	43-20 N.	66-20 W.	GENERAL	21	2
31/05/42	DINSDALE	BRITISH		CAPPELLINI	00-45 S.	29-50 W.	GASOLENE	44	13
01/06/42	BUSHRANGER	PAN.		U-107	18-15 N.	81-25 W.	BAUXITE	43	17
01/06/42	WESTMORELAND	BRITISH		U-566	35-55 N.	63-35 W.	GENERAL	68	3
01/06/42	HAMPTON ROADS	U.S.A.		U-106	22-45 N.	85-13 W.	PHOSPHATE	28	5
01/06/42	WEST NOTUS	U.S.A.		U-404	34-10 N.	68-20 W.	LINSEED	40	4
01/06/42	ALEGRETE	BRAZ.		U-156	13-40 N.	61-20 W.	GENERAL	64	0
02/06/42	TRITON	DUTCH		U-558	26-00 N.	59-34 W.	BAUXITE	36	6
02/06/42	ILLINOIS	U.S.A.		U-159	24-00 N.	60-00 W.	BAUXITE	38	32
02/06/42	MATTAWIN	BRITISH		U-553	40-34 N.	66-34 W.	GENERAL	71	0
02/06/42	KNOXVILLE CITY	U.S.A.		U-158	21-25 N.	83-50 W.	GENERAL	55	2
02/06/42	BERGANGER	NOR.		U-578	39-22 N.	70-00 W.	COFFEE	44	4
02/06/42	CITY OF ALMA	U.S.A.		U-172	23-00 N.	62-30 W.	BALLAST	39	29
03/06/42	ANNA	SWED.		U-404	34-10 N.	68-22 W.	COAL	25	0
03/06/42	M.F. ELLIOTT	U.S.A.		U-502	12-04 N.	63-49 W.	BALLAST	45	15
06/06/42	HOEGH GIANT	NOR.		U-126	06-52 N.	42-43 W.	BALLAST	39	0
04/06/42	GEMSTONE	BRITISH		A.M.C.	01-52 N.	26-38 W.	ORE	43	19
04/06/42	NIDARNES	NOR.		U-158	21-17 N.	85-07 W.	FUEL OIL	25	13
05/06/42	DELFINA	U.S.A.		U-172	20-20 N.	67-07 W.	BAUXITE	31	4
05/06/42	L.J. DRAKE	U.S.A.		U-68	15-40 N.	68-00 W.	FUEL OIL	41	41
05/06/42	VELMA LYKES	U.S.A.		U-158	21-21 N.	86-36 W.	GENERAL	32	15
							TOTALS	**2,092**	**530**

BARRWHIN - 15 DECEMBER 1941 TO 8 SEPTEMBER 1942

RECORD OF MERCHANT SHIPS SUNK IN ATLANTIC - 06/06/42 TO 23/06/42

DATE	SHIP	NAT.	CONVOY NO.	CAUSE OF LOSS	POSITION		CARGO	CASUALTIES CREW	DEAD
	BARRWHIN		SC86						
06/06/42	CASTILLA	HOND.		U-107	21-03 N.	83-30 W.	FLOUR	59	24
06/06/42	C.O. STILLMAN	U.S.A.		U-68	17-33 N.	67-55 W.	FUEL OIL	42	30
06/06/42	STANVAC CALCUTTA	PAN.		A.M.C.	05-00 S.	28-00 W.	BALLAST	51	14
07/06/42	CHILE	BRITISH		DA VINCI	04-17 N.	13-48 W.	GENERAL	44	5
07/06/42	EDITH	U.S.A.		U-159	14-33 N.	74-35 W.	GENERAL	31	2
07/06/42	GEORGE CLYMER	U.S.A.		A.M.C.	14-49 N.	18-30 W.	GENERAL	37	1
07/06/42	SUWIED	U.S.A.		U-107	20-05 N.	85-35 W.	BAUXITE	30	6
07/06/42	HERMIS	PAN.		U-158	23-08 N.	84-42 W.	GENERAL	51	1
08/06/42	ROSENBORG	BRITISH	RU71	U-386	18-47 N.	85-05 W.	BAUXITE	27	4
08/06/42	SICILIEN	U.S.A.		U-172	17-30 N.	71-29 W.	GENERAL	77	46
08/06/42	BRUXELLES	BELG.	TA5	U-502	11-05 N.	66-40 W.	GENERAL	48	1
08/06/42	TELA	HOND.		U-504	18-15 N.	85-20 W.	BALLAST	56	13
08/06/42	PLEASANTVILLE	NOR.		U-135	34-00 N.	68-00 W.	GENERAL	47	2
08/06/42	SOUTH AFRICA	NOR.		U-128	12-47 N.	49-44 W.	FUEL OIL	42	6
09/06/42	EMPIRE CLOUGH	BRITISH	ON100	U-94	51-30 N.	35-29 W.	BALLAST	49	5
09/06/43	RAMSAY	BRITISH	ON100	U-94	51-53 N.	34-59 W.	BALLAST	49	40
09/06/42	FRANKLIN K. LANE	U.S.A.	TA5	U-502	11-12 N.	66-39 W.	CRUDE OIL	41	4
10/06/42	ARDENVOHR	BRITISH		U-68	12-45 N.	80-20 W.	GENERAL	64	1
10/06/42	PORT MONTREAL	BRITISH		U-68	12-17 N.	80-20 W.	EXPL.	45	0
10/06/42	SURREY	BRITISH		U-68	12-45 N.	80-20 W.	GENERAL	67	12
10/06/42	MERRIMACK	U.S.A.		U-107	19-48 N.	85-55 W.		25	25
10/06/42	ALIOTH	DUTCH		DA VINCI	00-08 N.	18-52 W.	GENERAL	36	8
10/06/42	L.A. CHRISTENSEN	NOR.		U-129	27-44 N.	63-54 W.	BALLAST	31	0
11/06/42	FORT GOOD HOPE	BRITISH		U-159	10-12 N.	80-16 W.	WHEAT	47	2
11/06/42	GEO. H. JONES	U.S.A.		U-455	45-40 N.	22-40 W.	FUEL OIL	44	2
11/06/42	LYLEPARK	BRITISH		A.M.C.	14-00 S.	10-00 W.	GENERAL	46	23
11/06/42	PONTYPRIDD	BRITISH	ON100	U-569	49-50 N.	41-37 W.	BALLAST	48	2
11/06/42	AMERICAN	U.S.A.		U-504	17-58 N.	84-28 W.	ORE	38	4
11/06/42	F.W. ABRAMS	U.S.A.		U-701	34-52 N.	75-45 W.	FUEL OIL	36	0
11/06/42	CRLJNSSEN	NOR.		U-504	18-14 N.	82-11 W.		93	1
11/06/42	HAGAN	U.S.A.		U-157	22-00 N.	77-30 W.	MOLASSES	44	6
11/06/42	SHEHERAZADE	PAN.		U-158	28-41 N.	91-20 W.	BALLAST	59	1
11/06/42	AMERICAN	U.S.A.		U-504	17-58 N.	84-28 W.		38	4
12/06/42	DARTFORD	BRITISH	ON100	U-124	49-19 N.	41-33 W.	BALLAST	47	30
12/06/42	HARDWICKE GRANGE	BRITISH		U-129	25-45 N.	65-45 W.	GENERAL	81	3
12/06/42	CITY SERVICE TOLEDO	U.S.A.		U-158	29-02 N.	91-59 W.	CRUDE OIL	46	13
13/06/42	CLAN McQUARRIE	BRITISH		DA VINCI	05-30 N.	23-30 W.	BALLAST	90	1
13/06/42	SIXAOLA	U.S.A.		U-159	09-41 N.	81-10 W.	GENERAL	207	29
13/06/42	SOLON TURMAN	U.S.A.		U-159	10-45 N.	80-24 W.	GENERAL	53	1
14/06/42	ETRIB	BRITISH	HG84	U-552	43-18 N.	17-38 W.	GENERAL	40	4
14.06/42	PELAYO	BRITISH	HG84	U-552	43-18 N.	17-38 W.	GENERAL	42	21
14/06/42	LEBORE	U.S.A.		U-172	12-53 N.	80-40 W.	COAL	46	1
14/06/42	SCOTTSBURG	U.S.A.		U-502	11-51 N.	62-56 W.	GENERAL	50	11
14/06/42	REGENT	LATV.		U-504	17-50 N.	84-10 W.	GENERAL	25	11
14/06/42	SLEMDAL	NOR.	HG84	U-552	43-18 N.	17-38 W.	BALLAST	37	0
15/06/42	COLD HARBOR	PAN.		U-502	11-40 N.	62-55 W.		51	9
15/06/42	CITY OF OXFORD	BRITISH	HG84	U-552	43-32 N.	18-12 W.	GENERAL	44	1
15/06/42	THURSO	BRITISH	HG84	U-552	43-41 N.	18-02 W.	GENERAL	42	13
15/06/42	FRIMAIRE	FRENCH		U-68	11-50 N.	62-15 W.	FUEL OIL	50	50
15/06/42	WEST HARDAWAY	U.S.A.		U-502	11-50 N.	62-15 W.	GENERAL	50	0
15/06/42	BENNESTVET	NOR.		U-172	10-47 N.	82-12 W.	GENERAL	25	12
15/06/42	CARDINA	PAN.		ARCHIMEDE	04-45 N.	40-55 W.	LINSEED	34	0
16/06/42	PORT NICHOLSON	BRITISH	XB25	U-87	42-11 N.	69-25 W.	GENERAL	87	4
16/06/42	ARKANSAN	U.S.A.		U-126	12-07 N.	62-51 W.	GENERAL	40	4
16/06/42	CHEROKEE	U.S.A.	XB25	U-87	42-25 N.	69-10 W.	BALLAST	169	86
16/06/42	KAHUKU	U.S.A.		U-126	11-54 N.	63-07 W.	GENERAL	46	9
16/06/42	MANAGUA	NIC.		U-67	24-05 N.	81-40 W.	GENERAL	25	0
17/06/42	MOTOREX	BRITISH		U-172	10-10 N.	81-30 W.	FUEL OIL	21	1
17/06/42	SANTORE	U.S.A.		U-701	36-53 N.	75-49 W.	COAL	46	3
17/06/42	FLORA	DUTCH		U-159	11-55 N.	72-36 W.	GENERAL	36	1
17/06/42	MOIRA	NOR.		U-158	25-35 N.	96-20 W.	BALLAST	19	1
17/06/42	SAN BLAS	PAN.		U-158	25-26 N.	95-33 W.	BALLAST	47	33
18/06/42	TILLIE LYKES	U.S.A.		U-161	19-00 N.	85-00 W.		33	33
18/06/42	MILLINOCKET	U.S.A.		U-129	23-12 N.	79-28 W.	BAUXITE	35	11
18/06/42	SEATTLE SPIRIT	U.S.A.	ON102	U-124	50-24 N.	42-37 W.	BALLAST	55	4
19/06/42	ANTE MATKOVIC	YUGO.		U-159	12-05 N.	75-30 W.	COAL	29	6
21/06/42	WEST IRA	U.S.A.		U-128	12-28 N.	57-05 W.	GENERAL	49	1
22/06/42	RIO TERCERO	ARG.		U-202	39-15 N.	72-32 W.	GENERAL	42	5
22/06/42	E.J. SADLER	U.S.A.		U-159	15-36 N.	67-52 W.	KEROSENE	36	0
23/06/42	RAWLEIGH WARNER	U.S.A.		U-67	28-53 N.	89-15 W.			
23/06/42	ANDREA BROVIG	NOR.		U-128	12-10 N.	59-10 W.	FUEL OIL	38	0
23/06/42	HENRY GIBBONS	U.S.A.		U-158	24-42 N.	87-46 W.			
23/06/42	TORVANGER	NOR.		U-84	39-40 N.	41-30 W.	GENERAL	37	4
23/06/42	ARRIAGA	PAN.		U-68	13-08 N.	72-16 W.	GENERAL	25	1
							TOTALS	3,517	712

BARRWHIN - 15 DECEMBER 1941 TO 8 SEPTEMBER 1942

SHIP AND U-BOAT LOSSES - WHEN SERVING ON *BARRWHIN* - 25 MAY 1942 TO 23 JUNE 1942

GERMAN U-BOATS	SHIPS SUNK IN PERIOD					ENEMY U-BOAT LOSSES				
NUMBER	TOTALS		TOTAL	25/05/42 05/06/42	06/06/42 23/06/42		DETAILS OF LOSS			
	C/F	B/F					DATE	CAUSE	DEAD	SAVED
U-67			2		2	U-157	13/06/42	D/C	52	0
U-68			7	1	6	U-568	28/05/42	D/C	0	47
U-84			1		1	U-652	02/06/42	SCUT	0	45
U-87			2		2					
U-94			2		2					
U-103			2	2						
U-106			4	4						
U-107			4	1	3					
U-124			2		2					
U-126			3	1	2					
U-128			3		3					
U-129			3		3					
U-135			1		1					
U-155			2	2						
U-156			2	2						
U-157			1		1					
U-158			9	3	6					
U-159			8	1	7					
U-161			1		1					
U-172			7	3	4					
U-202			1		1					
U-386			1		1					
U-404			3	3						
U-432			1	1						
U-455			1		1					
U-502			7	2	5					
U-504			6	1	5					
U-506			2	2						
U-552			5		5					
U-553			1	1						
U-558			3	3						
U-566			1	1						
U-569			1		1					
U-578			2	2						
U-593			1	1						
U-703			1	1						
U-701			2		2					
U-753			1	1						
	1,063	957	106	39	67					

	C/F	B/F	TOTAL	25/05/42 05/06/42	06/06/42 23/06/42
HEAVY SHIPS	15	15	0		
RAIDERS	22	18	4	1	3
LIGHT WARSHIPS	6	6	0		
AIRCRAFT	64	58	6	6	
ITALIAN SUBMARINES	58	52	6	2	4
OTHER CAUSES	6	6	0		
	171	155	16	9	7

TOTALS	3	52	92
B/F	85	2,486	1,151
C/F	88	2,538	1,243

On the credit side, a semblance of a convoy system had been established in the sea areas adjacent to the U.S.A., and in the West Indies,
indicating that the American operational command was awaking to reality.

Barrwhin detached from the convoy in the North Channel, and made
passage north about Scotland, and south through the North Sea, arriving
at Immingham on 23 June 1942, where the ship paid off and signed on the
following day. During the month of the passage of *Barrwhin* from New
York to Immingham, only three U-Boats were sunk, two (U-157 and U-
568) by depth charge attack, and one (U-652) by scuttling. Allied aircraft
achieved no successes.

Successful U-Boats were: U-158 (nine ships), U-159 (eight ships), U-68,
U-172 and U-502 (seven ships), U-504 (six ships) and U-552 (five ships). U-
68 was commanded by one of the most successful and distinguished U-
Boat commanders, Karl-Friedrich Merten. He survived the war; and was
promoted to the rank of Kapitan. Over forty years later, I wrote to him,
and he was able to provide me with details of the loss of my own ship
later in the war. He was a professional seaman of the highest standing,
with a great respect and admiration for British seamen. He had a tough
and dirty job to do, but conformed to the highest code of conduct, unlike
some of his fellow U-Boat commanders.

Quite amazingly, none of the Sidney Cape Breton or Halifax Nova
Scotia homeward bound convoys were attacked during the months of
May and June. This was partly because the enemy concentrated the
main U-Boat strength in areas where merchant ship protection was
minimal, but also because of the huge volume of tanker traffic in those
areas.

We discharged part cargo in Immingham. The ship was berthed next
to a quay on which thousands of mines were stored, preparatory for mine
laying operations in the North Sea and other coastal areas. The mines
were not armed, but there is no doubt that a direct hit from a bomb
would have blown Immingham to pieces, and certainly the ships berthed
in the vicinity.

I was not permitted leave, but Betty was allowed to travel to
Immingham and live aboard the ship, together with the wives of other
officers. After a week in Immingham, the ship moved to Hull. This
required a passage down to near Spurn Point at the mouth of the River
Humber, and then up river to Hull. No authority had issued any instructions about ladies remaining aboard, so Betty stayed on the ship, under
strict instructions from me to keep out of sight. Regrettably, her curiosity

prompted her to show herself on deck, as were entering the lock gates in Hull. A diligent R.N.V.R. Naval Control officer, who observed her on deck, came aboard asserting that the ship did not have authority to take a female to sea during wartime. On reflection, it was not a very intelligent action, because the enemy had mined the Humber estuary on occasions previously. It was all swept under the carpet, and Betty returned to her home just before the ship left Hull.

During the period when *Barrwhin* was berthed in Immingham and Hull, Arctic convoy PQ17 sustained huge losses. A great deal has been written about the events that occurred during the passage of convoy PQ17. The men of the Merchant Navy have never held the officers and seamen of the Royal Navy to blame for the debacle, which was precipitated by misjudgements in the Admiralty, and not by the escorts at sea with the convoy.

Convoy ON110

Barrwhin put to sea, and joined outward northern route convoy ON110, via Methil and the Pentland Firth, making contact on about 8 July. This convoy of 32 ships put to sea from Liverpool on 6 July, destination Boston, and arrived without attack on 26 July. The month of July was unusually quiet on the North Atlantic, probably because the enemy had concentrated forces in the Arctic waters, and in the southern and western areas of the Atlantic. Very substantial losses were sustained by our merchant ships during the month, in particular in Arctic convoy PQ 17 and amongst the independently routed ships well to the south, of which 32 were American owned or manned. It was tragic.

During our Atlantic passage, the convoy encountered dense fog for about a week, and many of the ships became detached, to proceed independently to the designated rendezvous points. *Barrwhin* was enveloped in intermittent dense fog banks for several days.

A surfaced U-Boat close ahead!!

During one night watch at about 2200, the fog lifted for a short time, and I was astonished to see a U-Boat on the surface, fine on our port bow, and about 1,000 yards ahead. At our speed of about 11 knots, the ship could cover the distance in about three minutes. The U-Boat was almost athwart our course, moving slowly from starboard to port. Our helmsman was unable to see the U-Boat, his view ahead being obstructed by the foremast and rigging. I opened the weather wheel house door, so I could conn the ship, by altering course gradually to port, to keep the U-Boat directly ahead. We had reduced the distance to about 500 yards, when the fog was beginning to close down again. I heard a shout from the starboard side of the bridge "For Christ's sake, hard a starboard!" The Master had arrived on the navigating bridge for his usual visit prior to turning in, and sighted the now barely discernible silhouette of a vessel close ahead. His instinctive reaction was to avoid collision. Before I could explain, it was too late. The U-Boat must have seen us at almost the same time, turned hard a starboard as well, and passed along our port side, at a distance of about 25 yards. With a forepeak half full of concrete to resist the Arctic ice, *Barrwhin* would have made a mess of the U-Boat. I missed the opportunity of ramming the bugger by about a half a minute, and a distance of about 20 yards.

On reflection, the Master took the only action, which his experience and training could permit, when confronted by an unidentified silhouette so close ahead, in darkness and in indifferent visibility. If he had delayed his visit to the bridge, or arrived on the bridge several minutes earlier, the outcome would have been so different. The enemy U-Boat was by then several miles astern, in dense fog, and probably very relieved at the narrow escape. Probably the lookout and officer of the watch may have qualified for the firing squad, because apparently they had not seen our ship until it would have been too late.

We berthed in Boston on 30 July 1942, where we commenced loading the usual cargo of steel products in the lower holds, and cases and equipment in the upper holds and on deck. During our ocean passage, five convoys were attacked, with modest losses: OS33 (five ships), KS120 (one ship), OS34 (two ships), QS19 (one ship) and ON113 (three ships). The main casualties were 36 ships lost when on independent passage.

During a period of two months to 30 July 1942, 210 ships were sunk, the most disastrous losses having been incurred in the Arctic convoys and around the West Indies, and American coast. The American Merchant Marine suffered huge losses in ships and men, due to lack of protection in the western Atlantic, Caribbean Sea, Gulf of Mexico and the West Indies.

Casualties – Ships and Personnel
24 June to 30 July 1942

Ships sunk – 104 by 46 successful U-Boats.
One ship sunk by Italian submarine.
Fourteen ships sunk by aircraft.
Six ships sunk by mines off Iceland

Lost with all hands

Ljubica Matkovic, cargo sugar, 30 dead.
Empire Attendant, general cargo, 59 dead.
Empire Hawksbill, general cargo, 46 dead.

Lost with very heavy casualties

Moldanger, general cargo, 23 dead out of 44.
Raphael Semmes, general cargo, 19 dead out of 37.
Empire Mica, Cargo fuel oil, 33 dead out of 47.
Ruth, cargo iron ore, 35 dead out of 39.
Alexander McComb, general cargo, 15 dead out of 66.
Navarino, general cargo, 19 dead out of 42.
Avila Star, gereral cargo and passengers, 62 dead out of 196.
River Afton, cargo war materials, 26 dead out of 64.
Bayard, general cargo, 11 dead out of 32.
Hartlebury, cargo war materials, 38 dead out of 56.
Triglav, cargo iron ore, 24 dead out of 43.
Benjamin Brewster, cargo gasoline, 27 dead out of 42.
Cortina, general cargo, 32 dead out of 55.
Port Hunter, general cargo, 88 dead out of 91.
British Yeoman, cargo fuel oil, 43 dead out of 53.
Port Antonio, cargo coffee, 13 dead out of 24.
Garmula, cargo grain, 21 dead out of 98.
Robert E. Lee, general cargo and passengers, 25 dead out of 407.
Onondanga, cargo ron ore, 18 dead out of 32.
Telamon, cargo bauxite, 23 dead out of 37.
Leikanger, cargo iron ore, 18 dead out of 31.
Prescodoc, in ballast, 15 dead out of 21.

Merchant seamen and passengers killed – 1,011 out of 6,387,
a fatal casualty rate of 16 percent.

BARRWHIN - 15 DECEMBER 1941 TO 8 SEPTEMBER 1942

RECORD OF MERCHANT SHIPS SUNK IN ATLANTIC - 24/06/42 TO 06/07/42

BARRWHIN - SIGNED ARTICLES AT IMMINGHAM - 24/06/42 - BERTHED AT IMMINGHAM AND HULL - 24/06/42 TO 06/07/42

DATE	SHIP	NAT.	CONVOY NO.	CAUSE OF LOSS	POSITION		CARGO	CASUALTIES CREW	DEAD
24/06/42	WILLIMATIC	BRITISH		U-156	25-55 N.	51-58 W.	BALLAST	38	6
24/06/42	LJUBICA MATKOVIC	YUGO		U-404	34-30 N.	75-40 W.	SUGAR	30	30
24/06/42	MANUELA	U.S.A.		U-404	34-20 N.	75-40 W.	SUGAR	43	2
24/06/42	NORDAL	PAN.		U-404	34-20 N.	75-40 W.	ORE	32	0
25/06/42	ANGLO CANADIAN	BRITISH		U-153	25-12 N.	55-31 W.	BALLAST	49	0
26/07/42	PUTNEY HILL	BRITISH		U-203	24-20 N.	63-06 W.	BALLAST	38	3
26/06/42	JAGERSFONTAIN	DUTCH		U-107	32-02 N.	54-53 W.	GENERAL	67	0
26/06/42	PENDRINHAS	BRAZ.		U-203	23-07 N.	62-06 W.	GENERAL	48	0
27/07/42	TUXPAM	MEX.		U-129	20-15 N.	96-20 W.	BALLAST	39	8
27/06/42	LIVE ERIKSSON	NOR.		U-126	13-18 N.	59-57 W.	FUEL OIL	44	2
27/06/42	LAS CHOAPAS	MEX.		U-129	20-15 N.	96-20 W.	FUEL OIL	32	4
27/06/42	POLYBIUS	U.S.A.		U-128	10-55 N.	57-40 W.	ORE	44	4
27/06/42	POTLACH	U.S.A.		U-153	19-20 N.	53-18 W.	GENERAL	55	8
27/06/42	MOLDANGER	NOR.		U-404	38-03 N.	70-52 W.	GENERAL	44	23
28/06/42	RAPHAEL SEMMES	U.S.A.		U-332	29-30 N.	64-30 W.	GENERAL	37	19
28/06/42	WM. ROCKEFELLER	U.S.A.		U-701	35-07 N.	75-07 W.	FUEL OIL	50	0
28/06/42	SAM HOUSTON	U.S.A.		U-203	19-21 N.	62-22 W.	GENERAL	47	8
28/06/42	SEA THRUSH	U.S.A.		U-505	23-38 N.	60-59 W.	GENERAL	66	0
29/06/42	EMPIRE MICA	BRITISH		U-67	29-25 N.	85-17 W.	FUEL OIL	47	33
29/06/42	RUTH	U.S.A.		U-153	21-44 N.	74-05 W.	ORE	39	35
29/06/42	WAIWERA	BRITISH		U-754	45-56 N.	34-23 W.	GENERAL	85	8
29/06/42	THOMAS McKEAN	U.S.A.		U-505	22-00 N.	60-00 W.	GENERAL	60	5
29/06/42	EVERELDA	LATV.		U-158	31-00 N.	70-00 W.	BALLAST	36	0
30/06/42	TYSA	DUTCH		MOROSINI	25-33 N.	57-53 W.	ORE	43	0
30/06/42	MOSFRUIT	NOR.		U-458	56-10 N.	23-20 W.	GENERAL	36	0
01/07/42	CITY OF BIRMINGHAM	U.S.A.		U-202	35-10 N.	70-53 W.	GENERAL	381	12
01/07/42	CADMUS	NOR.		U-129	22-50 N.	92-30 W.	BANANAS	22	2
01/07/42	WARRIOR	U.S.A.		U-126	10-54 N.	61-02 W.	GENERAL	56	7
01/07/42	GUNDERSEN	NOR.		U-129	23-33 N.	92-35 W.	BANANAS	23	1
02/07/42	ALEXANDER MACOMB	U.S.A.		U-215	41-26 N.	66-46 W.	GENERAL	66	15
04/07/42	NAVARINO	BRITISH	PQ17	AIRCRAFT	75-57 N.	27-14 E.	GENERAL	42	19
04/07/42	CHRIS. NEWPORT	U.S.A.	PQ17	AIRCRAFT	75-49 N.	22-25 E.	GENERAL	50	3
04/07/42	WILLIAM HOOPER	U.S.A.	PQ17	AIRCRAFT	75-57 N.	27-15 E.	GENERAL	45	3
04/07/42	NORLANDIA	U.S.A.		U-575	19-33 N.	68-39 W.	BALLAST	30	9
04/07/42	TUAPSE	RUSS.	QP13	U-129	22-13 N.	86-06 W.	BALLAST	46	8
05/07/42	AVILA STAR	BRITISH		U-201	38-04 N.	22-45 W.	GENERAL	196	62
05/07/42	EARLSTON	BRITISH	PQ17	U-334	74-54 N.	37-40 E.	GENERAL	52	0
05/07/42	EMPIRE BYRON	BRITISH	PQ17	U-703	76-18 N.	33-30 E.	GENERAL	69	7
05/07/42	RIVER AFTON	BRITISH	PQ17	U-703	75-57 N.	43-00 E.	GENERAL	55	22
05/07/42	CARLTON	U.S.A.	PQ17	U-88	76-14 N.	40-00 E.	GENERAL	45	3
05/07/42	PETER KERR	U.S.A.	PQ17	AIRCRAFT	76-14 N.	40-00 E.	GENERAL	49	0
05/07/42	HONOMU	U.S.A.	PQ17	U-456	75-05 N.	38-00 E.	GENERAL	41	0
05/07/42	HEFFRON	U.S.A.	QP13	MINED			BALLAST		
05/07/42	EXTERMINATOR	PAN.	QP13	MINED			BALLAST		
05/07/42	HYBERT	U.S.A.	QP13	MINED			BALLAST		
05/07/42	BOLTON CASTLE	BRITISH	PQ17	AIRCRAFT	76-40 N.	36-30 E.	GENERAL	58	0
05/07/42	ZAAFARAN	BRITISH	PQ17	AIRCRAFT	75-08 N.	42-43 E.	BALLAST	60	1
05/07/42	DANIEL MORGAN	U.S.A.	PQ17	U-88	75-08 N.	45-06 E.	GENERAL	54	3
05/07/42	FAIRFIELD CITY	U.S.A.	PQ17	AIRCRAFT	74-40 N.	39-45 E.	GENERAL	40	8
05/07/42	ALDERSDALE	BRITISH	PQ17	AIRCRAFT	75-12 N.	43-03 E.	GENERAL	54	0
05/07/42	MASSMAR	U.S.A.	QP13	MINED			BALLAST		
05/07/42	PAN KRAFT	U.S.A.	PQ17	AIRCRAFT	76-50 N.	38-00 E.	GENERAL	47	2
05/07/42	RODINA	RUSS.	QP13	MINED			BALLAST		
05/07/42	PETER KERR	U.S.A.	PQ17	AIRCRAFT	74-30 N.	35-00 E.	GENERAL	49	0
05/07/42	WASHINGTON	U.S.A.	PQ17	AIRCRAFT	75-00 N.	45-00 E.	GENERAL	46	0
05/07/42	JOHN RANDOLPH	U.S.A.	QP13	MINED			BALLAST		
05/07/42	PAULUS POTTER	DUTCH	PQ17	AIRCRAFT	75-00 N.	45-00 E.	GENERAL	62	0
06/07/42	PAN KRAFT	U.S.A.	PQ17	AIRCRAFT	76-50 N.	38-00 E.	GENERAL	47	2
06/07/42	DINARIC	BRITISH	QS15	U-132	49-28 N.	69-28 W.	GENERAL	41	4
06/07/42	JOHN WITHERSPOON	U.S.A.	PQ17	U-255	70-30 N.	52-30 E.	GENERAL	49	1
06/07/42	HAINAUT	BELG.	QS15	U-130	49-13 N.	66-49 W.	GENERAL	43	1
06/07/42	ANASTASSIOS PATERAS	GREEK	QS15	U-132	49-30 N.	66-30 W.	GENERAL	29	3
06/07/42	PAN ATLANTIC	U.S.A.	PQ17	AIRCRAFT	70-30 N.	52-30 E.	GENERAL	49	1
06/07/42	BAYARD	NOR.		U-67	29-35 N.	88-44 W.	GENERAL	32	11
						TOTALS		3,177	408

UPON THEIR LAWFUL OCCASIONS

BARRWHIN - 15 DECEMBER 1941 TO 8 SEPTEMBER 1942

RECORD OF MERCHANT SHIPS SUNK IN ATLANTIC - 07/07/42 TO 30/07/42

BARRWHIN - BERTHED IN IMMINGHAM AND ON PASSAGE TO LOCH EWE

DATE	SHIP	NAT.	CONVOY NO.	CAUSE OF LOSS	POSITION		CARGO	CASUALTIES CREW	DEAD
07/07/42	HARTLEBURY	BRITISH	PQ17	U-355	70-17 N.	56-10 E.	GENERAL	56	38
07/07/42	ALDERSDALE	BRITISH	PQ17	U-457	75-00 N.	45-00 E.	GENERAL	54	0
07/07/42	ALCOA RANGER	U.S.A.	PQ17	U-255	71-20 N.	51-00 E.	GENERAL	40	0
07/07/42	OLOPANA	U.S.A.	PQ17	U-255	72-10 N.	51-00 E.	GENERAL	41	6
07/07/42	UMTATA	BRITISH		U-571	25-35 N.	80-02 W.	ORE	90	0
08/07/42	J.A. MOFFETT, Jr.	U.S.A.		U-571	24-45 N.	80-42 W	BALLAST	43	1
09/07/42	CAPE VERDE	BRITISH		U-203	11-32 N.	60-17 W.	GENERAL	42	2
09/07/42	EMPIRE EXPLORER	BRITISH		U-575	11-40 N.	60-55 W.	GENERAL	71	3
09/07/42	SANTA RITA	U.S.A.		U-172	26-11 N.	55-40 W.	GENERAL	60	3
09/07/42	NICHOLAS CUNEO	HOND.		U-571	23-54 N.	82-33 W.	GENERAL	20	1
09/07/42	TRIGLAV	YUGO.		U-66	26-47 N.	48-10 W.	ORE	43	24
09/07/42	HOOSIER	U.S.A.	PQ17	U-376	69-45 N.	38-35 E.	GENERAL	52	0
09/07/42	EL CAPITAN	PAN.	PQ17	U-251	69-23 N.	40-50 E.	GENERAL	50	0
	BARRWHIN		ON111						
10/07/42	BENJAMIN BREWSTER	U.S.A.		U-67	29-05 N.	90-05 W.	GASOLENE	42	27
11/07/42	CORTONA	BRITISH	OS33	U-116	32-30 N.	24-47 W.	GENERAL	55	32
11/07/42	PORT HUNTER	BRITISH	OS33	U-582	31-00 N.	24-00 W.	GENERAL	91	88
11/07/42	STANVAC PALEMBANG	PAN.		U-203	11-28 N.	60-23 W.	BALLAST	50	5
12/07/42	SHAFTESBURY	BRITISH	OS33	U-116	31-42 N.	25-32 W.	COAL	45	0
12/07/42	SIRIS	BRITISH		U-201	31-20 N.	24-48 W.	GENERAL	55	3
12/07/42	TACHIRA	U.S.A.		U-129	18-15 N.	81-54 W.	GENERAL	39	5
13/07/42	PAULUS POTTER	DUTCH		U-255	70-00 N.	52-00 E	GENERAL	40	0
13/07/42	SITHONIA	BRITISH	OS33	U-201	29-00 N.	25-00 W.	COAL	53	7
13/07/42	ANDREW JACKSON	U.S.A.		U-84	23-32 N.	81-02 W.	BALLAST	49	3
13/07/42	ONEIDA	U.S.A.		U-166	20-17 N.	74-06 W.	GENERAL	37	6
13/07/42	R.W. GALLAGHER	U.S.A.		U-67	28-32 N.	90-59 W.	FUEL OIL	52	8
14/07/42	BRITISH YEOMAN	BRITISH		U-201	26-42 N.	24-20 W.	FUEL OIL	53	43
15/07/42	EMPIRE ATTENDANT	BRITISH	OS33	U-582	23-48 N.	21-51 W.	GENERAL	59	59
15/07/42	CHILORE	U.S.A.	KS520	U-576	34-47 N.	75-22 W.	BALLAST	49	2
15/07/42	BLUEFIELDS	NIC.		U-576	34-46 N.	75-22 W.	GENERAL	24	0
16/07/42	FAIRPORT	U.S.A.		U-161	27-12 N.	64-30 W.	GENERAL	49	0
16/07/42	BEACONLIGHT	PAN.		U-160	10-59 N.	61-05 W.	BALLAST	41	1
18/07/42	CARMONA	PAN.		U-160	10-58 N.	61-20 W.	LINSEED	35	4
19/07/42	EMPIRE HAWKSBILL	BRITISH	OS34	U-564	42-29 N.	25-26 W.	GENERAL	46	46
19/07/42	LAVINGTON COURT	BRITISH	OS34	U-564	42-38 N.	25-28 W.	GENERAL	45	6
19/07/42	LEONIDAS M.	GREEK		U-332	37-52 N.	52-04 W.	IRON ORE	31	0
19/07/52	BAJA CALIFORNIA	HOND.		U-84	25-24 N.	82-27 W.	GENERAL	37	3
19/07/42	PORT ANTONIO	NOR.		U-129	23-39 N.	84-00 W.	COFFEE	24	13
20/07/42	FREDERICA LENSEN	BRITISH	QS19	U-132	49-22 N.	65-12 W.	BALLAST	47	4
21/07/42	DONOVANIA	BRITISH		U-160	10-56 N.	61-10 W.	BALLAST	50	5
22/07/42	HONOLULAN	U.S.A.		U-582	08-41 N.	22-04 W.	ORE	40	0
23/07/42	GARMULA	BRITISH		U-752	05-32 N.	14-45 W.	GRAIN	98	21
23/07/42	ONONDAGA	U.S.A.		U-129	22-40 N.	68-44 W.	ORE	32	18
24/07/42	TELAMON	DUTCH		U-160	09-15 N.	59-54 W.	BAUXITE	37	23
25/07/42	BROOMPARK	BRITISH	ON113	U-552	49-02 N.	40-26 W.	GENERAL	49	4
25/07/42	TANK EXPRESS	NOR.		U-130	10-05 N.	26-31 W.	BALLAST	39	0
26/07/42	EMPIRE RAINBOW	BRITISH	ON113	U-607	47-08 N.	42.57 W.	BALLAST	47	0
26/07/42	TAMANDARE	BRAZ.		U-66	11-34 N.	60-30 W.	GENERAL	52	4
26/07/42	OAXACA	MEX.		U-171	28-23 N.	96-08 W.	GENERAL	45	6
27/07/42	ELMWOOD	BRITISH		U-130	04-48 N.	22-00 W.	GENERAL	51	0
27/07/42	WEIRBANK	BRITISH		U-66	11-29 N.	58-51 W.	BALLAST	67	1
27/07/42	STELLA LYKES	U.S.A.		U-582	06-40 N.	25-05 W.	BALLAST	53	1
27/07/42	LEIKANGER	NOR.		U-752	04-00 N.	18-00 W.	ORE	31	18
28/07/42	BARBACENA	BRAZ.		U-155	13-10 N.	56-00 W.	CEREALS	62	6
28/07/42	PIAVE	BRAZ.		U-155	12-30 N.	55-49 W.	BALLAST	35	1
29/07/42	PRESCODOC	BRITISH		U-160	08-50 N.	59-05 W.	BALLAST	21	15
29/07/42	BILL	NOR.		U-155	12-50 N.	55-30 W.	GENERAL	24	1
30/07/42	PACIFIC PIONEER	BRITISH	ON113	U-132	43-32 N.	60-38 W.	BALLAST	67	0
30/07/42	ROBERT E. LEE	U.S.A.		U-166	28-40 N.	88-42 W.	GENERAL	407	25
30/07/42	CRANFORD	U.S.A.		U-155	12-17 N.	55-11 W.	ORE	47	11
30/07/42	DANMARK	BRITISH		U-130	07-00 N.	24-19 W.	BALLAST	46	0
							TOTALS	**3,210**	**603**

258

BARRWHIN - 15 DECEMBER 1941 TO 8 SEPTEMBER 1942

SHIP AND U-BOAT LOSSES - WHEN SERVING ON *BARRWHIN* - 24 JUNE 1942 TO 30 JULY 1942

GERMAN SUBMARINES			SHIPS SUNK IN PERIOD			ENEMY U-BOAT LOSSES				
NUMBER	TOTALS			24/06/42	07/07/42	DETAILS OF LOSS				
	C/F	B/F	TOTAL	06/07/42	30/07/42		DATE	CAUSE	DEAD	SAVED
U-66			3		3	U-90	24/07/42	D/C	44	0
U-67			4	2	2	U-126	11/06/42	D/C	45	0
U-84			2		2	U-136	11/07/42	D/C	45	0
U-88			2	2		U-153	13/06/42	D/C	52	0
U-107			1	1		U-158	30/06/42	AIR	54	0
U-116			2		2	U-215	03/07/42	D/C	48	0
U-126			2	2		U-502	06/07/42	AIR	52	0
U-128			1	1		U-576	15/07/42	GUN	45	0
U-129			8	5	3	U-701	07/06/42	AIR	39	17
U-130			4	1	3	U-751	17/07/42	AIR	44	0
U-132			4	2	2					
U-153			3	3						
U-155			4		4					
U-156			1	1						
U-158			1	1						
U-160			5		5					
U-161			1		1					
U-166			2		2					
U-171			1		1					
U-172			1		1					
U-201			4	1	3					
U-202			1	1						
U-203			5	3	2					
U-215			1	1						
U-251			1		1					
U-255			4	1	3					
U-332			2	1	1					
U-334			1	1						
U-355			1		1					
U-376			1		1					
U-404			4	4						
U-456			1	1						
U-457			1		1					
U-458			1	1						
U-505			2	2						
U-552			1		1					
U-564			2		2					
U-571			3		3					
U-575			2	1	1					
U-576			2		2					
U-582			4		4					
U-607			1		1					
U-701			1	1						
U-703			3	3						
U-752			2		2					
U-754			1	1						
	1,167	1,063	104	44	60	TOTALS	10	468	17	
						B/F	88	2,538	1,243	
						C/F	98	3,006	1,260	

HEAVY SHIPS	15	15	0		
RAIDERS	22	22	0		
LIGHT WARSHIPS	6	6	0		
AIRCRAFT	78	64	14	14	
ITALIAN SUBMARINES	59	58	1	1	
OTHER CAUSES	12	6	6	6	
	192	171	21	21	0

There was an amusing incident when we were in port. Our D.E.M.S. gunners, including a giant private in the Royal Maritime Artillery, went ashore for a booze-up. This private was about 6' 9" in height, and must have weighed over 20 stones or 300 pounds. He could lift two sacks of potatoes by the ears of the sacks, one in each hand, and hold them horizontally at arms length. Despite his huge bulk and phenomenal strength, he was a quiet man, and a model shipmate. He suffered from an impediment in speech, which caused him to stutter sometimes when agitated.

I was officer of the deck when the crew, including the gunners, went ashore; and about midnight was on deck when a number returned, some quite the worse for wear. One of the gunners reported to me, that they had been involved in a fracas in a bar with a number of American Marines. The report was, "I think the big fellow may have killed a f...... Yank, sir". They then went aft and turned in, including the huge gunner. About a half an hour later, a number of American Navy Police boarded the ship and reported to me. "Do you have a giant soldier aboard, sir?" It could have been none other than our gentle giant.

I told them to wait amidships, while I went aft to interview the gunners. All agreed on the story that they were having drinks in a bar when several American marines commenced taunting them, turning their main attentions on the big man. Then one of them called him a "f...... Limey." The giant responded with the words "I d-d-don't w-want to h-h-have any t-t-trouble with you f-f-f-fellows". When they persisted with their taunts, all hell broke loose; and three American marines were taken to hospital by ambulance. I asked the big fellow what had happened, and his answer was "They k-k-kept on c-c-calling me a f...... Limey, sir, so all I did was to t-t-tap them". A tap from him must have been worse than a kick from an elephant!

I returned to the military police, and told them that it appeared that their countrymen had provoked the fracas, and that I would not release any of our crew into their custody. I then learned that all three marines had sustained fractured skulls, and one had half the bones in his face broken, and was on the critical list in hospital. Despite this, I refused to allow them to attempt to arrest any of our men on a British ship and demanded that they report the matter to a senior officer. They left reluctantly. Several days later a U.S. Marine Corps officer boarded the ship to report that witnesses in the bar had verified the version of events given by our men; also that he had visited his men in hospital, and was happy to report that they were recovering. I think that after their tangle with one private in our Royal Maritime Artillery, anything that they would encounter from the enemy would be child's play in comparison.

During the time when we were loading in Boston, another homeward bound convoy, SC94, of 30 ships, departing from Sidney Cape Breton on 13 August 1942 bound for Liverpool, encountered a flotilla of six U-Boats, U-176, U-379, U-438, U-593 and U-660. The U-Boats mounted sustained attacks from 5 to 10 August, sinking 11 ships, namely the British ships *Anneberg, Cape Race, Empire Reindeer, Kelso, Oregon, Radchurch*, and *Trehata*, the Greek ships *Condylus* and *Mount Kassion*, and the American ship *Kaimoku. Trehata*, suffered the heaviest fatal casualties, once again testimony to the lethal character of steel cargoes. The following convoy, SC95 of 41 ships lost one American ship, *Balladier* to the attack of U705, with the loss of 11 officers and men.

During the period of 36 days, the most successful U-Boats were U-129 (eight ships): U-160 and U-203 (five ships each): and U-67, U-130, U-132, U-155, U-404 and U-582 (four ships each). Ten U-boats were destroyed, five by depth charge attack, one by depth charge and gunfire, and four by aircraft. Out of a total complement of 485 officers and other ranks, 468 were killed.

CONVOY SC97

We completed loading in the middle of August 1942, and departed for Halifax, where we joined convoy SC97 of 59 ships, which put to sea on 22 August, destination Liverpool. *Barrwhin* was second ship in the starboard outside column of the convoy. Escort was the destroyer *H.M.S. Bulldog* and some R.C.N. naval vessels. I am not certain of the exact composition of the escort, but believe it included two other destroyers and a number of corvettes. I now know that one of the Canadian escort vessels was *H.M.C.S. Morden*.

When we were three days on passage, we received frequent signals indicating a concentration of U-Boats in our area, and the convoy made many emergency turns. A sustained attack was made on outward bound convoy ON122 by at least 3 U-Boats, and during the night of 25 August four British ships in ballast were sunk: *Empire Breeze* by U176, *Katvaldis* and *Sheafmount* by U605, and *Trolla* by U438. *Sheafmount* suffered 31 men killed.

I was on the bridge during the night watch on either 24 or 25 August. There was no moon, the wind was gentle and the sea slight, and the ship was keeping station in the outer starboard column of the convoy. Suddenly, a dark silhouette appeared on the starboard quarter, closing rapidly, and slowed to our speed when abeam. It was one of the escorting destroyers. The loud hailer was switched on, and a cultured voice called us, by our position number, "I have just come in from an anti U-Boat sweep on the starboard wing of the convoy, and you have a bloody light showing amidships. Put the light out, officer of the watch".

I shouted some inadequate apology over our megaphone. Then the destroyer increased speed, and turned away. Before the destroyer was well away from us, the loud hailer boomed out again in the same cultured voice, "She's lit up like a f...... Christmas tree, No. 1!" The officer of the watch on the destroyer had omitted to switch off the loud hailer.

The standby man reported that the Chief Engineer had left his cabin during daylight to visit the Master for their usual evening drinks, leaving his door on the hook; so the door-operated light switch was in the "off position", but the light switch in the "on" position. He had forgotten to close and clip the porthole deadlights. When the First Mate had sent the standby man to check blackout security before dark, no light was seen in the cabin, because the door-operated switch was in the "off" position. The standby man failed to observe that the porthole deadlight was not closed and clipped. When the Chief Engineer returned to his dark cabin, probably with more than a few whiskies in him, he unclipped the door hook, closed the door, and the light switched on. We were lucky on that occasion, and it was a lesson to all of us.

Several days later, on 31 August 1942, during the forenoon watch, at 1005, I saw the tracks of several torpedoes, crossing our bows, diagonally from starboard to port. I altered course hard a starboard, to run down the tracks of the torpedoes. The Norwegian ship *Bronxville*, on our port beam in the next column, was stuck by a torpedo on the starboard side between No. 1 and No. 2 holds. There was a huge explosion and column of water, throwing debris high into the air. A fire broke out over No. 2 hold. She was carrying a part cargo of high explosives, and immediately broke out the "B" burgee. The ships in the adjacent columns took emergency action to steer out of the vicinity of what would have been a catastrophic explosion. The ship took a severe list to starboard and commenced sinking rapidly by the head. Less than a minute later, the Panamanian ship *Capira*, the rear ship in one of the middle columns, was struck by a torpedo on the starboard side between No. 4 and No. 5 holds, and settled rapidly by the stern. Then the trigger-happy Armed Guard gunners on a number of American ships unleashed a barrage of fire in every direction, some of the projectiles falling near the lifeboats from the sinking ships. They also opened fire with their Bofors and Oerlikan automatic weapons. It was bedlam for a short time. They were firing in all directions. Fortunately, their aim was as poor as their discipline.

Both ships remained afloat for about ten minutes and then sank. The attack was made from a submerged position, diagonally from outside the starboard wing of the convoy, by U-609, commanded by Kapitan-Leutnant Klaus Rudloff. The luck of U-609 ran out when the U-Boat was attacking convoy SC118 on 7 February 1943, and was destroyed by depth charges by the French corvette *Lobelia*. There were no survivors from her complement of 46.

During 1942, the number of American ships in our ocean convoys had increased, and in particular, the numbers of American ships in Arctic convoys exceeded the numbers of other nationalities. Although it was unnecessary, our "Consigs" (convoy signals) code books, which we had been using for three years, had the name changed to "Mersigs" (merchant ship signals). It was daft, because the books were otherwise fundamentally unaltered; but when the U.S.A. cracked the whip, we jumped through the hoop. Similarly, we were forced to adopt their phonetic alphabet when using radio telephone signals. Apple and Butter became Able and Baker, and so on through the alphabet. It was just another nuisance to endure, after using our phonetic alphabet for years.

During the night watch on 31 August 1942, when I was on the bridge at about 2200 hrs, I heard a constant throbbing sound, which appeared to be aboard our ship, somewhere on the starboard side. I sent the standby man to check the funnel guys to ascertain if there was a slack bottle screw. When he reported that they were all secure, I ordered him to check the lifeboat davit guys and griping bands, but they were also secure. It was a calm night with a slight sea, without any moonlight, and the darkness was overwhelming. The radio telephone earphones were hanging out through the chart room porthole, so I could hear any messages. At about seven bells, 2330, there was a message over the R/T. from the senior officer of the escort "All ships – illuminate Hitler, I repeat – illuminate Hitler".

I jerked the toggles of the starboard bridge "Snowflake" rocket launchers, and it seemed like all the 55 ships in the convoy, and our escort, did the same, turning the pitch black night into almost daylight. I rang the alarm bells to turn the gunners out, and called Captain Dixon to the bridge. The Second Mate and the middle watch had been called already at seven bells.

The intense light illuminated a surfaced U-Boat, conning tower just awash, which was about 50 yards away just abaft our starboard beam, and on a parallel course, travelling at convoy speed. The U-Boat engines were the origin of the throbbing noises that I had heard for about a half an hour. I opened fire with the starboard bridge twin Marlin machine gun, firing two belts at the conning tower, where we could clearly see the German crew. During the short time the U-boat was illuminated, the tracer bullets were ricocheting off her hull into the darkness. The ship astern of *Barrwhin* also opened fire with her bridge-mounted machine guns.

The U-Boat veered rapidly to starboard, and increased to full speed, and disappeared into the stygian darkness that had returned. I will never know what the U-Boat was doing so close to the convoy. It is possible that the commander was waiting for other units in the flotilla to join her for a surface attack, but no attack materialised.

The records show that U-756 (Kapitan-Leutnant Klaus Harney) reported an attack on convoy SC97, but gave no details. The recorded time was 2104 on 31 August 1942, U-Boat time. Allowing for an hour difference in the times, I can only assume that the surfaced U-Boat was U-756, which I heard first at about 2200. The commander must have been very inexperienced or very foolhardy. He was not to live long after his encounter with our convoy SC97. Our escort, *H.M.C.S. Morden* detected U-756 on the following day, 1 September 1942. The U-Boat was sunk by depth charge attack. There were no survivors from the U-Boat complement of 43. Certainly, if the commander of U-756 believed that his crazy action was attack, he was as misguided as he was foolish. One record states, "U-756 reported an attack in position AK2686, but gave no details".

In the early hours of 1 September, U-604, reported time 0328, position AK2839, Kapitan-Leutnant Horst Holtring, in U-604, made attack reports based on their hearing explosions, and claimed to have damaged a 5,000 ton ship. Two hours later at 0544, U-609 reported "one detonation after 4 min. 30 sec." In position AK3727." However, for almost the whole of the trans Atlantic passage of SC97, and in almost every ocean passage throughout the war, there had been frequent depth charge explosions, by day and night.

These reports appeared to have been cases of deluded optimism, because there were no further successful U-Boat attacks, due to the vigilance and expertise of our ocean escort group. U-604 was eventually caught by an American Liberator aircraft, and by the destroyer *U.S.S. Moffett*. The U-Boat was scuttled. The commanding officer survived, but 14 of his crew were lost.

The Second Mate had habitually relieved me late on almost every watch during the period of my service in *Barrwhin*, usually fifteen minutes after eight bells, but sometimes even later. He invariably slept in his bunk in pyjamas. After the encounter with the surfaced U-Boat, there was no sign of the Second Mate, fully 15 minutes after the commencement of his middle watch.

The Master had ordered the doubling of the watches by the officers. The Second Mate should have been on watch with him, while I was on watch with the First Mate. The Master asked, "Where the hell is the Second Mate?" I told him that he had been called at seven bells and again at one bell. "Then go down and drag the bugger out of his bunk". I found the Second Mate fast asleep again. He had slept though all the gunfire commotion, alarm bells, and the traffic over his head. I dragged him into a sitting position with his feet over the edge of his bunk, and went back on the bridge. Again he did not appear. Eventually, the First Mate left the bridge and returned with him, and all hell exploded on the bridge. The Master asked how long this had been going on, and I had to admit that it happened almost every middle watch. The Second Mate received a thorough roasting by the Master. He was a one off, but I had only a further week with him, as a fellow officer, thank God.

Convoy SC97 reached Liverpool on 7 September 1942, and we arrived in Cardiff late in the evening. I learned from the parson from the Missions to Seamen that Betty was undertaking voluntary work in a canteen near the dock gates. I was released from duty, and we walked home through the blackout for the commencement of my leave entitlement.

During the 17 days when the ship was berthed in Boston, and the 21 days on passage to Halifax and Cardiff, the pattern of U-Boat activity had changed dramatically. Out of the 51 ships sunk in the first period, 21 were sunk when in convoy, and 30 when on independent passage. However, a convoy system – of sorts – had been established in the western Atlantic. Two ships were sunk in convoy TAW12, a short distance north of Cuba and Haiti, and two ships were sunk in convoy PG6, in the Caribbean Sea north of Venezuela. Atlantic convoys lost quite heavily, ON15 losing three ships, SC94 (eleven ships), SC95 (two ships) and SL118 (one ship).

Within the second period, out of 55 ships sunk, 31 were lost in convoy, and 24 when on independent passage. Attacks continued on the western Atlantic convoys: in the Caribbean Sea convoy TAW13 lost four ships, and in the West Indies area there were losses in convoy TAW(S) (two ships), TAW 15 (four ships):, and T3 and GAT2 (one ship each). Ocean convoys also suffered: SL118 (three ships), ON122 (four ships), SL119 (three ships), SC97 (two ships), OS37 (one ship) and OS33 (three ships).

Seventeen U-Boats were sunk: four by depth charge, four by ramming (probably after depth charge attack), six by air attack, one by a submarine and two by collision. The encouraging factor for us was the increasing numbers of U-Boats destroyed by air attack. Of course, the seamen in the merchant ships were not aware of these facts at the time. All we knew was that hundreds of our ships were being sunk, and thousands of our fellow seamen were being slaughtered. We could detect no significant improvement, except for a temporary lull in U-Boat activity directed against Atlantic convoys for a period of about six months during 1942.

U-507 and U176 sank six ships each: U-66, U-130 and U517, five ships each: and U-109, U-155, U-162, four ships each. The circumstances of the sinking by U-507 of the Brazilian ships, *Baependy, Araraquara, Annibal Benevola*, and *Itagiba* are decidedly questionable. Out of a total of 802 passengers and crew, 611 were killed. *Baependy* and *Araraquara* were attacked in the hours of darkness, so the heavy loss of life may have been due to panic. However, *Annibal Benevolo* and *Itabiba* were sunk during daylight. We can feel no sense of regret that Korvetten-Kapitan Schacht and the entire crew of U-507 perished in an air attack on 13 January 1943.

When *Barrwhin* paid off on 8 September 1942, I had served on the ship for nearly nine months. Although Captain Dixon asked me to sign on again, I decided to take my full leave entitlement. *Barrwhin* was sunk with heavy loss of life on the following voyage.

Casualties – Ships and Personnel
31 July 1942 to 8 September 1942

Ships sunk – 106 by 47 U-Boats.
One ship sunk by a raider.
Five ships sunk by Italian submarines.

Lost with all hands

Manzanillo, general cargo 23 dead.
Louisiana, cargo fuel oil, 49 dead.
West Celina, general cargo, 44 dead.
Hamla, cargo iron ore, 38 dead.

Lost with very heavy casualties

Belgian Soldier, in ballast, 21 dead out of 53.
Tricula, cargo fuel oil, 47 dead out of 58.
Arletta, in ballast, 34 dead out of 39.
Trehata, cargo steel, 31 dead out of 56.
San Emiliano, cargo gasoline, 40 dead out of 48.
Mendenau, general cargo, 69 dead out of 85.
Malmanger, cargo fuel oil, 18 dead out of 34.
Vimeira, cargo fuel oil, 23 dead out of 45.
Santiago de Cuba, general cargo, 10 dead out of 29.
Everelza, cargo iron ore, 23 dead out of 37.
Baependy, general cargo and passengers, 284 dead out of 320.
Araraquara, passengers, 136 dead out of 143.
Annibal Benevolo, passengers, 159 dead out of 163.
Itagiba, general cargo and passengers, 32 dead out of 176.
Arara, cargo scrap steel, 20 dead out of 35.
Sheafmount, in ballast, 31 dead out of 59.
Viking Star, general cargo, 33 dead out of 69.
City of Cardiff, general cargo, 21 dead out of 84.
San Fabian, cargo fuel oil, 26 dead out of 59.
Topa Topa, general cargo, 25 dead out of 60.
West Lashaway, general cargo, 39 dead out of 56.
Jack Carnes, in ballast, 27 dead out of 56.
Winamac, cargo fuel oil, 30 dead out of 51.
Ilorin, general cargo, 32 dead out of 37.
Amatlan, in ballast, 10 dead out of 34.
Saganaga, cargo iron ore, 30 dead out of 44.
Tuscan Star, general cargo, 52 dead out of 114.

Merchant seamen and passengers killed – 1,732 out of 6,982,
a fatal casualty rate of 25 percent

UPON THEIR LAWFUL OCCASIONS

BARRWHIN - 15 DECEMBER 1941 TO 4 SEPTEMBER 1942

RECORD OF MERCHANT SHIPS SUNK IN ATLANTIC - 31/07/42 TO 17/08/42

BARRWHIN - BERTHED AT BOSTON - 31/07/42 TO 17/08/42

DATE	SHIP	NAT.	CONVOY NO.	CAUSE OF LOSS	POSITION		CARGO	CASUALTIES CREW	DEAD
01/08/42	KENTAR	DUTCH		U-155	11-53 N.	55-08 W.	ORE	79	3
01/08/42	CLAN MacNAUGHTON	BRITISH		U-155	11-54 N.	54-25 W.	COTTON	86	6
01/08/42	KASTOR	GREEK		TAZOLLI	11-06 N.	59-05 W.	GENERAL	35	4
02/08/42	MALDONALDO	URUG.		U-510	28-20 N.	63-10 W.	GENERAL	49	0
02/08/42	FLORA II	BRITISH		U-254	62-45 N.	19-07 W.	FISH	30	0
02/08/42	TREMINNARD	BRITISH		U-160	10-40 N.	57-07 W.	BALLAST	38	0
03/08/42	LOCHKATRINE	BRITISH	ON115	U-552	45-52 N.	46-44 W.	BALLAST	81	9
03/08/42	BELGIAN SOLDIER	BELG.	ON115	U-607	45-52 N.	47-13 W.	BALLAST	53	21
03/08/42	TRICULA	BRITISH		U-108	11-35 N.	56-51 W.	FUEL OIL	58	47
04/08/42	RICHMOND CASTLE	BRITISH		U-176	50-25 N.	25-05 W.	MEAT	64	14
04/08/42	EMPIRE ARNOLD	BRITISH		U-155	10-45 N.	52-30 W.	GENERAL	59	9
05/08/42	ARLETTA	BRITISH	ON115	U-458	44-44 N.	55-22 W.	BALLAST	39	34
05/08/42	SPAR	DUTCH	SC94	U-593	53-05 N.	43-38 W.	GENERAL	39	3
06/08/42	HAVSTEN	NOR.		TAZOLLI	11-18 N.	54-45 W.	BALLAST	33	2
06/08 42	ROZEWIE	PAL.		U-66	11-00 N.	57-30 W.	GENERAL	18	3
06/08/42	BRENAS	NOR.		U-108	10-20 N.	56-10 W.	GENERAL	34	1
06/08/42	DELFSHAVEN	DUTCH		U-572	07-24 N.	25-37 W.	GENERAL	39	1
07/08/42	ARTHUR W. SEWALL	NOR.		U-109	08-28 N.	34-21 W.	BALLAST	36	0
08/08/42	TREHATA	BRITISH	SC94	U-176	56-30 N.	32-14 W.	STEEL	56	31
08/08/42	KELSO	BRITISH	SC94	U-176	56-30 N.	32-14 W.	GENERAL	45	4
08/08/42	MOUNT KASSION	GREEK	SC94	U-176	56-30 N.	32-14 W.	GENERAL	54	0
08/08/42	KAIMOKU	U.S.A.	SC94	U-379	56-30 N.	32-14 W.	GENERAL	50	4
08/08/42	ANNEBERG	BRITISH	SC94	U-379	55-10 N.	33-10 W.	PULP	38	0
09/08/42	SAN EMILIANO	BRITISH		U-155	07-22 N.	54-08 W.	GASOLENE	48	40
09/08/42	RADCHURCH	BRITISH	SC94	U-176	56-15 N.	32-00 W.	IRON ORE	42	2
09/08/42	MENDENAU	DUTCH		U-752	04-45 N.	18-00 W.	GENERAL	85	69
09/08/42	MALMANGER	NOR.		U-130	07-13 N.	26-30 W.	FUEL OIL	34	18
09.08/42	DALHOUSIE	BRITISH		A.M.C.	20-22 S.	24-40 W.	BALLAST	36	0
10/08/42	MEDON	BRITISH		GUILIANI	09-26 N.	38-28 W.	BALLAST	64	0
10/08/42	CONDYLIS	GREEK	SC94	U-660	57-03 N.	22-59 W.	GRAIN	35	9
10/08/42	EMPIRE REINDEER	BRITISH	SC94	U-660	57-00 N.	22-30 W.	GENERAL	64	0
10/08/42	CAPE RACE	BRITISH	SC94	U-660	56-45 N.	22-30 W.	TIMBER	63	0
10/08/42	OREGON	BRITISH	SC94	U-438	57-05 N.	22-41 W.	GENERAL	42	11
11/08/42	MIRLO	NOR.		U-130	06-04 N.	26-53 W.	FUEL OIL	37	0
11/08/42	VIMEIRA	BRITISH		U-109	10-03 N.	28-55 W.	FUEL OIL	45	23
12/08/42	SANTIAGO DE CUBA	CUBAN		U-508	24-20 N.	81-50 W.	GENERAL	29	10
12/08/42	MANZANILLO	CUBAN		U-508	24-20 N.	81-50 W.	GENERAL	23	23
13/08/42	MEDEA	DUTCH		U-658	19-54 N.	76-16 W.	GENERAL	44	5
13/08/42	CRIPPLE CREEK	U.S.A.		U-752	04-55 N.	18-30 W.	GENERAL	52	1
13/08/42	EVERELZA	LATV.		U-600	19-55 N.	73-49 W.	ORE	37	23
13/08/42	DELMUNDO	U.S.A.		U-600	19-55 N.	73-49 W.	GENERAL	48	6
13/08/42	R.M. PARKER	U.S.A.		U-171	28-50 N.	90-42 W.	BALLAST	44	0
13/08/42	CALIFORNIA	U.S.A.		GUILIANI	09-21 N.	34-35 W.	ORE	36	1
14/08/42	MICHAEL JEBSEN	BRITISH	TAW 12	U-598	21-45 N.	76-10 W.	SUGAR	47	7
14/08/42	EMPIRE CORPORAL	BRITISH	TAW12	U-598	21-45 N.	76-10 W.	GASOLENE	55	6
14/08/42	SYLVIA DE LARRINAGA	BRITISH		GUILIANI	10-49 N.	33-35 W.	ORE	53	3
15/08/42	BALLADIER	U.S.A.	SC95	U-705	55-23 N.	24-32 W.	GENERAL	45	11
16/08/42	BAEPENDY	BRAZ.		U-507	11-50 S.	37-00 W.	GENERAL	320	284
16/08/42	ARARAQUARA	BRAZ.		U-507	12-00 S.	37-19 W.	GENERAL	143	136
16/08/42	ANNIBAL BENEVOLO	BRAZ.		U-507	11-41 S.	37-21 W.	GENERAL	163	159
16/08/42	SUECIA	SWED.	SC95	U-596	55-43 N.	25-58 W.	GENERAL	65	0
17/08/42	FORT LA REINE	BRITISH	PG6	U-658	18-80 N.	75-20 W.	GRAIN	44	3
17/08/42	SAMIR	EGYPT.	PG6	U-658	18-30 N.	75-20 W.	BALLAST		
17/08/42	ITAGIBA	BRAZ.		U-507	13-23 S.	38-41 W.	GENERAL	176	32
17/08/42	LOUISIANA	U.S.A.		U-108	07-24 N.	51-33 W.	FUEL OIL	49	49
17/08/42	ARARA	BRAZ.		U-507	13-20 S.	38-49 W.	SCRAP	35	20
17/08/42	TRITON	NOR.	SL118	U-566	39-31 N.	22-43 W.	GENERAL	43	0
								3,259	**1,147**

268

BARRWHIN - 15 DECEMBER 1941 TO 4 SEPTEMBER 1942

RECORD OF MERCHANT SHIPS SUNK IN ATLANTIC - 18/08/42 TO 08/09/42

BARRWHIN - ON PASSAGE TO SYDNEY CAPE BETON

DATE	SHIP	NAT.	CONVOY NO.	CAUSE OF LOSS	POSITION		CARGO	CASUALTIES CREW	DEAD
18/08/42	EMPIRE BEDE	BRITISH	TAW13	U-553	19-41 N.	76-50 W.	COTTON	44	2
18/08/42	BLANKAHOLM	SWED.	TAW13	U-553	19-41 N.	76-50 W.	BAUXITE	28	5
18/08/42	JOHN HANCOCK	U.S.A.	TAW13	U-553	19-41 N.	76-50 W.	SUGAR	49	0
18/08/42	BALINGKAR	NOR.	SL118	U-214	41-30 N.	19-19 W.	GENERAL	93	2
18/08/42	HATARANA	BRITISH	SL118	U-214	41-07 N.	20-32 W.	GENERAL	98	0
19/08/42	WEST CELINA	U.S.A.	TAW (S)	U-162	11-45 N.	62-30 W.	GENERAL	44	44
19/08/42	EMPIRE CLOUD	BRITISH	TAW13	U-564	11-58 N.	62-38 W.	BALLAST	54	3
19/08/42	CRESSINGTON COURT	BRITISH		U-510	07-58 N.	36-00 W.	GENERAL	44	8
19/08/42	BRITISH CONSUL	BRITISH	TAW (S)	U-564	11-58 N.	62-38 W.	BALLAST	41	2
19/08/42	CITY OF MANILA	BRITISH	SL118	U-406	43-21 N.	18-20 W.	GENERAL	96	1
21/08/42	CITY OF WELLINGTON	BRITISH		U-506	07-29 N.	14-52 W.	GENERAL	73	7
	BARRWHIN		SC97						
22/08/42	HAMMAREN	SWED.	OS36	U-507	13-00 S.	38-15 W.	GENERAL	31	5
23/08/42	HAMLA	BRITISH		U-506	04-00 S.	24-00 W.	ORE	38	38
24/08/42	KATVALDIS	BRITISH	ON122	U-605	48-55 N.	35-10 W.	BALLAST	47	3
24/08/42	SHEAF MOUNT	BRITISH	ON122	U-605	48-55 N.	35-10 W.	BALLAST	58	31
24/08/42	ABBEKERK	DUTCH		U-604	52-05 N.	30-50 W.	GENERAL	64	2
24/08/42	MOENA	DUTCH		U-162	13-30 N.	57-50 W.		87	4
24/08/42	TROLLA	NOR.	ON122	U-422	48-55 N.	35-10 W.	BALLAST	22	5
25/08/42	EMPIRE BREEZE	BRITISH	ON122	U-176	49-22 N.	35-52 W.	BALLAST	48	1
25/08/42	AMAKURA	BRITISH	TAW15	U-558	17-40 N.	75-52 W.	GENERAL	44	13
25/08/42	VIKING STAR	BRITISH		U-130	06-00 N.	14-00 W.	GENERAL	69	33
25/08/42	STAD AMSTERDAM	DUTCH	TAW15	U-164	16-39 N.	73-15 W.	GENERAL	38	3
26/08/42	BEECHWOOD	BRITISH		U-130	05-30 N.	14-04 W.	GENERAL	43	1
26/08/42	CLAN McWHIRTER	BRITISH	SL119	U-156	35-45 N.	18-45 W.	GENERAL	88	11
26/08/42	THELMA	NOR.		U-162	13-20 N.	58-10 W.	BALLAST	33	2
27/08/42	CHATHAM	U.S.A.		U-517	52-53 N.	55-48 W.	GENERAL	762	14
28/08/42	ARLYN	U.S.A.	SG6S	U-165	51-53 N.	55-48 W.	GENERAL	54	9
28/08/42	CITY OF CARDIFF	BRITISH	SL119	U-566	40-20 N.	16-02 W.	GENERAL	84	21
28/08/42	SAN FABIAN	BRITISH	TAW15	U-511	18-09 N.	74-38 W.	FUEL OIL	59	26
28/08/42	ROTTERDAM	DUTCH	TAW15	U-511	18-09 N.	74-38 W.	GASOLENE	51	10
28/08/42	ZUIDERKERK	DUTCH	SL119	U-566	40-20 N.	16-02 W.	GENERAL	68	0
29/08/42	TOPA TOPA	U.S.A.		U-66	10-16 N.	51-30 W.	GENERAL	60	25
30/08/42	WEST LASHAWAY	U.S.A.		U-66	10-30 N.	55-10 W.	GENERAL	56	39
30/08/42	JACK CARNES	U.S.A.		U-516	41-35 N.	29-01 W.	BALLAST	56	27
30/08/42	STAR OF OREGON	U.S.A.		U-162	11-48 N.	59-45 W.	GENERAL	55	1
30/08/42	VARDAAS	NOR.		U-564	11-35 N.	60-40 W.	BALLAST	41	0
30/08/42	SIR HUON	PAN.		U-66	10-52 N.	54-00 W.	GENERAL	46	0
31/08/42	WINAMAC	BRITISH	T3	U-66	10-36 N.	54-34 W.	FUEL OIL	51	30
31/08/42	BRONXVILLE	NOR.	SC97	U-609	57-13 N.	33-40 W.	GENERAL	39	0
31/08/42	CAPIRA	PAN.	SC97	U-609	57-13 N.	33-40 W.	GENERAL	54	5
01/09/42	ILORIN	BRITISH		U-125	05-00 N.	01-00 W.	GENERAL	37	32
02/09/42	OCEAN MIGHT	BRITISH	OS37	U-109	00-57 N.	04-11 W.	GENERAL	54	4
03/09/42	DONALD STEWART	BRITISH	LN7	U-517	50-32 N.	58-46 W.	GENERAL	20	3
03/09/42	HOLLINSIDE	BRITISH		U-107	38-00 N.	09-00 W.	BALLAST	46	9
03/09/42	PENROSE	BRITISH		U-107	38-00 N.	09-00 W.	BALLAST	45	2
04/09/42	AMATLAN	MEX.		U-171	23-27 N.	97-30 W.	BALLAST	34	10
05/09/42	MYRMIDON	BRITISH		U-506	00-45 N.	06-27 W.	GENERAL	235	0
05/09/42	LORD STRATHCONA	BRITISH		U-513	47-35 N.	52-59 W.	IRON ORE	44	0
05/09/42	SAGANAGA	BRITISH		U-513	47-35 N.	52-59 W.	IRON ORE	44	30
06/09/42	JOHN A. HOLLOWAY	BRITISH	GAT2	U-164	14-10 N.	71-30 W.	GENERAL	24	1
06/09/42	TUSCAN STAR	BRITISH		U-109	01-34 N.	11-39 W.	GENERAL	114	52
07/09/42	OAKTON	BRITISH	QS33	U-517	48-50 N.	63-46 W.	COAL	20	0
07/09/42	AEAS	GREEK	QS33	U-165	49-10 N.	66-50 W.	GENERAL	31	2
07/09/42	MOUNT PINDUS	GREEK	QS33	U-517	48-50 N.	63-46 W.	GENERAL	37	2
07/09/42	MOUNT TAYGETOS	GREEK		U-517	48-50 N.	63-46 W.	GENERAL	28	5
							TOTALS	**3,723**	**585**

BARRWHIN - 15 DECEMBER 1941 TO 8 SEPTEMBER 1942

SHIP AND U-BOAT LOSSES - WHEN SERVING ON *BARRWHIN* - 31 JULY 1942 TO 08 SEPTEMBER 1942

GERMAN U-BOATS	SHIPS SUNK IN PERIOD					ENEMY U-BOAT LOSSES				
NUMBER	TOTALS			31/07/42	18/08/42	DETAILS OF LOSS				
	C/F	B/F	TOTAL	17/08/42	08/09/42		DATE	CAUSE	DEAD	SAVED
U-66			5	1	4	U-94	28/08/42	RAM	19	26
U-107			2		2	U-162	03/09/42	RAM	2	49
U-108			3	3		U-166	01/08/42	AIR	52	0
U-109			4	2	2	U-210	06/08/42	RAM	6	37
U-125			1		1	U-213	31/07/42	D/C	50	0
U-130			5	3	2	U-222	02/09/42	COLL	42	4
U-155			4	4		U-335	03/08/42	SUB.	41	1
U-156			1		1	U-372	04/08/42	D/C	0	47
U-160			1	1		U-379	09/08/42	RAM	36	5
U-162			4		4	U-464	20/08/42	AIR	2	52
U-164			2		2	U-578	10/08/42	AIR	49	0
U-165			2		2	U-588	31/07/42	D/C	46	0
U-171			2	1	1	U-612	06/08/42	COLL.	1	44
U-176			6	5	1	U-669	05/10/42	AIR	44	0
U-214			2		2	U-705	03/09/42	AIR	45	0
U-254			1	1		U-754	31/07/42	AIR	44	0
U-379			2	2		U-756	01/09/42	D/C	43	0
U-406			1		1					
U-422			1		1					
U-438			1	1						
U-458			1	1						
U-506			3		3					
U-507			6	5	1					
U-508			2	2						
U-510			2	1	1					
U-511			2		2					
U-513			2		2					
U-516			1		1					
U-517			5		5					
U-552			1	1						
U-553			3		3					
U-558			1		1					
U-564			3		3					
U-566			3	1	2					
U-572			1	1						
U-593			1	1						
U-596			1	1						
U-598			2	2						
U-600			2	2						
U-604			1		1					
U-605			2		2					
U-607			1	1						
U-609			2		2					
U-658			3	3						
U-660			2	2						
U-705			1	1						
U-752			2	2						

	C/F	B/F	TOTAL	17/08/42	08/09/42
	1,273	1,167	106	51	55

								DEAD	SAVED
TOTALS							17	522	265
B/F							98	3,006	1,260
C/F							115	3,528	1,525

	C/F	B/F	TOTAL	17/08/42	08/09/42
HEAVY SHIPS	15	15	0		
RAIDERS	23	22	1	1	
LIGHT WARSHIPS	6	6	0		
AIRCRAFT	78	78	0		
ITALIAN SUBMARINES	64	59	5	5	
OTHER CAUSES	12	12	0		
	198	192	6	6	0

15

THE WAR AT SEA: OPERATION PEDASTAL

GIBRALTAR TO MALTA
10–13 AUGUST 1942

During the time when *Barrwhin* was loading prior to joining convoy SC97, we learned about the attacks sustained by, and the heavy losses incurred in "Operation Pedestal" convoy, despatched for the relief of Malta.

The convoy was comprised of 14 of the largest and most modern merchant ships, all capable of maintaining above average speeds, and protected by two battleships, *H.M.S. Nelson* and *Rodney*, the aircraft carriers, *H.M.S. Argus, Victorious, Eagle* and *Indomitable*, together with 7 cruisers and a large number of destroyers. The various accounts give the number of destroyers as between "two dozen" and 28. The convoy was comprised of: *Brisbane Star, Melbourne Star, Port Chalmers, Deucalion, Rochester Castle, Empire Hope, Clan Ferguson, Ohio, Wairangi, Dorset, Waimarama, Almeria Lykes, Santa Elisa, Glen Orchy.*

The Royal Navy suffered heavy losses during five days of sustained attacks by German and Italian high level, dive and torpedo bombers, destroyers, submarines and E-Boats, losing the aircraft carrier, *H.M.S. Eagle*, cruisers, *H.M.S. Manchester* and *Cairo*, and destroyer, *H.M.S. Foresight.* Many other warships suffered damage and casualties.

The convoy suffered catastrophic losses in ships, but personnel casualties were relatively light, except in *Waimarama*, which exploded and sank with heavy casualties. The ships lost were:

> *Deucalion*, 37 – 56 N, 08 – 40 E, 1 dead out of 153
> *Empire Hope* off Cape Bon, none dead out of 94
> *Clan Ferguson*, off Zembra Island, 18 dead out of 114

271

Wairangi, 36 – 34 N. 11 – 15 E., none dead out of 117
Glen Orchy, off Kelibia, 7 dead out of 81
Santa Elisa, 36 – 48 N. 11 – 23 E., 4 dead out of 94
Almeria Lykes, 36 – 40 N. 11 – 35 E., none dead out of 99
Waimarama, 36 – 25 N. 12 – 00 E., 83 dead out of 104
Dorset, 36 – 12 N. 12 – 49 E., none dead out of 101.
Ohio was badly damaged and made port, but sank in Malta harbour.
Two of her complement of 77 were killed.
Brisbane Star, Melbourne Star, Port Chalmers and *Rochester Castle* made port
in Malta.

My friend, Malcolm Hayes Thompson served in *Empire Hope* as Second Radio Officer at the age of nineteen, having qualified as a Radio Officer shortly after his eighteenth birthday in 1941. He has contributed his first hand account of his experiences prior to, during, and after the attacks on the Operation Pedestal convoy to Malta, presenting the viewpoint of events from the perspective of a Radio Officer.

I acknowledge with thanks his permission to reproduce his account.

An Account of Life at Sea from 1941 to 1945

Malcolm Hayes Thompson

From early childhood I was never happier than when messing about in boats. At the age of sixteen I decided I would like to join the Merchant Navy and set about applying to various shipping companies for an apprenticeship, eventually being accepted by the Donaldson Line. My elation was soon dashed when I received a communication advising me that due to the losses they had sustained they had a surplus of apprentices who would have to be found places on their surviving vessels. Shortly afterwards I learned that it was general policy amongst the majority of Shipping Companies not to indenture further apprentices for the time being.

It was suggested to me that, as there was a desperate need for Merchant Navy Radio Officers, I might enrol at the South Wales Wireless College at Swansea, which advice I took in January 1941.

I obtained the Post Master General's Special Radio Communications Certificate in the following July. There was no difficulty in finding employment with the Marconi Marine Radio Company and, on the 1st of August 1941 I joined my first ship, s.s. *Baron Dechmont* on the Thames at Poplar. The *Baron Dechmont* was a small tramp steamer owned by the Hogarth Line, generally referred to as "Hungry Hogarths". She had no refrigerator, fresh meat being kept in an ice box situated on the deck. After 7 to 10 days out of port and we were eating salt tack or tinned meat.

The *Baron Dechmont* sailed in convoy out of the Thames and up the East Coast, surviving an E-Boat attack on the first evening. We sailed mainly by night and anchored in protected waters during daylight. There were no further incidents and we arrived safely in Loch Ewe where an Atlantic Convoy was being assembled.

As was the usual practice at this time, the convoy disbursed half way across the Atlantic and we made our way alone to Charleston, Virginia, to replenish the bunkers. From Charleston we sailed to the West Indies, discharging general cargo at Barbados, Cuba and Trinidad, picking up a cargo of sugar at Jamaica. We returned to Greenock via Sydney Cape Breton, without incident.

My next ship was the m.v. *San Ernesto* which I joined at Avonmouth in December 1941. She was owned by the Eagle Oil Company, which had the reputation of operating the best fed ships in the British Merchant Navy. The contrast with "Hungry Hogarths" could not have been greater.

We were on voyage with an Atlantic Convoy when the Japanese attacked Pearl Harbour. The sailing orders were changed immediately and, instead of disbursing in mid Atlantic, the convoy was diverted to Boston, Maine.

From Boston we sailed South in the first ever convoy organised by the U.S. Navy. The escort consisted of a Navy Blimp and a Coastguard Cutter. Because none of the U.S. Merchant Vessels had been equipped with Aldis Lamps all signalling was carried out by means of semaphore. Chaos reigned!

A voyage on a Cruise Ship following the same route south from Boston taken by that convoy would have cost a fortune. We made our way via Cape Cod, Martha's Vineyard, Long Island Sound, the Inter Coastal Waterway, up the Delaware River, through the Delaware River Canal into Chesapeake Bay, then hugging the West Coast as far as Key West, where we were left to proceed unescorted across the Gulf of Mexico to our port of destination, Port Arthur in Texas.

This was just about the time when the German Submarine presence in the Gulf was intensified and we heard distress calls from ships being attacked all around us, some of them from ships that had accompanied us in the convoy.

I left the *San Ernesto* in July 1942, having made three voyages to the Gulf of Mexico. On July 29th 1942, I joined s.s. *Empire Hope* at Avonmouth. She was a brand new ship of 12,688 tons, capable of 17 knots, owned by the Ministry of War Transport and managed by the Shaw Saville and Albion Shipping Company. She was more heavily armed than any other Merchant Ship I had seen before, and it was obvious, from the deck cargo of Army Vehicles that she was on her way to a war zone.

We sailed from Avonmouth on July 30th 1942, and arrived at Greenock on August 1st, having joined a Coastal Convoy at Milford Haven. On the evening of August 2nd the convoy, consisting of fourteen merchant ships, each capable of a speed of 16 knots, sailed out into the Atlantic, by which time it had been confirmed to that our destination was Malta.

We passed through the Straits of Gibraltar during the night of 9th/10th of August 1942. Until then we had not been involved in any action other than practicing manoeuvres. The strength of the escort had, by now, grown to two Battleships, four Aircraft Carriers, seven Cruisers and twenty-eight Destroyers.

During the 10th August we experienced no enemy action and it was not until we were in the middle of our lunch on the morning of the 11th that we were awakened out of our complacency by four loud explosions that shook the *Empire Hope*. By the time we had rushed out on deck the Aircraft Carrier *H.M.S. Eagle* was already lying on its side, close enough for us to see members of the crew sliding down the flight deck into the water.

During the afternoon, the Carrier, *H.M.S. Furious* despatched thirty eight Spitfires destined for Malta, and in the evening there was an abortive attack from the air, which failed to penetrate the defence screen.

Next morning, the attack on the convoy by aircraft began in earnest. It was unwise to go out onto the open decks because of the volume of anti aircraft shrapnel falling from the skies. All morning and during the afternoon repeated attacks by enemy aircraft were repulsed by the heavy anti-aircraft barrage put up by the escort vessels. At one stage the battleships *Nelson* and *Rodney* began firing their 16" guns, leading us to believe that a surface attack was imminent. Years later I read that someone had discovered a supply of 16" shrapnel shells left over from the Dardanelles. The idea was conceived that these shells could be fired at approaching aircraft at very long range. It was said to prove most effective against Italian Torpedo Bombers.

It was not until the afternoon of 12th August that the first Merchant Ship was successfully attacked. It was the s.s. *Deucalion*. Shortly afterwards, the Aircraft Carrier, *Victorious* was hit by bombs but not seriously damaged. At tea-time we were heartened by seeing a submarine brought to the surface after being rammed by one of the escort vessels.

During the early evening enemy attacks concentrated on the Naval Force, the Aircraft Carrier *H.M.S. Indomitable* suffering serious damage. At about 6.30p.m., the main Naval Force retired, leaving an escort of four cruisers and eleven destroyers.

With dusk setting in I thought we would soon be safe from further attacks. However, at 7.55 p.m., I was standing on deck when there were four explosions, and I saw that the Cruisers *Nigeria* and *Cairo*, together with the Tanker *Ohio* had all been hit by a single salvo of torpedoes.

At about 8.30 p.m., the final air attack of the day occurred, during which some 50% of the Merchant ships in the convoy were lost or damaged. According to the account given in the book "Operation Pedestal" the *Empire Hope* seemed to have been singled out for special attention, with eighteen near misses counted around her. Eventually, the explosions from a stick of bombs, which fell close alongside where I was standing, blew a hole in her side which disabled the engines.

Two direct hits caused an explosion in No.4 Hold and ignited the aviation spirit being carried in No.1 Hold. The vessel was well ablaze when the order was given to abandon ship. It was my duty to load the emergency radio transmitter into my allocated lifeboat but when I went to collect it I found it buried under a great heap of coal that had blown off the hatch cover of the No.4 Hold. All hatch covers had sacks of coal covering them to act as "sand bags". Likewise, my allocated lifeboat was rendered useless because it was half full of coal.

The whole crew got away in the surviving lifeboats and it was not much more than fifteen minutes before we were rescued by the Destroyer, *H.M.S. Penn*, which then fired a torpedo into the *Empire Hope* in an unsuccessful attempt to sink her. When last seen she was nothing but a blazing hulk. It is more remarkable because the *Empire Hope*'s sister ship, the *Waimarama*, almost identically loaded, blew up and sank with great loss of life, immediately she was hit by a stick of bombs.

The rescued officers were accommodated in the Officers' Mess, which soon became extremely overcrowded as the *Penn* picked up further survivors. Naturally, whilst the *Penn* was heavily involved in the action, we were discouraged from going up on deck. It was not until the morning of August 14th, with *Penn* securely tied alongside the Tanker *Ohio*, that I was able to stretch my legs, having volunteered to join a party to accompany the Chief Steward of the *Ohio* to collect the contents of her medicine chest. By this time the *Penn* was rapidly running short of medical supplies.

As we neared Malta, ships were sent out to assist with the tow of the *Ohio*. One of these was an ancient paddle wheeled tug which took up a towing hawser from the bows. Unfortunately it was unable to keep up with the pace of the two destroyers lashed to the sides of the tanker. It slewed round on the end of its towing wire and was unable to release itself before crashing into the side of the *Penn*, striking her above the waterline, opening up a hole into the Officers' Mess-room. We were having tea at the time and I still vividly remember the scramble to get up the companion ladder leading to the deck.

The vision of our entry into the Grand Harbour at Valetta will remain with me as long as I live: the thousands of civilians and service personnel lining the harbour walls shouting and waving, with a military band play-ing. It can only be compared to the reception of a victorious rugby team returning with the World Cup.

The *Penn* docked alongside a warehouse into which the survivors were mustered, here our details were recorded and we were issued with a set of underwear, a cotton khaki shirt and a pair of khaki shorts, also basic toiletries. I was fortunate because I still had my "panic bag" containing my papers, personal items and money.

The Officers from the *Empire Hope* were accommodated in the Imperial Hotel at Sliema, a very comfortable billet in the circumstances. The first meal we were given consisted of goats' meat which none of us succeeded in eating. It was some while before we appreciated the sacri-fice made by the Maltese in slaughtering their goats to provide that meal. The majority of the islanders had not eaten meat of any sort for months.

On a recent visit to Malta I visited the Imperial Hotel. The front elevation is unchanged, as is the magnificent foyer with its double spiral marble staircase. Obviously the accommodation has been modernised and extended to the rear on what was a garden. It certainly brought back memories to see it.

I remained in Malta for about three weeks awaiting a passage out. Most of the ratings had been taken to Gibraltar on board the returning escort vessels. The Officers were flown out on Anson Aircraft by night in dribs & drabs, those who I met when I eventually arrived in Gibraltar had experienced a pretty horrific flight in the freezing cold dressed only in tropical kit.

My Chief Radio Officer and I spent most of our time sunbathing and swimming in Sliema Creek, the Third Radio Officer having been repatriated early. At the same time as I revisited the Imperial Hotel, I walked down to the Creek to view the spot where we swam and found it difficult to believe that I was ever capable of swimming across the bay to the other side and back, a distance of some five hundred yards.

Early in September, we were at the Creek swimming when a message came down from the hotel that we were to report to the Shipping Office as soon as possible. On our way we met a party of Engineers returning from the Office, who informed us that we were wasting our time, they had been offered a passage to Gibraltar by submarine which they had turned down.

My Chief and I discussed this information and concluded that we would never have another opportunity to experience a voyage on a submarine, whereas, after the war we could always pay fifteen shillings for a flight around an airfield.

The following day we joined *H.M.S. Clyde* which, together with her sister ships *Thames* and *Severn* were the largest and fastest submarines in the Royal Navy. She was armed with a large calibre gun and was capable of twenty knots on the surface. One of her battery rooms had been emptied and was used, we were informed, for carrying a cargo of powdered milk for the babies. We swallowed this story at the time but, I have read in a recent account, that she carried cased aviation spirit in that space. On the outward journey the empty battery room provided sufficient space for about twenty passengers, sleeping in hammocks.

To conserve battery power the *Clyde* lay on the bottom during daylight hours and proceeded on the surface, using her diesel engines during the night. The passage to Gibraltar took eight days, during which time none of the passengers were allowed on deck. However, we would stand at the base of the conning tower breathing fresh air whenever possible.

I stayed at Gibraltar for a week, during which I attended a gunnery course. Together with approximately 50 other survivors from the Malta Convoy, I joined the m.v. *Gudren Maersk*, which was a small Danish coastal vessel that had been converted to carry troops in accommodation built into its hold.

We were landed at Belfast from where I experienced a tedious journey via ferry to the Clyde, thence on an interminable succession of packed trains eventually ending up on the Mid Wales line from Shrewsbury to Swansea, travelling throughout the night.

Recently I was told by a fellow survivor who travelled to Swansea from

Malta by the same route as I did, that the *Gudren Maersk* left Belfast immediately after dropping her passengers, and sailed for Swansea, arriving twenty four hours before we did.

After two weeks survivors leave I was ordered to report at the Newcastle office of Marconi Marine where I was sent to North Shields to join s.s. *Empire Standard,* a brand new vessel in the final stages of completion. Here I witnessed, in a minor way, the stranglehold which the shipbuilding unions had over the employers. The cabins were being fitted with the usual wooden racks intended to hold a water bottle and two glasses. This simple task could not be carried out by one man, but involved three men from three different unions, one to mark the position of the screws, one to drill the holes and one to screw the racks to the bulkheads.

After undergoing sea trials the *Empire Standard* sailed from the Tyne to Leith where she loaded military supplies of all sorts, with a deck cargo of army trucks with yellow stars painted on their bonnets.

We had no indication of our final destination but after a few days at sea the news of the invasion of North Africa broke. The convoy met atrocious weather crossing the Bay of Biscay, and partially broke up, and to compound our troubles our steering engine failed and we were left floundering in heavy seas.

Fortunately, whilst in Leith the Navy fitted brand new Radio Telephone equipment. My training at the Wireless College included a course in R/T procedures, something with which the Chief Radio Officer was not familiar.

After the steering gear had been repaired I suggested we should contact the convoy by R/T for instructions. My chief did not want to know, having been brainwashed into the importance of maintaining radio silence on the ordinary marine bands. He strongly advised against this course of action.

The Captain listened to my argument that there was no point in having the Naval R/T set if it was not used. It was agreed that I should try to make contact with the Convoy. There was an immediate response and, after sending a coded message giving our estimated position, we were advised the course we should set to rejoin the convoy. The following day we were sighted by a corvette, which had been sent out to round up stragglers.

We reached our destination, Algiers, without further incident, by which time the port had been occupied and we were able to discharge our cargo alongside a jetty.

As a sequel, when attending the Convoy Conference for the return journey, the Chief Petty Officer Signals who was briefing the Radio Officers asked "Which of you gentlemen is Harry James Duff Five Four?" The call sign I had used when communicating with the outward bound escort. I raised my hand and my chief whispered "Now you've done it. We are in for a rocket for breaking radio silence". But, much to his surprise, and mine, the C.P.O. said "Well done, you have probably earned your Old Man an O.B.E.".

My next ship was s.s. *Fort Yale* which I joined at Southampton. Following an uneventful trip to Portland, Maine, I left her at Avonmouth in May 1943.

At the end of May I joined s.s. *Gloucester City* at Bristol Docks and remained with her until October 1945 after the fall of Japan.

The *Gloucester City* was a small, elderly, cargo vessel, nett tonnage 1,852, owned by Messrs Charles Hill of Bristol, known as the Bristol City Line. Her regular pre war trade was between Bristol and New York, carrying general cargo, including sherry from Harveys of Bristol, outward bound and returning with tobacco for the Bristol Tobacco Companies. Up to the date of my joining she had continued to carry on her normal trade throughout the war. She had seen her share of action in the North Atlantic and, like her sister ship; the *Bristol City* had earned the title of "Lifeboat of the Atlantic", on one occasion having landed over 200 survivors at St.John's Newfoundland.

For the first six months we kept to the old routine; then we were sent to the Spanish coast, discharging general cargo at Seville and Cadiz. From Cadiz we were ordered to Valencia to load a cargo of onions which was discharged at Naples. From Naples we returned to Seville where we loaded a part cargo of sherry. On leaving Seville we had on board two escaped British airmen and a secret agent from Czechoslovakia. The airmen boarded, acting as two very drunk firemen amongst a crowd of seamen returning from the local bar. They were hidden in the bunkers until we left territorial waters. The spy was brought aboard by the British Consul and members of his staff to attend a party given by the Captain. They left in small groups and with a lot of noise when the party was over so that it was difficult for the Spanish guards to count them.

The sherry loaded at Seville was destined for Dublin and the full cargo was completed at Lisbon. The reason for this unusual destination was that, during the spring of 1944 the British Government placed an embargo on Irish Free State shipping, confining their vessels to port to avoid the risk of spying on the preparations for V.E. Day.

At Dublin we loaded a cargo destined for Lisbon and again loaded at Lisbon for Dublin, by which time the Invasion of France was well under way and I suspect the embargo had been lifted.

Prior to the next trip we were fitted out with awnings and tropical equipment, after which we were sent to the West Coast of Africa, unloading at Accra, Lagos and Port Harcourt, and loading timber at Sapale in Nigeria, which entailed an interesting passage up a tributary of the river Osse using a native pilot and a young boy who acted as helmsman.

On our return to the U.K., we reverted to routine crossings between Bristol and New York.

Pat and I were married on April 26th 1945. We spent our honeymoon at Bristol. The day before we were due to sail Pat returned to Portland where she was stationed as a W.A.A.F. Radar Operator. The following day was D-Day. We sailed as far as the locks in the Cumberland Basin, where the firemen walked ashore en bloc, and refused to return on board. Having missed the tide a compromise was reached when it was agreed that we could remain in the basin until the next morning. Thus was it that I experienced the thrill of seeing the vast throng of people celebrating VE Day in Bristol City Centre that evening.

16

THE WAR AT SEA: START POINT

12 OCTOBER 1942– 7 JANUARY 1943

I had accumulated more than three weeks leave during my period of nearly nine months service in *Barrwhin*, and it was sheer luxury to sleep in a bed again, and to enjoy the comfort of life ashore, despite the queues and rationing. However, the idyllic life soon ended, and early in October 1942 I was ordered to report to Captain Skee in the Merchant Navy Officers Reserve Pool. He seemed to have mellowed since my last encounter with him.

I had visited his offices on more than one occasion before my term of leave expired. The first time I had asked what ships were available. I believe that one was called *Vin River*, a very old American ship acquired by the Ministry of War Transport. I have been unable to trace a ship of that name, so it is likely that the ship may have been on the point of re-registration. I have since ascertained that the *Vin River* existed, but have no details about the ship. On the second occasion, Betty and I had arranged to visit the cinema, and I called in at the Merchant Navy Officers Reserve Pool offices en route. Betty was allowed to join us in the interview room.

During the pre war era, all officers held certificates of competency of at least one rank higher. On many of the larger ships, all officers held certificates of competency as Master. Due to casualties and an accelerated shipbuilding programme, it was necessary to relax those standards in order to provide officers for our ships. A substantial number of cargo ships carried un-certificated Third Mates, many of whom had not served as apprentices or cadets. Quartermasters, able seamen and bosuns had been promoted from the forecastle to the bridge. I had served as a certificated Third Mate for five voyages and was looking for a berth as Second Mate.

Captain Skee greeted me with the question "How would you like a ship with a swimming pool?" I pondered upon the usefulness of a swimming pool in a convoy in the Atlantic. He gave me the name of the ship *Regent Panther,* which required a Third Mate. When the name "Regent" was mentioned, Betty conjured up visions of petrol and blazing ships, and started kicking my shins under the table, and whispering "Is she a tanker?" I did not share her apprehensions, because the steel cargoes carried by my previous ships, were in my opinion, at least as lethal as most bulk oils and gasoline, with the exception of high-octane fuels. However, I was still a few days within my leave, and was not enamoured with the prospects of a further six months as Third Mate.

Captain Skee consulted his list of berths for Second Mates, and assigned me to *Start Point*, due to sign on in Avonmouth several days later. He issued me with a railway voucher and wished me good luck. Before we visited the cinema, I went to offices of the Navigators and Engineer Officers Union, where I was permitted to peruse the records in Lloyd's Register of Ships. The name *Start Point* was not recorded, so I assumed that she was a relatively new ship built during wartime. The prospect of promotion to the rank of Second Mate on a new ship was encouraging.

I bade farewell to Betty and her family on Sunday 11 October 1942 and boarded the train for Bristol and Avonmouth. One of my fellow passengers in the carriage was another M.N. officer, and we struck up a conversation. That was the beginning of what was to develop into a lifetime friendship. Frank Bernard Howe had been posted to *Start Point* as Third Mate. During our conversation, I learned that he had survived the loss of four ships by enemy attack.

He was then in a state of what is now termed Post Traumatic Stress Disorder. This is now used as an excuse for massive fictitious claims for compensation, not only in industry and commerce, but even in our armed forces. If the sergeant major farts too loudly in the presence of a subordinate, a clever lawyer will claim for impaired hearing, and sue for massive compensation.

It is therefore appropriate – even essential – that I record in this narrative a record of the courage and fortitude of one officer of our Merchant Navy. Frank Bernard Howe was born in Cardiff on 18 June 1916. He served as an apprentice on the Bristol Channel pilot cutters from 1933

S.S. King Idwal, ex *War Coronet*, ex *Keramies*
Built in 1920, 5115 gross registered tonnage
Torpedoed and sunk by U-123 on 23 November 1940 in convoy OB244
(Photograph by A. Duncan, Cowes, I.O.W.)

until 1937. The apprentices undertook duties similar to those of apprentices on deep-sea ships, "learning the business of a seaman as practised on steamships." From later knowledge of Frank Howe, it seems clear that apprentices in Bristol Channel pilot cutters were just another example of the exploitation of cheap labour. They received practical training in deck work on small vessels; but it seems unlikely that training was extended into the syllabus of apprentices under the auspices of the tuition provided by the Merchant Navy Officers Training Board.

The pilot cutters operated mainly in Cardiff and Barry Roads, and were never out of sight of familiar landmarks. Therefore, apprentices gained no practical knowledge of deep-sea navigation, and many theoretical subjects such as meteorology, ship construction and stability and cargo work. It appears that the four-year term as an apprentice did not qualify immediately for the examinations for certificates of competency as Second Mate (Foreign Going Steamship), but probably as Mate (Home Trade Steamship.)

The first entry in the Certificate of Continuous Discharge (Discharge

Book) number 157356, issued to Frank Bernard Howe, is dated 21 October 1937, when he signed on *City of Tokio* as a quartermaster and able seamen. There is an endorsement "Eligible under Merchant Shipping Act 1906 for A.B. rating". He served in *City of Tokio* for four voyages until 26 January 1939. The next entry is an engagement as able seaman on *Stanwood* for one voyage from 17 May 1939 to 14 July 1939. He was promoted when he joined *Llanberis* on 10 August 1939 to Third Mate, and served three voyages on the ship until 25 July 1940.

The next entry reflects his signing on *King Idwal* on 15 August 1940, with the date of discharge as 23 November 1940 "at sea". This was the form adopted by the Ministry of War Transport, when ships were sunk by enemy action. All wages ceased on the date of loss of ship. *King Idwal* was torpedoed and sunk by U-123 on 23 November 1940, when outward bound in ballast in convoy OB244. *H.M.S. Sandwich* rescued the Master and 27 survivors. Twelve men were lost out of a complement of 40. The U-Boat records the attack at 0712. I was then serving in *Filleigh*, homeward bound in convoy HX91. The weather was very cold, but the severe gales of December 1940 were building up, so the survivors of *King Idwal* took to the lifeboats in very cold weather and rough seas.

Almost all the deaths occurred when the lifeboats were alongside the rescue ship, when the survivors were crushed between the heavy lifeboats and the ship. Frank Howe had vast experience of boarding ships in rough weather from small craft, and tried his best to discipline the survivors to jump for the scrambling nets on the high point of the waves. A number of men jumped when the lifeboat was in the trough of the seas and were crushed to death before they could climb the scrambling nets.

He recounted in vivid detail the horrifying sight of the scrambling nets covered with the mangled remains of his shipmates, with blood pouring into the sea. It was an enduring memory of a ghastly experience. The survivors were landed in Liverpool on 2 December 1940, the date of the first losses in the catastrophic attack on convoy HX90. It is significant to record that the pay of a Third Mate was a measly £ 20.00 per month. Survivors were allowed fourteen days unpaid survivor's leave from the date of loss of ship.

I had paid off from *Filleigh* on 22 December 1940, so our paths crossed briefly, when Frank Howe signed on as Third Mate of *Filleigh* in Cardiff on 30 December 1940, relieving me on the ship. Despite his horrifying ordeal after the loss of *King Idwal*, he was again on articles after a short time ashore. The compulsory period of six months on articles had commenced, so Frank Howe served in *Filleigh* for six months and nine days, on two voyages. The ship paid off on 8 July 1941. He qualified for eleven days paid leave, but remained ashore for three extra days unpaid leave.

He signed articles as Third Mate on *Aldergrove* on 22 July 1941. She was a small ship, of 1,974 gross registered tonnage, managed by David Alexander of Glasgow, built in 1919 as *Glenpark*, renamed *Elba* in 1932, and renamed *Aldergrove* in 1940. The ship was part of convoy OG71, which put to sea from Liverpool on 13 August 1941, destination Gibraltar. Records of the attacks on the convoy differ appreciably from the account given to me by Frank Howe. The commodore ship of the convoy was the small Yeoward Line passenger ship *Aguila*, which carried a crew of 76, 5 gunners, naval commodore and 5 staff, and 91 passengers, of whom many were W.R.N.S. (Womens' Royal Naval Service) personnel destined for service in Gibraltar.

The first casualties were the Norwegian destroyer, *Bath*, sunk by U-204 at 0205 on 19 August, followed by *Alva* (U-559), *Ciscar* (U-559), and *Aguila* (U-201). *Aldergrove* was close to *Aguila*, and Frank Howe recounted to me the horrific details of the catastrophic event. The ship caught fire, and in the flames 89 of the 91 passengers perished in almost indescribable circumstances, twenty being W.R.N.S. personnel. He never could forget this awful spectacle.

The accounts of following events differ appreciably. It is recorded that U-564 fired a salvo of four torpedoes at 2331 on 22 August, and it is assumed that the tug *Empire Oak* and *Clonlara* had been struck by the salvo. Later at 0214, U-201 reported firing a salvo of four torpedoes, claiming hits on *Stork* and *Aldergrove*. Frank Howe was clear in recounting that *Aldergrove* was sunk before *Empire Oak*, because he had been rescued by the tug, with a number of survivors from *Aguila*. His version of events was that most of the survivors were taken below decks on *Empire Oak*. He stayed on deck, in his words "To wait for the end of the fireworks." The records show that 13 crew of *Empire Oak* were lost, together with 6 survivors from *Aguila*.

His account was that he was sitting in his wet clothing and lifejacket on the engine room skylight when the torpedo explosion blew him into the water. He was rescued by one of the escorts and landed at Gibraltar on 25 August 1941. Seven ships were lost in the passage of convoy OG71 in several nights of appreciable chaos and confusion; hence the conflicting records of events. Three escorts were sunk as well.

Frank Howe remained in Gibraltar for ten days, and signed on *Margareta* as Third Mate on 4 September 1941. The ship was originally under the Finnish flag, with the name *Margarita*, but was seized at Gibraltar by the Ministry of War Transport and transferred to British registry with a slight change in name. *Margareta* was built in 1904, under the name *Atlantic*, 3,016 gross registered tonnage, with a deadweight cargo capacity of 5,500 tons and a designed speed of 8 knots. The ship joined homeward bound convoy HG73 of 29 ships, which put to sea from Gibraltar on 17 September 1941, destination Liverpool.

The commodore ship was the Yeoward liner *Avoceta*, with a crew of 66, naval commodore and 5 staff, 6 gunners and 82 passengers. The passengers included service personnel returning to the U.K. from Gibraltar, among them a number of W.R.N.S.

The first successful U-Boat attack was on 25 September, when U-124 torpedoed and sank *Empire Stream* at 0744. At 0031 on 26 September, U-203 fired a spread of four torpedoes, sinking *Varangberg, Avoceta* and *Cortes*, with fatal casualties of 175 in the three ships. The sinking of *Avoceta* was almost instantaneous, and out of a complement of 160 only 40 survived, including only 6 passengers. Two hours later, *Petrel* and *Lapwing* were sunk by U-124, with 49 killed out of their total complements of 65. Then U-124 struck again, at 2335 on the night of 26 September, sinking *Cervantes*, with the loss of 31 out of her complement of 36.

Frank Howe had witnessed the holocaust of the sinking of seven ships in convoy HG73. Then, a day later, U-201 fired a spread of five torpedoes, sinking the Norwegian ship *Siremalm* with all 27 crew, and *Margareta*, which suffered no fatal casualties. After the loss of nine ships, convoy HG73 arrived at Liverpool on 1 October 1941.

It was customary to allow fourteen days survivors' leave after the loss of a ship. I was never able to determine how this was assessed, nor whether Frank Howe received this leave for the loss of three ships in quick succession. The next entry in his discharge book was 2 January 1942, when he signed on as Third Mate of *King Arthur*. He signed off on 15 May 1942, and signed on *Empire Nightingale* on 10 June 1942, signing off on 11 September 1942. It is of great credit to him that he reported for further sea duty, and was assigned to *Start Point* a month later. This was the background of one courageous shipmate and friend.

Frank Howe and I hoped that *Start Point* would prove to be a ship of modern construction, in view of the fact that we had been unable to identify her in Lloyd's Register. We shared these thoughts during the short walk from the dock gates in Avonmouth to her berth, looking for the name of the ship. The awful truth dawned upon us when

S.S. Start Point, built in 1919, ex *War Warbler,* ex *Bretwalda,*
5293 gross registered tonnage.
Torpedoed and sunk by U-128 on 10 November 1942, one dead, two P.O.W.
The 44 survivors adrift for 13 days. One died
(*Photograph by National Maritime Museum*)

we saw the name *Start Point* on the bridge name board of the oldest
and most decrepit ship in the docks. We boarded the ship in the
afternoon of Sunday 11 October 1942, and reported to the Master and
First Mate.

Start Point was a typical long well-deck ship of 5,293 gross registered
tons, built during the shipbuilding programme of the Great War in 1919
under the name *War Warbler*. She was re-named *Bretwalda* in 1935, and was
acquired by the Ministry of War Transport, under the management of
John Cory & Sons Limited of Cardiff. The dimensions of the ship were:
length 412 feet, beam 52 feet 5 inches, draught 25 feet 3 inches, cargo
capacity 8,350 deadweight tons and designed speed 10.5 knots. I subsequently learned that the ship was not capable of exceeding 9 knots. My
accommodation was on the starboard side under the bridge, at the
forward end of the inboard working alleyway. We always referred to what

were termed "war built ships" as "built by the mile, and cut off to length." Many were distinguishable by their latticework steel fabricated cargo derricks, which were supplied because of a wartime shortage of tubular steel sections.

The Master was a native of Cardigan aged 49, and the First Mate was a native of Hull aged 53. I know nothing about their history or previous service. I found it rather surprising that a First Mate, 53 years of age, with a Certificate of Competency as Master, did not have his own command, three years after the declaration of war. Merchant Navy officers had returned to service after retirement, to fill the vacancies caused by war losses and the increase in shipbuilding, yet he had not been given command. Later, I was to learn the reason.

After three years of war, the Master in command, and the First Mate as second in command, such older officers must have been seriously affected, both physically and mentally, by the strains imposed by the war at sea. Both had been drinking heavily when we reported for duty, and the state of the ship was indicative of neglect and indiscipline. We were half their age, and therefore probably better able to withstand the stresses we all had been called upon to endure. However, it was not an auspicious start for my first voyage as Second Mate.

We reported to the Master, who took little interest in us, and told us to report to the First Mate. Although the names of the Master and First Mate are on record, I have deliberately not named them. We were ordered to "get on with our duties". The Third Mate and I agreed to spend our short time in Avonmouth in checking the most important items of equipment.

With the experience of the loss of four ships, Frank Howe immediately inspected the lifesaving equipment, which he found to be in a deplorable state. With my agreement, he visited the Board of Trade offices. Almost immediately after his visit, a surveyor boarded the ship, and condemned all four lifeboats as unserviceable. Within two days, four lifeboats were delivered along with all their equipment and stores. Four life rafts were also delivered, together with their launching platforms, which were attached to the mast shrouds. Our independent action did not find favour with the First Mate.

My concern, as the navigating and gunnery officer, was the state of our defensive weapons, and the charts. The 4.7-inch and anti-aircraft guns were in a filthy state. The four navy and three army D.E.M.S. personnel were unkempt and living like pigs in dirty accommodation. How the weapons and personnel had passed the customary inspection by the port

D.E.M.S. naval officer was a mystery. Those officers were relatively young and inexperienced R.N.V.R. officers, and many did not know one end of a ship from another. It was so easy for them to board the ship, complete their paperwork, and return to the comfort of their offices and billets ashore. I turned the scruffy gunners to, and ordered them to clean up themselves, their accommodation and their weapons. They were also given standing orders for routine and periodic gun drills. They did what they were told to do, but very truculently.

The chart room was a mess, with hundreds of Notices to Mariners spread around everywhere. We did not know our destination, so all I could do in the short time available was to sort the notices in date order, and correct the charts for the Bristol Channel, Irish Sea, and northern approaches. The remainder of the notices were reserved for our ocean passage, when I could correct the appropriate charts in my watches below. We were only a few days in Avonmouth, but had made a significant start in a short time. However, neither of us was ever in the favour of our superior officers from then on.

Start Point made passage to Barry Docks, where we loaded 6,280 tons of steam coal, and a part cargo of case oil and stores for the naval base at Freetown. Betty stayed aboard for one night, during which we were disturbed at night by the outbreak of a fire in the accommodation of the Third Mate, who had gone to sleep with a lighted cigarette in his mouth.

We put to sea in the evening of 21 October, destination Freetown via Milford Haven for convoy. When I commenced the middle watch, the night order book showed the word "DODGE" written in a large shaky scrawl diagonally across the page. It was a filthy night, with a strong westerly wind, heavy mist and intermittent rain squalls. The flood tide was running against the ship at between 4 and 5 knots strength. The ship was on slow speed and in a position well offshore in Carmarthen Bay, between Port Eynon Point and St. Govan's Head.

I descended the companion ladder between the chartroom and the Master's accommodation. He was lying on his settee, wearing thigh sea boots, and in an advanced state of inebriation. I asked him "Will you please explain what you mean by dodge, sir?" The answer was, "Surely you know the meaning of the word, Mr. Mate. Dodge for the whole of your watch between the Helwick and Scarweather Light Vessels." I tried to explain to him that at our reduced speed this would be almost impossible in the prevailing weather conditions and strong tidal currents, and asked him if he would come to the navigating bridge to see for himself. I also suggested anchoring the ship and waiting for daylight. His answer was that a decision to anchor was his prerogative; and he warned me that if he came to the bridge, he would relieve me of watch keeping duties. Miraculously, the ship "dodged" back and forth across Carmarthen Bay during my watch. How, I will never know.

There was a further problem at the end of the watch. The First Mate did not appear on the bridge at one bell, 0345, or eight bells, 0400, and, despite several visits by the standby man, he did not appear until well after 0500, and then very much under the influence of gin. My protests met with the response that it was the prerogative ot a senior officer to come on watch whenever he felt like it; and as a young junior officer, I had to wait until he arrived. I showed him where we were, passed over the night order book with its weird instruction, and went below. At just before 0730, the standby man wakened me with a request from the Third Mate, calling for my presence on the bridge. The Third Mate greeted me with the words, "For Christ's sake, check our position. I think the Old Man has gone mad!"

When I arrived on the navigating bridge, the Third Mate had relieved the First Mate, who was on the forecastle head preparing to anchor. The Master was lolling in the port wing of the bridge, issuing a stream of helm orders. The ship was on slow speed on a northerly course. Daylight was just beginning to show. A quick look at the chart showed what I identified as St. Ann's Head fine on our starboard bow; so I climbed to the "monkey island" and took several bearings on the standard compass with the azimuth mirror. Cross bearings of Linney Head, St. Ann's Head and Skokholm Island placed the ship well to the west of St. Ann's Head, and on a course directly for Gateholm Island. The Master had mistaken Skokholm Island for St. Ann's Head. We were on a course to go ashore.

When I pointed out the position to the Master, he berated me furiously and even refused to enter the chartroom where I had drawn the cross bearings on the chart. The only recourse in such an emergency was to take action. While he continued to issue helm orders, the Third Mate responded "Aye aye, sir", I conned the ship slowly to starboard from the wheelhouse. He was so drunk that he did not notice the alterations in course. The ship was brought to a course between St. Ann's head on the port side and Sheep Island on the starboard side, and into the approach channel to Milford Haven, where we anchored. The First Mate was by that time reasonably sober, so I suggested to him that his two junior officers would back him if he assumed command. His answer was "Let the bugger shit in his own nest."

As the Master staggered from the bridge, he remarked to me that he had brought the ship to safe anchorage without the benefit of my navigational help. He went ashore to the convoy conference, still unsteadily, and still wearing thigh sea boots. He returned from the convoy conference, and staggered to his cabin. I was summoned to his cabin, where he gave me all the documents appertaining to the convoy, whereupon he retired to his settee. He never came to the navigating bridge during my service in the ship.

When I perused the convoy instructions, I was horrified to learn that the Master had declared *Start Point* as capable of sustaining a service speed of 10 knots, to qualify for inclusion in a 9-knot convoy. It was well known then that ships should have been capable of about 3 knots in excess of the mean convoy speed. Many of the other ships in the convoy showed speeds of 12 knots and more. There is no doubt that our ship should have been delayed, in order to join a slow convoy. My protests to the Master were again ineffectual.

CONVOY ON141

Start Point put to sea in the morning of 22 October 1942 in convoy ON141 of 59 ships, bound for New York. Those ships on southbound passages would detach from the convoy in mid Atlantic, and proceed under orders, to be opened after detachment. Ships that became detached or straggled before reaching 15 degrees west longitude were instructed to return to Belfast.

The convoy instructions included orders for surface action target practice when clear of Milford Haven. Each ship was to open fire on a towed target in succession as the convoy left the anchorage in single column. Neither the Master nor the First Mate were on the bridge as we cleared harbour in the morning watch, the bridge being in charge of the Third Mate, while I was aft with the gun crew, preparing to fire our 4.7-inch gun. We fired several rounds with reasonable accuracy, straddling the target, and received a signal from the tug "Well done." A skeleton gun crew remained on duty to man the anti-aircraft weapon. The remainder stood down, and I returned to the bridge.

After passing through the Irish Sea and North Channel, the convoy formed into ocean passage order of columns abreast, and began a broad zig zag pattern. The commodore ordered 9 knots speed. The wind was westerly fresh to strong, with a rough head sea. *Start Point* was struggling to maintain 8 knots, and when fires were cleaned at the end of each watch, the speed reduced to about 7 knots, with thick smoke belching from the funnel.

During the first hour of the afternoon watch of 25 October, I was endeavouring to keep up with the convoy by steering a straight course to gain on the convoy zig zag. The first signal from the commodore was a flag hoist "The ship or ships indicated will reduce funnel smoke." Our convoy position number followed this signal. I called the commodore by Aldis lamp with the signal "Endeavouring to reduce smoke due to fire cleaning." This was acknowledged. About two hours later, an escort detached from the convoy and returned to our position, then several miles astern of the convoy. The signal by Aldis lamp was "Are you in difficulty?" My response was "No difficulty. Ship unable to maintain convoy speed." I entered all the signals in the log. The First Mate relieved me a half hour late at 1630 – earlier than usual for him – and I went below. Shortly afterwards the escort returned, with loud hailer orders for the ship to return to Belfast.

After I had been in my cabin for about five minutes, the standby man knocked on my cabin door with the order that the Master demanded my immediate presence in his cabin. The First Mate had brought the signal log to him, including the order for the ship to return to Belfast. He confronted me with the signal log and furiously demanded to know why I had sent the signals. My response was that the ship was unable to maintain convoy speed, and should therefore return to Belfast in accordance with convoy instructions.

Although he was partially inebriated, he was coherent enough to demand that I return to the bridge and send a signal "From Master. Vessel will maintain convoy speed." I was forced to obey his order. The convoy was then barely discernible in the failing light. When I stood the middle watch, I could see no ships, and in the morning, the horizon was clear. We had crossed 15 degrees west longitude; so proceeded in accordance with the courses laid down in our instructions. The Master had not left his cabin since returning from the convoy conference, and never again ascended the companion ladder to the navigating bridge. The First Mate not only relieved me well after the time of commencement of his watches, but took no part in the navigational duties. The Third Mate was an excellent watch-keeping officer, but had not been taught to take a sight or work out a position. His knowledge of chartwork was quite rudimentary. Hence, I found myself effectively in charge of the ship.

Straggler from Convoy ON141

The ship then conformed to the courses set out for stragglers, in accordance with instructions. The records show that the convoy arrived in New York on 10 November 1942. I have no record of the date when ships bound south were detached from the convoy, but it is probable that *Start Point* was by that time well east and south of the dispersal position.

During the time we were a part of convoy ON141, and the five days after being detached from the convoy, four convoys were attacked by concentrations of U-Boats. Our Chief Radio Officer, Thomas Maldwyn Jenkins, almost wore a groove in the deck bringing distress messages to the bridge.

Convoy ON136 had already lost two ships, and lost a further two, including *Empire Turnstone* with all hands. Convoy ON139 lost three ships. Freetown homeward bound convoy SL125 was decimated by the loss of 12 ships out of 42. The loss I felt the most was when I was handed the distress signal of my previous ship, *Barrwhin*, sunk by U-436 on 29 October 1942, with the loss of 24 men, among them my good friends, Neatby Nevers Stubbs the Chief Engineer, and Martin Benedict Preiera the Chief Steward. There were also a number of West African firemen, Jack Togba, Samuel Smallboy and Augustus Lindo. During my period of service in *Barrwhin*, I had written letters for them to their families. They were good men.

Barrwhin was an element in convoy HX212, which put to sea from Halifax on 18 October, and arrived in Liverpool on 2 November 1942. Attacks by the "Puma" group of U-boats, on station south of Iceland, commenced just before midnight on 27 October, when *Sourabaya*, a large general cargo and whale factory ship, owned by the South Georgia Co. Ltd, was torpedoed by U-436. The ship carried a cargo of oil and military stores, with invasion landing craft on deck, crew of 63, 8 gunners, 32 D.B.S (Distressed British Subjects – mainly merchant seamen) and 55 passengers, a complement of 158. There were no casualties when the ship sank, and all survivors were rescued, 81 by escort ships and 77 by *Bic Island*. It is reported that all survivors rescued by *Bic Island* were lost when the ship was sunk by U-224 two days later. Records show that all 40 of the crew of *Bic Island*, 77 survivors from *Sourabaya* and 43 survivors from *Gurney E. Newlin* were lost when *Bic Island* was sunk, a catastrophic loss of the lives of 160 men. Although we were not then fully aware of the statistics, it was almost inconceivable that Whitehall could be unaware of such enormous casualties, and fail to take positive steps to deal with such a crisis. The solution was clearly long-range air cover to keep the U-Boat groups away from convoys during the day.

During my period of service in *Barrwhin*, the whole of the after 'tween decks on both sides had been converted into accommodation. The account of her sinking in Lloyds' War Losses records her complement as 54 crew and 60 passengers. Another version records that *Barrwhin* accommodated 60 survivors from *Kosmos* II and *Abosso*. The survivors from *Abosso* could not have been rescued by *Barrwhin*, because *Abosso* was sunk in position 48 – 30 north latitude, 28 – 50 west longitude, at almost the same time as *Barrwhin* was sunk in position 55 – 02 north latitude, 22 – 45 west longitude. A distance 392 miles of latitude and about 150 miles of longitude separated the ships. *Abosso*, was on independent passage well south and east of convoy HX212. They were over 400 miles apart.

During the period when *Start Point* had been berthed in Avonmouth and Barry Docks, and on passage to Milford Haven, Sidney Cape Breton convoy SC104 was attacked by the eight U-Boats of the "Leopard" group, losing 8 ships out of 47. Casualties were exceptionally heavy. From a total complement of 426 in the ships sunk, 253 were lost, a fatal casualty rate of nearly 60 percent.

Start Point continued on the second leg of her independent passage to Freetown, maintaining a southerly course to pass west of the Azores. After the heavy losses in convoys SC104, SL125 and HX212, an even more severe attack developed on convoy SC107, which put to sea on 24 October, and was then north and west of our position. The "Vielchen" (Violet) group of 13 U-Boats attacked the convoy over a period of three days, sinking 15 of its 41 ships. One of the victims was *Empire Leopard* (ex *Onomea*, ex *Marian Otis Chandler,* ex *West Haven*, ex *War Flame*). This was the American ship that I had been detailed to join in New York in July 1940, only to be diverted to serve in the Yugoslav ship *Istok*. The fatal casualties in *Empire Leopard* were very heavy, with the loss of 37 out of her complement of 41. The loss of four tankers in convoy TAG18, and their precious cargoes of oil fuel, apparently was not enough to deviate our high command from their obsessive policy of the bombing German civilians. It was tragic.

Start Point followed a course set to pass west of the Azores and Cape Verde Islands. Sierra Leone convoy SL125 had suffered the loss of 12 ships between 26 October and 30 October. The U-Boat group had pursued the convoy from a latitude of 22 – 15 north to 38 – 08 north, when the attacks were discontinued. The Streitaxt (Battle Axe) group of eight U-Boats was stationed east and south of the Azores, about 500 miles south and east of the positions of our ship during the several days when we were inundated with their distress calls. It is likely that the U-Boats returned to the French Biscay ports after their successes against convoy SL125.

We had been diverted to the south of Halifax convoy HX212, which had sustained the loss of six ships in the attacks mounted by the Velchen (Violet) group of U-Boats, so when we received their distress messages we were almost due south of the positions of the attacks. The Natter (Viper) group of 12 U-Boats was stationed almost in mid North Atlantic, and the Puma group of 13 U-Boats was stationed south and west of the North Channel. *Start Point* and convoy ON141 had been diverted away from their operating areas. We had borne charmed lives. There is no doubt that many ships were diverted from U-Boat attack by the admirable efficiency and dedication of the personnel in the Admiralty Tracking Room under Lieutenant Commander Roger Winn R.N.V.R., and the personnel at Bletchley Park. Merchant seamen owe them an eternal debt of gratitude, and many of us are still alive to-day because of their expertise and dedication. We owe them a great deal.

During the time when our ship was detached from convoy ON141 and on independent passage, we received not only a substantial number of distress calls, but also information on U-Boat group positions. On a number of occasions, the Chief Radio Officer, Thomas Maldwyn Jenkins, called me to the wireless room, and allowed me to listen to the U-Boats signalling to each other, with his dry comments "Listen to the bastards. They are chattering like a flock of bloody Magpies." I marked every sinking on the chart with a cross, and every U-Boat with the replica of a submarine, a small oval with a vertical mark indicating a periscope. The chart was covered by the marks.

Undoubtedly, the whole of 1942, and into early 1943, marked the lowest point in the Battle of the Atlantic, and in particular the winter of 1942/1943. A great number of ships were sunk, but the casualties to their crews were enormous and unsustainable. Between 12 October 1942 (when I joined *Start Point*) and 9 January 1943 (when I joined *Pilar de Larrinaga*) the fatal casualties in the Atlantic were:

From 12 October to 31 October 1942 – 43.88% killed.
From 1 November to 10 November – 40.53% killed.
From 11 November to 9 December 1942 – 42.46% killed.
From 10 December 1942 to 9 January 1943 – 31.59% killed.

Out of a total of 14,371 seamen in the 291 ships sunk in the Atlantic, 5,481 were killed, an average fatal casualty rate of 38.14%.

Such casualty rates would never be sustained or tolerated in any Service units; but they were never publicised, or generally known. It was a disgrace, and indicative of inexcusable high-level indifference. We were being cut to ribbons, and could do nothing about the continuous slaughter in the Atlantic and Arctic waters.

Undoubtedly, the very severe weather that we encountered in the Atlantic and Arctic waters in the winter of 1942/1943, reduced the chances of survival for survivors. There was no way in which survivors in open boats could survive in the tempestuous seas, and the freezing cold of the almost continuous squalls of rain, sleet and snow. Moreover, even though rescue ships were incorporated in convoys, the weather was so atrocious that it would have been almost impossible for them to rescue survivors. Survivors in the water or in lifesaving craft just perished.

Casualties – Ships and Personnel
12 October 1942 to 31 October 1942

Ships sunk – 46 by 28 successful U-Boats.
One ship sunk in a minefield.

Lost with all hands

Ashworth, cargo bauxite, 49 dead.
Senta, cargo unknown, 37 dead.
Stornest, cargo coal, 48 dead.
Newton Pine, in ballast, 40 dead.
Empire Turnstone, in ballast, 46 dead.
Bic Island, general cargo, 40 dead.

Lost with very heavy casualties

Southern Empress, cargo fuel oil, 48 dead out of 125.
Fagersten, cargo lumber, 19 dead out of 29.
Susana, general cargo, 38 dead out of 59.
Nellie, cargo steel, 32 dead out of 37.
Nikolina Matkovik, cargo lumber 14 dead out of 35.
Empire Mersey, general cargo, 16 dead out of 55.
Caribou, general cargo and passengers, 136 dead out of 191.
Steel Navigator, in ballast, 16 dead out of 52.
Empire Star, general cargo, 41 dead out of 102.
Sourabaya, oil and war materials, 77 dead out of 158.
Stentor, general cargo and passengers, 44 dead out of 246.
Gurney E. Newlin, cargo petrol, 48 dead out of 60.

Nagpore, general cargo, 19 dead out of 92.

Kosmos II, cargo crude oil, and passengers, 40 dead out of 150.

Brittany, general cargo, 14 dead out of 58.

Abosso, general cargo and passengers, 340 dead out of 371.

Barrwhin, general cargo and survivors, 24 dead out of 114.

Pan New York, cargo clean oil, 40 dead out of 56.

Bullmouth, in ballast, 50 dead out of 55.

President Doumer, general and passengers, 260 dead out of 345.

Marylyn, general cargo, 15 dead out of 42.

Aldington Court, cargo war materials, 34 dead out of 44.

Merchant seamen and passengers killed – 1,682 out of 3,833,
a fatal casualty rate of 44 percent.

START POINT - 12 OCTOBER 1942 TO 7 JANUARY 1943

RECORD OF MERCHANT SHIPS SUNK IN ATLANTIC - 12/10/42 TO 31/10/42

START POINT - SIGNED ARTICLES AVONMOUTH - 12/10/42 - BERTHED AT AVONMOUTH AND BARRY

DATE	SHIP	NAT.	CONVOY NO.	CAUSE OF LOSS	POSITION		CARGO	CASUALTIES CREW	DEAD
13/10/42	ASHWORTH	BRITISH	SC104	U-221	53-55 N.	44-06 W.	BAUXITE	49	49
13/10/42	SOUTHERN EMPRESS	BRITISH	SC104	U-221	53-40 N.	40-40 W.	FUEL OIL	125	48
13/10/42	FAGERSTEN	NOR.	SC104	U-221	52-54 N.	43-55 W.	LUMBER	29	19
13/10/42	SENTA	NOR.	SC104	U-221	53-00 N.	44-00 W.		37	37
13/10/42	SUSANA	U.S.A.	SC104	U-221	53-41 N.	41-23 W.	GENERAL	59	38
13/10/42	STORNEST	BRITISH	ON136	U-706	54-25 N.	27-42 W.	COAL	48	48
14/10/42	NELLIE	GREEK	SC104	U-607	53-45 N.	40-45 W.	STEEL	37	32
14/10/42	NIKOLINA MATKOVIC	YUGO.	SC104	U-661	53-41 N.	42-23 W.	LUMBER	35	14
14/10/42	EMPIRE MERSEY	BRITISH	SC104	U-618	54-00 N.	40-30 W.	GENERAL	55	16
14/10/42	CARIBOU	BRITISH	NL9	U-69	47-19 N.	59-29 W.	PASS.	191	136
15/10/42	TRAFALGAR	NOR.		U-129	25-15 N.	50-00 W.	GENERAL	43	0
15/10/42	NEWTON PINE	BRITISH	ON136	U-410	55-00 N.	30-00 W.	BALLAST	40	40
16/10/42	CASTLE HARBOUR	BRITISH	T19	U-160	11-00 N.	61-10 W.	BALLAST	23	2
18/10/42	ANGELINA	U.S.A.	ON137	U-618	49-39 N.	30-20 W.	BALLAST	55	9
19/10/42	ROTHLEY	BRITISH		U-332	13-34 N.	54-34 W.	BALLAST	42	2
19/10/42	STEEL NAVIGATOR	U.S.A.	ON137	U-610	49-45 N.	31-30 W.	BALLAST	52	16
	START POINT		**ON 141**						
22/10/42	WINNIPEG II	BRITISH	ON139	U-443	49-51 N.	27-58 W.	GENERAL	192	0
22/10/42	DONAX	BRITISH	ON139	U-443	49-51 N.	27-58 W.	BALLAST	62	0
23/10/42	EMPIRE TURNSTONE	BRITISH	ON136	U-621	54-40 N.	28-00 W.	BALLAST	46	46
23/10/42	RUEBEN TIPTON	U.S.A.		U-129	14-33 N.	54-51 W.	GENERAL	52	3
23/10/42	EMPIRE STAR	BRITISH		U-615	48-14 N.	26-22 W.	GENERAL	102	41
24/10/42	HOLMPARK	BRITISH		U-516	13-11 N.	47-00 W.	BALLAST	50	1
25/10/42	PRIMERO	NOR.		U-67	13-38 N.	53-55 W.	BALLAST	39	2
26/10/42	ANGLO MAERSK	BRITISH	SL125	U-604	27-50 N.	22-15 W.	BALLAST	37	0
27/10/42	SOURABAYA	BRITISH	HX212	U-436	54-32 N.	31-02 W.	FUEL OIL	158	77
27/10/42	PACIFIC STAR	BRITISH	SL125	U-509	29-16 N.	20-57 W.	GENERAL	97	0
27/10/42	STENTOR	BRITISH	SL125	U-509	29-13 N.	20-53 W.	GENERAL	246	44
27/10/42	GURNEY E. NEWLIN	U.S.A.	HX212	U-436	54-51 N.	30-06 W.	PETROL	60	48
28/10/42	NAGPORE	BRITISH	SL125	U-509	31-30 N.	19-36 W.	GENERAL	92	19
28/10/42	KOSMOS II	NOR.	HX212	U-606	55-15 N.	28-10 W.	BLACK OIL	150	40
28/10/42	BRITTANY	NOR.	SL125	U-509	33-29 N.	18-32 W.	GENERAL	58	14
29/10/42	MACABI	PAN.		MINED	10-02 N.	61-55 W.		28	0
29/10/42	HOPECASTLE	BRITISH	SL125	U-509	31-35 N.	19-23 W.	GENERAL	46	5
29/10/42	ABOSSO	BRITISH		U-203	48-30 N.	28-50 W.	GENERAL	371	340
29/10/42	WEST KEBAR	U.S.A.		U-129	14-57 N.	53-57 W.	GENERAL	67	14
29/10/42	PRIMROSE HILL	BRITISH	ON139	UD-5	18-58 N.	28-40 W.	GENERAL	49	3
29/10/42	BARRWHIN	BRITISH	HX212	U-436	55-02 N.	22-45 W.	GRAIN	114	24
29/10/42	BIC ISLAND	BRITISH	HX212	U-224	55-05 N.	23-27 W.	GENERAL	40	40
29/10/42	PAN-NEW YORK	U.S.A.	HX212	U-624	54-58 N.	23-56 W.	CLEAN OIL	56	40
30/10/42	BULLMOUTH	BRITISH	SL125	U-409	33-20 N.	18-45 W.	BALLAST	55	50
30/10/42	TASMANIA	BRITISH	SL125	U-659	36-06 N.	16-59 W.	GENERAL	46	2
30/10/42	SILVER WILLOW	BRITISH	SL125	U-409	38-08 N.	16-44 W.	GENERAL	67	6
30/10/42	PRESIDENT DOUMER	BRITISH	SL125	U-604	38-08 N.	16-44 W.	GENERAL	345	260
30/10/42	BARON VERNON	BRITISH	SL125	U-604	36-06 N.	16-59 W.	IRON ORE	44	0
30/10/42	CORINALDO	BRITISH	SL125	U-509	33-20 N.	18-12 W.	MEAT	58	8
31/10/42	MARYLYN	BRITISH		U-174	00-40 S.	32-40 W.	GENERAL	42	15
31/10/42	ALDINGTON COURT	BRITISH		U-172	30-20 S.	02-10 W.	STORES	44	34
							TOTALS	**3,833**	**1,682**

During the attacks on convoys SC104, SL125 and HX212, ships that were sunk subsequently rescued the survivors from a number of ships. When assessing casualties, I have endeavoured to interpolate for this as accurately as possible.

By 31 October, *Start Point* had passed through an area of constant enemy attacks, during which period enormous losses had been inflicted on convoys SC104, SC107, SL125 and HX212, ON136, ON137, and ON139. The number of merchant seamen, D.E.M.S. gunners and supernumeraries killed in the ten days we had been on passage was 1,177, over three times the fatal casualties suffered by all forces in the Falklands War. This was equivalent to the extermination of one army battalion, or the crews of nearly 150 Lancaster bombers. Winston Churchill may have stated that the Battle of the Atlantic "frightened him", but he and Whitehall were doing nothing to prevent the losses.

The First Mate and Master did not participate in the navigation. The Master did not leave his cabin, except on one occasion. After leaving Milford Haven, I posted standing orders for the seven gunners. The basic instructions were that the defensive armament would be manned in the event of the alarm bells being sounded. The guns would be cleaned and maintained properly, and daily gun drill would take place at 1000. The reaction of the gunners was truculent and non-co-operative.

After several days of this routine, the standby man called me after breakfast with orders to go to the cabin of the Master. The Master was standing propped up in the doorway of his cabin on the lower bridge, talking to the seven gunners. He was under the influence, but just coherent. He told me that the gunners had complained about the daily hour of gun drill, with words to the effect that I had been "Riding them too hard. The previous Second Mate had not demanded daily gun drills. Was it necessary?" My answer was that it was decidedly necessary.

I told the Master that they were a sloppy group of swabs, and required a good shaking up. Despite my protests, he backed them up, and I was ordered to relax the regime I was trying to establish. Having served as the breech worker in the gun crew of *Appledore* as an apprentice, under the authority of a smart regular Royal Marine Colour Sergeant, I could not tolerate the attitude of the gunners. It was also unbelievable that the Master of a ship could demean the authority of one of his officers, by backing up such individuals, who were a disgrace to the Royal Navy and Royal Maritime Artillery. The Leading Seaman and Lance Corporal in joint command of the gunners were the ringleaders in the rebellion. However, they had succeeded in coercing the Master into over-ruling my authority.

The development of the D.E.M.S. (Defensively Equipped Merchant Ships) authority had been massive, when compared with the situation at the beginning of the war. Then, one gunner was appointed to each ship, the guns being manned by Merchant Navy gunners, trained volunteers. The gunners in charge were usually non-commissioned Royal Marines or Royal Navy leading seamen or petty officers. They were experts. When the numbers of gunners were increased to about seven in each ship, and more in larger ships, the Royal Maritime Artillery was formed, and ships carried both army and navy personnel. These were conscripts with a short period of training in their weaponry, and without the background of their predecessors. They were generally well-disciplined personnel, and many distinguished themselves in contact with the enemy.

However, as it became more generally known that casualties in attacks on merchant ships were likely to be very heavy, service in the D.E.M.S. lost its attraction. It was rumoured among Merchant Navy officers that some D.E.M.S. personnel were being drawn from the numbers of army and navy incorrigibles, bad conduct individuals who were sent to sea in merchant ships to escape the service prisons (glass houses). Certainly, the gunners who served in *Start Point* were no recommendation for the army and navy units from which they were drawn. They were the exception, in the nine ships in which I served.

Our passage south was relatively uneventful, despite the frequent distress messages and U-Boat reports. The First Officer continued to relieve me on watch between 30 minutes and one hour late, and never joined me in taking the customary sights at 0800 and 1200. The Master did not involve himself in the navigation at all. It was my custom to descend the companion ladder from the chart room to his cabin, with the dead reckoning positions, after I had worked out the longitude in the morning, and with the corrected position, when I had determined the accurate latitude at noon. He was given the positions for hourly intervals between noon of one day and noon of the next.

The same information was given to the Third and First Mates and the wireless room. I kept a copy in a waterproof bag in my uniform jacket, together with the declination of the sun for noon of each day for 30 days ahead, a notebook, pencil, and waterproof parchment charts of the North and South Atlantic Oceans. I made a water resistant canvas bag for my sextant and attached a stout lanyard, so that I could put the sextant in its box and sling the bag around my neck. My sextant was never far from me, either when I was on the bridge or when I was on watch below. I always kept a stout clasp knife on a lanyard around my neck.

My relationship with the First Mate was strained enormously by his inherent contempt for young officers trained in the more modern syllabus of the Merchant Navy Officers Training Board. This was aggravated by his consistently late arrival on the bridge to relieve me on watch, and his failure to participate in navigational duties. The only times we met each other were when he eventually arrived on the bridge to relieve me on watch or at meal times at the table. When on the bridge, our conversation was confined to course and speed, position of the ship, and perusal of the scrap log and signal log. He usually arrived, mostly after a session with the gin bottle, and I did not delay my departure after handing over the watch.

During meals, he was inclined to denigrate junior officers generally, and the Second Mate in particular. Typical remarks were, "Steward, give me a man's portion. I'll have twice as much curry and rice as the Second Mate. Men need more food than boys." On another occasion, when ox tails were served, "Steward, men need thicker pieces than boys. Give me the part nearest to the arse of the bull." I was conscious of the fact that he had been standing a watch on the bridge of a ship before I was born; but it was aggravating beyond measure to be reminded constantly of my relatively young age of 21, and comparative lack of experience.

There was no point in my attempting to retort to his perpetual snide comments. The needle had stuck in the groove. I was standing two five to five and a half hour watches a day due to his relieving me late on every watch, and was spending a further hour on navigation, correcting charts and supporting the Third Mate – who called me every time we received a signal ordering an alteration in course. After our evening meal, when the First Mate was on watch, the Third Mate and I played bridge with the wireless operators. This was a friendly interlude.

Start Point had not been fumigated for a long time. Rats are clever creatures, and many had escaped extermination during fumigation, by moving from hold to hold through the magnetic degaussing cable conduits around the ship. There were rats everywhere. When my mug of tea and sandwich were brought to the bridge, the mug and plate could not be left unguarded for even a short time. I made a practice of setting a break-back trap, baited with a piece of bread, in the wing of the bridge. Minutes after the trap had been set, there would be a crack, and a dead rat would be thrown into the sea. On one occasion, I set a treadle-actuated trap, which caught three rats simultaneously by the head. They invaded every part of the ship. *Start Point* would aptly fit the description of a "hell ship".

On 8 November 1942, we received a distress signal from the Norwegian ship *Maloja*, now recorded as having been sunk by U-128 in position 11 – 25 north 27 – 00 west. The U-Boat timed the attack at 1845. Our ship was approximately 120 miles north and west of the position. At a few minutes before 2230 (ship's apparent time), during the night watch on 9 October, we received a distress call from the tanker *Cerinthus*, also sunk by U-128, the position being 12 – 27 north, 27 – 45 west. The U-Boats appeared to be conforming to a time regime of one hour after G.M.T., so I timed the sinking of *Maloja* as 1745 G.M.T. on 8 November, and the sinking of *Cerinthus* as 2302 G.M.T. on 9 November. At about 2330 G.M.T. on 9 November 1942, the standby man brought me a message from the Third Mate, requesting my presence on the bridge. I was already awake and preparing for my middle watch. There was a signal from operational headquarters ordering a course of 127 degrees, which was an alteration of course of about 10 degrees to the south of the course I had set towards Freetown. At the time of the alteration of course, *Start Point* was about 100 miles north west of the position signalled by *Cerinthus* in her distress message. The diversion course would have placed *Start Point* in about the same position as where *Cerinthus* was sunk, about an hour before noon of 10 October 1942. The apparent time of ship, as calculated and corrected at noon each day, was one hour and thirty-five minutes behind G.M.T. We did not know whether one or more U-Boats had been responsible for the sinking of *Maloja* and *Cerinthus*. The likelihood was one U-Boat, patrolling slowly north and west on the route to Freetown. I calculated that our previous course direct to Freetown would have placed us north and east of the estimated patrol line. However, we were not to know whether other U-Boats were in the area. The problem was further complicated by the fact that our Master had declared a sustainable speed of 10 knots.

Cerinthus was a small tanker, built in 1920, with a designed speed of 10 knots, on passage in ballast to Freetown. She had been in company with *Start Point* in convoy ON141. Therefore, operational headquarters had to assume that both ships were near each other. They were not to know that *Cerinthus* had gained 100 miles during our respective ocean passages. I placed the position of the sinking of *Cerinthus*, and our position, on the chart, and took the positions to the Master. Contingency instructions permitted ships to make short high frequency wireless transmissions in code, in such cases of emergency.

I urged the Master to authorise a short signal to operational headquarters advising them that we were in imminent danger of attack, and requesting an immediate alteration of course. Alternatively, I requested permission to alter course to 090 degrees, which would have taken us well to the north and east of the position of threat. Both requests were denied. The Master even refused to go to the chart room, and his words to me were "If I go to the bridge, you will be divested of your authority and entered in the official log as being insubordinate." The Third Mate and I then woke the First Mate, to ask him to assume command, with our backing. He declined. We were powerless in such circumstances, apart from complete subordination.

In the traditional vernacular used at sea "We were up shit creek without a paddle." The only recourse was to send a short high frequency message to operational headquarters. The only authority for such action was an order from the Master. We knew the position of only one U-Boat. There could have been other U-Boats in a group disposed near our position. There was a possibility that the U-Boat or U-Boats could have left the area, and there was no longer a threat. Therefore, to take unauthorised action to alter course could have increased the dangers of an encounter with the enemy. My remarks to the Third Mate were that if the U-Boat had not moved far from its station, we would be likely to encounter the enemy within twelve hours. I prepared for the worst, as I stood the middle watch.

The German submarine U-128 was a type IXC built by AG Weser of Bremen, laid down on 10 July 1940, launched on 20 February 1941, and commissioned on 12 May 1941. Under the command of Kapitan-Leutnant Ulrich Heyse, U-128 put to sea from Kiel on 9 December 1941, and arrived at Lorient on 24 December 1941. The U-Boat left base at Lorient on 8 January for operations in the western Atlantic, and returned on 23 March 1942. On the first operational sortie, U-128 sank two American tankers off Cape Canaveral, *Pan Massachusetts* and *City Services Empire*, followed by a third, the Norwegian tanker *O.A. Knudsen*.

The second sortie lasted from 25 April to 22 July 1942. In the central Atlantic, U-128 attacked Sierra Leone convoy SL109, in company with U-126 and U-121, the only success in the attack being the British ship *Denpark*, sunk by U-128. The group of three U-Boats then moved south, where U-128 sank the tankers *South Africa, Andrea Brovig* and the cargo ships *West Ira* and *Polybius* in the West Indies. Moving south to the east coast of Brazil, U-128 sank *Steel Engineer*. The U-Boat left Lorient on 2 September 1942 and returned to base on 10 September 1942, presumably because of the necessity for repairs.

The third operational sortie commenced on 14 September 1942, and

U-128 returned to base on 15 January 1943. The U-Boat patrolled south-west off Freetown, encountering and sinking *Maloja* on 8 November and *Cerinthus* on 9 November 1942. Shortly afterwards, at noon on 10 November 1942, our paths crossed. As usual, the First Mate relieved me late for his morning watch on 10 November. I went below at about 0500, slept for three hours, and returned to the bridge at 0800 to take the morning sight for longitude. In accordance with usual custom, the Master was given the dead reckoning position, pending correction of the latitude by the noon sight. Following breakfast I corrected some charts, and went below for a wash and shave at about 1045.

Torpedoed by U-128! 10 November 1942

My sextant was always close at hand in its canvas bag and was left on my bunk. I had just completed my ablutions, when a torpedo struck the ship amidships, with a massive explosion, at 1130 ship's apparent time, 1305 G.M.T. The blast blew in the glass of my forward porthole with such force that the myriad fragments blew a jagged hole through the wooden bulkhead separating my cabin from the cabin of the Third Mate. By a miracle, I had just sat on my settee. If I had been standing in the centre of the cabin, I would have been cut to pieces.

The door to the working alleyway had jammed, but I had taken the precaution of leaving it partly ajar on its hook. Therefore, I was able to force it open. The after door of the alleyway was completely blocked by the wreckage of a derrick, so I crossed to the port working alleyway, through the connecting corridor, and made my way on deck amidships near No. 3 hatch. The whole of the amidships part of the ship between the bridge and the funnel was devastated. The torpedo must have been set at shallow depth, and struck the ship just below the waterline between the bridge and No. 3 hold, so the force of the explosion was concentrated above decks.

The whole of the port wing of the navigating bridge had been wrecked and collapsed. The port bridge lifeboat had been blown inboard with terrific force, and its bows driven through the steel bulkhead of the Master's cabin. Both No. 3 derricks had been blown from their mountings and crutches, and lay in a twisted mess on No. 3 hatch, with the end of the starboard derrick driven through the after door of the starboard working alleyway. The port Samson post and funnel rigging had been severed in the explosion, and both were bent severely to starboard. The port stokehold ventilator had been blown overboard and the starboard ventilator was severely bent. The ship had developed a heavy list to port, and was beginning to settle slowly by the head.

Fortunately, the torpedo struck the ship between the busy periods amidships. The afternoon watch of seamen and fireman had already drawn their meals from the galley, in the deckhouse immediately abaft No. 3 hatch, and had gone aft, except for one fireman, who had been severely injured. The food was being prepared for the meal for the officers and engineers, but the steward, cabin boy and mess room boy had not arrived at the galley to take the food to the respective mess rooms. Although the galley was badly damaged, the cook and galley boy had not been injured.

My first concern was my responsibility for the starboard lifeboats and rafts, particularly because of the heavy list to port. I made my way through the tangle of wreckage amidships to the starboard boat deck ladder. The severely injured fireman was climbing the ladder in front of me, with blood pouring from a large wound in his back. The blood covered my face and shoulders. The fireman reached the boat deck screaming with pain and holding his hand over the gaping hole in his back. Then, to add to the din, the exhaust valve in the boiler room started blowing steam. The steam whistle lanyard must have tightened, and actuated the whistle on the damaged funnel. It was a nightmare scenario.

There was one man on the boat deck, a fireman, who shouted to me asking if he could help. I ordered him to take off his singlet, and use it in an attempt to staunch the bleeding from the wound suffered by the injured man; and to help him into the lifeboat after it had been launched. There was no help on the boat deck to assist with the lowering of the starboard lifeboat; so I released the griping bands, left the falls with just two turns on the bollards, and found a secure seat on the sloping deck, with my feet propped against a mushroom ventilator. Grasping the after fall rope in my right hand and the forward fall rope in my left hand, I slacked away on the falls and lowered the boat from my precarious position.

The lifeboats were equipped with skids, to facilitate lowering in conditions of a heavy list to the opposite side. These helped in the lowering of the heavy boat to the water. I secured the painter. The uninjured fireman released the scrambling net, and assisted the injured man to board the lifeboat. There was pandemonium in the after well deck with about thirty men milling around, including the seven gunners. I shouted to the gunners to man the 4.7-inch gun, in case the U-Boat surfaced. The answer shouted above the din was "F... you, Mr. Mate. We are getting out of this bloody ship!" By then someone shouted to me for instructions. It sounded like the Third Mate, whom I had not seen. He was instructed to take the boat away from the ship, with as many survivors as possible, and boarded the boat with 29 men.

The appearance of the Third Mate on the starboard side was unexpected. The First and Third Mates were responsible for the port lifeboats. The boat on the port lower bridge had been smashed to matchwood. Later I learned that they arrived on the port side of the boat deck together. According to the account of the Third Mate, the First Mate was – as usual – far from steady on his feet; no doubt from his customary session with the gin bottle. He manned the forward fall rope, while the Third Mate manned the after fall rope. The lifeboat, a new large motor-powered craft with a capacity of 50 persons, had not been damaged in the explosion that had caused such damage amidships.

Unaccountably, the First Mate let go of the fall rope from its bollard. Whether this was due to his unsteadiness, or panic, or both, the result was that the heavy boat fell bows first into the sea. The ship was still carrying way, so the boat filled immediately and became a total wreck. Due to the incompetence of the First Mate, the port boat stuck the water bows down at a steep angle, with the after fall rope still on its bollard. The boat broke in two pieces, and floated away. This disaster should not have happened, especially when the lowering was in the charge of an officer with over 35 years sea experience. The ship was carrying way when I lowered the starboard lifeboat, but I controlled the falls in order that the boat would touch the water bows up.

I returned to the lower bridge, which was deserted, and lowered the smaller lifeboat in a similar manner, sitting on the deck, slacking away on both falls, securing the painter and releasing the scrambling net. Then the Chief Engineer, the bosun, carpenter and two able seamen arrived on the lower bridge. I ordered the bosun to take the boat away from the ship and stand by with as many of the remaining survivors as possible. The First Mate then arrived amidships carrying a pillowcase stuffed with cigarettes, cigarette papers and tobacco, and went over the side immediately. He gave no orders or spoke to me. His only concern was to abandon ship as quickly as possible with his precious pillowcase. He took charge of the boat with the Chief Engineer and 13 others aboard, and stood away from the ship. I remained aboard.

About 15 minutes had elapsed since the explosion of the torpedo. The ship was well down by the head, with the forecastle almost awash, and Nos. 1 and 2 hatches submerged. I ascended the starboard companion ladder to the navigating bridge, cleared the chart room of all confidential papers, placed them in the weighted box, returned to the wrecked port side of the lower bridge, where I retrieved the wireless signal code books from the severely damaged wireless cabin; and threw the box overboard. I then returned to the wireless cabin, where the Chief Radio Officer was calmly transmitting distress messages. We found that the connecting wire between the masthead aerials and wireless cabin had carried away, so between us we rigged a jury aerial to the partly wrecked port Samson post. I will never know whether it worked.

The "Sparks" then continued to transmit. All this time, I had my precious sextant slung around my neck in its waterproof bag. On my return to the bridge, he was still transmitting, and continued to transmit, as I went to the cabin of the Master, whom I had not seen on deck. The cabin was a shambles. The deck head had been ruptured, and a huge amount of the water thrown up by the explosion had poured through the deck head, partially flooding the cabin. The bow of the port bridge lifeboat had been driven through the bulkhead, and was partly in the cabin. There were gin bottles everywhere. The Master was lying on his settee in a partially dazed condition. I shouted to him "We have been bumped, sir. The ship won't last much longer!" This stimulated a reaction from him, and I managed to get him into a lifejacket, and helped him to the starboard lower bridge, where I held him upright for a short time.

Over 20 minutes had elapsed since the explosion, and the foredeck was then completely awash. I returned to the wireless cabin, and urged the "Sparks" to abandon ship, because there was nothing we could do then. He shouted that he would go aft to abandon ship. At about that time, U-128 must have fired a second torpedo.

After releasing the starboard bridge lifebelt and its flare from its housing on the bridge, I told the Master that I was going to jump overboard. The last thing he said to me was, "I am following you, Mr. Upton." I saw him following me as I descended the scrambling net and swam away from the ship, trailing my sextant behind me. The starboard bridge lifeboat, then in the command of the First Mate, picked me up after I had been in the water for a few minutes. During that time, I was burned by the spluttering particles of calcium thrown off by the flare attached to the lifebelt. These adhered to the skin of my chest, and scarred the skin severely, but healed later.

As I was being hauled into the lifeboat a second torpedo struck *Start*

Point on the port side, near Nos. 4 and 5 holds. The ship rolled over violently to starboard, the funnel struck the water with a huge splash and broke off, and the ship sank vertically by the stern. The bows stood up, the No. 1 hold ventilator covers blew off with the pressure, blowing out two spouts of black water, and the ship disappeared within 30 seconds. The time was 1155 ship's apparent time, 1330 G.M.T.

We searched the wreckage and could not find the Master. He had been seen on the scrambling net, shortly before the second torpedo exploded, so it was likely that he was caught in the net when the ship rolled over, and was taken down when *Start Point* sank.

Shortly afterwards two submarines surfaced, respectively flying German and Italian colours. Later, I learned that the U-Boat was U-128, commanded by Kapitan-Leutnant Ulrich Heyse. The identity of the Italian submarine has been obscure. Years later, I corresponded with Kapitan Karl Friedrich Mertens, the commander of U-68, who told me that the submarine was *Da Finzi*, commanded by a Captain Gazzara. The only commander I have been able to identify in the records is Gianfranco Gazzana-Priaroggia, in command of submarine *Leonardo da Vinci*. That submarine was then operating a thousand miles south of our position. Therefore, I believe that the Italian submarine was *Guiseppe Finzi,* which is recorded as having been operating west of Freetown in late 1942 to mid 1943. The commander was Mario Rossetto. It is likely that the Italian submarine was intending to relieve U-128, because her paintwork and condition indicated that she had not been at sea for very long, whereas U-128 was showing rust patches and weed growth.

Both submarines had surfaced about a half a mile from our lifeboats. The U-Boat silhouette was significantly different from the shapes of the Class II and Class VII types depicted in our silhouette books. U-128 was one of the first of the longer-range Type IX submarines. My sextant had kept dry in its waterproof bag, and my notebook, schedules of our positions, the noon declinations of the sun, and a pencil were also undamaged by the immersion in water. So I was able to make a quick sketch of the U-Boat as it approached. The boat was called alongside, and the commander hailed me from the bridge speaking in English, "Have you been drawing my submarine?" I shouted in reply that I was marking my position on my waterproof chart. I threw my sketch under a thwart

The commander ordered me to board the U-Boat. This was difficult, because there was a moderate sea running; and as I attempted to scramble aboard on the port side by the forward catwalk, I slipped on the seaweed that encrusted the bulge in the hull, and fell into the sea, with my legs inside the hull apertures. I had awful visions of being washed between the hulls and being trapped, but managed to crawl onto the fore deck catwalk. A seaman armed with a rifle stood over me as I crawled aboard. He then prodded me in the ribs with the muzzle of the gun as I made my way aft to the conning tower. I went aft gingerly, apprehensive that the seamen would stumble and pull the trigger of his rifle.

Five men, the commanding officer, officer of the watch, and two lookouts occupied the bridge of the conning tower, plus the seamen who stood guard over me. The lookouts were furnished with huge binoculars attached to platforms suspended from their necks, and constantly scanned the horizon to port and starboard. The commanding officer asked if I was one of the men who had stayed on board after the ship was struck by the first torpedo, and congratulated me for this. He told me that they had been watching for activity aboard, because of the possibility that we may have had a gun crew in hiding, ready to go into action if they surfaced. What a chance, with our gun crew of insubordinate swabs!

Previously, U-128 had sunk *Cerinthus* by torpedo and gunfire, and probably would have surfaced to finish off *Start Point* by gunfire, but was deterred by the fact that they could see men on deck after the two lifeboats had left the ship. He asked for the name of the ship and its cargo, but I gave my name and discharge book number R198560. They did not attempt to extract any information by force, and treated me well, but confiscated my waterproof chart. I carried two, so that did not worry me. The commanding officer told me, "Yesterday we killed an oil ship". I was in the conning tower for about a half an hour, with the muzzle of the gun digging into my ribs.

The lifeboat was then called alongside, and was secured close to the conning tower. The Chief Engineer was wearing his epaulettes of rank, and was immediately identified and ordered to board the U-Boat. The U-Boat commander called for the Master to identify himself. He was told that he had been lost with the ship. He then called for the next senior in command. The First Mate would not identify himself, and told the survivors in the lifeboat to identify me as the First Mate. He had never gained any respect in the forecastle, so he was identified by the crew, and ordered to board the U-Boat. In any case, I was wearing the epaulettes of rank of Second Mate, and was altogether too young to have been second in command of a merchant ship.

Kapitan Leutnant Ulrich Heyse then suggested that we strip the life rafts of anything useful, wished us luck, and allowed me to board the lifeboat. After my gruelling time on the U-Boat, I was enormously relieved to have escaped unharmed. Although at that time we did not know of the sinking of the passenger liner *Laconia*, and the resultant "Laconia Order" and "Rescue Ship Order" issued by Admiral Donitz, we had heard rumours of atrocities committed against survivors.

It just remains to account for the movements of the Chief Wireless Operator, the irrepressible Thomas Maldwyn Jenkins. After I left him by the wireless cabin, he returned and transmitted another distress message. He then collected the two heavy batteries for the lifeboat wireless transmitters that had been on charge, and carried them aft on the starboard side, just as the second torpedo exploded. He jumped clear of the ship as she sank, still carrying both batteries by their leather straps, and was dragged down when the ship sank.

His version in his Cardigan vernacular was, "The batteries were bloody heavy like, and they took me down and down where it was bloody dark. So I thought, I had better let one of them go!" Relieved of part of the weight, he surfaced near a raft, and dragged himself and one battery aboard. He was taken aboard the Italian submarine, where he distinguished himself by calling them a "Lot of bloody Dagoes", and eventually was taken aboard the lifeboat under the command of the Third Mate. Thomas Maldwyn Jenkins was an irrepressible character, and not easily frightened.

The submarines departed in company on the surface on an easterly course. The 44 survivors from *Start Point* were adrift in mid ocean in a position of unbelievable difficulty.

After we had collected into our lifeboats what was useful from the rafts, we moored together, and I told the survivors our position, the time I anticipated that we would be adrift, and the options available to us. My purpose was not to look for comments or action by committee, but to put the facts clearly before the survivors and to outline the course of action to be followed.

I explained to the survivors the several options. The position of the sinking of *Start Point* was approximately 180 miles south west of the Cape Verde Islands. The careless and incompetent destruction of our large motor lifeboat, made it virtually impossible to reach the islands. There was no way in which two heavily laden Class 1A lifeboats could beat against the prevailing northeast Trade Winds under sail. They would have been pointing in the direction of the islands and drifting westwards. Similar adverse conditions would have prevented an attempt to reach the west coast of Africa, about 1,000 miles away.

The boats should have made reasonable way on a due west course towards the Windward Islands, the distance being about 1,800 miles. However, this also presented problems. The area between the Equator and Tropic of Cancer generated fierce tropical revolving storms during November and December, and there would have been a likelihood of the boats being overwhelmed in such conditions.

I had no doubt about the course of action, and I made this clear to those under my command. We would set a course of about south south west towards St Paul Rocks, on the Equator north east of Brazil, and Cape Branco, the most easterly point in Brazil. The distance was 1,300 miles. At that time of the year, the Doldrums moved south of the Equator; so there was a good chance of carrying the North East Trade Winds the whole way. There was also the advantage of the westerly current of the Equatorial Drift that originated in the Gulf of Guinea. Moreover, ships on independent passage to South America usually passed west of St. Paul Rocks and east of Fernando Norohna, offering a faint possibility of rescue where their courses converged. I planned for our being adrift for at least 30 days.

I am now able to reflect on the circumstances that prevailed at the time, with the benefit of hindsight, and the records now available. The Third Mate was a competent practical seaman, but without comprehensive navigational training or experience. Moreover, the traumatic experiences he had suffered had eroded his confidence. There were 31 men in his lifeboat and 13 men in mine. My decision was that both lifeboats would remain together under one command. We would take advantage of the prevailing wind and ocean current, and attempt the passage of 1,300 miles towards Brazil.

The report of the loss of *Cerinthus*, sunk in almost the same position as *Start Point* bears out my decision. The boat commanded by the Master of *Cerinthus*, which originally carried 20 survivors, was found 55 days later on the same latitude, about 650 miles west, with one survivor and 6 bodies aboard. The boat of the First Mate of *Cerinthus*, with 19 survivors, was rescued by *H.M.S. Bridgewater* after being adrift 21 days. The position of the rescue is not shown in the records that I have examined. The boats of *Start Point*, in tow, covered a distance of nearly 600 miles in 12 days. My decision to keep the lifeboats together, and steer a southerly course, was undoubtedly the correct one.

When we had completed transferring the food and water from the two rafts, which were afloat and could be found, and the U-Boat and Italian submarine were out of sight, almost all the survivors in the two lifeboats were violently seasick. We all had eaten curry and rice for breakfast, and the residue from 44 stomachs was being vomited out in great quantities into the clear blue sea. I watched as the multitudes of grains of rice in my vomit slowly vanished into the deep, like a snowstorm. The bout of vomiting must have been caused by a combination of the violent motion of the small craft in the choppy sea, and the after effects of the experience that we had suffered. We had heard rumours of atrocities against survivors, and it was a great relief when the enemy behaved in such a civilised manner.

The immediate decision was to remain in the area for the night, sending distress signals on the lifeboat transmitter. We streamed the sea anchors, moored the boats end to end, and lay hove-to in a fresh wind and choppy sea, until the following morning.

During the period after the dispersal of convoy ON141, and during our independent passage south, attacks continued on convoys SC7, OP-FB, WB9, TAG18, TS23, TRIN24, TAG19 and ON142, with the loss of a further 32 ships, plus *Start Point* and *Cerinthus* from convoy ON141.

A further 925 merchant seamen were killed, almost another army battalion wiped out, or the crews of about 120 Lancaster bombers. Eighteen ships were sunk when on independent passage.

One of the ships lost was *Chulmleigh*, one of the more modern ships of the Tatem Line built in 1938. *Chulmleigh* was on independent passage from Philadelphia to Archangel. After attack by aircraft on 5 November 1942, and torpedoed by U-625, she was beached on Spitzbergen. Out of her crew of 58, 12 survived, the Master, Captain D.N. Williams, 3 crew and 9 gunners. Many of the 46 who died succumbed to frostbite in the freezing cold, while waiting for rescue on Spitzbergen, where they were isolated for 61 days.

Casualties – Ships and Personnel
1 November 1942 to 10 November 1942

Ships sunk – 47 by 25 successful U-Boats.
Four ships sunk by Italian submarines.
One ship sunk by aircraft.

Lost with all hands

Empire Sky, cargo war materials, 66 dead.

Lost with very heavy casualties

Empire Gilbert, cargo war materials, 63 dead out of 66.
Empire Leopard, cargo zinc, 37 dead out of 41.
Hartington, cargo wheat, 24 dead out of 47.
Maritima, general cargo, 32 dead out of 59.
Rose Castle, cargo iron ore, 24 dead out of 43.
Zaandam, iron ore and passengers, 135 dead out of 299.
Llandilo, cargo military stores, 24 dead out of 44.
Hobemma, general cargo, 28 dead out of 44.
Christian J. Kampmann, cargo sugar, 19 dead out of 27.
William Clark, general cargo, 30 dead out of 71.
Chulmleigh, general cargo, 45 dead out of 58.
City of Cairo, passengers, 104 dead out of 296.
Nathaniel Hawthorn, cargo bauxite, 38 dead out of 52.
Roxby, cargo coal, 34 dead out of 46.
Glenlea, cargo coal, 44 dead out of 48.
Lindenhall, cargo iron ore, 42 dead out of 48.
Nurmahall, in ballast, 14 dead out of 45.
Cerinthus, in ballast, 20 dead out of 39.

Merchant seamen and passengers killed – 925 out of 3,030,
a fatal casualty rate of 31 percent.

The most successful U-boats in the period from 12 October 1942 to 10
November 1942 were U-160 and U-509 (six ships each): U-129 (five
ships): and U-402 (four ships).

Fourteen U-Boats were sunk: nine by air attack: three by surface forces (two
by depth charges and one by ramming): and two from unknown causes.

THE WAR AT SEA: START POINT

START POINT - 12 OCTOBER 1942 TO 7 JANUARY 1943

RECORD OF MERCHANT SHIPS SUNK IN ATLANTIC - 01/11/42 TO 10/11/42

START POINT - DETACHED FROM CONVOY ON141 ON 31/10/42

DATE	SHIP	NAT.	CONVOY NO.	CAUSE OF LOSS	POSITION		CARGO	CASUALTIES CREW	DEAD
01/11/42	EMPIRE GILBERT	BRITISH	OP-FB	U-586	70-15 N.	13-50 E.	GENERAL	66	63
01/11/42	ELMDALE	BRITISH		U-174	17-30 N.	34-55 W.	STORES	42	6
01/11/42	EMPIRE LEOPARD	BRITISH	SC107	U-402	52-26 N.	45-25 W.	ZINC	41	37
01/11/42	EMPIRE ANTELOPE	BRITISH	SC107	U-402	52-26 N.	45-22 W.	GENERAL	50	0
01/11/42	HARTINGTON	BRITISH	SC107	U-521	52-30 N.	45-30 W.	WHEAT	47	24
01/11/42	EMPIRE SUNRISE	BRITISH	SC107	U-84	51-50 N.	46-25 W.	LUMBER	51	0
02/11/42	DALCROY	BRITISH	SC107	U-402	52-30 N.	45-30 W.	LUMBER	49	0
02/11/42	MARITIMA	BRITISH	SC107	U-522	52-20 N.	45-40 W.	GENERAL	59	32
02/11/42	MOUNT PELION	GREEK	SC107	U-522	52-20 N.	45-40 W.	GENERAL	39	7
02/11/42	RINOS	GREEK	SC107	U-402	52-30 N.	45-30 W.	GENERAL	31	8
02/11/42	EMPIRE ZEAL	BRITISH		DA VINCI	00-30 S.	30-45 W.	BALLAST	52	0
02/11/42	PLM 27	BRITISH	WB9	U-518	47-36 N.	52-58 W.	IRON ORE	49	12
02/11/42	ROSE CASTLE	BRITISH	WB9	U-518	46-36 N.	52-57 W.	IRON ORE	43	24
02/11/42	ZAANDAM	DUTCH		U-174	01-23 S.	36-22 W.	ORE	299	135
03/11/42	LLANDILO	BRITISH		U-172	27-03 S.	02-59 W.	STORES	44	24
03/11/42	HAHIRA	U.S.A.	SC107	U-521	54-15 N.	41-47 W.	FUEL OIL	56	3
03/11/42	THORSHAVET	NOR.	TAG18	U-160	12-16 N.	64-06 W.	CRUDE OIL	46	3
03/11/42	LEDA	PAN.	TAG18	U-160	12-16 N.	64-06 W.	FUEL OIL	48	0
03/11/42	HOBEMMA	DUTCH	SC107	U-132	55-55 N.	37-20 W.	GENERAL	44	28
03/11/42	PARTHENON	GREEK	SC107	U-522	53-30 N.	42-15 W.	GENERAL	29	6
03/11/42	EMPIRE LYNX	BRITISH	SC107	U-132	55-20 N.	40-01 W.	GENERAL	43	0
03/11/42	JEYPORE	BRITISH	SC107	U-89	55-30 N.	40-16 W.	GENERAL	91	1
03/11/42	HATIMURA	BRITISH	SC107	U-132	55-38 N.	39-52 W.	GENERAL	90	4
03/11/42	DAGOMBA	BRITISH	TS23	CAGNI	02-03 N.	19-00 W.	GENERAL	63	10
03/11/42	GYPSUM EMPRESS	BRITISH	TAG18	U-160	12-27 N.	64-04 W.	BAUXITE	40	0
03/11/42	CHRISTIAN J. KAMPMANN	BRITISH	TAG18	U-160	12-06 N.	62-42 W.	SUGAR	27	19
04/11/42	DEKABRIST	RUSSIAN		AIRCRAFT	75-30 N.	27-10 E.	GENERAL		
04/11/42	WILLIAM CLARK	U.S.A.	OP-FB	U-354	71-05 N.	13-20 W.	GENERAL	71	30
04/11/42	ANDREAS	GREEK		DA VINCI	02-00 S.	30-30 W.	GENERAL	47	10
04/11/42	OUED GROU	BRITISH		U-126	04-33 N.	04-49 E	BALLAST	39	5
04/11/42	DALEBY	BRITISH	SC107	U-89	57-00 N.	36-00 W.	GENERAL	47	0
05/11/42	NEW TORONTO	BRITISH		U-126	05-57 N.	02-30 E.	GENERAL	89	4
05/11/42	METON	U.S.A.	TAG18	U-129	12-21 N.	69-21 W.	FUEL OIL		
05/11/42	ASTRELL	NOR.	TAG18	U-129	12-21 N.	69-21 W.	CRUDE OIL	42	0
05/11/42	LA CORDILLERA	BRITISH		U-163	12-52 N.	58-00 W.	BALLAST	41	3
06/11/42	CHULMLEIGH	BRITISH		U-625			GENERAL	58	45
06/11/42	EMPIRE SKY	BRITISH	OP-FB	U-625	76-20 N.	17-30 E.	GENERAL	66	66
06/11/42	ARICA	BRITISH	TRIN24	U-160	10-58 N.	60-52 W.	GENERAL	67	12
06/11/42	OCEAN JUSTICE	BRITISH		U-505	10-06 N.	60-00 W.	ORE	56	0
06/11/42	CITY OF CAIRO	BRITISH		U-68	23-30 S.	05-30 W.	GENERAL	296	104
07/11/42	NATHANIEL HAWTHORN	U.S.A.	TAG19	U-508	11-34 N.	63-26 W.	BAUXITE	52	38
07/11/42	ROXBY	BRITISH	ON142	U-613	49-35 N.	30-32 W.	COAL	46	34
07/11/42	GLENLEA	BRITISH	ON142	U-566	50-00 N.	30-00 W.	COAL	48	44
07/11/42	LINDENHALL	BRITISH	TAG19	U-508	11-34 N.	63-26 W.	ORE	48	42
07/11/42	D'ENTRECASTEAUX	BRITISH		U-154	15-30 N.	57-00 W.	GENERAL	67	3
08/11/42	MALOJA	NOR.		U-128	11-25 N.	27-00 W.	COAL	41	2
08/11/42	WEST HUMHAW	U.S.A.		U-161	04-19 N.	02-44 W.	GENERAL	52	0
09/11/42	MARCUS WHITMAN	U.S.A.		DA VINCI	05-40 S.	32-40 W.	BALLAST	52	0
09/11/42	NURMAHAL	BRITISH		U-154	14-45 N.	55-45 W.	BALLAST	45	14
09/11/42	NIDARLAND	NOR.		U-67	11-41 N.	60-42 W.	ZINC	35	1
10/11/42	CERINTHUS	BRITISH	ON141	U128	12-27 N.	27-45 W.	BALLAST	39	20
10/11/42	**START POINT**	**BRITISH**	**ON141**	**U-128**	**13-12 N.**	**27-27 W.**	**COAL**	**47**	**2**
						TOTALS		**3,030**	**925**

START POINT -12 OCTOBER 1942 TO 7 JANUARY 1943

SHIP AND U-BOAT LOSSES - WHEN SERVING ON *START POINT*
12 OCTOBER 1942 TO 10 NOVEMBER 1942

GERMAN U-BOATS	SHIPS SUNK IN PERIOD				
NUMBER	TOTALS			12/10/42	01/11/42
	C/F	B/F	TOTAL	31/10/42	10/11/42
UD-5			1	1	
U-67			2	1	1
U-68			1		1
U-69			1	1	
U-84			1		1
U-89			2		2
U-126			2		2
U-128			3		3
U-129			5	3	2
U-132			3		3
U-154			2		2
U-160			6	1	5
U-161			1		1
U-163			1		1
U-172			2	1	1
U-174			3	1	2
U-203			1	1	
U-221			5	5	
U-224			1	1	
U-332			1	1	
U-354			1		1
U-402			4		4
U-409			2	2	
U-410			1	1	
U-436			3	3	
U-443			2	2	
U-505			1		1
U-508			2		2
U-509			6	6	
U-516			1	1	
U-518			2		2
U-521			2		2
U-522			3		3
U-566			1		1
U-586			1		1
U-604			3	3	
U-606			1	1	
U-607			1	1	
U-610			1	1	
U-613			1		1
U-615			1	1	
U-618			2	2	
U-621			1	1	
U-624			1	1	
U-625			2		2
U-659			1	1	
U-661			1	1	
U-706			1	1	
	1,366	1,273	93	46	47

HEAVY SHIPS	15	15	0		
RAIDERS	23	23	0		
LIGHT WARSHIPS	6	6	0		
AIRCRAFT	79	78	1		1
ITALIAN SUBMARINES	68	64	4		4
OTHER CAUSES	13	12	1	1	
	204	198	6	1	5

ENEMY U-BOAT LOSSES

DETAILS OF LOSS

	DATE	CAUSE	DEAD	SAVED
U-116	19/10/42	???	55	0
U-132	05/11/42	???	47	0
U-216	20/10/42	AIR	45	0
U-353	16/10/42	D/C	6	33
U-408	05/11/42	AIR	45	0
U-412	22/10/42	AIR	47	0
U-520	30/10/42	AIR	53	0
U-559	30/10/42	D/C	7	37
U-597	12/10/42	AIR	49	0
U-599	24/10/42	AIR	44	0
U-627	27/10/42	AIR	44	0
U-627	27/10/42	AIR	44	0
U-658	30/10/42	AIR	48	0
U-661	15/10/42	RAM	44	0

TOTALS	14	578	70
B/F	115	3,528	1,525
C/F	129	4,106	1,595

Adrift in open lifeboats –
10 to 23 November 1942

My log was kept in a notebook at first, but as I used all its pages it was continued on any scraps of paper available, including the wrappings from chocolate and malted milk tablets.

My log for the first day records:

> *Tuesday 10th November 1942. Latitude 13 – 35 north, longitude 27 – 27 west. At 1305 G.M.T., vessel struck by first torpedo. At 1335 G.M.T., second torpedo struck vessel, sinking her. Set course N.N.W. true, and burnt flares during the dark hours. Wind E.N.E. moderate, sea moderate.*

At daybreak on 11 November 1942 we hauled aboard the sea anchors. The boats then moored together end-to-end, on the two painters, and we prepared for what was likely to be a long and arduous ocean passage under sail. Firstly, it was essential that the survivors in the boats should be placed in positions in which would ensure consistent trim. The large boat carried 31 men, one severely injured. This equated to three watches of ten men, disposed in pairs of five. In the 25-foot length of the boat, it was possible to dispose the ten in each watch into two groups of five, lying fore and aft amidships. The remaining men were disposed: five forward of the mast, five abaft the mast, five forward of the stern sheets, two on each side on the stern sheet benches and one on the tiller.

Two of the men seated behind the mast were responsible for the jib sheet. Two of the men forward of the mast were detailed to man the yard halyard. Two on the stern sheet seats manned the lug sail sheet. The Third Mate always remained aft, with an able seaman Pascoe, an experienced seaman. At the end of each four-hour watch, the pairs of five men moved progressively aft, and the five at the stern went to the position forward of the bows. This ensured that duties were shared, and there were always ten men lying down off duty. Moreover, the regular movement helped to reduce cramp, particularly for those crammed in very uncomfortable positions between the mast and the bows.

The small 16-foot boat carried 13 men in very cramped positions. The men were disposed: four between the mast and bows, four lying fore and aft amidships, two on each side on the stern sheet seats and one on the tiller. I remained seated aft for a great deal of the time, but during moderate wind and sea conditions rested lying down amidships.

In order to make a fore and aft platform over the amidships thwarts, we removed the buoyancy tanks wooden cleading, and laid the members fore and aft across the thwarts in both boats. This served as a platform for those lying down, but had the even more important function of preventing unauthorised access to the emergency rations and water. We also lashed the boat hooks and oars outboard in the grab lines looped along the gunwales. This reduced the unnecessary hamper in the boats, but also helped to break the force of seas that came aboard.

As a final precaution, the men were ordered to throw all large sheath knives overboard. The two officers, bosun, carpenter and two able seamen retained strong clasp knives for culinary and emergency use. There would be no potentially offensive weapons available to those not vested with authority. Crowded lifeboats are not conducive to consistently friendly relations, particularly under the conditions that necessitated careful conservation of a meagre supply of food and water. The only way to ensure survival was by the rigid enforcement of discipline.

My 16-foot Class 1A lifeboat, carrying a dipping lug sail, soon proved to be very much faster on a wind than the 25-foot lifeboat in the charge of the Third Mate, which carried a standing lug sail and jib. We tried to reduce speed by towing a bucket, but this was impractical. This prompted my decision to connect the boats in tow, when the speed would be better than the speed of the slower.

Incredibly, there were no seamen who had any experience in handling boats under sail, including the Third Mate; so the first day was spent in instruction on the parts of the sails, and the drill orders for tacking, wearing, jibing and when running before the wind. With the painters connected end-to-end, we proceeded on our journey. The survivors who abandoned the ship in the small lifeboat included a number who had shown courage and resource, after the ship was struck by the torpedo. The bosun, Michael Patrick Casey, and able seamen William Gordon and Charles Hawden had acted without orders in releasing the life rafts. The bosun, was a great help. Although he had never trained in sailing a boat, he was an excellent seaman, and an apt pupil.

Although the dipping lug is a better sail than a standing lug, both on and before a wind, it was necessary to practise the drill of dipping the yard many times during the first day, in order to familiarise the seamen, especially the engine room and stokehold personnel. They would all have to take their turns on the halyards, tacks and sheets, as well as the tiller. This training had to be repeated with the survivors in the large boat, until a reasonable standard of proficiency was attained. Tacking and wearing with the standing lug on the large boat was easier, but the crew had the added drill of tending the jib.

It was almost certain that we would encounter strong winds and high seas, when prompt and efficient attention on the halyards and sheets would be critical. The time to train the survivors was at the earliest opportunity, and when we had the advantage of moderate weather. This proved to be a sound precaution.

The first day adrift, Wednesday 11 November 1942 was spent in consolidation, menu planning (if that could be regarded as an appropriate term), training and sail handling practice. We had our first meal in the morning, a biscuit each and three-quarters of a dipper of water. A full dipper would have been about equal to half a small whisky tumbler. I obtained a sight at noon. This was infinitely more difficult than I could have imagined. It was very difficult to hold a firm horizon at sea level, with waves constantly intervening. Standing in a boat that was moving violently, added to the discomfort and difficulty. Without a chronometer or accurate watch, it was necessary to stand for a long time waiting for the sun to reach its meridian. By the time I was able to sit, after this apparently endless torture, I was completely washed out and violently sick. There was nothing in my stomach after vomiting for most of the previous day, so I was unable to relieve myself by vomiting. My precaution of keeping a record of the declination of the sun for thirty days ahead in my notebook, proved to be invaluable.

Despite the difficulty of following the sun to its zenith, I obtained reasonably accurate latitude of 13 – 32 north, which was 3 miles north of the position I had calculated for noon on the previous day, when the ship was sunk. I had anticipated a westerly current of over 1 knot in strength, so our longitude at noon on 11 November 1942 would have been about 28 – 00 west. During the day, we steered a course of west north west, before a moderate wind and sea from the east north east on our starboard quarter. During the afternoon, we took the large boat in tow on the two painters joined end to end, in a freshening wind and rough sea. The small boat offered a freeboard of about 15 inches, waterline to gunwale, so took a great deal of water aboard. We sampled the pemmican meat and the condensed milk in our evening meal – a piece of pemmican about the size of an Oxo cube, and a teaspoon of milk – as well as two biscuits and a sip of water. This was something of a feast.

My log for the second day, records:

Wednesday 11th November 1942. *At daybreak set course W.N.W. true, wind E.N.E. gentle, sea moderate. Latitude at noon 13 – 32 north.*

Gave all hands three-quarters of a dipper of water, and one biscuit each for breakfast. Towards afternoon, wind fresher, with heavy swell. Boats lashed together, and making good way through the water. My boat taking a lot of water aboard. Third Mate's boat not such a good sailer as ours, but much drier. Had a picnic towards evening. Two biscuits, half-inch cube of pemmican, one half a dipper of water, one teaspoon of condensed milk. Spent a miserable night. Both boats taken aback during a squall.

The squall we encountered was a forerunner of the many sudden and tempestuous changes of wind direction and strength that we were to encounter. The training and practice in sail handling had been tested under severe conditions, and was successful. It was my intention to remain on approximately the same latitude for about 36 hours, just in case the naval base in Freetown had received our distress signals, and ordered an aircraft or surface search for the survivors of *Cerinthus* and *Start Point*. The hope of rescue was a very remote possibility. Ships were being sunk and seamen killed in such enormous numbers, that we were just statistics.

Course was set at south south west at daybreak, in a moderate easterly wind, sea and swell. Latitude at noon was 12 – 35 north. We had covered 57 miles in a southerly direction in 24 hours. The two boats in tow had maintained a speed of nearly 2.5 knots. Despite the fierce wind, we had not reefed our sails. We had our first encounter with the malted milk tablets. Although they were purported to be very nourishing, they exaggerated our severe thirst. They were not popular, but necessary.

We introduced the chocolate tablets into the diet during the third day adrift. They proved to be very good and not too sweet, and they did not increase our thirst. We had collected a small quantity of rain. During the night, the wind had varied in strength from moderate to fresh, and in direction all around the compass, during the frequent squalls. The sea was rough and confused, and the small boat took aboard a great deal of water. It was unbelievably uncomfortable, lying shivering in the cold water. The pump, balers and bucket kept us continuously at work. Even though we were in the temperate Horse Latitudes, it was very cold at night, sitting or lying in our soaking clothes.

My log for the third day records:

Thursday 12th November 1942. *Fine and clear. Wind easterly moderate, sea and swell moderate. Course S.S.W. true. Both boats making fair speed. Still towing Third Mate's boat. Latitude at noon 12 – 35 north. We have all got over our sea-sickness. Morning meal consisted of two* *biscuits, cube of pemmican, half a dipper of water with one teaspoon of milk, two chocolate tablets, two Horlicks tablets, which we have christened "Maltesers", and which are not popular, as they are conducive to thirst. Towards evening wind fresher with heavy rain squalls. Boat taking a lot of water. We are all soaked to the skin, and do not sleep very well.*

The fourth day was Friday the Thirteenth. The day dawned fine and clear with a moderate E.N.E. wind and rough sea. We were still in tow, and making good speed. My sight gave latitude of 11 – 52 north, a distance in a southerly direction of 43 miles. This was excellent, in view of the inconsistent wind direction and strength. I calculated roughly that we had made over 100 miles of latitude and possible 75 miles of longitude, or a distance of between 125 and 130 miles on our course. This would have placed us in about 28 – 45 west longitude. It was impossible to calculate longitude without a chronometer, and all the necessary tables; so I assumed that if we maintained a course of south south west, the drift of the ocean current would produce a true course of about south west.

Late in the afternoon, I boarded the large boat to assess the morale of the survivors. The boat had not shipped any water, and I found the men in quite good spirits. Certainly, they had always been dry, not having had to engage in the continuous hard work of pumping and baling out their boat. The small supply of antiseptic and dressings in the first aid kit had been exhausted. Despite the severity of his injury, the injured fireman, Norman Gillian, showed great fortitude. The singlet that was used to staunch the severe bleeding was stuck in the wound. We were forced to cast the boats apart, and resume the tow because of a freshening wind, and the onset of a very rough sea; but I decided to board the large boat again when the weather had moderated.

My log for the fourth day records:

Friday 13th November 1942. Fine and clear. Wind still E.N.E. moderate, sea rough. Boats making good way. Latitude at noon 11 – 52 north. Paid visit to Third Mate's boat, and found spirits to be good. Injured man in good spirits, and feeling better. We are now getting things properly organised. Food lasting well. Morning meal consisted of one biscuit, teaspoon of milk, two chocolate tablets, two Maltesers, three-quarters of a dipper of water. Towards evening heavy rain squalls and fresh wind. Boats racing along but my boat making very heavy weather of it. Towards midnight wind veered to the southward, with very heavy rain squalls. Everyone in our boat thoroughly drenched.

The fifth day dawned with a flat calm, smooth sea, but a heavy oily swell. I boarded the large boat to attend to the injured fireman. The makeshift dressing in the hole in his back had solidified with blood, grime and coal dust. It had to be removed. We heated sea water in a biscuit tin, lit a flare under the tin, and went to work with the very hot water, to soak the dressing. I carried out the operation as carefully as possible, but the pain must have been excruciating, because the dressing had penetrated so deeply into the huge wound. Eventually, after several applications of the hot sea water, the dressing softened, and could be removed. This revealed a hole about 5 inches in diameter on the back, between the floating ribs and pelvis. I probed the wound gently with my fingers, and found and removed several metal fragments. We then cauterised the wound with very hot sea water, and covered it with a makeshift dressing. During all this time the injured man hardly whimpered, despite his agony. He was 18-years old. I have no doubt that his survival was due to his young age, and his indomitable fortitude.

The calms and light airs, and almost smooth sea persisted throughout the day. I was unable to follow the sun to the meridian to obtain the latitude, due to the sun being occluded at noon. My log records that we had plenty of food. This was a relative term, when on a forecast of at least 30 days adrift. I am now certain that many men who were adrift must have perished because there might have been an optimistic estimate of the prospects of rescue, or of their making land. In cases of more relaxed discipline, it is probable that an unduly generous proportion of the available water and emergency rations might have been issued at an early stage, resulting in rapid depletion of the supply. In contrast, the discipline in our boats was draconian.

My log for the fifth day records:

Saturday 14th November 1942. *Calm, fine and clear. Smooth sea and heavy swell. Plenty of sharks and fish about. Boarded Third Mate's boat to have a look at the injured man's wound. Heated some sea water over flares and washed off the old dressing, which had stuck in the wound. Had a large piece of flesh torn out of his back, between floating ribs and pelvis. Abdominal wall had not been pierced, but was visible. The actual hole in the back was about four to five inches wide, and roughly round, and the wound was looking as healthy as could be expected; although it was beginning to smell, and probably was infected. Heated some more sea water to just under boiling point, and thoroughly cauterised the wound, and dressed it again. Increased the water ration, giving a mid-day meal. We have* *plenty of food. Towards evening had a very heavy rain squall, and collected a considerable amount of water. Wind freshened from the N.N.E., with a very heavy swell. Both boats making good speed. Cast off tow for a short while, but had to resume towing the Third Mate's boat, when the main tack parted during a heavy squall. A thoroughly miserable night with everyone soaked to the skin.*

During the afternoon, we sailed independently for a short time, but re-connected the tow for the night. The swell built up rapidly, and was accompanied by a steady fresh N.N.E. wind and rough sea. Despite the frequent drills, the large boat was taken aback in a violent squall, before the yard halyards could be released. The sail parted at the tack, and sustained a severe split. During the squalls, we lowered the sails and baled into the water breakers the rain that had collected. We also licked up the rain water that had collected on the boat. Our main concern continued to be the replenishment of the water supply. Despite collecting rain water, I did not permit any relaxation in the rigid rationing; each issue being restricted to either one half or three quarters of a dipper.

I boarded the Third Mate's boat at daybreak, in a light N.N.E. wind, slight sea and moderate swell. The mainsail was ripped, but was not very difficult to repair. The emergency kit included a palm and needle, and seaming twine. The sail was patched with a piece of the canvas lifeboat cover. The needle was rusty, and this made the work of sewing difficult. The Third Mate and I took turns on the flat seam of the large patch, and when the work was finished, our fingers were bleeding as the result of pulling the rusty needle through the canvas work. After about an hour both boats were again in tow, and making a fair speed in a freshening wind, and rough following sea on the port quarter. We carried full sail, despite the fact that seas broke over the small boat at frequent intervals.

My log for the sixth day records:

Sunday 15th November 1942. Cloudy and clear. Light N.N.E wind, slight sea and moderate swell, Latitude at noon 10 – 57 north. Went aboard other boat to effect repairs to the damaged sail, which was soon mended. Got away again at 0800 with both boats making fair speed. Becalmed during afternoon and evening. Heavy rain squall at 2300. Rode to sea anchor for a while, but got away close hauled on the starboard tack later on. Wind W.N.W. strong, sea rough. Our boat diving about a lot.

After a heavy rain squall before midnight, the wind backed rapidly to

W.N.W., increased to force 6 (strong wind), and kicked up a vicious rough sea. The small boat began to make heavy weather of it, and for a short time we lowered the sails, and rode to the sea anchors. I had taken a clear sight from the more stable platform of the Third Mate's boat, calculating latitude of 10 – 57 north at noon. We had covered 55 miles in 48 hours in an inconsistent weather pattern. The winds had varied from calms and light airs, to adverse strong westerly with violent squalls. The seas had varied from calms to very rough. Therefore, I was not dissatisfied with our progress of 158 miles of latitude in four sailing days.

The seventh day had opened with calms and light airs, fine and clear. The latitude at noon was 11 – 01 north, so we had drifted north during the day. The calms continued throughout the seventh day. We pulled the oars for short spells. It was desperately hard work in the fierce heat and in our weakened state. We were all constipated and a number of us were developing salt water boils. It was purgatory taking a sight, standing precariously on a thwart with two seamen holding me upright, as I waited for the sun to reach its meridian. After taking the sight, I was physically and mentally exhausted with the strain.

My log for the seventh day records:

> *Monday 16th November 1942. Calms and light airs during the day. Fine and clear. Latitude at noon 11 – 01 north. Rowed for a short while, and gave the hands extra water, which was collected during the night. About a dipper each extra. Cut down on food at tea time, because the calms are putting us behind in our schedule. A bit of a grumble from the hands, but that cannot be helped, and they will have to make the best of things in their own interests. Have now organised day and night watches. Working very well. Don't get much sleep myself though. When will this wind come? 870 miles to do. Will steer South True, and let the leeway and Equatorial Drift take me to the Westward. Evening meal the same as usual: two biscuits, cube of pemmican, teaspoon of milk, two Maltesers, three-quarters of a dipper of water. Calms and light airs during the night, with heavy E.N.E, swell. Third Mate's boat rowing with us in tow.*

The eighth day commenced with a light E.N.E. wind, slight sea but a very heavy swell from a north easterly direction. I had decided to have a sweep on the distance we had travelled, in an endeavour to stimulate better morale. We would issue a very small quantity of extra rations in the event of making 30 miles of southerly latitude in the day. There was no way in which the men could check on the accuracy, so I was able to adjust by adding or subtracting a few miles as appropriate. This was justifiable – but necessary – cheating.

Just after I had taken my noon sight, there would be the inevitable question "Do you think we have made 30 miles to-day, sir?" During calms, we would sometimes unship the oars, and pull the boat for a short time – just to make sure. Weather permitting; I would endeavour to take the sight from the large boat. It was a better platform, and my height of eye was marginally higher, and thus more advantageous. It was always a great effort to stand on the relatively unstable platform of a thwart, held upright by two men, and watch the sun as it reached its zenith on the meridian.

We took advantage of the moderate weather to clean up the boat, and count our stock of provisions. One problem was the supply of oil for the compass binnacle lamp and the hurricane lamp, which was clearly not adequate for an estimated period of 30 days. We had taken precautions to deal with the emergency of the tow painter parting during darkness. The large boat would immediately luff into the wind and show a hurricane lamp. The small boat would then wear around, and approach from the lee quarter of the large boat, when the rope would be thrown aboard one boat or the other, depending on where the tow rope had parted. We also took stock of the store of provisions, in order to review the level of rationing.

My log for the eighth day records:

Tuesday 17th November 1942. Light E.N.E. wind, slight sea and heavy E.N.E. swell, fine and clear. Got away again and took the other boat in tow. Latitude at noon 10 – 42 north. 835 miles to do. Took stock of food in the boat. 1200 biscuits, 44 tins of milk, 35 tins of pemmican, 1200 chocolate tablets, 3600 Maltesers, 20 gallons of water. Am working out for at least 20 more days, as we have to cross the Doldrums, and it will probably be about 30 or more if this weather holds. However it is obvious that wind is on the way following this swell. I now make a point of going aboard the other boat daily to try to keep up morale, which is not high. Take my sight from his boat, and have sweep on the day's run. If over 30 miles give the hands a small bonus of water.

One Maltese and one of the firemen a bit of a nuisance. Always grumbling. Towards afternoon wind freshening and both boats making fair speed through the water. Towards evening wind still freshening, with rough sea and heavy swell. We are towing the big boat.

There had been evidence of dissent in the Third Mate's boat. A

Maltese fireman had been drinking sea water, and his condition had deteriorated appreciably. He commenced occasional bouts of ranting and raving. The morale in the small boat was excellent, despite the fact that we had suffered appreciably greater discomfort and privation.

I obtained a good sight at noon, 10 – 42 north, giving a change in latitude of 26 miles in 24 hours. The men were told that we had just exceeded the magical number of 30 miles, and were issued with half a dipper of water each. This made them happy.

The bosun, Michael Patrick Casey, was always a great support. One irrepressible fireman, George Matthews, was always cheerful and optimistic, although over exuberant in his raucous rendition of the song "Cherry Ripe", which he seemed to sing continuously, to cries of "Put a sock in it George!" or "Turn the bloody record over!" The Third Mate, Frank Howe, had stood up to the trauma and rigours of losing a fifth ship, and the hardships of our eight days adrift, with remarkable fortitude and a consistent good humour.

Our ninth day adrift opened with a fresh to strong north east wind, rough sea and a very heavy confused swell. Although I had boarded the Third Mate's boat a number of times, it was becoming very hazardous, and I discontinued my visits. The noon sight from the small boat gave a latitude at noon of 9 – 49 north, a change of latitude of 46 miles, over 2 knots speed over the bottom. This was encouraging. The day was uneventful, except for the constantly increasing force of the wind and sea.

My log for the ninth day records:

Wednesday 18th November 1942. *Fresh N.E. Trade Winds, rough sea and heavy swell. Cloudy and clear. Boats still in tow. Have had several arguments re. going aboard the other boat in heavy weather. Have to swim across via the tow rope. Will not be able to go aboard if the present weather holds. Latitude at noon 9 – 49 north. Not too bad. Meals as usual and at the same times. Breeze constantly freshening with high seas and heavy swell. Our boat making water through the seams. Still in tow during the night. We are making a habit of dousing our heads under the water to keep cool during the day. We are getting pretty thin.*

The constant stresses of towing a heavy boat with 31 men aboard had imposed a severe strain on the stern post, and caused some of the planking strakes to open. It was serious.

The tenth day opened with a wind between forces 7 and 8, a huge breaking sea, and heavy confused swell, partly overcast, with violent squalls. The sea was a maelstrom. Under reefed canvas, we kept before the wind under indescribable conditions. Sometimes, the boats were on opposite sides of the huge waves, in the troughs of successive seas, imposing enormous stresses on the towing painters. Alternately, one boat would be in the trough of a sea, partly becalmed and commencing to mount the following sea, with the other boat at the crest of the following sea, and impelled by the full force of the wind. Then we were confronted by the sight of the heavy boat careening down the huge wave behind us, like a juggernaut. Frequently, we were forced close to each other beam to beam, or were in danger of collision. Despite this, we kept on under reefed canvas.

The tow rope parted twice in the morning, again in the afternoon, and twice during the night. The breakages always occurred close aboard either boat, either in the sternsheets of the small boat, or at the stem of the large boat. During the day, our manoeuvres of luffing the large boat and wearing the small boat around, to take position in its lee, were hazardous, but during the hours of darkness, it was a veritable nightmare. Despite the appalling conditions, I obtained a noon sight giving latitude of 8 – 41 north, a distance in 24 hours of 68 miles. This was incredible under the conditions, representing an average speed of over 3 knots.

We were suffering great privation, but making progress.

My log for the tenth day records:

Thursday 19th November 1942. Strong wind to moderate gale, very high breaking sea and heavy swell, cloudy and squally. Latitude at noon 8 – 41 north. Tow parted twice to-day, and the mast has started to crack. Have repaired same. Making a lot of water and jumping about a good deal. Still in company at noon when tow parted again. Gale continues during the day with similar conditions, and weather. Lost the other boat for a while when the tow parted again, but resumed towing when we made contact again. Tow parted twice again during the night, but was reconnected. We are getting good at this drill.

Even with reduced sail area, the strain on the mast had been enormous, and as a result the mast had started to crack, and was partially displaced from its housing on the keel. We rigged a heaving line from the stern post to the masthead, and created a Spanish windlass to tighten the makeshift backstay. It worked. The stern post was in a bad way; and we backed up the tow to the after thwart, to relieve the pressure on the ring bolt on the stern post, to which the tow rope was attached. This was also successful. It had been 24 hours of pure hell at daybreak of the eleventh day. My log for the eleventh day records a pathetic scenario:

Friday 20th November 1942. Gale continues with precipitous sea and heavy confused swell. Cloudy and squally. Tow parted again at noon. Latitude at noon 7 -42 north. Greaser Mizzi, in the other boat has gone mad. Several men drinking sea water. Wind continuing to freshen with heavy rain squalls. Miserable wet night with all hands soaked to the skin. Compass light continually going out, and we have run out of matches. Trying to steer by the stars, but some of the hands not too adept at this."

The storm had increased in strength during the eleventh day, with gale force winds, a precipitous breaking sea and heavy confused swell. Despite this, we kept on under reefed canvas. The noon position of 7 – 42 north latitude gave us a distance of 59 miles, another excellent achievement. This had been the worst day by far.

The morning of the twelfth day brought abatement in the strength of the wind, and the intensity of the seas. We were able to make way under full canvas. I was unable to obtain a sight at noon due to the sun being obscured by cloud. We collected an appreciable amount of water during frequent rain squalls. The red ochre used in tanning and preserving the sails contaminated the water, which was heavily tinged red. The condition of the small boat was now precarious; half filled with water: the stern post badly displaced: and making water through the strakes. The problems were compounded by the onset of a huge swell and sharp steep seas, a quite unusual phenomenon under conditions of reduced wind force. Clearly, the small boat would not be able to withstand much more punishment.

The Third Mate's boat then took up the tow, and we made very slow progress on a broad reach on a course of west south west. We reverted to towing the Third Mate's boat in the late afternoon. Mizzi was reported to have died during the night.

My log for the twelfth day records:

Saturday 21st November 1942. Strong E.N.E. wind, rough sea and heavy swell, cloudy and clear. Boats still in tow, and making good way through the water. Towards noon very heavy rain squalls. We collected about 13 gallons of water. Filled all tanks. Very heavy swell and rough confused sea rising. Other boat now towing us as we can carry no sail.

Making very bad weather of it. Have asked Third Mate if he will pick us up if we sink, which appears to be a certainty. Towards evening the sea is abating and the wind has gone S.E., gentle. Cannot make southerly course close hauled, so will make W.S.W. Again towing other boat towards evening. Wind and sea dropping. Mizzi reported to have died at around 2000.

The thirteenth day dawned with a light south east wind, slight sea, but a continuing heavy swell. The Third Engineer had preserved a naval prayer book. I boarded the Third Mate's boat to confirm whether Antonio Mizzi had died. He was lying in the bottom of the boat under one of the after thwarts, stiffened into a partially curled position by rigor mortis. We straightened his body and lashed him in a blanket. I read the burial service, and he was lowered over the side. Several sharks that had been keeping us company started to attack the corpse, so I ordered the oars to be unshipped, and we pulled away from the scene.

I obtained a sight at noon, 6 – 58 north. We had covered 46 miles of latitude in 48 hours of sailing, for an appreciable time on a W.N.W. course, so most of our progress was made during final day of the severe gale. It says a lot for the worthy boat builders of Devon that two of their Class 1A clinker built lifeboats had withstood nearly two weeks of tremendous buffeting in such tempestuous weather and enormous seas.

It was a sweltering hot day with a clear sky and burning sun. We could not make way in the calms and light airs, so we lowered the sails, created a canopy across some oars, and all hands in both boats had the morning and noon meals under the shade, with the benefit of the extra water ration from the amount collected the previous day. On occasions during our passage, the ever-hopeful Third Engineer had reported seeing ships and even aircraft; he was usually greeted with a reaction of "For Christ's sake, Third, not you again!" or something similar. At 1600, he raised the canopy, and shouted, "I can see a ship," receiving a response similar to those he had received on previous false alarms. When he continued to shout, several men lifted the canopy and looked in the direction in which he was pointing. Then the shout went up, "He's right. There is ship!"

The sighting proved to be a faint column of smoke bearing north east. I had a conference with the Third Mate and Chief Radio Officer, to make an estimate of our relative positions, and decide upon a course of action. If the ship was on a northerly course, there was no likelihood of our being seen or rescued. The position of our boats would have been well abaft the port beam of the ship. However, if the ship were steering a southerly course, we would have been in a position about four points on the starboard bow.

We did not have long to wait, because the ship appeared to be increasing in size; so I assumed that she was on a course of about south south west, making for the area between Cape Branco and St. Paul Rocks. I decided that we would steer a converging course of south south east, so that we could keep west and south of her, fine on her starboard bow. The early light south east wind had backed to the north east, so we were assisted by enough wind strength to sail on a broad port reach.

We unshipped the oars, and all hands were issued with chocolate and Horlicks tablets, condensed milk and water, to increase stamina. Then, with 43 men manning the oars of the two boats, in relays in short spells, we sailed, and pulled in the planned direction with all the strength that we could muster. We had enough life in the batteries to transmit a series of distress messages.

After a short time we could see the outline of the masts, funnel, and then the deck house of a ship, clearly on a southerly course. We were then about three points on her starboard bow, so we altered course to port, to close her more quickly. It was then about 1645, and the altitude of the sun was diminishing quickly. I remarked to the Third Mate that we should try to place ourselves between the ship and the setting sun, at the time when the officer of the watch should have been taking the usual amplitude of the sun from the upper navigating bridge. I expressed to Frank Howe my hope that the Third Mate would be on "Monkey Island" (the upper navigating bridge), and would see us from the higher vantage position. Traditionally on British ships, the Third Mate would relieve the First Mate for his evening meal during the first dog watch, at about 1700. The usual custom was for the Third Mate to take the amplitude of the sun at sunset. So I decided that just before sunset we would keep our boats about 100 yards apart, light a number of orange distress flares, and use the last of the battery life to transmit distress signals. The "Sparks" was given a position of 6 – 50 north, 31 – 30 west.

At about 1740, the form of the ship foreshortened. For a dreadful few minutes, we were uncertain whether she was turning towards or away from us. We soon realised that she had altered course almost due west, and was heading for us, at a distance of several miles. We altered course to steer towards her. When she was about a half a mile away, the ship altered course to starboard to make a lee for our boats, and reduced speed. We could see the men setting two boat ropes along the port side, secured to the bulwarks and rails in a series of loops. Several scrambling nets were released along the port side. A voice hailed us from the bridge, "I will not stop my ship. You have one chance to pick up our boat ropes." We made no mistake. My boat picked up the forward boat rope and made fast. The Third Mate's boat struck the ship head on with the momentum of her headway, and secured to the after boat rope. The ship towed both boats along at about slow speed.

The voice hailed us again. "Get your men aboard as quickly as you can, pull the plugs and cast off your boats." The Third Mate shouted, "We have a badly injured man aboard." A heaving line was lowered, and the injured fireman was hoisted aboard, followed by the rest of the survivors. The Third Mate and I unscrewed the plugs in the boats, cast off, and climbed aboard. My precious sextant was slung around my neck, and a record of our passage adrift was safe in its waterproof bag in my breast pocket. We had made it!

My log for the thirteenth day records:

> **Sunday 22nd November 1942.** *Light S.E. wind, slight sea and heavy swell, cloudy and clear. Latitude at noon 6 – 58 north. Went aboard the other boat at 0600 to perform last rites for Mizzi. Rigor Mortis had set in and his face was a mottled purple in colour. Read Burial Service and committed body to the sea. Commenced rowing. Meals as usual. At 1600 smoke sighted by the Third Engineer to the N.E., which proved to be a ship on an apparent southerly course. Commenced rowing to cross her bows and get between her and the setting sun. Two boats rowing independently and burning smoke flares alternately.*
>
> *Sending out wireless messages giving position of 6 – 50 north latitude, 31 – 30 assumed longitude west. At 1730 vessel turned towards us. At 1800 boarded "Eskdalegate" in darkness. Found that my latitude was correct to the mile, but longitude was 30 miles out to the westward.*

When we boarded *Eskdalegate* our sense of balance had been dramatically affected by nearly two weeks in the environment of violently pitching and rolling small boats. We reeled around the decks like drunken men. The Third Mate and I staggered to the navigating bridge to report to the Master, Captain Butterworth, an officer in his mid thirties. His first question was to ask us how long we had been adrift. He was surprised and somewhat relieved to learn that we had been adrift for 13 days. When they had sighted two lifeboats in close company, they had assumed that our ship had been sunk very recently, with the likelihood that the enemy warship would still be in the vicinity. They had found

S.S. Eskdale, built in 1930, 4250 gross registered tonnage
Rescued survivors from *S.S. Start Point*, 23 November 1942
(*Photograph by A. Duncan, Cowes, I..O.W.*)

accommodation for me in the spare cabin. Our officers were given berths in the cabins of their opposite numbers. I descended to the lower bridge, and leant on the after rails.

The deck hands of *Eskdalegate* were working on No. 3 hatch, spreading a tarpaulin over the derricks to make a tent to accommodate our deck and stokehold crew and the gunners. Through the stygian darkness, I heard orders being shouted, "Pull the puckin' tarpaulin across the puckin' derricks!" There could be no mistaking the voice of one, Hamat Bin Samat, the Malay serang who had been my tutor and mentor over four years before when I was an apprentice on *Appledore*. I called through the darkness, "Is that you, Hamat Bin Samat?" He climbed the companion ladder to the lower bridge, and the first feature that I could identify was his gleaming teeth shining in his pockmarked face. He greeted me with "Is it the crazy Canadian 'prentice?" It was a great joy to meet the wonderful character and superb seaman again.

The Steward arrived on the lower bridge to tell me that they had a spare cabin ready for me. I flopped on the bunk in the spare cabin, and fell into a sleep verging on suspended animation. I woke about 20 hours later, to find Captain Butterworth standing by the bunk, with the greeting "You will probably like to have a drink with the young man who sighted your lifeboats." The young Third Mate (who proved to be older than me) was standing by his side. Captain Butterworth held two large tumblers of whisky in his hand, and the Third Mate held one. I was given one digestive biscuit, and had a stiff peg of whisky with the Master and his Third Mate. Frank Howe and I had been right in our hopes that the Third Mate would be on "monkey island" to take the sunset amplitude of the sun.

When he brought the sun down with the azimuth mirror on to the face of the compass, to obtain the amplitude reading, he observed several columns of smoke showing against the image of the sun. The telescope showed up our lifeboats. The Master made the decision to rescue us after discussion with his officers.

The following day I was given clean underclothes and a shirt. My ragged khaki shorts had been washed clean of salt; but I continued to wear my patrol jacket, with its brass buttons and epaulettes, now green with verdigris. I washed from head to foot in the traditional style from a bucket of hot water on a platform across the bath. After standing for a short time, my legs and feet had swollen to almost twice their normal circumference, and it was impossible to wear shoes for several days.

Very foolishly, many of the ravenous men accommodated under the tarpaulins spread over the No. 3 derricks made gluttons of themselves on the food provided by the crew of *Eskdalegate*. After two weeks almost without food and water, they suffered as the result of their gluttony, and most of them vomited up the contents of their stomachs almost immediately. It was a pathetic display of lack of discipline. The gunners were the worst culprits.

I had soon recovered sufficiently to stand a watch on *Eskdalegate* with the Third Mate, and joined with the other officers in taking the sights in the morning and at noon. My precious Hughes "Three Circle" sextant was encrusted with salt. The cover of its wooden box had been broken by the violence of the explosion when *Start Point* was torpedoed, but the instrument was undamaged. However, there were deposits of verdigris on the metal parts and the whole instrument had to be cleaned thoroughly with a soft brush and colza oil. I also corrected for index error and parallax, and cleaned all the mirrors and shades.

The distance to Pernambuco (now named Recife) in Brazil, was about

900 miles. We arrived in the early morning of Friday 27 November 1942, and disembarked.

The injured fireman had been accommodated in the spare room used as a hospital. When I saw him, he had been thoroughly washed and was looking quite well and refreshed. After removing the makeshift dressing, Captain Butterworth had probed the wound with forceps and had removed jagged fragments of metal. The ship was well equipped with medical supplies, so the wound was dressed with antiseptics. The wound had become infected, and it was necessary to insert drainage gauze as part of the treatment. After my experience with my superiors on *Start Point*, it was refreshing beyond measure to be aboard an efficient ship under the command of such an exceptionally fine Master.

During the time when *Eskdalegate* was on passage to Pernambuco, I was able to reflect on the events during the time when we had been adrift. It had been proved to me that pessimism among survivors, in such cases of severe adversity, can spread like an epidemic, if not arrested by the imposition of rigid discipline. The seven gunners had demonstrated their lack of discipline before and after the enemy attack. Several survivors in the Third Mate's boat had been argumentative and trouble-some from the outset. Those individuals had been a liability, and could not be relied upon. The problems that they caused were overcome by the courage and fortitude of the men who displayed extraordinary ability and dedication.

The only time when we caught a seaman stealing water was halfway through our period in the lifeboats. The man had pulled the electric wire out of the rubber insulation of the flexible cable connecting the lifejacket light to its battery. He was then able to make a rubber tube with a tiny inside diameter. When lying down on the thwarts, he pushed his hand through the cleading boards, removed the plug from the water breaker, and sucked the water through this tube. The Third Mate discovered his action, and reported to me. When I boarded the Third Mate's boat, a trial was convened, and the culprit was found guilty of stealing water from his shipmates. When he admitted his guilt, the bosun was so overcome with fury that he struck him with blows from the tiller. The outcome was that he was told that if he repeated the heinous crime, he would be thrown overboard. This threat proved to be effective. I cannot say whether I would have given the order to kill a fellow survivor, but it would have been likely that the others would have had no hesitation in doing so.

After we had been rescued, the senior army and navy gunners

approached me with a request that I should not report their conduct to the D.E.M.S. authority, because "we had all suffered enough during our ordeal". They were unsuccessful, because such unreliable and insubordinate behaviour and actions could not be tolerated or excused. I do not know the extent of their punishment, if any. They were taken away.

We bade farewell to our friends on *Eskdalegate*, and were all accommodated in a run down hotel in Pernambuco. I was instructed to report to the offices of the British Consul. Here all the British members of the staff, from junior clerk to the most senior official, treated me with unbelievable discourtesy – almost to the point of contempt. The only one who showed any vestige of kindness was the Brazilian Pro Consul, who was an affable little man. I was asked to provide a list of survivors. They allowed me the use of a typewriter, and asked me to type the list for them, because I was not allowed the services of a stenographer.

When I was sitting at the typewriter, typing the list laboriously with two fingers, the Captain of a British "C" class anti aircraft cruiser in the port entered the offices. He saw me sitting at the desk using the typewriter, observed my epaulettes of rank, and asked me to identify myself. When he learned that I was the senior surviving officer of a merchant ship that had been sunk by the enemy, all hell broke loose. He berated the consul and his staff, and demanded that I leave the consulate with him to visit a clothing shop to be kitted out. We must have appeared to be an incongruous couple, as we walked along the streets of Pernambuco. A Royal Navy captain in immaculate white uniform, accompanied by an emaciated creature clad in a pair of ragged khaki shorts and bedraggled uniform patrol jacket; legs swollen like pumpkins, and the skin of the face and legs burnt raw by the blazing sun, and hanging in peeling strips. I must have been a sorry sight.

We entered a clothing shop, where I was fitted with a grey suit, and provided with clothing and footgear. We then visited a restaurant and bar, where we had a light meal and drinks. My stomach had not recovered sufficiently, and could cope only with very small meals. The captain then asked me to give him an account of events, to which he listened with interest. He expressed astonishment when he learned that we had kept two lifeboats in tow for over twelve days in such severe weather conditions, and congratulated me. When we parted, he remarked that we had acquitted ourselves well. Such an opinion from another professional officer was very gratifying.

I encountered another naval officer of a different type, during our stay in Pernambuco. Whether he was on the staff of the consulate, or from the Naval Control Office, is obscure. He was a lieutenant R.N.V.R., who interrogated me about the disposal of the confidential documents on *Start Point*. He asked if they had been thrown overboard, whether they had been placed in the weighted box, and if I had seen them sink. Finally, he demanded an assurance from me, as to whether the U-Boat may have been able to recover them from the bottom of the sea. Clearly, he did not know his arse from a hole in the ground, so I told him that the sea was several miles deep in the position where the ship sank in the Cape Verde Trench. This seemed to satisfy him.

I used one of the typewriters to copy my log into typescript, and the dog-eared copy that I typed 60 years ago has been photocopied and reproduced in this narrative. The consulate staff also assured me that a telegram had been sent to London, giving the authorities the list of survivors. Accordingly, none of the survivors sent to their next of kin the usual telegrams, reassuring them of their safe arrival at port of destination. My usual telegram would reflect just four words "Safe. Well. Love. Vernon."

Events proved that no telegram appears to have been received in London. Our relatives, including Betty, knew from experience that the time for the usual Atlantic passage was between 15 and 20 days. Frank Howe and I joined *Start Point* on 10 October 1942, and made monthly pay allotments. When Betty visited the offices to collect her allotment on or after 10 November, she was given the brusque response "Sorry, no money." Despite repeated requests, in an effort to ascertain whether the ship had been reported sunk or missing; Betty was faced with indifference and lack of co-operation. She was greeted with, "Anything can happen these days, Madam".

Here was a case of a 20-year old wife, without money, or any knowledge of what had happened to her husband or his ship; and no individual in any level of authority cared a bloody toss. Of course, the pay of a seaman ceased on the day when his ship was sunk. We knew all about that; but we never knew what had happened to the telegram that was alleged to have been sent, whether our distress message had been recorded, and what had gone awry in the system for communication with next of kin.

The attitudes shown at all levels of authority were examples of the low priority afforded to the Merchant Navy and its seamen. We had reason to be satisfied with our achievements. This was some consolation after the indifferent attitudes that we had always encountered. Our lifeboats had achieved something of a record in keeping in company in tow, sometimes under almost impossible conditions.

When *Start Point* was sunk off the Cape Verde Islands, our position was over 1,200 miles from the nearest point in Brazil. We had covered over 500 miles in under 10 days of hard sailing (having encountered 3 days of calms and baffling winds) in two heavily laden lifeboats, suffering the loss of only one man. When rescued, we were just about 750 miles from our intended destination. It is doubtful whether all the men in both boats would have survived. With the exception of a small number of sub-standard individuals, the men had behaved with great discipline. Some were exceptional.

During the period of time between the loss of *Start Point*, and the date when the survivors departed from Pernambuco, 21 ships were sunk when in convoy and 29 ships were sunk when on independent passage or detached from convoys. The convoys destined to and from the North African Mediterranean landing points suffered modest losses, 7 ships in 4 convoys. Outward bound Atlantic convoys lost 9 ships in 3 convoys, the most serious losses occurring in convoy ON144, which lost 5 ships. The homeward bound Halifax and Sidney Cape Breton convoys SC109, SC110, and HX217 lost 4 ships.

Disastrous loss of life occurred when the American ship *Coamo* was sunk by U-604 with the loss of all 186 on board. *Coamo* was a U.S. Army Transport, and was reported sunk 150 miles off Ireland on 2 December 1942. The only record I can find of the loss of this ship is in "The World's Merchant Fleets 1939", which records that the ship was on independent passage. I believe that there must be grave doubts about the circumstances of the loss of the ship and the actions of U-604. There must be similar doubts about the loss of the troopship *Ceramic*, sunk by U-515 west of the Azores when on independent passage. One account records only one survivor from her complement of 657, a soldier taken prisoner by the U-Boat and landed at Lorient. It is nothing short of incredible that the U-Boat surfaced to rescue and take prisoner only one man. This appears to be one more atrocity, covered up in enemy records.

The U-Boats had covered the area off West Africa, the Gulf of Guinea, the South Atlantic near the Brazilian coast and the West Indies. However, no ships were lost in the Caribbean Sea or the Gulf of Mexico. This indicated either that our countermeasures had improved dramatically, or that the U-Boat high command had changed to what they may have deemed more fruitful operational areas. Incredibly, there appears to have been no enemy activity in the approaches to the United Kingdom.

Although I am not certain of the exact date, I have marked 9 December 1942 as the date of our departure from Pernambuco. Before the date of our departure, I visited the severely injured fireman, Norman Gillian in hospital. He was undergoing a series of skin grafting surgical operations, to close the large hole in his back. By a remarkable coincidence, Betty and I encountered a couple in Queen Street in Cardiff quite some time later. They proved to be Norman Gillian and a lady friend, perhaps his fiancé or wife. He introduced me to the lady as "the man who saved my life". He saved his own life by his courage and indomitable spirit.

In the morning, we received instructions to board a train, without being informed of its destination. An unbelievably decrepit old engine, burning wood, pulled the train. The carriages were open at the sides, and we sat on hard wooden seats. We travelled during the day through what appeared to be a tropical jungle, in oppressive heat and discomfort, and arrived at our destination in the evening. We were exhausted, very hungry and covered from head to foot in thick layers of the dust thrown up by the funnel of the engine. We were transported by trucks to an American army air force landing strip in a jungle clearing, were given some food, and were accommodated in thatched huts set on wooden stilts. The site was near a town, because a Brazilian official, who I assumed might have been a pro consul, made contact with us.

The only way I have been able to identify our destination is by calculating the time of our journey and equating it to distance. The only two Brazilian towns in that large area are Natal and Fortaleza. Natal is about 150 miles from Pernambuco, and Fortaleza is about 450 miles distant. The train was travelling slowly, and stopping frequently, so it seems certain that we were near Natal. The wooden stilts on which our huts were built were wrapped in barbed wire, as protection for the occupants from venomous snakes.

We spent a hot and uncomfortable night in the huts; and were awakened at daybreak with instructions to board two Dakota aircraft that were waiting on the runway. We were given a meal of iron rations; and boarded the aircraft, seventeen men in one and eighteen in the other. We felt substantial apprehension, because it was for all of us our first flight. Our apprehensions were increased when we learned that the only parachutes aboard were the three provided for the three members of the aircraft crew.

Casualties – Ships and Personnel
11 November 1942 to 9 December 1942

Ships sunk – 50 by 38 successful U-Boats.
One ship sunk by an Italian submarine.

Lost with all hands

Widestone, cargo coal, 42 dead.
Ocean Crusader, general cargo, 45 dead.
Tjileboet, cargo unknown, 47 dead.
Coamo, cargo unknown, 186 dead.
Empire Dabchick, in ballast, 47 dead.
Berooskerk, cargo unknown, 73 dead.
Peter Maersk, general cargo, 67 dead.
James MacKay, general cargo, 62 dead.

Lost with very heavy casualties

City of Ripon, in ballast, 56 dead out of 78.
Warwick Castle, general cargo and passengers, 62 dead out of 263.
Scapa Flow, cargo iron ore, 33 dead out of 60.
President Sergent, in ballast, 20 dead out of 59.
Parisimina, in ballast, 22 dead out of 63.
Empire Sailor, general cargo, 22 dead out of 58.
Caddo, cargo fuel oil, 54 dead out of 60.
Benlomond, in ballast, 52 dead out of 53.
Barberrys, general cargo, 32 dead out of 53.
Clan MacFadyen, cargo sugar, 72 dead out of 92.
Empire Cromwell, cargo iron ore, 24 dead out of 49.
Besholt, general cargo, 14 dead out of 42.
Solon II, cargo iron ore, 75 dead out of 82.
Henry Stanley, general cargo, 63 dead out of 64.
Ceramic, troopship, 672 dead out of 673.
Charles L.D., general cargo, 36 dead out of 48.

Merchant seamen, passengers and troops killed – 1,961 out of 4,618,
a fatal casualty rate of 43 percent.

It is significant that the individual success rates of U-Boats had diminished dramatically, only 7 out of 38 U-Boats having sunk more than one ship. The more successful U-Boats were U-508 (six ships) and U-624 (four ships).

UPON THEIR LAWFUL OCCASIONS

START POINT - 12 OCTOBER 1942 TO 7 JANUARY 1943

RECORD OF MERCHANT SHIPS SUNK IN ATLANTIC - 11/11/42 TO 09/12/42

START POINT - SUNK ON 10/11/42 BY U-128 - 13-13 N. 27-27 W.

SURVIVORS FROM *START POINT* IN OPEN LIFEBOATS - 10/11/42 TO 22/11/42

DATE	SHIP	NAT.	CONVOY NO.	CAUSE OF LOSS	POSITION		CARGO	CASUALTIES CREW	DEAD
11/11/42	CITY OF RIPON	BRITISH		U-160	08-40 N.	59-20 W.	BALLAST	78	56
11/11/42	VEERHAVEN	DUTCH		DA VINCI	03-51 S.	29-22 W.	BALLAST	45	0
11/11/42	VICEROY OF INDIA	BRITISH	KMF1	U-406	36-26 N.	00-25 W.	PASS.	454	4
12/11/42	BROWNING	BRITISH	KMS2	U-593	35-52 N.	00-45 E.	GENERAL	62	1
12/11/42	BUCHANAN	PAN.		U-224	52-06 N.	25-54 W.	GENERAL	90	0
13/11/42	MARON	BRITISH		U-81	36-27 N.	00-55 W.	BALLAST	71	0
14/11/42	WARWICK CASTLE	BRITISH	MKF1	U-413	38-44 N.	13-00 W.	PASS.	263	62
14/11/42	SCAPA FLOW	PAN.		U-134	12-00 N.	30-00 W.	ORE	60	33
15/11/42	ETTRICK	BRITISH	MKF1	U-155	30-13 N.	07-54 W.	BALLAST	250	24
15/11/42	KING ARTHUR	BRITISH		U-67	10-30 N.	59-50 W.	COTTON	40	0
16/11/42	CLAN MacTAGGART	BRITISH	MKS1X	U-92	35-58 N.	07-29 W.	BALLAST	172	3
17/11/42	CITY OF CORINTH	BRITISH		U-68	10-55 N.	59-30 W.	GENERAL	87	11
17/11/42	MOUNT TAURUS	GREEK	ON144	U-264	54-30 N.	37-30 W.	BALLAST	40	2
17/11/42	WIDESTONE	BRITISH	ON144	U-184	54-30 N.	37-10 W.	COAL	42	42
18/11/42	PRESIDENT SERGENT	BRITISH	ON144	U-624	54-07 N.	38-26 W.	BALLAST	59	20
18/11/42	YAKA	U.S.A.	ON144	U-624	54-07 N.	38-26 W.	BALLAST	52	0
18/11/42	PARISIMINA	U.S.A.	ON144	U-624	54-07 N.	38-26 W.	BALLAST	63	22
18/11/42	TOWER GRANGE	BRITISH		U-154	06-20 N.	49-10 W.	GENERAL	47	6
18/11/42	BRILLIANT	U.S.A.	SC109	U-43	50-45 N.	45-53 W.	GAS OIL	60	0
18/11/42	TORTUGAS	NOR.		U-67	13-24 N.	55-00 W.	GENERAL	38	0
20/11/42	GRANGEPARK	BRITISH	KMS3G	U-263	35-55 N.	10-14 W.	GENERAL	69	3
20/11/42	PRINS HARALD	NOR.	KMS3G	U-263	35-55 N.	10-14 W.	GENERAL	56	3
21/11/42	EMPIRE SAILOR	BRITISH	ON145	U-518	43-53 N.	55-02 W.	GENERAL	58	22
21/11/42	EMPIRE STARLING	BRITISH		U-163	13-05 N.	56-20 W.	MEAT	55	0
22/11/42	APALOIDE	BRAZ.		U-163	13-28 N.	54-42 W.	COFFEE	56	5

SURVIVORS FROM *START POINT* RESCUED BY ESKDALEGATE - 22/11/42 TO 27/11/42

23/11/42	CADDO	U.S.A.		U-518	42-25 N.	48-27 W.	FUEL OIL	60	54
23/11/42	BENLOMOND	BRITISH		U-172	00-30 N.	38-45 W.	BALLAST	53	52
26/11/42	OCEAN CRUSADER	BRITISH	HX216	U-262	50-30 N.	45-30 W.	GENERAL	45	45
26/11/42	INDRA	NOR.		UD3	02-10 N.	28-52 W.	ORE	39	0
26/11/42	BARBERRYS	BRITISH	SC110	U-663	50-36 N.	47-10 W.	GENERAL	53	32
26/11/42	CLAN MacFADYEN	BRITISH		U-508	08-57 N.	59-48 W.	SUGAR	92	72
27/11/42	POLYDORUS	DUTCH		U-176	09-01 N.	25-32 W.	GENERAL	80	2

SURVIVORS FROM *START POINT* IN PERNAMBUCO - 27/11/42 TO 09/12/42

28/11/42	EMPIRE CROMWELL	BRITISH		U-508	09-00 N.	58-30 W.	ORE	49	24
28/11/42	ALASKAN	U.S.A.		U-172	02-38 N.	28-58 W.	ORE	46	5
28/11/42	TJILEBOET	DUTCH		U-161	05-34 N.	25-02 W.		47	47
30/11/42	TREVALGAN	BRITISH		U-508	09-40 N.	59-15 W.	BALLAST	43	0
02/12/42	CITY OF BATH	BRITISH		U-508	09-29 N.	59-30 W.	ORE	80	3
02/12/42	COAMO	U.S.A.		U-604				186	186
02/12/42	BESHOLT	NOR.		U-174	03-20 N.	30-20 W.	GENERAL	42	14
02/12/42	WALLSEND	BRITISH		U-552	20-08 N.	25-50 W.	GENERAL	41	4
02/12/42	SOLON II	BRITISH		U-508	07-45 N.	56-30 W.	ORE	82	75
03/12/42	EMPIRE DABCHICK	BRITISH	ON146	U-183	43-00 N.	58-17 W.	BALLAST	47	47
05/12/42	TEESBANK	BRITISH		U-128	03-33 N.	29-35 W.	BALLAST	62	1
06/12/42	SEROOSKERK	DUTCH	ON149	U-155	37-00 N.	35-00 W.		73	73
06/12/42	HENRY STANLEY	U.S.A.		U-103	40-35 N.	39-40 W.	GENERAL	64	63
06/12/42	CERAMIC	BRITISH	ON149	U-515	40-30 N.	40-20 W.	TROOPS	673	672
07/12/42	PETER MAERSK	BRITISH		U-158	39-47 N.	41-00 W.	GENERAL	67	67
08/12/42	NIGERIAN	BRITISH		U-508	09-17 N.	59-00 W.	GENERAL	60	5
08/12/42	JAMES McKAY	U.S.A.		U-600	57-50 N.	23-10 W.	GENERAL	62	62
08/12/42	EMPIRE SPENSER	BRITISH	HX217	U-524	57-04 N.	36-01 W.	GASOLENE	57	1
09/12/42	CHARLES L.D.	BRITISH	HX217	U-553	59-02 N.	30-45 W.	GENERAL	48	36
						TOTALS		**4,618**	**1,961**

START POINT - 12 OCTOBER 1942 TO 7 JANUARY 1943

SHIP AND U-BOAT LOSSES - AFTER LOSS OF *START POINT*
11 NOVEMBER 1942 TO 09 DECEMBER 1942

GERMAN U-BOATS	SHIPS SUNK IN PERIOD				ENEMY U-BOAT LOSSES				
NUMBER	TOTALS		TOTAL	11/11/42 09/12/42		DETAILS OF LOSS			
	C/F	B/F				DATE	CAUSE	DEAD	SAVED
UD-3			1	1	U-98	15/11/42	D/C	46	0
U-43			1	1	U-173	16/11/42	D/C	57	0
U-67			2	2	U-184	20/11/42	D/C	50	0
U-68			1	1	U-254	08/12/42	COLL	41	4
U-81			1	1	U-259	15/11/42	AIR	48	0
U-92			1	1	U-272	12/11/42	COLL	28	16
U-103			1	1	U-331	17/11/42	AIR	32	17
U-128			1	1	U-411	13/11/42	AIR	46	0
U-134			1	1	U-517	21/11/42	AIR	1	51
U-154			1	1	U-595	14/11/42	AIR	0	44
U-155			1	1	U-605	14/11/42	AIR	46	0
U-158			2	1	U-611	08/12/42	AIR	45	0
U-160			2	1	U-660	12/11/42	D/C	0	45
U-161			1	1					
U-163			1	2					
U-172			1	2					
U-174			1	1					
U-176			1	1					
U-183			1	1					
U-184			2	1					
U-224			1	1					
U-262			1	1					
U-263			1	2					
U-264			6	1					
U-406			1	1					
U-413			2	1					
U-508			1	6					
U-515			1	1					
U-517			2	2					
U-524			1	1					
U-552			1	1					
U-553			1	1					
U-593			1	1					
U-600			1	1					
U-604			4	1					
U-624			1	4					
U-663			0	1					

	C/F	B/F							
	1,416	1,366	50	50	TOTALS	13	440	177	
					B/F	129	4,106	1,595	
HEAVY SHIPS	15	15	0		C/F	142	4,546	1,772	
RAIDERS	23	23	0						
LIGHT WARSHIPS	6	6	0						
AIRCRAFT	79	79	0						
ITALIAN SUBMARINES	69	68	1	1					
OTHER CAUSES	13	13	0						
	205	204	1	1					

We flew for almost all day at 10,000 feet in freezing cold, sitting on aluminium benches facing each other; and landed in the late afternoon near Belem, in one of the Amazon deltas. The airstrip was in a jungle clearing near the town, with similar thatched huts as accommodation. Again, we were given a meal of iron rations. The night was even more uncomfortable than the previous night, with an almost unbearably hot atmosphere, and high humidity. We were awakened at daybreak, but no meal was provided. Then I was faced with a crew who steadfastly refused to move until food was provided. They sat under the wings of the aircraft and would not budge.

It was necessary to summon a Brazilian official, who bought some bananas, wine and locally baked bread, which we ate when sitting under the wings of the aircraft. We took off, and after another cold and uncomfortable flight, arrived late in the afternoon near Georgetown in British Guiana. Here the accommodation was in relatively comfortable huts, with basic washing and toilet facilities.

The following day we were again airborne early in the morning, and In the afternoon we arrived at the large American base in Puerto Rico, where we were accommodated in the barracks. Here again there were problems with a number of recalcitrant members of the crew. Our officers were berthed in the barracks of the American officers, and the crew were accommodated in the barracks for other ranks. The complaint that was made was that there should have been no differentiation between officers and other ranks.

The crew argued that we had all suffered similar privations, and should have been afforded identical privileges. An American colonel was called upon to intercede. I explained to him that there was no difference in the protocol covering accommodation for officers and other ranks in our mercantile marine, and the protocol that existed in the U.S. army. He agreed, and the potential mutiny was over. The only fundamental difference in the accommodation was the nameplates on the access doors,"Officers", "N.C.O.'s" and "Other Ranks". It was the fact that there was any form of discrimination , which provoked the militant elements in our crew. The protests were overruled, and they were accommodated in the "other ranks" accommodation.

The next morning we took off again, and arrived at Miami in the afternoon. The Duke of Windsor was then Governor of the Bahamas Islands, and was on a visit to Miami. When he learned that the survivors from a British ship had arrived, he arranged a meal and party, to which we were invited. We were given huge jugs, to drink the American beer, which was served in enamel buckets in enormous quantities. The actress and singer Dinah Shore provided the entertainment. A number of our crew distinguished themselves by getting thoroughly drunk. It was a most convivial evening.

The following day we boarded a train for the journey to New York, where we arrived in the afternoon of 16 December 1942, after seven days of arduous travelling from Brazil. All the officers were accommodated in the Woodstock Hotel, and other ranks elsewhere. It had been snowing, and the weather was very cold. Having arrived from a semi-tropical climate, we all felt the rapid change in the temperature very severely. Moreover, the clothing that had been issued to us was unsuitable for the freezing New York weather.

I sent Betty my usual telegram from the hotel immediately after arrival. She had not received any information about my whereabouts from the authorities, so, after two months without communication, she must have assumed the worst. By the most optimistic of estimates, we were five weeks overdue. On reflection, I should not have relied on the staff of the British Consulate to send notification of our safe arrival. To them we were just like so much dog shit. I should have made sure that Betty knew that I was safe.

After the luxury of an evening meal, a bath, and a night between sheets, I visited the hotel barber shop, to have my first haircut in over two months. When he was cutting my hair, the barber tactfully asked me if I had seen my scalp in the mirror. I had washed my hair several times since the date of our rescue, but had not examined my scalp. He parted my hair and held a mirror over my scalp, to reveal a mess. The blood that had poured over me from the wound of the injured fireman had congealed all over my scalp, together with coal dust and grime, and was caked in a black mass. No amount of washing could have removed the deposits. The barber worked on this for about an hour. Firstly, he massaged olive oil well into the scalp. Following this, he placed an electric heater over my head, and after about a half an hour the heat had softened the deposits. Then he scraped the scalp with a special steel comb, removing the caked black deposits. I was horrified when I saw the result. For an individual of fastidious habits, this was very embarrassing. However, the barber was not only tactful and kind, but also understanding, particularly when he learned about our ordeal.

A great many survivors from British ships were accommodated in New York. Many of the officers were accommodated in the Woodstock

Hotel in Manhattan. We were paid a daily subsistence allowance. Reserve Pools for officers and men had been established. There was a fine and well-furnished Officers' Club. There was a problem in finding working berths on ships, or passenger accommodation for repatriation, due to the numbers of survivors and shortage of vacancies. The only real measure of priority had to be on a chronological order basis. When we arrived, I would have been near the bottom of the list.

The first necessity was for suitable clothes for the freezing climate of New York. It was arranged for us to visit the local clothes emporia to be kitted out, in my case the department store of Abraham & Strauss. Here, I was furnished with a heavier suit of clothes, a fine warm overcoat, shoes, and other apparel.

The American people were, as ever, warm hearted and generous. Local individuals and organisations maintained liaison with our clubs, with offers of accommodation and entertainment. These were posted on the notice boards. On one occasion, I was delighted to accept the invitation of a wealthy family to join them in their box at the Metropolitan Opera House for "Manon", conducted by Sir Thomas Beecham.

Frank Howe and I were invited to the home of Jim Green and his family at West Hempstead on Long Island, where we spent several days during the Christmas holiday. The Green family consisted of Jim, his wife, teenage son and daughter and niece, all friendly and warm-hearted individuals. Frank Howe and I were accommodated in a large cosy attic furnished with camp beds. We spent two days at Christmas, and also over the New Year 1943 celebrations; both of which were convivial occasions, with large numbers of guests. All the males slept on the many camp beds in the attic and the females were spread around the bedrooms and living rooms.

Even though America had been at war for over a year, there was no sign of any element of austerity. It was rather comical. One American said to me, "We are all pulling our weight in austerity. We have a meatless Tuesday." When I endeavoured to sympathise with him, and asked what they ate on a Tuesday, the answer was "We have to make do with chicken or turkey!" Notwithstanding this, they were friendly, generous and hospitable hosts.

My one aim was to secure a passage home as quickly as possible. Many did not share this ambition, and would have been happy to enjoy life in the bars of Woodstock Hotel on their daily subsistence allowance, which was sufficient to fund all but extreme drinking habits. Hence, some who were offered accommodation or working berths on passenger ships for repatriation would defer to those eager to return home, and would post notices to that effect in the Officers' Club. I was always on the lookout for any offers.

The United States Navy had approached the Officers Reserve Pool for assistance in navigating Landing Ship Tanks (L.S.T.'s) to their operational destinations. The prospect was transfer on short-term loan to the United States Navy, to command small groups of L.S.T.'s destined for the Mediterranean area of operations. These large vessels were not usually transported on merchant ships, although a number of the smaller types were carried in sections aboard larger ships. The incentive was the rank and pay of a lieutenant commander U.S.N.

I have never ascertained the protocol involved in the transfer of a British Subject serving as an officer in the Merchant Navy, to the armed forces of a foreign power. All officers in the service of the U.S.A. are bound by an oath of allegiance to their country. Moreover, it was likely that each L.S.T. would be commanded by an officer with the rank of lieutenant or above in the regular, or more likely, reserve body of the United States Navy.

The U.S. Navy and Mercantile Marine had commenced a massive training program for officers, whom we designated "30-day wonders". These novice officers were taught only the rudiments of the profession which entailed for us four years of practical and theoretical training. There was no other way for the authorities to provide the officers and men for the huge numbers of ships being built. The expedient of using temporarily redundant experienced officers of the British Merchant Navy on a "one-voyage basis" seemed to be a practical solution. However, in conditions of wartime, when serving under the threat of enemy action, the question was, where did the levels of authority begin and end?

I have never known whether any of my fellow officers volunteered, or were ordered to serve as supernumeraries in the U.S. Navy or its reserve. After three weeks in New York, I was allocated a berth on a ship loading cargo for the United Kingdom.

On 5 January 1943, I learned in the Officers' Club of a berth as Second Mate on *Pilar de Larrinaga*, loading across the river in Hoboken. I visited the Reserve Pool offices, where they confirmed the information, and offered me the berth, subject to the acceptance of the Master. It seemed strange that many qualified officers, who enjoyed greater priority for berths, apparently had not been offered the berth. Notwithstanding this, on 7 January 1943 I travelled by bus through the tunnel under the Hudson River to Hoboken, and met the Master, Captain R.F. Rickenman. He engaged me, and I returned, and signed articles on the following day.

The following day, I learned the reason for the reluctance of the other officers to accept a passage home on *Pilar de Larrinaga*. They had learned that the ship would be carrying a part cargo of high explosives. A magazine for the explosives was being constructed in the 'tween decks over Number 2 and 3 holds.

When I boarded on 8 January 1943, the carpenters were working on a wooden magazine, which was constructed by lining the decks, bulkheads and deckheads with wooden planking, and encasing all stanchions and other steel members in wooden cladding. All fires on board had been extinguished. The workmen were wearing felt soled footwear, and used copper headed hammers and copper nails for fixing the wooden components

I took the view that you are just as dead if you are blown sky high, as when drowned in a ship carrying steel rails or iron ore. The important factor was that I had a berth on a ship making homeward passage, and that was all that mattered. I boarded *Pilar de Larrinaga* on 9 January 1943.

During the three months that had elapsed since the date when I joined *Start Point*, the unremitting slaughter in the Atlantic had continued with massive casualties in ships and merchant seamen.

Casualties – Ships and Personnel
10 December 1942 to 9 January 1943

Ships sunk – 49 by 29 successful U-Boats.
Four ships sunk by Italian submarines.
One ship sunk by a raider.
One ship sunk by a mine.

Lost with all hands

Oropos, in ballast, 34 dead.
Otina, in ballast, 60 dead.
Montreal City, general cargo, 39 dead.
Norse King, cargo coal, 35 dead.
Empire Wagtail, cargo coal, 39 dead.
Louise Lykes, cargo explosives, 83 dead.

Lost with very heavy casualties

City of Bombay, general cargo, 20 dead out of 150.
Orfor, cargo jute, 22 dead out of 58.
Bello, in ballast, 33 dead out of 41.
Emile Francqui, general cargo, 46 dead out of 87.
Observer, cargo iron ore, 66 dead out of 80.
King Edward, in ballast, 23 dead out of 48.
Oakbank, in ballast, 26 dead out of 63.
Treworlas, cargo iron ore, 38 dead out of 47.
Melmore Head, in ballast, 14 dead out of 49.
Empire Shackleton, general cargo, 37 dead out of 62.
Fidelity, cargo unknown, 45 dead out of 60.
Ingerferm, in ballast, 40 dead out of 41.
Empire March, general cargo, 30 dead out of 55.
British Vigilence, cargo fuel oil, 27 dead out of 54.
Oltenba II, cargo fuel oil, 17 dead out of 60.
Broad Arrow, cargo fuel oil, 23 dead out of 47.
Empire Lytton, cargo gasoline, 13 dead out of 47.

Merchant seamen killed – 913 out of 2,890,
a fatal casualty rate of 32 percent.

Successful U-Boats were U-124 (five ships): U-225 (four ships):
U-159, U-356, U-507 and U-591 (three ships each) and the Italian submarine *Enrico Tazzoli* with four ships.

Between 10 November 1942 (the date when *Start Point* was sunk) and
8 January 1943 (the date when I signed articles on *Pilar de Larrinaga*) 17 U-
Boats had been destroyed, 7 by depth charge attack, 8 by air attack, and 2
by collisions.

START POINT - 12 OCTOBER 1942 TO 7 JANUARY 1943

RECORD OF MERCHANT SHIPS SUNK IN ATLANTIC - 10/12/42 TO 09/01/43

SURVIVORS FROM *START POINT* TRAVELLING TO NEW YORK - 11/12/42 TO 17/12/42

DATE	SHIP	NAT.	CONVOY NO.	CAUSE OF LOSS	POSITION		CARGO	CASUALTIES CREW	DEAD
12/12/42	EMPIRE HAWK	BRITISH		TAZZOLI	05-56 N.	39-50 W.	GENERAL	51	0
12/12/42	RIPLEY	BRITISH		U-161	00-35 S.	32-17 W.	GENERAL	41	0
12/12/42	OMBILIN	DUTCH		TAZZOLI	07-25 N.	39-19 W.	GENERAL	81	0
13/12/42	SCANIA	SWED.		U-176	01-36 N.	32-22 W.	GENERAL	25	0
13/12/42	CITY OF BOMBAY	BRITISH		U-159	02-43 S.	29-06 W.	GENERAL	150	20
14/12/42	ORFOR	BRITISH		U-105	16-00 N.	50-00 W.	JUTE	58	22
14/12/42	ETNA	SWED.		U-217	17-50 N.	46-30 W.	GENERAL	27	0
15/12/42	ALCOA RAMBLER	U.S.A.		U-174	03-51 S.	33-08 W.	COAL	55	1
15/12/42	STAR OF SUEZ	EGYPT		U-159	00-42 S.	29-34 W.	GENERAL	42	2
16/12/42	BELLO	NOR.	ON153	U-610	51-45 N.	23-50 W.	BALLAST	41	33
16/12/42	EMILE FRANCQUI	BELG.	ON153	U-664	50-58 N.	24-42 W.	GENERAL	87	46
16/12/42	EAST WALES	BRITISH		U-159	00-24 N.	31-27 W.	COAL	45	17
16/12/42	OBSERVER	BRITISH		U-176	05-30 S.	31-00 W.	ORE	80	66

SURVIVORS FROM *START POINT* IN NEW YORK - 17/12/42 TO 09/01/43

DATE	SHIP	NAT.	CONVOY NO.	CAUSE OF LOSS	POSITION		CARGO	CASUALTIES CREW	DEAD
18/12/42	OROPOS	GREEK	ON152	U-621	51-00 N.	31-00 W.	BALLAST	34	34
18/12/42	BRETWALDA	BRITISH	MKS3Y	U-563	44-35 N.	16-28 W.	BALLAST	56	1
20/12/42	OTINA	BRITISH	ON153	U-621	47-40 N.	33-06 W.	BALLAST	60	60
21/12/42	MONTREAL CITY	BRITISH	ON152	U-591	50-23 N.	38-00 W.	GENERAL	39	39
21/12/42	QUEEN CITY	BRITISH		TAZZOLI	00-49 S.	41-34 W.	GENERAL	46	5
25/12/42	DONA AURORA	U.S.A.		TAZZOLI	02-02 S.	35-17 W.	GENERAL	73	7
26/12/42	EMPIRE UNION	BRITISH	ON154	U-356	57-00 N.	22-30 W.	GENERAL	69	6
27/12/42	MELROSE ABBEY	BRITISH	ON154	U-356	47-30 N.	24-30 W.	COAL	34	7
27/12/42	KING EDWARD	BRITISH	ON154	U-356	47-25 N.	25-20 W.	BALLAST	48	23
27/12/42	SOEKABOEMI	DUTCH	ON154	U-441	47-25 N.	25-20 W.	GENERAL	66	1
27/12/42	OAKBANK	BRITISH		U-507	00-46 S.	37-58 W.	BALLAST	63	26
28/12/42	TREWORLAS	BRITISH		U-124	10-52 N.	60-45 W.	ORE	47	38
28/12/42	NORSE KING	NOR.	ON154	U-591	43-27 N.	27-15 W.	COAL	35	35
28/12/42	MELMORE HEAD	BRITISH	ON154	U-225	43-27 N.	27-15 W.	BALLAST	49	14
28/12/42	VILLE DE ROUEN	BRITISH	ON154	U-662	43-25 N.	27-15 W.	GENERAL	71	0
28/12/42	EMPIRE WAGTAIL	BRITISH	ON154	U-260	43-17 N.	27-22 W.	COAL	39	39
28/12/42	PRESIDENT FRANCQUI	BELG.	ON154	U-225	43-23 N.	27-14 W.	BALLAST	49	5
28/12/42	ZARIAN	BRITISH	ON154	U-591	43-23 N.	27-14 W.	GENERAL	53	4
28/12/42	LYNTON GRANGE	BRITISH	ON154	U-225	43-23 N.	27-14 W.	GENERAL	52	0
28/12/42	BARON COCHRANE	BRITISH	ON154	U-123	43-23 N.	27-14 W.	COAL	44	2
28/12/42	EMPIRE SHACKLETON	BRITISH	ON154	U-225	43-20 N.	27-18 W.	GENERAL	62	37
30/12/42	FIDELITY	BRITISH	ON154	U-435	43-23 N.	27-07 W.		60	45
30/12/42	INGERFERM	NOR.		U-631	59-00 N.	21-00 W.	BALLAST	41	40
30/12/42	PADEREWSKI	POLISH		U-214	10-52 N.	60-25 W.	GENERAL	41	3
01/01/43	BRAGELAND	SWED.		U-164	00-19 N.	37-35 W.	GENERAL	28	0
01/01/43	EMPIRE PANTHER	BRITISH		MINE	BRISTOL CHANNEL		STEEL	48	6
02/01/43	EMPIRE MARCH	BRITISH		A.M.C.	35-00 S.	15-00 W.	GENERAL	55	30
03/01/43	BARON DECHEMONT	BRITISH		U-507	03-11 S.	38-41 W.	COAL	44	7
03/01/43	BRITISH VIGILANCE	BRITISH	TM1	U-514	20-58 N.	44-40 W.	FUEL OIL	54	27
08/01/43	YORKWOOD	BRITISH		U-507	04-10 S.	35-30 W.	GENERAL	48	1
08/01/43	OLTENIA II	BRITISH	TM1	U-436	27-59 N.	28-50 W.	FUEL OIL	60	17
08/01/43	ALBERT L. ELLSWORTH	NOR.	TM1	U-436	27-59 N.	28-50 W.	FUEL OIL	42	0
09/01/43	BROAD ARROW	U.S.A.	TB1	U-124	07-23 N.	55-48 W.	FUEL OIL	47	23
09/01/42	BIRMINGHAM CITY	U.S.A.	TB1	U-124	07-25 N.	55-48 W.	GENERAL	56	10
09/01/42	COLLINGSWORTH	U.S.A.	TB1	U-124	07-12 N.	55-37 W.	GENERAL	66	11
09/01/43	EMPIRE LYTTON	BRITISH	TM1	U-442	28-08 N.	28-20 W.	GASOLENE	47	13
09/01/43	MINOTAUR	U.S.A.	TB1	U-124	07-12 N.	55-37 W.	FUEL OIL	52	2
09/01/43	NORVIK	PAN.	TM1	U-522	28-08 N.	28-20 W.	FUEL OIL	45	2
09/01/43	MINISTER WEDEL	NOR.	TM1	U-522	28-08 N.	28-20 W.	FUEL OIL	38	0
09/01/43	LOUISE LYKES	U.S.A.		U-384	58-55 N.	23-40 W.	EXPLOSIVES	83	83
09/01/43	WILLIAM WILBERFORCE	BRITISH		U-511	29-20 N.	26-53 W.	GENERAL	63	3
							TOTALS	**2,890**	**913**

START POINT - 12 OCTOBER 1942 TO 7 JANUARY 1943

	SHIP AND U-BOAT LOSSES - AFTER LOSS OF *START POINT* 10 DECEMBER 1942 TO 09 JANUARY 1943								
GERMAN U-BOATS	**SHIPS SUNK IN PERIOD**				**ENEMY U-BOAT LOSSES**				
NUMBER	**TOTALS**		**TOTAL**	**10/12/42**		**DETAILS OF LOSS**			
	C/F	**B/F**		**09/01/43**		**DATE**	**CAUSE**	**DEAD**	**SAVED**
U-105			1	1	U-164	06/01/43	AIR	54	2
U-123			1	1	U-356	27/12/42	D/C	45	0
U-124			5	5	U-357	28/12/42	D/C.	37	7
U-159			3	3	U-626	15/12/42	D/C	47	0
U-161			1	1					
U-164			1	1					
U-174			1	1					
U-176			2	2					
U-214			1	1					
U-217			1	1					
U-225			4	4					
U-260			1	1					
U-356			3	3					
U-384			1	1					
U-435			2	2					
U-436			2	2					
U-441			1	1					
U-442			1	1					
U-507			3	3					
U-511			1	1					
U-514			1	1					
U-522			2	2					
U-563			1	1					
U-591			3	3					
U-610			1	1					
U-621			2	2					
U-631			1	1					
U-662			1	1					
U-664			1	1					
	1,465	**1,416**	**49**	**49**	**TOTALS**		**4**	**183**	**9**
					B/F		**142**	**4,546**	**1,772**
					C/F		**146**	**4,729**	**1,781**
HEAVY SHIPS	15	15	0						
RAIDERS	24	23	1	1					
LIGHT WARSHIPS	6	6	0						
AIRCRAFT	79	79	0						
ITALIAN SUBMARINES	73	69	4	4					
OTHER CAUSES	14	13	1	1					
	211	**205**	**6**	**6**					

17

THE WAR AT SEA: PILAR DE LARRINAGA

8 JANUARY– 23 FEBRUARY 1943

During the 31 days since our departure from Pernambuco 49 ships had been sunk in the Atlantic. Of these, 31 had been lost in convoy and 18 when on independent passage or detached from convoys. Astonishingly no homeward bound convoys suffered losses. The main enemy attacks were against outward bound convoy ON154, which lost 15 of its 46 ships, and convoy TM1, composed entirely of tankers, which lost 6 out of 9 ships. The small convoy TB1, composed of American ships with cargoes of fuel oil and war materials, also suffered the severe loss of 4 ships. Outward bound convoys ON152 and ON153 lost respectively 2 and 3 ships, and convoy MKS3Y one ship.

A total of 29 U-Boats were responsible for sinking most of the ships. One ship was lost by attack by a raider, and one ship struck a mine. The casualties were severe. The change in tactics to heavy attacks on outward bound convoys indicates the opportunist nature of the tactics of the enemy U-Boats. The reason for their failure to achieve successes against homeward bound Atlantic convoys for a month suggested that our counter measures must have been effective – even for a relatively short time.

Although we did not know the statistics when standing watch on the bridges of merchant ships, those on passage in the HX and SC convoys from Halifax and Sidney Cape Breton must have known that the U-Boat activity had been less effective – for a time. How long the respite would last was the question.

Seventeen U-Boats had been sunk during the 60 days between the loss of *Start Point* and my signing articles on *Pilar de Larrinaga*, 7 by depth

S.S. Pilar de Larrinaga, ex *War Nymph*, built in 1918, 7046 gross registered tonnage
(*Photograph by A. Duncan, Cowes, I.O.W.*)

charge attack, 8 by air attack and 2 by collisions. After forty months at war, this poor success rate for our anti U-Boat measures was disappointing.

We loaded the usual lower hold cargo (except for the magazine) of steel products, cases of foodstuffs and war materials. In the case of *Pilar de Larrinaga,* there was just considerably more of everything. She was a large ship built in 1917 as *War Nymph*, registered number 142675, and was distinguished by a tall natural draft funnel. She had a gross registered tonnage of 7,046 and a cargo capacity of 10,998 deadweight tons carried in seven holds. Her dimensions were

462 feet length, 58 feet 1 inch beam, and 26 feet 9 inches draft. Her designed loaded speed was 11 knots.

After we had finished loading the No. 2 lower hold, all lights were extinguished on board, and a special team of stevedores wearing felt soled shoes loaded the explosives. All equipment used was made of non-ferrous materials. We learned that we would be carrying nitro glycerine, T.N.T., amatol and other explosives. The No. 2 and No. 3 'tween deck magazines were then boarded up using copper hammers and nails, and the holds were battened down. The precautionary routine was relaxed. We remained at the berth in Hoboken for the remainder of the month of January 1943 for construction of the magazines, for the loading of the lower hold cargo and the explosive material, and finally for loading the deck cargo. This consisted of several landing ships in sections, secured on the forward and after hatches. These high sections increased the apparent size of *Pilar de Larrinaga* appreciably, and the huge natural draught funnel further exaggerated her silhouette. Convoy SC119 assembled off New York on 3 February 1943 and put to sea.

There had been intense enemy activity in the Atlantic during the period of 25 days between the date when I signed articles on *Pilar de Larrinaga* and the date when convoy SC119 put to sea. Fifteen ships had been sunk, 11 of them in convoy, and only 4 when on independent passage or detached from convoy. The ill-fated convoy TM1 lost another of its tankers, *British Dominion*, sunk by U-620 with the loss of 37 out of a complement of 54. Convoys SC115, TM1, HX222 and HX224 lost one ship each, SC117 and HX223 lost 2 ships each and UGS4 lost 3 ships. The casualties were heavy.

Miraculously convoy SC119 was not attacked, despite the continuing mayhem in the Atlantic during her passage to Liverpool. The ship did encounter what could have been a catastrophic mishap when en route. During my middle watch, when we were about a week from our destination, there was a shout from the helmsman "The bloody ship won't steer, sir!"

I rushed to the wheelhouse and found glycerine gushing from the Telemotor hydraulics that transmitted the steering wheel movements to the steering engine that turned the rudder. A hydraulic pipe had ruptured, probably in the 'tween decks.

The ship had veered rapidly to starboard, and was closing the next outside column. I switched on the two red lights that were permanently hoisted on the jackstay above the bridge, signifying "Vessel Not Under Command" rang the engine room telegraph to "stop", and then "full astern", and blew three blasts on the steam whistle. The Master came rushing up the companion ladder shouting, "What the hell is going on, Mr. Upton?" I told him that we had lost our steering and were not under control. His response was that he was unable to see clearly, and he left me to conn the ship. The First and Third Mates then arrived on the navigating bridge and were immediately ordered to go aft to supervise steering by the huge emergency steering wheel on the poop. I stopped the ship, and the Master took charge.

On the first veer to starboard, we had narrowly avoided colliding with our next abeam in the column to starboard, by taking the way off the ship by going full astern. The ships astern of *Pilar de Larrinaga* in our column avoided collision by altering to port. The danger lay in the risk of collision with the ships on our starboard quarter in the two outside columns. These acted with good seamanship by altering course to starboard together when they saw the red lights and heard our whistle signal. This left us stopped, and athwart the convoy course. They passed clear of us, and left us astern. The other ships knew the nature of the cargo that we carried in our magazines, and there had to be "Nicotine stains on the underpants" of the Masters and Mates of the ships in positions near us – as well as on our own underpants!

Fortunately, there were no American ships in our section of the convoy. Their inexperienced crews, particularly the Armed Guard Gunners, were in a perpetually trigger-happy state; so that if an emergency occurred, they were likely to open fire indiscriminately in any direction. With our part cargo of over 1,000 tons of high explosives, a stray projectile from a trigger-happy gun crew would have obliterated several columns of ships, and we would be the first men to land on the moon.

An escort was detached from the convoy and communicated with us by loud hailer. We gave them details of the steering malfunction and the action that we were taking. *Pilar de Larrinaga* was a fine, efficient ship, with an excellent Master and an efficient First Mate, who had ensured that the emergency steering gear was well maintained. Within a very short time, the ship was manageable from the stern steering position. Watches were doubled. For one watch the First Mate was on the bridge with the Third Mate aft, and for the other watch the Master was on the bridge and I was aft. We made full speed to rejoin the convoy, and took station astern of the middle columns, and ahead of the rear escort ship.

Thus, *Pilar de Larrinaga* covered the remainder of our passage from mid Atlantic to port in Liverpool. It was freezing cold for the officers and seamen stationed on the stern steering position, and very difficult to maintain a steady and accurate course, but we crossed the Bar in the Mersey, and docked in Liverpool without any further problems. I signed off articles on 23 February 1943, and travelled to Cardiff, where I arrived the following day. *Pilar de Larrinaga* was the only ship in which I undressed and slept in pyjamas, during the war. We stood no chance at all if struck amidships by a torpedo, so there was no point in taking the customary precautions of sleeping "fully booted and spurred".

It was my intention to apply for leave for refresher studies for the Certificate of Competency as First Mate (Foreign Going Steamship). However, I was short on qualifying sea time.

The qualifying time between the examinations for certificates of competency for Second and First Mate had been set at 18 months, or 78 weeks, on articles in full charge of a watch. I had served for 73 weeks and 5 days, leaving me exactly 30 days short on sea time. I applied for a remission of sea time, in view of the circumstances relating to the loss of *Start Point*, the period in charge of the lifeboats, the period spent keeping watch as a supernumerary on *Eskdalegate*, and my time on the register of the Reserve Pool in New York. After due consideration, my application was approved, and I was granted the qualifying period of service.

During the 19 days on passage in SC119, the enemy had returned to the attacks on the Atlantic convoys. Of the 44 ships sunk, 40 were lost in attacks on 10 convoys, and only 4 when on independent passage. The heaviest losses were incurred in outward bound convoy ON166, which lost 14 of its 48 ships, and Sidney Cape Breton homeward bound convoy SC118, in which 11 ships were sunk out of 61. Convoys MKS7, UC1 and ON165 lost 3 ships each, HX224 and KMS8, 2 ships each and SG19, RA52 and ON167 one ship each. It was a disastrous period, with massive casualties. Once again my ship, and its convoy, had passed unscathed through an area of massive enemy activity, on this occasion carrying enough high explosive to destroy every ship within two columns each way in our convoy.

The constant streams of distress signals were recorded, and the Radio Officers brought details to the bridge, where the officers of the watch entered the positions on the charts. The U-Boat dispositions that were regularly reported in Admiralty signals were also recorded on our charts. We owed a great deal to the scientists and mathematicians in the intelligence department in Bletchley Park for their dedicated work in cracking the enemy "Enigma" code, by which the Admiralty intelligence officers were able to identify the positions of the U-Boats. This enabled the convoy commodores and escort commanders to divert convoys away from the threat of attack. Thus, many ships were saved from attack, and the lives of a great number of seamen were preserved.

Therefore, we knew the extent of our losses in ships, and the positions where the attacks had occurred. However, none of us ever knew the extent of the fatal casualties, until statistics revealed them many years later. Had we known at the time, the effect on personnel morale would have been serious. It is fortunate that we did not know.

The catastrophic extent of our casualties is manifested in the following statistics. The total casualties of 2,099 men in 58 ships sunk represented a fatal casualty rate of 40 percent, an appreciably greater percentage than our army casualties on the Somme in 1916.

Viewing the heavy losses from the perspective of an officer who was at sea when the catastrophic loss of life was inflicted on Atlantic convoys, it is difficult to find a reason for the dramatic increase in fatal casualties. Only 8 ships had been sunk when on independent passage, *Roxburgh Castle, Cape Decision* and *Benjamin Smith* (all crew saved), Roger B. Taney (3 killed, 88 saved), *Braziloide*, (all 540 crew and passengers saved), *Rhexenor* (3 killed, 67 saved). The other two were *Ocean Courage* (45 killed, 7 saved), Neva (19 killed, 2 saved).

Therefore, the huge casualties were incurred in the 50 ships under the protection of escorts. Although the weather was moderate by North Atlantic winter standards, when *Pilar de Larrinaga* was on passage, it was bitterly cold, with very rough seas and frequent snow squalls. Therefore, survivors could not withstand such conditions for long in open lifesaving craft, and many must have died as the result of exposure, before rescue

Successful U-Boats were U-402 (six ships): U-118 (four ships): U-186 and U-606 (three ships each). Although the number of U-Boats on station had increased, the individual success rate had diminished appreciably. A total of 23 U-Boats were destroyed in the period of 45 days, 10 by air attack: 9 by surface warships: one by a British submarine: one by ramming: and 2 from unknown causes. This was an improvement. It was encouraging that the toll of U-Boats destroyed by air attack had increased significantly. This represented a dramatic improvement in the effectiveness of our countermeasures.

It was quite incredible that our convoy SC119 of 39 ships was on passage, without direct attack, for 19 days through a veritable holocaust in which 44 ships were sunk with massive loss of life. There were the usual alarms, and the dropping of depth charges; but no ships in the convoy were attacked. The only explanation must be that after the attacks on convoy TM1 in early January, and convoys HX222, HX223, HX224, followed by the sustained slaughter inflicted on convoy SC118, well ahead of convoy SC119, the U-Boats returned to base. Moreover, it is likely that convoy SC119 had been widely diverted from the area of the attacks.

The huge bulk of *Pilar de Larrinaga*, accentuated by her very tall natural draught funnel, and the deck cargo of invasion barges, would have made the ship a prime target. The substantial part cargo of the most volatile explosives could have resulted in a massive explosion, which would have destroyed a number of other ships, as well as sending us all sky high. We were all very lucky

Casualties – Ships and Personnel
10 January 1943 to 23 February 1943

Ships sunk – 58 by 38 successful U-Boats.
One ship sunk in a collision.

Lost with all hands

Mount Mycale, cargo grain, 47 dead.
Lackenby, cargo phosphate, 44 dead
Nortind, cargo fuel oil, 47 dead.
West Portal, general cargo, 77 dead.
Zeus, general cargo, 37 dead.
Empire Norseman, in ballast, 63 dead.
Radhurst, in ballast, 38 dead.
Stockport, rescue ship, 155 dead
Eulima, in ballast, 63 dead.

Lost with very heavy casualties

British Dominion, cargo gasoline, 37 dead out of 54.
Ocean Courage, cargo iron ore, 45 dead out of 52..
Neva, cargo coal, 19 dead out of 21.
Kollbjorg, cargo fuel oil, 12 dead out of 47.
J. Van Rensselaer, general cargo, 24 dead out of 70.
Cordelia, cargo fuel oil, 46 dead out of 47.
Inverilen, cargo clean oil, 31 dead out of 47.
Dorchester, general cargo and personnel, 695 dead out of 924.
Toward, rescue ship, 43 dead out of 70.
Afrika, general cargo, 23 dead out of 60.
Harmala, cargo iron ore, 53 dead out of 64.
Henry R. Mallory, general cargo and personnel, 272 dead out of 494.
Empire Mordred, in ballast, 15 dead out of 70.
Mary Slessor, general cargo, 32 dead out of 79.
Newton Ash, cargo grain, 34 dead out of 38.
Atlantic Sun, in ballast, 65 dead out of 66.
Rosario, in ballast, 33 dead out of 63.
Winkler, in ballast, 20 dead out of 51

Merchant seamen and personnel killed – 2,099 out of 5,275,
a fatal casualty rate 40 percent.

PILAR DE LARRINAGA - 8 JANUARY 1943 TO 23 FEBRUARY 1943

RECORD OF MERCHANT SHIPS SUNK IN ATLANTIC - 10/01/43 TO 23/02/43

PILAR DE LARRINAGA - SIGNED ARTICLES AT NEW YORK - 08/01/43

DATE	SHIP	NAT.	CONVOY NO.	CAUSE OF LOSS	POSITION		CARGO	CASUALTIES CREW	DEAD
10/01/43	OCEAN VAGABOND	BRITISH	SC115	U-186	57-17 N.	20-11 W.	GENERAL	47	1
11/01/43	BRITISH DOMINION	BRITISH	TM1	U-620	30-30 N.	19-55 W.	GASOLENE	54	37
15/01/43	OCEAN COURAGE	BRITISH		U-182	10-52 N.	23-28 W.	ORE	52	45
17/01/43	VESTVOLD	PAN.	HX222	U-268	61-25 N.	26-12 W.	FUEL OIL	75	19
22/01/43	NEVA	SWED.		U-358	61-35 N.	14-15 W.	COAL	21	19
22/01/43	MOUNT MYCALE	GREEK	SC117	U-413	52-00 N.	50-30 W.	GRAIN	47	47
23/01/43	BENJAMIN SMITH	U.S.A.		U-175	04-05 N.	07-50 W.	GENERAL	66	0
25/01/43	LACKENBY	BRITISH	SC117	U-624	55-00 N.	37-50 W.	PHOSPHATE	44	44
25/01/43	CITY OF FLINT	U.S.A.	UGS4	U-575	34-47 N.	31-30 W.	GENERAL	65	7
26/01/43	NORTIND	NOR.	HX223	U-358	58-40 N.	33-10 W.	FUEL OIL	47	47
26/01/43	KOLLBJORG	NOR.	HX223	U-594	55-40 N.	33-10 W.	FUEL OIL	47	12
27/01/43	CAPE DECISION	U.S.A.		U-105	22-57 N.	47-28 W.	GENERAL	77	0
27/01/43	CHARLES C. PINCKNEY	U.S.A.	UGS4	U-514	36-37 N.	30-55 W.	GENERAL	76	0
27/01/43	JULIA WARD HOWE	U.S.A.	UGS4	U-442	35-12 N.	30-29 W.	GENERAL	64	4
02/02/43	J. VAN RENSSELAER	U.S.A.	HX224	U-456	55-13 N.	28-52 W.	GENERAL	70	24
	PILAR DE LARRINAGA		**SC119**						
03/02/43	CORDELIA	BRITISH	HX224	U-632	56-37 N.	22-58 W.	FUEL OIL	47	46
03/02/43	INVERILEN	BRITISH	HX224	U-456	56-35 N.	23-20 W.	CLEAN OIL	47	31
03/02/43	RHEXENOR	BRITISH		U-217	24-59 N.	43-37 W.	COCOA	70	3
03/02/43	DORCHESTER	U.S.A.	SG19	U-223	49-22 N.	48-42 W.	GENERAL	924	695
03/02/43	GREYLOCK	U.S.A.	RA52	U-255	70-50 N.	00-48 W.	BALLAST	70	0
05/02/43	WEST PORTAL	U.S.A.	SC118	U-413	53-00 N.	33-00 W.	GENERAL	77	77
06/02/43	POLYKTOR	GREEK	SC118	U-266	53-04 N.	33-04 W.	GRAIN	45	2
06.02/43	TOWARD	BRITISH	SC118	U-402	54-55 N.	26-05 W.	RESCUE	70	43
07/02/43	AFRIKA	BRITISH	SC118	U-402	55-16 N.	26-31 W.	GENERAL	60	23
07/02/43	EMPIRE BANNER	BRITISH	KMS8	U-77	36-48 N.	01-32 E.	GENERAL	72	0
07/02/43	EMPIRE WEBSTER	BRITISH	KMS8	U-77	36-48 N.	01-25 E.	GENERAL	61	4
07/02/43	HARMALA	BRITISH	SC118	U-614	55-14 N.	26-37 W.	IRON ORE	64	53
07/02/43	HENRY R. MALLORY	U.S.A.	SC118	U-402	55-30 N.	29-33 W.	GENERAL	494	272
07/02/43	ROGER B. TANEY	U.S.A.		U-160	22-00 S.	07-45 W.	BALLAST	88	3
07/02/43	ROBERT E. HOPKINS	U.S.A.	SC118	U-402	55-13 N.	26-22 W.	FUEL OIL	57	0
07/02/43	KALLIOPI	GREEK	SC118	U-402	55-01 N.	26-35 W.	GENERAL	36	4
07/02/43	DAGHILD	NOR.	SC118	U-402	55-25 N.	26-12 W.	FUEL OIL	39	0
07/02/43	BALTONIA	BRITISH	MKS7	U-118	35-55 N.	05-57 W.	GENERAL	62	11
07/02/43	EMPIRE MORDRED	BRITISH	MKS7	U-118	35-58 N.	06-01 W.	BALLAST	70	15
07/02/43	MARY SLESSOR	BRITISH	MKS7	U-118	35-54 N.	05-59 W.	GENERAL	79	32
08/02/43	NEWTON ASH	BRITISH	SC118	U-118	56-25 N.	22-26 W.	GRAIN	38	34
08/02/43	ADAMAS	GREEK	SC118	COLLISION	56-35 N.	22-23 W.	GENERAL	37	0
15/02/43	ATLANTIC SUN	U.S.A.	ON165	U-607	51-00 N.	41-00 W.	BALLAST	66	65
18/02/43	BRAZILOIDE	BRAZ.		U-518	12-38 S.	37-57 W.	GENERAL	540	0
19/02/43	ZEUS	GREEK	ON165	U-525	49-28 N.	44-50 W.	GENERAL	37	37
21/02/43	RADHURST	BRITISH	ON165	U-525	48-50 N.	47-00 W.	BALLAST	38	38
21/02/43	EMPIRE TRADER	BRITISH	ON166	U-92	48-25 N.	30-10 W.	CHEMICALS	106	0
21/02/43	ROSARIO	U.S.A.	ON167	U-664	50-30 N.	24-38 W.	BALLAST	63	33
21/02/43	STIGSTAD	NOR.	ON166	U-332	49-26 N.	29-08 W.	BALLAST	37	3
21/02/43	H.H. ROGERS	U.S.A.	ON166	U-664	50-13 N.	24-48 W.	BALLAST	73	0
22/02/43	EMPURE REDSHANK	BRITISH	ON166	U-606	46-53 N.	34-32 W.	BALLAST	47	0
22/02/43	ROXBURGH CASTLE	BRITISH		U-107	39-12 N.	36-22 W.	GENERAL	64	0
22/02/43	CHATTANOOGA CITY	U.S.A.	ON166	U-606	46-53 N.	34-32 W.	BALLAST	52	0
22/02/43	EXPOSITOR	U.S.A.	ON166	U-606	46-52 N.	34-26 W.	BALLAST	60	6
22/02/43	N.T. NIELSON-ALONSO	NOR.	ON166	U-92	48-00 N.	24-00 W.	BALLAST	33	3
23/02/43	STOCKPORT	BRITISH	ON166	U-604	47-22 N.	34-10 W.	RESCUE	155	155
23/02/43	EXPOSITOR	U.S.A.	ON166	U-303	46-52 N.	34-26 W.	BALLAST	60	6
23/02/43	ATHELPRINCESS	BRITISH	UC1	U-552	32-02 N.	24-30 W.	BALLAST	51	1
23/02/43	EMPIRE NORSEMAN	BRITISH	UC1	U-382	31-18 N.	27-20 W.	BALLAST	53	0
23/02/43	EULIMA	BRITISH	ON166	U-186	46-48 N.	36-18 W.	BALLAST	63	63
23/02/43	ESSO BATON ROUGE	U.S.A.	UC1	U-202	31-15 N.	27-22 W.	BALLAST	68	3
23/02/43	HASTINGS	U.S.A.	ON166	U-186	46-48 N.	36-24 W.	BALLAST	62	9
23/02/43	GLITTRE	NOR.	ON166	U-628	47-00 N.	36-20 W.	BALLAST	37	3
23/02/43	WINKLER	PAN.	ON166	U-628	46-48 N.	36-18 W.	BALLAST	51	20
							TOTALS	**5,275**	**2,099**

PILAR DE LARRINAGA - 8 JANUARY 1943 TO 23 FEBRUARY 1943

SHIP AND U-BOAT LOSSES - WHEN SERVING ON *PILAR DE LARRINAGA*
10 JANUARY 1943 TO 23 FEBRUARY 1943

GERMAN U-BOATS	SHIPS SUNK IN PERIOD				ENEMY U-BOAT LOSSES			
NUMBER	TOTALS		TOTAL	10/01/43		DETAILS OF LOSS		
	C/F	B/F		23/02/43		DATE	CAUSE	DEAD	SAVED

NUMBER	C/F	B/F	TOTAL	10/01/43 23/02/43		DATE	CAUSE	DEAD	SAVED
U-77			2	2	U-69	17/02/43	RAM	46	0
U-92			2	2	U-187	04/02/43	D/C	9	45
U-105			1	1	U-201	17/02/43	D/C	49	0
U-107			1	1	U-205	17/02/43	D/C	8	42
U-118			4	4	U-224	13/01/43	D/C	44	1
U-160			1	1	U-225	15/02/43	AIR	46	0
U-175			1	1	U-265	03/03/43	AIR	45	0
U-182			1	1	U-268	19/02/43	AIR	45	0
U-186			3	3	U-301	21/01/43	SUB.	45	1
U-202			1	1	U-337	16/01/43	AIR	47	0
U-217			1	1	U-442	12/02/43	AIR	48	0
U-223			1	1	U-443	23/02/43	D/C	48	0
U-255			1	1	U-507	13/01/43	AIR	54	0
U-266			1	1	U-519	10/02/43	AIR	50	0
U-268			1	1	U-522	23/02/43	D/C	51	0
U-303			1	1	U-529	15/02/43	???	48	0
U-332			1	1	U-553	22/01/43	???	47	0
U-358			2	2	U-562	19/02/43	D/C	49	0
U-382			1	1	U-606	22/02/43	D/C	36	12
U-402			6	6	U-609	07/02/43	D/C	46	0
U-413			2	2	U-620	13/02/43	AIR	46	0
U-442			1	1	U-623	21/02/43	AIR	46	0
U-456			2	2	U-624	07/02/43	AIR	45	0
U-514			1	1					
U-518			1	1					
U-525			2	2					
U-552			1	1					
U-575			1	1					
U-594			1	1					
U-604			1	1					
U-606			3	3					
U-607			1	1					
U-614			1	1					
U-620			1	1					
U-625			1	1					
U-628			2	2					
U-632			1	1					
U-664			2	2					

	C/F	B/F	TOTAL	10/01/43–23/02/43
	1,523	1,465	58	58

HEAVY SHIPS	15	15	0	
RAIDERS	24	24	0	
LIGHT WARSHIPS	6	6	0	
AIRCRAFT	79	79	0	
ITALIAN SUBMARINES	73	73	0	
OTHER CAUSES	15	14	1	1
	212	211	1	1

		DEAD	SAVED
TOTALS	23	998	101
B/F	146	4,729	1,781
C/F	169	5,727	1,882

18

BETWEEN SHIPS FOR EXAMINATIONS

CERTIFICATE OF COMPETENCY – FIRST MATE

Betty had received no allotments or any funds during the period between 10 October 1942 and 23 February 1943 (when I signed off articles on *Pilar de Larrinaga*). I do not know the formula used to calculate the pay, war bonus, leave pay, allowances and deductions, for the period of over four months. There were allowances for survivors' leave, loss of kit, subsistence pay, replacement of sextant, etc. It was all too complicated, and when I was finally paid, I took the cash and left the Shipping Office, just relieved that I was still had some funds. It was also a bonus to be alive; after the ordeals that we had suffered.

After my statutory period of leave had expired, I reported to the Merchant Navy Officers' Reserve Pool, and applied for the customary study leave (unpaid of course), which was approved. I then enrolled for the course of study at the Smith Nautical School of Navigation and Seamanship. The syllabus for the examination for First Mate included as particular subjects, more advanced Ship Construction and Stability and Cargo Work, as well as more advanced Navigation, Chartwork, and the other subjects covered by the examination for Second Mate. The Ministry of War Transport Examiner was a fearsome Scot, Captain Logan, with an awesome reputation. His pet subject was lifeboat handling. In mid March 1943, I commenced the preparatory course of study.

Shortly after my return to Cardiff, I was summoned to the offices of the Receiver of Wreck. They already had a copy of the report that I had submitted to the Naval Control Officer. The original of the report that I typed in the British Consulate in Pernambuco is too tattered to reproduce by copying, and is copied as follows:

Report by V.G.A. Upton, 2nd Officer S.S. Start Point

Tuesday 10th November 1942.

At 1305 G.M.T., 1130 a.m. S.A.T. in D.R. position 13-35 North, 27-27 West, course 127 degrees true, speed 9 knots. Vessel struck in port side after end number two hold by one torpedo. Force of explosion blew away fore part port side of bridge: port jolly boat and port number three derrick smashed. Port lifeboat smashed while being lowered under the supervision of Chief Officer. Vessel listing to port, and going down slowly by the head.

I immediately superintended lowering of starboard lifeboat, which got away from vessel in charge of 3rd Officer (30 men were in this boat). Then proceeded to lower starboard bridge lifeboat, assisted by Chief Engineer (14 men, including the Chief Officer and Chief Engineer got into this boat.) Then disposed of all confidential papers and documents before leaving vessel at 1325 G.M.T. 1150 a.m. S.A.T.

The Master appeared to be dazed and would not leave the vessel although I made several attempts to get him over the side into the boat. When last seen he was on the lower bridge.

1st Radio Officer remained on board to re-transmit the distress message and his conduct was highly commendable throughout.

The Bosun, M.P. Casey and an A.B., W.H. Gordon, showed great coolness in getting rafts away from the vessel and their conduct in the lifeboats was very good.

At 1330 G.M.T., 1155 S.A.T., the vessel was struck by a second torpedo in number four hold, and went down within two minutes. The 1st Radio Officer managed to get away in one of the rafts, but Master was not found although 3rd Officer made a thorough search of the wreckage. A submarine then broke surface and approached the boat I was in, then in charge of the Chief Officer. This submarine proved to be Italian and appeared to have been on station for a short period of time, judging by the condition of her hull and paintwork. Shortly afterwards, a submarine flying German colours broke surface and approached. We brought the boat alongside the German submarine under orders from her commander and the Chief Engineer and Chief Officer were ordered to board her. The German submarine had by then drawn abeam of the Italian, and it appeared from the condition and paintwork that she had been on station for a considerable period of time. A member of the crew of the German submarine told us that they had sunk an oil tanker the previous day.

The crew of the Italian submarine appeared to be in good health and spirits and not unfriendly towards us. Relations between German and Italian crews appeared to be good. All members of both crews including the commanders were very young. Both submarines appeared to be of the 750-ton class. The Italian mounted a 3 or 4 inch gun on the after deck and a light anti aircraft, possibly 20-mm. on the foredeck. The German mounted no heavy gun, but had two light weapons of the type previously mentioned, one forward and one aft.

We were ordered to cast off from the submarine and the Chief Officer and Chief Engineer were detained aboard. I then went alongside the rafts and transferred all stores and provisions to my boat while the 3rd Officer did the same to the stores in the damaged motor boat, which was still afloat. Both submarines were last seen heading east in company.

We then set course N.N.W. true, close hauled on the starboard tack, wind E.N.E. moderate, sea moderate: and steered this course for the night, burning red distress flares at intervals of one hour. At daybreak I decided to strike west to take advantage of the prevailing winds, as it would have been difficult to make any headway to the eastward in the face of the fresh E'ly winds then prevailing. My object was to make the north coast of Brazil at the same time crossing the route for southbound ships.

One fireman, Norman Gillian, age 19, had been badly injured when the vessel was torpedoed and was in the 3rd Officer's boat. He had a severe wound in the right side over the pelvis, which was bleeding profusely. This wound was dressed by the Chief Steward and Cook, under the supervision of the 3rd Officer and the bleeding was partially stemmed. He was made as comfortable as possible and kept warm. The dressing was changed on several occasions and the wound was washed with warm sea water and painted with iodine. The conduct of this man was an inspiration to all in the boat. Although badly injured as he was he never made any complaint and was cheerful at all times. Throughout the 12-day passage we kept the boats lashed together with my boat towing the 3rd Officer's, as mine was the faster.

With the exception of four days of calms and baffling winds, we experienced fresh and strong east to N.E. winds, at times reaching gale force. We had great difficulty in keeping my small boat afloat in the high seas and at times had to lay to the sea anchor. The boat was almost swamped on several occasions and it is only due to the willingness of my crew and the co-operation I received from the inexperienced members from the engine room department, notably fireman G.A. Matthews, that we kept the boat afloat. Despite the fact that everyone was constantly soaked spirits were remarkably high and morale good and an example to the crew of the larger boat, who were not suffering such hardship.

The 3rd Officer reports on the good conduct of the crew in general, and the exceptionally good conduct of the 1st Radio Officer, T. Jenkins, 4th Engineer H. Marshall, A.B. S. Pascoe, A.B. J. Williams, Cook, J. Daniel, and Chief Steward L. Hendry.

We had provisions in both boats to last approximately 30 days and collected considerable amounts of rainwater during squalls. The men kept regular watches and had regular meal times. The 3rd Officer and I also saw that they washed or soused their bodies regularly and thus absorbed moisture through their pores. During calms regular rowing watches were kept and extra water and food given out.

Antonio Mizzi, greaser, caused trouble from the outset and was gradually going insane during the passage. He died between 9 P.M. and midnight on Saturday 21st November I examined him on the morning of the 22nd at 6 A.M. Rigor mortis had set in, his body was hunched up and his face a mottled purple colour. No response from pulse of heart. He was suffering from piles before death. I read a burial service over his body and buried him at 6-15 A.M.

At 4-0 P.M. on the 22nd, smoke was sighted bearing N.E. and course was altered towards it. We burnt smoke flares and sent a distress message by W/T. At 5-30 P.M. the vessel altered course towards us and we were taken aboard at 6-0 P.M. All hands were treated with the utmost kindness by the Master, officers and crew of this vessel. During the passage I had been able to ascertain our daily latitude with some degree of accuracy, having saved my sextant, and this did much to keep up the morale of the boats' crews.

An experienced master mariner interrogated me. My report had stated that the Master of *Start Point* had "appeared to be in a dazed condition". This did not seem to satisfy the Receiver of Wreck, who finally stated that the drinking habits of both the Master and First Mate had been a matter of record, and asked, "Had the senior officers been drinking? It will do no harm if you tell the truth." Under such circumstances, I was bound to give him a full report on the circumstances, as they are related in this narrative.

Following this, I received orders to report at the Admiralty offices in Whitehall, and Betty and I travelled to London, where we stayed for two days and nights. I was interviewed by a number of senior naval officers, the most notable being Admiral Sir Max Horton, V.C. They questioned me on the circumstances of the loss of *Start Point*, and particularly the passage of our lifeboats under tow, showing particular interest in the fact that the boats had remained together for nearly two weeks. I was then congratulated on our achievement. It was very gratifying that such senior naval officers considered our achievement to be commendable.

My body weight had reduced dramatically, as the result of the privations that we had suffered. When I arrived at Cardiff General station, Betty had arranged to meet me in the waiting hall. I arrived very late in the evening, and stood in the dimly lit hall for quite some time, until a figure appeared through the darkness and I heard the words "Is that you, Vern?" Betty had been standing at a short distance away, but was not certain that the thin, emaciated figure was her husband. Later, she reflected on her reactions after we had met, and were sitting in the taxi, "My God, do I have to go home and sleep with that scarecrow?"

As ever, the time spent on leave was over all too quickly. Even though we suffered a strict rationing regime, the combination of being able to sleep between sheets in a bed, the daily exercise of walking to and from the technical college, and regular meals stimulated an increase in weight, and an improvement in health.

I presented myself at the examination rooms on Monday 3 May 1943, after the usual ten weeks preparatory study programme, and sat the written examinations from Monday to Thursday. On Friday 14 May 1943, I stood before the dreaded Captain Logan for my oral examination. His first words were "Well, Upton, are you expecting me to question you about lifeboat handling?" My response was that I had heard that lifeboat handling was a subject of some importance to him. His answer was that the Receiver of Wreck had briefed him, and that lifeboat handling was a subject he proposed to omit in my case. He concentrated comprehensively on the clearing of a foul hawse, throwing coins on the table to indicate the port and starboard anchors. When I had the temerity to ask him "How many turns of chain cable are there in the foul hawse?" his answer was, "As many turns as you like." I told him that I had never encountered a foul hawse, and the only way I had learned to clear the chain cable was by the instructions in "Nicholl's Seamanship and Nautical Knowledge". He then proceeded to show me his way. He followed this with exhaustive questions on the handling of bulk cargoes, particularly rice, and then the stowage factors of various cargoes. When he came to case oil, I had to admit that I did not know its stowage factor, evoking the question "Why the hell not?" My answer was that I would refer to "Thomas's Stowage", the encyclopaedia on the subject, rather than attempt to commit stowage factors to memory.

I am bound to conclude that much of this was a psychological game plan to test the reactions of examinees. Captain Logan was a very perceptive judge of human character and reactions, and behind the brusque and fearsome demeanour, for which he was well known, there resided a keen mind, not lacking in humour. After the usual several hours in the oral examination room, he told me that I had passed the oral examination, and instructed me to return on Monday 10 May 1943, to find out if I had passed the written section of the examination. My Certificate of Competency as First Mate of a Foreign Going Steamship No. 50177 confirms that I passed the examination on 10 May, and is signed on 19 May 1943. My certificate as Second Mate No. 46226 was duly surrendered.

19

THE WAR AT SEA: OCEAN VAGRANT

12 JUNE– 23 OCTOBER 1943

I bade farewell to Betty and her family on 12 June 1943, and signed articles as Second Mate of *Ocean Vagrant* in Swansea on that date. The Master of *Ocean Vagrant* was Captain A. Pauling. The ship was managed by W.H. Cockerline & Co. on behalf of the Ministry of War Transport. Cockerline ships were colloquially known as "The Whitby Ships". *Ocean Vagrant* was a newly completed ship of the class now known as "Liberty Ships", which were constructed in massive numbers in American and Canadian ship-yards. The American-built "Liberty", "Sam" and "Ocean", and Canadian "Fort" nomenclature ships were based on a common hull design and dimensions. The fundamental difference between the American-manned ships, and the "Ocean" and "Fort" classes, manned by British personnel, was that the officers and other ranks on American ships were accommo-dated together amidships, whereas the officers were segregated from other ranks in the "Ocean" and "Fort" class of ships; officers in the bridge accommodation and other ranks in the traditional forecastles aft. Later, the "Sam" ships under British colours accommodated all hands amidships.

The gross registered tonnages varied marginally from ship to ship, but the common denominator was between 7,100 and 7,250 G.R.T. The ships were manufactured in sections and assembled by advanced welding processes in a great number of shipyards. One of my close friends, Eric Dunnett, was the welding supervisor in the Burrard Drydock in North Vancouver, where a substantial number of the "Fort" class of ships were built. He and his colleagues encountered major problems in welding together the large sections, particularly in the areas of stress relief. As a result, many of the ships built in the earlier stages developed cracks along

S.S. Ocean Vagrant, built in 1942, 7146 gross registered tonnage
Ship depicted in post-war livery as *S.S. Atlantic Vagrant*
(*Photograph by A. Duncan, Cowes, I.O.W.*)

or adjacent to welded joints. He was one of the pioneers in the process of sequence welding, which helped to relieve weld stresses.

The "Liberty" ships were, in their way, the Model "T" motor cars of the sea, designed and produced in the ingenuity of American mass production techniques. A substantial number gave good service for many years after the war, an excellent testimony to their quality and durability. The all welded hull construction tended to make the ships roll more easily and heavily than ships of overlapping riveted hull plate construction; and *Ocean Vagrant* was no exception. The ship also carried a weld stress crack in the deck plates amidships on the port side abreast of the funnel. This was welded over on a number of occasions, but after the ship was working in a seaway, the crack re-appeared. It was quite alarming, because the crack and the repairs eventually extended over a length of about 10 feet of deck, and about 4 feet up a bulkhead. Even when a patch was welded over the crack, the fissure would re-appear alongside the area that had been strengthened. We lived with the prospect that the ship would break apart if we encountered very severe weather. Fortunately, that did not happen.

CONVOY ON190

After over a week in Swansea, the ship put to sea in ballast, and joined convoy ON190 of 87 ships that left Liverpool on 24 June 1943, destination New York. The passage was uneventful, and we detached from the convoy and berthed in Baltimore on 10 July 1943. On arrival at Baltimore, a telegram awaited me from my family informing me that I had been awarded the George Medal, and on 13 July I received a similar telegram from Betty. The official notification from the Director General of the Ministry of War Transport was dated 5 July, and the award was published in the London Gazette on 6 July 1943.

I never saw the entry in the London Gazette, or a copy, until over 30 years later, when my secretary was determined to obtain details. She telephoned the London Gazette, and obtained a copy for the sum of two shillings. I was not aware at the time when I was notified of the award, that the Third Mate, Frank Bernard Howe, and Senior Radio Officer, Thomas Maldwyn Jenkins, had been awarded the M.B.E., and the irrepressible fireman, George Alfred Matthews, and the cook, Percy Daniel had been awarded the B.E.M. The courageous and determined Bosun, Michael Patrick Casey, was awarded a King's Commendation.

During the period between signing articles in Swansea, and arriving at Baltimore, in a period of 28 days, 28 ships were sunk in the Atlantic and North African coast of the Mediterranean. Only 7 ships were sunk in convoy, three of these in convoy KMS18B off the coast of Algeria. The British ship *Yoma*, carrying troops, suffered the loss of 484 men. The homeward bound New York/Halifax and Sidney Cape Breton, and the outward bound ocean convoys made passage unscathed.

CONVOY UGS13

The ship remained in Baltimore for 17 days, loading a mixed cargo of war materials: Sherman tanks and army trucks, food, beer and clothing, all destined for the build up to the invasion of Italy. We put to sea on 27 July and arrived off Algiers about 19 August 1943, where the ship anchored for several days. There were sporadic enemy air attacks on the port and shipping. The ship then moved to the port of Bone. The port had been devastated by incessant bombing attacks, and a number of ships had been sunk in the harbour and alongside.

During the period when the ship was loading cargo in Baltimore, and

Rose Upton
Relaxing in her garden

From left
Aircraftman Franklyn N. Upton,
R.C.A.F.

Lieut. Gordon N. R. Upton
R.C.N.V.R.

Private Alan G. Upton,
Royal Canadian Signals

on passage in convoy UGS13, 26 ships were sunk in the Atlantic and Mediterranean, none when in convoy. The heaviest loss of life occurred when *Timothy Pickering*, carrying 192 crew and service personnel, was bombed by aircraft off Algiers with the loss of 159 officers and other ranks. *Fort Pelly* was bombed and caught fire off the Sicilian port of Augusta, with the loss of 38 out of her complement of 70. The enemy forces were suffering severely, and had lost 61 U-Boats. We were beginning to beat the buggers.

We berthed alongside the only lifting equipment capable of handling the 32-ton Sherman tanks, which comprised the main cargo in Nos. 2 and

4 holds. This was achieved with the assistance of our 16-ton Jumbo derricks serving Nos. 2 and 4 holds. The discharge of cargo was in the hands of men of the Pioneer Corps, assisted by Arab labourers. On one occasion, we nearly suffered a serious mishap when one of the heavy tanks was slung by the relatively fragile towing lugs, instead of the stronger lifting lugs. Fortunately, only one lug broke away with the tank in suspension, but the other three held.

The Royal Army Service Corps officer detailed to check quantities was something of an oaf. He read his instructions as orders for the rejection of all parcels that had been broached, or contained fewer than the numbers shown on the labels. There had been modest petty pilfering of cargo by the American stevedores; mainly army shirts, bush jackets, canned beer and tinned fruit and meat. Even if one item was missing out of a parcel marked 100 items, the officer refused to allow it to go ashore. Broached cargo was placed in a spare storeroom, and there it remained. Consequently, the ship acquired hundreds of shirts, bush jackets and tins of food and beer. It was an unexpected bonus. We were all dressed in khaki shirts and bush jackets, and fed on the American army food.

Shortly after we started to discharge the cargo, there was a sound of plaintive wailing from the area of the port No. 2 'tween deck. We found an American stevedore, who had gone to sleep on the job in Baltimore; and was overlooked by the rest of his gang, who had stacked cases of food and beer around him. There he remained, battened down below decks for nearly three weeks. He had sustained himself by breaking open cases of Canadian Black Horse canned beer with his stevedore's crowbar, and drinking himself into a drunken stupor. He also broke open cases of Del Monte fruit salad. He must have been shitting himself when he heard the explosions of depth charges, when he was entombed in the cargo.

I had my first experience of lower deck mutiny when in Bone. I was officer of the deck one evening when the aggressive little Third Engineer boarded the ship, his right hand covered in blood. Shortly afterwards he was followed up the companion ladder by an able seaman, with blood all over his face and clothes, and his lips split severely. The two protagonists had entered into an argument in one of the sleazy bars in the remains of the town.

The Third Engineer had waited for an opportunity to attack the A.B., by waiting half way up the companionway, on the first platform. When the A.B arrived on the ladder and was attempting to stagger aboard, with both hands grasping the ropes, the cowardly Third Engineer dealt the virtually defenceless man several fierce blows to the face, causing severe injury. I forced the semi drunken engineer into the chartroom and locked the door.

Some of the seamen took the injured A.B. aft, and put him in his bunk. All appeared to be quiet for a time, so I took a first aid kit aft, and dressed the severe gash on the injured man's face, swabbed the area with hydrogen peroxide to prevent infection, and placed a dressing on the wound. Shortly afterwards a number of semi drunk seamen returned to the ship, and went aft. About six of their number returned amidships shortly afterwards, and demanded retribution against the Third Engineer. I told them that I knew the facts, and that proper action would be taken when the Master returned to the ship. They were on the point of returning aft, when the Master and First Mate boarded the ship. The Master immediately demanded to know what was going on, and I told him that there was no doubt that the Third Engineer had been the aggressor, and had been locked in the chartroom for his own safety. The Master immediately went to his cabin, and returned with a revolver, from which he fired several shots into the air. He was shouting,"I'll have no bloody mutiny on my ship!" Mistakenly assuming that the crew would attack the officers, the First Mate removed his Boy Scout belt from his waist, and began to belabour the seamen nearest to him with the heavy buckle. This provoked a melee, in which about six angry and partly drunk seamen surrounded the Master and two officers. I protected myself with a marlin spike.

Then a detachment of Red Cap military police arrived after hearing the shots, and marched all the seamen to the military prison, where they were locked up in the "glass house" until the ship was ready to put to sea. The Third Engineer, who was undoubtedly the cause of it all, had his name entered in the Official Log. His discharge book would have been endorsed "DR" (Decline to Report).

The aggressive and cowardly Third Engineer should have been the individual to suffer imprisonment, rather than the seamen, whose only crime was being drunk, and remaining loyal to a shipmate who had been viciously attacked. I felt that the Master had been precipitate, unfair and unreasonable, but Captain Pauling was a man who demanded – and got – his own way.

Another event occurred several days later when I was officer of the deck. One of our gunners was armed and always posted at the top of the companion ladder to identify all who boarded the ship. A colonel in the United States Army arrived aboard and asked to speak to the officer of the watch. He behaved in a courteous and gentlemanly manner. He asked if he would be permitted to have breakfast in the officers' mess. I replied that I was certain that we would be pleased to entertain him, and escorted him to the mess, where my fellow officers and the Master were on our traditional breakfast middle course of curry and rice.

I introduced him to Captain Pauling, whose reaction was astonishing. With a mouthful of rice, he shouted, "Get off my ship. You'll get no bloody breakfast here!" In his fury, he was spattering rice in all directions. I was ordered to escort the American army officer back to the gangway; and all I could do was to proffer my own profound apologies. After the kindness that had always been shown to me by the American people, and their great generosity, I could not understand the reason for such an unfriendly attitude. When I was relieved of duty and entered the mess, I told the Master that I felt that a senior officer in the army of our ally should have been treated with hospitality. The Master then berated me with the words, "Don't allow any of those buggers aboard my ship. I hate them all!" He was a very volatile individual. It was impossible to reason with him. I never ascertained the reason for his fierce antipathy towards the Americans.

I was by then experiencing violent stomach pains, and finding it diffi-cult to prevent vomiting after eating even light meals. The only foods that I could manage were tinned fruit, and rice puddings made with condensed milk. Fortunately, our cargo had contained Del Monte tinned peaches and fruit cocktail, and our store of broached cargo contained many hundreds of tins, on which I subsisted. By avoiding normal ship food, I managed to carry out my duties, both at sea and in port. On reflection, the digestive malfunctions must have been caused by the red oxide paint used to tan the sails of the lifeboats of *Start Point*, which were dark red in colour from the dye. We used the sails to collect the rain water, which became heavily tinged with the red ochre dye. It had been a case of our either drinking the contaminated water or dying of thirst.

It had been arranged that I would relieve my fellow officers for meals in port and at sea, because there was no point in sitting in the mess room looking at them eating food that I could not digest. This was a conven-ient arrangement, because the Steward was able to serve food that would not induce me to vomit, after the others had finished their meals. I could manage rice pudding, and potatoes mashed in condensed milk and water. In port, we could obtain fresh fish.

The port and town of Bone were oppressively hot, with constant thick dust, and millions of aggressive flies. Decomposing human and animal corpses were surfacing, and floating in the water. The stench was sometimes almost overpowering. This aggravated the vomiting and nausea. There was some respite when we completed discharging our cargo, and put to sea for the short passage to Bizerta, where we anchored among a forest of sunken ships. It was refreshingly cool and clean after the stench and dust of Bone. We put to sea on 24 September 1943, when we made passage to Gibraltar.

During our short stay at anchor off Gibraltar, the Italians were still maintaining attacks on Allied shipping by frogmen carrying limpet explosive devices. The Italian mother ship for these activities was anchored in the safety of Algeciras Bay, and there is no doubt that the Italians had the passive support of the Spanish authorities. There was no way in which the Spanish government could have been unaware of aggressive warlike activities that were being undertaken from the safe haven of their professed neutrality. It was quite disgraceful, and we would have been justified in blowing the mother ship out of the water.

The officers of the deck on our ships were issued with small grenades that we carried around the decks and threw overboard at regular intervals. These were pressure detonated, and, hopefully, may have been a deterrent, even if they did not blow any frogmen to bits. They killed a great number of fish.

CONVOY GUS16

The convoy put to sea from Alexandria on 19 September 1943, and arrived at Hampton Roads on 15 October 1943. Our passage to New York was without incident, and we arrived on 17 October 1943. I then received the news that I had been awarded the Lloyd's War Medal for Bravery at sea. The Committee of Lloyds had notified Betty of the award in a letter dated 13 October 1943. My family received the news from the Vancouver Daily Province, and my father sent me a telegram on 13 November 1943. By that time, I would have traded all the medals for some relief from the violent pains in my abdomen, and the almost constant spells of vomiting.

My gastric malfunction was by then serious, and I was examined by an American Doctor David Matus, who diagnosed either a gastric or duodenal ulcer, but more likely severe gall bladder disease. He recommended hospitalisation for barium meals and ex-ray, and certified that I was unfit for sea duties. I did not welcome the prospects of indefinite hospitalisation in the U.S.A., and requested repatriation for further medical examination in the U.K. There were then limited berths for D.B.S. on homeward bound ships; so, once again I was on a waiting list, this time for a berth as a passenger.

I had always thought that the term D.B.S. meant "Distressed British Seaman", but only recently, my misconception of the term has been corrected. It appears that the term is "Distressed British Subject", and does not apply specifically to seafarers. In any case, I was paid off on 25 October 1943, unfit for sea service, and found accommodation in the Great Northern Hotel, where I remained for nearly four weeks. *Ocean Vagrant* returned to the Mediterranean in support of the landings in Italy.

On 21 November, I was summoned to the offices of the authority in charge of D.B.S. repatriation and asked if I would agree to being accommodated in the troop deck of a passenger ship. This was subject to my signing an affidavit to the effect that I was accepting a berth in accommodation not designated for officers. I was then feeling so ill that I would have accepted a berth in a lavatory; so, I signed the disclaimer. I was not told the name of the ship. The following day I was issued with the appropriate vouchers. I boarded a taxi, and found myself alongside *R.M.S. Queen Mary* in the late afternoon.

Repatriation on passage in R.M.S. Queen Mary

It was all very efficient. I was issued with a round coloured badge, and directed by arrows of the same colour into the bowels of the ship, to my designated berth in a small cabin. Shortly afterwards about 15,000 American service personnel boarded, all with their badges of different colours, and were directed to their sections of the ship marked by their own specific colours.

This all happened with great speed and phenomenal efficiency, and we put to sea in the evening. Shortly after departure, we were called to meals. We filed through a number of alleyways, in which all signs and notices were in the same colour as our badges, and arrived at the kitchens, where we were issued with aluminium plates, with a number of sections for the food items. The only food that I selected from the self- service counters was mashed potato with some gravy, and a cup of coffee. Hundreds of us sat at the mess tables, where we ate our food, deposited our trays and utensils, and filed through the interminable corridors, miraculously to arrive at our berths in the small cabin. The standing orders were that anyone who strayed out of his allocated coloured zone would be arrested

R.M.S. Queen Mary, built in 1936, 81,235 gross registered tonnage
The author served as supernumery watchkeeping officer when on passage
home as D.B.S. in November 1943
(*Photograph by A. Duncan, Cowes, I.O.W.*)

by the military police, regardless of rank.

I shared the cramped accommodation with a number of young American soldiers. They were puzzled to find an individual not in army uniform in their midst, particularly a "Limey"; and were inquisitive about my identity. When they learned that I was a seaman who had experienced over four years sea service during the war, I was bombarded with naïve questions. What were the Germans like, had I seen action, had I been wounded, and so on? Most importantly, "Have you been awarded the Purple Heart?" Some of these conscripts, mainly the non-commissioned ranks, were already adorned with more medals and badges than regular British veterans with experience of many campaigns. They were ingenuous, but pleasant and friendly company.

My sextant in its box was placed on my bunk, and I went to find the shower room, wearing only a towel around my waist. When I returned shortly afterwards, one of the officers of *Queen Mary* was waiting for my return. He had passed the cabin while on routine inspection rounds, and saw my sextant on the bunk. He asked me to explain how an American G.I. could own a sextant. I told him the story; whereupon he departed and returned with a senior officer, possibly the Staff Captain. I was told that I would be moved to the ships' officers' accommodation on one of the top decks. They then asked if I would share a bridge watch, which I accepted with alacrity.

The huge ship made the journey to the U.K. at a speed of 29 knots, maintaining a broad zig zig. I kept a regular watch on the bridge and messed with the officers, where I enjoyed food that was more acceptable to my damaged digestive system. It was a most memorable experience.

During the period of 93 days between leaving Bizerta and arriving in the U.K., 51 ships had been sunk in the Atlantic and Mediterranean, 36 by U-Boats, 12 by aircraft, and 3 by mines. The U-Boats had returned to the attacks on convoys, in which 21 ships were sunk. Thirteen convoys were attacked, the most serious loss occurring in convoy ON202 that lost 5 ships.

On the credit side, 60 U-Boats had been destroyed with 2,608 of their officers and men, so the fatal casualties in merchant ships were substantially fewer that those suffered by our enemy. The most encouraging feature was that air attacks had accounted for 35 of the 60 U-Boats sunk.

Incredibly, late in 1942 and early 1943 the message had finally penetrated through to Whitehall. They were beginning to learn that the best way to win the war was by sinking the U-Boats by air attack, instead of concentrating on burning German women and children to death, and of wasting aircraft and many brave men in attempting to obliterate the almost impregnable U-Boat pens. During the month of May 1943, the first 17 very long range Liberator aircraft of No. 120 Squadron R.A.F., equipped with A.S.V. centimetric radar, became operational in Northern Ireland. Centimetric radar was a newer development, but large four-engine bombers had been available for several years, and could and should have been modified and released for anti U-Boat service two years previously. The failure of those in Whitehall to appreciate the strategic situation was a tragedy.

Even the youngest deck boy or apprentice on merchant ships had known for a long time that the only way to reduce convoy attacks was "to make the buggers keep their heads down." The reaction of the officers and other ranks in the merchant ships, suffering consistently enormous casualties, must have been that it took a hell of a long time to institute the measures that we all knew were necessary to arrest the menace of the U-Boats. I suppose it was a case of "better late than never."

During my Atlantic passage in *Queen Mary*, when standing a watch with her officers, I was told about the tragic collision between the huge ship and the anti aircraft cruiser *H.M.S. Curacoa* on 2 October 1942. Queen

Mary was on a broad zig zag at her speed of 29 knots, with Curacoa in close company. Inexplicably, *Curacoa* appeared to have attempted to cross the bows of Queen Mary, and was struck amidships by the massive liner. *Curacoa* was rolled under by the huge mass of *Queen Mary*, and sank quickly. The Court of Inquiry that was held after the war found the officer of the watch of the cruiser to be responsible for the collision.

I disembarked from Queen Mary on 27 November 1943, and arrived in Cardiff on 28 November 1943. By then, the battle against the U-Boats had been won decisively. During a period of five and a half months, the U-Boat successes had been modest compared with their enormous losses. The U-Boats had sunk 74 ships with the loss of 2,833 seamen, but had suffered the loss of 121 of their number with 5,057 of their crews. Air attacks had accounted for 87 U-Boats, or 72 percent of the total destroyed. This proved beyond measure what the officers and men in the merchant ships and their surface escorts had known for several years. For the first time, more U-Boats were sunk than merchant ships, and air attacks had proved to be the decisive factor.

When I returned to my home, I was beginning to suffer severely from the effects of over four years of almost constant wartime sea service, and was thoroughly exhausted and washed out. I had crossed the Atlantic on twenty five passages under the almost constant threat of enemy attack.

One severe problem suffered by most Merchant Navy officers and other ranks was almost constant insomnia. We slept fully clothed on our settees, listening for the sound of explosions and alarm bells, and under constant stress. During the night, it was a relief to walk around the decks like sleepwalkers, rather than remain confined in our cabins. During attacks we took benzadrine stimulants, and when in port resorted to pheno-barbitone tablets to induce sleep. It was very difficult to acclimatise myself to the unreal atmosphere of life ashore, without the familiar sounds of shipboard life. It was like living in another world. Although I was not aware of it at the time, this was the beginning of the end of my career as an officer in the Merchant Navy.

Casualties – Ships and Personnel
12 June 1943 to 27 November 1943

Ships sunk – 74 by 34 successful U-Boats.
One ship sunk by an Italian midget submarine.
Twenty seven ships sunk by aircraft.
Three ships sunk by mines.

Lost with all hands

Eldena, general cargo, 66 dead.
Baron Semple, cargo iron ore, 62 dead.

Lost with very heavy casualties

Yoma, troopship, 484 dead out of 1961.
Brinkburn, general cargo, 27 dead out of 29.
Lot, cargo fuel oil, 23 dead out of 134.
Devis, general cargo and personnel, 52 dead out of 343.
B.P. Newton, cargo gasoline, 23 dead out of 47.
Manchester Citizen, in ballast, 15 dead out of 67.
California, in ballast with personnel, 46 dead out of 316.
Timothy Pickering, general and personnel, 159 dead out of 192.
Fort Pelly, general cargo, 38 dead out of 70.
Fishpool, general cargo, 28 dead out of 53.
Rosalia, cargo crude oil, 24 dead out of 37.
Bage, general cargo, 48 dead out of 135.
Empire Kestrell, general cargo, 11 dead out of 41.
Thomas W. Weld, in ballast, 33 dead out of 98.
Itapage, general cargo, 20 dead out of 97.
Christian Michelson, general cargo, 47 dead out of 50.
Yorkmar, general cargo, 13 dead out of 67.
Penolver, cargo iron ore, 27 dead out of 41.
Campos, in ballast, 16 dead out of 68.
Hallfried, cargo iron ore, 31 dead out of 34.
Carlier, general cargo, 72 dead out of 91.
Pompoon, general cargo, 23 dead out of 27.

Merchant seamen and personnel killed, 2,833 out of 11,624,
a fatal casualty rate of 24 percent.

Four Russian ships were sunk in the Kara Sea,
but no details of casualties have been published

A total of 121 U-Boats were sunk, of which 87 were sunk
by air attack, and 5,057 officers and other ranks
manning U-Boats were killed, and 1,109 were saved.

UPON THEIR LAWFUL OCCASIONS

OCEAN VAGRANT - 12 JUNE 1943 TO 27 NOVEMBER 1943

RECORD OF MERCHANT SHIPS SUNK IN ATLANTIC AND MEDITERRANEAN - 12/06/43 TO 19/08/43

OCEAN VAGRANT -SIGNED ARTICLES AT SWANSEA - 12/06/43

DATE	SHIP	NAT.	CONVOY NO.	CAUSE OF LOSS	POSITION		CARGO	CASUALTIES CREW	DEAD
15/06/43	ATHELMONARCH	BRITISH		U-97	32-20 N.	34-39 E.	FUEL OIL	47	4
17/06/43	YOMA	BRITISH	QTX2	U-81	33-03 N.	22-04 E.	TROOPS	1,961	484
21/06/43	BRINKBURN	BRITISH		U-73	36-53 N.	02-22 E.	GENERAL	29	27
21/06/43	VENEZIA	SWED.		U-513	25-50 S.	38-38 W.	GENERAL	27	0
22/06/43	LOT	FRENCH	UGS10	U-572	23-56 N.	43-10 W.	FUEL OIL	134	23
23/06/43	VOLTURNO	BRITISH		AIRCRAFT	CAPE ST. VINCENT		GENERAL	83	9
23/06/43	SHETLAND	BRITISH		AIRCRAFT	CAPE ST. VINCENT		GENERAL	34	4
	OCEAN VAGRANT		**ON190**						
25/06/43	EAGLE	U.S.A.		U-513	21-07 S.	41-53 W.	BALLAST	52	0
27/06/43	MICHALIOS	GREEK		U-81			GENERAL	35	1
28/06/43	VERNON CITY	BRITSH	KMS16	U-172	04-20 S.	27-20 W.	COAL	52	0
01/07/43	TUTOYA	BRAZ.		U-513	24-40 S.	47-05 W.	GENERAL	37	7
02/07/43	EMPIRE KOHINOOR	BRITISH		U-618	06-20 N.	16-30 W.	GENERAL	88	6
02/07/43	BLOODY MARSH	U.S.A.		U-66	31-33 N.	78-57 W.	FUEL OIL	78	3
03/07/43	ELIHU S. WASHBURNE	U.S.A.		U-513	24-03 S.	45-11 W.	COFFEE	70	0
04/07/43	PELATSLOIDE	BRAZ.		U-590	00-30 S.	47-25 W.	COAL	44	5
04/07/43	ST. ESSYLT	BRITISH	KMS18B	U-375	36-44 N.	01-31 E.	GENERAL	79	1
04/07/43	CITY OF VENICE	BRITISH	KMS18B	U-375	36-44 N.	01-31 E.	GENERAL	170	11
05/07/43	DEVIS	BRITISH	KMS18B	U-593	37-01 N.	04-10 E.	GENERAL	343	52
05/07/43	MALTRAN	U.S.A.		U-759	18-11 N.	74-57 W.	GENERAL	35	0
06/07/43	POELAU ROEBIAH	DUTCH		U-759	17-55 N.	76-03 W.	ORE	87	2
07/07/43	JAMES ROBERTSON	U.S.A.		U-185	04-05 S.	35-58 W.	GENERAL	68	1
07/07/43	THOMAS SINNICKSON	U.S.A.		U-185	03-51 S.	36-22 W.	ORE	69	0
07/07/43	WM. BOYCE THOMPSON	U.S.A.		U-185	04-05 S.	35-58 W.	BALLAST	57	4
08/07/43	B.P. NEWTON	NOR.		U-510	05-05 S.	50-20 W.	GASOLENE	47	23
08/07/43	ELDENA	U.S.A.		U-510	05-05 S.	50-20 W.	GENERAL	66	66
09/07/43	DE LA SALLE	FRENCH		U-508	05-50 N.	02-22 E.	GENERAL	150	8
09/07/43	MANCHESTER CITIZEN	BRITISH	ST71	U-508	05-50 N.	02-22 E.	BALLAST	67	15
09/07/43	SCANDINAVIA	SWED.		U-510	08-21 N.	48-30 W.	GENERAL	25	0
	OCEAN VAGRANT	**- BERTHED AT BALTIMORE - 10/07/43 TO 27/07/43**							
11/07/43	CALIFORNIA	BRITISH		AIRCRAFT	41-15 N.	15-24 W.	BALLAST	316	46
11/07/43	DUCHESS OF YORK	BRITISH		AIRCRAFT	41-15 N.	15-24 W.	PASS.	281	11
11/07/43	BAARN	DUTCH		AIRCRAFT	36-55 N.	15-13 E.	GENERAL	72	0
12/07/43	AFRICAN STAR	U.S.A.		U-172	25-46 S.	40-35 W.	GENERAL	83	1
12/07/43	OCEAN PEACE	BRITISH		AIRCRAFT	36-55 N.	15-13 E.	GENERAL	78	0
12/07/43	ROBERT ROWAN	U.S.A.		AIRCRAFT	36-55 N.	15-13 E.	GENERAL	73	0
13/07/43	TIMOTHY PICKERING	U.S.A.		AIRCRAFT	36-55 N.	15-13 E.	GENERAL	192	159
15/07/43	HARMONIC	BRITISH		U-572	23-00 S.	33-00 W.	LINSEED	47	1
16/07/43	RICHARD CASWELL	U.S.A.		U-513	28-10 S.	46-30 W.	ORE	67	11
18/07/43	INCOMATI	BRITISH		U-508	03-09 N.	04-15 E.	GENERAL	158	1
20/07/43	FORT PELLY	BRITISH		AIRCRAFT	AT AUGUSTA		GENERAL	70	38
21/07/43	EMPIRE FLORIZEL	BRITISH		AIRCRAFT	AT AUGUSTA		GENERAL	83	9
24/07/43	FORT CHILCOTIN	BRITISH		U-172	15-03 S.	32-35 W.	IRON ORE	57	4
24/07/43	HENZADA	BRITISH		U-199	25-15 S.	44-08 W.	CHEMICALS	64	2
25/07/43	FISHPOOL	BRITISH		AIRCRAFT	OFF SYRACUSE		GENERAL	53	28
26/07/43	EL ARGENTINO	BRITISH		AIRCRAFT	39-50 N.	15-36 W.	BALLAST	104	4
	OCEAN VAGRANT		**UGS13**						
27/07/43	HALIZONES	BRITISH		AIRCRAFT	38-04 N.	12-59 W.	GENERAL	90	0
28/07/43	ROSALIA	DUTCH		U-615	12-07 N.	69-13 W.	CRUDE OIL	37	24
01/08/43	BAGE	BRAZ.		U-185	11-29 S.	36-58 W.	GENERAL	135	48
04/08/43	HARRISON GRAY OTIS	U.S.A.		MIDGET SUB	GIBRALTAR		BALLAST	60	1
06/08/43	FORT HALKETT	BRITISH		U-185	09-30 S.	26-50 W.	BALLAST	59	0
07/08/43	FERNHILL	NOR.		U-757	06-58 N.	19-15 W.	GENERAL	44	4
07/08/43	CONTRACTOR	BRITISH	GTX5	U-371	37-15 N.	07-21 E.	GENERAL	83	5
13/08/43	FRANCIS W. PETTYGROVE	U.S.A.	MKS21	U-371	36-15 N.	02-23 W.	BALLAST	71	0
15/08/43	WARFIELD	BRITISH		AIRCRAFT	39-59 N.	12-58 W.	GENERAL	96	2
16/08/43	EMPIRE KESTREL	BRITISH		AIRCRAFT	37-10 N.	04-35 E.	STORES	41	11
							TOTALS	**6,548**	**1,166**

OCEAN VAGRANT - 12 JUNE 1943 TO 27 NOVEMBER 1943

SHIP AND U-BOAT LOSSES - WHEN SERVING ON *OCEAN VAGRANT*
12 JUNE 1943 TO 19 AUGUST 1943

GERMAN U-BOATS	SHIPS SUNK IN PERIOD				ENEMY U-BOAT LOSSES				
NUMBER	TOTALS		TOTAL	12/06/43		DETAILS OF LOSS			
	C/F	B/F		19/08/43		DATE	CAUSE	DEAD	SAVED
U-66			1	1	U-36	05/08/43	COLL	4	25
U-73			1	1	U-43	30/07/43	AIR	55	0
U-81			2	2	U-67	16/07/43	AIR	48	3
U-97			1	1	U-97	16/06/43	AIR	27	21
U-172			3	3	U-106	02/08/43	AIR	22	27
U-185			5	5	U-117	07/08/43	AIR	62	0
U-199			1	1	U-118	12/06/43	AIR	43	16
U-371			2	2	U-119	24/06/43	RAM	55	0
U-375			2	2	U-126	03/07/43	AIR	55	0
U-508			3	3	U-135	15/07/43	D/C	5	51
U-510			3	3	U-159	15/07/43	AIR	53	0
U-513			5	5	U-160	14/07/43	AIR	57	0
U-572			2	2	U-194	24/06/43	AIR	54	0
U-590			1	1	U-199	31/07/43	AIR	49	12
U-593			1	1	U-200	24/06/43	AIR	62	0
U-615			1	1	U-232	08/07/43	AIR	47	0
U-618			1	1	U-334	14/06/43	D/C	47	0
U-757			1	1	U-359	28/07/43	AIR	47	0
U-759			2	2	U-375	30/07/43	D/C	45	0
					U-383	01/08/43	AIR	52	0
	1,561	1,523	38	38	U-388	20/06/43	AIR	47	0
					U-403	17/08/43	AIR	49	0
HEAVY SHIPS	15	15	0		U-404	28/07/43	AIR	50	0
RAIDERS	24	24	0		U-409	12/07/43	D/C	22	35
LIGHT WARSHIPS	7	6	1	1	U-435	09/07/43	AIR	48	0
AIRCRAFT	94	79	15	15	U-449	24/06/43	D/C	49	0
ITALIAN SUBMARINES	73	73	0		U-454	01/08/43	AIR	32	13
OTHER CAUSES	15	15	0		U-459	24/07/43	AIR	19	36
					U-461	30/07/43	AIR	53	0
	228	212	16	16	U-462	30/07/43	AIR	1	53
					U-468	11/08/43	AIR	42	7
					U-487	13/07/43	AIR	31	33
					U-489	04/08/43	AIR	1	53
					U-504	30/07/43	D/C	53	0
					U-506	12/07/43	AIR	54	6
					U-509	15/07/43	AIR	54	0
					U-513	19/07/43	AIR	46	7
					U-514	08/07/43	AIR	54	0
					U-525	11/08/43	AIR	54	0
					U-527	23/07/43	AIR	42	13
					U-535	05/07/43	AIR	55	0
					U-558	20/07/43	AIR	41	5
					U-561	12/07/43	M.T.B.	42	0
					U-564	14/06/43	AIR	28	21
					U-572	03/08/43	AIR	47	0
					U-590	09/07/43	AIR	45	0
					U-591	30/07/43	AIR	19	28
					U-598	23/07/43	AIR	43	2
					U-604	11/08/43	AIR	9	38
					U-607	13/07/43	AIR	45	7
					U-613	23/07/43	D/C	49	0
					U-614	29/07/43	AIR	49	0
					U-615	07/08/43	AIR	4	43
					U-622	24/07/43	AIR	??	??
					U-628	03/07/43	AIR	49	0
					U-647	04/08/43	??	48	0
					U-662	21/07/43	AIR	44	3
					U-664	09/08/43	AIR	7	40
					U-706	02/08/43	AIR	42	5
					U-759	26/07/43	AIR	47	0
					U-951	07/07/43	AIR	46	0
					TOTALS	61		2,449	603
					B/F	169		5,727	1,882
					C/F	230		8,176	2,485

UPON THEIR LAWFUL OCCASIONS

OCEAN VAGRANT - 12 JUNE 1943 TO 27 NOVEMBER 1943

RECORD OF MERCHANT SHIPS SUNK IN ATLANTIC AND MEDITERRANEAN - 20/08/43 TO 27/11/43

OCEAN VAGRANT - BERTHED AT ALGIERS. BONE AND BIZERTA - 19/08/43 TO 24/09/43

DATE	SHIP	NAT.	CONVOY NO.	CAUSE OF LOSS	POSITION		CARGO	CASUALTIES CREW	DEAD
26/08/43	JOHN BELL	U.S.A.	UGS14	U-410	37-15 N.	08-24 E.	GENERAL	69	1
26/08/43	RICHARD HENDERSON	U.S.A.	UGS14	U-410	37-15 N.	08-24 E,	GENERAL	70	0
13/09/43	FORT BABINE	BRITISH		AIRCRAFT	41-31 N.	14-39 W.	BALLAST	23	7
13/09/43	NEWFOUNDLAND	BRITISH		AIRCRAFT	40-14 N.	13-20 E.	HOSPITAL	106	4
15/09/43	BUSHROD WASHINGTON	U.S.A.		AIRCRAFT	40-40 N.	14-43 E.	GENERAL	75	4
20/09/43	ST. USK	BRITISH		U-161	16-30 S.	29-28 W.	GENERAL	47	0
20/09/43	FREDERICK DOUGLASS	U.S.A.	ON202	U-238	57-03 N.	28-08 W.	BALLAST	70	0
20/09/43	THEODORE D. WELD	U.S.A.	ON202	U-238	57-03 N.	28-08 W.	BALLAST	98	33
21/09/43	WILLIAM H. GERHARD	U.S.A.		U-593	40-50 N.	14-07 E.	GENERAL	267	2
22/09/43	RICHARD OLNEY	U.S.A.	KMS26	MINED	37-25 N.	09-54 E.	GENERAL	80	2
23/09/43	FORT JEMSEG	BRITISH	ON202	U-238	53-18 N.	40-24 W.	BALLAST	54	1
23/09/43	STEEL VOYAGER	U.S.A.	ONS18	U-952	53-34 N.	40-40 W.	BALLAST	63	0
23/09/43	OREGON EXPRESS	NOR.	ON202	U-238	53-40 N.	39-50 W.	BALLAST	45	8
23/09/43	SKJELBRED	NOR.	ON202	U-238	53-18 N.	40-24 W.	BALLAST	43	0
	OCEAN VAGRANT	**GUS16**							
26/09/43	ITAPAGE	BRAZ.		U-161	10-00 S.	35-45 W.	GENERAL	97	20
26/09/43	CHRISTIAN MICHELSON	NOR.	UGS17	U-410	37-12 N.	08-26 E.	GENERAL	50	47
30/09/43	EMPIRE COMMERCE	BRITISH	MKS26	U-410	37-19 N.	06-40 E.	BALLAST	51	0
30/09/43	FORT HOWE	BRITISH	MKS26	U-410	37-19 N.	06-40 E.	BALLAST	71	2
01/10/43	STANMORE	BRITISH	KMS27	U-223	36-41 N.	01-10 E.	GENERAL	49	0
01/10/43	METAPAN	U.S.A.		MINED	37-22 N.	10-37 E.	GENERAL	73	0
04/10/43	MARIT	NOR.	XT4	U-596	37-57 N.	21-11 E.	FUEL OIL	54	2
04/10/43	FORT FITZGERALD	BRITISH	UGS18	AIRCRAFT	36-42 N.	01-17 E.	GENERAL	56	5
05/10/43	ARCHENGELSK	RUSS.		U-302	IN KARA SEA		GENERAL		
05/10/43	DIKSON	RUSS.		U-302	IN KARA SEA		GENERAL	30	0
05/10/43	SERGEI KIROV	RUSS.		U-703	IN KARA SEA		GENERAL		
05/10/43	TBILISI	RUSS.		MINED	IN KARA SEA		GENERAL		
09/10/43	YORKMAR	U.S.A.	SC143	U-645	56-38 N.	20-30 W.	GENERAL	67	13
15/10/43	ESSEX LANCE	BRITISH	ONS20	U-426	57-53 N.	28-00 W.	COAL	52	0
15/10/43	JAMES RUSSELL LOWELL	U.S.A.	GUS18	U-371	37-22 N.	07-08 E.	BALLAST	75	0

OCEAN VAGRANT - BERTHED AT NEW YORK - 16/10/43 TO 25/10 43 - PAID OFF - D.B.S. - 25/10/43

DATE	SHIP	NAT.	CONVOY NO.	CAUSE OF LOSS	POSITION		CARGO	CASUALTIES CREW	DEAD
16/10/43	ESSEX LANCE	BRITISH	ONS20	U-426	57-53 N.	28-00 W.	COAL	52	0
19/10/43	PENOLVER	BRITISH	WB65	U-220	47-19 N.	52-27 W.	ORE	41	27
19/10/43	DELISLE	U.S.A.		U-220	47-19 N.	52-27 W.	GENERAL	39	0
21/10/43	SALTWICK	BRITISH		AIRCRAFT	36-55 N.	01-36 E.	GENERAL	51	0
21/10/43	TITIVES	U.S.A.		AIRCRAFT	36-55 N.	01-30 E.	GENERAL	80	2
22/10/43	LITIOPA	NOR.		U-68	06-18 N.	11-55 W.	BALLAST	35	0
23/10/43	CAMPOS	BRAZ.		U-170	24-07 S.	45-50 W.	BALLAST	68	16
24/10/43	STRANGER	NOR.		U-155	00-00 N.	38-45 W.	GENERAL	37	0

ASHORE D.B.S. IN NEW YORK AWAITING PASSAGE TO U.K - 25/10/43 TO 21-11/43

DATE	SHIP	NAT.	CONVOY NO.	CAUSE OF LOSS	POSITION		CARGO	CASUALTIES CREW	DEAD
31/10/43	NEW COLUMBIA	BRITISH		U-68	04-05 N.	05-03 E.	GENERAL	65	0
02/11/43	HALLFRIED	NOR.		U-262	46-05 N.	20-26 W.	ORE	34	31
02/11/43	MONT VISO	FRENCH	KMS30	U-593	36-45 N.	01-55 E.	UNKNOWN	UNKNOWN	
02/11/43	BARON SEMPLE	BRITISH		U-848	05-00 S.	21-00 W.	ORE	62	62
11/11/43	BIRCHBANK	BRITISH		AIRCRAFT	36-13 N.	00-06 W.	GENERAL	65	2
11/11/43	INDIAN PRINCE	BRITISH		AIRCRAFT	36-10 N.	00-06 W.	GENERAL	61	1
11/11/43	NIVOSE	FRENCH		AIRCRAFT	36-13 N.	00-05 W.	FUEL OIL	UNKNOWN	
11/11/43	CARLIER	BELG.		AIRCRAFT	36-13 N.	00-05 W.	GENERAL	91	72
12/11/43	POMPOON	PAN.		U-516	11-00 N.	75-00 W.	GENERAL	27	23
18/11/43	EMPIRE DUNSTAN	BRITISH		U-81	39-24 N.	17-40 E.	GENERAL	39	2
21/11/43	MARSA	BRITISH		AIRCRAFT	46-40 N.	18-18 W.	ORE	48	1

RETURN PASSAGE ON R.M.S. *QUEEN MARY* AS A SUPERNUMERARY - 22/11/43 TO 27/11/43

DATE	SHIP	NAT.	CONVOY NO.	CAUSE OF LOSS	POSITION		CARGO	CASUALTIES CREW	DEAD
23/11/43	ELIZABETH KELLOGG	U.S.A.		U-516	11-10 N.	80-42 W.	FUEL OIL	48	10
24/11/43	MELVILLE E. STONE	U.S.A.		U-516	10-36 N.	80-19 W.	GENERAL;	66	15
26/11/43	ROHNA	BRITISH		AIRCRAFT	36-56 N.	05-20 E.	TROOPS	2,232	1,162
							TOTALS	**5,076**	**1,577**

OCEAN VAGRANT - 12 JUNE 1943 TO 27 NOVEMBER 1943

SHIP AND U-BOAT LOSSES - WHEN SERVING ON *OCEAN VAGRANT*
20 AUGUST 1943 TO 27 NOVEMBER 1943

GERMAN U-BOATS	SHIPS SUNK IN PERIOD				ENEMY U-BOAT LOSSES				
NUMBER	TOTALS		TOTAL	20/08/43		DETAILS OF LOSS			
	C/F	B/F		27/11/43		DATE	CAUSE	DEAD	SAVED
U-68			2	2	U-84	24/08/43	AIR	46	0
U-81			1	1	U-97	20/08/43	AIR	67	0
U-155			1	1	U-134	24/08/43	AIR	46	0
U-161			2	2	U-161	27/09/43	AIR	53	0
U-170			1	1	U-185	24/08/43	AIR	43	36
U-220			2	2	U-197	20/08/43	AIR	67	0
U-223			1	1	U-211	19/11/43	AIR	54	0
U-238			5	5	U-220	28/10/43	AIR	56	0
U-262			1	1	U-221	27/09/43	AIR	50	0
U-302			2	2	U-226	06/11/43	D/C	51	0
U-371			1	1	U-229	22/09/43	D/C	50	0
U-410			5	5	U-274	23/10/43	D/C	48	0
U-426			2	2	U-279	04/10/43	AIR	48	0
U-516			3	3	U-280	16/11/43	AIR	49	0
U-593			2	2	U-282	29/10/43	D/C	48	0
U-596			1	1	U-306	31/10/43	D/C	51	0
U-645			1	1	U-336	04/10/43	AIR	50	0
U-703			1	1	U-338	20/09/43	AIR	51	0
U-848			1	1	U-340	02/11/43	D/C	1	48
U-952			1	1	U-341	19/09/43	AIR	50	0
					U-346	20/09/43	??	37	0
	1,597	1,561	36	36	U-378	20/10/43	AIR	52	0
					U-389	05/10/43	AIR	50	0
HEAVY SHIPS	15	15	0		U-402	13/10/43	AIR	50	0
RAIDERS	24	24	0		U-405	01/11/43	D/C	49	0
LIGHT WARSHIPS	7	7	0		U-419	08/10/43	AIR	48	1
AIRCRAFT	106	94	12	12	U-420	26/10/43	AIR	49	0
ITALIAN SUBMARINES	73	73	0		U-422	04/10/43	AIR	49	0
OTHER CAUSES	18	15	3	3	U-458	22/08/43	D/C	8	43
					U-460	04/10/43	AIR	62	0
	243	228	15	15	U-470	16/10/43	AIR	46	2
					U-508	12/11/43	AIR	57	0
					U-523	25/08/43	D/C	16	37
					U-536	20/11/43	D/C	38	17
					U-538	21/11/43	D/C	55	0
					U-540	17/10/43	AIR	55	0
					U-566	24/10/43	AIR	0	49
					U-584	31/10/43	AIR	53	0
					U-600	25/11/43	D/C	54	0
					U-610	08/10/43	AIR	51	0
					U-617	12/09/43	AIR	0	49
					U-631	17/10/43	D/C	53	0
					U-634	30/08/43	D/C	47	0
					U-639	25/08/43	SUB.	47	0
					U-643	08/10/43	AIR	30	21
					U-648	23/11/43	D/C	50	0
					U-669	07/09/43	AIR	52	0
					U-670	20/08/43	COLL	21	26
					U-718	18/11/43	COLL.	43	0
					U-732	31/10/43	D/C	31	19
					U-760	08/09/43	AIR	0	47
					U-768	20/11/43	COLL.	49	0
					U-841	17/10/43	D/C	26	27
					U-842	10/11/43	AIR	8	39
					U-844	16/10/43	AIR	53	0
					U-847	27/08/43	AIR	62	0
					U-848	05/11/43	AIR	63	0
					U-849	25/11/43	AIR	63	0
					U-964	16/10/43	AIR	47	3
					U-983	08/09/43	COLL.	5	42
					TOTALS	60	2,608	506	
					B/F	230	8,176	2,485	
					C/F	290	10,784	2,991	

20

ON LEAVE FOR MEDICAL TREATMENT

I can remember little about disembarking from *Queen Mary*. My discharge book was stamped and returned to me on Tuesday 30 November 1943, so I would have travelled home on Saturday 27 November 1943.

When I arrived home, a letter dated 27 November 1943, from the Central Chancery of Knighthoods, awaited me. This summoned me to attend at Buckingham Palace for an Investiture, to be held at 10.15 a.m. on Tuesday 7 December 1943. After acknowledging the letter, I visited the Mercantile Marine Offices, where I was issued with rail vouchers for Betty and myself, and paid the statutory subsistence allowance.

We travelled to London on Monday 6 December 1943, and stayed overnight at the Russell Hotel, prior to the investiture on the following morning. When we arrived at Buckingham Palace, Betty was escorted to the seats allocated for spectators, and I was directed to a room where recipients of awards were assembled, briefed, and directed to their places in their respective lines.

We were informed that, due to the indisposition of His Majesty the King, H.R.H. the Duke of Gloucester would preside at the Investiture. From then on everything happened with great efficiency and speed, after moving along what seemed like a maze of corridors, and having my name checked on a number of occasions, I found myself before the royal personage. He mumbled some unintelligible words, and I replied with the name of my ship, the date and theatre of operations. I was then ushered along more corridors, and, quite miraculously, was re-united with Betty. She was ecstatic with the experience, sitting in comfort, sipping coffee and listening to the band. My priority was to find a toilet to relieve myself after having partaken of several drinks before the event.

Outside the palace, we were photographed, and returned to our hotel.

CENTRAL CHANCERY OF
THE ORDERS OF KNIGHTHOOD,
ST JAMES'S PALACE, S.W.1

27th November, 1945.

Sir,

    The King will hold an Investiture at Buckingham Palace
on   Tuesday, the 7th Dec. 1945 at which your attendance is
requested.

    It is requested that you should be at the Palace not
later than 10.15 o'clock a.m.

DRESS-Service Dress, Morning Dress or Civil Defence Uniform.

    This letter should be produced on entering the Palace,
as no further card of admission will be issued.

    Two tickets for relations or friends to witness the
Investiture may be obtained on application to this Office
and you are requested to state your requirements on the
form enclosed.

    Please complete the enclosed form and return immediately
to the Secretary, Central Chancery of the Orders of
Knighthood, St. James's Palace, London, S.W.1.

       I am, Sir,

          Your obedient Servant,

Vernon G. A. Upton, Esq.,
         G.M.

                             Secretary.

Betty and Vernon Upton
After investiture at Buckingham Palace
7th December 1943

We returned to Cardiff the following day.

The following week, after being examined by the Shipping Federation doctor, I was admitted to the Royal Hamadryad Hospital, where I remained a patient for about a week. It was suspected that I was suffering from a gastric ulcer, with the probability that my gall bladder and kidneys had suffered damage. There were also problems with my liver, resulting from a build up of salt in my system. During the day, salt encrustations would work out of the pores of my feet, and the white deposits would permeate through my shoes. I had to eliminate salt from my diet completely, even in the water used for cooking food.

I was then transferred to the Rookwood Ministry of Pensions hospital, for a barium meal and ex-rays. The diagnosis was "severe dyspepsia – result of exposure". A strict salt-free diet of milk, eggs and fish was prescribed, and I was certified as unfit for sea service. I received no pay, disability or subsistence allowances, and the authorities just left Betty and me to subsist as best we could. Although I had been contributing to the Merchant Navy Officers Pension Fund, that body did not fund war disability pensions. I did not want to apply to the Ministry of Pensions, because I hoped to be able to return to sea duty. There was no option but to seek employment.

There was a vacancy in the Cardiff City Council for an Assistant Port Health Officer. One of the requirements was knowledge of shipping. The pay was poor and the conditions were awful. Two Assistant Port Health Officers served Cardiff Docks, working the two daily tides, from four hours before flood tide to two hours after, the times when ships would dock. The coasters were berthed in the West and East Docks, and the deep-sea ships were accommodated in the Roath and Queens Docks. The distance between the extreme boundaries, represented by the West Dock locks and the Queens Dock Pierhead was considerable. A bicycle was the means of transport. I bought one second hand for £ 5.

The duties of the Assistant Port Health Inspector were to board the ships as soon as possible, preferably in the first lock of entry, interview the Master and, if the ship was healthy, grant clearance. With four locks to cover, the ideal scenario was for the ships to enter port one at a time, but this rarely happened. We sheltered either in a midway position at the Low Water Pier, or in the Customs hut on the Queens Dock Pierhead.

One of my companions was Charlie the rat catcher. I learned a great deal about the habits of rodents from Charlie, and a great deal about the methods he used to dispose of the vermin. Quite often, he kept a live rat in one of the capacious pockets of his tattered old army greatcoat. He was a wealth of knowledge on the subject of rats, after a lifetime spent in disposing of them.

We whiled the time away by playing "shove ha'penny" in a shed on the Queens Dock entrance, or yarning with the keeper of the Low Water Pier, a character named Freddie Hayes. There were always several officials waiting to board the ships, but none would be permitted to board until after I had certified that the ship was healthy. Among those were the D.E.M.S. and Naval Control officers, H.M. Customs, port officials and agents.

I encountered trouble from only one person, an officious Naval Control R.N.V.R. lieutenant. I believe that his name was Lieutenant Windybanks. He did not endear himself to me because he treated his W.R.N.S. driver with lack of consideration and courtesy. He boarded the ship before me and claimed priority of interview with the Master. When I intervened, and found out that there had been a death aboard, I placed the ship in quarantine. The Naval Control Officer was then forced to remain aboard at the quarantine berth until the Port Medical Officer had cleared the ship, despite his vehement protestations. The Naval Control Officer had learned his lesson.

An amusing incident occurred, when a very small ship with a crew of six arrived from the Bristol Channel port of Portishead, a small port in the Bristol Channel, about thirty miles away. The ship was entering the Queens Dock locks during a violent gale and torrential rain. I boarded the ship and asked the Master, "Is your ship healthy?" On receiving his assurance that the ship was healthy, I gave the ship clearance and went ashore. The Customs Watcher was standing next to me, with a megaphone in his hand. He shouted through the roar of the wind to the Master, firstly "What is the name of your ship? Then "Where from?" The answer was "Portishead". The Customs Watcher wrote laboriously in his notebook "Port Said." The next shouted question from the Customs Watcher was "When did you leave, Captain?" The reply was, "Two hours ago." The Customs Watcher, who was as thick as a plank, turned to me with the words, "He came f.....g quick, didn't he?"

The ideal conditions rarely, if ever, happened. On many occasions several ships were blowing their whistles signifying the dock they would enter: one blast for West Dock, two for East Dock, three for Roath Dock, four for Queens Dock, and "cock-a-doodle-do" for tugs – all signals being made as the ships rounded Penarth Head. In the event of the simultaneous arrival of more than one ship, one would be boarded in the locks and the others after they had berthed.

This involved a cycle ride of several miles, in the night watches in the blackout. On a busy watch, probably 20 miles would be covered by bicycle in six hours, often in pitch darkness without lights, and usually in weather that varied from severe to bloody diabolical. The only reason why I put up with it was because I was not fit enough to follow my profession; and I needed the money desperately, to pay for our household expenses, modest though they were.

On one occasion, I had boarded and cleared a ship in the West Dock, when I heard a ship signalling by whistle for the Queens Dock, four blasts on the whistle. A strong westerly gale was blowing, with heavy rain and sleet squalls. I was trying to pedal as fast as I could along the road, wearing oilskins, a sou'wester pulled down over my eyes, bent double over the handlebars, and endeavouring to make laborious progress against the fierce wind, all in pitch darkness.

A violent gust blew me off course, and I veered off the road to starboard and rode at great speed down the stone pitching, through the barbed wire emplacements, and headlong into the tideway. Recovering from this, drenched, and festooned with mud and seaweed, I re-mounted my damaged bicycle and rode to the locks, only to find that the ship had moved to the top end of the Queens Dock. This was an additional journey of about a mile and a half, on a bicycle with a partly buckled front wheel. Then, after the watch was over, a journey of about four miles home, the wheels of the bicycle clanking at every turn of the pedals. I began to believe that it would have been an easier life if I had remained aboard my ship, vomiting my guts out.

During the period of time when I was working for the Cardiff Council Port Health Authority, I learned that my good friend and former shipmate, Frank Bernard Howe, had suffered the loss of his sixth ship. We had gone our separate ways when I left Frank Howe in the Woodstock Hotel in New York on 8 January 1943, and joined *Pilar de Larrinaga*. Very shortly afterwards, on 12 January 1943, he was detailed to join *Imperial Transport* as Third Mate. *Imperial Transport* was a motor ship built in 1931 and owned by a subsidiary of Houlder Brothers & Co. Ltd, with a gross registered tonnage of 8,022 and a deadweight cargo capacity of 12,460 tons.

Imperial Transport made a safe passage across the Atlantic, and paid off on 6 March 1943. Frank Howe and I were then ashore at the same time, and were offered berths as Third and Second Mates respectively of *Fort St. Nicholas*, then building in North Vancouver. This would have been an ideal berth for me, because the crew would have been standing by the ship not far from the home of my parents in North Vancouver. Regrettably, I was unable to join the crew for the journey to Vancouver, due to the fact that I was in school preparing for the examination for First Mate (Foreign Going Steamship). It was a great disappointment.

On her second voyage, *Fort St. Nicholas* was on passage from Hull to Naples via Augusta in Sicily, with war materials to support the landings on the Italian coast. The ship was torpedoed by U-410, on 15 February 1944, and sank close to the island of Capri. The Master, Captain Howard Pengelly, had been Third Mate of *Appledore* when I had spent two weeks aboard the ship in 1935 (before I joined in 1936). He and his crew of 48 and 14 gunners were rescued and landed at Salerno. Frank Howe never recovered sufficiently to return to sea service; and was discharged on 11 October 1944, certified as physically unfit for sea service. Like so many of us, after five years of almost constant strain, he was worn out.

My main ambition was to return to sea duty, and I underwent a number of further medical examinations, all without success. Then a breakthrough occurred in June 1944, after about six months of the purgatory of the work on Cardiff Docks. Following the invasion of the Normandy coast, I learned that officers were required for ships supporting the supply chain. I was examined by the Shipping Federation doctor, who pronounced that I was fit for sea service, subject to the condition that it was advisable to serve in conditions of a temperate climate. The semi tropical climate of North Africa had aggravated the bouts of sickness and vomiting. In view of the fact that the call was for volunteers to serve in ships serving the Normandy landing areas, he seemed satisfied, and gave me clearance to report to the Merchant Navy Officers Reserve Pool. They must have been desperate for officers then.

I was ordered to report at the offices of the Merchant Navy Officers' Reserve Pool, where Captain Skee was still behind his desk. I told him about the conditions suggested by the doctor. He told me that *Empire Spey* was loading in Barry, destined for the landing areas, and I was detailed to join the ship as First Mate. It was for me a wonderful bonus to be allocated a berth as First Mate, with a certificate of rank, at the age of 23.

During the period when I was ashore undergoing medical treatment, an event occurred which I learnt about many years later, when I became acquainted with Captain Pierre Payne, M.B.E. Pierre was born on 24 January 1915; and commenced his apprenticeship when he was sixteen years old in 1931. On the date of the event, he was the First Mate of

British Chivalry, a tanker in the fleet of the British Tanker Co. Ltd. We first met in 1960, when he was still serving as a Master at sea; and have been close friends for over forty years. I am indebted to Captain Pierre Payne, M.B.E. for allowing me to recount his experiences and to reproduce his log of this event.

British Chivalry was a large ship by the standards of the era, built in 1929: 7,118 gross registered tonnage, 11,220 tons cargo capacity, 456 feet long, 57 feet 1 inch beam, loaded draught of 27 feet 8 inches and designed loaded speed of 10 knots.

On 22 February 1944, the Japanese submarine I-37, commanded by the villainous Hajime Nakagawa, torpedoed *British Chivalry*, when on passage in the Indian Ocean from Melbourne to Abadan in ballast. There follow the accounts of the event.

I have recorded the experiences of Captain Pierre Payne, M.B.E. exactly as typed by him, and have not entered any punctuation marks or amendments in the script. I believe that it is a remarkable story. His experiences are similar to my own, but in many ways different. The main difference is that the lifeboats of *British Chivalry* encountered moderate weather conditions for all except one day during their time adrift in the Indian Ocean, whereas the lifeboats of *Start Point* had been beset by weather approaching tumultuous conditions for almost the whole time they were adrift.

Copy of the entry in the Official Log of British Chivalry
10-30 a.m., 22nd February 1944, Indian Ocean
Latitude 00-50 S,, Longitude 68-00 E. approximately

This is to certify that on February 22nd 1944 at sea in the Indian Ocean at 10-30 a.m., the vessel received a direct hit by torpedo in the engine room. Something in the water aft had been reported to the bridge a few minutes previously and the Third Officer sighted the track of two torpedoes approaching the starboard quarter. He immediately attempted to take avoiding action. One torpedo passed harmlessly astern but the other struck in way of the engine room immediately below the galley. An attempt to send a radio message was made but it was found that the apparatus was beyond repair.

An attempt to ascertain the extent of the damage was made but within three or four minutes of the explosion the engine room filled with water sufficient to cover the upper platforms. The two after boats were rendered useless and the crew came aft amidships and orders were given to clear away two midship boats and four rafts on main decks.

After considering the condition of the vessel, which had been rendered totally incapable of proceeding under her own power, the Master decided to abandon ship temporarily in order to prevent further loss of life should another attack be made. Although very much down by the stern, the vessel did not appear to be going to founder and it was thought we might return aboard later.

The two boats with all survivors left the ship and as they drew away the enemy submarine was sighted coming to the surface. One of the boats, a motor boat in charge of the Chief Officer passed the boat under oars in charge of the Master and received instructions to round up the rafts, which were floating away. About five minutes later the submarine commenced shelling and according to reports the shots were in line with the Master's boat. Later, attention appeared to be made more of shelling the ship and not until the submarine was within about a quarter of a mile of the ship did she score any direct hits.

About 20 rounds in all were fired and the ship finally sank by a third torpedo on her port side. The ship finally sank at about 11-30 a.m.

During the sinking of the ship a roll call was made and casualties were found to be:

S. Morrison	*4th Engineer*	*No. 24 in Agreement*
J. Gallagher	*Fireman*	*No. 6 in Agreement (From 1.2.44)*
J. Sayers	*Ships' Cook*	*No. 41 in Agreement*
K. Bagshaw	*Apprentice*	*No. 6 (on page 7 of Agreement)*
R. O'Neil	*Fireman*	*No 58 in Agreement*
P. Byrne	*Fireman*	*No. 32 in Agreement*
G. Robbins	*Galley Boy*	*No. 40 in Agreement*

After sinking the vessel the submarine then opened fire on the two lifeboats with light machine gun fire. A white flag of truce was displayed from the Master's boat and machine-gunning ceased. Attempts to communicate by semaphore were made. The submarine closed the boats and waved us alongside. It was noted that the submarine was manned by Japanese. They intimated that they required the Master to board her, which he did. The boats were then ordered to carry on and the submarine moved off.

After the boats had been proceeding for about 5 minutes in company, the submarine suddenly altered course and steered for them and, on passing, heavy machine-gunning of the boats commenced. Most of the crew dived into the water and some lay down in the boats. The machine-gunning lasted until about 2 p.m., when one boat containing radio equipment etc. had been sunk and the other left in a sinking condition. The submarine then made off in a S.W'ly direction.

Strenuous efforts were then made by the surviving members of the crew to bale out the remaining boat and at about 5 p.m. had been made in a condition to be of use. Rafts and survivors in the water were then gathered together and a consultation was held among the officers. Another roll call was made and the names of those killed by machine-gunning were as follows:

W. Dickinson	Chief Engineer	No 21. in Agreement
C. Kennedy	1st Radio Officer	No. 5 in Agreement
T. Beighton	Deck Hand	No. 47 in Agreement
B. Penfold	Deck Hand	No. 83 in Agreement
D. Merrill	Deck Hand	No. 87 in Agreement
J. Mitchell	Greaser	No. 3 in Agreement
C. Mann	2nd Engineer	No. 22 in Agreement
C. Cooksley	Chief Steward	No. 35 in Agreement
R. Saunders	Deck Hand	No. 65 in Agreement
M. King	Deck Hand	No. 40 in Agreement
C. Keneally	A.B.	No. 5 in Agreement
J. Gillan	Greaser	No. 32 in Agreement

Wounded were as follows:

J. Sloan,	Deck Hand,	No. 77. Lacerations, from bullet right shoulder under chin and back of neck.
J. Taylor,	Asst. Steward,	No. 37. Bullet wounds in chest and right arm.
P. Hesnan,	D.B.S.,	No. 2. Lacerations from bullet under chin.
L. Morris,	A.B.,	No. 18. Lacerations from bullet in hand and bullet hole in right forearm.
L. Abbott,	Deck Hand,	No. 70. Bullet in buttock near anus – bullet extracted in boat.

Others had various cuts and abrasions

After considering the chances of rescue it was decided that it would be hopeless to remain in the area. The boat in company with one raft and all available provisions moved off in an attempt to make land using the most favourable conditions of wind, weather and currents etc. Plans were made for making roughly a 1500-mile passage and a scale of rations calculated accordingly.

At 11-30 p.m. on 23rd February 1944 Able Seaman L. Morris, No. 18 on Agreement suffering from wounds as described above lost his life by drowning. His wounds were of such a character that he had been rendered insane and efforts were made by the survivors on the raft to restrain him. He proved to be too violent to hold and during the struggling evaded the others, jumped overboard and disappeared from view before rescue could be effected.

On Friday 25th February, the engine rendered useless by seawater was dumped overboard and the occupants of the raft were transferred to the boat.

The subsequent proceedings of this report are such as might be expected during a period of great hardship and suffering of 38 men cast adrift for 37 days in an overcrowded boat. During this period, morale in the boat was excellent and the conduct and bearing of the men at all times cheerful and courageous.

Special mention may here be made of three men, Mr. J. Edwards, 3rd Engineer, No. 23 on Agreement for calm bearing and cheerful influence on all. Petty Officer Frank Alder, Donkeyman, No. 28 on Agreement for valuable work rendered in first aid and the care of the sick and wounded. Able Seaman Harry Belcher, No. 8 on Agreement (from 1.2.44) for his outstanding ability and brilliant seamanship.

On Wednesday 29th March at 1114 G.M.T. the boat was sighted by M.V. Delane and rescue was effected.

Signed P.Payne 1st Mate
R.W. Mountain 2nd Mate
2.4.44 10.00 a.m. aboard M.V. Delane at sea

This is to certify that on this day it was found in questioning various members of the surviving crew of this vessel that G. Robbins, Galley Boy, No. 40 in agreement was killed by machine gunning in lifeboats instead of torpedoing as previous entry dated 2nd April 1944 entered wrongly on that date. See page 53 line 27.

Date of this entry 4.4.44

Log of the period adrift in lifeboats
British Chivalry
24 February 1944 to 29 March 1944
Kept by Pierre Payne, M.B.E., First Mate

The British Chivalry an oil tanker of 4,237 Nett Registered Tons carried about 9,500 tons of cargo and belonged to the British Tanker Company, a subsidiary of Anglo Persian Oil Company now the B.P.

Sailing from Greenock under the command of Captain Walter Hill of Dublin at the beginning of July 1943 after a voyage across the North Atlantic was posted to the Middle East with the intention that she would later proceed to the Far Eastern theatre of war.

After carrying a cargo from Abadan in the Persian Gulf to South Africa, orders were received to load at Abadan for Melbourne where, after discharge, the ship was overhauled and drydocked as a matter of routine.

Early in February 1944 the British Chivalry left Melbourne in ballast but carried about 450 tons of bagged grain for her destination again Abadan. Some passengers including two ladies were barred from travelling at the last moment and later it was felt with great relief that they were not allowed to accompany us.

After an uneventful journey of about 14 days the ship was well out in the middle of the Indian Ocean and nearing the equator. The track was almost due North and well off the direct track from Australia to the Gulf.

During the day of 21st February a radio message purporting to come from the Commander-in-Chief, Colombo was received requesting our position. This in itself was not surprising but Mr. C. Kennedy, the Chief Radio Officer, a native of Caithness in Scotland, appeared to have great difficulty in contacting the radio station in Colombo. The transmitter, a spark-gap type, caused enough noise around the ship to keep all hands aware that he was transmitting, a practice normally prohibited during an ocean passage such as we were making. This proceeded to well into the evening at 10-00 p.m. I personally went to the radio room to enquire when he was going to cease. We already knew that enemy submarines were in the area and we later wondered whether the original message had perhaps emanated from one, which had possibly obtained our codes and was using them to identify us. Later, possibly early next morning, a message was received ordering us to cease zigzagging and to proceed on our course as direct as possible.

It was with some misgivings that as Chief Officer, when daylight broke on the morning of the 22nd February 1944 I explained to the quar-

termaster that orders had been received to cease zigzagging. The sea was calm and visibility was perfect. I came off watch at 8-00 a.m. and handed over to the Third Officer. Mr. John Dahl was very concerned at this obviously dangerous procedure of maintaining a straight course.

At breakfast at 8-30 a.m. – a lovely meal of bacon eggs and chips – an altercation blew up with the Captain regarding the incident of the night before and the steering of the straight course. Mr. Dickinson, the Chief Engineer, thoroughly agreed with my own view. The feeling became so strained that I pushed my own breakfast aside not feeling able to eat it. That action was regretted later.

At 9-00 a.m. the Boatswain, Mr. Geoge Dunsby, came to me with a request that during the morning he should go down to the after cofferdam which separated the cargo carrying space from the engine room and use a hose to wash out any traces of sediment which might be at the bottom. As this compartment had been well washed for going into drydock in Melbourne it was felt that there would be no oil and the sediment would not leave any track. After setting the men to work, the operation to wash the cofferdam was commenced. The boatswain tried desperately to get me to allow him to go down to the bottom but I felt it was too dangerous in view of what had already occurred.

Shortly before 10-30 a.m. I heard a shout. Frantically I hauled on the lifeline, which had been secured in such a manner that he was only below the deck level and shouted to him to come out.

His body was only half way over the hatch coaming when a torpedo exploded in the engine room only feet away. We were covered in rubbish thrown up. By the time we had disconnected the lifeline I saw the Captain coming along the flying bridge and he called to ask whether I had seen the damage. As I had not, I climbed the ladder to the poop deck and running aft to the engine room door I saw that the engine room was already full of water. The starboard after door had been blown away and one of the four deck apprentices, Kenneth Bagshaw, who had been painting the boat was never seen again. Neither was the cook Mr. J. Sayers, who had apparently rushed from the galley to his room below to collect his gear. Two rafts were being released from the after shrouds as I returned amidships.

As I reached the lower bridge I noted the Radio Officers attacking the teak door to the radio room with a fire axe. Apparently it had jammed in the explosion and the radio equipment was wrecked. The ship was in a position 00-50 S 68-00 E and about 300 miles west of Addu Attoll where an R.A.F. base was situated and we feel sure it would have picked up any distress message transmitted.

The two boats amidships were being launched and my own on the port side suffered a nasty gash in the bottom when someone too hurriedly let go the falls. Whilst repairing the damage a number of cans of petrol were loaded into the boat, as this was the only one to have a motor. Having lowered the boat to the water I nipped over to the starboard side to enquire whether the ship was being abandoned and received permission to do so from Captain Hill from his vantage point in his boat already some 50 yards away. Our crew then descended and we cast off, proceeding forwards, and rounding the stem, met up with the other boat. It was then that Mr. Mountain, the 2nd Officer shouted to me "February again, Mate!" The reason for this was that he had remembered that February was my unlucky month. In February 1940 I had been in British Triumph when it was mined in the North Sea and in February 1942 I had been in the British Motorist when that ship was bombed and sunk in Port Darwin.

A roll call was taken and six men were found to be missing. They comprised the 4th Engineer, Chief Cook, three firemen and one deck apprentice. Just then the submarine surfaced and after a short while commenced shelling the ship. Several shots fell close to us and we wondered whether that was caused by their bracketing or just merely bad shots. Eventually it circled the ship and sank it with another torpedo.

Attention was then turned on us in the boats and very neatly tracer bullets could be seen coming towards us. We all huddled down rather frightened. These were the Japs we had heard about! Frequently I heard the Captain calling from the other boat. He knew that I was quite good at semaphore and he was telling me to ask them what it was they wanted us to do. Frankly, I was at a loss as to how to semaphore in Japanese: should I stand on my head and waggle my feet? In any case it didn't look too healthy to expose oneself to this sort of action. However, I stood up and started to wave my arms. Many tracer bullets shot past me but I couldn't see each four between each tracer so it didn't look too bad. In all fairness, when I started to send the message "What do you want us to do?" the shooting ceased.

Perhaps they were wondering, "What sort of an idiot is this standing up to be shot at?" Perhaps it took them by surprise but I got away with it.

All this time the submarine had been drawing closer and now we could hear them calling "Kapitan. We want the Kapitan." So waving to them we turned our boat and I went over to the Captain's boat in which he was standing up. I asked him if he wished me to go aboard myself and tell them a story of him not being there but Captain Hill said, "No. I'll go. Give me a tow." We therefore towed his boat over to the submarine, left it along-

side, and backed off to about a hundred yards distant. We saw the Captain climb aboard and soon after we saw his boat being rowed towards us. As they drew near the 2nd Officer shouted to us that we were to take them in tow and go off in a Westerly direction. We took their painter and set off steering approximately due West. We noted that the submarine had turned to head Eastwards.

We had been travelling for about four or five minutes when suddenly amongst the wreckage a figure jumped off a raft and commenced swimming towards us. Seeing this, I altered a few degrees and ordered the engines to be stopped and gave instructions for those at the forward end of the boat to haul him in. The man turned out to be the 3rd Officer Mr. John Dahl who later gave me a satisfactory explanation of why he had gone off by himself. His mother, sister and brother lived in Norway and he feared repercussions on them if he should be taken prisoner.

As he was being pulled over the bow, Mr. Dunsby, the boatswain, sitting near me at the stern suddenly cried out, "Look out, the submarine!" Glancing over my shoulder I saw the submarine spinning like a top, and, heading towards us, came up at good speed. Hurriedly I told the others, "If he opens fire, everybody over the side!" We were all wearing lifejackets so non-swimmers would not sink. Just as we imagined, as he came up to the other boat he opened fire with both machine guns. In our boat we went over the side like a school of porpoises. In the other boat, which bore the initial burst they were not so quick. Indeed, I don't think that they had decided to do anything and consequently had more people killed. Coming on towards us the two machine guns on his deck blazed away again. We saw a man with a camera on a tripod filming the incident.

The time was now about 12 o'clock noon. Drawing ahead, the submarine turned and came at us again and as he passed, once more blazed at us. He turned again and raking both boats with both guns as he passed. Cruising backwards and forwards he made every effort to destroy both boats and men. We played hide and seek with him using the boat as a shelter, dodging around it each time he passed. After about an hour and a half I realised we were playing a losing battle, if battle it could be called, certainly a one-sided effort, so I decided to pass the word around for the men to gradually clear away from the boats and get as far as possible away from it at the same time to play "dead" in the water.

As he passed we would sink as far as our lifejackets would allow. We would loll about and keep face down. Actually, my eardrums ached with the crack of bullets flying past my head so I must have been a very lucky soul.

Evidently spotting a cluster of men in the water it appeared to several of us that the submarine deliberately turned to bring his propellers in amongst them. This was done a number of times and several must have been killed in this shameful tactic. Things were getting very bad indeed; not from exhaustion but a dreadful feeling that our adversary did not intend to leave many alive. During this episode one man paddled slowly past me and called, "Hullo! I thought you were dead long ago!" "No!" I called back, "Still alive and well!" Shortly after, I passed another man who was looking towards me quite cheerfully, smiling in the middle of all this torment. I called to him the same as the other man had done to me, "Thought you were dead long ago!" The words were hardly out of my mouth when he rolled over and I could see there was no back to his head. I saw another man who was still in the Captain's boat suddenly jump up and scream for his mother as a hail of bullets mowed him down.

Then, suddenly, all was quiet. The time, registered by the Boatswain's watch was 2 p.m. and the submarine had disappeared from view. Perhaps he felt that he had wiped us all out. Certainly, he had used up a lot of ammunition but remarkable as it may seem, he had only killed a third of the number who survived. Thirteen men died in that onslaught and 39 were alive although one man died later from severe wounds received. It was Able Seaman L. Morris.

Immediately we realised the submarine had departed the uppermost thought in my mind was "Survival". We hadn't really a sporting chance before the shooting but here now it was somewhat desperate to say the least! My own boat was still afloat, the kapok in the buoyancy tanks doing a splendid job. The other boat sank as we watched. Unfortunately the 3rd Radio Officer didn't realise he was letting go a splendid chance of us being picked up. The emergency radio was in that boat but he was only a very young man and he could be forgiven after all he had been through for allowing it to go down with the boat. So we concentrated on my own boat. Gathering as many together as possible, one man was told to get in the boat and search for the bucket and start baling, another was told to find a bag of plugs and oakum for stopping up the bullet holes and the rest of us kept diving to plug them. I believe about seventeen were found and filled with something. We worked like beavers and at long last, after three hours, it was now 5 p.m. we had what we called a seaworthy boat. True, I doubt whether it would have been passed by a Board of Trade Inspector but there weren't any B.O.T. Inspectors there to worry about!

The first job to be done was to call a muster of those surviving. As we did this Mr. C. Cookesley, the Chief Steward, died of wounds and was buried at once. There were 39 men remaining. We then decided on a plan of action. No message had been got away so there was no good point served in trying to remain where we were. The nearest mainland, Africa, was about 1200 miles away. Our weather map indicated that we should be just north enough to be inside the drift to the West. Putting 10 men on a raft in charge of the 2nd Officer, the others were gathered into the boat. Darkness would soon be upon us, the weather was calm and the sea smooth. Actually we were in the Doldrums of which one hears so much but seldom sees. Taking it in turns we rowed westward all night towing the raft but when daylight came it was obvious we should not be able to keep this up for long.

Able Seaman L. Morris who had been shot through the head and through the forearm became very delirious and eventually jumped off the raft where the 9 other men had been trying to look after him. He was the only man to die on our journey.

Our boat, which, as mentioned before, had an engine in it, had been thought as being our saviour but all attempts at starting the engine now proved fruitless. Having been submerged it was completely unusable despite the efforts of Mr. J. Edwards, the 3rd Engineer. After deciding it would be of no further use, a plan was evolved whereby if we could dismantle it we could utilise the space available and bring the men on the raft into the boat thus keeping everyone together. I had heard of this before when boats and rafts drifted apart. I was determined that if one was to be saved, all would be saved. Our bag of tools was pretty pitiful, however the main objective was to loosen the holding down bolts and these were pretty hefty affairs. By dint of hammering with the screwdriver being used as a chisel, all six were unscrewed. I would imagine the nuts were at least two inches in diameter. The next job was to get rid of the engine. Weighing 5 cwt. Mr. Thorneycroft, the maker, would have wrung his hands to see the excited group, which let go and watched it plummet through the beautifully clear sea.

Getting rid of the engine was a major step forward in our survival. All were now in the boat. True, it was very cramped. I think I am right in saying it was only 28 feet long by about seven feet wide, possibly less than that. We had three severely injured men. Young Taylor, a boy of only 17 years had a gaping hole in his chest and later, in hospital, a bullet was extracted from under his armpit. He was thrilled to bits to show me the bullet. The Pump Man, an Australian lad had terrible lacerations to his throat. Indeed, whilst swimming in the water I had told this man to hold the flesh up to his throat as the windpipe was exposed. A third man, Sloan, an Army gunner was also terribly injured. The ball and socket of his shoul-

der was exposed through a gaping wound down his arm, there was a furrow across the front of his head and a hole in the back of his neck. Another, more fortunate than the rest of the wounded complained of a pain in his rear parts. After a quick examination I reached for the pliers and deftly withdrew the offending item, a bullet which had lodged near the anus, which he evidently had received when diving in the water to avoid being hit. The man was as happy as a sand boy and loudly proclaimed he was the only one in the boat with two holes in his behind, or words to that effect.

Watches were set. A deck officer and an A.B. on together took the tiller for one-hour spells. Three men were appointed lookouts forward in charge of the Carpenter. The remainder had to sit as best as they could in the waist of the boat. Canopies were rigged over the middle section and the sail hoisted. Oars were placed fore and aft along the middle of the boat, partly to let the men rest on it and partly to keep the two sides of the boat separated so that in the event of an emergency one side would not crowd over to the other side. The freeboard was about ten inches so too much listing could not be tolerated. We had gathered as many stores from the raft as we could find and a steady scheme of rationing was compiled. I had calculated on a month's voyage. After that I would have to plan again. For the first fortnight the rations were as follows:

Breakfast. 8-30 a.m. 1 Horlicks tablet 2 $^{1/2}$ oz. water
Dinner. 1-00 p.m. 1 Horlicks tab. 1 chocolate tab. 2 $^{1/2}$ oz. Water.
Tea. 5-30 p.m. 1 biscuit (the size of a Marie tea biscuit)
1/3 oz. (2 spoons) Pemmican. 2 $^{1/2}$ oz. Water.

During the shooting up of the boats most of the biscuit containers had been pierced and therefore, as the boat filled with water the biscuits in those cans were soaked in seawater. Later, after it rained, by placing a pile of biscuits on top of the canopy, a lot of the salt was taken out of them but I used this much to help out. Using the flat top of the first aid kit tin, about 9 ins. long by about 4 ins. wide I mixed this biscuit with half a tin of Pemmican and very carefully cut the mixture into 38 very equal parts and spread each part on top of half a biscuit. They were very equal parts when one realises that 74 other eyes were watching!

Thereafter, for 22 days the rations were:

Breakfast. 2 Horlicks tablets, 1 spoon (1/6 oz.) Pemmican, 2 $^{1/2}$ oz. Water.
Dinner. 1 Horlicks tablet, 1 spoon Pemmican. (3 or 4 times a week)

	and always on Sundays we made beasts of ourselves. 1 choco-
	late tablet.
Tea.	*1 Horlicks tablet, 1 portion mixed paste on 1/2 biscuit,*
	1 chocolate tablet, 2 1/2 oz. Water.

After 36 days adrift rations had to be cut to 1 Horlicks tablet for breakfast, no chocolate for dinner and no Horlicks tablet for tea. I estimated then that we could last for another 28 days. Advice had been given in survival kits that it was not necessary to restrict the taking of rations as if one got into a boat one had an 80% chance of being picked up. Unfortunately our chances were by no means as good and I still feel that those rations were just sufficient to live.

We all became terribly weak. For the first fortnight we used to go over the side swimming but the strict rule was that the boat would not turn back for anybody. Strict discipline had to be maintained. In fact our discipline was so strict it would probably be frowned on by people ashore. However, we had a fair idea that we were better off than those poor souls in the hands of the enemy. If a man "accidentally" dropped a tablet into the bilges, he would not receive a tablet for himself. Those tablets had to be passed by hand right up the length of the boat and the men at the bow expected to receive theirs. The sun blazed down upon us and we were thankful for the canopies even though it was awfully hot under them.

We had no rain for the first six days, which brought us to the 1st of March, to Welshmen, St. David's Day. As the 3rd Engineer came from Carmarthen and I lived in Cardiff, it was decided after breakfast that he and I should stand up in the boat and sing "Mae Hen Wlad Fy Nhadau" the Welsh National Anthem. It was burning with the heat from the sun but we got to our feet and gave a jolly good rendering despite our parched throats. When we stood up there was not a cloud in the sky. We had not sat down but a few minutes when the heavens seemed to open and we were deluged with rain. Everybody was allowed to drink his fill and we caught rainwater in empty tins we had saved and thereafter, whenever it rained we had what we wanted and any over was put in the water breakers to conserve our resources. Water from the metal containers gathered from the raft was very bitter, rainwater was rather flat but the water from the wooden casks or breakers tasted like fresh spring water.

Each noon we endeavoured to "fix" our position but one day the Boatswain's watch stopped and we had to set it again by the rising sun as we recorded this event each day. Nerves began to become frayed and arguments broke out.

We all talked about food and what we would eat when we were picked up, preferably by an American ship, which would have plenty of food aboard. Our swimming over the side ceased when one day, looking like a great mud bank astern a tremendous shark followed our boat for a while. We got rid of our unwelcome visitor by putting out the oars and rowing discretely away. We saw a whale blowing and again sheered away from this entertainment. I manufactured a net out of the copper piping that led the fuel to the engine. Constructing a framework, I used a skein of twine to make the mesh. Fish were all around us and lying alongside the boat. When all was ready I quietly put the net in the water and scooped up three fish. They were delightful eaten raw but they were small fish but never mind, they were skinned and cut up into 38 equal parts. I think we were all reminded of the story in the Bible when Christ fed so many on so little. Porpoises would jump out of the water and spray us continually with their splashing. Clearly they were enjoying it but we did not mind so much because we knew they would keep away the sharks and porpoises are friendly towards humans. We contemplated what we should do with one if it fell into the boat. I shudder now to think of the damage it would have done.

One night a squall struck us. With it came a strong wind. We used to lower the sail at night so that gave us no trouble but as the waves increased we had to get out the sea anchor and lie to it to keep heading into the weather. As it was, some water was shipped which had to be bailed out. With all this going on a fight broke out. Being prepared for such an emergency I grabbed the only torch we had and shone it onto those concerned. It did the trick: everybody stopped in their tracks and there were yells of "Put out that light!" In a very loud voice I told them I would settle everything I the morning. When daylight broke all were very subdued knowing full well that I meant what I said. I waited until 8-00 a.m. and then held what must indeed have been termed a "court martial." Five troublesome ones were each made to come separately to me in the after end. Each was told his faults and each was told the penalty if it happened again. I knew that I had the backing of every other one in the boat and at least two were told that should they commit the same offence again it would be "over the side." It was really meant. I don't know how I should have fared had I had to put it into practice. The Authorities in the U.K. would probably have taken stern action against me but when needs must the Devil drives. There were a lot of other men's lives at stake. By the Grace of God it never had to be put into effect. This took about an hour and I thought it was ended but one naval rating who had been an *optician in civvy street wished to speak and he suggested that instead of quarrelling all the time, why not ask God's help in the form of prayer and would I as Officer in Charge please lead them in just that. I must confess this took me rather aback but not to turn them down I suggested a show of hands of those who wished me to do this. Every man put his hand up so here I was now, with a parson's job on my hands and as tough a congregation as any parson ever had!*

I thought it over quickly and said, "Right, I'll lead you all in prayer each morning before breakfast and when we are picked up. (It was never if we are picked up but when we are picked up.) I will lead you all to say the Lord's Prayer after me." I continued to say that it was all very well to pray now, but remember to do the same for the rest of their lives.

The Lord's Prayer was said, and each day before breakfast a short prayer was given. Eventually I said, "Now we'll have breakfast" and a great roar of delight went up.

This is an outline of the manner in which we existed. Then one day, on the 29th March to be precise, during the afternoon, hot and calm, Chippy, the Carpenter, was sitting talking to Able Seaman Arthur Light. Chippy was facing aft and Arthur was facing forwards. Quite casually, Chippy said to Arthur, "There's a ship over there." So Arthur said nothing. Again Chippy said, "There's a ship over there." Arthur said, "Don't be daft you're seeing things." Chippy said, "There's a ship over there and I'm not daft." So Arthur looked over his shoulder and said, "So there is." Then lightness dawned on him.

This was the moment I had been waiting for. Immediately I drew my whistle and blew it as pandemonium broke out. Fair enough, they all went about their tasks as they had been instructed. In fact it would seem as though it was quite a natural thing for a ship to be there. Two got out oars, one each side and started rowing. Another reached for the smoke floats the first of which was damp. Another took the hand rockets and holding one up allowed it to fire. It was rather a pity that the A.B. whose job this was failed to count five separate stars and after the fourth I was looking down the barrel. Knocking it out of his hand the fifth star shot into the sea. The canopies came down and also the sail. The canopies still covered most of those in the middle of the boat. It must have been a good ten minutes before I was able to turn and look at the ship. Then my heart fell. I could not recognise this outline yet something nagged at the back of my mind that I had indeed seen it before but where?

During our period adrift we had all come up with the same idea that if a Japanese submarine or ship should appear we would all go over the side and drown rather than be taken aboard. I told the men that I did not recognise this ship and reminded them of what we had agreed. Everybody was still of the same mind. As we rowed closer, standing up near the mast I shouted out "What nationality?" Men were standing alongside the rail and back came the answer "British!" When we heard it we nearly all went mad with joy. American ships and their food were forgotten. Here was a British ship to pick us up after all we had endured.

The ship was the Delane, one of Lamport & Holt's half way on a voyage from Calcutta to Cape Town. It appeared that somewhere about 3-00 p.m. the 2nd Officer on the bridge had spotted what he thought was a periscope. (Just as I had visualised) and sounding the alarm bells had rung for emergency full ahead and with increased speed the engines had stopped. They had manned their guns and indeed the anti submarine gun was loaded with shell. It appears that they had seen us long before we saw them. The Chief Officer, Mr. Jones from North Wales, went to the bridge and having been shipwrecked himself through enemy action and took a pair of glasses and persuaded the Captain that it was not a submarine but a lifeboat.

As we climbed up the rope ladder one after the other the 2nd and 3rd Officers on the bridge became somewhat alarmed at the number coming out from under the canopies. It could well have been a decoy with a boarding party coming to seize the ship. However, it soon became apparent that we were not invaders.

We had an Australian seaman, Harry Belcher, a tough fellow and an excellent seaman. He held back and when all but us two had climbed the ladder he said to me, "Up you go, Mr. Mate." "No", I said. "That is my privilege to be last up." He tried hard but in the end said, "Well you know that half bottle of brandy left over from the night we had the storm." "Oh, yes," I said. "Go on then, take it." So Harry laid his hands on the very place it was kept and withdrawing the cork put it to his lips and drank the lot. He then scrambled up the ladder like a lark.

Up on deck the climb had beaten us and we couldn't walk, only crawl. Presently the Boatswain crawled over to me and reminded me of what I had promised I would do on the ship that picked us up. Without any more ado I called out "Every man down on his knees and repeat after me." Then very sadly and gratefully we all said the Lord's Prayer. Never could it have been said with more meaning.

We were all treated very well on board the Delane and later \I remembered the nagging at the back of my mind when I first saw it. The Delane had been next to us in the British Triumph on our first convoy from

Freetown to the U.K. in late 1939.

Ten days later, with a change of orders, the Delane landed us at Durban where we rested until a passage home came our way. Four days after being landed in Durban I weighed myself. I was four stones four pounds! So we all must have been close to starvation when we were picked up.

Whilst on board the Delane the Chief Officer had our boat repaired and having it swung out on a derrick we used it for ourselves when lifeboat drill was held. It must be remembered that we almost outnumbered their own crew and we were quite happy to use it for ourselves.

When we landed at Durban the local people were most kind and we all had a very nice time. Many invited us to their homes for long weekends and we could not wish for better treatment and kindness shown to us. Our lifeboat had been landed when the Delane sailed and although we did not see it for ourselves, it appears that it was placed on a trailer and towed around to various parts of the country and raised a considerable amount of money for War Charity efforts.

Many months later after I had returned home and then rejoined another ship I happened to be in Birkenhead. A gentleman came into my room and laughing fit to bust told me how a ship down the river had come in, and of the story they were telling about some survivors they had picked up and the man in charge had made them all get down on their knees and recite the Lords Prayer. "Of course, you can take that with a pinch of salt", he said. I asked him if the name of the ship was Delane. "Yes", he replied, "it was". "How do you know?" By the time I had finished with him he was dying to rush out of my room."

I found the account to be fascinating. It emphasises indelibly the value of the draconian training regime under which Merchant Navy officers learned their profession, and the value of such training in times of danger, difficulty and emergency. It is the story of a brave and resourceful officer.

21

THE WAR AT SEA: EMPIRE SPEY

27 JUNE– 16 OCTOBER 1944

The Master of *Empire Spey* was Captain B.J. Rush, an elderly seaman, but an excellent commander. We developed a cordial and fruitful relationship. As a young officer in my first berth as second in command, I could not have served under a better Master. Neither of the junior officers was qualified, and from the beginning, they were an unknown quantity.

After I joined the ship, I learned that I had been misled about the destination of *Empire Spey*. We were to proceed to Augusta in Sicily, to support the military operations in Italy. It was too late to do anything about it; but I was so happy to be on board ship again, and away from the awful tedium of the work as an Assistant Port Health Officer. I would take my chances with the Mediterranean weather, as the lesser of two evils.

Empire Spey was built in 1929 under the name *Blairspey*, for Northern Navigation Co. Ltd, a subsidiary of George Nisbet & Co. Ltd of Glasgow. With a gross registered tonnage of 4,155 and a deadweight cargo capacity of 6,800 tons, her leading dimensions were: length 385 feet 3 inches, beam 51 feet 3 inches, loaded draught 22 feet 11 inches and her designed loaded speed 10 knots. *Blairspey* was a typical "three island" ship of her time with long well decks fore and aft. The ship was an element in the ill-fated convoy SC7 of 34 ships that left Sidney Cape Breton on 5 October 1940, and suffered severe attacks by a pack of U-Boats, losing 20 ships. Several torpedoes fired by U-100 and U-101 struck *Blairspey*. The fore part of the ship sank, taking 18 men with it, but the after part remained afloat, due to the cargo of timber. The after part was towed to the Clyde and beached; and subsequently was married to a new bow section in February 1942.

S.S. Empire Spey, built in 1929 as *S.S. Blairspey,* 4155 gross registered tonnage
Ship depicted in wartime livery in North Africa, either *Bone* or *Sfax*
(Photograph by National Maritime Museum)

The ship was re-named *Empire Spey* under the Ministry of War Transport, and managed by her original owners. She was a handy little ship, with exceptional sea-keeping quality, particularly in a following wind and sea.

When I joined the ship the loading of cargo had commenced, mainly Welsh steam coal. We also loaded food, stores, ammunition, and drinking water. The Master ordered me to trim the ship 12 inches by the stern. We loaded about 6,000 tons of coal in the four lower holds, and the remainder of the cargo in the 'tween decks. It was my first attempt at being in sole charge of loading and trimming a ship, and I was happy that the ship was down to her marks and trimmed by the stern, as ordered by the Master.

Shortly after putting to sea, the Master called me to his cabin for a conference. He was not happy with the abilities of the junior officers, and asked for my opinion. He had decided that they should be under supervision when on watch. I agreed with him. It was decided that we would double the bridge watches, and work watch and watch, four hours on and four hours off – just as a precaution. The Second Mate shared a watch with the Master, and the Third Mate shared with me.

CONVOY OS82

Empire Spey joined convoy OS82 of 26 ships on 1 July 1944. The convoy amalgamated with a Mediterranean convoy, and made passage to Augusta in Sicily, via Gibraltar and Algiers, arriving on 23 July 1944. The ship anchored in the bay. There we received orders to act as a supply ship for a flotilla of Royal Navy escort trawlers of the "Dance" class. The supply of the trawlers was my responsibility for the following two months. The names of the trawlers were *H.M.S. Waltz, Foxtrot, Quickstep, Gavotte, Minuet, Tango,* and other names of dances.

We rigged the port and starboard derricks of Nos. 1 and 2, 4 and 5 holds outboard, set the winches in single gear and rove rope runners through the derrick head blocks and down to the drum ends of the winches for whipping the coal aboard the trawlers. We were provided with about a hundred wicker baskets to transfer the bunker coal from ship to ship.

After the trawler or trawlers moored alongside, the seamen donned dirty gear and worked in the holds shovelling the coal into the baskets, and aboard their own ships, trimming the coal into the bunkers. We could, and did on some occasions, accommodate four trawlers alongside at the same time. Speed of discharge was of the essence, and we improved the turn round of our little fleet substantially with experience. We also supplied ammunition, stores and water. Most of these small naval craft were manned by R.N.R. ex fisherman, and commanded by an R.N.R. ex trawler Skipper. They were fine seamen, and we developed a friendly relationship with them.

The work kept me constantly on duty when we had the little naval craft alongside. It was vitally important that four holds were available at all times, in case we had to supply four trawlers at a time. Therefore, the amount of available bunker coal had to be monitored carefully to maintain consistently adequate quantities in each hold. The trim of the ship was also an important element in the calculations. This responsibility could not be delegated to un-certificated and relatively inexperienced junior officers. Within about three weeks, we had exhausted our bunker coal supplies; and were ordered to the Sardinian port of Antioco, to load a further cargo.

During our stay at anchor off Augusta, there was a serious accident to one of the young gunners. As he left the door of the after accommodation, the seamen were sliding the heavy steel-shod hatch boards off the poop towards No. 5 hatch. A hatch board struck the gunner on the head just above the scalp, and virtually tore his scalp from his head in a huge flap. With blood pouring from the ghastly injury, he was brought forward and I examined him in the room that we used as a hospital. The Cingalese steward was endeavouring to staunch the bleeding. He and I worked together in attempts to render first aid. We had no anaesthetic; so as a substitute, we gave the gunner a half a bottle of brandy, which rendered him quite inebriated. I stood alongside him, and as the steward and I attempted to shave the hair from the flap of scalp, the injured gunner gripped my leg and asked, "Am I going to die, sir?" We managed to shave the scalp, and swabbed the bleeding scalp and flap of skin with hydrogen peroxide, which created a froth of blood and bubbles. The steward then handed me the sutures, and we put in about 30 stitches, starting from the nape of the neck, over the top of the head to the forehead, and around over the crown of the head again, to the nape of the neck on the opposite side. By this time the gunner had fainted, and we finished off with a substantial length of bandage wrapped around his head. Both of us were covered with blood and perspiration. The Cingalese steward was a gem.

The Master had been ashore. When he returned he inspected our handiwork, which he deemed satisfactory, under the circumstances. However, as a precaution the gunner was taken ashore in a jolly boat, where he was seen by an army doctor in a military clearing station, and given an anti tetanus injection. The wound was dressed again and bandaged by an experienced nurse, but the doctor complimented us on our attempts with the needle and sutures, which satisfied him.

The Italian forces had surrendered on 8 September 1944. We made passage to Sardinia and anchored off the port of Antioco after a two-day passage from Augusta. We possessed no up-to-date charts of the approaches to Cagliari and Antioco, and certainly had no knowledge of likely minefields or wrecks.

The Master decided that I would take a boat ahead to ascertain soundings, while the ship followed slowly, and by that means we made port and berthed. We were the first of their previous enemies to land in Sardinia; and were greeted by the Mayor of Cagliari and a host of local dignitaries. We immediately commenced loading from the piles of coal on the dockside. The easiest way to get the stevedores to pull their fingers out was by bribing them with our cigarettes, in tins of 50. This achieved a relatively fast rate of loading.

When loading was nearly completed and we were trimming by alternately loading in Nos. 1 and 5 holds, I made the mistake of entrusting to the Second Mate the duty of supervising the trimming during the night. I gave strict instructions that he was to wake me at a specified time, so that I could supervise the move of the loading from No.1 hold to No. 5 hold. I woke hours after the designated time to be confronted by the sight of a huge pyramid of coal on No. 1 hold, spilling overboard into the sea and on the dockside, with the ship massively down by the head. The Second Mate was fast asleep in his bunk.

The bloody fool stevedores had just continued to tip coal, despite the cock up by the negligent Second Mate. The only recourse was to bribe the foreman stevedore with several tins of cigarettes; whereupon he brought some grabs into action and partly discharged No. 1 cargo, which was deposited on the dockside. We then moved the ship forward, and by the time the Master was on deck prior to breakfast, the ship was loaded and trimmed. He never knew what had happened, and I did not tell him.

The rest of our stay on the Italian coast was routine. We made passage to Bari, then Barletta, on the Adriatic coast, where we continued to discharge coal into small naval vessels and barges. We were then ordered to put to sea, destination the port of Bone in North Africa, to load a cargo of iron ore.

Our stay in Bone was not without interesting incident. We were berthed close to an American Liberty ship. The First mate boarded our ship, and asked to see me. The gunner on gangway duty brought him to my cabin, where I entertained him to a few stiff glasses of Scotch whiskey, which he accepted gratefully, because most American ships were dry. His request was, "Have you such a thing as some red oxide paint, Mister Mate?" My answer was "How many tons do you require?" On a British ship – food – NO – red oxide paint – YES!

He asked if I could spare a hundredweight and asked, "What can I give you in return?" My answer was "What about Kellogs Corn Flakes?" Now it was his turn to ask "How many tons?" The result was a sling load of cartons of corn flakes came aboard *Empire Spey*, and a keg of red oxide went aboard the American ship. We became quite chummy, and spent many a happy interlude over a bottle of Scotch. I also received as presents a superb pair of sunglasses and an American steel helmet.

Then there was a misunderstanding with the stevedore. I had worked out the tonnages of iron ore to be loaded in the five holds, to put the ship down to her marks and trimmed a foot by the stern, and ordered the Second and Third Mates to supervise the trimming in No. 1 and No. 5 holds. When the loading was completed the Second Mate brought me the

S.S. Empire Spey in post-war livery and re-named *S.S. Blairspey*
Built in 1929 as *S.S. Blairspey*, 4155 gross registered tonnage
Torpedoed by U-100 and U-101 on 18/19 October 1940, in convoy SC7
Towed to port and rebuilt as *S.S. Empire Spey*
(Photograph by A. Duncan, Cowes, I.O.W.)

draught readings, which showed that we were about 12 inches under our marks. I thought that the ship had touched bottom, so we sounded all round. There was plenty of water under the ship. Then I checked with the Chief Engineer to determine whether he had given me incorrect information on the state of his bunker coal reserves. He verified his calculations.

I told the stevedore that I would not sign the Bills of Lading until he had loaded the ship to its marks, but he refused. Therefore, I signed the bills of lading under protest. It was soon clear that I had made my calculations in Imperial long tons, whereas the stevedore had loaded in metric tons of 1,000 kilos or 2,024.6 pounds. My calculations in long tons of 2,240 lbs, resulted in a difference of 215.4 pounds per ton. On a cargo of 6,000 long tons, the difference would have been about 575 tons, or over 12 inches according to our tons per inch immersion characteristics. Despite my attempts to reconcile the differences with the French stevedore, he could not be moved, and we put to sea short of our marks.

Convoys MKS63, MKS63G and SL172

Empire Spey joined convoy MKS 63, which put to sea from Port Said on 26 September, making rendezvous off Bone on 30 September, and arriving at Gibraltar on 8 October 1944. The convoy was reformed as MKS63G, and joined homeward bound Freetown convoy SL172 on 9 October, arriving at Liverpool on 16 October 1944. *Empire Spey* had been detached from the convoy in the Irish Sea, to arrive at Glasgow on the same day, where the ship paid off.

I had suffered spasmodic problems with occasional vomiting, but this had not impaired my ability to undertake my duties on *Empire Spey*. Later, when I was on leave a mild spell of vomiting brought traces of blood. It was deemed advisable for me to have another barium meal and ex-ray. The disappointing verdict of the doctors was that I was not fit enough to return to duty on *Empire Spey*. Although I remained on the register of the Reserve Pool for six weeks in the forlorn hope that the condition would improve, further examination by the Shipping Federation doctor confirmed their previous diagnoses, and resulted in my discharge book being endorsed "Discharged from M.N.R. Pool Physically unfit – C.R.S.8." The certificate was dated 8 December, and the C.R.S.8. Certificate of Discharge from Merchant Navy Service was issued and signed on 9 December 1944.

During the period of 112 days of my service in *Empire Spey* the losses of ships in the Atlantic were negligible, when compared with the earlier ocean passages. The losses amounted to 12 ships sunk by 8 successful U-Boats, and 2 by mines.

The price the enemy paid for these modest successes was the loss of 64 U-Boats together with 2,660 of their officers and other ranks. I am glad to reflect on the fact that I had seen it through until the U-Boats had been beaten.

Casualties – Ships and Personnel
27 June 1944 to 16 October 1944

Ships sunk – 12 by 8 successful U-Boats.
Two ships sunk by mines.

Lost with all hands

Robin Goodfellow, in ballast, 68 dead.

Lost with very heavy casualties

Jacksonville, cargo gasoline, 76 dead out of 78.
Livingston, general cargo, 14 dead out of 28.
Empire Heritage, cargo fuel oil, 114 dead out of 162.
Pinto, in ballast, 23 dead out of 62.

Merchant seamen killed – 319 out of 968,
a fatal casualty rate of 33 percent.

Despite the fact that the enemy U-Boats finally had been beaten, and victory in Europe was in sight; the awful casualty rate among the seamen in merchant ships remained at over 30 percent.

Of the 64 U-Boats destroyed, 25 were sunk by depth charges: 25 by air attack: 9 by mines: 2 by submarines: 1 by ramming: 1 by FIDO.

EMPIRE SPEY - 27 JUNE 1944 TO 16 OCTOBER 1944

RECORD OF MERCHANT SHIPS SUNK IN ATLANTIC - 27/06/44 TO 16/10/44

EMPIRE SPEY - SIGNED ARTICLES AT BARRY - 27/06/44

DATE	SHIP	NAT.	CONVOY NO.	CAUSE OF LOSS	POSITION		CARGO	CASUALTIES CREW	DEAD
02/07/44	BODEGRAVEN	DUTCH		U-547	04-14 N.	11-00 W.	GENERAL	111	9
	EMPIRE SPEY		OS82						
07/07/44	ESSO HARRISBURG	U.S.A.		U-516	13-20 N.	71-15 W.	CRUDE OIL	72	8
20/07/44	NORFALK	BRITISH		MINED	49-39 N.	01-06 W.	SAND	40	0
24/07/44	WILLIAM GASTON	U.S.A.		U-861	26-42 S.	46-12 W.	GRAIN	67	0
24/07/44	AUK	BRITISH		MINED	43-29 N.	13-33 E.	PETROL	35	0
EMPIRE SPEY - BERTHED AT AUGUSTA. ANTIOCO. BARI. BARLETTA AND BONE - 23/07/44 TO 30/09/44									
25/07/44	ROBIN GOODFELLOW	U.S.A.		U-862	20-03 S.	14-21 W.	BALLAST	68	68
08/08/44	EZRA WESTON	U.S.A.		U-567	50-42 N.	05-30 W.	GENERAL	79	0
30/08/44	JACKSONVILLE	U.S.A.	CU36	U-482	55-30 N.	07-30 W.	GASOLENE	78	76
02/09/44	FJORDHEIM	NOR	ON251	U-482	55-20 N.	09-58 W.	COAL	38	3
03/09/44	LIVINGSTON	BRITISH	ON251	U-541	46-15 N.	58-05 W.	GENERAL	28	14
08/09/44	EMPIRE HERITAGE	BRITISH	HX 305	U-482	55-27 N.	08-01 W.	FUEL OIL	162	114
08/09/44	PINTO	BRITISH	HX305	U-482	55-27 N.	08-01 W.	BALLAST	62	23
29/09/44	SAMSUVA	BRITISH	RA60	U-310	72-58 N.	23-59 E.	TIMBER	60	3
29/09/44	EDWARD H. CROCKETT	U.S.A.	RA60	U-310	72-59 N.	24-26 E.	ORE	68	1
	EMPIRE SPEY		MKS63G						
	EMPIRE SPEY		SL172						
								968	319

THE WAR AT SEA: EMPIRE SPEY

EMPIRE SPEY - 27 JUNE 1944 TO 16 OCTOBER 1944

SHIP AND U-BOAT LOSSES - WHEN SERVING ON *EMPIRE SPEY*
27 JUNE 1944 TO 16 OCTOBER 1944

GERMAN U-BOATS	SHIPS SUNK IN PERIOD					ENEMY U-BOAT LOSSES				
NUMBER	TOTALS		TOTAL	27/06/44			DETAILS OF LOSS			
	C/F	B/F		16/10/44			DATE	CAUSE	DEAD	SAVED
U-310			2	2		U-107	18/08/44	AIR	58	0
U-482			4	4		U-129	18/08/44	SCUTT.	0	47
U-516			1	1		U-154	03/07/44	D/C	57	0
U-541			1	1		U-168	06/10/44	SUB.	23	27
U-547			1	1		U-180	22/08/44	MINE	56	0
U-667			1	1		U-198	12/08/44	D/C	66	0
U-861			1	1		U-212	21/07/44	D/C	49	0
U-862			1	1		U-214	26/07/44	D/C	48	0
						U-233	05/07/44	RAM	31	29
	1,609	**1,597**	**12**	**12**		U-243	08/07/44	AIR	12	38
						U-247	01/09/44	D/C	52	0
HEAVY SHIPS	15	15	0			U-250	30/07/44	D/C	49	6
RAIDERS	24	24	0			U-270	13/08/44	AIR	10	71
LIGHT WARSHIPS	7	7	0			U-317	26/06/44	AIR	50	0
AIRCRAFT	106	106	0			U-319	15/07/44	AIR	50	0
ITALIAN SUBMARINES	73	73	0			U-333	31/07/44	D/C	45	0
OTHER CAUSES	20	18	2	2		U-344	22/08/44	AIR	50	0
						U-347	17/07/44	AIR	49	0
	245	**243**	**2**	**2**		U-354	22/08/44	AIR	51	0
						U-361	17/07/44	AIR	52	0
ITALIAN SUBMARINES						U-362	05/09/44	D/C	51	0
						U-385	11/08/44	AIR	1	41
ARCHIMEDE	1	1	0			U-390	05/07/44	D/C	47	1
DANDOLO	1	1	0			U-394	02/09/44	D/C	50	0
BRIN	2	2	0			U-407	19/09/44	D/C	5	47
CAGNI	1	1	0			U-413	20/08/44	D/C	45	1
MALASPINA	2	2	0			U-415	14/07/44	MINE	2	47
EMO	2	2	0			U-445	24/08/44	D/C	52	0
BAGNOLINI	2	2	0			U-478	30/06/44	AIR	52	0
BARACCA	2	2	0			U-484	09/09/44	D/C	52	0
BARBARIGO	3	3	0			U-543	02/07/44	FIDO	58	0
PIETRO CALVI	5	5	0			U-547	13/08/44	MINE	50	0
GUISEPPE FINZI	3	3	0			U-565	24/09/44	AIR	5	45
GUILIANI	3	3	0			U-586	05/07/44	AIR	50	0
GUGLIELMO MARCONI	3	3	0			U-608	10/08/44	AIR	51	0
MOROSINI	5	5	0			U-618	15/08/44	D/C	51	0
ENRICO TAZZOLI	17	17	0			U-621	18/08/44	D/C	54	0
CAPPELLINI	3	3	0			U-642	05/07/44	AIR	50	0
LEONARDO DA VINCI	9	9	0			U-667	25/08/44	MINE	45	0
LUIGI TORELLI	3	3	0			U-671	04/08/44	D/C	47	6
NANI	1	1	0			U-672	18/07/44	D/C	0	46
OTARIO	1	1	0			U-678	06/07/44	D/C	52	0
ARGO	1	1	0			U-719	26/06/44	D/C	52	0
VENERIO	2	2	0			U-703	30/09/44	MINE	54	0
MOCENIGO	1	1	0			U-736	06/08/44	D/C	28	26
						U-741	15/08/44	D/C	48	1
	73	**73**	**0**	**0**		U-742	18/07/44	AIR	52	0
						U-743	15/09/44	D/C	50	0
						U-855	18/09/44	MINE	56	0
						U-859	23/09/44	SUB.	47	18
						U-863	29/09/44	AIR	69	0
						U-865	19/09/44	MINED	59	0
						U-867	19/09/44	AIR	61	0
						U-871	24/09/44	AIR	69	40
						U-921	30/09/44	AIR	50	0
						U-925	02/09/44	MINE	51	0
						U-981	12/08/44	AIR	12	40
						U-984	20/08/44	D/C	45	0
						U-988	30/06/44	AIR	50	0
						U-1006	16/10/44	D/C	7	44
						U-1062	30/09/44	AIR	55	0
						U-1122	11/07/44	AIR	56	0
						U-1229	20/08/44	AIR	17	41
						U-2323	26/07/44	MINE	2	12
						TOTALS	64		2,660	627
						B/F	290		10,784	2,991
						C/F	354		13,444	3,618

22

AFTER THE WAR
REFLECTIONS OF A
MERCHANT NAVY OFFICER

I counted myself as being fortunate to be alive after having served at sea, mainly on the Atlantic, for most of the war. I had participated in 27 Atlantic crossings, and it was difficult to absorb the realisation that it was now over for me.

This has been emphasised, now that I have been able to undertake research into the casualties during my time on the articles of nine ships. The statistics have been produced, and are attached to this narrative. They embrace the numbers of seamen killed respectively in British, Greek, Norwegian, Dutch, American and Panamanian ships, and ships of other nationalities, mainly neutral countries. The astonishing element in the statistics has been the consistent running average of fatal casualties of between 30 and 32 percent, regardless of nationality. It underlines the contribution of our allies in the conflict; and the cost that they bore in terms of human suffering and death.

The Battle of the Atlantic lasted from 3 September 1939 to 8 May 1945, the date when the enemy capitulated in Europe, a period of 2,075 days. An analysis of my records shows that I was borne on the articles of nine ships for 1,320 days. During the war, I was on leave when not on articles for two periods, 47 days. Study and training leave absorbed two periods ashore, 192 days. Medical treatment for injuries and privation kept me ashore for 101 days in the early part of the war, but for most of the last year of the war.

The records of ship losses and U-Boat activity, and the summaries that I have produced cover only the period when I was borne on articles, and appertain mainly to the Atlantic theatre of war.

During my time on articles, 1,609 ships had been sunk by U-Boats, 15 by heavy surface ships, 7 by light surface forces, 24 by raiders, 106 by aircraft, 73 by Italian submarines, and 20 by other causes, a total of 1,854 ships of all nationalities. The German forces had lost 354 U-Boats sunk, and 13,344 of their crews.

Therefore, casualties that occurred in the Mediterranean Sea, Indian Ocean, Far Eastern waters, and around the U.K. coast, have not been recorded. I have set out the fatal casualties suffered by the British Merchant Navy, and the mercantile marines of other ships, during the period when I was borne on the articles of nine ships, a total of 1,320 days.

RECORD OF WARTIME SERVICE AT SEA

ANALYSIS OF SERVICE AT SEA - 03 SEPTEMBER 1939 TO 08 MAY 1945				
	FROM	TO	NUMBER OF DAYS	NUMBER OF DAYS
SERVICE IN *APPLEDORE*	03/09/39	08/07/40	310	
SHORE LEAVE	09/07/40	23/07/40		15
SERVICE IN *ONOMEA/ISTOK*	24/07/40	08/10/40	77	
SERVICE IN *FILLEIGH*	09/10/40	22/12/40	75	
SHORE LEAVE FOR TRAINING AND STUDY	23/12/40	17/03/41		85
SERVICE IN *HADLEIGH*	18/03/41	04/09/41	171	
SHORE LEAVE FOR MEDICAL ATTENTION	05/09/41	14/12/41		101
SERVICE IN *BARRWHIN*	15/12/41	08/09/42	268	
LEAVE BETWEEN SHIPS	09/09/42	11/10/42		32
SERVICE IN *START POINT*	12/10/42	09/11/42	29	
SURVIVORS FROM *START POINT* IN LIFEBOATS	10/11/42	23/11/42	14	
SURVIVORS FROM *START POINT*	24/11/42	07/01/43	45	
SERVICE IN *PILAR DE LARRINAGA*	08/01/43	23/02/43	47	
SHORE LEAVE FOR TRAINING AND STUDY	24/02/43	11/06/43		107
SERVICE IN *OCEAN VAGRANT*	12/06/43	25/10/43	136	
REPATRIATION AS D.B.S.	26/10/43	30/11/43	36	
SHORE LEAVE FOR MEDICAL ATTENTION	01/12/43	26/06/44		209
SERVICE IN *EMPIRE SPEY*	26/06/44	15/10/44	112	
DISCHARGED - MEDICALLY UNFIT FOR SEA SERVICE	16/10/44	08/05/45		205
			1,320	754

SEAMEN KILLED IN BRITISH SHIPS

	CASUALTIES IN MERCHANT SHIPS DURING PERIODS ON ARTICLES - 1939 TO 1945								

	SEAMEN KILLED IN BRITISH SHIPS								
NAME OF SHIP	**ON ARTICLES DATES**		**NUMBER OF DAYS**	**FATAL CASUALTY STATISTICS**					**TOTAL %'AGE DEAD**
	FROM	**TO**		**CREW**	**DEAD**	**%'AGE DEAD**	**TOTAL CREWS**	**TOTAL DEAD**	
APPLEDORE	03/09/39	07/12/39	96	3,753	585	15.59%	3,753	585	15.59%
APPLEDORE	08/12/39	12/04/40	127	670	119	17.76%	4,423	704	15.92%
APPLEDORE	13/04/40	08/07/40	87	3,270	1,178	36.02%	7,693	1,882	24.46%
ISTOK	24/07/40	30/08/40	38	2,825	246	8.71%	10,518	2,128	20.23%
ISTOK	31/08/40	08/10/40	39	3,388	1,213	35.80%	13,906	3,341	24.03%
FILLEIGH	09/10/40	13/11/40	36	2,736	851	31.10%	16,642	4,192	25.19%
FILLEIGH	14/11/40	22/12/40	39	3,354	1,713	51.07%	19,996	5,905	29.53%
HADLEIGH	18/03/41	06/05/41	50	4,274	1,361	31.84%	24,270	7,266	29.94%
HADLEIGH	07/05/41	06/06/41	31	2,916	534	18.31%	27,186	7,800	28.69%
HADLEIGH	07/06/41	05/07/41	29	2,680	954	35.60%	29,866	8,754	29.31%
HADLEIGH	06/07/41	04/09/41	61	1,861	713	38.31%	31,727	9,467	29.84%
BARRWHIN	15/12/41	13/02/42	61	1,711	1,062	62.07%	33,438	10,529	31.49%
BARRWHIN	14/02/42	06/03/42	21	1,046	571	54.59%	34,484	11,100	32.19%
BARRWHIN	07/03/42	25/03/42	19	962	393	40.85%	35,446	11,493	32.42%
BARRWHIN	26/03/42	13/04/42	19	1,573	305	19.39%	37,019	11,798	31.87%
BARRWHIN	14/04/42	07/05/42	24	1,135	244	21.50%	38,154	12,042	31.56%
BARRWHIN	08/05/42	21/05/42	14	1,164	167	14.35%	39,318	12,209	31.05%
BARRWHIN	22/05/42	07/06/42	17	931	183	19.66%	40,249	12,392	30.79%
BARRWHIN	08/06/42	23/06/42	16	936	167	17.84%	41,185	12,559	30.49%
BARRWHIN	24/06/42	06/07/42	13	948	203	21.41%	42,133	12,762	30.29%
BARRWHIN	07/07/42	30/07/42	24	1,352	377	27.88%	43,485	13,139	30.22%
BARRWHIN	31/07/42	17/08/42	18	1,197	249	20.80%	44,682	13,388	29.96%
BARRWHIN	18/08/42	08/09/42	22	1,760	364	20.68%	46,442	13,752	29.61%
START POINT	12/10/42	31/10/42	20	2,980	1,336	44.83%	49,422	15,088	30.53%
START POINT	01/11/42	10/11/42	10	2,000	620	31.00%	51,422	15,708	30.55%
START POINT	11/11/42	09/12/42	29	3,336	1,390	41.67%	54,758	17,098	31.22%
START POINT	10/12/42	07/01/43	29	1,736	575	33.12%	56,494	17,673	31.28%
PILAR DE LARRINAGA	08/01/43	23/02/43	47	1,466	818	55.80%	57,960	18,491	31.90%
OCEAN VAGRANT	12/06/43	16/08/43	66	4,633	865	18.67%	62,593	19,356	30.92%
OCEAN VAGRANT	17/08/43	30/11/43	106	3,160	1,276	40.38%	65,753	20,632	31.38%
EMPIRE SPEY	27/06/44	16/10/44	112	387	154	39.79%	66,140	20,786	31.43%

			1,320	**66,140**	**20,786**				**31.43%**

By reference to official statistics, I have been able to estimate that my analyses have covered very close to five-eighths of the realistic totals, or 67.5 percent. From this I have been able to interpolate a reasonably accurate statistical record of casualties in merchant ships of all nations. The approximate numbers of fatal casualties in non-British ships have been calculated by interpolation, and are shown as follows:

British ships – official record of 30,248 men killed.
Dutch ships – approximately 1,320 men killed.
Greek ships – approximately 1,400 men killed.

SEAMEN KILLED IN DUTCH SHIPS

CASUALTIES IN MERCHANT SHIPS DURING PERIODS ON ARTICLES - 1939 TO 1945									
SEAMEN KILLED IN DUTCH SHIPS									
NAME OF SHIP	ON ARTICLES DATES FROM	TO	NUMBER OF DAYS	CREW	DEAD	FATAL CASUALTY STATISTICS %'AGE DEAD	TOTAL CREWS	TOTAL DEAD	TOTAL %'AGE DEAD
APPLEDORE	03/09/39	07/12/39	96	35	26	74.29%	35	26	74.29%
APPLEDORE	08/12/39	12/04/40	127	171	0	0.00%	206	26	12.62%
APPLEDORE	13/04/40	08/07/40	87	153	37	24.18%	359	63	17.55%
ISTOK	24/07/40	30/08/40	38	0	0	0.00%	359	63	17.55%
ISTOK	31/08/40	08/10/40	39	61	32	52.46%	420	95	22.62%
FILLEIGH	09/10/40	13/11/40	36	110	6	5.45%	530	101	19.06%
FILLEIGH	14/11/40	22/12/40	39	103	43	41.75%	633	144	22.75%
HADLEIGH	18/03/41	06/05/41	50	159	15	9.43%	792	159	20.08%
HADLEIGH	07/05/41	06/06/41	31	329	38	11.55%	1,121	197	17.57%
HADLEIGH	07/06/41	05/07/41	29	184	43	23.37%	1,305	240	18.39%
HADLEIGH	06/07/41	04/09/41	61	83	19	22.89%	1,388	259	18.66%
BARRWHIN	15/12/41	13/02/42	61	0	0	0.00%	1,388	259	18.66%
BARRWHIN	14/02/42	06/03/42	21	27	0	0.00%	1,415	259	18.30%
BARRWHIN	07/03/42	25/03/42	19	111	53	47.75%	1,526	312	20.45%
BARRWHIN	26/03/42	13/04/42	19	72	16	22.22%	1,598	328	20.53%
BARRWHIN	14/04/42	07/05/42	24	183	40	21.86%	1,781	368	20.66%
BARRWHIN	08/05/42	21/05/42	14	113	14	12.39%	1,894	382	20.17%
BARRWHIN	22/05/42	07/06/42	17	149	54	36.24%	2,043	436	21.34%
BARRWHIN	08/06/42	23/06/42	16	72	9	12.50%	2,115	445	21.04%
BARRWHIN	24/06/42	06/07/42	13	172	0	0.00%	2,287	445	19.46%
BARRWHIN	07/07/42	30/07/42	24	77	23	29.87%	2,364	468	19.80%
BARRWHIN	31/07/42	17/08/42	18	286	81	28.32%	2,650	549	20.72%
BARRWHIN	18/08/42	08/09/42	22	308	19	6.17%	2,958	568	19.20%
START POINT	12/10/42	31/10/42	20	0	0	0.00%	2,958	568	19.20%
START POINT	01/11/42	10/11/42	10	343	163	47.52%	3,301	731	22.14%
START POINT	11/11/42	09/12/42	29	248	122	49.19%	3,549	853	24.03%
START POINT	10/12/42	07/01/43	29	147	1	0.68%	3,696	854	23.11%
PILAR DE LARRINAGA	08/01/43	23/02/43	47	0	0	0.00%	3,696	854	23.11%
OCEAN VAGRANT	12/06/43	16/08/43	66	196	26	13.27%	3,892	880	22.61%
OCEAN VAGRANT	17/08/43	30/11/43	106	0	0	0.00%	3,892	880	22.61%
EMPIRE SPEY	27/06/44	16/10/44	112	111	9	8.11%	4,003	889	22.21%
			1,320	4,003	889				22.21%

Norwegian ships – approximately 2,650 men killed.
U.S.A/Panamanian ships – approximately 8,000 men killed.
Non-belligerent ships – approximately 4,300 men killed.

If the additional year of the war in the Pacific is added into the calculations, it appears that over 50,000 merchant seamen were killed during the war, not including the catastrophic losses in several troop carrying ships, particularly *Lancastria*.

During some periods covered by the analysis, the fatal casualty rate increased dramatically: during the violent winter storms and tempestuous weather of November and December 1940 (over 51 percent): during the

SEAMEN KILLED IN GREEK SHIPS

CASUALTIES IN MERCHANT SHIPS DURING PERIODS ON ARTICLES - 1939 TO 1945									
SEAMEN KILLED IN GREEK SHIPS									
NAME OF SHIP	ON ARTICLES DATES		NUMBER OF DAYS	FATAL CASUALTY STATISTICS					TOTAL %'AGE DEAD
	FROM	TO		CREW	DEAD	%'AGE DEAD	TOTAL CREWS	TOTAL DEAD	
APPLEDORE	03/09/39	07/12/39	96	69	25	36.23%	69	25	36.23%
APPLEDORE	08/12/39	12/04/40	127	180	56	31.11%	249	81	32.53%
APPLEDORE	13/04/40	08/07/40	87	359	62	17.27%	608	143	23.52%
ISTOK	24/07/40	30/08/40	38	161	58	36.02%	769	201	26.14%
ISTOK	31/08/40	08/10/40	39	187	27	14.44%	956	228	23.85%
FILLEIGH	09/10/40	13/11/40	36	183	28	15.30%	1,139	256	22.48%
FILLEIGH	14/11/40	22/12/40	39	135	87	64.44%	1,274	343	26.92%
HADLEIGH	18/03/41	06/05/41	50	95	7	7.37%	1,369	350	25.57%
HADLEIGH	07/05/41	06/06/41	31	60	28	46.67%	1,429	378	26.45%
HADLEIGH	07/06/41	05/07/41	29	257	187	72.76%	1,686	565	33.51%
HADLEIGH	06/07/41	04/09/41	61	0	0	0.00%	1,686	565	33.51%
BARRWHIN	15/12/41	13/02/42	61	131	75	57.25%	1,817	640	35.22%
BARRWHIN	14/02/42	06/03/42	21	40	26	65.00%	1,857	666	35.86%
BARRWHIN	07/03/42	25/03/42	19	150	33	22.00%	2,007	699	34.83%
BARRWHIN	26/03/42	13/04/42	19	0	0	0.00%	2,007	699	34.83%
BARRWHIN	14/04/42	07/05/42	24	23	14	60.87%	2,030	713	35.12%
BARRWHIN	08/05/42	21/05/42	14	33	0	0.00%	2,063	713	34.56%
BARRWHIN	22/05/42	07/06/42	17	0	0	0.00%	2,063	713	34.56%
BARRWHIN	08/06/42	23/06/42	16	0	0	0.00%	2,063	713	34.56%
BARRWHIN	24/06/42	06/07/42	13	29	3	10.34%	2,092	716	34.23%
BARRWHIN	07/07/42	30/07/42	24	37	0	0.00%	2,129	716	33.63%
BARRWHIN	31/07/42	17/08/42	18	124	13	10.48%	2,253	729	32.36%
BARRWHIN	18/08/42	08/09/42	22	96	9	9.38%	2,349	738	31.42%
START POINT	12/10/42	31/10/42	20	37	32	86.49%	2,386	770	32.27%
START POINT	01/11/42	10/11/42	10	146	31	21.23%	2,532	801	31.64%
START POINT	11/11/42	09/12/42	29	40	2	5.00%	2,572	803	31.22%
START POINT	10/12/42	07/01/43	29	34	34	100.00%	2,606	837	32.12%
PILAR DE LARRINAGA	08/01/43	23/02/43	47	309	99	32.04%	2,915	936	32.11%
OCEAN VAGRANT	12/06/43	16/08/43	66	35	1	0.00%	2,950	937	31.76%
OCEAN VAGRANT	17/08/43	30/11/43	106	0	0	0.00%	2,950	937	31.76%
EMPIRE SPEY	27/06/44	16/10/44	112	0	0	0.00%	2,950	937	31.76%
			1,320	2,950	937				31.76%

winter of 1941/1942 (62 and 55 percent): and again in January and February 1943 (56 percent). This underlined the fact that severe and particularly cold weather affected the chances of survival.

After the war, the Medical Research Council commissioned a research study into Merchant Navy war casualties. The results were published under the authorship of R.A. McCance, C.C. Ungley, J.W.L. Crosfill and E.M. Widdowson in a booklet with the title *The Hazards to Men in Ships Lost at Sea, 1940-44*. I was contacted by one of the joint authors, Doctor C.C. Ungley, who specialised in Peripheral Vasoneuropathy after chilling, and Immersion Foot Syndrome, and published papers in the Lancet and elsewhere.

SEAMEN KILLED IN NORWEGIAN SHIPS

CASUALTIES IN MERCHANT SHIPS DURING PERIODS ON ARTICLES - 1939 TO 1945

SEAMEN KILLED IN NORWEGIAN SHIPS

NAME OF SHIP	ON ARTICLES DATES FROM	TO	NUMBER OF DAYS	CREW	DEAD	%'AGE DEAD	TOTAL CREWS	TOTAL DEAD	TOTAL %'AGE DEAD
APPLEDORE	03/09/39	07/12/39	96	104	21	20.19%	104	21	20.19%
APPLEDORE	08/12/39	12/04/40	127	151	43	28.48%	255	64	25.10%
APPLEDORE	13/04/40	08/07/40	87	247	25	10.12%	502	89	17.73%
ISTOK	24/07/40	30/08/40	38	146	50	34.25%	648	139	21.45%
ISTOK	31/08/40	08/10/40	39	256	71	27.73%	904	210	23.23%
FILLEIGH	09/10/40	13/11/40	36	130	35	26.92%	1,034	245	23.69%
FILLEIGH	14/11/40	22/12/40	39	131	112	85.50%	1,165	357	30.64%
HADLEIGH	18/03/41	06/05/41	50	124	14	11.29%	1,289	371	28.78%
HADLEIGH	07/05/41	06/06/41	31	168	35	20.83%	1,457	406	27.87%
HADLEIGH	07/06/41	05/07/41	29	148	55	37.16%	1,605	461	28.72%
HADLEIGH	06/07/41	04/09/41	61	178	24	13.48%	1,783	485	27.20%
BARRWHIN	15/12/41	13/02/42	61	451	218	48.34%	2,234	703	31.47%
BARRWHIN	14/02/42	06/03/42	21	432	235	54.40%	2,666	938	35.18%
BARRWHIN	07/03/42	25/03/42	19	157	84	53.50%	2,823	1,022	36.20%
BARRWHIN	26/03/42	13/04/42	19	299	86	28.76%	3,122	1,108	35.49%
BARRWHIN	14/04/42	07/05/42	24	135	51	37.78%	3,257	1,159	35.58%
BARRWHIN	08/05/42	21/05/42	14	230	18	7.83%	3,487	1,177	33.75%
BARRWHIN	22/05/42	07/06/42	17	174	26	14.94%	3,661	1,203	32.86%
BARRWHIN	08/06/42	23/06/42	16	369	26	7.05%	4,030	1,229	30.50%
BARRWHIN	24/06/42	06/07/42	13	201	39	19.40%	4,231	1,268	29.97%
BARRWHIN	07/07/42	30/07/42	24	118	32	27.12%	4,349	1,300	29.89%
BARRWHIN	31/07/42	17/08/42	18	217	21	9.68%	4,566	1,321	28.93%
BARRWHIN	18/08/42	08/09/42	22	228	9	3.95%	4,794	1,330	27.74%
START POINT	12/10/42	31/10/42	20	356	112	31.46%	5,150	1,442	28.00%
START POINT	01/11/42	10/11/42	10	164	6	3.66%	5,314	1,448	27.25%
START POINT	11/11/42	09/12/42	29	175	17	9.71%	5,489	1,465	26.69%
START POINT	10/12/42	07/01/43	29	232	143	61.64%	5,721	1,608	28.11%
PILAR DE LARRINAGA	08/01/43	23/02/43	47	133	59	44.36%	5,854	1,667	28.48%
OCEAN VAGRANT	12/06/43	16/08/43	66	91	27	29.67%	5,945	1,694	28.49%
OCEAN VAGRANT	17/08/43	30/11/53	106	298	88	29.53%	6,243	1,782	28.54%
EMPIRE SPEY	27/06/44	16/10/44	112	38	3	7.89%	6,281	1,785	28.42%
			1,320	6,281	1,785				28.42%

When I signed off the articles of *Empire Spey* on 16 October 1944, I entertained the hope that I would be able to return to my career at sea after rest and medical care. The medical examination established that this had been a forlorn hope; and that I had to reconcile myself to the prospect that I would have to seek employment ashore.

Betty had saved part of the pay allotment during my service in *Empire Spey*, so she had a small amount of savings in the Post Office Savings Bank. My pay during the four months service in the ship would have produced about £ 180, so we were left with less than about £ 100. We paid a contribution of ten shillings a week for the tiny bed sitting room, so with stringent economy we would be able to survive financially for

SEAMEN KILLED IN UNITED STATES AND PANAMANIAN SHIPS

CASUALTIES IN MERCHANT SHIPS DURING PERIODS ON ARTICLES - 1939 TO 1945									
SEAMEN KILLED IN UNITED STATES AND PANAMANIAN SHIPS									
NAME OF SHIP	ON ARTICLES			FATAL CASUALTY STATISTICS					
	DATES		NUMBER						TOTAL
	FROM	TO	OF DAYS	CREW	DEAD	%'AGE DEAD	TOTAL CREWS	TOTAL DEAD	%'AGE DEAD
APPLEDORE	03/09/39	07/12/39	96						
APPLEDORE	08/12/39	12/04/40	127						
APPLEDORE	13/04/40	08/07/40	87	58	3	5.17%	58	3	5.17%
ISTOK	24/07/40	30/08/40	38	30	21	70.00%	88	24	27.27%
ISTOK	31/08/40	08/10/40	39	34	8	23.53%	122	32	26.23%
FILLEIGH	09/10/40	13/11/40	36	0	0	0.00%	122	32	26.23%
FILLEIGH	14/11/40	22/12/40	39	52	2	3.85%	174	34	19.54%
HADLEIGH	18/03/41	06/05/41	50	0	0	0.00%	174	34	19.54%
HADLEIGH	07/05/41	06/06/41	31	46	0	0.00%	220	34	15.45%
HADLEIGH	07/06/41	05/07/41	29	0	0	0.00%	220	34	15.45%
HADLEIGH	06/07/41	04/09/41	61	27	24	88.89%	247	58	23.48%
BARRWHIN	15/12/41	13/02/42	61	483	216	44.72%	730	274	37.53%
BARRWHIN	14/02/42	06/03/42	21	694	296	42.65%	1,424	570	40.03%
BARRWHIN	07/03/42	25/03/42	19	820	229	27.93%	2,244	799	35.61%
BARRWHIN	26/03/42	13/04/42	19	1,237	314	25.38%	3,481	1,113	31.97%
BARRWHIN	14/04/42	07/05/42	24	1,121	271	24.17%	4,602	1,384	30.07%
BARRWHIN	08/05/42	21/05/42	14	939	269	28.65%	5,541	1,653	29.83%
BARRWHIN	22/05/42	07/06/42	17	1,273	370	29.07%	6,814	2,023	29.69%
BARRWHIN	08/06/42	23/06/42	16	1,520	341	22.43%	8,334	2,364	28.37%
BARRWHIN	24/06/42	06/07/42	13	1,617	150	9.28%	9,951	2,514	25.26%
BARRWHIN	07/07/42	30/07/42	24	1,308	126	9.63%	11,259	2,640	23.45%
BARRWHIN	31/07/42	17/08/42	18	324	72	22.22%	11,583	2,712	23.41%
BARRWHIN	18/08/42	08/09/42	22	1,238	164	13.25%	12,821	2,876	22.43%
START POINT	12/10/42	31/10/42	20	433	170	39.26%	13,254	3,046	22.98%
START POINT	01/11/42	10/11/42	10	377	105	27.85%	13,631	3,151	23.12%
START POINT	11/11/42	09/12/42	29	763	425	55.70%	14,394	3,576	24.84%
START POINT	10/12/42	07/01/43	29	477	139	29.14%	14,871	3,715	24.98%
PILAR DE LARRINAGA	08/01/43	23/02/43	47	2,681	1,166	43.49%	17,552	4,881	27.81%
OCEAN VAGRANT	12/06/43	16/08/43	66	1,041	246	23.63%	18,593	5,127	27.57%
OCEAN VAGRANT	17/08/43	30/11/43	106	1,267	105	8.29%	19,860	5,232	26.34%
EMPIRE SPEY	27/06/44	16/10/44	112	432	153	35.42%	20,292	5,385	26.54%
			1,320	20,292	5,385				26.54%

about six months.

The Certificate of Discharge from the Merchant Navy Service reflects on the reverse a "Notice to Seamen", referring those suffering from a disablement to the Local Officer of the Ministry of Pensions. This states that he "will assist you in making an application". The notice omitted the words "everyone in the Ministry of Pensions is trained to treat applicants like so much dog shit". Certainly, I encountered no officer or employee in that government body who appeared to possess even the smallest degree of humanity or decency.

Frank Howe and I had resumed contact with each other after his discharge on 10 October 1944. His medical condition was termed

SEAMEN KILLED IN SHIPS OF NON BELLIGERENT COUNTRIES

CASUALTIES IN MERCHANT SHIPS DURING PERIODS ON ARTICLES - 1939 TO 1945

SEAMEN KILLED IN SHIPS OF NEUTRAL AND NON-BELLIGERENT NATIONALITIES

NAME OF SHIP	ON ARTICLES DATES FROM	TO	NUMBER OF DAYS	CREW	DEAD	%'AGE DEAD	TOTAL CREWS	TOTAL DEAD	TOTAL %'AGE DEAD
APPLEDORE	03/09/39	07/12/39	96	263	63	23.95%	263	63	23.95%
APPLEDORE	08/12/39	12/04/40	127	460	210	45.65%	723	273	37.76%
APPLEDORE	13/04/40	08/07/40	87	323	70	21.67%	1,046	343	32.79%
ISTOK	24/07/40	30/08/40	38	1,646	442	26.85%	2,692	785	29.16%
ISTOK	31/08/40	08/10/40	39	139	39	28.06%	2,831	824	29.11%
FILLEIGH	09/10/40	13/11/40	36	182	14	7.69%	3,013	838	27.81%
FILLEIGH	14/11/40	22/12/40	39	205	117	57.07%	3,218	955	29.68%
HADLEIGH	18/03/41	06/05/41	50	332	163	49.10%	3,550	1,118	31.49%
HADLEIGH	07/05/41	06/06/41	31	90	17	18.89%	3,640	1,135	31.18%
HADLEIGH	09/06/41	05/07/41	29	276	75	27.17%	3,916	1,210	30.90%
HADLEIGH	06/07/41	04/09/41	61	53	2	3.77%	3,969	1,212	30.54%
BARRWHIN	15/12/41	13/02/42	61	190	135	71.05%	4,159	1,347	32.39%
BARRWHIN	14/02/42	06/03/42	21	249	42	16.87%	4,408	1,389	31.51%
BARRWHIN	07/03/42	25/03/42	19	310	148	47.74%	4,718	1,537	32.58%
BARRWHIN	26/03/42	13/04/42	19	73	22	30.14%	4,791	1,559	32.54%
BARRWHIN	14/04/42	07/05/42	24	288	38	13.19%	5,079	1,597	31.44%
BARRWHIN	08/05/42	21/05/42	14	358	59	16.48%	5,437	1,656	30.46%
BARRWHIN	22/05/42	07/06/42	17	199	30	15.08%	5,636	1,686	29.91%
BARRWHIN	08/06/42	23/06/42	16	275	86	31.27%	5,911	1,772	29.98%
BARRWHIN	24/06/42	06/07/42	13	274	51	18.61%	6,185	1,823	29.47%
BARRWHIN	07/07/42	30/07/42	24	318	45	14.15%	6,503	1,868	28.73%
BARRWHIN	31/07/42	17/08/42	18	1,111	711	64.00%	7,614	2,579	33.87%
BARRWHIN	18/08/42	08/09/42	22	93	20	21.51%	7,707	2,599	33.72%
START POINT	12/10/42	31/10/42	20	35	14	40.00%	7,742	2,613	33.75%
START POINT	01/11/42	10/11/42	10	0	0	0.00%	7,742	2,613	33.75%
START POINT	11/11/42	09/12/42	29	56	5	8.93%	7,798	2,618	33.57%
START POINT	10/12/42	07/01/43	29	299	56	18.73%	8,097	2,674	33.02%
PILAR DE LARRINAGA	08/01/43	23/02/43	47	571	19	3.33%	8,668	2,693	31.07%
OCEAN VAGRANT	12/06/43	16/08/43	66	552	91	16.49%	9,220	2,784	30.20%
OCEAN VAGRANT	17/08/43	30/11/43	106	286	108	37.76%	9,506	2,892	30.42%
EMPIRE SPEY	27/06/44	16/10/44	112	0	0	0.00%	**9,506**	**2,892**	**30.42%**
			1,320	**9,506**	**2,892**				**30.42%**

"Psycho Neurosis". My condition was termed "Dyspepsia – Result of Exposure". We visited the office of the Ministry of Pensions, and received similar treatment. After sitting for hours in a large cold waiting room with many other victims, we were summoned to the presence of one of a number of medical practitioners. These shared common characteristics of lack of any vestige of humour, kindness or consideration. They all seemed to be imbued with the intention to seek out malingerers and those making false claims; and reject their applications.

The first examinations for us resulted in our being assessed as 40 percent disabled, for which we qualified for the standard disability allowance of ten shillings a week for officers, subject to regular "Review

SEAMEN KILLED IN SHIPS OF ALL NATIONALITIES

					CASUALTIES IN MERCHANT SHIPS DURING PERIODS ON ARTICLES - 1939 TO 1945					

SEAMEN KILLED IN SHIPS OF ALL NATIONALITIES

NAME OF SHIP	ON ARTICLES DATES FROM	TO	NUMBER OF DAYS	CREW	FATAL CASUALTY STATISTICS DEAD	%'AGE DEAD	TOTAL CREWS	TOTAL DEAD	TOTAL %'AGE DEAD
APPLEDORE	03/09/39	07/12/39	96	4,224	720	17.05%	4,224	720	17.05%
APPLEDORE	08/12/39	12/04/40	127	1,632	428	26.23%	5,856	1,148	19.60%
APPLEDORE	12/04/40	08/07/40	87	4,410	1,375	31.18%	10,266	2,523	24.58%
ISTOK	24/07/40	30/08/40	38	4,808	817	16.99%	15,074	3,340	22.16%
ISTOK	31/08/40	08/10/40	39	4,065	1,390	34.19%	19,139	4,730	24.71%
FILLEIGH	09/10/40	13/11/40	36	3,341	934	27.96%	22,480	5,664	25.20%
FILLEIGH	14/11/40	22/12/40	39	3,980	2,074	52.11%	26,460	7,738	29.24%
HADLEIGH	18/03/41	06/05/41	50	4,984	1,560	31.30%	31,444	9,298	29.57%
HADLEIGH	07/05/41	06/06/41	31	3,609	652	18.07%	35,053	9,950	28.39%
HADLEIGH	07/06/41	05/07/41	29	3,545	1,314	37.07%	38,598	11,264	29.18%
HADLEIGH	06/07/41	04/09/41	61	2,202	782	35.51%	40,800	12,046	29.52%
BARRWHIN	15/12/41	13/02/42	61	2,966	1,706	57.52%	43,766	13,752	31.42%
BARRWHIN	14/02/42	06/03/42	21	2,488	1,170	47.03%	46,254	14,922	32.26%
BARRWHIN	07/03/41	25/03/42	19	2,510	940	37.45%	48,764	15,862	32.53%
BARRWHIN	26/03/42	13/04/42	19	3,254	743	22.83%	52,018	16,605	31.92%
BARRWHIN	14/04/42	07/05/42	24	2,885	658	22.81%	54,903	17,263	31.44%
BARRWHIN	08/05/42	21/05/42	14	2,837	527	18.58%	57,740	17,790	30.81%
BARRWHIN	22/05/42	07/06/42	17	2,726	663	24.32%	60,466	18,453	30.52%
BARRWHIN	08/06/42	23/06/42	16	3,172	629	19.83%	63,638	19,082	29.99%
BARRWHIN	24/06/42	06/07/42	13	3,241	446	13.76%	66,879	19,528	29.20%
BARRWHIN	07/07/42	30/07/42	24	3,210	603	18.79%	70,089	20,131	28.72%
BARRWHIN	31/07/42	17/08/42	18	3,259	1,147	35.19%	73,348	21,278	29.01%
BARRWHIN	18/08/42	08/09/42	22	3,723	585	15.71%	77,071	21,863	28.37%
START POINT	12/10/42	31/10/42	20	3,841	1,664	43.32%	80,912	23,527	29.08%
START POINT	01/11/42	10/11/42	10	3,030	925	30.53%	83,942	24,452	29.13%
START POINT	11/11/42	09/12/42	29	4,618	1,961	42.46%	88,560	26,413	29.82%
START POINT	10/12/42	07/01/43	29	2,925	948	32.41%	92,485	27,361	29.58%
PILAR DE LARRINAGA	08/01/43	23/02/43	47	5,160	2,161	41.88%	97,645	29,522	30.23%
OCEAN VAGRANT	12/06/43	16/08/43	66	6,548	1,256	19.18%	104,193	30,778	29.54%
OCEAN VAGRANT	17/08/43	30/11/43	106	5,011	1,577	31.47%	108,204	32,355	29.90%
EMPIRE SPEY	27/06/44	16/10/44	112	968	319	32.95%	109,172	32,674	29.93%
			1,320	109,172	32,764				29.93%

Boards". Frank Howe was fortunate in not requiring hospitalisation; and obtained employment as a junior clerk in a factory on a pittance of a wage. I was referred to the Ministry of Pensions hospitals for examination and treatment, and was hospitalised first in the Royal Hamadryad Hospital for Seamen, and then for a short time in the Rookwood Hospital.

The Medical Boards were held at frequent intervals, and recipients of disability allowances had to attend. This involved a loss of earnings for those on hourly or daily rates of pay; in most cases the loss of pay being greater than the disability allowance. Eventually, his employers told Frank

Howe that they would not release him for the frequent medical boards; so he forfeited the disability allowance.

I attended as an outpatient at the Ministry of Pensions Rookwood Hospital in Cardiff, where I underwent further examination followed by a barium meal and ex-ray. Despite the fact that I was vomiting tinges of blood, it appeared that the tests were not conclusive. Then, I was instructed to attend the Sutton Emergency Hospital in Surrey, for indefinite in-patient treatment.

The Sutton Emergency Hospital had been a hospital for the mentally ill, but had been commandeered by the Ministry of Pensions for the assessment and treatment of cases of Psycho Neurosis. The Medical Superintendent was a Doctor Minski and the medical practitioner responsible for our section was Doctor Sands. I was accommodated in a ward for Merchant Navy Officers. An adjacent ward accommodated other ranks. There were about 40 officers and 120 other ranks. The first intimation I received that I was not to be treated for a severe gastric disorder, was when I was told that I would commence "insulin shock treatment" the following morning. That was shock enough, but the treatment was even more shocking.

The treatment consisted of an injection of a substantial dose of insulin, delivered into a buttock by a tough V.A.D. nurse at 6.00 a.m. in the morning, in a freezing cold ward with the windows open. This produced a state of coma that lasted for several hours, and was intended to create a carbohydrate starvation. A huge tureen of mashed potatoes was then wheeled into the ward, and placed on a central table: whereupon the patients would attack the huge pile and devour it, like a pack of starving wolves. About 12 patients received this treatment. The food played hell with my stomach, and caused a recurrence of vomiting. This meant nothing to the medical staff or nurses. They did what they were ordered to do. Their main concern appeared to be keeping the bedclothes tidy, and the beds aligned with precision, for inspection by a dragon of a Matron. The V.A.D. nurses were equally dreadful. A bed out of alignment by an inch constituted a catastrophe for the matron.

To add to our discomfort, all the windows were opened at 6.00 a.m., so the unheated wards were like refrigerators, when we bared our buttocks to the hypodermic needles. The same needle was used for each victim, and I recall the remarks of the individual in the next bed, an officer named Shand, "For Christ's sake nurse, you are ramming a bloody marlin spike in my arse!" Those on the end of the line received the blunt needles.

A number of more serious cases (in the opinion of the Ministry of

Pensions) were on what was termed "Narcosis" treatment. The injections they received induced what appeared to be a long-term coma. The most severe treatment was what we termed "the knocker". A plate was placed on each side of the head, and an electric shock passed through the brain. Patients were required to sign an affidavit absolving the hospital from liability. We were given no option but to suffer this experimentation.

There were about a thousand patients from the Services and Merchant Navy in Sutton Emergency Hospital. We were not allowed to leave our ward, so did not fraternise with the prisoners in the other wards. There were no physical barriers, but we were expected to stay within the confines of our ward. Those who were able to do so were permitted to leave the hospital, subject to a curfew. My aunt and uncle lived a short bus ride away in Carshalton Beeches; so I visited their home, where they gave me food that was suitable for my gastric condition.

I was hospitalised for most of January and February 1945; and every day was worse than the previous one. It was a hell on earth. There were no amenities, or any form of recreation: just a bare, cold ward, with two long rows of camp beds: a nail on the wall by each bed, on which to hang a suit on a wire hanger: a small wooden locker for personal possessions. The officers used a small toilet and washroom close to similar facilities for the other ranks.

Then Doctor Sands decided on what he termed "occupational therapy". The officers and other ranks were established in a mixed rota for the cleaning of wards, including both toilet facilities. The officers refused to undertake the duties, which were demeaning. Doctor Sands relented, but we were put to cleaning our own facilities. I refused, and was reported to Doctor Minski.

Shortly afterwards, when I was trying to sleep, I was awakened by a pair of hands clenched about my throat, by a very strong man who was intent on choking me. He was a man named Nicholson, from the R.A.F. section of the hospital, who had run amok and was pursued by a tiny nurse. The nurse was clinging to his back and screaming, "Stop it Nicky!" He released his grip on my throat, turned, and struck the poor nurse so violently that she was knocked unconscious. He then raced off, pursued by several male nurses with a straight jacket. Eventually, he was cornered and caught, as he was attempting to climb into the bell tower.

The next day, I visited my relatives for some peace and quiet and a meal of edible food. V1 and V2 rockets were bombarding London, and an air raid alert was in progress as I was returning to the hospital. The bus service had been discontinued, so I had to walk to the hospital, where I arrived about a half an hour after curfew time. When I signed in, I was told that I would be reported for returning late.

The following day, when I attempted to sign out for another visit to the home of my relatives, the gatekeeper attempted to refuse to allow me to leave. He had received an instruction from Doctor Sands, cancelling any leave for me from the hospital for an unspecified period. I told him to bugger off, and continued on my way, returning later. This was the final indignity. Firstly, Doctor Sands, attempted reprimand me, for my insubordination. I told him to go to hell. I then walked into the office of Doctor Minski, and demanded the immediate issue of a railway ticket voucher for the journey from Sutton to Cardiff. He refused. I sat in his office for several hours, and eventually told him that I intended to give his prison for medical experimentation the maximum publicity; through the medium of the Navigators and Engineer Officers' Union.

He eventually relented, and wrote out a second-class rail voucher, which I refused. I left in the late afternoon with a first-class voucher, and was relieved to crawl into my bed at home in the early hours of the next morning.

I wrote to the Navigators and Engineer Officers Union, giving an account of the quite appalling conditions in the hospital, and my apprehensions that it was a centre for medical experimentation for the Ministry of Pensions. The General Secretary responded, promising to take action with the Ministry of Pensions at the highest level. Shortly afterwards, I received a letter from Shand, the occupant of the next bed to mine in the prison. All patients had been provided with wooden wardrobes. The opening of all the ward windows at 6.00 a.m. and the cleaning of toilets by the patients had been discontinued. The stringent regime that had governed the release of patients into civilisation during the day had been relaxed.

However, the Ministry of Pensions exacted their immediate retribution upon me. Shortly afterwards, I received a letter from them, informing me that in view of the fact that I had refused treatment, the ten shillings a week disability allowance, was discontinued with immediate effect. They sent me a remittance for paltry £ 26 as a gratuity. Fifty years later in May 1995 a friend told me that he had been awarded a war disability pension for impaired hearing caused by naval gunfire. He was a medical practitioner, who had served as a Surgeon Lieutenant in the Royal Navy. On his recommendation I applied to the War Pensions Agency, the successor to the Ministry of Pensions. There had been improvements in the government body. The War Pensions Agency conformed to what was termed the "Citizen's Charter". My application was processed with courtesy and an acceptable standard of efficiency. After a number of medical examinations they finally assessed the disability at 20 percent, embracing "Injury left shoulder – 1941: injury left arm – 1941: dyspepsia – 1942." They diagnosed my insomnia as "Post traumatic stress disorder." Further ex-rays were undertaken and an examination by a specialist orthopaedic surgeon. This added "Severe damage to lower spine." The disability was re-assessed as 40 percent in 1996, fifty years after the war. The War Pensions Agency has now adopted the title of the Veterans Agency. The organisation is managed efficiently, and veterans are treated with courtesy and kindness.

Frank Howe and I remained close friends for thirty years. He had been affected enormously by his traumatic experiences in the sinking of six ships, suffering severely from insomnia and acute depression. He committed suicide by taking a massive overdose of sleeping tablets on 14 March 1977. There is no doubt that he was a casualty of the war, just as if he had been drowned burnt alive, or blown to pieces..

In 1996 I applied to the War Pensions Agency on behalf of his wife, Mary Howe, for a War Widow's Pension. Remarkably, they processed the claim within six months of the date of application, and awarded her a pension as a War Widow. The passage of fifty years had indeed wrought a transformation in that government body.

In 1945 it was clear to me that there was likely to be no help forthcoming from what was then termed a "grateful country", or any of the government bodies. My gastric disorder necessitated a strict diet of milk, eggs and fish. The severe insomnia was alleviated by the prescription of increasing doses of Pheno Barbitone. This induced drowsiness during the day. The doctor prescribed Benzadrine to overcome the drowsiness. Both drugs are habit forming, and required increased dosage to remain effective. Eventually, I decided to throw them all down the toilet, and get on with my life.

My first employment was as a sales representative for the local agent for the supply of machine tools. The pay was £ 3 per week and commission of $2^{1/2}$ %. I bought a bicycle for £ 12, and cycled about 40 miles a day in the locality, with my briefcase containing catalogues hanging from the handlebars. When I obtained an order for £ 700 for milling cutters for a local factory, I was overjoyed at the prospect of having earned £ 17-10s-0d in commission. My reward was to be informed that my employment had been terminated, and the son of my employer would be employed in my place. He had been demobilised after a short period of non-combatant military service. I never received the commission, on the grounds that it would be paid on delivery of the merchandise, but only if I was an employee then.

Fortunately, I was immediately employed as a sales representative for an electrical wholesaler at a pay of £ 4-10s-0d per week plus commission of 21/2 % on new business and one percent on existing accounts. This required a motor car. We scraped together the deposit, and I bought an Austin Seven Ruby saloon of 1937 vintage on hire purchase. The cost was £ 105. The car allowance was one penny a mile. This Baby Austin was traded in for a 1935 Austin Ten Lichfield Saloon, which was traded in for a 1936 Austin Twelve Ascot Saloon.

Our accommodation was improved by the addition of what was termed a "middle room and conservatory". This was improved by many hours of amateur plastering, electrical work and decorating in the evenings and over weekends. Our son, Robert was born in 1951 into the environment of this basic accommodation. Although I suffered from occasional recurrences of the after effects of malaria, my health had been improved by careful diet. Despite the poverty of our circumstances, I never applied for state-assisted financial aid. We were without debt and happy in our little family. Our income was then about £ 12 per week, and we had saved £ 60.

With this capital, we formed a partnership and obtained agencies for a number of manufacturers. One manufacturer of pumps and acid inhibitors, Ian Merrill of Sheffield, showed sufficient confidence to pay a retainer of £ 100 per annum, and commission on receipt of order. Ian Merrill was a gentleman, and we owe a great deal to him, because he helped us over the first critical three months of our business. He had lost an eye during service in the army in the 1914 to 1918 war, and had made a success by ability and perseverance in the face of adversity.

After encountering and overcoming many difficulties in the following years, we limited the liability of our partnership into a registered company in 1966. Our activities developed and prospered into a substantial business organisation in the fields of manufacturing: warehousing: transport: equipment rental: and industrial and commercial property. Thirty years later we retired from business. Betty and I had made it to modest success without any handouts from the State.

Looking back to the day when I joined *Appledore* sixty-seven years ago as a naïve 15-year old junior apprentice, I reflect that I would not have deviated from that decision. Life in the half deck of a British merchant ship was hard and unremitting. However, it brought me into contact with unforgettable individuals, who not only helped to teach me in learning "the business of a Seaman as practised in steamships", but also contributed by their fine examples in the building of character. I am proud to have served as an officer in the British Merchant Navy during peace and war; and have no regrets that this was my chosen profession. Those sentiments are exemplified in the words of Francis Bacon:

"Every man is a debtor to his profession, from which, as men do seek to receive countenance and reward, so ought they, by way of amends, to endeavour to be a credit and an ornament thereto."

In the opening of this narrative, I paid tribute to the loving care and support of my wife Betty. During our sixty years of marriage she has never changed in her steadfast courage and happy disposition. It is therefore appropriate that I close this narrative with a further expression of appreciation for this wonderful person, who has meant so much to me. I have been a fortunate man.

When I Have Crost the Bar

Sunset and evening star,
And one clear call for me,
And may there be no moaning of the bar,
When I put out to sea,
But such a tide as moving seems asleep,
Too full for sound and foam,
When that which drew from out the boundless sleep
Turns again .. .. .. home.

TWILIGHT and evening bell,
And after that the dark,
And may there be no sadness of farewell,
When I embark,
For, tho' from out our bourne of time or place,
The flood may bear me far,
I hope to see my Pilot face to face,
When I have crost the bar.

APPENDIX 1
INDEX OF SHIP LOSSES

APPENDIX I

UPON THEIR LAWFUL OCCASIONS

APPENDIX 1

APPENDIX 1

APPENDIX 1

441

Appendix 2
Index of U-boat losses

U-BOAT	PAGE	U-BOAT	PAGE	U-BOAT	PAGE	U-BOAT	PAGE
U-413	415	U-529	357	U-606	357	U-702	235
U-415	415	U-535	379	U-607	379	U-703	415
U-419	381	U-536	381	U-608	415	U-705	270
U-420	381	U-538	381	U-609	357	U-706	379
U-422	381	U-540	381	U-610	381	U-718	381
U-433	223	U-543	415	U-611	339	U-719	415
U-434	223	U-547	415	U-612	270	U-732	381
U-435	379	U-551	195	U-613	379	U-736	415
U-442	357	U-553	357	U-614	379	U-741	415
U-443	357	U-556	203	U-615	379	U-742	415
U-445	415	U-557	223	U-617	381	U-743	415
U-449	379	U-558	379	U-618	415	U-751	259
U-451	223	U-559	314	U-619	270	U-754	270
U-452	203	U-561	379	U-620	357	U-756	270
U-454	379	U-562	357	U-621	415	U-759	379
U-458	381	U-564	379	U-622	379	U-760	381
U-459	379	U-565	415	U-623	357	U-768	381
U-460	381	U-566	381	U-624	357	U-841	381
U-461	379	U-567	223	U-626	347	U-842	381
U-462	379	U-568	252	U-627	314	U-844	381
U-464	270	U-570	203	U-628	379	U-847	381
U-468	379	U-572	379	U-631	381	U-848	381
U-470	381	U-573	247	U-634	381	U-849	381
U-478	415	U-574	223	U-639	381	U-855	415
U-484	415	U-576	259	U-642	415	U-859	415
U-487	379	U-577	223	U-643	381	U-863	415
U-489	379	U-578	270	U-647	379	U-865	415
U-501	203	U-580	223	U-648	381	U-867	415
U-502	259	U-581	223	U-651	203	U-871	415
U-503	235	U-583	223	U-652	252	U-921	415
U-504	379	U-584	381	U-655	235	U-925	415
U-506	379	U-585	235	U-656	235	U-951	379
U-507	357	U-586	415	U-658	314	U-964	381
U-508	381	U-587	235	U-660	339	U-981	415
U-509	379	U-588	270	U-661	314	U-983	381
U-513	379	U-590	379	U-662	379	U-984	415
U-514	379	U-591	379	U-664	379	U-988	415
U-517	339	U-595	339	U-667	415	U-1006	415
U-519	357	U-597	314	U-669	381	U-1062	415
U-520	314	U-598	379	U-670	381	U-1122	415
U-522	357	U-599	314	U-671	415	U-1229	415
U-523	381	U-600	381	U-672	415	U-2323	415
U-525	379	U-604	379	U-678	415		
U-527	379	U-605	339	U-701	259		